## IMPERIAL UNITS

| | |
|---|---|
| ac | acre |
| bbl | barrel |
| cu ft | cubic foot |
| cu in. | cubic inch |
| cu yd | cubic yard |
| cwt | hundred weight |
| fbm | foot board measure |
| ft | foot or feet |
| gal | gallon(s) |
| in. | inch(es) |
| lb | pound |
| lf | linear foot (feet) |
| mi | mile(s) |
| mph | miles per hour |
| psi | pounds per square inch |
| sq ft | square foot (feet) |
| sq in. | square inch(es) |
| sq yd | square yard(s) |
| mf bm | thousand foot board measure |
| m gal | thousand gallons |
| yd | yard(s) |

## METRIC UNITS

| | |
|---|---|
| C | Celsius |
| cm | centimeter |
| ha | hectare |
| kg | kilogram(s) |
| km | kilometer(s) |
| kN | kilonewton(s) |
| kPa | kilopascal(s) |
| L | liter(s) |
| m | meter(s) |
| $m^2$ | square meter |
| $m^3$ | cubic meter |
| mm | millimeter(s) |
| t | tonne |

# SURVEYING
## Principles and Applications

*Sixth Edition*

**Barry F. Kavanagh**
**Seneca College Emeritus**

Prentice
Hall

Upper Saddle River, New Jersey
Columbus, Ohio

**Library of Congress Cataloging-in-Publication Data**

Kavanagh, Barry F.
    Surveying: principles and applications/Barry F. Kavanagh.—6th ed.
        p.; cm.
    Includes bibliographical references and index.
    ISBN 0-13-099582-7
    1. Surveying. I. Title.
TA545 .K37 2003
526.9—dc21

2002018843


**Editor in Chief:** Stephen Helba
**Editor:** Ed Francis
**Production Editor:** Holly Shufeldt
**Design Coordinator:** Diane Ernsberger
**Cover Designer:** Bryan Huber
**Cover photo:** Courtesy of MicroSurvey Software Inc., Westbank, British Columbia, Canada.
**Production Manager:** Matt Ottenweller
**Marketing Manager:** Mark Marsden


This book was set in Times Roman by The Clarinda Company, and was printed and bound by R. R. Donnelley & Sons Company. The cover was printed by Phoenix Color Corp.


Pearson Education Ltd.
Pearson Education Australia Pty. Limited
Pearson Education Singapore Pte. Ltd.
Pearson Education North Asia Ltd.
Pearson Education Canada, Ltd.
Pearson Educación de Mexico, S.A. de C.V.
Pearson Education—Japan
Pearson Education Malaysia Pte. Ltd.
Pearson Education, *Upper Saddle River, New Jersey*

10 9 8 7 6 5 4 3
ISBN: 0-13-099582-7

# Preface

This text has been extensively revised since the fifth edition. The text is now divided into three parts:

Part I  *Surveying Principles* includes chapters on Basics of Surveying, Distance Measurement (Taping), Leveling, Angles and Directions, Theodolites, Traverse Surveys, Electronic Surveying Measurement, Topographic Surveying and Mapping, Geographic Information Systems, Control Surveys, and Global Positioning Systems (GPSs).

Part II  *Remote Sensing* (Chapter 12) includes 29 sections on the topics of satellite imagery and airborne imagery.

Part III  *Surveying Applications* includes chapters on Highway Curves, Construction Surveys, Land Surveying, and Hydrographic Surveys.

Part I continues the approach of covering the basics in clear, understandable language. Many illustrations and examples clarify and reinforce the chapter topics. Updated isogonic charts, epoch 2000, are included for North America and the entire globe. Geographic information systems (GISs) are now included as a separate chapter, and in Chapter 10, Control Surveys, on-line and interactive techniques for computing grid and geographic coordinates are illustrated using NGS tools (www.ngs.noaa.gov/TOOLS/).

Part II includes the topics of satellite imagery and airborne imagery. The sections on satellite imagery cover techniques of remote sensing, multispectral scanning, image analysis, and ground-truthing, and brief descriptions of many of the internationally sponsored satellites presently used for earth-study purposes. The sections on airborne imagery cover the fundamentals of aerial surveying and photogrammetry and also introduce students to the latest in imaging techniques using lidar mapping techniques.

Part III covers practical approaches for applications in the engineering, hydrographic, and land surveying fields. As with the earlier parts of the text, material here is presented in a clear and logical fashion, a style that reflects the many years of field experience accumulated by the authors. S. J. Glenn Bird (1933–1989), academic, land surveyor, photogrammetric engineer, and hydrographer, wrote for the first two editions sections covering land surveying, hydrographic surveying, and photogrammetry; his impact on the text is still evident.

The appendixes have been expanded. New entries are included in the glossary and in the surveying and mapping website index. Four-screw instruments (dumpy level and engineer's transit) are covered in a separate appendix. Also new to this edition is an appendix describing field projects that accompany classroom work. These projects have been developed and refined over 25 years of college experience.

Comments and suggestions about this text are welcomed by the author at barry_kavanagh@sympatico.ca.

Barry F. Kavanagh

## Acknowledgments

The author is grateful for the comments and suggestions received from those who adopted previous editions of this text and from the faculty of the Center for the Built Environment at Seneca College.

In addition, particular thanks are due to Gary L. Backer, Minneapolis, Minnesota, and Carl Hillyard, Pennsylvania, for their assistance with the sixth edition text review.

The following surveying, engineering, and equipment manufacturers have provided generous assistance:

- American Congress on Surveying and Mapping, Bethesda, Maryland
- American Society for Photogrammetry and Remote Sensing
- Bird and Hale, Ltd., Toronto, Ontario
- Canadian Institute of Geomatics, Ottawa, Ontario
- Canadian Space Agency, Ottawa, Ontario
- Carl Zeiss Inc., Thornwood, New York
- CST/Berger, Watseka, Illinois
- Environmental Systems Research Institute, Inc. (ESRI), Redlands, California
- Geomagnetic Laboratory, Geological Survey of Canada, Ottawa—Larry Newitt
- International Systemap Corp., Vancouver, British Columbia
- Leica Canada Ltd., Toronto, Ontario
- Leica Geosystems Inc., Norcross, Georgia
- L H Systems, San Diego, California—Suzanne Hallam
- MicroSurvey International, Kelowna, British Columbia
- National Geodetic Survey (NGS), Rockville, Maryland
- Nikon Inc., Melville, New York
- OPTECH, Toronto, Ontario—Jim Green
- Pentax Canada, Toronto—Harry Otani
- Position Inc., Calgary, Alberta
- Sokkia Corporation, Olathe, Kansas
- Texas DOT—Kathleen Chavez
- Topcon Instrument Corp., Paramus, New Jersey
- Topcon Positioning Systems—Chuck Neely
- Trimble, Sunnyvale, California
- U.S. Geological Survey, Denver, Colorado—John M. Quinn
- U.S. Geological Survey, Sioux Falls, South Dakota—Ron Beck

# Contents

Contents

FIELD NOTE INDEX

| Page # | Figure # | Description |
|--------|----------|-------------|
| 76 | 3.15 | Level notes, with arithmetic check |
| 79 | 3.18 | Profile field notes |
| 81 | 3.21 | Cross-section notes (municipal format) |
| 82 | 3.22 | Cross-section notes (highway format) |
| 86 | 3.28 | Survey notes for three-wire leveling |
| 126 | 5.6 | Field notes for angles by repetition |
| 133 | 5.11 | Field notes for directions |
| 148 | 6.3 | Field notes for open traverse |
| 226 | 7.22 | Field notes for Total Station graphics descriptors |
| 263 | 8.12 | Topographic field notes for single baseline; split baseline |
| 352 | 10.22 | Control point directions and distances |
| 353 | 10.23 | Prepared polar coordinate layout notes |
| 368 | 10.33 | Field notes for Polaris observation |
| 400 | 11.19 | Station visibility diagram |
| 402 | 11.20 | GPS field log |
| 557 | 14.5 | House survey (plat) |
| 558 | 14.6 | Property markers used to establish center line |
| 619 | 15.11 | Original township notes (chains) |
| 630 | 15.14 | Rural land survey techniques and note forms |
| 639 | 15.16 | Title or mortgage survey notes |
| 714 | G.1 | Field note layout |
| 715 | G.2 | Sample field notes for taping building dimensions—Project #1 |
| 716 | G.3 | Sample field notes for Project #3 (traverse distances) |
| 719 | G.4 | Sample field notes for Project #4 (differential leveling) |
| 721 | G.5 | Sample field notes for Project #5 (traverse angles) |
| 723 | G.6 | Sample field notes for Project #6 (topography tie-ins) |
| 724 | G.7 | Sample field notes for Project #6 (topography cross sections) |
| 725 | G.9 | Sample field notes for Project #6 (topography by theodolite/EDM) |
| 726 | G.10 | Sample field notes for Project #6 (topography by total station) |
| 729 | G.11 | Sample field notes for Project #7 (building layout) |

PART

I Surveying Principles

# 1 Basics of Surveying

## 1.1 Surveying Defined

Surveying is the art of measuring distances, angles, and positions on or near the surface of the earth. It is an art because only a surveyor who possesses a thorough understanding of surveying techniques will be able to determine the most efficient methods required to obtain optimal results over a wide variety of surveying problems. Surveying is also scientific because rigorous mathematical techniques are used to analyze and adjust the field survey data. The accuracy and thus the reliability of the survey depend not only on the field expertise of the surveyor, but also on the surveyor's understanding of the scientific principles underlying and affecting all forms of survey measurement.

Figure 1.1 is an aerial photo of undeveloped property. Figure 1.2 is an aerial photo of the same property after development. The straight and circular lines that have been added to the postdevelopment photo, showing modifications and/or additions to roads, buildings, highways, residential areas, commercial areas, property boundaries, and so on, are all the direct or indirect result of surveying.

## 1.2 Types of Surveys

*Plane surveying* is that type of surveying in which the surface of the earth is considered to be a plane for all $X$ and $Y$ dimensions. All $Z$ dimensions (height) are referenced to the mean spherical surface of the earth (mean sea level). Most engineering and property surveys are plane surveys, although some of these surveys that cover large distances (for example, highways and railroads) will have corrections applied at regular intervals (e.g., 1 mile) to correct for the earth's curvature.

*Geodetic surveying* is that type of surveying in which the surface of the earth is considered to be spherical (actually an ellipsoid of revolution) for $X$ and $Y$ dimensions. As in plane surveying, the $Z$ dimensions (height) are referenced to the mean surface of the earth (mean sea level). Traditional geodetic surveys were very precise surveys of great magnitude (e.g., national boundaries, control networks, etc.). Modern surveys (data gathering, control, and layout) utilizing the global positioning system (satellite surveying) are also

**FIGURE 1.1** Aerial photograph of undeveloped property.

based on the geometric shape of the earth. Such measurements must be mathematically translated to be of use in leveling and other local surveying projects.

## 1.3 Classes of Surveys

The *preliminary survey* (data gathering) is the gathering of data (distances, position, and angles) to locate physical features (for example, trees, rivers, roads, structures, or property markers) so that the data can be plotted to scale on a map or plan. Preliminary surveys also include the determination of differences in elevation (vertical distances) so that elevations and contours can also be plotted.

**FIGURE 1.2**  Aerial photograph of same property after development.

**Layout surveys** involve marking on the ground the features shown on a design plan. Wood stakes, iron bars, aluminum and concrete monuments, nails, spikes, and so on, can be used to make these markings. The layout can be for property lines, as in subdivision surveying, or it can be for a wide variety of engineering works (for example, roads, pipelines, bridges). The latter group is known as construction surveys. In addition to marking the proposed horizontal ($X$ and $Y$ dimensions) location of the designed feature, reference will also be given to the proposed elevations ($Z$ dimensions).

**Control surveys** are used to reference both preliminary and layout surveys. Horizontal control can be placed arbitrarily, but it is usually tied directly to property lines, roadway center lines, or coordinated control stations. Vertical control is a series of benchmarks—permanent points whose elevation above mean sea level have been carefully determined.

It is accepted practice to take more care in control surveys with respect to precision and accuracy. Great care is also taken to ensure that the control used for a preliminary survey can be easily reestablished later, whether it be needed for further preliminary work or for a related layout survey.

## 1.4 Definitions

1. Topographic surveys: preliminary surveys used to tie in the natural and constructed surface features of an area. The features are located relative to one another by tying them all into the same control lines or control grid.

2. Hydrographic surveys: preliminary surveys used to tie in underwater features to a surface control line. Usually shorelines, marine features, and water depths are shown on a hydrographic map.

3. Route surveys: preliminary, layout, and control surveys that range over a narrow but long strip of land. Typical projects that require route surveys are highways, railroads, electricity transmission lines, and channels.

4. Property surveys: preliminary, layout, and control surveys involved in determining boundary locations or in laying out new property boundaries (also known as *cadastral* or *land surveys*).

5. Aerial surveys: preliminary and final surveys using traditional aerial photography and aerial imagery. Aerial imagery includes the use of digital cameras, multispectral scanners, Lidar, and radar.

6. Construction surveys: layout surveys for engineering works.

7. Final ("as built") surveys: similar to preliminary surveys. Final surveys tie in features that have just been constructed to provide a final record of the construction and to check that the construction has proceeded according to the design plans.

## 1.5 Surveying Instrumentation

The simple instruments most often used in surveying are (1) the *transit* or theodolite, which is used to establish straight or curved lines and to measure horizontal and vertical angles (see Figures 1.3 and 1.4); (2) the *level* and *rod,* which are used to measure differences in elevation (see Figure 1.5); and (3) the *steel* tape, which is used to measure horizontal and slope distances (see Figure 1.6). Once the simpler instruments have been learned, you may then be introduced to more advanced instrumentation such as *total station* instruments (Chapter 7) and *global positioning system (GPS)* receivers (Chapter 11).

*Total stations* measure horizontal and vertical angles as well as horizontal and vertical distances. All data can be captured into *electronic field books* or onboard storage as the data are received. *GPS* receivers capture data from several *NAVSTAR* satellites to determine position coordinates (north, east, and elevation) of a survey station. See Figure 1.7(a) and (b).

**FIGURE 1.3** Optical theodolite and engineers' (American) transit.

# 1.6 Survey Geographic Reference

It has already been mentioned that surveying involves measuring the location of physical land features relative to one another and relative to a defined reference on the surface of the earth. In the broadest sense, the earth's reference system is composed of the surface divisions denoted by geographic lines of latitude and longitude. The latitude lines run east and west and are parallel to the equator. The latitude lines are formed by projecting the latitude angle out from the center of the earth to its surface. The latitude angle itself is measured (90° maximum) at the earth's center, north or south from the equatorial plane.

The longitude lines all run north and south and converge at the poles. The lines of longitude (meridians) are formed by projecting the longitude angle out to the surface of the earth at the equator. The longitude angle itself is measured at the earth's center, east or west (180° maximum) from the plane of 0° longitude, which has been arbitrarily placed through Greenwich, England (see Figures 1.8 and 1.9).

This system of geographic coordinates is used in navigation and geodesy, but those engaged in plane surveying normally use either coordinate grid systems or the original township fabric as a basis for referencing.

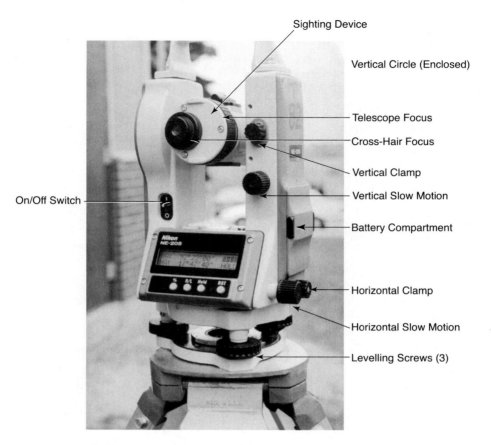

Sighting Device

Vertical Circle (Enclosed)

Telescope Focus

Cross-Hair Focus

Vertical Clamp

Vertical Slow Motion

Battery Compartment

On/Off Switch

Horizontal Clamp

Horizontal Slow Motion

Levelling Screws (3)

**FIGURE 1.4**   Electronic theodolite.

## 1.7   Survey Grid Reference

All states and provinces have adopted a grid system best suited to their needs. The grid itself is limited in size so that no serious errors will accumulate when the curvature of the earth is ignored. Advantages of the grid systems are the ease of calculation (plane geometry and trigonometry) and the availability of one common datum for $X$ and $Y$ dimensions in a large area, usually thousands of square miles. The coordinates in most grid systems can be referenced to the central meridian and to the equator so that translation to geographic coordinates is always easily accomplished. This topic is discussed in more detail in Chapter 10.

## 1.8   Survey Legal Reference

Public lands in North America were originally laid out for agricultural use by the settlers. In the United States and parts of Canada, the townships were laid out in 6-mile squares;

Level Rod (Foot)

**FIGURE 1.5** Level and rod. (Courtesy of Sokkia Co. Ltd.)

**FIGURE 1.6** Measuring to a water-main access frame using a steel tape.

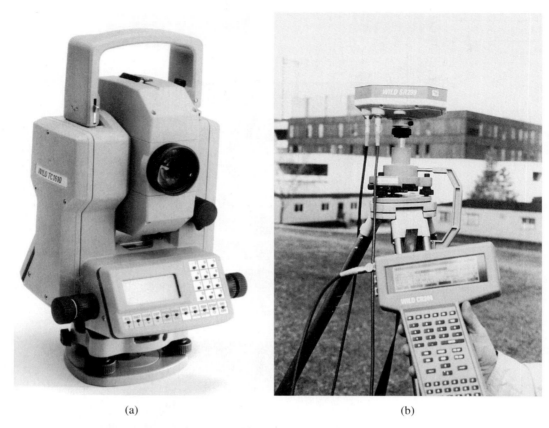

(a)                             (b)

**FIGURE 1.7**   (a) Total station. (Courtesy of Leica, Heerbrugg) (b) Global positioning system receiver. (Courtesy of Leica, Toronto)

however, in the first established areas of Canada, a wide variety of township patterns exist—reflecting both the French and English heritage.

The townships themselves were subdivided into sections and ranges (lots and concessions in Canada), each uniquely numbered. The basic township sections or lots were either 1 mile square or some fraction thereof. Eventually, the townships were (and still are) further subdivided in real-estate developments. All developments are referenced to the original township fabric, which has been reasonably well preserved through ongoing resurveys. This topic is discussed in detail in Chapter 15.

## 1.9 Survey Vertical Reference

The previous sections described how the $X$ and $Y$ dimensions (horizontal) of any feature can be referenced for plane surveying purposes. Although vertical dimensions can be referenced to any datum, the reference datum most used is that of mean sea level (MSL). Mean sea level is assigned an elevation of 0.000 feet (ft) (or meters), and all other points on

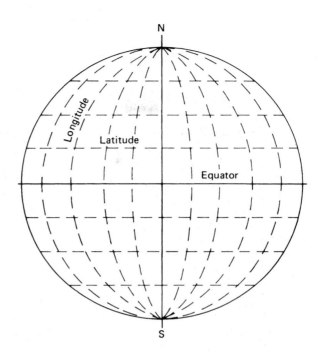

**FIGURE 1.8** Sketch of earth showing lines of latitude and longitude.

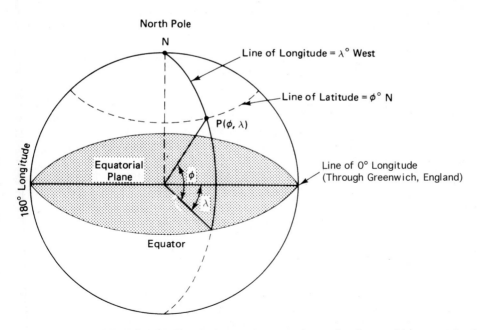

**FIGURE 1.9** Sketch showing location of point *P*, referenced by geographical coordinates.

the earth can be described as being elevations above or below zero. Permanent points whose elevations have been precisely determined (*benchmarks*) are available in most areas for survey use. See Chapters 10 and 11 for further discussion of this topic.

## 1.10   Distance Measurement

Distances between two points can be horizontal, slope, or vertical and are recorded in feet (foot units) or meters (SI units) (see Figure 1.10). **Horizontal** and **slope distances** can be measured with a fiberglass or steel tape or with an electronic distance measuring device. In surveying, the horizontal distance is always required (for plan plotting and design purposes); if a slope distance between two points has been taken, it must then be converted to its horizontal equivalent. Slope distances can be trigonometrically converted to horizontal distances by using either the slope angle or the difference in elevation (vertical distance) between the two points. **Vertical distances** can be measured with a tape, as in construction work, with a surveyors' level and leveling rod (see Figure 1.11), or with a total station (see Chapter 7).

## 1.11   Units of Measurement

The many different measuring units have caused no end of confusion. An attempt to standardize weights and measures led to the creation of the metric system in the 1790s. It was agreed that the standard unit of length would be the meter. The length of the meter was supposed to be one ten-millionth of the distance from the North Pole to the equator. In 1866, the U.S. Congress made the use of metric weights and measures legal. The meter was equal to 39.37 inches; or 1 foot (U.S. survey foot) equaled 0.3048006 meters. In 1959, the United States officially adopted the International Foot, whereby 1 foot equals 0.3048 meters exactly. One U.S. survey foot equals 1.000002 International feet. In 1960, the metric system was modernized and called the Système International d'Unites (SI). (See Table 2.1 for selected unit comparisons.) As of 1999, the large number of U.S. federal and state metric initiatives already taken seemed to indicate that the complete adoption of metric units is only a matter of time; however, the complete changeover to the metric system will probably take many years, perhaps several generations. The impact is that, from now on, most surveyors will have to be proficient in both the foot and metric systems. Additional equipment costs in this dual system are limited mostly to measuring tapes and leveling rods.

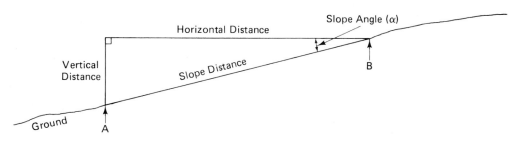

**FIGURE 1.10**   Distance measurement.

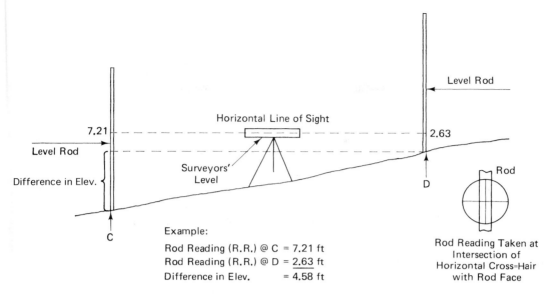

**FIGURE 1.11** Leveling technique.

SI units were a modernization (1960) of the long-used metric units. This modernization included a redefinition of the meter and the addition of some new units. One example is the Newton (see Table 2.1). With the United States committed to switching to metric units, all industrialized nations are now using the metric system.

Table 1.1 describes and contrasts metric and foot units. Degrees, minutes, and seconds are used almost exclusively in both metric and foot systems for angular measurement. In some European countries, however, the circle has also been graduated into 400 gon (also called grad). Angles in that system are expressed to four decimals (that is, a right angle = 100.0000 gon).

## 1.12 Location Methods

A great deal of surveying effort is spent in measuring points of interest relative to some reference line so that these points may be shown later on a scaled plan. The illustrations in Figure 1.12 show some common location techniques. Point $P$ in Figure 1.12(a) is located relative to known line $AB$ by determining $CB$ or $CA$, the right angle at $C$, and distance $CP$. This is known as the **right-angle offset tie** or the **rectangular tie.** Point $P$ in Figure 1.12(b) is located relative to known line $AB$ by determining the angle ($\theta$) at $A$ and the distance $AP$. This is known as the **angle-distance tie** or the **polar tie.** Point $P$ in Figure 1.12(c) can also be located relative to known line $AB$ by determining **either** the angles at $A$ and $B$ to $P$ **or** by determining the distances $AP$ and $BP$. Both methods are **intersection** techniques.

Alternately, a point can be tied-in using positioning techniques. For example, Point $P$ can be located by simply holding a pole-mounted GPS receiver/antenna directly on the

**Table 1.1** MEASUREMENT DEFINITIONS AND EQUIVALENCIES

| Linear measurements | Foot units |
|---|---|
| 1 mile = 5,280 feet<br>= 1,760 yards<br>= 320 rods<br>= 80 chains | 1 foot = 12 inches<br>1 yard = 3 feet<br>1 rod = 16½ feet<br>1 chain = 66 feet<br>1 chain = 100 links |

1 acre = 43,560 ft$^2$ = 10 square chains

| Linear measurement | Metric (SI) units | |
|---|---|---|
| 1 kilometer | = | 1,000 meter |
| 1 meter | = | 100 centimeter |
| 1 centimeter | = | 10 millimeter |
| 1 decimeter | = | 10 centimeter |
| 1 hectare (ha) | = | 10,000 m$^2$ |
| 1 square kilometer | = | 1,000,000 m$^2$ |
| | = | 100 hectares |

Foot-to-metric conversion

| | | |
|---|---|---|
| 1 ft = | 0.3048 m (exactly) | 1 inch = 25.4 mm (exactly)[a] |
| 1 km = | 0.62137 miles (approx.) | |
| 1 hectare (ha) = | 2.471 acres (approx.) | |
| 1 km$^2$ = | 247.1 acres (approx.) | |

Angular measurement

1 revolution = 360°
1 degree = 60′
1 minute = 60″ seconds

[a]Prior to 1959, the United States used the relationship 1 m = 39.37 in. This resulted in a U.S. survey foot of approximately 0.3048006 m.

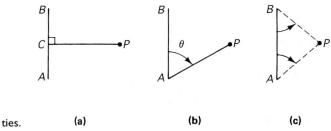

**FIGURE 1.12** Location ties.　　(a)　　　　　　(b)　　　　　　(c)

point and then waiting until a sufficient number of measurements indicate that the point has been located (coordinates determined) to the required level of precision.

## 1.13 Accuracy and Precision

*Accuracy* is the relationship between the value of a measurement and the "true" value (see Section 1.14 for "true" values) of the dimension being measured. *Precision* describes the refinement of the measuring process and the ability to repeat the same measurement with consistently small variations (that is, no large discrepancies) in the measurements. The following figure depicts targets with hit marks for both a rifle and a shotgun and illustrates the concepts of precision and accuracy.

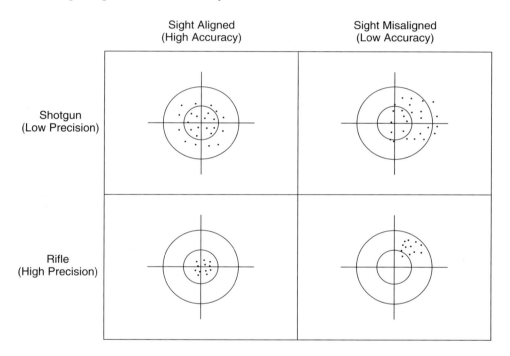

The concepts of accuracy and precision are also illustrated in the following example. A building wall known to be 157.22 ft long is measured by two methods. In the first case, the wall is measured very carefully using a fiberglass tape graduated to the closest 0.1 ft. The result of this operation is a measurement of 157.3 ft. In the second case, the wall is measured with the same care, but with a more precise steel tape graduated to the closest 0.01 ft. The result of this operation is a measurement of 157.23 ft. In this example, the more precise method (using the steel tape) resulted in the more accurate measurement:

| | "TRUE" DISTANCE | MEASURED DISTANCE | ERROR |
|---|---|---|---|
| Cloth tape | 157.22 | 157.3 | 0.08 |
| Steel tape | 157.22 | 157.23 | 0.01 |

It is conceivable, however, that more precise methods can result in less accurate answers. In the preceding example, if the steel tape had previously been broken and then incorrectly repaired (say, that an even foot had been dropped), the results would still be relatively precise but very inaccurate.

## 1.14 Accuracy Ratio

The *accuracy ratio* of a measurement or series of measurements is the ratio of error of closure to the distance measured. The *error of closure* is the difference between the measured location and the theoretically correct location. The theoretically correct location can be determined from repeated measurements or mathematical analysis. Since relevant systematic errors and mistakes can and should be eliminated from all survey measurements, the error of closure will be composed of random errors. To illustrate, a distance was measured and found to be 250.56 ft. The distance was previously known to be 250.50 ft. The error is 0.06 ft in a distance of 250.50 ft.

$$\text{Accuracy ratio} = 0.06/250.50 = 1/4{,}175 = 1/4{,}200$$

The accuracy ratio is expressed as a fraction whose numerator is unity and whose denominator is rounded to the closest 100 units.

Survey specifications are discussed in Chapter 10. Many land and engineering surveys have been performed in the past at 1/5,000 or 1/3,000 levels of accuracy. With the trend to polar layouts from coordinated control, accuracy ratios on the order of 1/10,000 and 1/20,000 are now often specified. It should be emphasized that **for each of these specified orders of accuracy, the techniques and instrumentation used must also be specified.** See Chapter 10 for survey specifications.

## 1.15 Errors

It can be said that no measurement (except for counting) can be free of error. For every measuring technique used, a more precise and potentially more accurate method can be found. For purposes of calculating errors, the "true" value is determined statistically after repeated measurements. In the simplest case, the true value for a distance is taken as the mean value for a series of repeated measurements. This topic is discussed further in Appendix A.

*Systematic errors* are defined as those errors whose magnitude and algebraic sign can be determined. The fact that these errors can be determined allows the surveyor to eliminate them from the measurements and thus improve the accuracy. An error due to the effects of temperature on a steel tape is an example of a systematic error. If the temperature is known, the shortening or lengthening effects on a steel tape can be determined precisely.

*Random errors* are associated with the skill and vigilance of the surveyor. Random (also known as accidental) errors are introduced into each measurement mainly because no human being can perform perfectly. Some random errors, by their very nature, tend to cancel themselves; when surveyors are skilled and careful in measuring, random errors will be of little significance except for high-precision surveys. However, random errors resulting from unskilled or careless work do cause problems. As noted earlier, random errors, even large random errors, tend to cancel themselves mathematically; this does not result in accurate work, only in work that appears to be accurate. Even if the random errors canceled exactly, the final averaged measurement will be imprecise.

## 1.16 Mistakes

Mistakes are blunders made by survey personnel. Examples of mistakes include transposing figures (recording a tape value of 68 as 86), miscounting the number of full tape lengths in a long measurement, measuring to or from the wrong point, and the like. Students should be aware that mistakes **will** occur. Mistakes must be discovered and eliminated, preferably by the people who made them. All survey measurements are suspect until they have been verified. Verification may be as simple as repeating the measurement, or verification can result from geometric or trigonometric analysis of related measurements. As a rule, **every** measurement is immediately checked or repeated. This immediate repetition enables the surveyor to eliminate most mistakes and, at the same time, improve the precision of the measurement.

## 1.17 Stationing

In surveying, measurements are sometimes taken along a baseline and at right angles to that baseline. Distances along a survey baseline are referred to as stations or chainages, and distances at right angles to the baseline (offset distances) are simple dimensions. The beginning of the survey baseline, the zero end, is denoted by 0 + 00; a point 100 ft (m) from the zero end is denoted as 1 + 00; a point 131.26 ft (m) from the zero end is 1 + 31.26; and so on. If the stationing is extended back of the 0 + 00 mark (rarely), the stations would be 0 − 50, − 1 + 00, and so on.

In the preceding discussion, the full stations are 100 ft (m) and the half-stations would be at even 50-ft intervals. In the metric system, 20-m intervals are often used as partial stations. With the changeover to metric units, most municipalities have kept the 100-unit station (that is, 1 + 00 = 100 meters), whereas many highway agencies have adopted the 1,000-unit station (i.e., 1 + 000 = 1,000 meters).

Figure 1.13 shows a building tied into the centerline (℄) of Elm Street. It also shows the ℄ (baseline) distances as stations and the offset distances as simple dimensions. The sketch also shows that 0 + 00 is the intersection of the centerlines of the two streets.

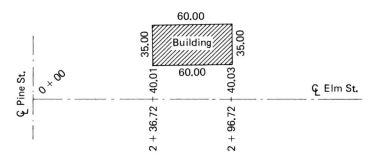

**FIGURE 1.13** Baseline stations and offset distances.

## 1.18 Field Notes

One of the most important aspects of traditional surveying is the taking of accurate, neat, legible, and complete field notes. After the survey has been completed, a plan is drawn from the survey notes, and the notes are then filed, often under lock and key. Modern surveys, employing electronic data collectors, automatically store point positioning angles and distances that will later be transferred to the computer. Surveyors have discovered that reliable field notes are also invaluable for these modern surveys. See Section 8.10 for more on this topic.

An experienced surveyor's notes will be complete, without redundancies, well arranged to aid in comprehension, and neat and legible to ensure that the correct information is conveyed. The surveyor will use sketches whenever necessary to aid in comprehension and in the ordering of data. Some students and inexperienced surveyors may find, at first, that it is very difficult to make accurate and neat field notes. The first few attempts at note keeping can be quite embarrassing to otherwise gifted students. There is a real temptation to scribble the notes on scraps of paper and then later, in a quiet and peaceful environment, to transcribe the scribbled notes neatly onto field note paper. This temptation must be resisted. **Notes cannot be copied without the occurrence of mistakes.**

Copied notes are not field notes and, as such, are outlawed in the surveying profession. Property and engineering surveyors sometimes find themselves in court testifying to the results of a survey. If the notes referred to in court are copied notes, the surveyor would, no doubt, be quickly excused from further participation in the proceedings. It may be a relatively rare occurrence to have to appear in court, but total reliance on the integrity of field notes is a daily requirement for surveyors and their associates. When surveyors are found to be copying or otherwise "cooking" notes, they are soon working elsewhere.

It is sometimes necessary to copy from field notes for other survey purposes. When notes are legitimately copied, they are placed on different-colored notepaper or similar notepaper with the word "copy" prominently placed on each page.

The field notes themselves are placed in bound field books or in loose-leaf field binders. The pages in bound field books are usually lined and columned on the left leaf and squared on the right leaf. The loose-leaf pages can be lined and columned or squared or in fact in any format required by the surveyor. A considerable advantage to using loose-leaf notebooks is that the notes for one project can be filed under that project heading. If a bound book is used for several projects, filing becomes difficult because several cross-references are required just to locate one set of project notes. Bound books are used to advantage on large projects such as highways and other heavy construction operations.

### BOUND BOOKS

1. Name, address, and phone number in ink on inside or outside cover.
2. Pages numbered throughout, right leaf only (most bound books have about 80 pages).
3. Room is left at the front of each book for the title, index, and diary.
4. Each project must show the date, title, surveyors' names, and instrument numbers.

**LOOSE-LEAF BOOKS**

1. Name, address, and phone number in ink on the binder.

2. Each page must be titled and dated, with identification by project number and surveyors' names, and instrument numbers.

**ALL FIELD NOTES**

1. Entries are to be in pencil in the range 2H to 4H. The harder pencil (4H) is more difficult to use but will not smear. The softer pencil (2H) is easy to use for most people but will smear somewhat if care is not exercised. Most surveyors use 2H or 3H lead. Pencils softer than 2H are not used in field notes.

2. All entries are neatly printed. Uppercase lettering can be reserved for emphasis, or it is sometimes used throughout.

3. All arithmetic computations are to be checked and signed.

4. Sketches are used to clarify the field notes. Although the sketches are not scale drawings, they are usually drawn roughly to scale to help order the inclusion of details.

5. Sketches are not freehand. Straightedges and curve templates are used for all line work.

6. Sketches are properly oriented by the inclusion of a north arrow (preferably pointing to the top of the page or to the left).

7. Avoid crowding information onto the page. This practice is one of the chief causes of poor notes.

8. Mistakes in the entry of **measured data** are to be carefully lined out, **not erased.**

9. Mistakes in entries other than measured data (for example, descriptions, sums, or products of measured data) may be erased and reentered neatly.

10. Show the word "COPY" at the top of copied pages.

11. Lettering on sketches is to be read from the bottom of the page or from the right side.

12. Measured data are to be entered in the field notes at the time the measurements are taken.

13. The note-keeper verifies all data by repeating them aloud as he or she is entering them in the notes. The surveyor who originally gave the data to the note-keeper will listen and respond to the verification call-out.

14. If the data on an entire page are to be voided, the word "VOID," together with a diagonal line, is placed on the page. A reference page number is shown for the location of the new data.

# 1.19    Field Management

Survey crews (parties) often comprise a party chief, an instrument operator, and one or two survey assistants; two-person crews are more common when modern electronic equipment is being used. The party chief is responsible for the operation of the survey crew and for the integrity of the work performed. The instrument operator is responsible for the operation and care of the instruments being used. He or she should be vigilant to ensure that any instrument maladjustment is immediately noted and corrected. The survey assistant helps perform the taping (chaining) measurements and the rod or prism work and maintains all equipment. In three-person crews, the party chief usually takes the lead in tape measurements and directs the operations in all types of surveys.

With the introduction of advanced electronic surveying techniques, however, the traditional survey crew is being considerably downsized. For example, total station surveys (Chapter 7) require only a surveyor (party chief), who operates the instrument and routinely "books" the survey data electronically, and an assistant, who holds the prism rod in the required locations. "Robotic" or motorized total stations can really be operated effectively with just one surveyor, who holds the prism rod and controls the motorized instrument with the remote controller. GPS surveys (see Chapter 11) can be carried out effectively by two surveyors, and in some applications, by just one roving surveyor.

## 1.20    Evolution of Surveying

Surveying is a profession with a very long history. Since the time when people first owned property, boundary markers have been required to distinguish one property from another. Historical records dating back almost 5,000 years show evidence of surveyors in China, India, Babylon, and Egypt. The Egyptian surveyor, called "harpedonapata" (rope-stretcher), was in constant demand because the Nile River flooded more or less continuously, destroying boundary markers in those fertile farmlands. The surveyors used ropes with knots tied at set graduations to measure distances.

Ropes were also used to lay out right angles. The early surveyors discovered that the 3:4:5 ratio provided right-angle triangles. To lay out *XZ* at 90 degrees to *XY* (see Figure 1.14), a 12-unit rope would have knots tied at 3- and 7-unit positions, as shown in the figure. One surveyor held the 3-unit knot at *X;* the second surveyor held the 7-unit knot at *Y.* The third surveyor held both loose ends of the rope and stretched the rope tightly, resulting in the location of point *Z*. These early surveyors knew that multiples of 3:4:5 (for example, 30:40:50) would produce more accurate positioning.

Another ancient surveying instrument consisted of three pieces of wood in the form of an isosceles triangle, with the base extended in both directions (see Figure 1.15). A plumb bob suspended from the apex of the frame would line up with a notch in the midpoint of the base—but only when the base was level. These levels came in various sizes, depending on the work being done.

It is presumed that the great pyramids were laid out with knotted ropes, the levels described here, and various forms of water trough levels for the foundations. These Egyptian surveying techniques were empirical solutions that were field-proven. It remained for the Greeks to provide the mathematical reasoning and proofs to explain why the field techniques worked. Pythagoras was one of many famous Greek mathematicians; he and his school developed theories of geometry and numbers (about 550 B.C.). They were also among the first to deduce that the earth is spherical by noting the shape of the earth's shadow cast on the moon. The word "geometry" derives from Greek, "geometria," meaning "to measure the earth," which shows clearly the relationship between mathematics and surveying. In fact, the history of surveying is closely related to the history of mathematics and astronomy.

By 250 B.C., Archimedes had recorded in a book known as the *Sand Reckoner* that the circumference of the earth is 30 myriads of stadia (that is, 300,000 stadia). He had

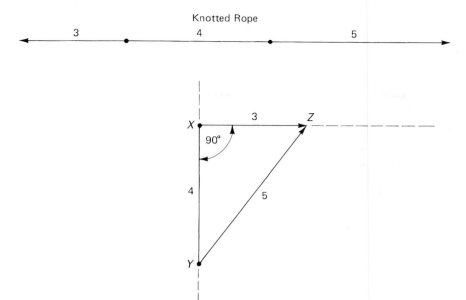

**FIGURE 1.14** Rope knotted at 3:4:5 ratio—used to place point Z at 90 degrees to point X from line XY.

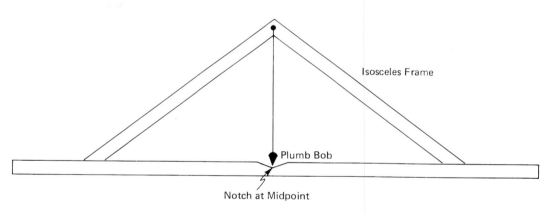

**FIGURE 1.15** Early Egyptian level.

received some support for this value from a friend, Eratosthenes, who was a mathematician and a librarian at the famous library of Alexandria in Egypt. According to some reports, Eratosthenes knew that a town called Syene (Aswan) was 5,000 stadia due south of Alexandria. He also knew that at summer solstice (around June 21), the sun was directly over Syene at noon because there were no shadows. The absence of shadows was demonstrated by noting that the sun's reflection was exactly centered in the water of a well.

Eratosthenes apparently reasoned that at the summer solstice, the sun, the towns of Syene and Alexandria, and the center of the earth all lay in the same plane (see Figure 1.16). At noon on the summer solstice, the elevation of the sun was measured at Alexandria at 82⅘ degrees, and the angle from the top of a rod to the sun was then calculated as 7⅕ degrees. Since the sun is such a long distance from the earth, it can be assumed that the sun's rays are parallel as they reach earth. With that assumption, it can be deduced that the angle from the top of the rod to the sun is the same as the angle at the earth's center: 7⅕ degrees. Because 7⅕ degrees is one-fiftieth of 360 degrees, it follows that the circular arc subtending 7⅕ degrees (the distance from Syene to Alexandria) is one-fiftieth of the circumference of the earth. The circumference of the earth is thus determined to be 250,000 stadia. If the stadium being used was one-tenth of a mile (different values for the

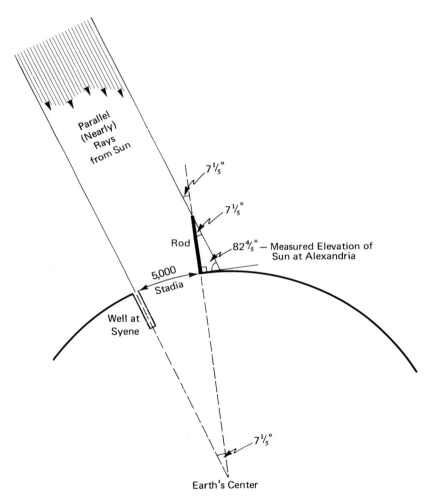

**FIGURE 1.16** Illustration of Eratosthenes' technique for computing the earth's circumference.

stadium existed, but one value was roughly one-tenth of our mile), then it is possible that Eratosthenes calculated the earth's circumference to be 25,000 miles. Using the Clarke ellipsoid with a mean radius of 3,960 miles, the circumference of the earth would actually be $C = 2 \times 3.1416 \times 3,960 = 24,881$ miles. Regardless of the accuracy of Eratosthenes' calculation, it does show an ingenious approach to the problem.

After the Greeks, the Romans made good use of practical surveying techniques to construct roadways, aqueducts, and military camps for many centuries. Some Roman roads and aqueducts remain to this day. For leveling, the Romans used a "chorobate," a 20-ft wooden structure with plumbed end braces and a 5-ft groove for a water trough (see Figure 1.17). Linear measurements were often made with wooden poles 10 to 17 ft long. With the fall of the Roman Empire, surveying and most other intellectual endeavors became lost arts in the Western world.

Renewed interest in intellectual pursuits may have been fostered by explorers, who needed navigational skills. The lodestone, a naturally magnetized rock (magnetite), was first used to locate magnetic north. Later, the compass would be used for navigation on land and water. In the mid-1500s, the surveyors' chain was first used in the Netherlands, and an Englishman, Thomas Digges, first used the term "theodolite" to describe an instrument, graduated in 360 degrees, that was used to measure angles. By 1590, the *Plane Table* (a combined positioning and plotting device) was created by Jean Praetorius. It wasn't very different from the plane tables used in the early 1900s. The telescope was invented in 1609 by Galileo (among others). The telescope, attached to a quadrant (an angle-measuring device), allowed triangulation (see Section 5.14), a simple method of determining long distances. Jean Picard (1620–1682) was apparently the first to use a spider-web cross hair in

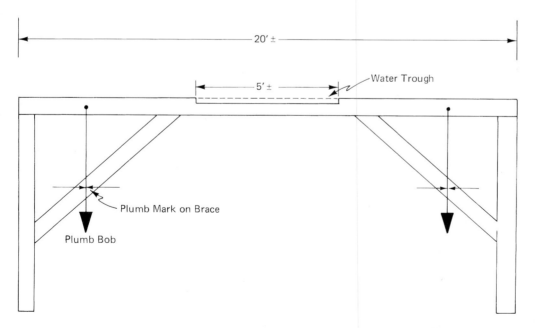

**FIGURE 1.17**   Roman level (chorobate).

a telescope. He also used vernier scales to improve the precision of angular measurement. James Watt (1736–1819), who invented the steam engine, is also credited with being the first to install stadia hairs in the survey telescope.

The first dumpy levels were devised in the first half of the 1700s by combining a telescope with a bubble level. The repetition style of theodolite (see Section H.2.2) was seen in Europe in the mid-1800s, but it soon lost favor because scale imperfections were causing large cumulative errors. Direction theodolites were favored because high accuracy could be achieved by reading angles at different positions on the scales, thus eliminating the effect of scale imperfections. Refinements to theodolites continued over the years with better optics, micrometers, coincidence reading, lighter materials, and so on. Heinrich Wild is credited with many significant improvements to theodolites in the early 1900s. These improvements had a great impact on the designs of most European survey instruments produced by the Wild, Kern, and Zeiss companies.

Meanwhile, in the United States, William J. Young of Philadelphia invented the transit in 1831. The shortened telescope of this instrument permitted the telescope to revolve (transit) on its axis. This simple but brilliant adaptation permitted the surveyor to produce straight lines accurately simply by sighting the backsight and transiting the telescope forward (see Section 5.11). When this technique was repeated—once with the telescope in the normal position and once with the telescope inverted—many of the potential errors (scale graduation imperfections, cross-hair misalignment, standards, etc.) in the instrument could be removed by averaging.

Use of a repeating instrument meant that angles could be quickly and accurately accumulated (see Section 5.8). The transit proved to be superior for North American surveying needs. If the emphasis in European surveying was on precise control surveys, the emphasis in North America was on enormous railroad and canal construction projects and vast public land surveys, all occasioned by the influx of immigrants. The American repeating transit—fast to use, practical, and accurate—was thus a significant factor in the development of North America (see Appendix H). It wasn't until the 1950s and 1960s that this vernier transit received strong competition from European and Japanese repeating instruments, which were characterized by micrometer or scale readouts (most with 10- or 20-second least count) and optical plummets. These optical instruments are now being replaced by electronic theodolites and total stations.

Electronic distance measurement (EDM) was first introduced by Geodimeter, Inc., in the 1950s. It and GPS have almost completely replaced triangulation for control-survey distance measurements and the steel tape for all but short distances in boundary and engineering surveys. Aerial surveys became very popular after World War II. This technique is a very efficient method of performing large-scale topographic surveys and is used for most of them, although total station surveys now are competitive at lower levels of detail density.

In the late 1980s, the total station instrument was thought to be the ultimate in surveying instrumentation. It meant electronic data collection of angles, distances, and descriptive data with transfer to a computer and plans drawn by a digital plotter could occur on the same day. Now, with the wider use of global positioning system (GPS) receivers, many more applications are being introduced. (See Chapter 12 for this remarkable procedure.)

# 2 Distance Measurement (Taping)

## 2.1 Methods of Distance Determination

There are two ways to locate the position of a topographic feature in relation to other topographic features. First, the position of each feature can be directly captured using GPS techniques and/or by remote sensing data capture (see Chapters 11 and 12). Second, topographic features can be related to each other by measuring between them or by measuring from any number of topographic features to some common baseline or control net. This chapter focuses on the latter technique using a steel tape. We saw in Chapter 1 that the early Egyptians used knotted ropes to measure property lines *directly* after each flooding of the Nile River. That technique illustrates the direct application of a measuring standard against the distance to be measured; more recent measuring techniques employ fiberglass or steel tapes to measure a distance directly. In addition to these direct methods of distance determination, there are several *indirect* (or *tacheometric*) methods of determining distances. These techniques (also discussed briefly below) use related measurements to deduce the required distance. Distances can also be determined using geometric or trigonometric computations working with related distance and angle measurements. Finally, ground distances can be roughly determined by simply measuring distances on a scaled map or plan and then converting the scaled distances to their ground equivalents.

## 2.2 Distance Measurement: General Background

### 2.2.1 Pacing

Pacing is a very useful (although imprecise) technique of distance measurement. Surveyors can determine the length of pace that, for them, can be comfortably repeated. An individual's length of pace can be determined by repeatedly pacing between two marks a set distance apart (say, 100 ft or 30 m). Pacing is particularly useful when looking for previously set survey markers. The plan distance from a found marker to another marker can be paced off so that the marker can be located, either visually using a magnetic or electronic bar locator or by digging with a shovel. Pacing is also very useful when checking the positions of property and construction layout markers. When carefully done on a horizontal surface, pacing can result in accuracies of 1:100.

## 2.2.2 Odometer

When beginning a survey, the surveyor often has to distinguish between fence lines adjacent to a road. The automobile odometer can be quite useful in measuring directly from a known corner to the fence-marked property lines that define the area to be surveyed. Also, a measuring wheel (12″–24″ diameter) equipped with an odometer can be used in traffic investigations to measure distances at an accident scene. Such measuring wheels are used by assessors and other real-estate personnel to record property frontages and areas.

## 2.2.3 Electronic Distance Measurement (EDM)

EDM instruments send a light wave or microwave along the path to be measured and then measure the phase differences between the transmitted and received signals. In the case of microwaves, identical instruments (one transmitting and one receiving) are positioned at each end of the line to be measured. In the case of light waves, only one instrument is required, with a reflecting prism located at the other end of the line. Over short distances in some applications, light waves can be reflected back to the instrument right from the measured object itself. Many of these instruments employ pulsed laser emissions, and the distance determination here depends on the measurement of the time sequence between transmission and reception of the laser signals. Figure 2.1 shows a handheld laser instrument

**FIGURE 2.1** Handheld laser. (Courtesy Leica Geosystems, Markham, Ontario)

(Leica's Disto) that utilizes a visible laser beam to measure distances indoors or outdoors up to a range of 100 m, with accuracies approaching 3 mm. See Chapter 7 for more discussion of EDM techniques.

## 2.3 Tacheometry

Tacheometry is a general term used to describe techniques of indirect measurement using angle-measuring instruments (e.g., theodolites) and graduated rods or bars.

### 2.3.1 Stadia

Stadia is a form of indirect measurement that uses a telescopic cross-hair configuration to assist in determining distances. Additional cross hairs (stadia hairs) are positioned in the telescope an equal distance above and below the main cross hair so that when the interval (as measured on a leveling rod) between the upper and lower stadia hairs is multiplied by a constant (usually 100), the ground distance is determined. Additional treatment is required for inclined sightings.

### 2.3.2 Subtense Bar

A subtense bar is a tripod-mounted bar with targets precisely 2.000 meters apart. The subtense bar is set over a point, leveled, and then turned so that it is precisely perpendicular to the sight from a precise (one-second angle reading minimum) theodolite. The bar has a sighting device that permits the theodolite operator to determine perpendicularity. The device is reasonably accurate over short ($\leq$ 500 ft) distances. Figure 2.2 shows the geometry involved in this indirect distance determination. The horizontal distance $= 1/\tan \frac{1}{2}\alpha = \cot \frac{1}{2}\alpha$. Since the angle $\alpha$ is the measurement between the vertical planes containing the subtense bar targets, the distance obtained is always the horizontal distance, regardless of the angle of inclination to the targets. EDM instruments have now replaced the subtense bar for field measurements, but the device continues to be useful as a calibration tool in electronic three-dimensional positioning. This advance uses electronic theodolites, interfaced to a computer, to position manufacturing components (e.g., welding robots) precisely on assembly lines.

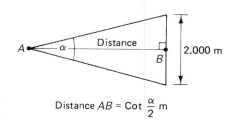

Distance $AB = \text{Cot } \frac{\alpha}{2}$ m

**FIGURE 2.2** Subtense bar.

## 2.4 Gunter's Chain

When North America was first surveyed (in the 18th and 19th centuries), the distance measuring device in use was the Gunter's chain. It was 66 ft long and was comprised of 100 links. The length of 66 ft was apparently chosen because of its relationships to other units in the Imperial System:

$$80 \text{ chains} = 1 \text{ mile}$$
$$10 \text{ square chains} = 1 \text{ acre } (10 \times 66^2 = 43{,}560 \text{ ft}^2)$$
$$4 \text{ rods} = 1 \text{ chain}$$

Many of North America's old plans and deeds contain measurements in chains and links, so surveyors occasionally have to convert these distances to feet or meters for current projects.

> ■ **EXAMPLE 2.1**
> An old plan shows a dimension of 3 chains, 83 links. Convert this value to (a) feet and (b) meters.
> **Solution**
> (a) $3.83 \times 66 = 252.78$ ft
> (b) $3.83 \times 66 \times 0.3048 = 77.047$ m

## 2.5 Taping

### 2.5.1 Fiberglass and Cloth Tapes

For precise tape measuring, steel tapes are always used. For the many applications where a lower precision is acceptable, however, various types of tapes are used. In the past, cloth tapes (some with copper strand reinforcement) were used for this type of measurement. Cloth tapes tended to stretch somewhat when wet, but they were still acceptable for less precise measurements (for example, topographic tie-ins, fencing measurements, etc.). More recently, the fiberglass tape has become popular due to its ruggedness and consistency (see Figure 2.3).

### 2.5.2 Steel Tapes

Steel tapes are manufactured in both foot and metric units and come in various lengths, markings, and weights. In foot units, tapes come in many lengths, but the 100-ft length is the most commonly used. Tapes are also used in 200-ft and 300-ft lengths for special applications. In metric units, the most commonly used tape length is 30 meters, although lengths of 20 m, 50 m, and 100 m can also be obtained.

Steel tapes come in two common cross sections: heavy duty is 8 mm × 0.45 mm, or $\frac{5}{16}$ in. × 0.18 in.; normal usage is 6 mm × 0.30 mm, or $\frac{1}{4}$ in. × 0.012 in. Metric tapes are now being introduced for some applications in the United States; in Canada, they have

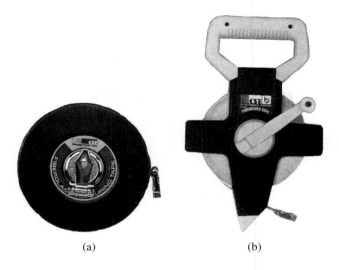

(a)                                    (b)

**Graduated in 10ths and Metric**

| 7 | 8 | 9 | 1 | F | 1 |

| 0·2 | ▲ | 0·3 |

Printed on two sides—one side in 10ths and 100ths of a foot; the second side in metric with increments in meters, cm, and 2 mm.

**Graduated in 8ths and Metric**

| 8 | 9 | 10 | 11 | 1 | F | 1 |

| 0·2 | ▲ | 0·3 |

Printed on two sides—one side in feet, inches, and 8ths; the second side in metric with increments in meters, cm, and 2 mm.

(c)

(d)

**FIGURE 2.3**   Fiberglass tapes. (a) Closed case. (b) Open reel. (c) Tape graduations. (d) Steel tape and plumb bob. (Courtesy of CST/Berger, Illinois)

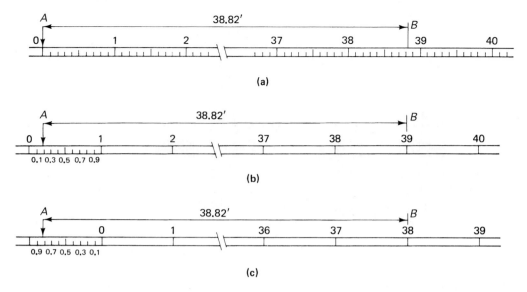

**FIGURE 2.4** Various tape markings (hundredth marks not shown). (a) Fully graduated tape. (b) Cut tape. (c) Add tape.

been in full use for several decades. The 100-ft tape and the 30-m tapes have similar handling characteristics (see Section 2.8).

Generally, the heavy-duty tapes (drag tapes) are used in route surveys (e.g., highways, railroads) and are designed for use off the reel. Leather thongs are tied through the eyelets at both ends of the tape to aid in measuring. The lighter-weight tapes can be used on (usually) or off the reel and are usually found in municipal and structural surveys. If they are used on the reel, the wind-up handle can be flipped over to contact the handle-frame and serve as a brake, thus assisting in the measuring process [see Figures 2.3(b) and 2.3(d)].

Steel tapes are usually graduated in one of three ways (see Figure 2.4):

1. Preferred by many, this tape is graduated throughout in feet and hundredths (0.01) of a foot or in meters and millimeters; see Figures 2.4(a) and 2.3(d).
2. The cut tape is marked throughout in feet, with the first and last foot graduated in tenths and hundredths of a foot; see Figure 2.4(b). The metric tape is marked throughout in meters and decimeters, with the first and last decimeters further graduated in millimeters. A measurement is made between two points with the cut tape by one surveyor holding that even foot (decimeter) mark on one point, which allows the other surveyor to read the graduations on the first foot (or decimeter) on the other point. For example, in Figure 2.4(b), the distance from $A$ to $B$ is determined by holding 39 ft at $B$ and reading 0.18 at $A$. Distance $AB = 38.82$ ft (i.e., 39 ft "cut" 0.18 = 38.82). Each measurement involves this "cut" subtraction from the even foot or meter mark being held at the far end of the measurement. Extra care is needed here to avoid subtraction mistakes.

3. The add tape is similarly marked, except that an additional foot or decimeter is placed before the zero mark at the beginning of the tape. In Figure 2.4(c), the distance from A to B is determined by holding 38 ft at B and reading 0.82 at A. Thus, distance AB is 38.82 ft (i.e., 38 "add" 0.82).

## 2.6 Taping Accessories

### 2.6.1 Plumb Bob

Plumb bobs are normally made of brass and weigh from 8 oz to 18 oz, with the 10 oz and 12 oz plumb bobs most widely used [see Figure 2.3(d)]. Plumb bobs came with about six ft of string and a sharp, replaceable screw-on point. Plumb bobs are used in taping to permit the surveyor to hold the tape horizontal when the ground is sloping. A graduation mark on the horizontal tape can be transferred down to a point on the ground using the plumb bob string. A graduation can be read on the tape as the plumb bob string is moved until the plumb bob is directly over the ground mark being measured. (See Figure 2.5.) Also, a plumb bob (with or without a string-mounted target) can be used to provide precise theodolite sightings.

### 2.6.2 Hand Level

Hand levels [see Figure 2.6(a)] are small rectangular or cylindrical sighting tubes equipped with tubular bubbles and horizontal cross hairs that permit the surveyor to make low-precision horizontal sightings. The bubble location and the cross hair can be viewed together via a 45° mounted mirror. Hand levels can be used to assist the surveyor in keeping the tape horizontal while the tape is held off the ground. The hand level is held by the surveyor at the lower elevation and a sight is taken on the uphill surveyor, who is used as a measuring standard. For example, if the lower elevation surveyor is sighting horizontally at the other surveyor's waist, and if both are roughly the same height, then the surveyor with the hand level is lower than his or her partner by the distance from his eye to his waist. See Figure 2.6(b). The low end of the tape is held up in the air that distance (say, 1.8 ft or 0.55 m) and, using a plumb bob, the distance is measured and recorded.

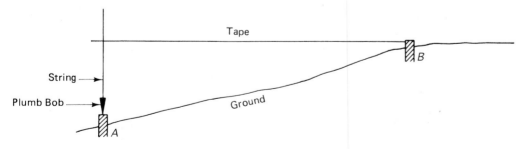

**FIGURE 2.5** Use of a plumb bob.

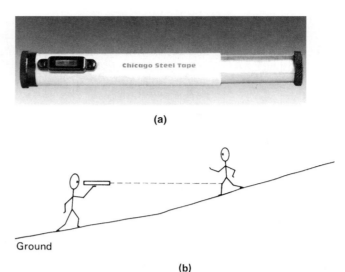

**FIGURE 2.6** (a) Hand level. Ground
(b) Hand-level application.
(Courtesy of CST/Berger)

(a)

(b)

## 2.6.3 Clinometer

The clinometer is essentially a hand level with an attached protractor, which permits the determination of low-precision (closest 10 minutes of arc) angle readings. The clinometer can be used as a hand level or it can be used to determine slope angles [see Figure 2.7(a)].

■ **EXAMPLE 2.2**

How can you determine the height of a building using a clinometer and a tape?

**Solution**

To determine the height of a building, set 45° on the protractor scale and then move backward or forward until the top of the structure is sighted on the cross hair. At the same time, the bubble (mounted on the protractor) will appear to be superimposed on the cross hair. Refer to Figure 2.7(b), where you can see that the height of the building is $h_1 + h_2$. Also, from trigonometry, we know that the tan of 45° is 1 (this is an isosceles triangle), so the distance from the observer's eye to the building wall is equal to $h_1$. This distance can be measured with a tape and then added to the tape-measured distance from the eye-height mark on the wall down to the ground ($h_2$) to arrive at the overall building height. Similar techniques can be used to determine electrical conductor heights.

The clinometer is also useful when working on route surveys where long tapes (e.g., 300 ft or 100 m) are being used. The long tape can be held, mostly supported, on the ground and the slope angle can be taken for each tape length. By having the long tape mostly supported, the tension requirements can be reduced to a comfortable level. See Figure 2.7(c).

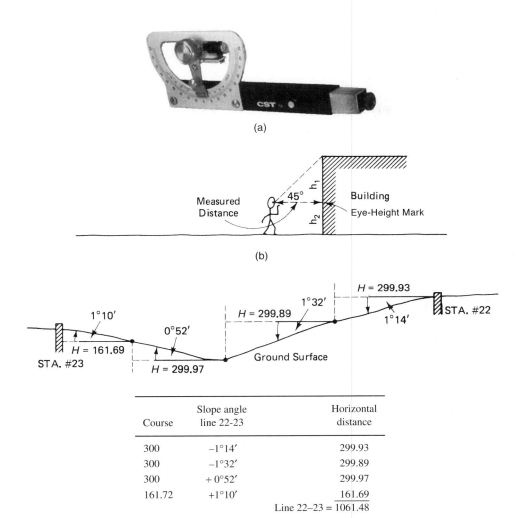

(a)

(b)

(c)

| Course | Slope angle line 22-23 | Horizontal distance |
|--------|------------------------|---------------------|
| 300 | −1°14′ | 299.93 |
| 300 | −1°32′ | 299.89 |
| 300 | + 0°52′ | 299.97 |
| 161.72 | +1°10′ | 161.69 |
| | Line 22–23 = | 1061.48 |

**FIGURE 2.7**  (a) Abney hand level; scale graduated in degrees with a vernier reading to 10 minutes. (Courtesy of Keuffel & Esser Co.). (b) Abney hand-level application in height determination. (c) Abney hand-level typical application in taping.

## 2.6.4  Additional Accessories

Range poles are 6-ft or 8-ft wood or steel poles with steel points. These poles are usually painted alternately red and white in 1-ft sections [see Figure 2.8(a)]. These poles can be used in taping to help with alignment for distances longer than one tape length. The pole is set behind the measurement terminal point. The rear tape person can keep the forward tape person on line by simply sighting on the pole and then moving the forward tape person left

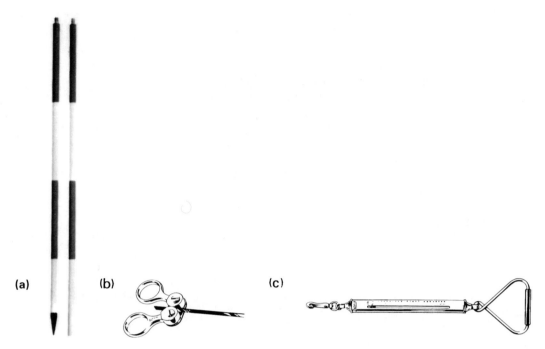

**(a)**　　　**(b)**　　　　　　　　　　**(c)**

**FIGURE 2.8**　Taping accessories. (a) Two-section range pole. (b) Tape clamp handle. (c) Tension handle.

or right until she or he is on line. The range pole can be used to provide a transit/theodolite sighting for angle and line work.

The clamp handle [see Figure 2.8(b)] helps the surveyor to grip the tape at any intermediate point without kinking the tape. The tension handle [see Figure 2.8(c)] is used in precise work to ensure that the correct tension is being applied. It is usually graduated to 30 lbs in ½-lb increments. With metric tapes, the relationship 50 N = 11.24 lbs is useful.

Chaining pins (marking arrows) come in a set of eleven. They are painted alternately red and white and are 14 to 18 in. long. Chaining pins are used to mark intermediate points on the ground while making long measurements. The chaining pin is set sloping 45° to the ground and at right angles to the direction of measurement. Sloping the pin permits precise measurement with a plumb bob to the point where the pin enters the ground.

## 2.7　Taping Techniques

The measurement begins with the head surveyor carrying the zero end of the tape forward toward the final point, until the tape has been unwound. At this point, the rear surveyor calls "tape" to alert the head surveyor to stop walking and to prepare for measuring. If a drag tape is used, the tape is removed from the reel and a leather thong is attached to the reel end to facilitate measuring. If the tape is not designed to come off the reel, the winding handle is folded to the lock position and the reel is used to help hold the tape. The head surveyor is put on line by the rear surveyor, who is sighting forward to a range pole or other target that has been erected at the final mark. In very precise work, the intermediate marks can be aligned by transit. The rear surveyor holds the appropriate graduation (e.g., 100.00 ft or 30.000 m) against the mark from which the measurement is being taken. The head surveyor, after ensuring that the tape is straight, slowly increases tension to the proper amount and then marks the ground with a chaining pin or other market. Once the mark has been made, both surveyors repeat the measuring procedure to check the measurement. If necessary, adjustments are made and the check procedure is repeated. See Figure 2.9.

If the ground is not level (determined by estimation or by the use of a hand level), one or both surveyors must use a plumb bob (see Figure 1.5). Normally, the only occasion when both surveyors have to use plumb bobs is when the ground rises or obstacles exist between the two surveyors (see Figure 2.10). Because of the additional random errors introduced when plumbing, plumb bobs are not used unless it is necessary. Figure 2.11 shows the relationship of the slope and the horizontal and vertical distances between any two points.

When plumbing, the tape is usually held at waist height, although any height between the shoulders and the ground is common. Holding the tape above shoulder height

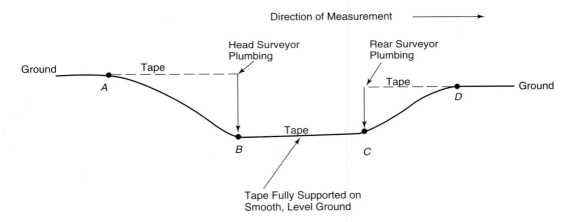

**FIGURE 2.9**  Horizontal taping; plumb bob used at one end.

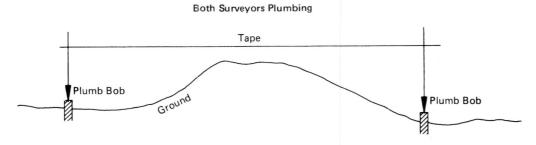

**FIGURE 2.10**  Horizontal taping; plumb bob used at both ends.

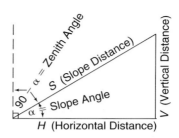

**FIGURE 2.11** Relationship among slope, horizontal, and vertical distances.

creates more chance for error because the surveyor must move his or her eyes up and down to include the ground mark and tape graduation in the field of view. The plumb bob string is usually held on the tape with the left thumb (in the case of right-handed people). You must take care not to cover the graduation mark completely. As the tension is increased, it is common for the surveyor to sometimes take up some of the tension with the left thumb, causing it to slide along the tape. If the graduations have been covered with the left thumb, the surveyor is often not aware that the thumb (and string) has moved, resulting in an erroneous measurement. When plumbing, it is advisable to hold the tape close to the body and thus provide good leverage for applying or holding tension and to transfer accurately from tape to ground, and vice versa.

If the rear surveyor is using a plumb bob, he or she shouts out "tape," "mark," or some other sign that, at that instant, the plumb bob is steady and over the mark. If the head surveyor is also using a plumb bob, he or she must wait to take a reading until both plumb bobs are simultaneously over their respective marks.

You will discover that plumbing is a challenging aspect of taping. You will likely encounter difficulty in holding the plumb bob steady over the point and at the same time applying appropriate tension. To help steady the plumb bob, it is held only a short distance above the mark and is repeatedly touched down. This momentary touching down will dampen the plumb bob oscillations and generally steady the plumb bob. Don't allow the plumb bob to rest on the point because this will result in an erroneous measurement.

In practice, most measurements are taken with the tape held horizontally. If the slope is too great to allow an entire tape length to be employed, shorter increments will be measured until all the required distance has been measured. This operation is known as *breaking tape* (see Figure 2.12). The sketch shows distance AB, composed of increments *AL LM*, and *MB*. The exception to the foregoing occurs when preliminary route surveys (for example, electricity transmission lines) are performed using a 300-ft (100-m) steel tape. It is customary to measure slope distances, which allows the surveyors to keep this

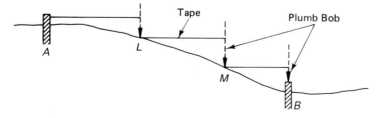

**FIGURE 2.12** Breaking tape.

relatively heavy tape more or less fully supported on the ground. To allow for reduction to the horizontal, each tape length is accompanied by its slope angle, usually determined by using a clinometer (also known as an Abney hand level). See Figure 2.7(c).

In summary, the rear surveyor handles the following tasks:

1. Visually aligns the head surveyor by sighting to a range pole or other target placed at the forward station.
2. Holds the tape on the mark, either directly or with the aid of a plumb bob. If a plumb bob is being used, the rear surveyor will repeatedly call out "tape," "mark," or a similar word to signify to the head surveyor that, for that instant in time, the plumb bob (tape mark) is precisely over the station.
3. Calls out the station and tape reading for each measurement and listens for verification from the head surveyor as the information is being entered in the field book or data collector.
4. Keeps a count of all full tape lengths included in each overall measurement.
5. Maintains the equipment (e.g., wipes the tape clean at the conclusion of the day's work or as conditions warrant).

The head surveyor is responsible for these tasks:

1. Carries the tape forward and ensures that the tape is free of loops, which could lead to tape breakage.
2. Prepares the ground surface for the mark (e.g., clears away grass, leaves, etc.).
3. Applies proper tension after first ensuring that the tape is straight.
4. Places marks (chaining pins, wood stakes, iron bars, nails, rivets, cut crosses, etc.).
5. Takes and records measurements of distances, temperature, and other factors.

## 2.8 Standard Conditions for the Use of Steel Tapes

Since steel tapes can give different measurements when used under various tension, support, and temperature conditions, it is necessary to provide standards for their use. Standard taping conditions are shown below:

**FOOT SYSTEM, 100-FT STEEL TAPE**
1. Temperature = 68°F
2. Tape fully supported
3. Tape under a tension of 10 lbs

**METRIC SYSTEM, 30.000-M STEEL TAPE**
1. Temperature = 20°C
2. Tape fully supported
3. Tape under a tension of 50 N (Newtons) Since a 1 lb force = 4.448 N, 50 N = 11.24 lbs.

In the real world of field surveying, the above noted standard conditions seldom occur at the same time. The temperature is usually something other than standard, and in many instances the tape cannot be fully supported (one end of the tape is often held off the ground to keep it horizontal). If the tape is not fully supported, the tension of 10 lbs does not apply. When standard conditions are not present, systematic errors will be introduced into the tape measurements. The following sections illustrate how these systematic errors and random errors are treated.

## 2.9   Taping Corrections: General Background

As noted in Chapter 1, no measurements can be performed perfectly, so all measurements (except for counting) must contain some errors. Surveyors must use measuring techniques that will minimize random errors to acceptable levels, and they must make corrections to systematic errors that can affect the accuracy of the survey. Typical taping errors are summarized below:

| SYSTEMATIC TAPING ERRORS | RANDOM TAPING ERRORS |
|---|---|
| 1. Slope | 1. Slope |
| 2. Erroneous length | 2. Temperature |
| 3. Temperature | 3. Tension and Sag |
| 4. Tension and sag | 4. Alignment |
| | 5. Marking and Plumbing |

## 2.10   Systematic Slope Corrections

As noted in the previous section, taping is usually performed by keeping the tape horizontal. In some situations, however, distances are deliberately measured on a slope and then converted to their horizontal equivalents. To convert slope distances to horizontal distances, either the slope angle ($\alpha$) or the vertical distance (difference in elevation) must also be known (see Figure 2.11).

$$\frac{H \,(\text{horizontal})}{S \,(\text{slope})} = \cos \alpha \qquad \text{or} \qquad H = S \cos \alpha \qquad (2.1)$$

$$\frac{H}{S} = \sin (90 - \alpha) \qquad \text{or} \qquad H = S \sin (90 - \alpha) \qquad (2.1a)$$
$$(\text{where } (90 - \alpha) \text{ is the zenith angle})$$

When the vertical distance or difference in elevation is known, the expression becomes:

$$H^2 = S^2 - V^2 \qquad \text{or} \qquad H = \sqrt{S^2 - V^2} \qquad (2.2)$$

Slope can also be expressed as a *gradient*, or rate of grade. The gradient is expressed as a ratio of the vertical distance over the horizontal distance. When this ratio is multiplied by 100, it is called a percentage gradient. For example, if the ground rises 1 ft (m) in 100 ft (m), it is said to have a +1% slope (i.e., 1/100 × 100 = 1). If the ground falls 2.6 ft (m) in 195.00 ft (m), it is said to have a slope of −1.33%. If the elevation of a point on a gradient is known, the elevation of any other point on the gradient can be calculated. See Example 2.3.

## ■ EXAMPLE 2.3

A road centerline (℄) gradient falls from station 0 + 00 (elevation = 564.22 ft) to station 1 + 50 at a rate of −2.5%. What is the ℄ elevation at station 1 + 50?

**Solution**

| Station | Elevation |
|---------|-----------|
| 0 + 00 | 564.22 ft |
| (Gradient = −2.5%) | |
| 1 + 50 | Required |

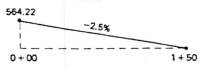

Difference in elevation = 150 (2.5/100) = −3.75

Elevation at 1 + 50 = (564.22 − 3.75) = 560.47 ft

If the elevations of at least two points on a grade line are known, as well as the distances between them, the slope gradient can be determined:

## ■ EXAMPLE 2.4

A road ℄ runs from station 1 + 00 (elevation = 471.37 ft) to station 4 + 37.25 (elevation = 476.77 ft). What is the slope of the ℄ grade line?

**Solution**

| Station | Elevation |
|---------|-----------|
| 1 + 00 | 471.37 |
| 4 + 37.25 | 476.77 |

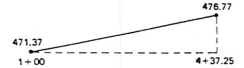

Elevation difference = +5.40

Distance = 337.25

Gradient = (+5.40/337.25)100 = +1.60%

## ■ EXAMPLE 2.5 *Slope Corrections*

(a) The slope distance (S) and slope angle (α), or the zenith angle (90° − α) are given. A slope distance between two points is 78.22 ft and the slope angle is 1° 20′ (the equivalent zenith angle is 88° 40′). What is the corresponding horizontal distance?

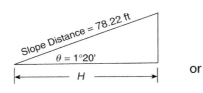

or

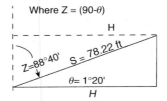

(b) The slope distance (S) and the gradient (slope percentage) are given. A slope rises from one point, a distance of 156.777 m, to another point at a rate of +1.5%, What is the corresponding horizontal distance (H) between the points?

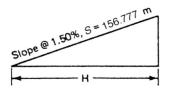 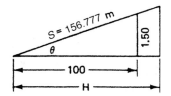

(c) The slope distance (S) and difference in elevation (V) are given. Calculate the horizontal distance (H).

(d) The slope distance between two points is found to be 83.52 ft, and the vertical distance is found to be 3.1 ft. What is the horizontal distance between the two points?

**Solution**

(a) $H/S = \cos \alpha$      $H/S = \sin Z$

 $H = S \cos \alpha$      $H = S \sin Z$

 $H = 78.22 \cos 1° 20'$    $H = 78.22 \sin 88° 40'$

 $H = 78.20$ ft      $H = 78.20$ ft

(b) $1.50/100 = \tan \alpha$

 $\alpha = 0.85937°$

 $H/156.777 = \cos 0.85937°$

 $H = 156.777 \cos 0.85937°$

 $H = 156.759$ m

(c) The slope distance between two points is measured to be 199.908 m and the vertical distance between the points (i.e., the difference in elevation) is +2.435 m. What is the horizontal distance (H) between the points?

 $H^2 = S^2 = V^2$

 $H = \sqrt{199.908^2 - 2.435^2}$

 $H = 199.893$ m

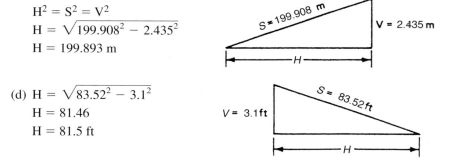

(d) $H = \sqrt{83.52^2 - 3.1^2}$

 $H = 81.46$

 $H = 81.5$ ft

Usually, the solution is rounded to the same number of decimals shown in the least precise measurement.

# 2.11   Erroneous Tape Length Corrections

For all but precise work, tapes supplied by the manufacturer are considered to be correct under standard conditions. Through extensive use, tapes do become kinked and stretched, and in need of repair. The length can become something other than that specified. When this occurs, the tape must be corrected, or the measurements taken with the erroneous tape must be corrected.

### ■ EXAMPLE 2.6

A measurement was recorded as 171.278 m with a 30-m tape that was only 29.996 m under standard conditions. What is the corrected measurement?

**Solution**

Correction per tape length $= -0.004$

Number of times the tape was used $= 171.278/30$

Total correction $= -0.004 \times 171.278/30$

$\qquad\qquad\qquad = -0.023$ m

Corrected distance $= 171.278 - 0.023 = 171.255$ m

or

$$= 29.996/30 \times 171.278 = 171.255 \text{ m}$$

### ■ EXAMPLE 2.7

You must lay out the front corners of a building: a distance of 210.08 ft. The tape to be used is known to be 100.02 ft under standard conditions.

**Solution**

Correction per tape length $= 0.02$ ft

Number of times that the tape is to be used $= 2.1008$

Total correction $= 0.02 \times 2.1008 = +0.04$ ft

When the problem involves a layout distance, the sign of the correction must be reversed before being applied to the layout measurement. We must find the distance that, when corrected by $+0.04$, will give 210.08 ft, i.e., $210.08 - 0.04 = 210.04$ ft. This is the distance to be laid out with that tape (100.02 ft) so that the corner points will be exactly 210.08 ft apart.

You will discover that four variations of this problem are possible: correcting a measured distance while using (1) a long tape or (2) a short tape, or precorrecting a layout distance using (3) a long tape or (4) a short tape. To minimize confusion about the sign of the correction, you must consider the problem with the distance reduced to only one tape length (100 ft or 30 m).

In Example 2.6, a recorded distance of 171.278 m was measured with a tape only 29.996 m long. The total correction was found to be 0.023 m. If doubt exists about the sign of 0.023, ask yourself what the procedure would be for correcting only one tape length. In Example 2.6, after one tape length had been measured, it would have been recorded that 30 m had been measured. If the tape were only 29.996 m long, then the field book entry of

30 m must be corrected by −0.004 m. The magnitude of the tape error is determined by comparing the tape with a tape that has been certified (National Bureau of Standards, Gaithersburg, Maryland; or the National Research Council, Ottawa, Ontario, Canada). In practice, tapes that require corrections for ordinary work are either repaired or discarded.

## 2.12 Temperature Corrections

Section 2.6 notes the conditions under which tape manufacturers specify the accuracy of their tapes. One of these standard conditions is that of temperature. In the United States and Canada, tapes are standardized at 68°F, or 20°C. Temperatures other than standard result in an erroneous tape length.

The thermal coefficient of the expansion of steel (k) is 0.00000645 per unit length per degree Fahrenheit (°F), or 0.0000116 per unit length per degree Celsius °C. The general formula is:

$$C_t = k(T - T)L$$

For foot units, the formula is:

$$C_t = 0.00000645(T - 68)L$$

where $C_t$ = correction due to temperature, in feet
   $T$ = temperature of tape (°F) during measurement
   $L$ = distance measured, in feet

For metric units, the formula is:

$$C_t = 0.0000116(T - 20)L$$

where $C_t$ = correction due to temperature, in meters
   $T$ = temperature of tape (°C) during measurement
   $L$ = distance measured, in meters

### ■ EXAMPLE 2.8

A distance was recorded as being 471.37 ft at a temperature of 38°F. What is the distance when corrected for temperature?

**Solution**

$$C_t = 0.00000645(38 - 68)471.37 = -0.09$$

$$\text{Corrected distance} = 471.37 - 0.09 = 471.28 \text{ ft}$$

### ■ EXAMPLE 2.9

You must lay out two points in the field that will be exactly 100.000 m apart. Field conditions indicate that the temperature of the tape is 27°C. What distance will be laid out?

**Solution**

$$C_t = 0.0000116(27 - 20)100.000 = +0.008 \text{ m}$$

Since this is a layout (precorrection) problem, the correction sign must be reversed. In other words, we are looking for the distance that, when corrected by +0.008, will give us 100.000 m: Layout distance is 100.000 − 0.008 = 99.992 m.

For most survey work, accuracy requirements do not demand precision in determining the actual temperature of the tape. Usually, it is sufficient to estimate air temperature. However, for more precise work (say, 1:15,000 and higher), care is required in determining the actual temperature of the tape, which can be significantly different than the temperature of the air.

## 2.13 Invar Steel Tapes

High-precision surveys require the use of steel tapes that have a low coefficient of thermal expansion. Such tapes are composed of a nickel-steel alloy with a thermal expansion ranging from 0.0000002 to 0.00000055 per degree Fahrenheit ($3.60 \times 10^{-7}$ to $5.50 \times 10^{-7}$ per degree Celsius). Since the temperature of the tape can be significantly different from that of the surrounding air, it is customary to attach thermometers directly to the invar tapes. Electronic distance measurement (EDM) and GPS positioning have largely replaced invar tapes for precise distance measurements.

## 2.14 Tension and Sag Corrections

The three conditions under which tapes are normally standardized are given in Section 2.6. If a tension other than standard is applied, a tension (pull) error exists. The tension correction formula is

$$C_P = \frac{(P - P_s)L}{AE}$$

If a tape has been standardized while fully supported and is being used without full support, an error called *sag* will occur. The force of gravity pulls the center of the unsupported section downward in the shape of a catenary, thus creating an error $B'B$.

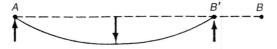

The sag correction formula is

$$C_s = \frac{-w^2L^3}{24P^2} = \frac{-W^2L}{24P^2}$$

**Table 2.1** CORRECTION FORMULA TERMS DEFINED (FOOT, METRIC, AND METRIC [SI] UNITS)

| Unit | Description | Foot | Metric (old) | Metric (SI) |
|------|-------------|------|--------------|-------------|
| $C_P$ | Correction due to tension per tape length | ft | m | m |
| $C_s$ | Sag correction per tape length | ft | m | m |
| $L$ | Length of tape under consideration | ft | m | m |
| $P_s$ | Standard tension | lb (force) | kg (force) | N (newtons) |
| | Typical standard tension | 10 lb (f) | 4.5–5 kg (f) | 50 N |
| $P$ | Applied tension | lb (f) | kg (f) | N |
| $A$ | Cross-sectional area | in.$^2$ | cm$^2$ | m$^2$ |
| $E$ | Average modulus of elasticity of steel tapes | $29 \times 10^6$ lb (f)/in.$^2$ | $21 \times 10^5$ kg (f)/cm$^2$ | $20 \times 10^{10}$ N/m$^2$ |
| | Average modulus of elasticity of invar tapes | $21 \times 10^6$ lb (f)/in.$^2$ | $14.8 \times 10^5$ kg (f)/cm$^2$ | $14.5 \times 10^{10}$ N/m$^2$ |
| $w$ | Weight of tape per unit length | lb (f)/ft | kg (f)/m | N/m |
| $W$ | Weight of tape | lb (f) | kg (f) | N |

Table 2.1 defines the terms in the tension and sag correction formulas.

From Table 2.1, 1 newton is the force required to accelerate a mass of 1 kg by 1 meter/s$^2$:

$$\text{Force} = \text{mass} \times \text{acceleration}$$
$$\text{Weight} = \text{mass} \times \text{acceleration due to gravity (g)}$$
$$g = 32.2 \text{ ft/s}^2 = 9.807 \text{ m/s}^2$$

That is, 1 kg(f) = 9.807 N.

Because some tension spring balances are graduated in kilograms, and because standard tensions are expressed in newtons by tape manufacturers, some students must be prepared to work in both old metric and (SI) units.

## 2.14.1 Examples of Tension Corrections

### ■ EXAMPLE 2.10

A 100-ft tape is used with a 20-lb force pull, instead of the standard tension of 10 lbs. If the cross-sectional area of the tape is 0.003 in., what is the tension error for each tape length used?

**Solution**

$$C_p = \frac{(20 - 10)100}{29,000,000 \times 0.003} = +0.011 \text{ ft}$$

If a distance of 421.22 ft had been recorded, the total correction would be:

$$4.2122 \times 0.011 = +0.05 \text{ ft.}$$

The corrected distance would be 421.27 ft.

### ■ EXAMPLE 2.11

A 30-m tape is used with a 100-N force, instead of the standard tension of 50 N. If the cross-sectional area of the tape is 0.02 cm$^2$, what is the tension error per tape length?

**Solution**

$$C_p = \frac{(100 - 50)30}{0.02 \times 21 \times 10^5 \times 9.807} = +0.0036 \text{ m}$$

If a distance of 182.716 m had been measured under these conditions, the total correction would be

$$\text{Total } C_p = \frac{182.716}{30} \times 0.0036 = +0.022 \text{ m}$$

The corrected distance would be 182.738 m.

## 2.14.2  Notes on Tension Corrections

The cross-sectional area of the tape can be measured with a micrometer or taken from manufacturer's specifications, or it can be determined by using the following expression:

$$\text{Tape length} \times \text{tape area} \times \text{specific weight of tape steel} = \text{weight}$$

or

$$\text{Tape area} = \frac{\text{weight}}{\text{length} \times \text{specific weight}}$$

### ■ EXAMPLE 2.12

A tape is weighed and found to be 1.95 lb. The overall length of the 100-ft tape (end to end) is 102 ft. The specific weight of steel is 490 lb/ft$^3$. What is the cross-section area of the tape?

**Solution**

$$\frac{102 \text{ ft} \times 12 \text{ in.} \times \text{area (in.}^2)}{1,728 \text{ in.}^3} \times 490 \text{ lb/ft}^3 = 1.95 \text{ lb}$$

$$\text{Area} = \frac{1.95 \times 1728}{102 \times 12 \times 490} = 0.0056 \text{ in.}^2$$

Tension errors are usually quite small and as such have relevance only for very precise surveys. Even for precise surveys, it is seldom necessary to calculate tension corrections because the availability of a tension-spring balance allows the surveyor to apply standard tension and thus eliminates the necessity of calculating a correction.

## 2.14.3 Sag Corrections

The sag correction formula is repeated here for easy reference while you complete Examples 2.13 and 2.14.

$$C_s = \frac{-w^2 L^3}{24 P^2} = \frac{-W^2 L}{24 P^2}$$

where $W^2 = w^2 L^2$

$w$ = weight of tape per unit length

$W$ = weight of tape between supports

$L$ = length of tape between supports

### ■ EXAMPLE 2.13

A 100-ft steel tape weighs 1.6 lb and is supported only at the ends with a force of 10 lb. What is the sag correction?

**Solution**

$$C_s = \frac{-1.6^2 \times 100}{24 \times 10^2} = -0.11 \text{ ft}$$

If the force were increased to 20 lb, the sag is reduced to:

$$C_s = \frac{-1.6^2 \times 100}{24 \times 20^2} = -0.03 \text{ ft}$$

### ■ EXAMPLE 2.14

Calculate the length between two supports if the recorded length is 42.071 m, the mass of the tape is 1.63 kg, and the applied tension is 100 N.

**Solution**

$$C_p = \frac{-(1.63 \times 9.807)^2 \times 42.071}{24 \times 100^2} = -0.045 \text{ m}$$

Therefore, the length between supports = $42.071 - 0.045 = 42.026$ m.

## 2.14.4 Normal Tension

The error in a measurement due to sag can be eliminated by increasing the tension. Although sag cannot be eliminated entirely, the tape can be stretched to compensate for the residual sag. Tension that eliminates sag errors is known as *normal tension*. It ranges from 19 lb (light 100-ft tapes) to 31 lb (heavy 100-ft tapes). The following formula gives a value for $P_n$ that will eliminate the error caused by sag.

$$P_n = \frac{0.204 \sqrt{AE}}{\sqrt{P_n - P_s}}$$

The formula is solved by making successive approximations for $P_n$ until the equation is satisfied. This equation is seldom used in field practice.

## 2.14.5 Experiment to Determine Normal Tension

Normal tension can be determined experimentally for individual tapes. The most popular steel tapes (100 ft) require a normal tension of about 24 lb. For most 30-m tapes (lightweight), a normal tension of 90 N (20 lb or 9.1 kg) is appropriate. To determine the normal tension for a 100-ft steel tape:

1. Lay out the tape on a flat, horizontal surface; an indoor corridor is ideal.
2. Select (or mark) a well-defined point on the surface at which the 100-ft mark is held.
3. Attach a tension handle at the zero end of the tape; apply standard tension, say, 10 lb; and mark the surface at 0.00 ft.
4. Repeat the process, switching personnel duties to ensure that the two marks are in fact exactly 100.00 ft apart.
5. Raise the tape off the surface to a comfortable height (waist). The surveyor at the 100-ft end holds a plumb bob over the point. At the same time, the surveyor(s) at the zero end slowly increases tension (a third surveyor could perform this function) until the plumb bob is over the zero mark on the surface. The tension is then read off the tension handle.

This process is repeated several times until a set of consistent results is obtained.

## 2.15 Random Errors Associated with Systematic Taping Errors

As mentioned in Section 2.9, random errors can coexist with systematic errors. For example, when dealing with the systematic error caused by variations in temperature, the surveyor can determine the prevailing temperature in several ways:

1. The air temperature can be estimated.
2. The air temperature can be taken from a pocket thermometer.
3. The actual temperature of the tape can be determined by a tape thermometer held in contact with the tape.

For an error of 15°F in temperature, the error in a 100-ft tape would be:

$$C_t = 0.00000645(15)100 = 0.01 \text{ ft}$$

Since $0.01/100 = 1/10,000$, even an error of 15°F would be significant only for higher-order surveys. If metric equipment were being used, a comparable error would be 8½°C; that is,

$$C_t = 0.0000116(8.5)30 = 0.003 \text{ m}$$

For precise work, however, random errors in determining temperature will be significant. Tape thermometers are recommended for precise work because of difficulties in estimating and because of the large differentials possible between air temperature and the actual temperature of the tape on the ground.

Consider the treatment of systematic errors dealing with slope versus horizontal dimensions. For a slope angle of 2°40′ read with an Abney hand level (clinometer) to the closest 10 minutes, we can say that an uncertainty of 5 minutes exists.

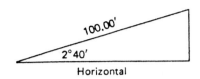

Horizontal

$$\text{Horizontal distance} = 100 \cos 2°40' = 99.89 \text{ ft}$$

In this case, an uncertainty of 5 minutes in the slope angle introduces an uncertainty of only 0.01 ft in the answer.

$$\text{Horizontal distance} = 100 \cos 2°45' = 99.88 \text{ ft}$$
$$= 100 \cos 2°35' = 99.90 \text{ ft}$$

Once again, this error (1/10,000) would be significant only for higher-order surveys.

Consider the sag for a light 100-ft tape weighing 1 lb, with $A = 0.003$ and $E = 30,000,000$. Normal tension in Trial 1 would be:

$$20 = 0.204 \times \frac{1.0\sqrt{0.003 \times 30,000,000}}{\sqrt{20 - 10}}$$
$$= \frac{61.2}{3.16} = 19.35$$

Normal tension in Trial 2 would be:

$$19.7 = \frac{61.2}{\sqrt{9.7}} = 19.7 \qquad \text{(okay for normal tension)}$$

If a tension of 25 lb were exerted instead of 19.7 lbs, the following error would occur:

$$C_p = \frac{(P - P_n)L}{AE}$$
$$C_p = \frac{(25 - 19.7)100}{0.003 \times 30,000,000} = 0.006 \text{ ft}$$

Once again, this error (1/16,700), by itself, is not significant for ordinary taping.

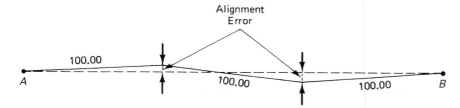

**FIGURE 2.13** Alignment errors.

## 2.16  Random Taping Errors

In addition to the systematic and random errors already discussed, random errors associated directly with the skill and care of the surveyors sometimes occur. These errors result from the inability of the surveyor to work to perfection in the areas of alignment, plumbing, and marking, and when estimating horizontal.

**Alignment errors** occur when the tape is inadvertently aligned off the true path (see Figure 2.13). Under ordinary surveying conditions, the rear surveyor can keep the head surveyor on line by sighting a range pole marking the terminal point. It would take an alignment error of about 1.5 ft to produce an error of 0.01 ft in 100 ft. It is not difficult to keep the tape aligned by eye to within a few tenths of a foot (0.2 to 0.3 ft), so alignment is not usually a major concern. It should be noted that although most random errors are compensating, alignment errors are cumulative. Misalignment can occur randomly on the left or on the right, but in both cases the result of the misalignment is to make the measured course too long. Alignment errors can be nearly eliminated on precise surveys by using a transit or theodolite to align all intermediate points.

**Marking and plumbing errors** are the most significant of all random errors. Even experienced surveyors must exercise great care to place a plumbed mark accurately to within 0.02 ft of true value over a distance of 100 ft. Horizontal measurements taken with the tape fully supported on the ground can be determined more accurately than measurements taken on a slope requiring the use of plumb bobs. Rugged terrain conditions that require many breaks in the taping process will cause these errors to multiply significantly.

Errors are also introduced when surveyors **estimate the horizontal position** of a plumbed measurement. The effect of this error is identical to that of the alignment error previously discussed, although the magnitude of these errors is often larger than that of alignment errors. Skilled surveyors can usually estimate a horizontal position to within 1 ft (0.3 m) over a distance of 100 ft (30 m). However, even experienced surveyors can be seriously in error when measuring across side-hills, where one's perspective with respect to the horizon can be seriously distorted. These errors can be nearly eliminated by using a hand level.

## 2.17  Techniques for Ordinary Taping Precision

Ordinary taping precision is referred to as precision that can result in 1:5,000 accuracy. The techniques used for ordinary taping, once mastered, can easily be maintained. It is possible to achieve an accuracy level of 1:5,000 with little more effort than is required to attain the 1/3,000 level. Since the bulk of all engineering surveying need only be either at the 1:3,000 or 1:5,000 level, experienced surveyors will often use 1:5,000 techniques even for the 1:3,000 level work. This practice permits good measuring work habits to be reinforced continually without appreciably increasing survey costs.

Modern electronic surveying equipment can routinely attain levels of precision and accuracy well beyond the 1:3,000 and 1:5,000 levels. You are advised, however, to keep in mind the project needs in these areas. How much precision and accuracy are really needed for mapping projects, road construction, resource surveys, structural surveys, etc.? If greater precision and accuracy can be achieved with available equipment, all well and good; but if high-precision equipment (e.g., precise GPS equipment) is rented at high cost just to perform drainage surveys, money will be wasted.

Because of the wide variety of field conditions that exist, absolute specifications cannot be prescribed. The specifications in Table 2.2 can be considered as typical for ordinary 1:5,000 taping.

**Table 2.2**  SPECIFICATION FOR 1/5,000 ACCURACY

| | Maximum effect on one tape length | |
|---|---|---|
| Source of error | 100 ft | 30 m |
| Temperature estimated to closest 7°F (4°C) | ±0.005 ft | ±0.0014 m |
| Care is taken to apply at least normal tension (lightweight tapes) and tension is known within 5 lb (20 N) | ±0.006 ft | ±0.0018 m |
| Slope errors are no larger than 1 ft/100 ft or 0.30 m/30 m | ±0.005 ft | ±0.0015 m |
| Alignment errors are no larger than 0.5 ft/100 ft or 0.15 m/30 m | ±0.001 ft | ±0.0004 m |
| Plumbing and marking errors are at a maximum of 0.015 ft/100 ft or 0.0046 m/30 m | ±0.015 ft | ±0.0046 m |
| Length of tape is known within ±0.005 ft (0.0015 m) | ±0.005 ft | ±0.0015 m |

To determine the total random error ($\Sigma e$) in one tape length, take the square root of the sum of the squares of the individual maximum errors (see Appendix A):

| **FOOT** | **METRIC** |
|---|---|
| $0.005^2$ | $0.0014^2$ |
| $0.006^2$ | $0.0018^2$ |
| $0.005^2$ | $0.0015^2$ |
| $0.001^2$ | $0.0004^2$ |
| $0.015^2$ | $0.0046^2$ |
| $0.005^2$ | $0.0015^2$ |
| 0.000337 | 0.000031 |

$$\Sigma e = \sqrt{0.000337} = 0.018 \text{ ft} \qquad \text{or} \qquad \sqrt{0.000031} = 0.0056 \text{ m}$$

$$\text{Accuracy} = \frac{0.018}{100} = \frac{1}{5,400} \qquad \text{or} \qquad \frac{0.0056}{30} = \frac{1}{5,400}$$

In this calculation, it is understood that corrections due to systematic errors have already been applied.

## 2.18  Mistakes in Taping

If errors are associated with inexactness, mistakes must be thought of as blunders. Whereas errors can be analyzed and even predicted to some degree, mistakes are totally unpredictable. Just one undetected mistake can nullify the results of an entire survey, so it is essential to perform the work so that the opportunity for mistakes to develop will be minimized and verification of the results can occur.

**The opportunities for the occurrence of mistakes are minimized by setting up and then rigorously following a standard method of performing the measurement.** The more standardized and routine the measurement manipulations, the more likely it is that the surveyor will immediately spot a mistake. The immediate double-checking of all measurement manipulations reduces the opportunities for mistakes to go undetected and at the same time increases the precision of the measurement. In addition to the immediate checking of all measurements, the surveyor looks constantly for independent methods of verifying the survey results. Gross mistakes can often be detected by comparing the survey results with distances scaled from existing plans. The simple check technique of pacing can be an invaluable tool for rough verification of measured distances, especially construction layout distances. The possibilities for verification are limited only by the surveyor's diligence and imagination.

Common mistakes in taping are:

1. Measuring to or from the wrong marker. All members of the survey crew must be vigilant in ensuring that measurements begin or end at the appropriate permanent or temporary marker. Markers include legal steel bars, construction stakes or steel bars, nails, and the like.

2. Reading the tape incorrectly. Mistakes are sometimes made by reading. Transposing figures is a common mistake (e.g., reading or writing 56 instead of 65).

3. Losing proper count of the full tape lengths involved in a measurement. The counting of full tape lengths is primarily the responsibility of the rear surveyor and can be as simple as counting the chaining pins that have been collected as the work progresses. If the head surveyor is also keeping track of full tape lengths, mistakes such as failing to pick up all chaining pins can be spotted and corrected easily.

4. Recording the values in the notes incorrectly. The note-keeper sometimes hears the rear surveyor's call-out correctly but then transposes the figures as they are being entered in the notes. This mistake can be eliminated if the note-keeper calls out the value as it is recorded. The rear surveyor listens for this call-out to ensure that the values called out are the same as the data originally given.

5. Calling out values ambiguously. The rear surveyor can call out 20.27 as twenty (pause) two, seven. This might be interpreted as 22.7. To avoid mistakes, this value should be called out as twenty, decimal (point), two, seven.

6. Not identifying the zero point of the tape correctly when using cloth, fiberglass, or steel tapes. This mistake can be avoided if the surveyor checks unfamiliar tapes before use. The tape itself can be used to verify the zero mark.

7. Making arithmetic mistakes in sums of dimensions and in error corrections (e.g., for temperature and slope). These mistakes can be identified and corrected if each crew member is responsible for checking (and signing) all survey notes.

## Problems

**2.1** How do random systematic errors differ?

**2.2** Describe three surveying applications where the measurements could be made with a cloth or fiberglass tape.

**2.3** What measuring or positioning techniques would you use in the following examples? Explain your choice.
  **(a)** Topographic survey of a large tract of land ($>$ 100 acres)
  **(b)** Topographic survey for a proposed factory or shopping mall
  **(c)** Construction layout survey for a row of houses
  **(d)** Measurements for payment for new concrete curb construction
  **(e)** Measurements for payment for the laying of sod or the clearing of trees

**2.4** The following distances were measured with a Gunter's chain. Convert these distances to feet and meters.
  **(a)** 177 chains, 31 links
  **(b)** 66 chains, 30 links
  **(c)** 141.09 chains
  **(d)** 1 chain, 90 links

**2.5** Give two examples of a suitable use for each of the following measuring techniques or instruments.
  **(a)** Pacing
  **(b)** Steel tape
  **(c)** EDM
  **(d)** Remote sensing
  **(e)** Subtense
  **(f)** Scaling
  **(g)** Fiberglass tape
  **(h)** Odometer

**2.6** A 100-ft cut steel tape was used to measure between two property markers. The rear surveyor held 61 ft, while the head surveyor cut 0.17 ft. What was the distance between the markers?

**2.7** The slope measurement between two points is 29.303 m and the slope angle is $1°50'$. Compute the horizontal distance.

**2.8** A distance of 122.57 ft was measured along a 2% slope. Compute the horizontal distance.

**2.9** The slope distance between two points is 49.989 m and the difference in elevation between the points is 2.148 m. Compute the horizontal distance.

**2.10** To determine the ground clearance of an overhead electrical cable, surveyor B is positioned directly under the cable (surveyor B can make a position check by sighting past the string of a plumb bob held in his or her outstretched hand, to the cable); surveyor A sets the clinometer to 45° and then backs away from surveyor B until the overhead electrical cable is on the cross hair of the leveled clinometer. At this point, surveyors A and B determine the distance between them to be 52.6 ft. Surveyor A then sets the clinometer to 45° and sights surveyor B. This horizontal line of sight cuts surveyor B at the knees, a distance of 3.1 ft above the ground. Determine the ground clearance of the electrical cable.

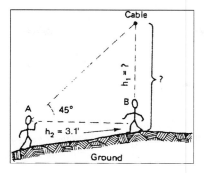

**2.11** A 100-ft steel tape known to be only 99.97 ft long (under standard conditions) was used to record a measurement of 365.28 ft. What is the distance corrected for the erroneous tape?

**2.12** A 30-m steel tape known to be 30.004 m (under standard conditions) was used to record a measurement of 137.888 m. What is the distance corrected for the erroneous tape length?

**2.13** You must lay out a rectangular commercial building 118.00 ft wide and 200.00 ft long. If the steel tape is 100.02 ft long (under standard conditions), what distances would be laid out?

**2.14** A survey distance of 274.62 ft was recorded when the field temperature was 91°F. What is the distance corrected for temperature?

**2.15** Station 8 + 62.63 must be marked in the field. If the steel tape to be used is only 99.98 (under standard conditions), and if the temperature will be 90°F at the time of the measurement, how far from the existing station mark at 10 + 45.26 will the surveyor have to measure back to locate the new station?

**2.16** The point of intersection of the centerline of Elm Road with the centerline of First Street was originally recorded as being at 9 + 77.210. How far from existing station mark 9 + 00 on First Street would a surveyor have to measure along the centerline to reestablish the intersection point when the temperature is −8°C and the tape is 29.996 under standard conditions?

For Problems 2.17 through 2.21, compute the corrected horizontal distance.

| | Temperature | Tape length | Slope data | Slope measurement |
|---|---|---|---|---|
| **2.17** | −04°F | 99.98 ft | Difference in elevation = 4.62 ft | 249.45 ft |
| **2.18** | 53°F | 100.00 ft | Slope angle 2°10 | 126.00 ft |
| **2.19** | 27°C | 29.992 m | Slope angle −3°42′ | 206.482 m |
| **2.20** | 0°C | 30.003 m | Slope at 1.50% | 500.000 m |
| **2.21** | 100°F | 100.02 ft | Slope at −0.80% | 488.38 ft |

For Problems 2.22 through 2.26, compute the required layout distance.

|  | Temperature | Tape length | Required horizontal distance |
|---|---|---|---|
| **2.22** | 38°F | 99.98 ft | 179.91 ft |
| **2.23** | 28°C | 30.012 m | 111.111 m |
| **2.24** | 15°C | 29.990 m | 600.000 m |
| **2.25** | 20°F | 100.02 ft | 200.00 ft |
| **2.26** | 100°F | 100.04 ft | 194.67 ft |

**2.27** A 50-m tape is used to measure between two points. The average weight of the tape per meter is 0.320 N. The measured distance is 48.888 m, with the tape supported at the ends only and with a tension of 100 N. Find the corrected distance.

**2.28** A 30-m tape has a mass of 544 g and is supported only at the ends with a force of 80 N. What is the sag correction?

**2.29** A 100-ft steel tape, weighing 1.8 lb and supported only at the ends with a tension of 24 lb, is used to measure a distance of 471.16 ft. What is the distance corrected for sag?

**2.30** A distance of 72.55 ft is recorded using a steel tape supported only at the ends, with a tension of 15 lb and weighing 0.016 lb per foot. Find the distance corrected for sag.

# CHAPTER 3 Leveling

## 3.1 General Background

Leveling is the procedure for determining differences in elevation between points that are some distance from each other. An *elevation* is the vertical distance above or below a reference datum. In surveying, the reference datum that is universally employed is that of *mean sea level (MSL)*. In North America, 19 years of observations at tidal stations in 26 locations on the Atlantic, Pacific, and Gulf of Mexico shorelines were reduced and adjusted to provide the National Geodetic Vertical Datum (NGVD) of 1929. This datum has been further refined to reflect gravimetric and other anomalies in the 1988 general control readjustment (North American Vertical Datum [NAVD 88]). Although the NAVD datum does not agree precisely with mean sea level at some specific points on the earth's surface, the term *mean sea level* is generally used to describe the datum. MSL is assigned a vertical value (elevation) of 0.000 ft or 0.000 m. See Figure 3.1. Specifications for vertical control in the United States and Canada are shown in Tables 3.1 and 3.2.

A *vertical line* is a line from the surface of the earth to the earth's center. It is also referred to as a plumb line or a line of gravity.

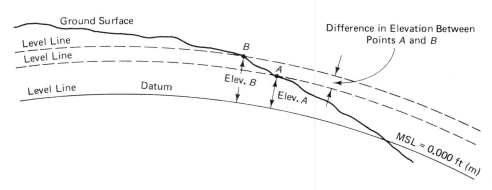

**FIGURE 3.1** Leveling concepts.

**Table 3.1** NATIONAL OCEAN SURVEY, U.S. COAST AND GEODETIC SURVEYS: CLASSIFICATION, STANDARDS OF ACCURACY, AND GENERAL SPECIFICATIONS FOR VERTICAL CONTROL

| Classification | First order Class I, Class II | Second order — Class I | Second order — Class II | Third order |
|---|---|---|---|---|
| *Principal uses:* Minimum standards; higher accuracies may be used for special purposes | Basic framework of the National Network and of metropolitan area control Extensive engineering projects Regional crustal movement investigations Determining geopotential values | Secondary control of the National Network and of metropolitan area control Large engineering projects Local crustal movement and subsidence investigations Support for lower-order control | Control densification, usually adjusted to the National Network. Local engineering projects Topographic mapping Studies of rapid subsidence Support for local surveys | Miscellaneous local control; may not be adjusted to the National Network. Small engineering projects Small-scale topographic mapping Drainage studied and gradient establishment in mountainous areas |
| *Recommended spacing of lines:* | | | | |
| National Network | Net A: 100 to 300 km, *Class I* Net B: 50 to 100 km, *Class II* | Secondary network: 20 to 50 km | Area control: 10 to 25 km | As needed |
| Metropolitan control | 2 to 8 km | 0.5 to 1 km | As needed | As needed |
| Other purposes | As needed | As needed | As needed | As needed |
| *Spacing of marks along lines* | 1 to 3 km | 1 to 3 km | Not more than 3 km | Not more than 3 km |
| *Gravity requirement*[a] | $0.20 \times 10^{-3}$ gpu | — | — | — |
| Instrument standards | Automatic or tilting levels with parallel plate micrometers; invar scale rods | Automatic or tilting levels with optical micrometers or three-wire levels; invar scale rods | Geodetic levels and invar scale rods | Geodetic levels and rods |
| Field procedures | Double-run; forward and backward, each section | Double-run; forward and backward, each section | Double- or single-run | Double- or single-run |
| Section length | 1 to 2 km | 1 to 2 km | 1 to 3 km for double-run | 1 to 3 km for double-run |
| Maximum length of sight | 50 m *Class I;* 60 m *Class II* | 60 m | 70 m | 90 m |

*Field procedures*[b]

| | | | | |
|---|---|---|---|---|
| Max. difference in lengths of forward and backward sights | | | | |
| Per setup | 2 m *Class I*; 5 m *Class II* | 5 m | 10 m | 10 m |
| Per section (cumulative) | 4 m *Class I*; 10 m *Class II* | 10 m | 10 m | 10 m |
| Max. length of line between connections | Net A: 300 km / Net B: 100 km | 50 km | 50 km double-run; 25 km single-run | 25 km double-run; 10 km single-run |
| *Maximum closures*[c] | | | | |
| Section; forward and backward | 3 mm $\sqrt{K}$ *Class I*; 4 mm $\sqrt{K}$ *Class II* | 6 mm $\sqrt{K}$ | 8 mm $\sqrt{K}$ | 12 mm $\sqrt{K}$ |
| Loop or line | 4 mm $\sqrt{K}$ *Class I*; 5 mm $\sqrt{K}$ *Class II*[a] | 6 mm $\sqrt{K}$ | 8 mm $\sqrt{K}$ | 12 mm $\sqrt{K}$ |

[a]See text for discussion of instruments.

[b]The maximum length of line between connections may be increased to 100 km double run for second order, class II, and to 50 km for double run for third order in those areas where the first-order control has not been fully established.

[c]Check between forward and backward runnings where $K$ is the distance in kilometers.

Notes:

1. $K$ = kilometers, $m$ = miles = the one-way distance between benchmarks measured along the leveling route.
2. To maintain the specified accuracy, long narrow loops should be avoided. The distance between any two benchmarks measured along the actual route should not exceed four times the straight-line distance between them.
3. Branch, spur, or open-ended lines should be avoided because of the possibility of undetected gross errors.
4. For precise work, the sections should be leveled once forward and once backward independently using different instruments and, if possible, under different weather conditions and at different times of the day.
5. A starting BM must be checked against another independent BM by two-way leveling before the leveling survey can commence. If the check is greater than the allowable discrepancy, both BMs must be further checked until the matter is resolved.
6. When a parallel-plate micrometer is used for special- or first-order leveling, double-scale invar rods must be used; the spacing of the smallest graduations must be equivalent to the displacement of the parallel-plate micrometer. When the three-wire method is used for first- or second-order leveling, rods with the checkerboard design must be used.
7. Line of sight not less than 0.5 m above the ground (special and first order).
8. Alternate reading of backsight and foresight at successive setups.
9. Third- and lower-order surveys should use the two-rod system; read only one wire and try to balance backsight and foresight distances.
10. Results equivalent to fourth-order spirit leveling can sometimes be obtained by measurement of vertical angles in conjunction with traverses, trilateration, or triangulation. Best results are obtained on short (<16 km) lines with simultaneous (within the same minute) measurement of the vertical angles at both ends of the line, using a 1-second theodolite.

*Source:* Tables A.7, A.8, A.9, and A.11 are taken from the 1974 publication *Classification, Standards of Accuracy, and General Specifications of Geodetic Control Surveys*. Detailed specifications related to these tables are available in the publication *Specifications to Support Classification, Standards of Accuracy, and General Specifications of Geodetic Control Surveys* by the Federal Geodetic Control Committee. Both publications may be obtained from U.S. Department of Commerce, National Oceanic and Atmospheric Administration, National Ocean Survey, Rockville, Maryland.

**Table 3.2** CLASSIFICATION, STANDARDS OF ACCURACY, AND GENERAL SPECIFICATIONS FOR VERTICAL CONTROL

| Classification | Special order | First order | Second order (first-order procedures recommended) | Third order | Fourth order |
|---|---|---|---|---|---|
| Allowable discrepancy between forward and backward levelings | $\pm 3$ mm $\sqrt{K}$ $\pm 0.012$ ft $\sqrt{m}$ | $\pm 4$ mm $\sqrt{K}$ $\pm 0.017$ ft $\sqrt{m}$ | $\pm 8$ mm $\sqrt{K}$ $\pm 0.035$ ft $\sqrt{m}$ | $\pm 24$ mm $\sqrt{K}$ $\pm 0.10$ ft $\sqrt{m}$ | $\pm 120$ mm $\sqrt{K}$ $\pm 0.5$ ft $\sqrt{m}$ |
| *Instruments* | | | | | |
| Self-leveling high-speed compensator | Equivalent to 10″/2 mm level vial | Equivalent to 10″/2 mm level vial | Equivalent to level vial 20″/mm | Equivalent to sensitivity below 40″ to 50″/2 mm | Equivalent to sensitivity below 40″ to 50″/2 mm |
| Level vial telescopic magnification | 10″/2 mm 40× | 10″/2 mm 40× | 20″/2 mm 40× | | |
| Parallel plate micrometer | | | | | |
| Sun shade and instrument cover | | | | Graduations on wood, metal, alloy, or fiber glass are satisfactory | |
| *Rods* | | | | | |
| Invar and double scale | × | × × | × × | | |
| Invar-checkerboard footplates or steel pins for turning points | | | | | |
| Circular bubble attached to rod | × | × | × | | |
| Rod supports | × | × | × | | |
| Difference between backsight and foresight distances and their total for the section not to exceed: | 5 m | 10 m | 10 m | Balanced | Balanced |
| *Maximum length of sight* | | | | | |
| 1-mm-wide rod mark | 50 m | × | × | | |
| 1.6 mm-wide rod mark | 60 m | | | | |
| Parallel-plate method | | 80 m | 80 m | N/A[a] | N/A |
| Three-wire method | | 110 m | 110 m | N/A | N/A |

[a]N/A, not applicable.

*Source:* Adapted from "Specifications and Recommendations for Control Surveys and Survey Markers." Surveys and Mapping Branch, Department of Energy, Mines, and Resources, Ottawa, Ontario, Canada, 1973.

A *level line* is a line in a level surface. A level surface is a curved surface parallel to the mean surface of the earth. A level surface is best visualized as being the surface of a large body of water at rest.

A *horizontal line* is a straight line perpendicular to a vertical line.

## 3.2 Theory of Differential Leveling

*Differential leveling* is used to determine differences in elevation between points that are some distance from each other by using a surveyors' level together with a graduated measuring rod. The surveyors' level consists of a cross-hair telescope and an attached spirit level tube, all of which are mounted on a sturdy tripod. The surveyor can sight through the telescope to a rod graduated in feet or meters and determine a measurement reading at the point where the cross hair intersects the rod. See Figure 3.2. If the rod reading at $A = 6.27$ ft and the rod reading at $B = 4.69$ ft, the difference in elevation between $A$ and $B$ is $6.27 - 4.69 = 1.58$ ft. If the elevation of $A$ is 61.27 ft (above MSL), then the elevation of $B$ is $61.27 + 1.58 = 62.85$ ft. That is, 61.27 (elevation $A$) + 6.27 (rod reading at $A$) − 4.69 (rod reading at $B$) = 62.85 (elevation $B$).

Figure 3.3 shows a potential problem. Whereas elevations are referenced to level lines (surfaces), the line of sight through the telescope of a surveyors' level is, in fact,

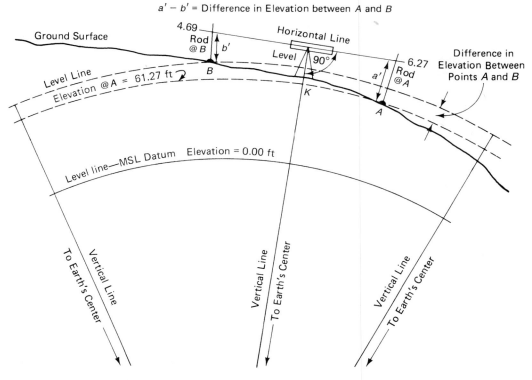

**FIGURE 3.2** Leveling process.

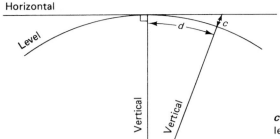

Horizontal

Level

Vertical

Vertical

*d*

*c*

*c* is the amount by which a level line and a horizontal line diverge over distance *d*

**FIGURE 3.3**   Relationship between a horizontal line and a level line.

almost a horizontal line. All rod readings taken with a surveyors' level will contain an error *c* over a distance *d*. I have greatly exaggerated the curvature of the level lines shown in Figures 3.1 through 3.3 for illustrative purposes. In fact, the divergence between a level line and a horizontal line is quite small. For example, over a distance of 1,000 ft, the divergence is 0.024 ft, and for a distance of 300 ft, the divergence is only 0.002 ft (0.0008 m in 100 in.).

## 3.3   Curvature and Refraction

The previous section introduced the concept of curvature error, that is, the divergence between a level line and a horizontal line over a specified distance. When considering the divergence between level and horizontal lines, one must also account for the fact that all sight lines are refracted downward by the earth's atmosphere. Although the magnitude of the refraction error depends on atmospheric conditions, it is generally considered to be about one-seventh of the curvature error. You can see in Figure 3.4 that the refraction error of *AB* compensates for part of the curvature error of *AE,* resulting in a net error due to curvature and refraction (*c* + *r*) of *BE*.

From Figure 3.4, the curvature error can be computed as follows:

$$(R + c)^2 = R^2 + KA^2$$
$$R^2 + 2Rc + c^2 = R^2 + KA^2$$
$$c(2R + c) = KA^2$$

$$c = \frac{KA^2}{2R + c} \approx \frac{KA^2}{2R} \tag{3.1}$$

In the term (2$R$ + $c$), $c$ is so small, when compared to $R$, that it can be safely ignored. Consider $R$ = 6370 km:

$$c = \frac{KA^2}{2 \times 6{,}370} = 0.0000785\ KA^2\ \text{km} = 0.0785\ KA^2\ \text{m}$$

Refraction (*r*) is affected by atmospheric pressure, temperature, and geographic location but, as noted earlier, it is usually considered to be about one-seventh of the curvature error

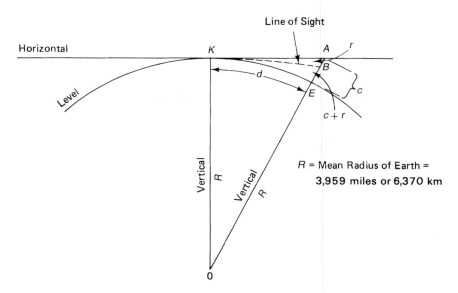

**FIGURE 3.4** Effects of curvature and refraction.

(c). If $r = 0.14c$, $c + r = 0.0675\,K$, where $K = KA$ (Figure 3.4) and is the length of sight in kilometers. The combined effects of curvature and refraction $(c + r)$ can be determined from the following formulas:

$$(c + r)_m = 0.0675K^2 \qquad (c + r)_m \text{ in meters} \qquad K \text{ in kilometers} \qquad (3.2)$$

$$(c + r)_{ft} = 0.574K^2 \qquad (c + r)_{ft} \text{ in feet} \qquad K \text{ in miles} \qquad (3.3)$$

$$(c + r)_{ft} = 0.0206M^2 \qquad (c + r)_{ft} \text{ in feet} \qquad M \text{ in thousands of feet} \qquad (3.4)$$

### ■ EXAMPLE 3.1

Calculate the error due to curvature and refraction for the following distances:

- (a) 2500 ft
- (b) 400 ft
- (c) 2.7 miles
- (d) 1.8 km

**Solution**

- (a) $(c + r) = 0.0206 \times 2.5^2 = 0.13$ ft
- (b) $(c + r) = 0.0206 \times 0.4^2 = 0.003$ ft
- (c) $(c + r) = 0.574 \times 2.7^2 = 4.18$ ft
- (d) $(c + r) = 0.0675 \times 1.8^2 = 0.219$ m

You can see from the values in Table 3.3 that $(c + r)$ errors are relatively insignificant for differential leveling. Even for precise leveling where distances of rod readings are seldom

**Table 3.3**  SELECTED VALUES FOR $(c + r)$ AND DISTANCE

| Distance (m) | $(c + r)_m$ | Distance (ft) | $(c + r)_{ft}$ |
|---|---|---|---|
| 30 | 0.0001 | 100 | 0.000 |
| 60 | 0.0002 | 200 | 0.001 |
| 100 | 0.0007 | 300 | 0.002 |
| 120 | 0.001 | 400 | 0.003 |
| 150 | 0.002 | 500 | 0.005 |
| 300 | 0.006 | 1000 | 0.021 |
| 1 km | 0.068 | 1 mi | 0.574 |

in excess of 200 ft (60 m), it would seem that this error is of only marginal importance. We will see in Section 3.11 that the field technique of balancing the distances of rod readings (from the instrument) effectively cancels out this type of error.

## 3.4  Types of Surveying Levels

### 3.4.1  Automatic Level

The automatic level (see Figure 3.5) employs a gravity-referenced prism or mirror compensator to orient the line of sight (line of collimation) automatically. The instrument is quickly leveled when a circular spirit level is used. When the bubble has been centered (or nearly so), the compensator takes over and maintains a horizontal line of sight, even if the telescope is slightly tilted (see Figure 3.5).

Automatic levels are extremely popular in present-day surveying operations and are available from most survey instrument manufacturers. They are easy to set up and use, and can be obtained for use at almost any required precision. A word of caution: all automatic levels employ a compensator referenced by gravity. This operation normally entails freely moving prisms or mirrors, some of which are hung by fine wires. If a wire or fulcrum breaks, the compensator will become inoperative, and all subsequent rod readings will be incorrect.

The operating status of the compensator can be verified by tapping the end of the telescope or by slightly turning one of the leveling screws (one manufacturer provides a push button), causing the telescopic line of sight to veer from horizontal. If the compensator is operative, the cross hair will appear to deflect momentarily before returning to its original rod reading. Constant checking of the compensator will avoid costly mistakes caused by broken components.

Most levels (most new surveying instruments) now come equipped with a three-screw leveling base. Whereas the support for a four-screw leveling base is the center bearing, the three-screw instruments are supported entirely by the foot screws themselves. Adjustment of the foot screws of a three-screw instrument effectively raises or lowers the height of the instrument line of sight. Adjustment of the foot screws of a four-screw instrument does not affect the height of the instrument line of sight because the instrument is supported by the center bearing. The surveyor should be aware that adjustments made to a three-screw level in the midst of a setup operation will effectively change the elevation of

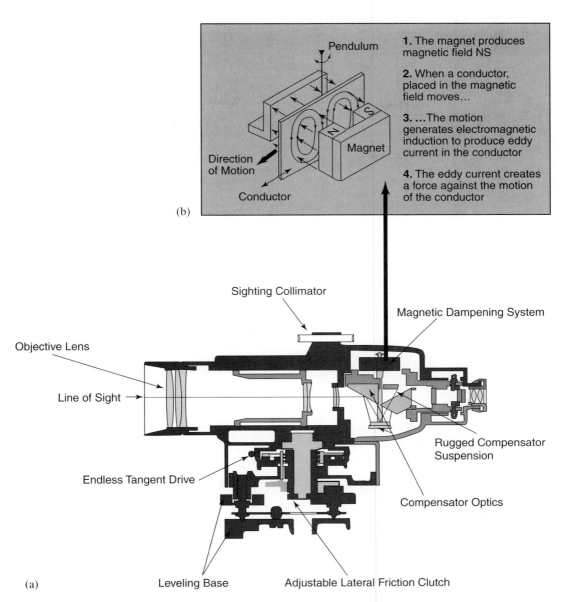

**Pendulum**

**1.** The magnet produces magnetic field NS

**2.** When a conductor, placed in the magnetic field moves…

**3.** …The motion generates electromagnetic induction to produce eddy current in the conductor

**S**

**N**

**Magnet**

**Direction of Motion**

**4.** The eddy current creates a force against the motion of the conductor

**Conductor**

(b)

Sighting Collimator

Magnetic Dampening System

Objective Lens

Line of Sight →

Rugged Compensator Suspension

Endless Tangent Drive

Compensator Optics

(a)

Leveling Base

Adjustable Lateral Friction Clutch

**FIGURE 3.5**   (a) Schematic of an engineer's automatic level. (b) Magnetic dampening system. (Courtesy of Sokkia Corp., Overland Park, Kansas)

the line of sight and could cause significant errors on very precise surveys (e.g., benchmark leveling or industrial surveying).

The bubble in the circular spirit level is centered by adjusting one or more of the three independent screws. Figure 3.6 shows the positions for a telescope equipped with a tube level when using three leveling foot screws. If you think of this configuration when

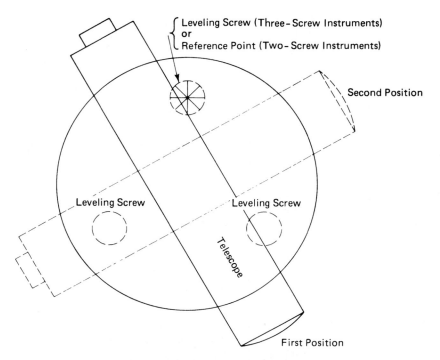

**FIGURE 3.6**  Telescope positions when leveling a two- or three-screw instrument.

you are leveling the circular spirit level, you can easily predict the movement of the bubble. Some manufacturers have provided levels and transits with only two leveling screws. Figure 3.6 shows that the telescopic positions are identical for both two- and three-screw instruments.

Levels used to establish or densify vertical control are designed and manufactured to give precise results. The magnifying power, setting accuracy of the tubular level or compensator, quality of optics, and so on, are all improved to provide for precise rod readings. The least count on leveling rods is 0.01 ft or 0.001 m. Precise levels are usually equipped with optical micrometers so that readings can be determined one or two places beyond the rod's least count.

Many automatic levels utilize a concave base that, when attached to its domed-head tripod top, can be roughly leveled by sliding the instrument on the tripod top. This rough leveling can be accomplished in a few seconds. If the bull's-eye bubble is nearly centered by this maneuver and the compensator is activated, the leveling screws may not be needed at all to level the instrument.

## 3.4.2  Digital Level

Figure 3.7 shows a digital level and bar-code rod. This level features digital, electronic image-processing for determining heights and distances with the automatic recording of

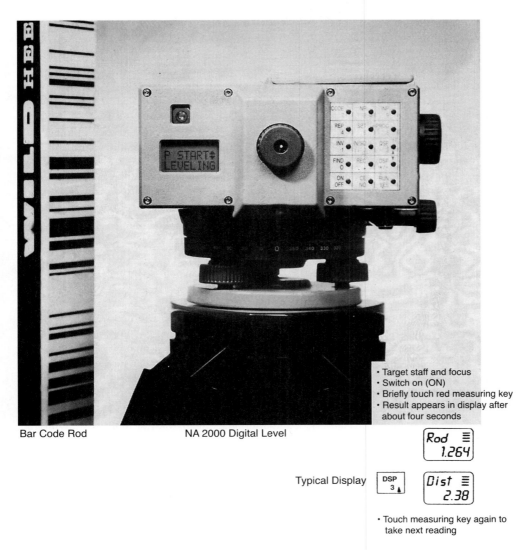

Bar Code Rod        NA 2000 Digital Level

- Target staff and focus
- Switch on (ON)
- Briefly touch red measuring key
- Result appears in display after about four seconds

Rod ≡
1.264

Typical Display    DSP 3▲    Dist ≡
2.38

- Touch measuring key again to take next reading

**FIGURE 3.7** Wild NA 2000 Digital level and bar-code rod. (Courtesy of Leica Co., 3.7 Toronto)

data for later transfer to the computer. The digital level is an automatic level (pendulum compensator) capable of normal optical leveling with a rod graduated in feet or meters. When used in electronic mode with the rod face graduated in bar code, this level will, with the press of a button, capture and process the image of the bar-code rod. This processed image of the rod reading is then compared with the image of the whole rod, which is stored permanently in the level's memory module, to determine height and distance values. The rod shown in Figure 3.11 is 4.05 m long; it is graduated in bar code on one side and in either feet or meters on the other side.

After the instrument has been leveled, the image of the bar code must be focused properly by the operator. Next, the operator presses the measure button to begin the image processing, which takes about 4 seconds (see Figure 3.11 for typical displays). Although the heights and distances are automatically determined and recorded (if desired), the horizontal angles must be read and recorded manually with this instrument.

Preprogrammed functions include level loop survey, two-peg test, self-test, set time, and set units. Coding can be the same as that used with total stations (see Chapter 7), which means that the processed leveling data can be transferred directly to the computer data base. The bar code can be read in the range of 1.8 to 100 m away from the instrument, optically the rod can be read as close as 0.5 cm. If the rod is not plumb or is held upside down, an error message will flash on the screen. Other error messages include "instrument not level," "low battery," and "memory almost full." Rechargeable batteries are said to last for 2,000 measurements. Distance accuracy is in the range of 1/2,500 to 1/3,000, whereas leveling accuracy is stated as having a standard deviation for a 1-km double run of 1.5 mm for electronic measurement and 2.0 mm for optical measurement.

## 3.4.3  Tilting Level

The tilting level is roughly leveled by observing the bubble in the circular spirit level. Just before each rod reading is to be taken, and while the telescope is pointing at the rod, the telescope is precisely leveled by manipulating a tilting screw, which effectively raises or lowers the eyepiece end of the telescope. The level is equipped with a tube level that is precisely leveled by operating the tilting screw. The bubble is viewed through a separate eyepiece or, as is the case in Figure 3.8, through the telescope. The image of the bubble is longitudinally split in two and viewed with the aid of prisms. One-half of each end of the bubble can be seen (see Figure 3.12), and after adjustment, the two half-ends are brought to coincidence and appear as a continuous curve. When coincidence has been achieved, the telescope has been precisely leveled.

It has been estimated by Leica Ltd. that the accuracy of centering a level bubble with reference to the open tubular scale graduated at intervals of 2 mm is about one-fifth of a division, or 0.4 mm. With coincidence-type (split bubble) levels, however, this accuracy increases to about one-fortieth of a division, or 0.05 mm. As you can see, these levels are useful where a relatively high degree of precision is required; however, if tilting levels are used on ordinary work (e.g., earthwork), the time and expense involved in setting the split bubble to coincidence for each rod reading can scarcely be justified. These levels have by now been replaced mostly by automatic levels.

The level tube is used in many levels; it is a sealed glass tube filled mostly with alcohol or a similar substance with a low freezing point. The upper (and sometimes lower) surface has been ground to form a circular arc. The degree of precision possessed by a surveyor's level is partly a function of the sensitivity of the level tube; the sensitivity of the level tube is related directly to the radius of curvature of the upper surface of the level tube. The larger the radius of curvature, the more sensitive is the level tube.

Sensitivity is usually expressed as the central angle subtending one division (usually 2 mm) marked on the surface of the level tube. The sensitivity of many engineer's levels is 30″; that is, for a 2-mm arc, the central angle is 30″ ($R = 13.75$ m or 45 ft) (see Figure 3.9).

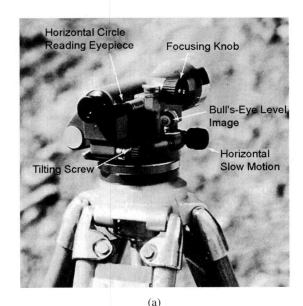

Horizontal Circle
Reading Eyepiece

Focusing Knob

Bull's-Eye Level
Image

Horizontal
Slow Motion

Tilting Screw

(a)

Before Coincidence          After Coincidence

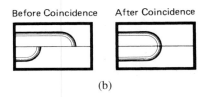

(b)

**FIGURE 3.8** (a) Kern engineering tilting level, GK 23 C. (b) Split bubble, before and after coincidence. (Courtesy of Kern Instruments—Leica)

The sensitivity of levels used for precise work is usually $10''$, that is, $R = 41.25$ m or 135 ft.

In addition to possessing more sensitive level tubes, precise levels have improved optics, including a greater magnification power. The relationship between the quality of the optical system and the sensitivity of the level tube can be simply stated: for any observable movement of the bubble in the level tube, there should be an observable movement of the cross hair on the leveling rod.

## 3.5 Leveling Rods

Leveling rods are manufactured from wood, metal, or fiberglass and are graduated in feet or meters. The foot rod can be read directly to 0.01 ft, whereas the metric rod can usually be read directly only to 0.01 m, with millimeters being estimated. Metric rod readings are normally booked to the closest $1/3$ cm or $1/2$ cm (i.e., 0.000, 0.003, 0.005, 0.007, and 0.010); more precise values can be obtained by using an optical micrometer. One-piece rods are used for more precise work. The most precise work requires the face of the rod to be an invar strip held in place under temperature-compensating spring tension (invar is a metal that has a very low rate of thermal expansion).

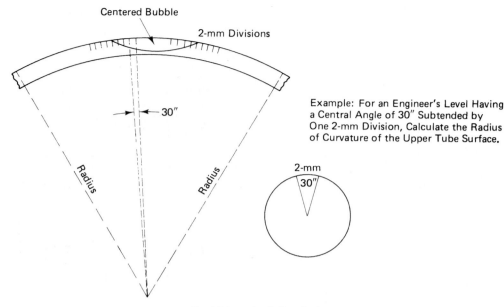

Centered Bubble

2-mm Divisions

30″

Radius

Radius

Example: For an Engineer's Level Having a Central Angle of 30″ Subtended by One 2-mm Division, Calculate the Radius of Curvature of the Upper Tube Surface.

2-mm

30″

Establish an Angle/Arc Ratio

$$\frac{30''}{360°} = \frac{0.002}{2\pi R} \; , \; R = \frac{360}{0.00833} \times \frac{0.002}{2\pi} \; , \; R = 13.75 \text{ m (or 45 ft.)}$$

**FIGURE 3.9**   Level tube showing the relationship between the central angle per division and the radius of curvature of the level tube upper surface. (Courtesy of Leica, Switzerland)

Most leveling surveys utilize two- or three-piece rods graduated in either feet or meters. The sole of the rod is a metal plate that will withstand the constant wear and tear of leveling. The zero mark is at the bottom of the metal plate. The rods are graduated in a wide variety of patterns, all of which readily respond to logical analysis. The surveyor is well advised to study an unfamiliar rod at close quarters prior to leveling to ensure that the graduations are thoroughly understood. See Figure 3.10 for a variety of graduation markings.

The rectangular sectioned rods are of either the folding (hinged) or the sliding variety. Newer fiberglass rods have oval or circular cross sections and fit telescopically together for heights of 3, 5, and 7 m, from a stored height of 1.5 m (equivalent foot rods are also available). Benchmark leveling utilizes folding (one-piece) rods or invar rods, both of which have built-in handles and rod levels. When the bubble is centered, the rod is plumb. All other rods can be plumbed by using a rod level (see Figure 3.11).

## 3.6   Definitions for Differential Leveling

The following list of definitions is helpful in differential leveling:

- A *benchmark (BM)* is a permanent point of known elevation. Benchmarks are established by using precise leveling techniques and instrumentation. Benchmarks are

# Level Rod Faces

Rod faces pictured are approximately one-half actual size.

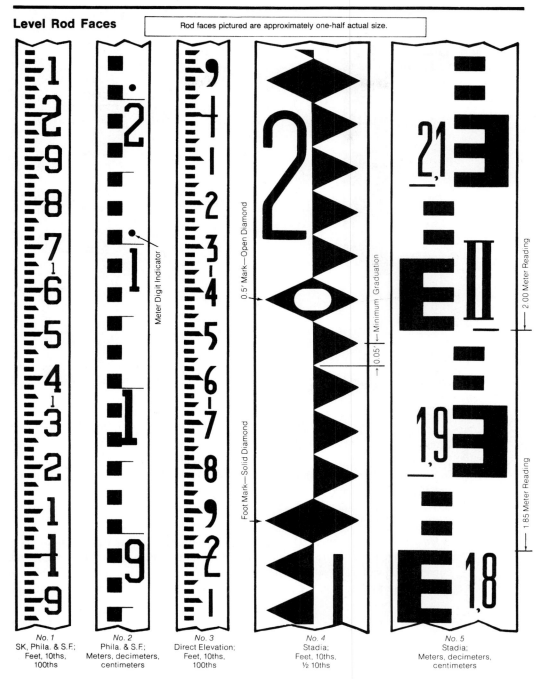

| No. 1 | No. 2 | No. 3 | No. 4 | No. 5 |
|---|---|---|---|---|
| SK, Phila. & S.F.;<br>Feet, 10ths,<br>100ths | Phila. & S.F.;<br>Meters, decimeters,<br>centimeters | Direct Elevation;<br>Feet, 10ths,<br>100ths | Stadia;<br>Feet, 10ths,<br>½ 10ths | Stadia;<br>Meters, decimeters,<br>centimeters |

**FIGURE 3.10** Traditional rectangular cross-section leveling rods showing a variety of graduation markings. (Courtesy of Sokkia Co. Ltd.)

(a)

**FIGURE 3.11** (a) Circular rod level. (Courtesy of Keuffel & Esser Co.) (b) Circular level, shown with a leveling rod.

(b)

bronze disks or plugs usually set into vertical wall faces. It is important that the benchmark be placed in a structure that has substantial footings (at least below minimum frost depth penetration) that will resist vertical movement due to settling or upheaval. Benchmark elevations and locations are published by federal, state or provincial, and municipal agencies and are available to surveyors for a nominal fee. See Figure 3.15.

- A *temporary benchmark (TBM)* is a semipermanent point of known elevation. TBMs can be flange bolts on fire hydrants, nails in the roots of trees, top corners of concrete culvert headwalls, and so on. The elevations of TBMs are not normally published, but they are available in the field notes of various surveying agencies. See Figure 3.12.

- A *turning point (TP)* is a point temporarily used to transfer an elevation (see Figure 3.14 on page 75).

- A *backsight (BS)* is a rod reading taken on a point of known elevation to establish the elevation of the instrument line of sight. See Figure 3.12.

- The *height of instrument (HI)* is the elevation of the line of sight through the level (i.e., elevation of BM + BS = HI). See Figure 3.12.

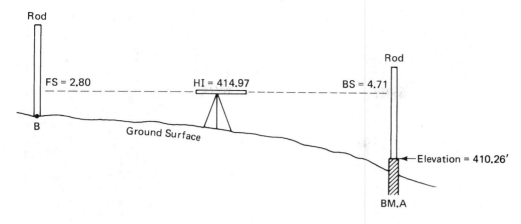

**FIGURE 3.12** Leveling procedure: one setup.

- A *foresight (FS)* is a rod reading taken on a turning point, benchmark, or temporary benchmark to determine its elevation [i.e., HI − FS = elevation of TP (or BM or TBM)]. See Figure 3.12.
- An *intermediate foresight (IS)* is a rod reading taken at any other point where the elevation is required (see Figure 3.20); that is, HI − IS = elevation.

Most engineering leveling projects are initiated to determine the elevations of intermediate points (as in profiles, cross sections, etc.). The addition of backsights to elevations to obtain heights of instrument and the subtraction of foresights from heights of instrument to obtain new elevations are known as note reductions.

## 3.7 Techniques of Leveling

In leveling, as opposed to theodolite work, the instrument can usually be set up in a relatively convenient location. If the level has to be set up on a hard surface, such as asphalt or concrete, the tripod legs will be spread out to provide a more stable setup. When the level is to be set up on a soft surface (e.g., turf), the tripod is first set up so that the tripod top is nearly horizontal, and then the tripod legs are firmly pushed into the earth. The tripod legs are snugly tightened to the tripod top so that a leg, when raised, will fall back only under the force of its own weight. Undertightening can cause an unsteady setup, just as overtightening can cause an unsteady setup due to torque strain. On hills, it is customary to place one leg uphill and two legs downhill; the instrument operator stands facing uphill while setting up the instrument. The tripod legs can be adjustable or straight leg. The straight-leg tripod is recommended for leveling because it contributes to a more stable setup. After the tripod has been set roughly level, with the feet firmly pushed into the ground, the instrument can be leveled.

Three-screw instruments are attached to the tripod via a threaded bolt that projects up from the tripod top into the leveling base of the instrument. The three-screw instrument, which usually has a circular bull's-eye bubble level, is leveled as described in Section 3.4.1

and Figure 3.6. Unlike the four-screw instrument, the three-screw instrument can be manipulated by moving the screws one at a time, although experienced surveyors will usually manipulate at least two at a time. After the bubble has been centered, the instrument can be revolved to check that the circular bubble remains centered. For techniques used with four-screw instruments, see Appendix H.

Once the level has been set up, preparation for the rod readings can take place. The eyepiece lenses, [E] are focused by turning the eyepiece focusing ring until the cross hairs are as black and as sharp as possible. (It helps to have the telescope pointing to a light-colored background for this operation.) Next, the rod is brought into focus by turning the telescope focusing screw until the rod graduations are as clear as possible. If both of these focusing operations have been carried out correctly, the cross hairs will appear to be superimposed on the leveling rod. If either focusing operation (eyepiece or rod focus) has not been carried out properly, the cross hair will appear to move slightly up and down as the observer's head moves slightly up and down. The apparent movement of the cross hair can cause incorrect readings. If one or both focus adjustments have been made improperly, the resultant error is known as *parallax*.

Figure 3.12 shows one complete leveling cycle; actual leveling operations are no more complicated than what you see in the figure. Leveling operations typically involve numerous repetitions of this leveling cycle, with some operations requiring that additional (intermediate) rod readings be taken at each instrument setup.

$$\text{Existing elevation} + \text{BS} = \text{HI} \qquad (3.5)$$

$$\text{HI} - \text{FS} = \text{new elevation} \qquad (3.6)$$

These two equations completely describe the differential leveling process.

When you are leveling between benchmarks or turning points, the level is set approximately midway between the BS and FS locations to eliminate (or minimize) errors due to curvature and refraction (Section 3.3) and errors due to a faulty line of sight (Section 3.11). To ensure that the rod is plumb, either a rod level (Figure 3.11) is used, or the surveyor gently "waves the rod" toward and away from the instrument. The correct rod reading will be the lowest reading observed. The surveyor must ensure that the rod does not sit up on the back edge of the base and effectively raise the zero mark on the rod off the BM (or TP). The instrument operator is sure that the rod has been properly waved if the readings decrease to a minimum value and then increase in value (see Figure 3.13).

Refer again to Figure 3.12. To determine elevation of *B*:

| | |
|---|---|
| Elevation BM *A* | 410.26 |
| Backsight rod reading at BM *A* | + 4.71 BS |
| Height (elevation) of instrument line of sight | 414.97 HI |
| Foresight rod reading at TBM *B* | −2.80 FS |
| Elevation TBM *B* | 412.17 |

After the rod reading of 4.71 is taken at BM *A,* the elevation of the line of sight of the instrument is known to be 414.97 (410.26 + 4.71). The elevation of TBM *B* can be determined by holding the rod at *B,* sighting the rod with the instrument, and reading the rod (2.80 ft). The elevation of TBM *B* is therefore 414.97 − 2.80 = 412.17 ft. In addition to

(a)

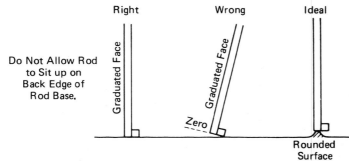

Right

Graduated Face

Do Not Allow Rod to Sit up on Back Edge of Rod Base.

Wrong

Graduated Face

Zero

Ideal

Rounded Surface

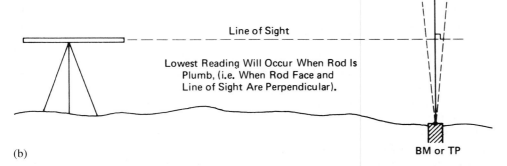

Line of Sight

Lowest Reading Will Occur When Rod Is Plumb, (i.e. When Rod Face and Line of Sight Are Perpendicular).

BM or TP

(b)

**FIGURE 3.13** (a) Waving the rod. (b) Waving the rod slightly to and from the instrument allows the instrument operator to take the most precise (lowest) reading.

determining the elevation of TBM *B,* the elevations of any other points lower than the line of sight and visible from the level can be determined in a similar manner.

The situation depicted in Figure 3.14 shows the technique used when the point whose elevation is to be determined (BM 461) is too far from the point of known elevation (BM 460) for a one-setup solution. The elevation of an intermediate point (TP 1) is determined, allowing the surveyor to move the level to a location where BM 461 can be "seen." Real-life situations may require numerous setups and the determination of the elevation of many intermediate points before getting close enough to determine the elevation of the desired point. When the elevation of the desired point has been determined, the surveyor must then either continue the survey to a point (BM) of known elevation or return (loop) the survey to the point of commencement. The survey must be closed onto a point of known elevation so that the accuracy and acceptability of the survey can be determined. If the closure is not within allowable limits, the survey must be repeated.

The arithmetic can be verified by performing the *arithmetic check* (page check). All BSs are added and all FSs are subtracted. When the sum of BS is added to the original elevation and then the sum of FS is subtracted from that total, the remainder should be the same as the final elevation calculated (see Figure 3.15).

$$\text{Starting elevation} + \Sigma \text{BS} - \Sigma \text{FS} = \text{ending elevation}$$

In the 1800s and early 1900s, leveling procedures like the one described here were used to survey locations for railroads that traversed North America between the Atlantic Ocean and the Pacific Ocean.

## 3.8   Benchmark Leveling (Vertical Control Surveys)

Benchmark leveling is the type of leveling employed when a system of benchmarks is to be established or when an existing system of benchmarks is to be extended or densified. For example perhaps a benchmark is required in a new location, or perhaps an existing benchmark has been destroyed and a suitable replacement is required. Benchmark leveling is typified by the relatively high level of precision specified, both for the instrumentation and for the technique itself.

The specifications shown in Tables 3.1 and 3.2 cover the techniques of precise leveling. Precise levels with coincidence tubular bubbles of a sensitivity of 10 seconds per 2-mm division (or equivalent for automatic levels) and with parallel-plate micrometers are used almost exclusively for this type of work. Invar-faced rods, together with a base plate (see Figure 3.16), rod level, and supports, are used in pairs to minimize the time required for successive readings.

Tripods for this type of work are longer than usual, enabling the surveyor to keep the line of sight farther above the ground and thus minimizing interference and errors due to refraction. Ideally the work is performed on a cloudy, windless day, although work can proceed on a sunny day if the instrument is protected from the sun and its possible differential thermal effects.

At the national level, benchmarks are established by federal agencies utilizing first-order methods and first-order instruments. The same high requirements are also specified for state and provincial grids. But as work proceeds from the whole to the part (i.e., down to municipal or regional grids), the rigid specifications are relaxed somewhat. For most engineering works, benchmarks are established (from the municipal or regional grid) at

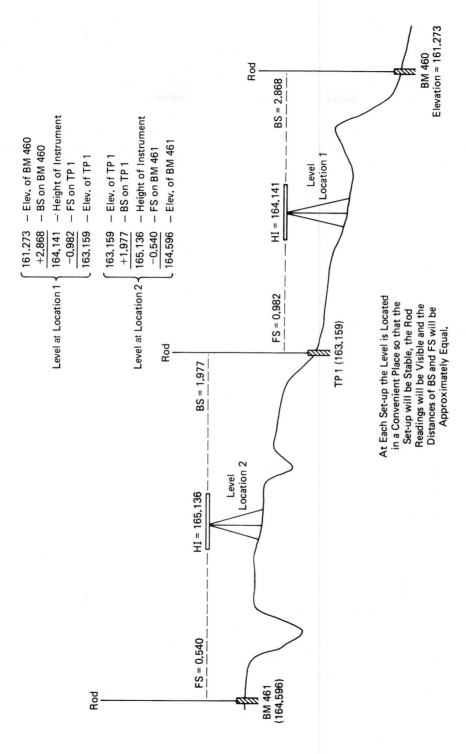

Level at Location 1 { 
161.273 — Elev. of BM 460
+2.868 — BS on BM 460
164.141 — Height of Instrument
−0.982 — FS on TP 1
163.159 — Elev. of TP 1

Level at Location 2 {
163.159 — Elev. of TP 1
+1.977 — BS on TP 1
165.136 — Height of Instrument
−0.540 — FS on BM 461
164.596 — Elev. of BM 461

Rod

BS = 2.868

Level Location 1

HI = 164.141

BM 460
Elevation = 161.273

FS = 0.982

TP 1 (163.159)

At Each Set-up the Level is Located in a Convenient Place so that the Set-up will be Stable, the Rod Readings will be Visible and the Distances of BS and FS will be Approximately Equal.

Rod

BS = 1.977

Level Location 2

HI = 165.136

FS = 0.540

BM 461 (164.596)

Rod

**FIGURE 3.14** Leveling procedure: more than one setup.

75

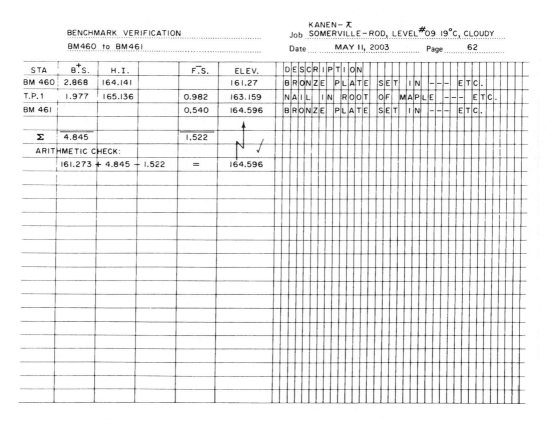

**FIGURE 3.15** Leveling field notes and arithmetic check (data from Figure 3.14).

third-order specifications. Benchmarks established to control isolated construction projects may be at even lower orders of accuracy.

It is customary in benchmark leveling at all orders of accuracy to verify first that the starting benchmark's elevation is correct. This can be done by two-way leveling to the closest adjacent benchmark. This check is particularly important when the survey loops back to close on the starting benchmark and no other verification is planned.

## 3.9 Profile and Cross-Section Leveling

In engineering surveying, we often consider a route (road, sewer pipeline, channel, etc.) from three distinct perspectives. The *plan view* of route location is the same as if we were in an aircraft looking straight down. The *profile* of the route is a side view or elevation (see Figures 3.17 and 3.18) in which the longitudinal surfaces are highlighted (e.g., road, top and bottom of pipelines). The *cross section* shows the end view of a section at a station (0 + 60 in Figure 3.19 and 2 + 60 in Figures 3.20 and 3.21) and is at right angles to the centerline. Together, these three views (plan, profile, and cross section) completely define the route in *X, Y,* and *Z* coordinates.

(a)

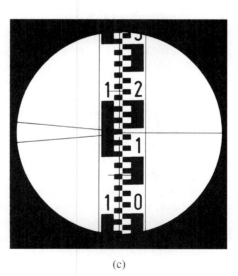

(b)

(c)

**FIGURE 3.16** (a) Invar rod, also showing the footplate, which ensures a clearly defined rod position. (Courtesy of Kern Instruments Ltd.) (b) Philadelphia rod, which can be read directly by the instrument operator or the rod holder after the target has been set (Courtesy of Keuffel & Esser Co.); Frisco rod, with two or three sliding sections having replaceable metal scales. (c) Metric rod; horizontal cross-hair reading on 1.143 m. (Courtesy of Leica, Switzerland Co. Ltd.)

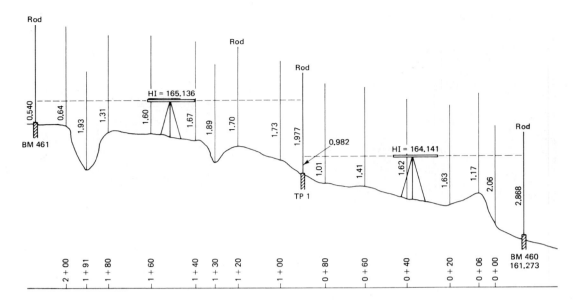

**FIGURE 3.17**  Example of profile leveling; see Figure 3.18 for survey notes.

Profile levels are taken along a path that holds interest for the designer. In roadwork, preliminary surveys often profile the proposed location of the centerline (℄ see Figure 3.17). The proposed ℄ is staked out at an even interval (50 to 100 ft or 20 to 30 m). The level is set up in a convenient location so that the benchmark, and as many intermediate points as possible, can be sighted. Rod readings are taken at the even station locations and at any other point where the ground surface has a significant change in slope. When the rod is moved to a new location and it cannot be seen from the instrument, a turning point is necessary so that the instrument can be moved ahead and the remaining stations leveled.

The turning point can be taken on a wood stake, the corner of a concrete step or concrete headwall, a lug on the flange of a hydrant, and so on. The turning point should be a solid, well-defined point that can be described precisely and, it is hoped, found again in the future. In the case of leveling across fields, it usually is not possible to find turning point features of any permanence. In that case, stakes are driven in and then abandoned when the survey is finished. In the example shown in Figure 3.18, the survey was closed acceptably to BM 461. Had there been no benchmark at the end of the profile survey, the surveyor would have looped back and closed into the initial benchmark.

The intermediate sights (ISs) in Figure 3.18 are shown in a separate column, and the elevations at the intermediate sights show the same number of decimals as are shown in the rod readings. Rod readings on turf, ground, and the like, are usually taken to the closest 0.1 ft or 0.01 m. Rod readings taken on concrete, steel, asphalt, and so on, are usually taken to the closest 0.01 ft or 0.003 m. It is a waste of time and money to read the rod more precisely than conditions warrant. Refer to Chapter 8 for details on plotting the profile.

When the final route of the facility has been selected, further surveying is required. Once again the ℄ is staked (if necessary), and cross sections are taken at all even stations. In roadwork, rod readings are taken along a line perpendicular to ℄ at

SMITH—NOTES
BROWN—$\pi$
PROFILE OF PROPOSED          JONES—ROD

ROAD 0 + 00 to 2 + 00

Job  21 °C — SUNNY   LEVEL  L–14

Date          AUG 3 2003          Page          72

| STA. | B.S. | H.I. | I.S | F.S. | ELEV. | DESCRIPTION |
|---|---|---|---|---|---|---|
| BM 460 | 2.868 | 164.141 | | | 161.273 | BRONZE PLATE SET IN --- ETC. |
| 0 + 00 | | | 2.06 | | 162.08 | ℄ |
| 0 + 06 | | | 1.17 | | 162.97 | ℄ -TOP OF BERM |
| 0 + 20 | | | 1.63 | | 162.51 | ℄ |
| 0 + 40 | | | 1.62 | | 162.52 | ℄ |
| 0 + 60 | | | 1.41 | | 162.73 | ℄ |
| 0 + 80 | | | 1.01 | | 163.13 | ℄ |
| T.P. 1 | 1.977 | 165.136 | | 0.982 | 163.159 | NAIL IN ROOT OF MAPLE --- ETC. |
| 1 + 00 | | | 1.73 | | 163.41 | ℄ |
| 1 + 20 | | | 1.70 | | 163.44 | ℄ |
| 1 + 30 | | | 1.89 | | 163.25 | ℄ BOTTOM OF GULLY |
| 1 + 40 | | | 1.67 | | 163.47 | ℄ |
| 1 + 60 | | | 1.60 | | 163.54 | ℄ |
| 1 + 80 | | | 1.31 | | 163.83 | ℄ |
| 1 + 91 | | | 1.93 | | 163.21 | ℄ BOTTOM OF GULLY |
| 2 + 00 | | | 0.64 | | 164.50 | ℄ |
| BM 461 | | | | 0.540 | 164.596 | BRONZE PLATE SET IN --- ETC. |

164.591 - PUBLISHED ELEV.

$\Sigma = 4.845$     $\Sigma = 1.522$     E = 164.596

ARITHMETIC CHECK: 161.273 + 4.845 −1.522     164.591

= 164.596     0.005

ALLOWABLE ERROR (3$^{RD}$ ORDER)

= 12 mm $\sqrt{K}$, = .012 $\sqrt{.2}$ = .0054 m

ABOVE ERROR (.005) SATISFIES 3$^{RD}$ ORDER.

**FIGURE 3.18**   Profile field notes.

each even station. The rod is held at each significant change in surface slope and at the limits of the job. In uniformly sloping land areas, rod readings required at each cross-sectioned station are often at ℄ and the two street lines (for roadwork). Chapter 7 shows how the cross sections are plotted and then utilized to compute volumes of cut and fill.

Figure 3.20 illustrates the rod positions required to define the ground surface suitably at 2 + 60, at right angles to ℄. Figure 3.21 is shown the field notes for this typical cross section, in a format favored by municipal surveyors. Figure 3.22 shows the same field data entered in a cross-section note form favored by many highway agencies. Note that the HI (353.213) has been rounded to two decimals (353.21) in Figures 3.21 and 3.22 to facilitate reduction of the two-decimal rod readings. The rounded value is placed in brackets to distinguish it from the correct HI, from which the next FS will be subtracted, or from which any three-decimal inter-mediate rod readings are subtracted.

Road and highway construction often requires the location of granular (sand, gravel) deposits for use in the highway roadbed. These *borrow pits* (gravel pits) are surveyed to determine the volume of material "borrowed" and transported to the site. Before any excavation takes place, one or more reference baselines are established, and two benchmarks

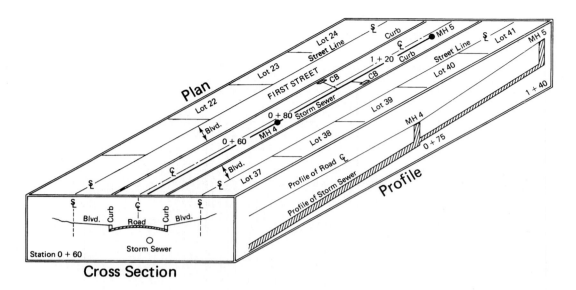

**FIGURE 3.19** Relationship of plan, profile, and cross-section views.

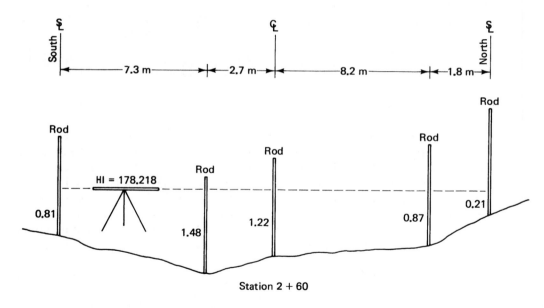

**FIGURE 3.20** Cross-section surveying.

CROSS-SECTIONS FOR PROPOSED

LOCATION OF DUNCAN ROAD

SMITH—NOTES  
BROWN—π  
JONES—ROD  
TYLER—TAPE  
LEVEL #6

Job 14 °C   CLOUDY

Date   NOV 24 2000   Page   23

| STA. | B.S. | H.I. | I.S. | F.S. | ELEV. | DESCRIPTION |
|------|------|------|------|------|-------|-------------|
| BM 28 | 2.011 | 178.218 | | | 176.207 | BRONZE PLATE SET IN SOUTH WALL 0.50m. |
| | | (178.22) | | | | ABOVE GROUND, CIVIC #2242, 23RD AVE. |
| | | | | | | |
| 2 + 60 | | | | | | |
| 10 m LT | | | 0.81 | | 177.41 | S. £ |
| 2.7 m LT | | | 1.48 | | 176.74 | BOTTOM OF SWALE |
| £ | | | 1.22 | | 177.00 | £ |
| 8.2 m RT | | | 0.87 | | 177.35 | CHANGE IN SLOPE |
| 10 m RT | | | 0.21 | | 178.01 | N. £ |
| | | | | | | |
| 2 + 80 | | | | | | |
| 10 m LT | | | 1.02 | | 177.20 | S. £ |
| 3.8 m LT | | | 1.64 | | 176.58 | BOTTOM OF SWALE |
| £ | | | 1.51 | | 176.71 | £ |
| 7.8 m RT | | | 1.10 | | 177.12 | CHANGE IN SLOPE |
| 10 m RT | | | 0.43 | | 177.79 | N. £ |

**FIGURE 3.21**  Cross-section notes (municipal format).

(at minimum) are located in convenient locations. The reference lines are located in secure locations where neither the stripping and stockpiling of topsoil nor the actual excavation of the granular material will endanger the stake (see Figure 3.23). Cross sections are taken over (and beyond) the area of proposed excavation. These **original** cross sections will be used as data against which interim and final survey measurements will be compared to determine total excavation. The volumes calculated from the cross sections (see Chapter 8) are often converted to tons (tonnes) for payment purposes. In many locations, weigh scales are located at the pit to aid in converting the volumes and as a check on the calculated quantities.

The original cross sections are taken over a grid at 50-ft (20-m) intervals. As the excavation proceeds, additional rod readings (in addition to 50-ft grid readings) for the top and bottom of the excavation are required. Permanent targets can be established to assist in the visual alignment of the cross-section lines running perpendicular to the baseline at each 50-ft station. If permanent targets have not been erected, a surveyor on the baseline can keep the rod on line by using a prism or estimated right angles.

CROSS–SECTIONS FOR PROPOSED
LOCATION OF DUNCAN HIGHWAY

SMITH–NOTES          JONES–ROD
BROWN–π              TYLER–TAPE
Job 14 °C   CLOUDY   LEVEL 6
Date       NOV 24 2003   Page   23

| STA. | B.S. | H.I. | I.S | F.S. | ELEV. | | | | | |
|------|------|------|-----|------|-------|---|---|---|---|---|
| | 2.011 | 178.218 | | | 176.207 | BRONZE PLATE SET IN SOUTH WALL | | | | |
| | | (178.22) | | | | 0.50 ABOVE GROUND, CIVIC #2242, 23RD AVE. | | | | |
| | | | | | | LEFT | | ℄ | RIGHT | |
| | | | | | | 10.0 | 2.7 | | 8.2 | 10.0 |
| 2 + 60 | | | | | | 0.81 | 1.48 | 1.22 | 0.87 | 0.21 |
| | | | | | | 177.41 | 176.74 | 177.00 | 177.35 | 178.01 |
| | | | | | | 10.0 | 3.8 | | 7.8 | 10.0 |
| 2 + 80 | | | | | | 1.02 | 1.64 | 1.51 | 1.10 | 0.43 |
| | | | | | | 177.20 | 176.58 | 176.71 | 177.12 | 177.79 |

**FIGURE 3.22**  Cross-section notes (highway format).

# 3.10  Reciprocal Leveling

Section 3.7 advises the surveyor to keep BS and FS distances roughly equal so that instrumental and natural errors will cancel out. In some situations, such as river or valley crossings, it is not always possible to balance BS and FS distances. The reciprocal leveling technique is illustrated in Figure 3.24. The level is set up, and readings are taken on TP 23 and TP 24. Precision can be improved by taking several readings on the far point (TP 24) and then averaging the results. The level is then moved to the far side of the river, and the process is repeated. The differences in elevation thus obtained are averaged to obtain the final result. The averaging process will eliminate instrumental errors and natural errors, such as curvature. Errors due to refraction can be minimized by ensuring that the elapsed time for the process is kept to a minimum.

# 3.11  Peg Test

The purpose of the peg test is to check that the line of sight through the level is horizontal (i.e., parallel to the axis of the bubble tube). The line of sight axis is defined by the location

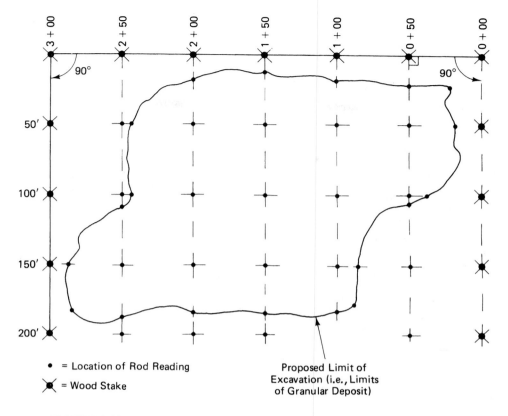

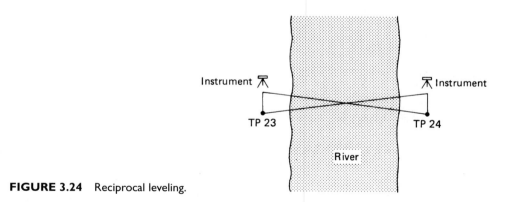

- • = Location of Rod Reading
- ✖ = Wood Stake

Proposed Limit of
Excavation (i.e., Limits
of Granular Deposit)

**FIGURE 3.23** Baseline control for a borrow pit survey.

**FIGURE 3.24** Reciprocal leveling.

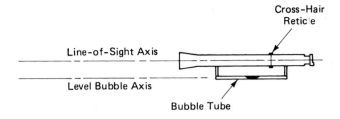

**FIGURE 3.25** Optical axis and level tube axis.

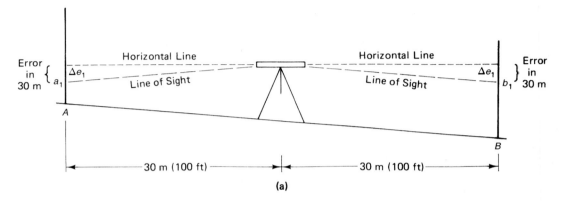

**(a)**

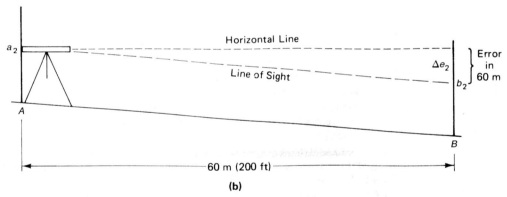

**(b)**

**FIGURE 3.26** Peg test.

of the horizontal cross hair (see Figure 3.25). Refer to Chapter 5 for a description of the horizontal cross-hair orientation adjustment.

To perform the peg test, the surveyor first places two stakes at a distance of 200 to 300 ft (60 to 90 m) apart. The level is set up midway (paced) between the two stakes, and rod readings are taken at both locations (see Figure 3.26, first setup). If the line of sight through the level is not horizontal, the errors in rod readings ($\Delta e_1$) at both points $A$ and $B$ will be identical because the level is halfway between the points. Because the errors are identical, the calculated difference in elevation between points $A$ and $B$ (difference in rod readings) will be the **true** difference in elevation. The level is then moved to one of the points (A) and set up so that the eyepiece of the telescope just touches the rod as it is being held plumb at point A. The rod reading ($a_2$) can be determined by sighting backward through the objective lens at a pencil point that is being moved slowly up and down the rod. The pencil point can be centered precisely, even though the cross hairs are not visible, because the circular field of view is relatively small. Once that reverse rod reading has been determined and booked, the rod is held at B and a normal rod reading is obtained. (The reverse rod reading at A will not contain any line-of-sight error because the cross hair was not used to obtain the rod reading.) If the surveyor cannot look backward through the telescope, the instrument is set up 5 or 6 ft (2 m) from A with the rod read normally. Any error generated over that short distance will be relatively insignificant.

### ■ EXAMPLE 3.2

What is the error in the line of sight for the level used to take the following readings?

**Solution**

First setup:

$$\text{Rod reading at } A, a_1 = 1.075$$
$$\text{Rod reading at } B, b_1 = \underline{1.247}$$
$$\text{True difference in elevations} = 0.172$$

Second setup:

$$\text{Rod reading at } A, a_2 = 1.783$$
$$\text{Rod reading at } B, b_1 = \underline{1.946}*$$
$$\text{Apparent difference in elevation} = 0.163$$

$$\text{Error } (\Delta e_2) \text{ in 60 m} = 0.009$$

This is an error of $-0.00015$ m/m. Therefore, the **collimation correction** (C factor) $= +0.00015$ m/m.

In Section 3.7, you were told to try to keep the BS and FS distances equal. The peg test illustrates clearly the benefits to be gained by use of this technique. If the BS and FS distances are kept roughly equal, errors due to a faulty line of sight simply do not have the opportunity to develop. For example, if the level used in the peg test of Example 3.2 is used in the field with a BS distance of 80 m and an FS distance of 70 m, the net error in the rod readings will be $10 \times 0.00015 = 0.0015$ (0.002); that is, for a relatively large differential between BS and FS distances and a large line-of-sight error (0.009 for 60 m), the effect on the survey is negligible for ordinary work. The peg test can also be accomplished by using the techniques of reciprocal leveling (Section 3.10).

## 3.12  Three-Wire Leveling

Leveling can be performed by utilizing the stadia cross hairs found on most levels of all theodolites (see Figure 3.27). Each backsight (BS) and foresight (FS) is recorded by reading the stadia hairs in addition to the horizontal cross hair. The three readings thus obtained are averaged to obtain the desired value. The stadia hairs (wires) are positioned an equal

---

*Had there been no error in the instrument line sight, the rod reading at $b_2$ would have been 1.955; i.e., 1.783 + 0.172.

Multiplication Factor of 100 { Stadia Hair (Upper) / Cross-Hair / Stadia Hair (Lower)

**FIGURE 3.27**  Reticle cross hairs.

100 X Stadia Hair Interval = Distance

B.M. LEVELING—3 WIRE
B.M. 17 to B.M. 201
(RETURN RUN ON P.48)

JONES—NOTES
SMITH—$\overline{x}$
BROWN—ROD
GREEN—ROD

Job ROD 19,  INST. L.33  8 °C, CLOUDY
Date  MAR 3, 2002  Page  47

| STA. | B.S. | DIST. | F.S. | DIST. | ELEV. | DESCRIPTION |
|------|------|-------|------|-------|-------|-------------|
| BM 17 |  |  |  |  | 186.2830 | BRONZE PLATE SET IN WALL --- ETC. |
|  | 0.825 |  | 1.775 |  |  |  |
|  | 0.725 | 10.0 | 1.673 | 10.2 | + 0.7253 |  |
|  | 0.626 | 9.9 | 1.572 | 10.1 | 187.0083 |  |
|  | 2.176 | 19.9 | 5.020 | 20.3 | −1.6733 |  |
|  | +0.7253 |  | −1.6733 |  |  |  |
| TP 1 |  |  |  |  | 185.3350 | N .LUG TOP FLANGE FIRE HYD. N/S |
|  | 0.698 |  | 1.750 |  |  | MAIN ST. OPP. CIVIC #181. |
|  | 0.571 | 12.7 | 1.620 | 13.0 | + 0.5710 |  |
|  | 0.444 | 12.7 | 1.490 | 13.0 | 185.9060 |  |
|  | 1.713 | 25.4 | 4.860 | 26.0 | −1.6200 |  |
|  | +0.5710 |  | −1.6200 |  |  |  |
| TP 2 |  |  |  |  | 184.2860 | N. LUG TOP FLANGE FIRE HYD. N/S |
|  | 1.199 |  | 2.509 |  |  | MAIN ST. OPP. CIVIC #163. |
|  | 1.118 | 8.1 | 2.427 | 8.2 | + 1.1180 |  |
|  | 1.037 | 8.1 | 2.343 | 8.4 | 185.4040 |  |
|  | 3.354 | 16.2 | 7.279 | 16.6 | −2.4263 |  |
|  | +1.1180 |  | −2.4263 |  |  |  |
| BM 201 |  |  |  |  | 182.9777 | BRONZE PLATE SET IN ESTLY FACE |
|  |  |  |  |  |  | OF RETAINING WALL --- ETC. |
| Σ | +2.4143 | 61.5m | −5.7196 | 62.9m |  |  |
|  |  |  |  |  | 182.9777 |  |

ARITHMETIC CHECK: 186.283 + 2.4143 − 5.7196 = ✓

**FIGURE 3.28**  Survey notes for three-wire leveling.

distance above and below the main cross hair and are spaced to give 1.00 ft (m) of interval for each 100 ft (m) of horizontal distance that the rod is away from the level. The recording of three readings at each sighting enables the surveyor to perform a relatively precise survey while utilizing ordinary levels. Readings to the closest thousandth of a foot (mm) are estimated and recorded. The leveling rod used for this type of work should be calibrated to ensure its integrity. Use of an invar rod is recommended.

Figure 3.28 shows typical notes for benchmark leveling. A realistic survey would include a completed loop or a check into another BM of known elevation. If the collimation correction as calculated in Section 3.11 (+0.00015 m/m) is applied to the survey shown in Figure 3.28, the correction to the elevation is as follows:

$$C = +0.00015 \times (62.9 - 61.5) = +0.0002$$
$$\text{Sum of FS corrected to } 5.7196 + 0.0002 = 5.7198$$

To calculate to elevation of BM 201 from Figure 3.31, see the following:

$$
\begin{aligned}
\text{Elev. BM 17} &= 186.2830 \\
+\Sigma\text{BS} &= \underline{+2.4143} \\
& \phantom{=} 188.6973 \\
-\Sigma\text{FS (corrected)} &= \underline{-5.7198} \\
\text{Elev. BM 201} &= 182.9775 \text{ (corrected for collimation)}
\end{aligned}
$$

When levels are used for precise purposes, it is customary to determine the collimation correction at least once each day.

## 3.13    Trigonometric Leveling

The difference in elevation between $A$ and $B$ (Figure 3.29) can be determined if the vertical angle $(\alpha)$ and the slope distance $(S)$ are measured.

$$V = S \sin \alpha \tag{3.7}$$

$$\text{Elevation at } \overline{\wedge} + \text{hi} \pm V - RR = \text{elevation at rod} \tag{3.8}$$

The hi in this case is not the elevation of the line of sight, as it is in differential leveling. Instead, hi here refers to the distance from point $A$ up to the optical center of the theodolite, measured with a steel tape or rod.

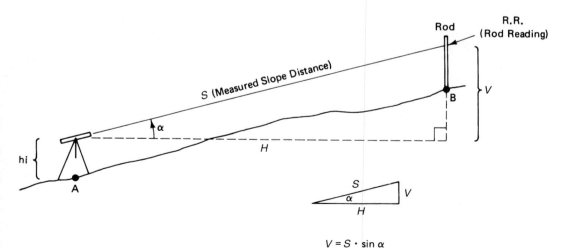

**FIGURE 3.29**   Trigonometric leveling.

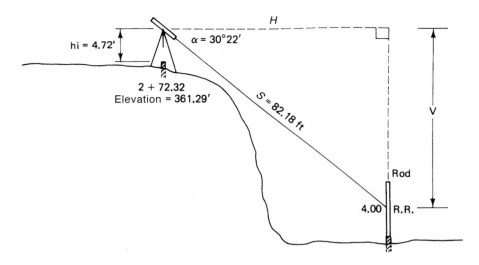

**FIGURE 3.30**  Example of trigonometric leveling (see Section 3.13).

Trigonometric leveling can be used where it is not feasible to use a level, or as an alternative to leveling. For example, a survey crew running a ℄ profile for a route survey comes to a point where the ℄ runs off a cliff. In that case, a theodolite can be set up on the ℄ with the angle and distance measured to a ℄ station at the lower elevation.

The slope distance can be determined by using a steel tape or EDM methods (Chapter 7). The angle is normally measured by use of a theodolite, but for lower-order surveys, a clinometer (Section 2.6.3) can be used. For long distances (associated with EDM), curvature and refraction errors must be eliminated. These matters are discussed in Chapter 7. Section 7.10 discusses total station techniques of trigonometric leveling. Instruments with dual-axis compensators can produce very accurate results.

### ■ EXAMPLE 3.3

Use Figure 3.30 and Equations 3.7 and 3.8 to determine the elevation of the instrument.

**Solution**

$$V = S \sin a$$
$$= 82.18 \sin 30°22'$$
$$= 41.54 \text{ ft}$$

Elevation at $\overline{\wedge}$ + hi $\pm$ V − RR = elevation at rod
$$361.29 + 4.72 - 41.54 - 4.00 = 320.47$$

Note that the RR could have been 4.72, the value of the hi. If that reading had been visible, the surveyor would have sighted on it to eliminate +hi and −RR from the calculation; that is,

$$\text{Elevation at } \overline{\wedge} - V = \text{elevation at rod} \tag{3.8a}$$

In example 3.3, the station (chainage) of the rod station could also be determined.

## 3.14 Level Loop Adjustments

We noted in Section 3.7 that level surveys had to be closed within acceptable tolerances or the survey would have to be repeated. The tolerances for various orders of surveys are shown in Tables 3.1 and 3.2. If a level survey were performed to establish new benchmarks, it would be desirable to proportion any acceptable error suitably throughout the length of the survey. Since the error tolerances shown in Tables 3.1 and 3.2 are based on the distances surveyed, adjustments to the level loop will be based on the relevant distances, or on the number of instrument setups, which is a factor directly related to the distance surveyed.

### ■ EXAMPLE 3.4

A level circuit is shown in Figure 3.31. A survey is needed for local engineering projects. It starts at BM 20; the elevations of new benchmarks 201, 202, and 203 were determined; and then the level survey was looped back to BM 20, the point of commencement (the survey could have terminated at any established BM). What is the permissible error?

**Solution**

According to Table 3.1, the allowable error for a second-order, class II (local engineering projects) survey is $0.008 \sqrt{K}$. Thus, $0.008 \sqrt{4.7} = 0.017$ m is the permissible error. The error in the survey was found to be $-0.015$ m over a total distance of 4.7 km, in this case an acceptable error. This acceptable error must be distributed suitably over the length of the survey. The error is proportioned according to the fraction of cumulative distance over total distance, as in Table 3.4. More complex adjustments are normally performed by computer, using the adjustment method of least squares.

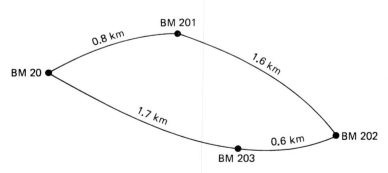

**FIGURE 3.31** Level loop.  Total Distance Around Loop is 4.7 km.

**Table 3.4** LEVEL LOOP ADJUSTMENTS

| BM | Loop distance: cumulative (km) | Elevation | Correction: $\dfrac{\text{Cumulative distance}}{\text{Total distance}} \times E^*$ | Adjusted elevation |
|---|---|---|---|---|
| 20 | | 186.273 (fixed) | | 186.273 |
| 201 | 0.8 | 184.242 | $+0.8/4.7 \times 0.015 = +0.003 =$ | 184.245 |
| 202 | 2.4 | 182.297 | $+2.4/4.7 \times 0.015 = +0.008 =$ | 182.305 |
| 203 | 3.0 | 184.227 | $+3.0/4.7 \times 0.015 = +0.010 =$ | 184.237 |
| 20 | 4.7 | 186.258 | $+4.7/4.7 \times 0.015 = +0.015 =$ | 186.273 |

$^*E = 186.273 - 186.258 = -0.015$ m

## 3.15 Suggestions for Rod Work

The following list of suggestions will help to ensure accurate rod work:

1. The rod should be properly extended and clamped. Take care to ensure that the bottom of the sole plate does not become encrusted with mud, dirt, and so on, which could result in mistaken readings. If a rod target is being used, ensure that it is properly positioned and that it cannot slip.

2. The rod should be held plumb for all rod readings. Either a rod level will be used, or the rod will be waved gently to and from the instrument so that the lowest (indicating a plumb rod) reading can be determined. This practice is particularly important for all backsights and foresights.

3. Ensure that all points used as turning points are suitable, in other words, describable, identifiable, and capable of having the elevation determined to the closest 0.01 ft or 0.001 m. The TP should be nearly equidistant from the two proposed instrument locations.

4. Make sure that the rod is held in precisely the same position for the backsight as it was for the foresight for all turning points.

5. If the rod is held temporarily near, but not on, a required location, the face of the rod should be turned away from the instrument so that the instrument operator cannot take a mistaken reading. This type of mistaken reading usually occurs when the distance between the two surveyors is too far to allow for voice communication and sometimes even for good visual contact.

## 3.16 Suggestions for Instrument Work

The following list offers suggestions to ensure that your instrument work is accurate:

1. Use a straight-leg (nonadjustable) tripod, if possible.

2. Tripod legs should be tightened so that when one leg is extended horizontally, it falls slowly back to the ground under its own weight.

3. The instrument can be comfortably carried resting on one shoulder. If tree branches or other obstructions (e.g., door frames) threaten the safety of the instrument, it should be cradled under one arm with the instrument forward, where it can be seen.

4. When setting up the instrument, gently force the legs into the ground by applying weight on the tripod shoe spurs. On rigid surfaces (e.g., concrete), the tripod legs should be spread farther apart to increase stability.

5. When the tripod is to be set up on a side hill, two legs should be placed downhill and the third leg placed uphill. The instrument can be set up roughly level by careful manipulation of the third, uphill leg.

6. The location of the level setup should be chosen so that you can "see" the maximum number of rod locations, particularly BS and FS locations.

7. Prior to taking rod readings, the cross hair should be focused sharply. It helps to point the instrument toward a light-colored background (e.g., the sky).

8. When the surveyor observes apparent movement of the cross hairs on the rod (parallax), he or she should carefully check the cross-hair focus adjustment and the objective focus adjustment for consistent results.

9. The surveyor should read the rod consistently, at either the top or the bottom of the cross hair.

10. Never move the level before a foresight is taken; otherwise, all work done from that HI will have to be repeated.

11. Check that the level bubble remains centered or that the compensating device (in automatic levels) is operating.

12. Rod readings (and the line of sight) should be kept at least 18 in. (0.5 m) above the ground surface to help minimize refraction errors when you perform a precise level survey.

# 3.17 Mistakes in Leveling

Mistakes in level loops can be detected by performing arithmetic checks, and also by closing in on the starting BM or on any other BM whose elevation is known. Mistakes in rod readings that do not form part of a level loop, such as in intermediate sights taken in profiles, cross sections, or construction grades, are a much more irksome problem. It is bad enough to discover that a level loop contains mistakes and must be repeated. It is a far more serious problem, however, to have to redesign a highway profile because a key elevation contains a mistake, or to have to break out a concrete bridge abutment (the day after the concrete was poured) because the grade stake elevation contained a mistake. Since intermediate rod readings cannot be inherently checked, it is essential that the opportunities for mistakes be minimized.

Common mistakes in leveling include the following: misreading the foot (meter) value, transposing figures, not holding the rod in the correct location, entering the rod readings incorrectly (i.e., switching BS and FS), giving a correct rod reading the wrong station identification, and making mistakes in the note reduction arithmetic. Mistakes in arithmetic can be eliminated almost completely by having the other crew members check the reductions and initial each page of notes checked. Mistakes in the leveling operation cannot be eliminated totally, but they can be minimized if the crew members are aware that mistakes can (and probably will) occur. All crew members should be constantly alert to the possible occurrence of mistakes, and all crew members should try to develop rigid routines for doing their work so that mistakes, when they do eventually occur, will be all the more noticeable.

## Problems

**3.1** Compute the error due to curvature and refraction for the following distances:
   **(a)** 500 ft
   **(b)** 1500 ft
   **(c)** 200 m
   **(d)** 3.5 miles
   **(e)** 2500 m
   **(f)** 6 kilometers

**3.2** Determine the rod readings indicated on the foot and metric rod illustrations in Figure 3.32. The foot readings are to the closest 0.01 ft, and the metric readings are to the closest one-half or one-third centimeter.

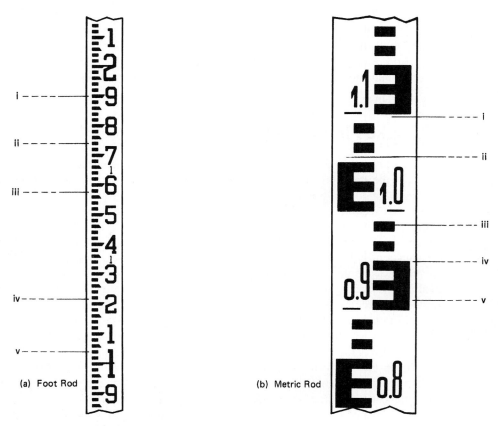

**FIGURE 3.32** (a) Foot rod. (b) Metric rod.

*(continued)*

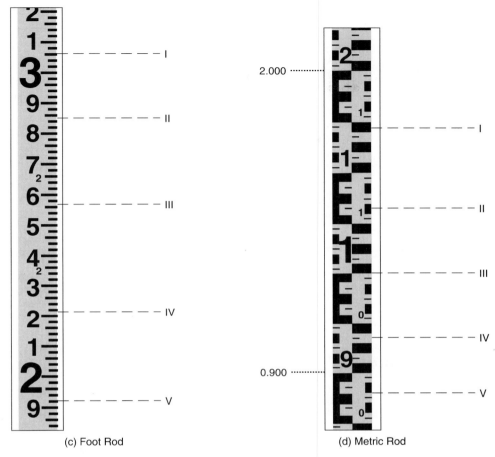

(c) Foot Rod                                          (d) Metric Rod

**FIGURE 3.32 *(continued)*** (c) Foot rod. (d) Metric rod.

**3.3** An offshore drilling rig is being towed out to sea. What is the maximum distance away that the navigation lights can still be seen by an observer standing at the shoreline? The observer's eye height is 5'6", and the uppermost navigation light is 250 ft above the water.

**3.4** Prepare a set of level notes for the survey in Figure 3.33. Show the arithmetic check.

**FIGURE 3.33**

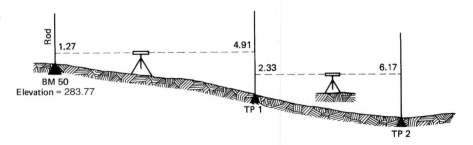

**3.5** Prepare a set of profile leveling notes for the survey in Figure 3.34. In addition to computing all elevations, show the arithmetic check and the resulting error in closure.

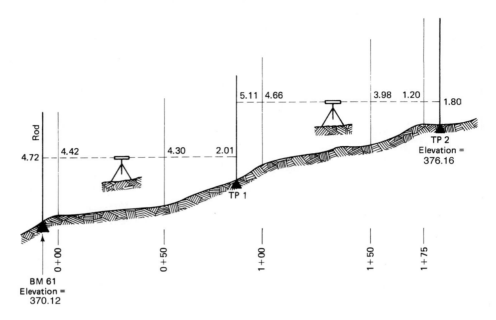

**FIGURE 3.34**

**3.6** Complete the set of differential leveling notes in Table 3.5, and perform the arithmetic check.

**Table 3.5**

| Station | BS | HI | FS | Elevation |
|---------|------|----|------|-----------|
| BM 100 | 2.71 | | | 611.79 |
| TP 1 | 3.62 | | 4.88 | |
| TP 2 | 3.51 | | 3.97 | |
| TP 3 | 3.17 | | 2.81 | |
| TP 4 | 1.47 | | 1.62 | |
| BM 100 | | | 1.21 | |

**3.7** If the loop distance in Problem 3.6 is 1,000 ft, at what order of survey do the results qualify? Use Table 3.1 or Table 3.2.

**3.8** Reduce the set of differential leveling notes in Table 3.6, and perform the arithmetic check.

**Table 3.6**

| Station | BS | HI | IS | FS | Elevation |
|---------|------|-----|------|------|-----------|
| BM 20 | 8.27 | | | | 133.33 |
| TP 1 | 9.21 | | | 2.60 | |
| 0 + 00 | | | 11.3 | | |
| 0 + 50 | | | 9.6 | | |
| 0 + 61.48 | | | 8.71 | | |
| 1 + 00 | | | 6.1 | | |
| TP 2 | 7.33 | | | 4.66 | |
| 1 + 50 | | | 5.8 | | |
| 2 + 00 | | | 4.97 | | |
| BM 21 | | | | 3.88 | |

**3.9** If the distance leveled in Problem 3.8 is 1,000 ft, for what order of survey do the results qualify? See Tables 3.1 and 3.2.

**3.10** Reduce the set of profile notes in Table 3.7, and perform the arithmetic check.

**Table 3.7**

| Station | BS | HI | IS | FS | Elevation |
|---------|-------|-----|-------|-----|-----------|
| BM 21 | 1.203 | | | | 146.212 |
| 0 + 00 | | | | | |
| ℄ | | | 1.211 | | |
| 10 m left, ℄ | | | 1.430 | | |
| 10 m right, ℄ | | | 1.006 | | |
| 0 + 20 | | | | | |
| 10 m left, ℄ | | | 2.93 | | |
| 7.3 m left | | | 2.53 | | |
| 4 m left | | | 2.301 | | |
| ℄ | | | 2.381 | | |
| 4 m right | | | 2.307 | | |
| 7.8 m right | | | 2.41 | | |
| 10 m right, ℄ | | | 2.78 | | |

**Table 3.7  Continued**

| Station | BS | HI | IS | FS | Elevation |
|---|---|---|---|---|---|
| 0 + 40 | | | | | |
| 10 m left, ℄ | | | 3.98 | | |
| 6.2 m left | | | 3.50 | | |
| 4 m left | | | 3.103 | | |
| ℄ | | | 3.187 | | |
| 4 m right | | | 3.100 | | |
| 6.8 m right | | | 3.37 | | |
| 10 m right | | | 3.87 | | |
| TP 1 | | | | 2.773 | |

**3.11** Reduce the set of municipal cross-section notes in Table 3.8.

**Table 3.8**

| Station | BS | HI | IS | FS | Elevation |
|---|---|---|---|---|---|
| BM 41 | 4.11 | | | | 341.41 |
| TP 13 | 4.10 | | | 0.89 | |
| 12 + 00 | | | | | |
| 50 ft left | | | 3.9 | | |
| 18.3 ft left | | | 4.6 | | |
| ℄ | | | 6.33 | | |
| 20.1 ft right | | | 7.9 | | |
| 50 ft right | | | 8.2 | | |
| 13 + 00 | | | | | |
| 50 ft left | | | 5.0 | | |
| 19.6 ft left | | | 5.7 | | |
| ℄ | | | 7.54 | | |
| 20.7 ft right | | | 7.9 | | |
| 50 ft right | | | 8.4 | | |
| TP 14 | 7.39 | | | 1.12 | |
| BM S.22 | | | | 2.41 | |

**3.12** Complete the set of highway cross-section notes in Table 3.9.

**Table 3.9**

| Station | BS | HI | FS | Elevation | Left | | ₵ | Right | |
|---------|------|----|------|-----------|------------------|------------------|------|------------------|------------------|
| BM 37 | 7.20 | | | 448.20 | | | | | |
| 5 + 50 | | | | | 50'  26.7' | 4.6  3.8 | 3.7 | 28.4'  50' | 3.0  2.7 |
| | | | | | | | | | |
| 6 + 00 | | | | | 50'  24.1' | 4.0  4.2 | 3.1 | 25.0'  50' | 2.7  2.9 |
| | | | | | | | | | |
| 6 + 50 | | | | | 50'  26.4' | 3.8  3.7 | 2.6 | 23.8'  50' | 1.7  1.1 |
| | | | | | | | | | |
| TP #1 | | | 6.71 | | | | | | |

**3.13** Complete the set of highway cross-section notes in Table 3.10.

**Table 3.10**

| Station | BS | HI | FS | Elevation | Left | | ₵ | Right | |
|---------|------|----|-------|-----------|------------------|------------------|------|------------------|------------------|
| BM 107 | 7.71 | | | 336.86 | | | | | |
| 80 + 50 | | | | | 60'  28' | 9.7  8.0 | 5.7 | 32'  60' | 4.3  4.0 |
| | | | | | | | | | |
| 81 + 00 | | | | | 60'  25' | 10.1  9.7 | 6.8 | 30'  60' | 6.0  5.3 |
| | | | | | | | | | |
| 81 + 50 | | | | | 60'  27' | 11.7  11.0 | 9.2 | 33'  60' | 8.3  8.0 |
| | | | | | | | | | |
| TP 1 | | | 10.17 | | | | | | |

**3.14** A level is set up midway between two wood stakes that are about 300 ft apart. The rod reading on stake A is 8.72 ft, and it is 5.61 ft on stake B. The level is then moved to point *B* and set up so that the eyepiece end of the telescope is just touching the rod as it is held plumb on the stake. A reading of 5.42 ft is taken on the rod at B by sighting backward through the telescope. The level is then sighted on the rod held on stake A, where a reading of 8.57 ft is noted.

(a) What is the correct difference in elevation between the tops of stakes A and B?

(b) If the level had been in perfect adjustment, what reading would have been observed at A from the second setup?

(c) What is the line-of-sight error in 300 ft?

(d) Describe how you would eliminate the line-of-sight error from the telescope.

**3.15** A pre-engineering baseline was run down a very steep hill (see Figure 3.35). Rather than measure horizontally downhill with the steel tape, the surveyor measures the vertical angle with a theodolite and the slope distance with a 200-ft steel tape. The vertical angle is −21°26′ turned to a point on a plumbed range pole is 4.88 ft above the ground. The slope distance from the theodolite to the point on the range pole is 148.61 ft. The theodolite's optical center is 4.66 ft above the upper baseline station at 110 + 71.25.

   **(a)** If the elevation of the upper station is 829.76, what is the elevation of the lower station?

   **(b)** What is the chainage of the lower station?

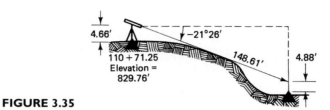

**FIGURE 3.35**

**3.16** You must establish the elevation of point $B$ from point $A$ (elevation 187.298 m). $A$ and $B$ are on opposite sides of a 12-lane highway. Reciprocal leveling is used, with the following results:

> Setup at A side of highway:
> Rod reading on $A$ = 0.673 m
> Rod readings on $B$ = 2.416 and 2.418 m
> Setup at B side of highway:
> Rod reading on $B$ = 2.992 m
> Rod readings on $A$ = 1.254 and 1.250 m

   **(a)** What is the elevation of point $B$?

   **(b)** What is the leveling error?

**3.17** Reduce the set of differential leveling notes in Table 3.11, and perform the arithmetic check.

   **(a)** Determine the order of accuracy (see Table 3.1 or 3.2).

   **(b)** Adjust the elevation of BM K110. The length of the level run was 780 m, with setups that are equally spaced. The elevation of BM 132 is 140.416 m.

**Table 3.11**

| Station | BS | HI | FS | Elevation |
|---------|-------|----|-------|-----------|
| BM 130 | 0.702 | | | 141.444 |
| TP 1 | 0.970 | | 1.111 | |
| TP 2 | 0.559 | | 0.679 | |
| TP 3 | 1.744 | | 2.780 | |
| BM K110 | 1.973 | | 1.668 | |
| TP 4 | 1.927 | | 1.788 | |
| BM 132 | | | 0.888 | |

# 4 Angles and Directions

## 4.1 General Background

We noted in Section 1.11 that the units of angular measurement employed in North American practice are degrees, minutes, and seconds. For the most part, angles in surveying are measured with a transit/theodolite or total station, although angles can be measured with clinometers, sextants (hydrographic surveys), or compasses.

## 4.2 Reference Directions for Vertical Angles

Vertical angles, which are used in slope distance corrections (Section 2.10) or in height determination (Section 3.13), are referenced to the (1) the horizon by plus (up) or minus (down) angles, (2) zenith, or (3) nadir (see Figure 4.1). *Zenith* and *nadir* are terms describing points on a celestial sphere (i.e., a sphere or infinitely large radius with its center at the center of the earth). The zenith is directly above the observer and the nadir is directly below the observer; the zenith, nadir, and observer are all on the same vertical line (see also Figure 10.29).

## 4.3 Meridians

A line on the mean surface of the earth joining the north and south poles is called a *meridian*. In Section 1.6, we noted that surveys could be referenced to lines of latitude and longitude. All lines of longitude are meridians. The term *meridian* can be more precisely defined by noting that it is the line formed by the intersection with the earth's surface of a plane that includes the earth's axis of rotation. The meridian, as described, is known as the *geographic meridian*. Magnetic meridians are parallel to the directions taken by freely moving magnetized needles, as in a compass. Whereas geographic meridians are fixed, magnetic meridians vary with time and location. *Grid meridians* are lines that are parallel

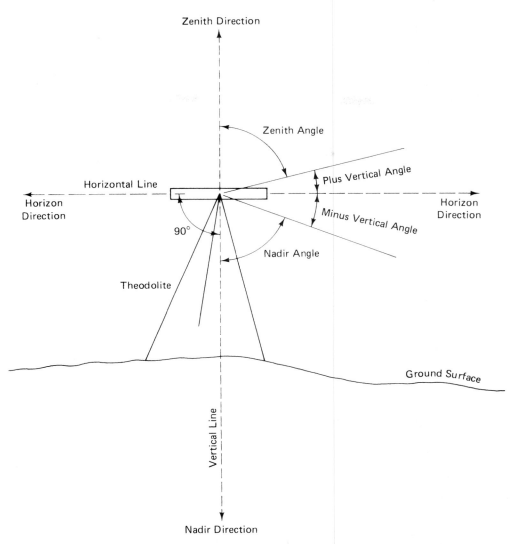

**FIGURE 4.1**  The three reference directions for vertical angles: horizontal, zenith, and nadir.

to a grid reference meridian (central meridian). The concept of a grid for survey reference was introduced in Section 1.7 and is described in detail in Chapter 10.

Figure 4.2 shows *geographic meridians,* which all converge to meet at the pole, and grid meridians, which are all parallel to the central (geographic) meridian. In the case of a small-scale survey of only limited importance, meridians are sometimes assumed, and the survey is referenced to that assumed direction. We saw in Section 4.2 that vertical angles were referenced to a horizontal line (plus or minus) or to a vertical line (from either the zenith or nadir direction). In contrast, we now see that all horizontal directions are referenced to meridians.

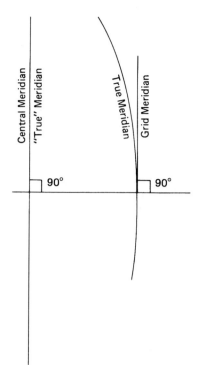

**FIGURE 4.2** Relationship between "true" meridians and grid meridians.

## 4.4 Horizontal Angles

Horizontal angles are usually measured with a theodolite or total station whose precision can range from 1 second to 20 seconds of arc. These instruments are described in detail in Chapters 5 and 7. Angles can be measured between lines forming a closed traverse, between lines forming an open traverse, or between a line and a point so that the point's location can be determined.

For all closed polygons of $n$ sides, the sum of the interior angles will be $(n - 2)180°$; the sum of the exterior angles will be $(n + 2)180°$. In Figure 4.3 the interior angles of a five-sided closed polygon have been measured. For a five-sided polygon, the sum of the interior angles must be $(5 - 2)180° = 540°$; the angles shown in Figure 4.3 do, in fact, total 540°. In practical field problems, however, the total is usually marginally more or less than $(n - 2)180°$, and it is then up to the surveyor to determine if the error of angular closure is within tolerances as specified for that survey. The adjustment of angular errors is described in Chapter 6.

Note that the exterior angles at each station in Figure 4.3 could have been measured instead of the interior angles, as shown. (The exterior angle at $A$ of 272°55′ is shown.) Generally, exterior angles are measured to serve only occasionally as a check on the interior angle. Refer to Chapter 5 for the actual field techniques used in the measurement of angles.

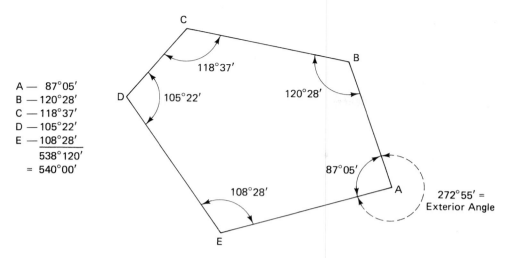

A — 87°05'
B — 120°28'
C — 118°37'
D — 105°22'
E — 108°28'
538°120'
= 540°00'

118°37'

105°22'

120°28'

87°05'

108°28'

272°55' =
Exterior Angle

**FIGURE 4.3** Closed traverse showing the interior angles.

An open traverse is illustrated in Figure 4.4(a). The *deflection angles* shown are measured from the prolongation of the back line to the forward line. The angles are measured either to the left (L) or to the right (R) of the projected line. The direction (L or R) must be shown along with the numerical value. It is also possible to measure the change in direction [see Figure 4.4(b)] by directly sighting the back line and turning the angle left or right to the forward line.

## 4.5 Azimuths

An *azimuth* is the direction of a line as given by an angle measured clockwise (usually) from the north end of a meridian. Azimuths range in magnitude from 0° to 360°. Values in excess of 360°, which are sometimes encountered in computations, are simply reduced by 360° before final listing. Figure 4.5 illustrates the concept of azimuths by showing four line directions in addition to the four cardinal directions (N, S, E, and W).

## 4.6 Bearings

A *bearing* is the direction of a line as given by the acute angle between the line and a meridian. The bearing angle, which can be measured clockwise or counterclockwise from the north or south end of the meridian, is always accompanied by letters that locate the quadrant in which the line falls (NE, NW, SE, or SW). Figure 4.6 illustrates the concepts of bearings and shows the proper designation for the four lines shown. In addition, the four cardinal directions are usually designated by the terms due north, due south, due east, and due west. Due west, for example, can also be designated as N 90° W (or S 90° W).

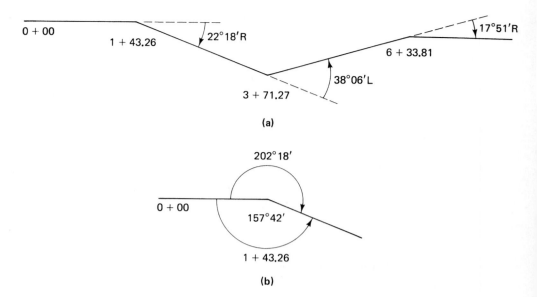

(a)

(b)

**FIGURE 4.4**    (a) Open traverse showing deflection angles. (b) Same traverse showing angle right (202°18′) and angle left (157°42′).

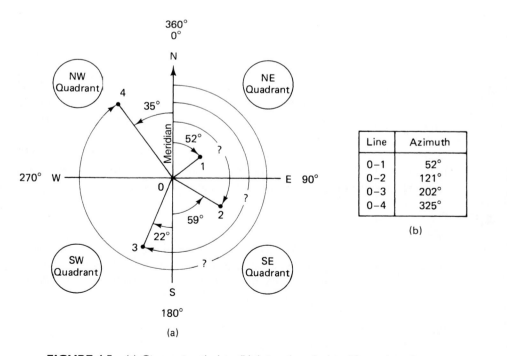

| Line | Azimuth |
|------|---------|
| 0–1 | 52° |
| 0–2 | 121° |
| 0–3 | 202° |
| 0–4 | 325° |

(b)

(a)

**FIGURE 4.5**    (a) Given azimuth data. (b) Azimuths calculated from given data.

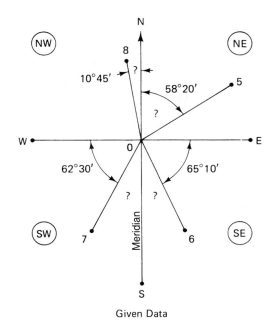

| Line | Bearing |
|------|---------|
| 0–5 | N 58°20′ E |
| 0–6 | S 24°50′ E |
| 0–7 | S 27°30′ W |
| 0–8 | N 10°45′ W |

Answers

Given Data

**FIGURE 4.6**  Bearings calculated from given data.

# 4.7  Relationships Between Bearings and Azimuths

Refer again to Figure 4.5. You can see that azimuth and bearing directions in the NE quadrant are numerically equal. That is, for line 0–1, the azimuth is 52° and the bearing is N 52° E. In the SE quadrant, you can see that 0–2, which has an azimuth of 121°, will have a bearing (acute angle from meridian) of S 59° E. In the SW quadrant, the azimuth of 0–3 is 202° and the bearing will be S 22° W. In the NW quadrant, the azimuth of 0–4 is 325° and the bearing will be N 35° W.

To convert from azimuths to bearings, first, determine the proper quadrant letters (see Figure 4.5):

1. For 0° to 90°, use NE (quadrant 1 in most software programs).
2. For 90° to 180°, use SE (quadrant 2 in most software programs).
3. For 180° to 270°, use SW (quadrant 3 in most software programs).
4. For 270° to 360°, use NW (quadrant 4 in most software programs).

Then the numerical value is determined by using the following relationships:

1. NE quadrant: bearing = azimuth
2. SE quadrant: bearing = 180° − azimuth
3. SW quadrant: bearing = azimuth − 180°
4. NW quadrant: bearing = 360° − azimuth

Now convert from bearing to azimuths by using these relationships:

1. NE quadrant: azimuth = bearing
2. SE quadrant: azimuth = 180° − bearing
3. SW quadrant: azimuth = 180° + bearing
4. NW quadrant: azimuth = 360° − bearing

## 4.8  Reverse Directions

It can be said that every line has two directions. The line shown in Figure 4.7 has direction *AB* or it has direction *BA*. In surveying, a direction is called **forward** if it is oriented in the direction of fieldwork or computation staging. If the direction is the reverse of that, it is called a **back** direction. The designations of forward and back are often arbitrarily chosen, but if more than one line is being considered, the forward and backward designations must be consistent for all adjoining lines.

In Figure 4.8, the line *AB* has a bearing of N 62°30′ E, whereas the line *BA* has a bearing of S 62°30′ W; that is, **to reverse a bearing, simply reverse the direction letters.** In this case, N and E become S and W, and the numerical value (62°30′) remains unchanged. In Figure 4.9, the line *CD* has an azimuth of 128°20′. Analysis of the sketch leads quickly to the conclusion that the azimuth of *DC* is 308°20′; that is, **to reverse an azimuth, simply add 180° to the original direction.** If the original azimuth is greater than 180°, 180° can be subtracted from it to reverse its direction. The key factor to remember is that a forward and back azimuth must differ by 180°.

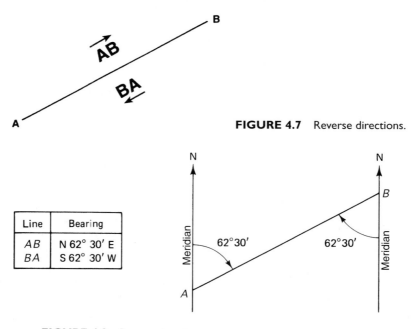

**FIGURE 4.7**  Reverse directions.

| Line | Bearing |
|------|-------------|
| AB | N 62° 30′ E |
| BA | S 62° 30′ W |

**FIGURE 4.8**  Reverse bearings.

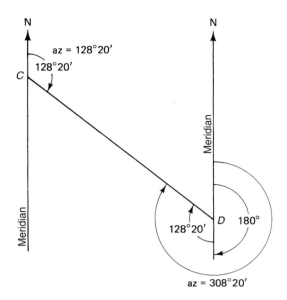

| Line | Azimuth |
|------|---------|
| CD | 128°20′ |
| DC | 308°20′ |

**FIGURE 4.9** Reverse azimuths.

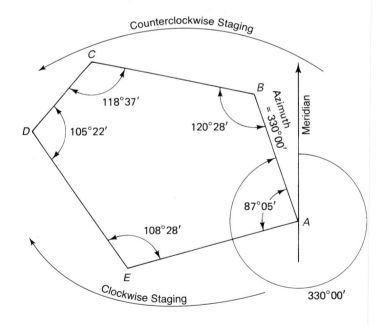

**FIGURE 4.10** Sketch for azimuth calculations. Computations can be staged to proceed clockwise or counterclockwise.

## 4.9 Azimuth Computations

The data in Figure 4.10 will be used to illustrate the computation of azimuths. Before azimuths or bearings are computed, it is important to check that the figure is geometrically closed: that the sum of the interior angles = $(n - 2)180$. In Figure 4.10, the five angles do add to 540°00′ and *AB* has a given azimuth of 330°00′. At this point, a decision must be made about how the computation will proceed. Using the given azimuth and the angle at *B*, the azimuth of *BC* can be computed (counterclockwise direction); or using the given azimuth and the angle at *A*, the azimuth of *AE* can be computed (clockwise direction). Once a direction for solving the problem has been established, all the computed directions must be consistent with that general direction. A neat, well-labeled sketch should accompany each step of the computation.

Analysis of the preceding azimuth computations gives the following observations:

1. If the computation is proceeding in a **counterclockwise direction, add the interior angle to the back azimuth of the previous course.**
2. If the computation is proceeding in a **clockwise direction, subtract the interior angle from the back azimuth of the previous course.**

If the bearings of the sides are also required, they can now be derived from the computed azimuths.

**Table 4.1**

COUNTERCLOCKWISE
SOLUTION

| Course | Azimuth | Bearing |
|--------|---------|---------|
| BC | 270° 28′ | N 89° 32′ W |
| CD | 209° 05′ | S 29° 05′ W |
| DE | 134° 27′ | S 45° 33′ E |
| EA | 62° 55′ | N 62° 55′ E |
| AB | 330° 00′ | N 30° 00′ W |

CLOCKWISE SOLUTION

| Course | Azimuth | Bearing |
|--------|---------|---------|
| AE | 242° 55′ | S 62° 55′ W |
| ED | 314° 27′ | N 45° 33′ W |
| DC | 29° 05′ | N 29° 05′ E |
| CB | 90° 28′ | S 89° 32′ E |
| BA | 150° 00′ | S 30° 00′ E |

Note the following points about azimuth calculations:

1. For reversal of direction (i.e., clockwise versus counterclockwise), the azimuths for the same side differ by 180°, whereas bearings for the same side remain numerically the same and have the letters (N/S, E/W) reversed.
2. The bearings calculated from azimuths have no built-in check. The only way that the correctness of the calculated bearings can be verified is to double-check the computation. **Constant reference to a good problem diagram will help reduce the incidence of mistakes.**

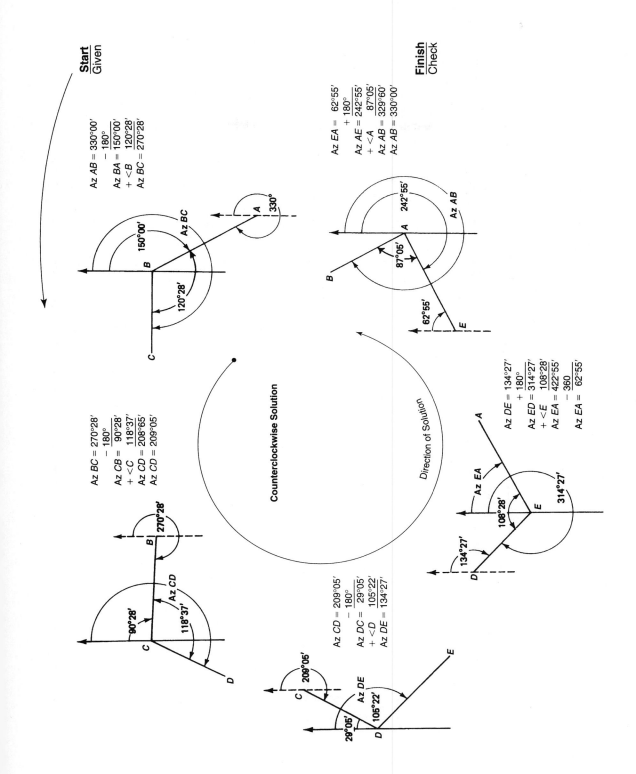

Az AB = 330°00'
      − 180°
Az BA = 150°00'
  + <B 120°28'
Az BC = 270°28'

150°00'

Az BC

330°

B

120°28'

A

C

Az BC = 270°28'
      − 180°
Az CB = 90°28'
  + <C 118°37'
Az CD = 208°65'
Az CD = 209°05'

270°28'

B

Az CD

90°28'

118°37'

C

D

**Counterclockwise Solution**

*Direction of Solution*

Az CD = 209°05'
      − 180°
Az DC = 29°05'
  + <D 105°22'
Az DE = 134°27'

209°05'

C

Az DE

29°05'

105°22'

D

E

Az DE = 134°27'
      + 180°
Az ED = 314°27'
  + <E 108°28'
Az EA = 422°55'
      − 360
Az EA = 62°55'

Az EA

314°27'

108°28'

E

134°27'

D

A

Az EA = 62°55'
      + 180°
Az AE = 242°55'
  + <A 87°05'
Az AB = 329°60'
Az AB = 330°00'

242°55'

A

Az AB

87°05'

B

62°55'

E

109

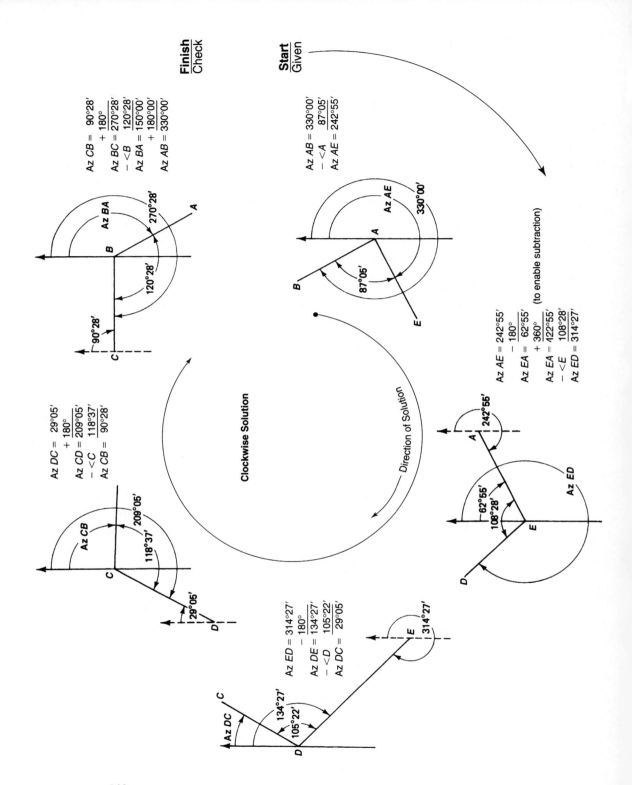

## 4.10  Bearing Computations

As with azimuth computations, the solution can proceed in a clockwise or counterclockwise manner. In Figure 4.11, side *AB* has a given bearing of N 30°00′ W, and the bearing of either *BC* or *AE* may be computed first. Because there is no systematic method of directly computing bearings, each bearing computation will be regarded as a separate problem. **It is essential that a neat, well-labeled diagram accompany each computation.** The sketch of each individual bearing computation will show the appropriate interior angle together with one bearing angle. The required bearing angle should also be shown clearly.

In Figure 4.12(a), the interior angle (*B*) and the bearing angle (30°) for side *BA* is shown; the required bearing angle for side *BC* is shown as a question mark. Analysis of the sketch shows that the required bearing angle (?) = 180° − 90°28′; i.e., (120°28′ − 30°00′) = 89°32′ and that the quadrant is NW. The bearing of *BC* = N 89°32′ W.

In Figure 4.12(b), the bearing for *CB* is shown as S 89°32′ E, which is the reverse of the bearing that was just calculated for side *BC*. When the meridian line is moved from *B* to *C* for this computation, it necessitates the reversal of direction. Analysis of the completely labeled sketch shows that the required bearing angle for *CD* (?) = (118°37′ − 89°32′) = 29°05′ and that the direction is SW. The bearing of *CD* is S 29°05′ W.

Analysis of Figure 4.12(c) shows that the bearing angle of line *DE* (?) = 180° − (105°22′ + 29°05′) = 45°33′ and that the direction of *DE* is SE. The bearing of *DE* is

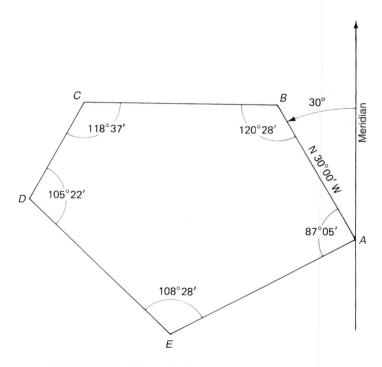

**FIGURE 4.11**  Sketch for bearing computations.

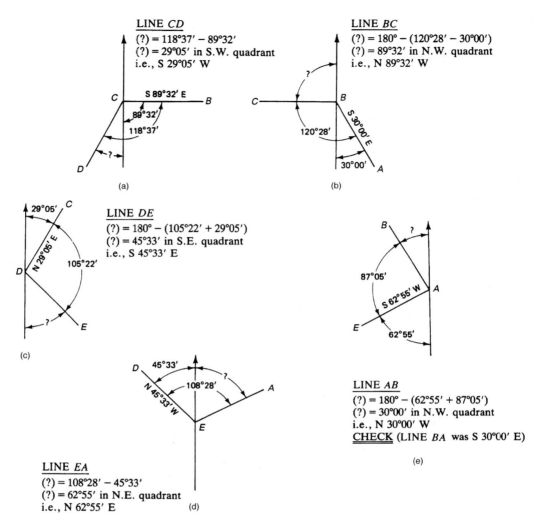

**LINE *CD***
(?) = 118°37′ − 89°32′
(?) = 29°05′ in S.W. quadrant
i.e., S 29°05′ W

**LINE *BC***
(?) = 180° − (120°28′ − 30°00′)
(?) = 89°32′ in N.W. quadrant
i.e., N 89°32′ W

(a)

(b)

**LINE *DE***
(?) = 180° − (105°22′ + 29°05′)
(?) = 45°33′ in S.E. quadrant
i.e., S 45°33′ E

(c)

**LINE *AB***
(?) = 180° − (62°55′ + 87°05′)
(?) = 30°00′ in N.W. quadrant
i.e., N 30°00′ W
<u>CHECK</u> (LINE *BA* was S 30°00′ E)

(e)

**LINE *EA***
(?) = 108°28′ − 45°33′
(?) = 62°55′ in N.E. quadrant
i.e., N 62°55′ E

(d)

**FIGURE 4.12**  Sketches for each bearing calculation for the discussion of Section 4.10.

S 45°33′ E. Analysis of Figure 4.12(d) shows that the bearing angle of line *EA* (?) is (108°28′ − 45°33′) = 62°55′ and that the direction is NE. The bearing of *EA* is N 62°55′ E.

The problem's original data included the bearing of *AB* as being N 30°00′ W. The bearing of *AB* will now be computed using the interior angle at *A* and the bearing just computed for the previous course (*EA*). The bearing angle of *AB* = 180° − (62°55′ + 87°05′) = 30°00′ and the direction is NW. The bearing of *AB* is N 30°00′ W [see Figure 4.12(e)]. This last computation serves as a check on all our computations.

## 4.11   Comments on Bearings and Azimuths

Both bearings and azimuths may be used to give the direction of a line. North American tradition favors the use of bearings over azimuths; most legal plans (plats) show directions in bearings. In the previous sections, bearings were derived from computed azimuths (Section 4.9), or bearings were computed directly from the given data (Section 4.10). The **advantage** of computing bearings directly from the given data in a closed traverse, is that the final computation (of the given bearing) provides a check on all the problem computations, ensuring (normally) the correctness of all the computed bearings. In contrast, if bearings are derived from computed azimuths, there is no intrinsic check on the correctness of the derived bearings.

The **disadvantage** associated with computing bearings directly from the data in a closed traverse is that there is no systematic approach to the overall solution. Each bearing computation is unique, requiring individual analysis. It is sometimes difficult to persuade people to prepare neat, well-labeled sketches for computations involving only intermediate steps in a problem. Without neat, well-labeled sketches for each bearing computation, the potential for mistakes is quite large. And when mistakes do occur in the computation, the lack of a systematic approach to the solution often means that much valuable time is lost before the mistake is found and corrected. In contrast, the computation of azimuths involves a highly systematic routine: **add (subtract) the interior angle from the back azimuth of the previous course.** If the computations are arranged as shown in Section 4.9, mistakes that may be made in the computation will be found quickly. See Figure 4.13 for a summary of results.

With the widespread use of computers and sophisticated handheld calculators, it is expected that azimuths will be used more and more to give the direction of a line. It is easier to deal with straight numeric values rather than the alphanumeric values associated with bearings, and it is more efficient to have the algebraic sign generated by the calculator or computer rather than trying to remember if the direction was north, south, east, or west.

We will see in Chapter 6 that bearings or azimuths are used in calculating the geometric closure of a closed survey. The absolute necessity of having mistakes eliminated from the computation of line directions will become more apparent in that chapter. You will see that the computation of direction (bearings or azimuths) is only the first step in what can be a very involved computation.

## 4.12   Magnetic Direction

A freely moving magnetized compass needle will always point in the direction of magnetic north. Because the magnetic north pole is some distance from the geographic north pole,

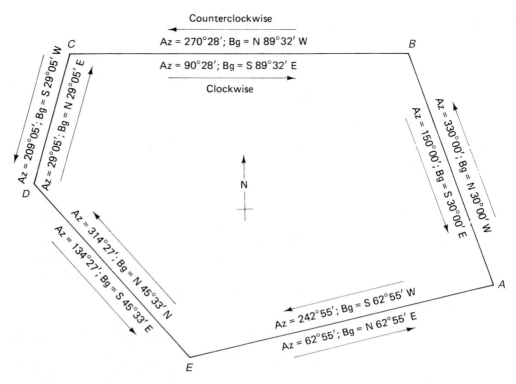

**FIGURE 4.13** Summary of results from clockwise and counterclockwise approaches.

the magnetized needle does not, for the most part, point exactly to geographic north. The horizontal angle between the direction taken by the compass needle and geographic north is the *magnetic declination*. In North America, the magnetic declination ranges from about 15° east on the west coast to about 15° west on the east coast. The magnetic declination thus varies with location and also with time.

Careful records have been kept over the years so that, although magnetic variations are not well understood, it is possible to predict magnetic declination over a short span of time. Many countries issue isogonic charts, usually every five or ten years, on which lines (isogonic lines) are drawn that join points of the earth's surface having equal magnetic declination. See Figure 4.14 for two examples. Additional lines shown on the chart join points on the earth's surface that are experiencing equal annual changes in magnetic declination. Due to the uncertainties of determining magnetic declination and the effects of local attraction (e.g., ore bodies) on the compass needle, magnetic directions are not employed for any but the lowest order of surveys. Also, due to the difficulty in long-term predictability of magnetic influences, you are cautioned about applying annual change corrections beyond five years from the epoch of the current isogonic chart.

Isogonic charts are a valuable aid for retracing original surveys (magnetic). Most original township surveys in North America were magnetically referenced. When magnetically referenced surveys are to be retraced, it is necessary to determine the magnetic declination for that area at the time of the survey and at the time of the retracement survey.

Declination data are also available at www.ngdc.noaa.gov. Inputs are zip codes (where relevant) and latitudes and departures.

### ■ EXAMPLE 4.1

A magnetic bearing was originally recorded for a specific lot line (AB) in Seattle as being N 10°30′ E. The magnetic declination at that time was 15°30′ east. You must retrace the survey from the original notes during the first week of September 2001.

(a) What compass bearing will be used for the same specific lot line during the retracement survey?

(b) What will be the geographic bearing for the same survey line in the retracement survey?

**Solution**

Using the isogonic chart Figure 4.14(a), the following data are scaled for the Seattle area:

$$\text{Declination } (2000.0) = 18° \, 50' \text{ E}$$

$$\text{Annual change} = 08' \text{ W}$$

$$\begin{aligned}\text{Declination September, 2001} &= 18°50' - (08' \times 1.75)\\ &= 18° \, 36' \text{ E}\end{aligned}$$

$$\text{Declination during original survey} = \underline{15° \, 30'E}$$

$$\text{Difference in declination} = 3° \, 06'$$

$$\text{Geographic bearing} = 10°30' + 15° \, 30' = \text{N } 26° \, 00' \text{ E}$$

$$\text{Magnetic bearing, September 2001} = 10°30' - 3°36' = \text{N } 7°24' \text{ E}$$

or

$$\text{Magnetic bearing, September 2001} = 26°00' - 18°36' = \text{N } 7°24' \text{ E}. \text{ See Figure 4.15.}$$

Other situations when modern surveyors need a compass are determining the meridian by observation of the North Star, Polaris (see Chapter 10), or preparing station visibility diagrams for GPS surveys (see Figure 11.19). A variety of compasses are available, from the simple to the more complex Figure 4.16 shows a **Brunton** compass, which is popular with many surveyors and geologists. It can be handheld or mounted on a tripod. It can also be used as a clinometer, with vertical angles read to the closest 5 minutes.

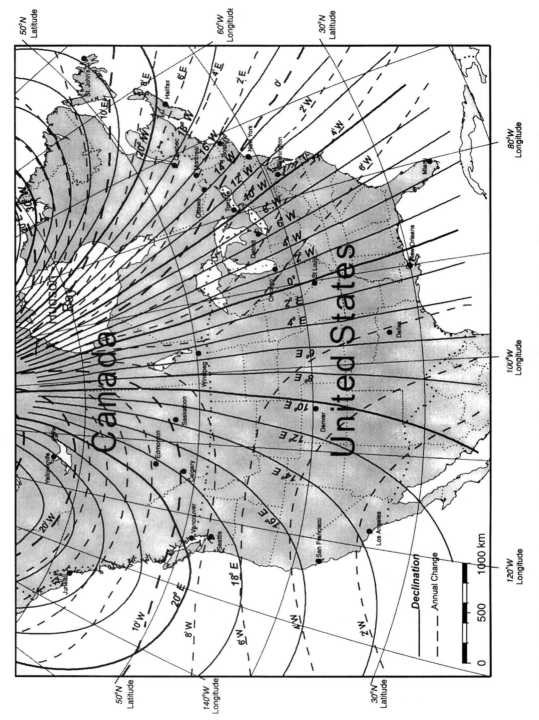

**FIGURE 4.14** (a) Isogonic map of North America, Epoch 2000. (Compilation by Natural Resources Canada, Geomagnetic Laboratory, Ottawa) (b) United States/United Kingdom world magnetic chart—declination, Epoch 2000. (Courtesy U.S. Department of the Interior, U.S. Geological Survey, Denver, Colo.)

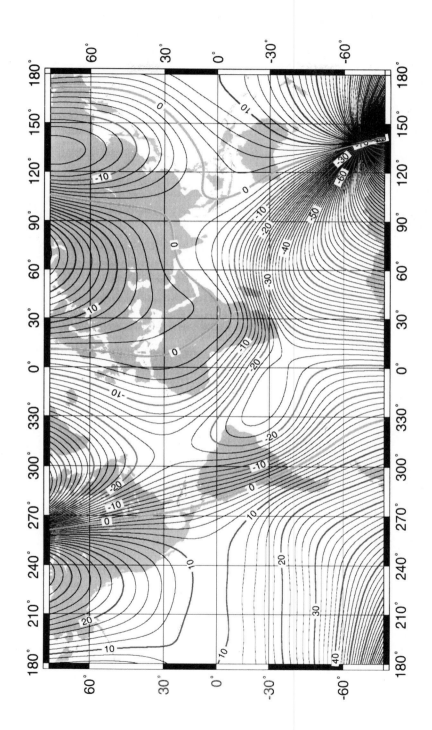

117

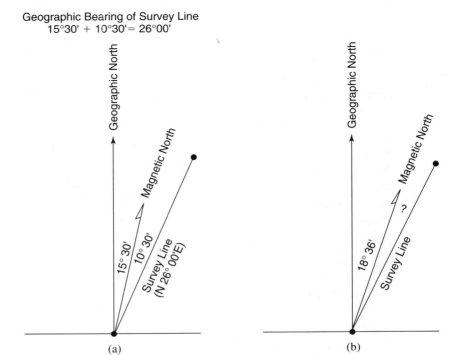

Geographic Bearing of Survey Line
15°30' + 10°30' = 26°00'

(a)

(b)

**FIGURE 4.15** Magnetic delination problem. (a) Original survey. (b) Retracement survey.

**FIGURE 4.16** Pocket transit, combining the features of a sighting compass, prismatic compass, hand level, and clinometer. Can be staff-mounted for more precise work. (Courtesy of Keuffel & Esser Co.)

# Problems

**4.1**  A closed five-sided field traverse has the following interior angles: $A = 127°30'00''$, $B = 118°11'30''$, $C = 83°20'00''$, $D = 85°33'30''$. Find the angle at $E$.

**4.2**  Convert the following azimuths to bearings.
(a) 200°58'  (b) 136°51'  (c) 127°43'  (d) 272°49'
(e) 8°08'  (f) 317°27'  (g) 199°10'

**4.3**  Convert the following bearings to azimuths.
(a) N 42°46' E  (b) N 2°21' W  (c) S 9°41' E  (d) S 77°52' W
(e) N 80°10' E  (f) S 5°30' W  (g) S 44°44' E

**4.4**  Convert the azimuths given in Problem 4.2 to reverse (back) azimuths.

**4.5**  Convert the bearings given in Problem 4.3 to reverse (back) bearings.

**4.6**  An open traverse that runs from $A$ through $H$ has the following deflection angles: $B = 6°25'$R, $C = 3°54'$R, $D = 11°47'$R, $E = 20°02'$L, $F = 7°18'$L, $G = 1°56'$R. If the bearing of $AB$ is N 32°51' E, compute the bearings of the remaining sides.

**4.7**  Closed traverse $ABCD$ has the following bearings: $AB =$ N 65°24' E, $BC =$ S 46°26' E, $CD =$ S 14°30' W, $DA =$ N 66°43' W. Compute the interior angles and provide a geometric check for your work.

Use the interior angles of Figure 4.17 for Problems 4.8 through 4.11.

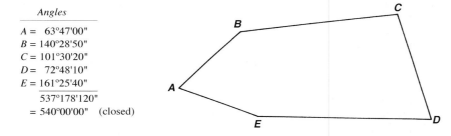

| Angles | |
| --- | --- |
| $A =$ | 63°47'00" |
| $B =$ | 140°28'50" |
| $C =$ | 101°30'20" |
| $D =$ | 72°48'10" |
| $E =$ | 161°25'40" |
| | 537°178'120" |
| $=$ | 540°00'00"  (closed) |

**FIGURE 4.17**  Sketch of interior angles for Problems 4.8 through 4.11.

**4.8**  If the bearing of $AB$ is N 44°44'40" E, compute the bearings of the remaining sides. Provide two solutions: one solution proceeding clockwise and the other proceeding counterclockwise.

**4.9**  If the azimuth of $AB$ is 44°44'40", compute the azimuths of the remaining sides. Provide two solutions: one solution proceeding clockwise and the other proceeding counterclockwise.

**4.10**  If the bearing of $AB$ is N 49°49' E, compute the bearings of the remaining sides proceeding in a clockwise direction.

**4.11**  If the azimuth of $AB$ is 49°49', compute the azimuths of the remaining sides proceeding in a counterclockwise direction.

**4.12**  On January 2, 2000, the compass reading on a survey line in the Seattle, Washington, area was N 39°30' E. Use Figure 4.14(a) to determine:
(a) The compass reading for the same survey line on July 2, 2004.
(b) The astronomic bearing of the survey line.

# 5 Theodolites

## 5.1 General Background

As noted in Section 1.5, the term **theodolite** or **transit** (transiting theodolite) can be used to describe those survey instruments designed to measure horizontal and vertical angles precisely. In addition to measuring horizontal and vertical angles, transits and theodolites can be used to mark out straight and curved lines in the field. During the 20th century, theodolites and transits have gone through three distinct evolutionary stages:

- The open-face, vernier-equipped engineers' transit (American transit). See the example in Figure H.4.
- The enclosed, optical read-out theodolites with direct digital read-outs or micrometer-equipped read-outs (for more precise readings). See Figure 5.2.
- The enclosed electronic theodolite with direct read-outs. See Figure 5.1.

Most recently manufactured transits are electronic, but many of the earlier optical instruments and even a few vernier instruments still survive in the field (and in the classroom), no doubt a tribute to the excellent craftsmanship of the instrument-makers. In past editions of this text, the instruments were introduced chronologically, but in this edition the vernier transits are introduced last (in Appendix H), in recognition their fading importance.

The electronic theodolite will probably be the last in the line of transits and theodolites. Because of the versatility and lower costs of electronic equipment, future field instruments will be more like the total station (see Chapter 7), which combines all the features of a transit with the additional capabilities of measuring horizontal and vertical distances electronically and storing all measurements along with relevant attribute data for future transfer to the computer. Future "transits" may even include a global positioning system (GPS) receiver (see Chapter 11) to permit precise positioning in both the horizontal and vertical planes.

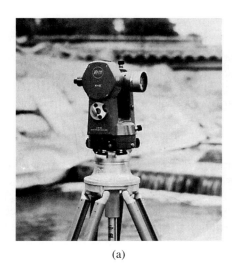

(a)

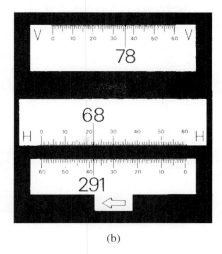

(b)

**FIGURE 5.1**   (a) Kern KI-S half-minute engineers' scale theodolite with optical plummet and direct reading scales. (b) Scale readings for KI-S theodolite. (Courtesy of Kern Instruments—Leica)

**FIGURE 5.2**   Electronic theodolite.

## 5.2  Electronic Theodolites

Electronic theodolites operate like optical theodolites; one major difference is that these instruments usually have only one motion (upper) and accordingly have only one horizontal clamp and slow-motion screw. Angle read-outs can be to 1″, with precision ranging from 0.5″ to 20″. The surveyor should check the specifications of new instruments to determine their precision, rather than simply accept the lowest read-out as relevant (some instruments with 1″ read-outs may be capable of only 5″ precision).

Digital read-outs eliminate the uncertainty associated with the reading and interpolation of scale and micrometer settings. Electronic theodolites have zero-set buttons for quick instrument orientation after the backsight has been taken (any angular value can be set for the backsight). Horizontal angles can be turned left or right, and repeat-angle averaging is available on some models. Figures 5.3, 5.4, and 5.5 are typical of the theodolites introduced more recently. The display windows for horizontal and vertical angles are located at both the front and rear of the instruments for easy access.

The instruments shown in Figures 5.3 and 5.4 are basic electronic theodolites, whereas the instrument shown in Figure 5.5 has additional capabilities, including expansion to total station capability with the inclusion of modular components such as EDM and data collection. Figure 5.3 also shows the operation keys and display area typical of many of these instruments. After turning on some instruments, the operator must activate the vertical circle by turning the telescope slowly through the horizon; newer instruments do not require this referencing action. The vertical circle can be set with zero at the zenith or at the horizon. The factory setting of zenith can be changed by setting the appropriate dip switch as described in the instrument's manual. The status of the battery charge can be monitored on the display panel, giving the operator ample warning of the need to replace and/or recharge the battery.

To turn an angle twice ("doubling"), first, press the hold button after turning the first angle. After that angle has been read and booked, the clamp is loosened (and the telescope transited), with the original angle staying in the read-out until after the backsight has been resighted. Finally, to turn the double angle, simply press (release) the hold button just prior to releasing the clamp. See Figure 5.6 for typical field notes.

Typical specifications for electronic theodolites include:

Magnification: $26\times$ to $30\times$
Field of view: $1.5°$
Shortest viewing distance: 1.0 m
Angle read-out, direct: 10″ to 20″
Angle measurement, electronic and incremental: see Figure 5.7(b)
Level sensitivity:
    plate bubble vial—40″/2 mm
    circular bubble vial—10′/2 mm

These simple electronic theodolites are quickly replacing optical transits and theodolites (which replaced the vernier transit). They are simpler to use and less expensive to purchase and repair, and their use of electronic components indicates a continuing drop in both purchase and repair costs. Some of these instruments have various built-in functions

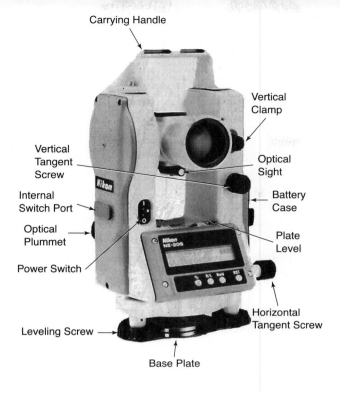

Carrying Handle

Vertical Clamp

Vertical Tangent Screw

Optical Sight

Internal Switch Port

Battery Case

Optical Plummet

Plate Level

Power Switch

Leveling Screw

Horizontal Tangent Screw

Base Plate

(a)

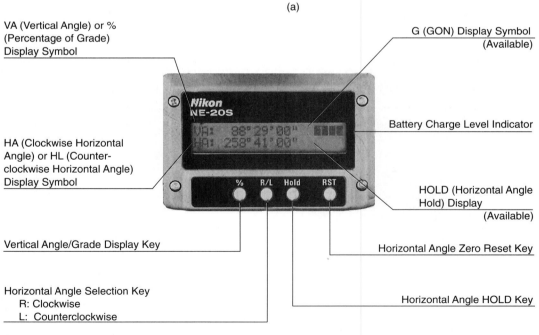

VA (Vertical Angle) or % (Percentage of Grade) Display Symbol

G (GON) Display Symbol (Available)

Battery Charge Level Indicator

HA (Clockwise Horizontal Angle) or HL (Counter-clockwise Horizontal Angle) Display Symbol

HOLD (Horizontal Angle Hold) Display (Available)

Vertical Angle/Grade Display Key

Horizontal Angle Zero Reset Key

Horizontal Angle Selection Key
R: Clockwise
L: Counterclockwise

Horizontal Angle HOLD Key

(b)

**FIGURE 5.3** Nikon NE-20S electronic digital theodolite. (a) Theodolite. (b) Operation keys and display. (Courtesy of Nikon Inc., Melville, N.Y.)

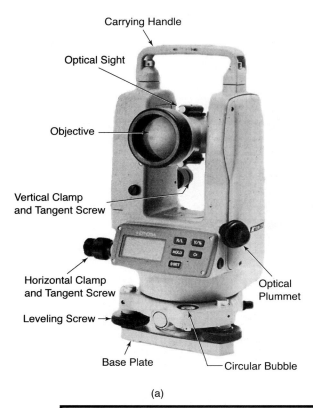

Carrying Handle

Optical Sight

Objective

Vertical Clamp
and Tangent Screw

Horizontal Clamp
and Tangent Screw

Leveling Screw →

Optical
Plummet

Base Plate

Circular Bubble

(a)

**FIGURE 5.4** Topcon DT-05 electronic digital theodolite. (a) Theodolite. (b) Encoder system for angle read-outs. (Courtesy of Topcon Instrument Corp., Paramus, N.J.)

## ROTARY ENCODER SYSTEM FOR ELECTRONIC THEODOLITES AND TRANSITS

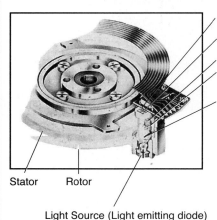

Photoelectric converter A

Photoelectric converter B

Slit A ⎡ A phase difference of 1/4th pitch or
Slit B ⎣ 90° exists between slits A and B

Collimator lens

Stator    Rotor

Light Source (Light emitting diode)

Topcon electronic theodolites (ETL-1 and DT-05/05A) and electronic transit (DT-30) measure horizontal and vertical angles with an incremental encoder detection system that reads to 1, 5, 10 or 30 seconds. Alternate dark and light patterns etched on the circles are detected by a light source and received by a photo detector, converting the beam into an electrical signal.

The signal is converted to a pulse signal corresponding to the angle turned and the pulse signal is passed on to the microprocessor, which displays an angle on the LCD.

(b)

**FIGURE 5.5** Leica T-1600 digital electronic theodolite. This instrument has keyboards front and back, an angle accuracy of 1.5″, automatic error monitoring, some surveying programs (e.g., "free stationing"), and interfaces that permit the addition of a data storage module and an electronic distance measurement device. (Courtesy of Leica Canada Co.)

that enable the operator to perform other theodolite operations, such as "remote object elevation," and "distance between remote points" (see Chapter 7). The instrumentation technology is evolving so rapidly that most instruments now on the market have been in production for only a year or two.

## 5.3 Theodolite Setup

The steps in a typical setup procedure for optical and electronic theodolites are listed below:

1. Place the instrument over the point with the tripod plate as level as possible and with two tripod legs on the downhill side, if applicable.
2. Stand back a pace or two and see if the instrument appears to be over the station; if it does not, adjust the location and check again from a pace or two away.
3. Move to a position 90° opposed to the original inspection location and repeat step 2. (This simple act of "eyeing-in" the instrument from two directions, 90° opposed, takes only seconds but could save a great deal of time in the long run.)
4. Check that the station point can now be seen through the optical plummet (or that the laser plummet spot is reasonably close to the setup mark). Then push in the tripod legs firmly by pressing down on the tripod shoe spurs. If the point is now not visible in the optical plumb sight, leave one leg in the ground, lift the other two legs, and rotate the

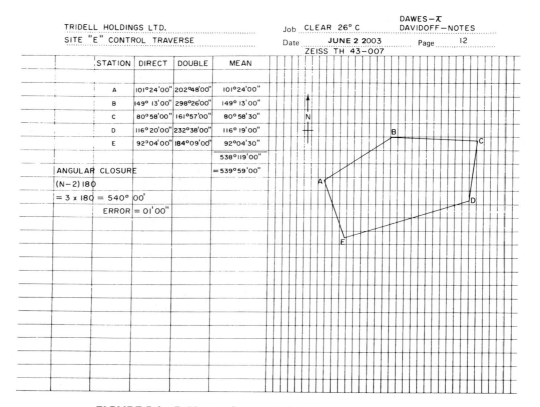

| | STATION | DIRECT | DOUBLE | MEAN |
|---|---|---|---|---|
| | A | 101°24'00" | 202°48'00" | 101°24'00" |
| | B | 149°13'00" | 298°26'00" | 149°13'00" |
| | C | 80°58'00" | 161°57'00" | 80°58'30" |
| | D | 116°20'00" | 232°38'00" | 116°19'00" |
| | E | 92°04'00" | 184°09'00" | 92°04'30" |
| | | | | 538°119'00" |
| ANGULAR CLOSURE | | | | = 539°59'00" |
| (N−2)180 | | | | |
| = 3 x 180 = 540° 00' | | | | |
| ERROR = 01'00" | | | | |

TRIDELL HOLDINGS LTD.

SITE "E" CONTROL TRAVERSE

Job CLEAR 26° C

Date JUNE 2 2003 Page 12

DAWES−π

DAVIDOFF−NOTES

ZEISS TH 43−007

**FIGURE 5.6** Field notes for repeated angles.

instrument, all the while looking through the optical plumb sight. When the point is sighted, carefully lower the two legs to the ground, keeping the station point in view.

5. While looking through the optical plumb (or at the laser spot), manipulate the leveling screws (one, two, or all three at a time) until the cross hair (bull's-eye) of the optical plummet or the laser spot is directly on the station mark.

6. Level the theodolite circular bubble by adjusting the tripod legs up or down. This is accomplished by noting which leg, when slid up or down, moves the circular bubble into the bull's-eye. Upon adjusting that leg, the bubble will either move into the circle (the instrument is level) or it will slide around until it is exactly opposite another tripod leg. That leg should then be adjusted up or down until the bubble moves into the circle. If the bubble does not move into the circle, adjust the leg until the bubble

is directly opposite another leg and repeat the process. If this manipulation has been done correctly, the bubble will be centered after the second leg has been adjusted; it is seldom necessary to adjust the legs more than three times. Comfort can be taken from the fact that these manipulations take less time to perform than they do to read about.

7. Perform a check through the optical plummet or note the location of the laser spot to confirm that it is still quite close to being over the station mark.

8. Turn one (or more) leveling screws to be sure that the circular bubble is now exactly centered (if necessary).

9. Loosen the tripod clamp bolt a bit and slide the instrument on the flat tripod top (if necessary) until the optical plummet or laser spot is exactly centered on the station mark. Retighten the tripod clamp bolt and reset the circular bubble, if necessary. When sliding the instrument on the tripod top, do not twist the instrument, but move it in a rectangular fashion. This ensures that the instrument will not go seriously off level if the tripod top itself is not close to being level.

10. The instrument can now be precisely leveled by centering the tubular bubble. Set the tubular bubble so that it is aligned in the same direction as two of the foot screws. Turn these two screws (together or independently) until the bubble is centered. Then turn the instrument 90°, at which point the tubular bubble will be aligned with the third leveling screw. Next, turn that third screw to center the bubble. The instrument now should be level, although it is always checked by turning the instrument through 180°.

Theodolite setup has been made easier with the introduction of laser plummets to the newer optical and electronic instruments. These plummets display a laser dot on the ground directly under the instrument.

# 5.4 Repeating Optical Theodolites

Optical theodolites are characterized by three-screw leveling heads, optical plummets, light weight, and glass circles read either directly or with the aid of a micrometer. Angles (0° to 360°) are normally read in the clockwise direction (see Figures 5.2 and 5.7). In contrast with the American engineer's transit, most theodolites do not come equipped with compasses or telescope levels. Most theodolites are now equipped with a compensating device that automatically indexes the horizontal direction when the vertical circle has been set to the horizontal setting of 90° (or 270°). The horizontal angular setting (in the vertical plane) for theodolites is 90° (270°); whereas for the transit, it is 0°. A word of caution: although all theodolites have a horizontal setting of 90° direct or 270° inverted, some theodolites have their zero set at the nadir, while others have the zero set at the zenith. The method of graduation can be ascertained quickly in the field by simply setting the telescope in an upward (positive) direction and noting the scale reading. If the reading is less than 90°, the zero has been referenced to the zenith direction; if the reading is more than 90°, the zero has been referenced to the nadir direction.

The graduations of both the vertical and horizontal circles are projected, by means of prisms and lenses, to one location just adjacent to the telescope eyepiece, where they are

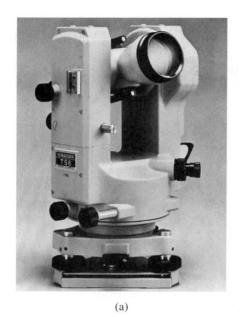

(a)

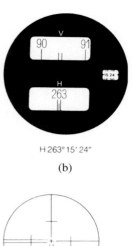

H 263° 15′ 24″

(b)

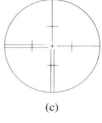

(c)

**FIGURE 5.7** (a) Six-second repeating micrometer theodolite. (b) Horizontal circle and micrometer reading. (c) Cross-hair reticle pattern. (d) A variety of tribrach-mounted traverse targets. Targets and theodolites can be easily interchanged to save setup time (forced centering system). (Courtesy of Sokkia Co. Ltd.)

read by means of a microscope. Light, which is necessary in the circle-reading procedure, is controlled by an adjustable mirror located on one of the standards. Light required for underground or night work is directed through the mirror window by attached lamps powered by battery packs.

The theodolite tripod has a flat base through which a bolt is threaded up into the three-screw leveling base (tribrach), thus securing the instrument to the tripod. Most theodolites have a tribrach release feature that permits the alidade and circle assemblies to be lifted from the tribrach and interchanged with a target or prism [see Figure 5.7(d)]. When the theodolite (minus its tribrach) is placed on a tribrach vacated by the target or prism, it will be instantly over the point and nearly level. This system, called *forced centering,* speeds up the work and reduces centering errors associated with multiple setups.

Optical plummets can be mounted in the alidade or in the tribrach. Alidade-mounted optical plummets can be checked for accuracy simply by revolving the alidade around its vertical axis and noting the location of the optical plummet cross hairs (bull's-eye) with respect to the station mark. Tribrach-mounted optical plummets can be checked by means of a plumb bob. Adjustments can be made by manipulating the appropriate adjusting screws, or the instrument can be sent out for shop analysis and adjustment.

Typical specifications for repeating micrometer optical theodolites are listed below:

Magnification: 30×
Clear objective aperture: 1.6 in. (42 mm)
Field of view at 100 ft (100 m): 2.7 ft (2.7 m)
Shortest focusing distance: 5.6 ft (1.7 m)
Stadia multiplication constant: 100
Bubble sensitivity
    Circular bubble: 8 ft per 2 mm
    Plate level: 30 in. per 2 mm
Direct circle reading: 01 in. to 06 in. (20 in. in older versions) from 0° to 360°

Like the engineer's transit (see Appendix H), many repeating theodolites have two independent motions (upper and lower), which necessitates upper and lower clamps, with their attendant tangent screws. However, some theodolites come equipped with only one clamp and one slow-motion or tangent screw; these instruments have a lever or switch that transfers clamp operation from upper to lower motion and thus probably reduces the opportunity for mistakes due to wrong-screw manipulation.

When some tribrach-equipped lasers are used in mining surveys, the alidade (upper portion of the instrument) can be released from the tribrach with the laser plummet projecting upward to ceiling stations. After the tribrach is centered properly under the ceiling mark, the alidade is then replaced in the tribrach, and the instrument is ready for final settings. This visual plumb line helps the surveyor to position the instrument over (under) the station mark more quickly than when he or she is using an optical plummet. Some manufacturers place the laser plummet in the alidade portion of the instrument, which permits an easy check on the beam's accuracy because the instrument can be simply rotated and the surveyor can observe whether the beam stays on the point. (Upward plumbing is not possible with alidade-mounted lasers.)

## 5.5 Angle Measurement with an Optical Theodolite

The technique for turning and doubling (repeating) an angle is the same as that described for a transit (Section H.2.8). The only difference in procedure is that of zeroing and reading the scales. In the case of the direct reading optical scale [see Figure 5.2(b)], zeroing the circle is simply a matter of turning the circle until the zero-degree mark lines up approximately with the zero-minute mark on the scale. Once the upper clamp has been tightened, the setting can be accomplished precisely by manipulation of the upper tangent screw. The scale is read directly as illustrated in Figure 5.2(b).

In the case of the optical micrometer instruments (see Figures 5.7 and 5.8), it is important first to set the micrometer to zero, and then to set the horizontal circle to zero. When the angle has been turned, you will note that the horizontal (or vertical) circle index mark is not directly over a degree mark. The micrometer knob is turned until the circle index mark is set to a degree mark. Movement of the micrometer knob also moves the micrometer scale; the reading on the micrometer scale is then added to the even degree reading taken from the circle. The micrometer scale does not have to be reset to zero for subsequent angle readings unless a new reference backsight is taken. Figure 5.7 shows a micrometer graduated to the closest 06′, which is a refinement of instruments that were formerly graduated to the closest 20′ (Figure 5.8). The vertical circle is read in the same way, using the same micrometer scale. If the vertical index is not automatically compensated (as it is for most repeating theodolites), the vertical index coincidence bubble must be centered by rotating the appropriate screw when vertical angles are being read.

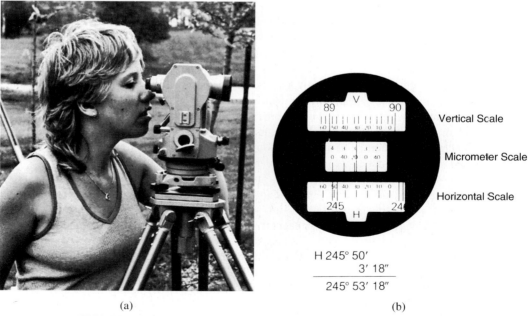

H 245° 50′
3′ 18″
―――――――
245° 53′ 18″

(a)                                 (b)

**FIGURE 5.8**  (a) Twenty-second micrometer theodolite, the Sokkia TM 20. (b) Horizontal and vertical scales with micrometer scale.

## 5.6 Direction Optical Theodolites

The essential difference between a direction optical theodolite and a repeating optical theodolite is that the direction theodolite has only one motion (upper), whereas the optical repeating theodolite has two motions (upper and lower). Because it is difficult to set angle values precisely on this type of instrument, angles are usually determined by reading the initial direction and the final direction, and then by determining the difference between the two.

Direction optical theodolites are generally more precise. For example, the Wild T-2 shown in Figure 5.9 reads directly to 01" and by estimation to 0.5", whereas the Wild T-3 shown in Figure 5.10 reads directly to 0.2" and by estimation to 0.1". In the case of the Wild T-2 (Figure 5.9) and the other 1-second theodolites, the micrometer is turned to force the index to read an even 10" (the grid lines shown above [beside] the scale are brought to coincidence), and then the micrometer scale reading (02'44") is added to the circle reading (94°10') to give a result of 94°12'44". In the case of the T-3 (see Figure 5.10), both sides of the circle are viewed simultaneously; one reading is shown erect, the other inverted. The micrometer knob is used to align the erect and inverted circle markings precisely. Each division on the circle is 04'. But if the lower scale is moved half a division, the upper also moves half a division, once again causing the markings to align, **with a movement of only 02'**. The circle index line is between the 73° and 74° mark, indicating that the value being read is 73°. Minutes can be read on the circle by counting the number of divisions from the

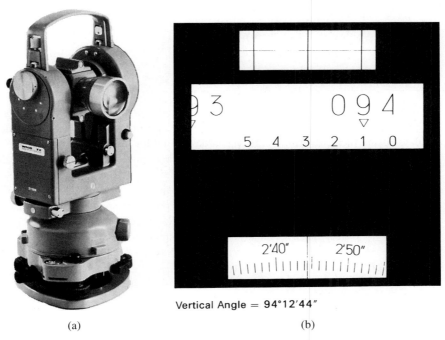

Vertical Angle = 94°12'44"

(a)                (b)

**FIGURE 5.9** (a) Wild T-2, a 1-second optical direction theodolite. (b) Vertical circle reading. (Courtesy of Leica Canada Co.)

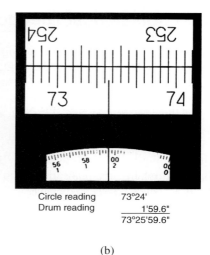

| Circle reading | 73°24' |
|---|---|
| Drum reading | 1'59.6" |
| | 73°25'59.6" |

(a) (b)

**FIGURE 5.10**   (a) Wild T-3 precise theodolite for first-order surveying. (b) Circle reading (least graduation is 4 minutes) and micrometer reading (least graduation is 0.2 seconds). (Courtesy of Leica Canada Co.) On the micrometer, a value of 01'59.6" can be read. The reading is, therefore, 73°25'59.6".

erect 73° to the inverted value that is 180° different than 73° (i.e., 253°). In this case, the number of divisions between these two numbers is 13, each having a value of 02' (i.e., 26'). These optical instruments have been superceded by precise electronic theodolites.

## 5.7   Angles Measured with a Direction Theodolite

As noted earlier, it is not always possible to set angles on a direction theodolite scale precisely, so directions are observed and then subtracted one from the other to determine angles. Furthermore, if several sightings are required for precision purposes, it is customary to distribute the initial settings around the circle to minimize the effect of circle graduation distortions. If you are using a directional theodolite where both sides of the circle are viewed simultaneously, the initial settings (positions) would be distributed per 180/$n$, where $n$ is the number of settings required by the precision specifications. (Specifications for precise surveys are published by the National Geodetic Survey in the United States, and by the Geodetic Surveys of Canada.) To be consistent, not only should the initial settings be distributed uniformly around the circle, but the range of the micrometer scale should be noted as well and appropriately apportioned.

Using the scales shown in Figure 5.8, the initial settings for four positions would be near 0°, 45°, 90°, and 135° on the circle and near 00'00", 02'30", 05'00", and 07'30" on the micrometer. For the instruments shown in Figures 5.9 and 5.10, the settings would be those given in Table 5.1. These initial settings are accomplished by setting the micrometer to zero (02'30", 05'00", 07'30"), and then setting the circle as close to zero as possible using the tangent screw. Precise coincidence of the zero (45, 90, 135) degree mark is achieved

**Table 5.1** APPROXIMATE INITIAL SCALE SETTINGS FOR FOUR POSITIONS

| 10-minute micrometer, Wild T-2 | 2-minute micrometer, Wild T-3 |
|---|---|
| 0°00′00″ | 0°00′00″ |
| 45°02′30″ | 45°00′30″ |
| 90°05′00″ | 90°01′00″ |
| 135°07′30″ | 135°01′30″ |

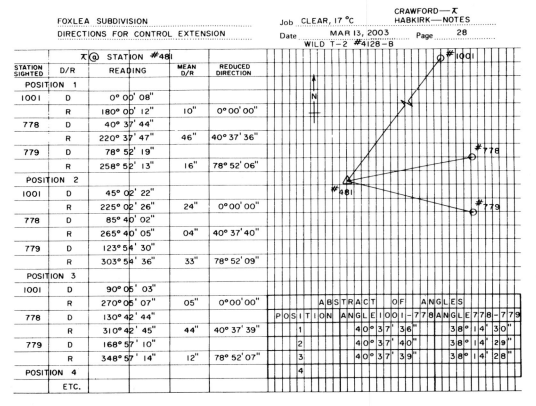

**FIGURE 5.11** Field notes for directions.

using the micrometer knob, which moves the micrometer scale slightly off zero (2′30″, 5′00″, 7′30″, etc.).

The direct readings are taken first in a clockwise direction. The telescope is then transited (plunged), and the reverse readings are taken counterclockwise. In Figure 5.11, the last entry at position 1 is 180°00′12″ (R). If the angles (shown in the abstract) do not meet the required accuracy, the procedure is repeated while the instrument still occupies that station.

## 5.8 Geometry of the Theodolite

The vertical axis of the theodolite goes up through the center of the spindles and is oriented over a specific point on the earth's surface. The circle assembly and alidade revolve about this axis. The horizontal axis of the telescope is perpendicular to the vertical axis, and the telescope and vertical circle revolve about it. The line of sight (line of collimation) is a line joining the intersection of the reticle cross hairs and the center of the objective lens. The line of sight is perpendicular to the horizontal axis and should be truly horizontal when the telescope level bubble is centered and when the vertical circle is set at 90°/270°, or 0° for vernier transits.

## 5.9 Adjustment of the Theodolite

Figure 5.12 shows the geometric features of the theodolite. The most important relationships are as follows:

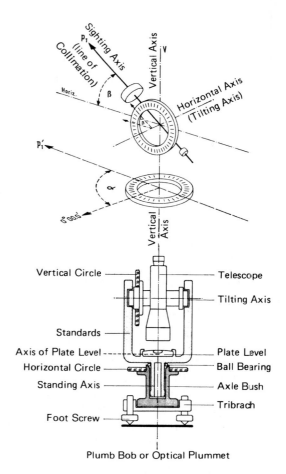

**FIGURE 5.12** Geometry of the theodolite. (Courtesy of Leica Co. Ltd.)

Chap. 5    Theodolites

1. The vertical cross hair should be perpendicular to the horizontal axis (tilting axis).
2. The axis of the plate bubble should be in a plane perpendicular to the vertical axis.
3. The line of sight should be perpendicular to the horizontal axis.
4. The horizontal axis should be perpendicular to the vertical axis (standards adjustment).

In addition, the following secondary features must be considered:

5. The axis of the telescope and the axis of the telescope bubble should be parallel.
6. The vertical circle vernier zero mark should be aligned with the vertical circle zero mark when the plate bubbles and the telescope bubble are centered.

These listed features are discussed in the following paragraphs. See Appendix H for additional adjustments applicable to the engineer's transit.

## 5.9.1 Vertical Cross Hair

If the vertical cross hair is perpendicular to the horizontal axis, all parts of the vertical cross hair can be used for line and angle sightings. This adjustment can be checked by sighting a well-defined distant point and then clamping the horizontal movements. The telescope is now moved up and down so that the point sighted appears to move on the vertical cross hair. If the point appears to move off the vertical cross hair, an error exists. The cross-hair reticle must then be rotated slightly until the sighted point appears to stay on the vertical cross hair as it is being revolved. The reticle can be adjusted slightly by loosening two adjacent capstan screws, rotating the reticle, and then retightening the same two capstan screws.

This same cross-hair orientation adjustment is performed on the level, but in the case of the level, the horizontal cross hair is of prime importance. The horizontal cross hair is checked by sighting a distant point on the horizontal cross hair with the vertical clamp set, and then moving the telescope left and right, checking to see that the sighted point remains on the horizontal cross hair. The adjustment for any maladjustment of the reticle is performed as described previously.

## 5.9.2 Plate Bubbles

We noted that after a bubble has been centered, its adjustment is checked by rotating the instrument through 180°; if the bubble does not remain centered, it can be properly set by bringing the bubble halfway back using the foot screws. For example, if you check a tubular bubble accuracy position and find that it is out by four division marks, the bubble can now be set properly by turning the foot screws until the bubble is only two division marks off center. The bubble should remain in this off-center position as the telescope is rotated, indicating that the instrument is, in fact, level. Although the instrument can now be used safely, it is customary to remove the error by adjusting the bubble tube.

The bubble tube can now be adjusted by turning the capstan screws at one end of the bubble tube until the bubble becomes centered precisely. The entire leveling and adjusting procedure is repeated until the bubble remains centered as the instrument is rotated and checked in all positions. All capstan screw adjustments are best done in small increments; that is, if the end of the bubble tube is to be lowered, first loosen the lower capstan screw a slight turn (say, one-eighth). Then tighten (snug) the top capstan screw to close the gap. This incremental adjustment is continued until the bubble is centered precisely.

### 5.9.3  Line of Sight

**5.9.3.1  Vertical cross hair**  The vertical line of sight should be perpendicular to the horizontal axis so that a vertical plane is formed by the complete revolution of the telescope on its axis. The technique for this testing and adjustment is very similar to the surveying technique of *double centering,* which is described in Section 5.11. The testing and adjustment procedure is described in the following steps:

**TEST**

1. The theodolite is set up at point $A$ [see Figure 5.13(a)].
2. A backsight is taken on any well-defined point $B$ (a well-defined point on the horizon is best).
3. The telescope is transited (plunged) and a point $C$ is set on the opposite side of the theodolite 300 to 400 ft away, at roughly the same elevation as the theodolite station.
4. After loosening the upper or lower horizontal plate clamp, and with the telescope still inverted from step 3, sight point $B$ again.
5. After sighting on point $B$, transit the telescope and sight in the direction of the previously set point $C$. Because it is highly probable that the line of sight will not fall precisely on point $C$, set a new point—point $D$— adjacent to point $C$.
6. With a steel tape, measure between point $D$ and point $C$ and set point $B'$ midway between them. Point $B'$ will be the correct point—the point established precisely on the projection of line $BA$. These six steps describe double centering—a surveying technique for producing a straight line. (See also Section 5.11.)

**ADJUSTMENT**

7. Since the distance $CB'$ or $B'D$ is double the sighting error, the line of sight correction is accomplished by first setting point $E$ midway between $B'$ and $D$ (or one-quarter of the way from $D$ to $C$).
8. After sighting the vertical cross hair on point $E$, the vertical cross hair correction adjustment is performed by adjusting the left/right capstan screws [see Figure H.2(a)] until the vertical cross hair is positioned directly on point $B'$. The capstan screws are adjusted by first loosening one screw a small turn and then immediately tightening the opposite capstan screw to take up the slack. This procedure is repeated until the vertical cross hair is positioned precisely on point $B'$.

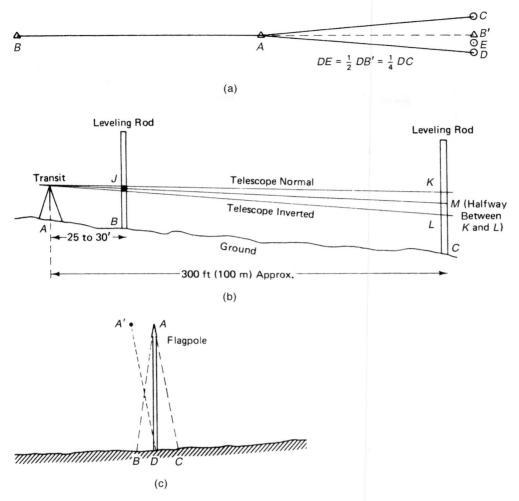

$$DE = \tfrac{1}{2} DB' = \tfrac{1}{4} DC$$

(a)

(b)

(c)

**FIGURE 5.13** Instrument adjustments. (a) Line of sight perpendicular to horizontal axis. (b) Horizontal cross-hair adjustment. (c) Standards adjustment.

**5.9.3.2 Horizontal cross hair** The horizontal cross hair must be adjusted so that it lies on the optical axis of the telescope. To test this relationship, set up the theodolite at point $A$ [see Figure 5.13(b)], and place two stakes $B$ and $C$ in a straight line, $B$ about 25 ft away and $C$ about 300 ft away. With the vertical motion clamped, take a reading first on $C(K)$ and then on $B(J)$. Transit (plunge) the telescope and set the horizontal cross hair on the previous rod reading ($J$) at $B$ and then take a reading at point $C$. If the transit is in perfect adjustment, the two rod readings at $C$ will be the same; if the cross hair is out of adjustment, the rod reading at $C$ will be at some reading $L$ instead of $K$. To adjust the cross hair, adjust the cross-hair reticle up or down by first loosening and then tightening the appropriate opposing capstan screws until the cross hair lines up with the average of the two readings ($M$).

### 5.9.7 Circular Level

Optical and electronic theodolites use a circular level for rough leveling as well as plate level(s) for fine leveling. After the plate level has been set and adjusted, as described in Section 5.9.2, the circular bubble can be adjusted (centered) by turning one or more of the three adjusting screws around the bubble.

### 5.9.8 Optical Plummet

The optical axis of the plummet is aligned with the vertical axis of the theodolite if, when the instrument is revolved through 180°, the reticle of the optical plummet stays superimposed on the ground mark. If the reticle does not stay on the mark, the plummet can be adjusted in the following manner. The reticle is placed over the ground mark by adjusting the leveling screws [see Figure 5.14(a)]. If the plummet is not in adjustment, the reticle will appear to be in a new location (X) after the theodolite is turned about 180°; point P is marked halfway between the two locations. The adjusting screws [see Figure. 5.14(b)] are turned until the reticle image is over P, indicating that the plummet is now in adjustment.

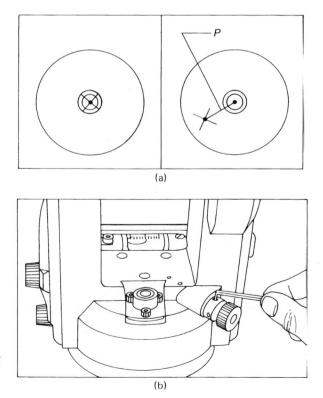

(a)

**FIGURE 5.14** Optical plummet adjustment. (a) Point P is marked halfway between the original position (·) and the 180° position (X). (b) Plummet adjusting screws are turned until X becomes superimposed on P. (Courtesy of Nikon Inc., Melville, N.Y.)

(b)

## 5.10 Laying Off Angles

### 5.10.1 Case 1

The angle is to be laid out no more precisely than the least count of the transit or theodolite. Assume a route survey where a deflection angle (31°12′ R) has been determined from aerial photos to position the ℄ (centerline) clear of natural obstructions [see Figure 5.15(a)]. The surveyor sets the instrument at the point of intersection (PI) of the tangents and sights the back line with the telescope reversed and the horizontal circle set to zero. Next, the surveyor transits (plunges) the telescope, turns off the required deflection angle, and sets a point on line. The deflection angle is 31°12′ R and a point is set at $a'$. The surveyor then loosens the lower motion (repeating instruments), sights again at the back line, transits the telescope, and turns off the required value (31°12′ × 2 = 62°24′). It is very likely that this line of sight will not match the first precise

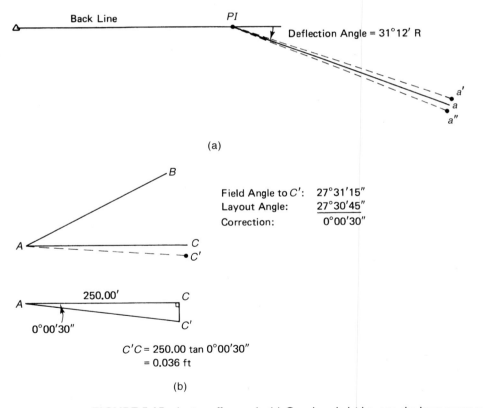

(a)

Field Angle to $C'$:    27°31′15″
Layout Angle:        27°30′45″
Correction:           0°00′30″

$C'C$ = 250.00 tan 0°00′30″
      = 0.036 ft

(b)

**FIGURE 5.15** Laying off an angle. (a) Case I, angle laid out to the least count of the instrument. (b) Case 2, angle to be laid out more precisely than the least count that the instrument will permit.

sighting at $a'$. If the line does not cross $a'$, a new mark $a''$ is made, and the instrument operator is given a sighting on the correct point $a$, which is midway between $a'$ and $a''$.

## 5.10.2  Case 2

The angle is to be laid out more precisely than the least count of the instrument will permit directly. Assume that an angle of 27°30′45″ is required in a heavy construction layout, and that a 01-minute transit is being used. In Figure 5.15(b), the transit is set up at $A$ zeroed on $B$, with an angle of 27°31′ turned to set point $C'$. The angle is then repeated to point $C'$ a suitable number of times so that an accurate value of that angle can be determined.

Let's assume that the scale reading after four repetitions is 110°05′, giving a mean angle value of 27°31′15″ for angle $BAC'$. If the layout distance of $AC$ is 250.00 ft, point $C$ can be located precisely by measuring from $C'$ a distance $C'C$:

$$C'C = 250.00 \tan 0°00'\ 30''$$
$$= 0.036 \text{ ft}$$

After point $C$ has been located, its position can be verified by repeating angles to it from point $B$.

## 5.11  Prolonging a Straight Line

Prolonging a straight line (also known as *double centering*) is a common survey procedure used every time a straight line must be prolonged. The best example of this requirement would be in route surveying, where straight lines are routinely prolonged over long distances and often over very difficult terrain. The technique of reversion (the same technique used in repeating angles) is used to ensure that the straight line is properly prolonged.

In Figure 5.16, the straight line $BA$ is to be prolonged to $B'$ [see also Figure 5.13(a)]. With the instrument at $A$, a sight is made carefully on station $B$. The telescope is transited, and a temporary point is set at $C$. The transit is revolved back to station $B$, and a new sighting is made (the telescope is in a position reversed to the original sighting). The telescope is transited, and a temporary mark is made at $D$, adjacent to $C$. The correct location of station $B'$ is established midway between $C$ and $D$ by measuring with a steel tape.

Over short distances, well-adjusted transits will show no appreciable displacement between points $C$ and $D$. Over the longer distances normally encountered in this type of work, however, all transits will display a displacement between direct and reversed sightings; the longer the forward sighting, the greater the displacement.

**FIGURE 5.16**  Double centering to prolong a straight line.

## 5.12   Bucking-In (Interlining)

It is sometimes necessary to establish a straight line between two points that themselves are not intervisible (i.e., a transit set up at one point cannot, because of an intervening hill, be sighted at the other required point). It is usually possible to find an intermediate position from which both points can be seen. In Figure 5.17 points $A$ and $B$ are not intervisible, but point $C$ is in an area from which both $A$ and $B$ can be seen. The **interlining** procedure is as follows. The transit is set up in the area of $C$ (at $C_1$) and as close to line $AB$ as is possible to estimate. The transit is roughly leveled and a sight is taken on point $A$. Then the telescope is transited and a sight taken toward $B$. The line of sight will, of course, not be on $B$ but on point $B_1$, some distance away. Noting roughly the distance $B_1B$ and the position of the transit between $A$ and $B$ (e.g., halfway, one-third, or one-quarter of the distance $AB$), an estimate is made about how far proportionately the instrument is to be moved and thus be on the line $AB$. The transit is once again roughly leveled (position $C_2$), and the sighting procedure is repeated.

This trial-and-error technique is repeated until, after sighting $A$, the transited line of sight falls on point $B$ or close enough to point $B$ so that it can be set precisely by shifting the transit on the leveling head shifting plate. When the line has been established, a point is set at or near point $C$ so that the position can be saved for future use. The entire procedure of interlining can be accomplished in a surprisingly short period of time. All but the final instrument setups are only roughly leveled, and at no time does the instrument have to be set up over a point.

## 5.13   Intersection of Two Straight Lines

The intersection of two straight lines is also a very common survey technique. In municipal surveying, street surveys usually begin $(0 + 00)$ at the intersection of the centerlines of two streets, and the station and angle of the intersections of all subsequent street centerlines are routinely determined.

Figure 5.18(a) illustrates the need for intersecting points on a municipal survey, and Figure 5.18(b) illustrates just how the intersection point is located. In Figure 5.18(b), with the instrument set on a Main Street station and a sight taken also on the Main Street ℄ (the

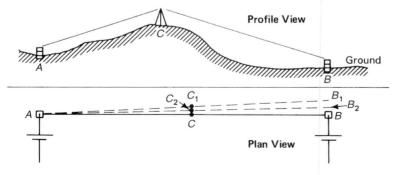

**FIGURE 5.17**   Bucking-in, or interlining.

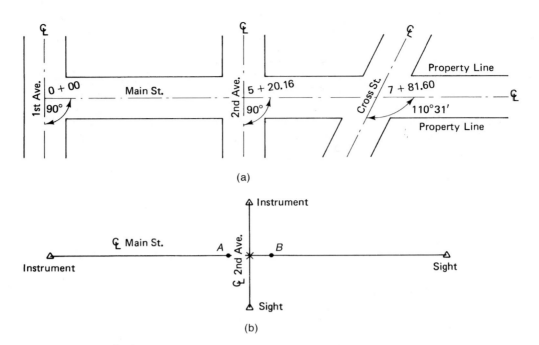

**FIGURE 5.18** Intersection of two straight lines. (a) Example of the intersection of the centerlines of streets. (b) Intersecting technique.

longer the sight, the more precise the sighting). Two points (2 to 4 ft apart) are established on the Main Street ℄, one point on either side of where the surveyor estimates that 2nd Avenue ℄ will intersect. The instrument is then moved to a 2nd Avenue station, and a sight is taken some distance away, on the far side of the Main Street ℄. The surveyor can stretch a plumb bob string over the two points (*A* and *B*) established on the Main Street ℄, and the instrument operator can note where on the string the 2nd Avenue ℄ intersects. If the two points (*A* and *B*) are reasonably close together (2 to 3 ft), the surveyor can use the plumb bob itself to take a line from the instrument operator on the plumb bob string; otherwise, the instrument operator can take a line with a pencil or any other suitable sighting target.

The intersection point is then suitably marked (e.g., nail and flagging on asphalt, wood stake with tack on ground), and then the angle of intersection and the station (chainage) of the point can be determined. After marking the intersection point, the surveyors remove temporary markers *A* and *B*.

# 5.14 Prolonging a Measured Line by Triangulation over an Obstacle

In route surveying, obstacles such as rivers or chasms must be traversed. Whereas the alignment can be conveniently prolonged by double centering, the station (chainage) may be deduced from the construction of a geometric figure. In Figure 5.19, the distance from

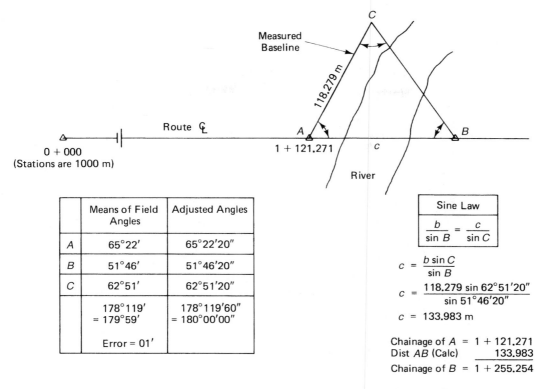

Route ₵

0 + 000
(Stations are 1000 m)

1 + 121.271

Measured Baseline

118.279 m

C

A

B

c

River

| | Means of Field Angles | Adjusted Angles |
|---|---|---|
| A | 65°22′ | 65°22′20″ |
| B | 51°46′ | 51°46′20″ |
| C | 62°51′ | 62°51′20″ |
| | 178°119′ = 179°59′ | 178°119′60″ = 180°00′00″ |
| | Error = 01′ | |

Sine Law

$$\frac{b}{\sin B} = \frac{c}{\sin C}$$

$$c = \frac{b \sin C}{\sin B}$$

$$c = \frac{118.279 \sin 62°51′20″}{\sin 51°46′20″}$$

$$c = 133.983 \text{ m}$$

Chainage of $A$ = 1 + 121.271
Dist $AB$ (Calc)           133.983
Chainage of $B$ = 1 + 255.254

**FIGURE 5.19**  Prolonging a measured line over an obstacle by triangulation.

1 + 121.271 to the station established on the far side of the river can be determined by solving the constructed triangle (triangulation).

The ideal (strongest) triangle is one having angles close to 60° (equilateral), although angles as small as 20° may be acceptable. The presence of rugged terrain and heavy tree cover adjacent to the river often results in a less than optimal geometric figure. The baseline and a minimum of two angles are measured so that the missing distance can be calculated. The third angle (on the far side of the river) should also be measured to check for mistakes and to reduce errors.

## 5.15  Prolonging a Line past an Obstacle

In property surveying, obstacles such as trees often block the path of the survey. In route surveying, it is customary for the surveyor to cut down the offending trees (later construction will require them to be removed in any case). In property surveying, however, the owner would be quite upset to find valuable trees destroyed just so the surveyor could establish a boundary line. Accordingly, the surveyor must find an alternative method of providing distances and/or locations for blocked survey lines.

Figure 5.20(a) illustrates the technique of right-angle offset. Boundary line *AF* cannot be run because of the wooded area. The survey continues normally to point *B* just clear

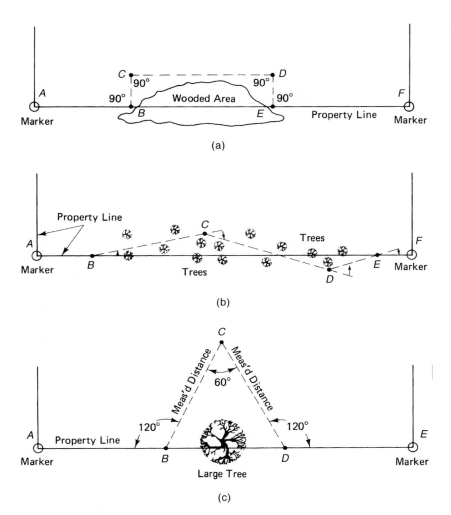

**FIGURE 5.20** Prolonging a line past an obstacle. (a) Right-angle offset method. (b) Random-line method. (c) Triangulation method.

of the wooded area. At *B,* a right angle is turned (and doubled), and point *C* is located a sufficient distance away from *B* to provide a clear parallel line to the boundary line. The transit is set at *C* and sighted at *B* (great care must be exercised because of the short sighting distance). An angle of 90° is turned to locate point *D.* Point *E* is located on the boundary line using a right angle and the offset distance used for *BC.* The survey can then continue to *F.* If distance *CD* is measured, then the required boundary distance (*AF*) is *AB* + *CD* + *EF.*

If intermediate points are required on the boundary line between *B* and *E* (e.g., fencing layout), a right angle can be turned from a convenient location on *CD,* and the offset distance (*BC*) can be used to measure back to the boundary line. Use of a technique like this minimizes the destruction of trees and other obstructions. In Figure

5.20(b), trees are scattered over the area, preventing the establishment of a right-angle offset line. In this case, a random line (open traverse) is run (by deflection angles) through the scattered trees. The distance *AF* is the sum of *AB, EF,* and the resultant of *BE.* (See Chapter 6 for appropriate computation techniques for "missing-course" problems such as this one.)

In Figure 5.20(c), the line must be prolonged past an obstacle, a large tree. In this case, a triangle is constructed with the three angles and two distances measured as shown. As noted earlier, the closer the constructed triangle is to equilateral, the stronger is the calculated distance (*BD*). Also, as noted earlier, the optimal equilateral figure cannot always be constructed due to topographic constraints, and angles as small as 20° are acceptable for many surveys.

We noted that the technique of right-angle offsets has a larger potential for error because of the weaknesses associated with several short sightings. At the same time, however, this technique gives a simple and direct method for establishing intermediate points on the boundary line. In contrast, the random-line and triangulation methods provide for stronger geometric solutions to the missing property line distances, but they also require less direct and much more cumbersome calculations for the placement of intermediate line points (e.g., fence layout).

## 6.1 General Background

A *traverse* is usually a control survey and is employed in all forms of legal, mapping, and engineering surveys. Essentially, a traverse is a series of established stations tied together by angle and distance. The angles are measured using theodolites, or total stations, whereas the distances can be measured using steel tapes or electronic distance-measurement instruments (EDMs). Traverses can be open, as in route surveys, or closed, as in a closed geometric figure (see Figures 6.1 and 6.2). Boundary surveys, which constitute a consecutive series of established (or laid out) stations, are usually described as being traverse surveys (e.g., retracement of the distances and angles of a section of property).

In engineering work, traverses are used as control surveys (1) to locate topographic detail for the preparation of plans, (2) to lay out (locate) engineering works, and (3) for the processing and ordering of earthwork and other engineering quantities. Traverses can also provide horizontal control for aerial surveys in the preparation of photogrammetric mapping (see Chapter 13).

## 6.2 Open Traverse

Simply put, an open traverse is a series of measured straight lines (and angles) that do not geometrically close. This lack of geometric closure means that there is no geometric verification possible with respect to the actual positioning of the traverse stations. Thus, the measuring technique must be refined to provide for field verification. At a minimum, distances are measured twice (sometimes once in each direction), and angles are doubled.

In route surveys, open traverse stations can be verified by computation from available tied-in field markers as shown on property plans, by scale from existing topographic plans, or through the use of global positioning system (GPS) receivers (see Chapter 11). Directions can be verified by scale from existing plans; by observation on the sun or Polaris; or by tie-ins to preset, coordinated monuments. Many states and provinces are now providing densely placed third- and fourth-order horizontal control monuments as an extension of their coordinate grid systems. It is now

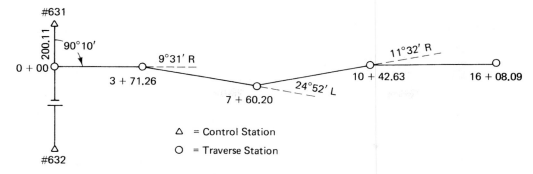

**FIGURE 6.1** Open traverse.

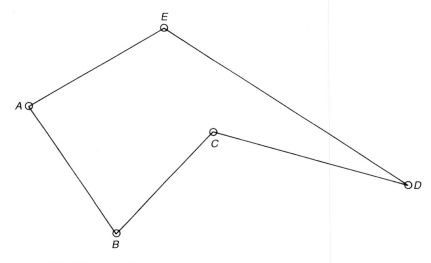

**FIGURE 6.2** Closed traverse (loop).

often possible to tie in the initial and terminal stations of a route survey to coordinate grid monuments whose positions have been accurately determined. In this case, the route survey becomes a closed traverse and is subject to geometric verification and analysis. As we noted in Section 4.4, open traverses are tied together angularly by deflection angles, and distances are shown in the form of stations that are cumulative measurements referenced to the initial point of the survey (0 + 00) (see Figure 6.3).

## 6.3 Closed Traverse

A closed traverse is one that either begins and ends at the same point or one that begins and ends at points whose positions have been previously determined (see Section 6.2). In both cases, the angles can be closed geometrically, and the position closure can be determined mathematically.

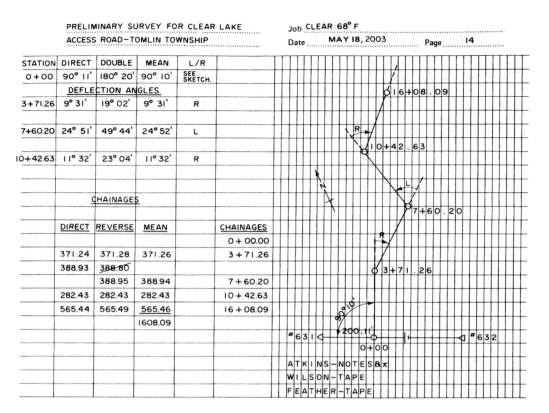

**FIGURE 6.3** Field notes for open traverse. (Note: The terms **chainages** and **stations** are interchangeable.)

A closed traverse that begins and ends at the same point is known as a loop traverse (see Figure 6.2). In this case, the distances are measured from one station to the next (and verified) by using a steel tape or EDM. The interior angle is measured at each station (and doubled). The loop distances and angles can be obtained by proceeding consecutively around the loop in a clockwise or counterclockwise manner. In fact, the data can be collected in any order convenient to the surveyor. As noted in the previous chapter, however, the angles themselves (by convention) are always measured from left to right.

## 6.4   Balancing Angles

In Section 4.4, we noted that the geometric sum of the interior angles in an $n$-sided closed figure is $(n - 2)180°$. For example, a five-sided figure would have $(5 - 2)180° = 540°$; a seven-sided figure would have $(7 - 2)180° = 900°$.

When all the interior angles of a closed field traverse are summed, they may or may not total the number of degrees required for geometric closure because of systematic and random errors associated with setting the transit over a point and with sighting. Before

**Table 6.1** TWO METHODS OF ADJUSTING FIELD ANGLES

| Station | Field angle | Arbitrarily balanced | Equally balanced |
|---------|-------------|----------------------|------------------|
| A | 101° 24′00″ | 101° 24′00″ | 101° 24′ 12″ |
| B | 149° 13′00″ | 149° 13′00″ | 149° 13′ 12″ |
| C | 80° 58′30″ | 80° 59′00″ | 80° 58′ 42″ |
| D | 116° 19′00″ | 116° 19′00″ | 116° 19′ 12″ |
| E | 92° 04′30″ | 92° 05′00″ | 92° 04′ 42″ |
| | 538°119′00″ | 538°120′00″ | 538°118′120″ |
| | = 539° 59′00″ | = 540° 00′00″ | = 540° 00′ 00″ |
| | Error = 01′ | Balanced | Balanced |

$$\text{Correction/angle} = \frac{60}{5} = 12''$$

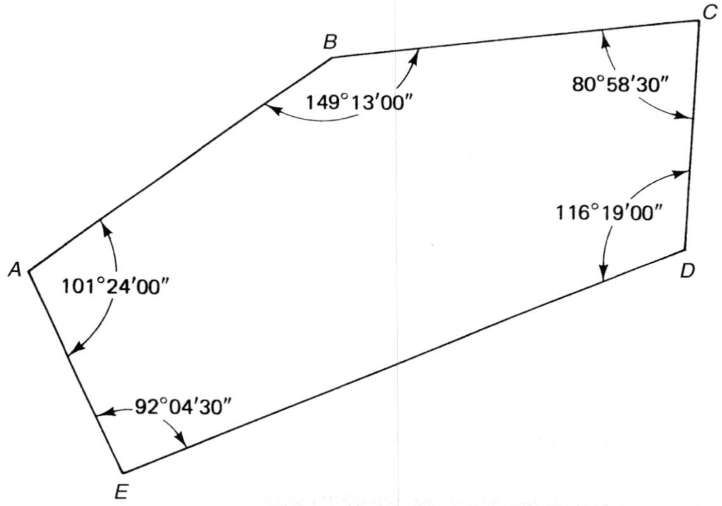

**FIGURE 6.4** Example 6.1 (closed traverse problem) field angles.

mathematical analysis of the traverse can begin, even before the bearings can be calculated, the field angles must be adjusted so that their sum equals the correct geometric total. The angles can be balanced by distributing the angular error evenly to each angle (if all angles were measured with the same precision), or one or more angles can be adjusted to force the closure. The acceptable total error of angular closure is usually quite small (i.e., < 03′); otherwise, the fieldwork will have to be repeated. The actual size of the allowable angular error is governed by the specifications used for that specific traverse.

The angles for the traverse example (Section 6.6) are shown in Table 6.1 and Figure 6.4. If one of the traverse stations had been in a particularly suspect location (e.g., a swamp), a larger proportion of the angle correction could be assigned to that one station. In all balancing operations, however, a certain amount of guesswork is involved because we don't know with certainty if any of the balancing procedures give us values closer to the true value than did the original field angle. The important point is that the overall angular closure is not larger than that specified.

## 6.5   Latitudes and Departures

In Section 1.12, we noted that a point could be located by polar ties (direction and distance) or by rectangular ties (two distances at 90°). In Figure 6.5(a), point $A$ is located, with respect to point $D$, by direction (bearing) and distance. In Figure 6.5(b), point $A$ is located, with respect to point $D$, by a distance north $(\Delta y)$ and a distance east $(\Delta x)$.

By definition, **latitude is the north/south rectangular component of a line.** To differentiate direction, north is considered plus, whereas south is considered minus. Similarly, **departure is the east/west rectangular component of a line,** and to differentiate direction, east is considered plus, whereas west is considered minus. When working with azimuths, the plus/minus designation is directly given by the appropriate trigonometric function:

$$\text{Latitude } (\Delta y) = \text{distance } (H) \cos \alpha \tag{6.1}$$

$$\text{Departure } (\Delta x) = \text{distance } (H) \sin \alpha \tag{6.2}$$

where $\alpha$ is the bearing or azimuth of the traverse course, and distance $(H)$ is the horizontal distance of the traverse course.

Latitudes (lats) and departures (deps) can be used to calculate the precision of a traverse by noting the plus/minus closure of both latitudes and departures. If the survey has been perfectly performed (angles and distances), the plus latitudes will equal the minus latitudes, and the plus departures will equal the minus departures.

In Figure 6.6, the computation direction has been approached in a counterclockwise mode (all signs would simply be reversed for a clockwise approach). Latitudes *CD, DA,* and *AB* are all positive and should precisely equal (if the survey were perfect) the latitude of *BC,* which is negative. Similarly, the departures of *CD* and *DA* are positive, and they should equal the departures of *AB* and *BC,* which are both negative.

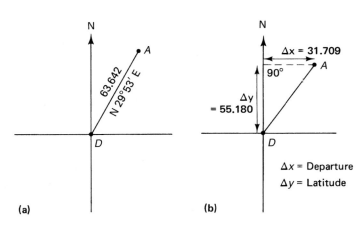

**FIGURE 6.5**   Location of a point.
(a) Polar ties. (b) Rectangular ties.   **(a)**                    **(b)**

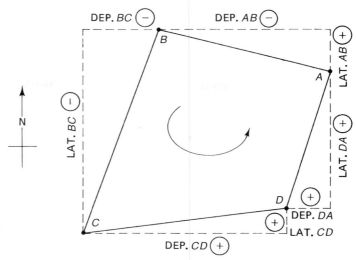

**FIGURE 6.6** Closure of latitudes and departures (counterclockwise approach).

As noted earlier, when using bearings for directions, the north and east directions are positive, whereas the south and west directions are negative. Figure 6.7 shows these relationships. The figure also shows that **for azimuth directions, the algebraic sign is governed by the algebraic sign of the appropriate trigonometric function (cos or sin).**

## 6.6  Computation of Latitudes and Departures

We will compute latitudes and departures to determine the error of closure and the precision of a traverse. The following sections summarize the steps in the process.

**Step 1: Balance the angles**  Use the data introduced in Section 6.4 for this computation, and the angles resulting from equal distribution of the error among the field angles. These balanced angles are shown in Figure 6.8.

**Step 2: Compute the azimuths**  Starting with the given direction of $AB$ (N51°22′00″E), the directions of the remaining sides are computed. The computation can be solved going counterclockwise (see Figure 6.9) or clockwise (see Figure 6.10) around the figure. Use the techniques developed in Section 4.9 (counterclockwise approach) for this example.

Refer to Figure 6.9:

$$
\begin{aligned}
\text{Bg } AB &= \quad \text{N } 51°\ 22′00″ \text{ E} \\
\text{Az } AB &= \qquad 51°\ 22′00″ \\
+ <A &\qquad 101°\ 24′12″ \\
\text{Az } AE &= \qquad 152°\ 46′12″ \\
&\quad +180° \\
\text{Az } EA &= \qquad 332°\ 46′12″
\end{aligned}
$$

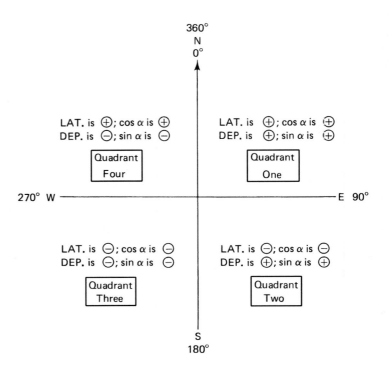

**FIGURE 6.7** Algebraic signs of latitudes and departures by trigonometric functions (where α is the azimuth).

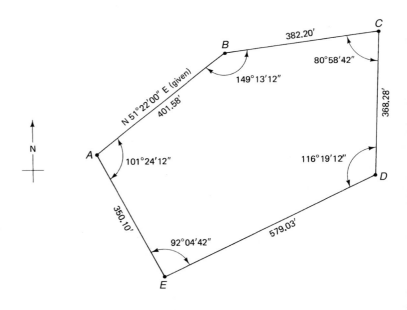

**FIGURE 6.8** Distances and balanced angles for Example 6.1.

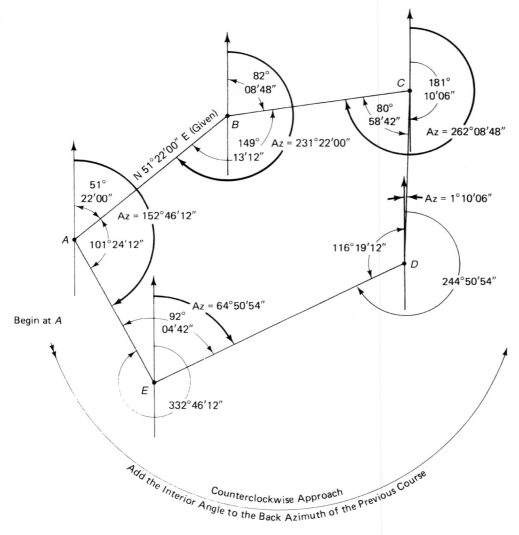

**FIGURE 6.9** Section 6.6: azimuth computation, counterclockwise approach.

$$
\begin{aligned}
+ <E \quad & 92°\ 04'42'' \\
\text{Az } ED = \quad & 424°\ 50'54'' \\
& -360° \\
\text{Az } ED = \quad & 64°\ 50'54'' \\
& +180° \\
\text{Az } DE = \quad & 244°\ 50'54'' \\
+ <D \quad & 116°\ 19'12'' \\
\text{Az } DC = \quad & 361°\ 10'06''
\end{aligned}
$$

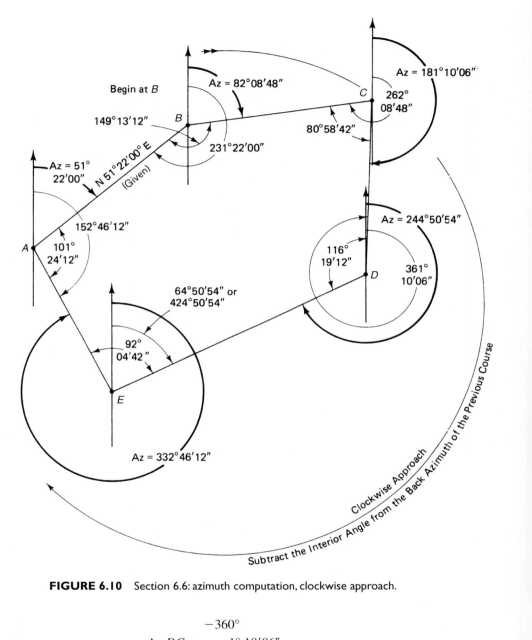

**FIGURE 6.10** Section 6.6: azimuth computation, clockwise approach.

$$
\begin{aligned}
&\phantom{\text{Az } DC =\ } -360° \\
&\text{Az } DC = \phantom{-}1°\ 10'06'' \\
&\phantom{\text{Az } DC =\ } +180° \\
&\text{Az } CD = \phantom{-}181°\ 10'06'' \\
&+ \angle C \phantom{=\ } 80°\ 58'42'' \\
&\text{Az } CB = \phantom{-}262°\ 08'48''
\end{aligned}
$$

$$-180°$$

| | |
|---|---|
| Az $BC$ = | 82° 08'48" |
| + < $B$ | 149° 13'12" |
| Az $BA$ = | 231° 22'00" |

$$-180°$$

| | | |
|---|---|---|
| Az $AB$ = | 51° 22'00" | |
| Bg $AB$ = | N 51° 22'00" E | Check |

For comparative purposes, the clockwise approach is also shown (refer to Figure 6.10):

| | | |
|---|---|---|
| Bg $AB$ = | N 51° 22'00" E | |
| Az $AB$ = | 51° 22'00" | |
| | +180° | |
| Az $BA$ = | 231° 22'00" | |
| − < $B$ | 149° 13'12" | |
| Az $BC$ = | 82° 08'48" | |
| | +180° | |
| Az $CB$ = | 262° 08'48" | |
| − < $C$ | 80° 58'42" | |
| Az $CD$ = | 181° 10'06" | |
| | +180° | |
| Az $DC$ = | 361° 10'06" | |
| − < $D$ | 116° 19'12" | |
| Az $DE$ = | 244° 50'54" | |
| | −180° | |
| Az $ED$ = | 64° 50'54" | |
| | +360° 00'00"* | |
| Az $ED$ = | 424° 50'54" | |
| − < $E$ | 92° 04'42" | |
| Az $EA$ = | 332° 46'12" | |
| | −180° | |
| Az $AE$ = | 152° 46'12" | |
| − < $A$ | 101° 24'12" | |
| Az $AB$ = | 51° 22'00" | [Check] |

### Step 3: Compute the latitudes ($\Delta y$) and departures ($\Delta x$)

Table 6.2 shows the format for a typical traverse computation. The table shows both the azimuth and the bearing for each course (usually only the azimuth or the bearing is included). Note that the algebraic sign for both latitude and departure is given directly by the calculator (computer) for each azimuth angle. In the case of the bearings, as noted earlier, latitudes are plus if the

*To permit subtraction of the next interior angle—$< E$.

| Course | Distance (ft) | Azimuth | Bearing | Latitude | Departure |
|--------|--------------|---------|---------|----------|-----------|
| AE | 350.10 | 152°46′12″ | S 27°13′48″E | −311.30 | +160.19 |
| ED | 579.03 | 64°50′54″ | N 64°50′54″E | +246.10 | +524.13 |
| DC | 368.28 | 1°10′06″ | N 1°10′06″E | +368.20 | +7.51 |
| CB | 382.20 | 262°08′48″ | S 82°08′48″W | −52.22 | −378.62 |
| BA | 401.58 | 231°22′00″ | S 51°22′00″W | −250.72 | −313.70 |
| | $P = 2081.19$ | | | $\Sigma$ lat $= +0.06$ | $\Sigma$ dep $= -0.49$ |

$$E = \sqrt{\Sigma\ \text{lat}^2 + \text{dep}^2} = \sqrt{0.06^2 + 0.49^2} = 0.49$$

$$\text{Precision ratio} = \frac{E}{P} = \frac{0.49}{2081.19} = \frac{1}{4247} \approx \frac{1}{4200}$$

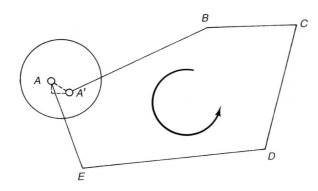

Closure Error = $A'A$

Closure Correction = $AA'$

Solution Proceeds Counterclockwise Around the Traverse beginning at A.

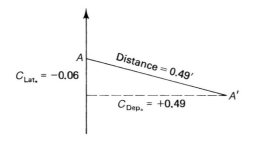

$$AA' = \sqrt{C_{\text{Lat.}}^2 + C_{\text{Dep.}}^2} = 0.494'$$

Bearing of $AA'$ Can Be Computed from the Relationship:

$$\tan \text{Bearing} = \frac{C_{\text{Dep.}}}{C_{\text{Lat.}}} = \frac{0.49}{-0.06}$$

Bearing Angle = 83.0189° = 83°01′

Bearing $AA'$ = S 83°01′ W

**FIGURE 6.11** Closure error and closure corrections.

bearing is north and minus if the bearing is south; similarly, departures are positive if the bearing is east and negative if the bearing is west. For example, course AE has an azimuth of 152°46′12″ (cos is negative, sin is positive; see Figure 6.7), meaning that the latitude will be negative and the departure positive. Similarly, AE has a bearing of S 27°13′48″ E, which, results in a negative latitude (south) and a positive departure (east), as expected.

Table 6.2 shows that the latitudes fail to close by +0.06 ($\Sigma$ lat) and the departures fail to close by −0.49 ($\Sigma$ dep). Figure 6.11 shows graphically the relationship between the

*C* lat and *C* dep.* *C* lat and *C* dep are opposite in sign to $\Sigma$ lat and $\Sigma$ dep and reflect the direction consistent (in this example) with the counterclockwise approach to the problem. The traverse computation began at *A* and concluded at *A'*. The *linear error of closure* is given by the line *A'A*, and the correction closure is given by *AA'*. *C* lat and *C* dep are in fact the latitude and departure of the required correction course.

The length of *AA'* is the square root of the sum of the squares of the *C* lat and *C* dep:

$$AA' = \sqrt{C \text{ lat}^2 + C \text{ dep}^2} = \sqrt{0.06^2 + 0.49^2}$$

It is sometimes advantageous to know the bearing of the closure correction (misclosure). Figure 6.11 shows that *C* dep/*C* lat = tan bearing: bearing *AA'* = S 83°01'E.

The error of closure (linear error of closure) is the net accumulation of the random errors associated with the measurement of the traverse angles and traverse distances. In this example, the total error is showing up at *A* simply because the computation began at *A*. If the computation had commenced at any other station, the identical linear error of closure would have shown up at **that** station.

The error of closure is compared to the perimeter (*P*) of the traverse to determine the precision ratio. In the example of Table 6.2, the precision ratio is *E/P* = 0.49/2,081 (rounded).

$$\text{Precision ratio} = \frac{1}{4,247} = \frac{1}{4,200}$$

The fraction of *E/P* is always expressed so that the numerator is 1, and the denominator is rounded to the closest 100 units. In the example shown, both the numerator and denominator are divided by the numerator (0.49).

The concept of an accuracy ratio was introduced in Section 1.14. Many states and provinces have precision ratios legislated for minimally acceptable surveys for boundaries. The values vary from one area to another, but usually the minimal values are 1/5,000 to 1/7,500. It is logical to assign more precise values (e.g., 1/10,000) to high-cost urban areas. Engineering surveys are performed at levels of 1/3,000 to 1/10,000, depending on the importance of the work and the types of materials used. For example, a gravel highway could well be surveyed at a 1/3,000 level of precision, whereas overhead rails for a monorail facility could well require levels of 1/7,500 to 1/10,000. As noted earlier, control surveyors for both legal and engineering projects must locate their control points at a much higher level of precision and accuracy than is necessary for the actual location of the legal or engineering project markers surveyed from those control points.

If the precision using latitudes and departures computed from field measurements is not acceptable as determined by the survey specifications (see Chapter 10), additional fieldwork must be performed to improve the level of precision. (Fieldwork is never undertaken until all calculations have been double-checked.) When fieldwork is to be checked, usually the distances are checked first because the angles have already been verified [i.e., $(n - 2)180°$].

If a large error (or mistake) has been made on one side, it will significantly affect the bearing of the linear error of closure. If a check on fieldwork is necessary, the surveyor first

---

*$\Sigma$ lat is the error in latitudes; $\Sigma$ dep is the error in departures; *C* lat is the required correction in latitudes; *C* dep is the required correction in departures.

computes the bearing of the linear error of closure and checks that bearing against the course bearings. If a similarity exists ($\pm 5°$), that course is the first course remeasured in the field. If a difference is found in that course measurement (or any other course), the new course distance is immediately substituted into the computation to check whether the required precision level has then been achieved.

A quick summary of initial traverse computations follows:

1. Balance the angles.
2. Compute the bearings and/or the azimuths.
3. Compute the latitudes and departures, the linear error of closure, and the precision ratio of the traverse.

If the precision ratio is satisfactory, further treatment of the data is possible (e.g., coordinates and area computations). If the precision ratio is unsatisfactory (e.g., a precision ratio of only 1/4,000 when a ratio of 1/5,000 was specified), complete the following steps:

1. Double-check all computations.
2. Double-check all field-book entries.
3. Compute the bearing of the linear error of closure and check to see if it is similar to a course bearing ($\pm 5°$).
4. Remeasure the sides of the traverse, beginning with a course having a similar bearing to the linear error of closure bearing (if there is one).
5. When a correction is found for a measured side, try that value in the latitude-departure computation to determine the new level of precision.

## 6.7  Traverse Precision and Accuracy

The actual accuracy of a survey as suggested by the precision ratio of a closed traverse can be misleading. The opportunity exists for significant errors to cancel out, which can result in "high-precision" closures from relatively inaccurate field techniques. In the case of a closed-loop traverse, untreated systematic errors will have been largely balanced during the computation of latitudes and departures. For example, in a square-shaped traverse, untreated systematic taping errors (long or short tape) will be completely balanced and beyond mathematical detection. Therefore, for high precision to reflect favorably on accuracy, control of field practice and techniques is essential.

If a traverse has been closed to better than 1/5,000, the taping should have conformed to the specifications shown in Table 2.2. Figure 6.12 shows that, for consistency, the survey should be designed so that the maximum allowable error in angle ($E_a$) should be roughly equal to the maximum allowable error in distance ($E_d$). If the linear error is 1/5,000, the angular error should be consistent:

$$1/5,000 = \tan \theta'$$
$$\theta' = 0°00'41''$$

See Table 6.3 for additional linear and angular error relationships. The overall allowable angular error in an $n$-angled closed traverse would be $E_a\sqrt{n}$. (Random errors accumulate

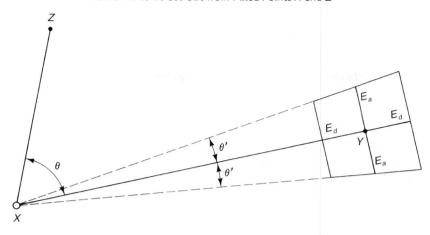

Point $Y$ is to Be Set Out from Fixed Points $X$ and $Z$

For the Line $XY$

$E_d$ is the Possible Error in Distance Measurement and $E_a$ is the Position Error Resulting from a Possible Angle Error of $\theta'$ in an Angle of $\theta$.

**FIGURE 6.12**   Relationship between errors in linear and angular measurements.

**Table 6.3**   LINEAR AND ANGULAR ERROR RELATIONSHIPS

| Linear accuracy ratio | Maximum angular error, $E_a$ | Least count of total station or theodolite scale or read-out |
|---|---|---|
| 1/1,000 | 0°03'26" | 01' |
| 1/3,000 | 0°01'09" | 01' |
| 1/5,000 | 0°00'41" | 30" |
| 1/7,500 | 0°00'28" | 20" |
| 1/10,000 | 0°00'21" | 20" |
| 1/20,000 | 0°00'10" | 10" |

as the square root of the number of observations.) Thus, for a five-sided traverse with a specification for precision of 1/3,000, the maximum angular misclosure would be $01'\sqrt{5} = 02'$ (to the closest minute). For a five-sided traverse with a specification for precision of 1/5,000, the maximum misclosure of the field angles would be $30''\sqrt{5} = 01'$ (to the closest 30 seconds).

# 6.8   Traverse Adjustments

Latitudes and departures can be used for the computation of coordinates or the computation of the area enclosed by the traverse. In addition, the station coordinates can then be used to establish control for additional survey layout. Before any further use can be made of these latitudes and departures, however, they must be adjusted so that their errors are suitably distributed, and the algebraic sums of the latitudes and departures are each zero. If done properly, these adjustments will ensure that the final position of each traverse station, as given by the station coordinates, is optimal with respect to the true station location.

Current surveying practice favors either the compass rule (Bowditch) adjustment or the least squares adjustment. The compass rule (an approximate method) is applied in most calculator solutions, with the least squares method being reserved for large, precise traverses (e.g., extension of a state or province coordinate grid) and for most computer software solutions. Although the least squares method requires extensive computations, advances in computer technology are now allowing the surveyor to use the least squares technique with the help of a desktop computer or even a handheld calculator.

## 6.9 Compass Rule Adjustment

The *compass rule* is used in many survey computations to distribute the errors in latitudes and departures. The compass rule distributes the errors in latitude and departure for each traverse course in the same proportion as the course distance is to the traverse perimeter; that is, generally:

$$\frac{C \text{ lat } AB}{\Sigma \text{ lat}} = \frac{AB}{P} \qquad \text{or} \qquad C \text{ lat } AB = \Sigma \text{ lat} \times \frac{AB}{P} \qquad (6.3)$$

where $C$ lat $AB$ = correction in latitude $AB$
$\Sigma$ lat = error of closure in latitude
$AB$ = distance $AB$
$P$ = perimeter of traverse

and

$$\frac{C \text{ dep } AB}{\Sigma \text{ dep}} = \frac{AB}{P} \qquad \text{or} \qquad C \text{ dep } AB = \Sigma \text{ dep} \times \frac{AB}{P} \qquad (6.4)$$

where $C$ dep $AB$ = correction in departure $AB$
$\Sigma$ dep = error in closure in departure
$AB$ = distance $AB$
$P$ = perimeter of traverse

In both cases, the sign of the correction is opposite from that of the error.

Table 6.2 from the traverse example in Section 6.6 has been expanded in Table 6.4 to provide space for traverse adjustments. The magnitudes of the individual corrections are shown next:

$$C \text{ lat } AE = \frac{0.06 \times 350.10}{2,081.19} = 0.01 \qquad C \text{ lat } CB = \frac{0.06 \times 383.20}{2,081.19} = 0.01$$

**Table 6.4** TRAVERSE ADJUSTMENTS: COMPASS RULE, SECTION 6.6

| Course | Distance (ft) | Bearing | Latitude | Departure | C lat | C dep | Balanced latitudes | Balanced departures |
|---|---|---|---|---|---|---|---|---|
| AE | 350.10 | S 27°13'48" E | −311.30 | +160.19 | −0.01 | +0.08 | −311.31 | +160.27 |
| ED | 579.03 | N 64°50'54" E | +246.10 | +524.13 | −0.02 | +0.14 | +246.08 | +524.27 |
| DC | 368.28 | N 1°10'06" E | +368.20 | +7.51 | −0.01 | +0.09 | +368.19 | +7.60 |
| CB | 382.20 | S 82°08'48" W | −52.22 | −378.62 | −0.01 | +0.09 | −52.23 | −378.53 |
| BA | 401.58 | S 51°22'00" W | −250.72 | −313.70 | −0.01 | +0.09 | −250.73 | −313.61 |
| | P = 2081.19 | | Σ lat = +0.06 | Σ dep = −0.49 | $C_{lat}$ = −0.06 | $C_{dep}$ = +0.49 | 0.00 | 0.00 |

$$C \text{ lat } ED = \frac{0.06 \times 579.03}{2,081.19} = 0.02 \qquad C \text{ lat } BA = \frac{0.06 \times 401.58}{2,081.19} = 0.01$$

$$C \text{ lat } DC = \frac{0.06 \times 368.28}{2,081.19} = 0.01 \qquad \text{Check: } \Sigma C \text{ lat} = 0.06$$

$$C \text{ dep } AE = \frac{0.49 \times 350.10}{2,081.19} = 0.08 \qquad C \text{ dep } CB = \frac{0.49 \times 382.20}{2,081.19} = 0.09$$

$$C \text{ dep } ED = \frac{0.49 \times 579.03}{2,081.19} = 0.14 \qquad C \text{ dep } BA = \frac{0.49 \times 401.58}{2,081.19} = 0.09$$

$$C \text{ dep } DC = \frac{0.49 \times 368.28}{2,081.19} = 0.09 \qquad \text{Check: } \Sigma C \text{ dep} = 0.49$$

When these computations are performed on a handheld calculator, the constants 0.06/2,081.19 and 0.49/2,081.19 are often entered into storage for easy retrieval and thus quick computations.

It remains now only for the algebraic sign to be determined. Quite simply, the corrections are opposite in sign to the errors. Therefore, for this example, the latitude corrections are negative and the departure corrections are positive. The corrections are now added algebraically to arrive at the balanced values. For example, in Table 6.4, the correction for latitude $AE$ is $-0.01$, which is to be "added" to the latitude $AE$, $-311.30$. Since the correction is the same sign as the latitude, the two values are added to get the answer. In the case of course $ED$, the latitude correction ($-0.02$) and the latitude ($+246.10$) have opposite signs, indicating that the difference between the two values is the desired value (i.e., subtract to get the answer).

To check your work, the balanced latitudes and balanced departures are added to see if their respective sums are zero. Sometimes the balanced latitude or balanced departure totals fail to equal zero by one last-place unit (0.01 in this example). This discrepancy is probably caused by rounding off and is normally of no consequence. This discrepancy is removed by arbitrarily changing one of the values and thus forcing the total to zero.

Note that when the error (in latitude or departure) to be distributed is quite small, the corrections can be assigned arbitrarily to appropriate courses. For example, if the error in latitude (or departure) were only 0.03 ft in a five-sided traverse, it would be appropriate to apply corrections of 0.01 ft to the latitude of each of the three longest courses. Similarly, in Section 6.6, where the error in latitude for that five-sided traverse is $+0.06$, it would have been appropriate to apply a correction of $-0.02$ to the longest course latitude and a correction of $-0.01$ to each of the remaining four latitudes, the same solution provided by the compass rule. See Appendix A for additional discussion on error adjustments.

## 6.10 Effects of Traverse Adjustments on the Original Data

Once the latitudes and departures have been adjusted, the original polar coordinates (distance and direction) will no longer be valid. In most cases, the adjustment required for the polar coordinates is too small to warrant consideration. But if the data are to be used for

**Table 6.5**  ADJUSTMENT OF BEARINGS AND DISTANCES USING BALANCED LATITUDES AND
DEPARTURES: SECTION 6.6

| Course | Balanced latitude | Balanced departure | Adjusted distance (ft) | Adjusted bearing | Original distance (ft) | Original bearing |
|---|---|---|---|---|---|---|
| AE | −311.31 | +160.27 | 350.14 | S 27°14′26″ E | 350.10 | S 27°13′48″ E |
| ED | +246.08 | +524.27 | 579.15 | N 64°51′21″ E | 579.03 | N 64°50′54″ E |
| DC | +368.19 | +7.60 | 368.27 | N 1°10′57″ E | 368.28 | N 1°10′06″ E |
| CB | −52.23 | −378.53 | 382.12 | S 82°08′38″ W | 382.20 | S 82°08′48″ W |
| BA | −250.73 | −313.61 | 401.52 | S 51°21′28″ W | 401.58 | S 51°22′00″ W |
| | 0.00 | 0.00 | $P = 2081.20$ | | $P = 2081.19$ | |

layout purposes, the **corrected** distances and directions should be used. The following
relationships are inferred from Figures 6.5 and 6.11:

$$\text{Distance } AD = \sqrt{\text{lat } AD^2 + \text{dep } AD^2} \tag{6.5}$$

$$\text{Tan bearing } AD = \frac{\text{dep } AD}{\text{lat } AD} \tag{6.6}$$

Next, we use the values from Table 6.4. The solution for course AE is shown in the following equations:

$$\text{Distance } AE = \sqrt{311.31^2 + 160.27^2} = 350.14 \text{ ft}$$

$$\text{Tan bearing } AE = \frac{+160.27}{-311.31}$$

$$\text{Bearing } = \text{S } 27°14′26″\text{E}$$

The remaining corrected bearings and distances are shown in Table 6.5

# 6.11  Omitted Measurements

The techniques developed in the computation of latitudes and departures can be
used to supply missing course information on a closed traverse. They can also be
used to solve any surveying problem that can be arranged in the form of a closed
traverse.

### ■ EXAMPLE 6.1
A missing course in a closed traverse is illustrated in Figure 6.13 and the data are tabulated in Table 6.6. The data can be treated in the same manner as in a closed traverse.
When the latitudes and departures are totaled, they will not balance. Both the latitudes
and departures will fail to close by the amount of the latitude and departure of the missing course, DA.

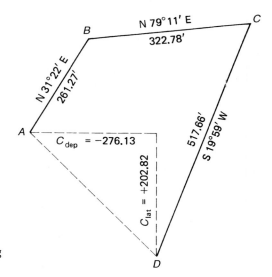

**FIGURE 6.13** Example 6.1: missing course computation.

**Table 6.6** MISSING COURSE: EXAMPLE 6.1

| Course | Distance | Bearing | Latitude | Departure |
|--------|----------|---------|----------|-----------|
| AB | 261.27 | N 31°22′ E | +223.09 | +135.99 |
| BC | 322.78 | N 79°11′ E | +60.58 | +317.05 |
| CD | 517.66 | S 19°59′ W | −486.49 | −176.91 |
|  |  |  | Σ lat = −202.82 | Σ dep = +276.13 |
| DA |  |  | C lat = +202.82 | C dep = −276.13 |

**Solution**

The length and direction of *DA* can be computed by using Equations 6.5 and 6.6:

$$\text{Distance } DA = \sqrt{\text{lat } DA^2 + \text{dep } DA^2}$$

$$= \sqrt{202.82^2 + 276.13^2}$$

$$= 342.61 \text{ ft}$$

$$\text{Tan bearing } DA = \frac{\text{dep } AD}{\text{lat } AD}$$

$$\text{Tan bearing } DA = \frac{-276.13}{+202.82}$$

Bearing *DA* = N 53°42′ W (rounded to closest minute)

Note that this technique does not permit a check on the accuracy ratio of the fieldwork. Since this is a closure course, the computed value will also contain all accumulated errors.

### ■ EXAMPLE 6.2

Figure 6.14 illustrates an intersection jog-elimination problem that occurs in many municipalities. For various reasons, some original streets do not intersect other original

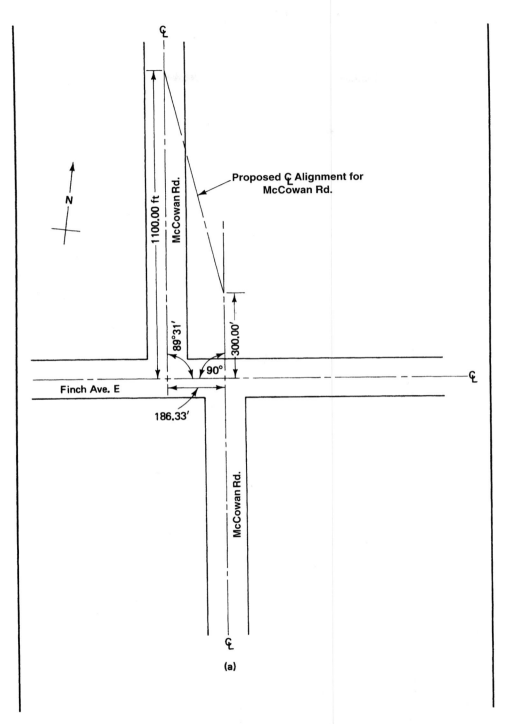

**FIGURE 6.14** (a) jog elimination, missing course problem. (*continued*)

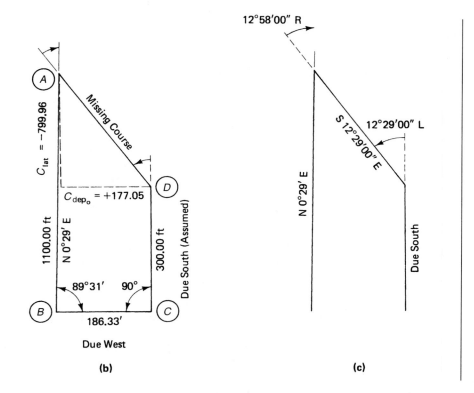

**FIGURE 6.14 (continued)**  (b) Distances and bearings. (c) Determination of deflection angles.

streets directly. They jog a few feet to a few hundred feet before continuing. Figure 6.14(a) indicates that, in this case, the entire jog will be taken out on the north side of the intersection. The designer has determined that if the McCowan Road ℄ (south of Finch) is produced northerly 300 ft of the ℄ of Finch Avenue E, it can then be joined to the existing McCowan Road ℄ at a distance of 1,100 ft northerly from the ℄ of Finch Avenue E. Presumably, these distances will allow for the insertion of curves that will satisfy the geometric requirements for the design speed and traffic volumes. The problem here is to compute the length of $AD$ and the deflection angles at $D$ and $A$ [see Figure 6.14(b) and Table 6.7].

**Solution**

Assume a bearing for line $DC$ of due south. The bearing for $CB$ is therefore due west, and obviously the bearing of $BA$ is N 0°29′ E. The problem is then set up as a missing course problem, and the corrections in latitude and departure are the latitude and departure of $AD$ (see Table 6.7).

$$\text{Distance } AD = \sqrt{799.96^2 + 177.05^2} = 819.32 \text{ ft}$$

**Table 6.7**   MISSING COURSE: EXAMPLE 6.2

| Course | Distance | Bearing | Latitude | Departure |
|--------|----------|---------|----------|-----------|
| DC | 300.00 | S 0°00′ E(W) | −300.00 | 0.00 |
| CB | 186.33 | S 90°00′ W | 0.00 | −186.33 |
| BA | 1100.00 | N 0°29′ E | +1099.96 | +9.28 |
| | | | Σ lat = 799.96 | Σ dep = −177.05 |
| AD | | | C lat = −799.96 | C dep = +177.05 |

$$\text{Tan bearing } AD = \frac{177.05}{-799.96}$$

Bearing $AD$ = S 12°29′00″E (to the closest 30″)

The bearings are shown in Figure 6.14(c), which leads to the calculation of the deflection angles as shown.

There are obviously many other situations in which the missing course techniques can be used. If one bearing and one distance (not necessarily on the same course) are omitted from a traverse, the missing data can be solved. In some cases, it may be necessary to compute intermediate cutoff lines and use cosine and sine laws in conjunction with the latitude/departure solution.

# 6.12   Rectangular Coordinates of Traverse Stations

## 6.12.1   Coordinates Computed from Balanced Latitudes and Departures

*Rectangular coordinates* define the position of a point with respect to two perpendicular axes. Analytic geometry uses the concepts of a $Y$ axis (north-south) and an $X$ axis (east-west), concepts that are obviously quite useful in surveying applications.

In universal transverse Mercator (UTM) coordinate grid systems, the $X$ axis is often the equator, and the $Y$ axis is a central meridian through the middle of the zone in which the grid is located (see Chapter 10). Uppercase $X$ and $Y$ are used for assigned axes. For surveys of a limited nature, where a coordinate grid has not been established, the coordinate axes can be assumed. If the axes are to be assumed, values are chosen so that the coordinates of all stations will be positive (that is, all stations will be in the northeast quadrant).

The traverse tabulated in Table 6.4 will be used for illustrative purposes. Values for the coordinates of station $A$ are assumed to be 1,000.00 ft north and 1,000.00 ft east. To calculate the coordinates of the other traverse stations, it is simply a matter of applying the **balanced** latitudes and departures to the previously calculated coordinates. In Figure 6.15, the balanced latitude and departure of course $AE$ are applied to the assumed coordinates of station $A$ to determine the coordinates of station $E$, and so on. These simple computations

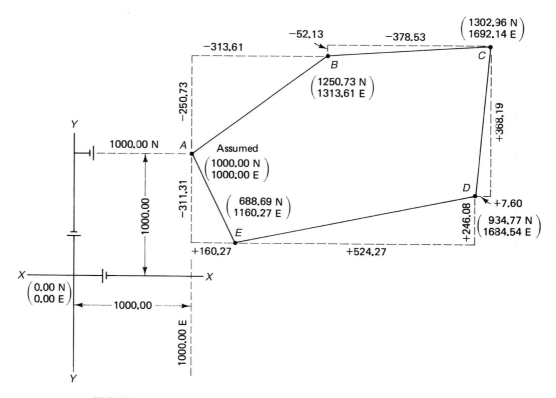

**FIGURE 6.15** Station coordinates, using balanced latitudes and departures.

are shown in Table 6.8. A check on the computation is possible by using the last latitude and departure (*BA*) to recalculate the coordinates of station *A*.

The use of coordinates to define the positions of boundary markers has been steadily increasing over the years (see Chapter 10). The storage of property-corner coordinates in large-memory civic computers will, in the not-so-distant future, permit lawyers, municipal authorities, and others to have instant retrieval of current land registration information, assessment, and other municipal information, such as census data and the availability of municipal services. Although such use is important, the truly impressive impact of coordinate use will result from (1) the coordination of topographic detail (digitization) so that plans can be prepared by computer-assisted plotters, and (2) the coordination of all legal and engineering details so that not only will the plans be produced by computer-assisted plotters, the survey layout will be accomplished using sets of computer-generated coordinates (rectangular and polar) fed either manually or automatically into total stations (see Chapter 7). Complex layouts can then be accomplished quickly by a few surveyors from one or two centrally located control points with a higher level of precision and a lower incidence of mistakes.

**Table 6.8**  COMPUTATION OF COORDINATES USING BALANCED LATITUDES AND DEPARTURES

| Course | Balanced latitude | Balanced departure | Station | North | | East | |
|--------|-------------------|--------------------|---------|-------|--|------|--|
| | | | A | **1000.00** | (assumed) | **1000.00** | (assumed) |
| AE | −311.31 | +160.27 | | −311.31 | | +160.27 | |
| | | | E | **688.69** | | **1160.27** | |
| ED | +246.08 | +524.27 | | +246.08 | | +524.27 | |
| | | | D | **934.77** | | **1684.54** | |
| DC | +368.19 | +7.60 | | +368.19 | | +7.60 | |
| | | | C | **1302.96** | | **1692.14** | |
| CB | −52.23 | −378.53 | | −52.23 | | −378.53 | |
| | | | B | **1250.73** | | **1313.61** | |
| BA | −250.73 | −313.61 | | −250.73 | | −313.61 | |
| | | | A | **1000.00** | **Check** | **1000.00** | **Check** |

# 6.12.2 Adjusted Coordinates Computed from Raw-Data Coordinates

Section 6.9 demonstrated the adjustment of traverse errors by the adjustment of the individual latitudes and departures for each traverse course using the compass rule. Although this traditional technique has been favored for many years, because of the recent wide use of the computer in surveying solutions, coordinates are now often first computed from raw (unadjusted) bearing and distance data and then adjusted using the compass rule or least squares technique. Since we are now working with coordinates and not individual latitudes ($\Delta Y$'s) and departures ($\Delta X$'s), the distance factor to be used in the compass rule must be cumulative. This technique will be illustrated using the same field data from Section 6.6.

Corrections (C) to raw-data coordinates (see Tables 6.9 and 6.10): $C\Delta Y =$ correction in northing (latitude), and $C\Delta X =$ correction in easting (departure).

### STATION E

$$C\Delta Y \text{ is } [AE/P] \, \Sigma\Delta Y: = [350.10/2081.19]0.06 = 0.01$$
$$C\Delta X \text{ is } [AE/P] \, \Sigma\Delta X: = [350.10/2081.19]0.49 = 0.08$$

### STATION D

$$C\Delta Y \text{ is } [(AE + ED)/p] \, \Sigma\Delta Y = [(350.10 + 579.03)/2081.19] \, 0.06 = 0.03$$
$$C\Delta X \text{ is } [(AE + ED)/p] \, \Sigma\Delta X = [(350.10 + 579.03)/2081.19] \, 0.49 = 0.22$$

### STATION C

$$C\Delta Y \text{ is } [(AE + ED + DC)/p] \, \Sigma\Delta Y = [(350.10 + 579.03 + 368.28)/2081.19] \, 0.06 = 0.04$$
$$C\Delta X \text{ is } [(AE + ED + DC)/p] \, \Sigma\Delta X = [(350.10 + 579.03 + 368.28)/2081.19] \, 0.49 = 0.31$$

### STATION B

$$C\Delta Y \text{ is } [(AE + ED + DC + CB)/p] \, \Sigma\Delta Y = [(350.10 + 579.03 + 368.28 + 382.20)/2081.19] \, 0.06 = 0.05$$

**Table 6.9** COMPUTATION OF RAW-DATA COORDINATES

| Station/ course | Azimuth | Distance | $\Delta Y$ | $\Delta X$ | Coordinates (raw-data) | |
|---|---|---|---|---|---|---|
| | | | | | Northing | Easting |
| A | | | | | 1,000.00 | 1,000.00 |
| AE | 152°46′12″ | 350.10 | −311.30 | 160.19 | | |
| E | | | | | 688.70 | 1,160.19 |
| ED | 64°50′54″ | 579.03 | 246.10 | 524.13 | | |
| D | | | | | 934.80 | 1,684.32 |
| DC | 1°10′06″ | 368.28 | 368.20 | 7.51 | | |
| C | | | | | 1,303.00 | 1,691.83 |
| CB | 262°08′48″ | 382.20 | −52.22 | −378.62 | | |
| B | | | | | 1,250.78 | 1,313.21 |
| BA | 231°22′00″ | 401.58 | −250.72 | −313.70 | | |
| A | | | $\Sigma\Delta Y = 0.06$ | $\Sigma\Delta X = -0.49$ | 1,000.06 | 999.51 |

$C\Delta X$ is $[(AE + ED + DC + CB)/p]\ \Sigma\Delta X$: $[(350.10 + 579.03 + 368.28 + 382.20)/2081.19]\ 0.49 = 0.40$

**STATION A**

$C\Delta Y$ is $[(AE + ED + DC + CB + BA)/p]\ \Sigma\Delta Y = [(350.10 + 579.03 + 368.28 + 382.20 + 401.58)/2081.19]\ 0.06 = 0.06$

$C\Delta X$ is $[(AE + ED + DC + CB + BA)/p]\ \Sigma\Delta X$: $[(350.10 + 579.03 + 368.28 + 382.20 + 401.58)/2081.19]\ 0.49 = 0.49$

■ **EXAMPLE 6.3**

Review Problem

Figure 6.16 shows the field data for a five-sided closed traverse.

(a) Balance the angles.

(b) Compute the azimuths and bearings.

(c) Compute the linear error of closure and the precision ratio of the traverse.

(d) If the precision ratio is equal to or greater than 1/4,000, balance the latitudes and departures using the compass rule.

(e) If the coordinates of station B are (1,000.000 N, 1,000.000 E), compute the coordinates of the remaining stations.

**Table 6.10** COMPUTATION OF ADJUSTED COORDINATES, DISTANCES AND DIRECTIONS

| Station/course | Coordinates (raw-data) | | CΔy[a] | CΔx[a] | Adjusted coordinates | | Adjusted ΔY | Adjusted ΔX | Adj. dist. | Adj. brg. |
| --- | --- | --- | --- | --- | --- | --- | --- | --- | --- | --- |
| | Northing | Easting | | | Northing | Easting | | | | |
| A | 1,000.00 | 1,000.00 | | | 1,000.00 | 1,000.00 | | | | |
| AE | | | | | | | −311.31 | 160.27 | 350.14 | S 27°14′26″E |
| E | 688.70 | 1,160.19 | −0.01 | +0.08 | 688.69 | 1,160.27 | | | | |
| ED | | | | | | | 246.08 | 524.27 | 579.15 | N 64°51′31″E |
| D | 934.80 | 1,684.32 | −0.03 | +0.22 | 934.77 | 1,684.54 | | | | |
| DC | | | | | | | 368.19 | 7.60 | 368.27 | N 1°10′57″E |
| C | 1,303.00 | 1,691.83 | −0.04 | +0.31 | 1,302.96 | 1,692.14 | | | | |
| CB | | | | | | | −52.23 | −378.53 | 382.12 | S 82°08′38″W |
| B | 1,250.78 | 1,313.21 | −0.05 | +0.40 | 1,250.73 | 1,313.61 | | | | |
| BA | | | | | | | −250.73 | −313.61 | 401.52 | S 51°21′28″W |
| A | 1,000.06 | 999.51 | −0.06 | +0.49 | 1,000.00 | 1,000.00 | | | | |

[a]Correction is opposite in sign to the error.

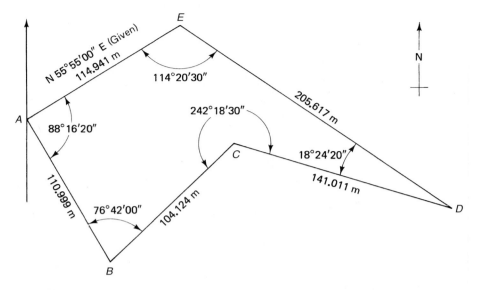

**FIGURE 6.16** Traverse sketch for Example 6.3 showing mean field distances and interior angles.

**Solution**

(a)  | **FIELD ANGLES** | | **BALANCED ANGLES** | |
|---|---|---|---|
| A | 88°16′20″ | A | 88°16′00″ |
| B | 76°42′00″ | B | 76°41′40″ |
| C | 242°18′30″ | C | 242°18′10″ |
| D | 18°24′20″ | D | 18°24′00″ |
| E | 114°20′30″ | E | 114°20′10″ |

538°120′00″ = 540°00′100″     538°119′60″ = 540°00′00″

$$(n - 2)180 = 540°$$
$$\text{Error in angular closure} = 100″$$
$$\text{Correction per angle} = -20″$$

(b) See Figure 6.17.

| | | |
|---|---|---|
| Az *AE* = | 55°55′00″ | (see Figure 6.16 and Table 6.11) |
| + <A | 88°16′00″ | |
| Az *AB* = | 144°11′00″ | |
| | +180° | |
| Az *BA* = | 324°11′00″ | |
| + <B | 76°41′40″ | |
| Az *BC* = | 400°52′40″ | |
| | −360° | |
| Az *BC* = | 40°52′40″ | |
| | +180° | |
| Az *CB* = | 220°52′40″ | |
| + <C | 242°18′10″ | |

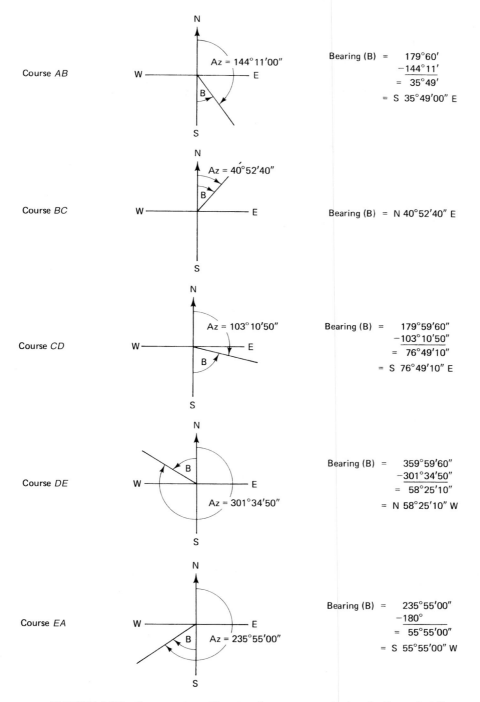

**FIGURE 6.17** Computation of bearings from computed azimuths, Example 6.3.

**Table 6.11** AZIMUTHS AND BEARINGS

| Course | Azimuths (clockwise) | Bearings (clockwise) computed from clockwise azimuths |
|--------|----------------------|------------------------------------------------------|
| AB | 144°11′00″ | S 35°49′00″E |
| BC | 40°52′40″ | N 40°52′40″ E |
| CD | 103°10′50″ | S 76°49′10″ E |
| DE | 301°34′50″ | N 58°25′10″ W |
| EA | 235°55′00″ | S 55°55′00″ W |

**Table 6.12** COMPUTATION OF LINEAR ERROR OF CLOSURE ($E$) AND THE ACCURACY RATIO $E/P$ OF THE TRAVERSE IN EXAMPLE 6.7

| Course | Azimuth | Bearing | Distance | Latitude | Departure |
|--------|---------|---------|----------|----------|-----------|
| AB | 144°11′00″ | S 35°49′00″E | 110.999 | −90.008 | +64.956 |
| BC | 40°52′40″ | N 40°52′40″ E | 104.124 | +78.729 | +68.144 |
| CD | 103°10′50″ | S 76°49′10″ E | 141.011 | −32.153 | +137.296 |
| DE | 301°34′50″ | N 58°25′10″ W | 205.617 | +107.681 | −175.166 |
| EA | 235°55′00″ | S 55°55′00″ W | 114.941 | −64.413 | −95.197 |
| | | | $P = 676.692$ | $E_L = -0.164$ | $E_D = +0.033$ |

$$E = \sqrt{E \text{ lat}^2 + E \text{ dep}^2} = \sqrt{0.164^2 + 0.033^2} = 0.167 \text{ m}$$

$$\text{Precision ratio of traverse} = \frac{0.167}{676.692} = \frac{1}{4052} = \frac{1}{4100}$$

$$
\begin{aligned}
\text{Az } CD &= 463°10′50″ \\
&\quad -360° \\
\text{Az } CD &= 103°10′50″ \\
&\quad +180° \\
\text{Az } DC &= 283°10′50″ \\
+ <D &\quad 18°24′00″ \\
\text{Az } DE &= 301°34′00″ \\
&\quad -180° \\
\text{Az } DE &= 121°34′50″ \\
+ <E &\quad 114°20′10″ \\
\text{Az } EA &= 235°55′00″ \\
&\quad -180° \\
\text{Az } AE &= 55°55′00″ \quad \text{Check}
\end{aligned}
$$

(c) In Table 6.12, the latitudes and departures are computed by using either the azimuths or the bearings and the distances. (Both azimuths and bearings are shown here only for comparative purposes.) Because the precision ratio (1/4,000) meets the specifications noted, the computations can continue.

(d) Use Equations 6.3 and 6.4:

$$C \text{ lat } AB = \Sigma \text{ lat} \times \frac{\text{distance } AB}{\text{perimeter}}$$

**Table 6.13** COMPUTATION OF BALANCED LATITUDES AND DEPARTURES USING THE COMPASS RULE

| Course | Latitude | Departure | C lat | C dep | Balanced latitude | Balanced departure |
|--------|----------|-----------|-------|-------|-------------------|--------------------|
| AB | −90.008 | +64.956 | +0.027 | −0.005 | −89.981 | +64.951 |
| BC | +78.729 | +68.144 | +0.025 | −0.005 | +78.754 | +68.139 |
| CD | −32.153 | +137.296 | +0.034 | −0.007 | −32.119 | +137.289 |
| DE | +107.681 | −175.166 | +0.050 | −0.010 | +107.731 | −175.176 |
| EA | −64.413 | −95.197 | +0.028 | −0.006 | −64.385 | −95.203 |
| | $E_L = -0.164$ | $E_D = +0.033$ | +0.164 | −0.033 | 0.00 | 0.00 |

$$C \text{ dep } AB = \Sigma \text{ dep} \times \frac{\text{distance } AB}{\text{perimeter}}$$

For the example problem:

$$C \text{ lat } AB = 0.164 \times \frac{111}{677} \text{ (values rounded)} = 0.027 \text{ m}$$

$$C \text{ dep } AB = 0.033 \times \frac{111}{677} = 0.005 \text{ m}$$

As a check, the algebraic sum of the balanced latitudes (and balanced departures) should be zero.

(e) The **balanced** latitudes and departures (Table 6.13) are used to compute the coordinates (see Figure 6.18). The axes are selected so that B is 1,000.000 N, 1,000.000 E. If the computation returns to B with values of 1,000.000 N and 1,000.000 E, the computation is verified. See Table 6.14.

# 6.13 Summary of Traverse Computations

1. Balance the field angles.
2. Correct (if necessary) the field distances (e.g., for temperature).
3. Compute the bearings and/or azimuths.
4. Compute the linear error of closure and the precision ratio of the traverse.
5. Compute the balanced latitudes ($\Delta Y$) and balanced departures ($\Delta X$).
6. Compute the coordinates.
7. Compute the area.

Allied topics, such as plotting by rectangular coordinates and the computation of land areas by other methods, are covered in Chapter 8.

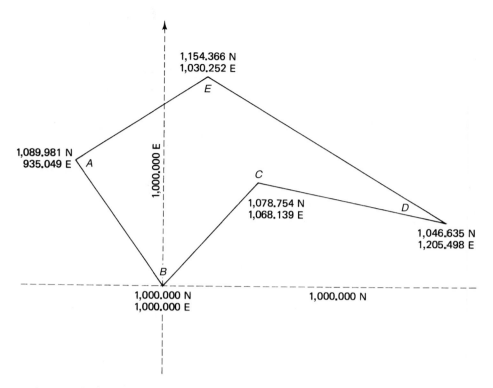

**FIGURE 6.18** Station coordinates, Example 6.3.

**Table 6.14** COORDINATES FOR EXAMPLE 6.7

| Station | North | | East | |
|---|---|---|---|---|
| B | **1,000.000** | | **1,000.000** | |
| | +78.754 (lat BC) | | +68.139 (dep BC) | |
| C | **1,078.754** | | 1,068.139 | |
| | −32.119 (lat CD) | | +137.289 (dep CD) | |
| D | **1,046.635** | | **1,205.428** | |
| | +107.731 (lat DE) | | −175.176 (dep DE) | |
| E | **1,154.366** | | **1,030.252** | |
| | −64.385 (lat EA) | | −95.203 (dep EA) | |
| A | **1,089.981** | | **935.049** | |
| | −89.981 (lat AB) | | +64.951 (dep AB) | |
| B | **1,000.000** | **Check** | **1,000.000** | **Check** |

# 6.14  Area of a Closed Traverse by the Coordinate Method

When the coordinates of the stations of a closed traverse are known, it is a simple matter to compute the area within the traverse, either by computer or handheld calculator. Figure 6.19(a) shows a closed traverse 1, 2, 3, 4 with appropriate $X$ and $Y$ coordinate distances. Figure 6.19(b) illustrates the technique used to compute the traverse area. You can see in Figure 6.19(b) that the desired **area of the traverse is, in effect, area 2 minus area 1**. Area 2 is the sum of the areas of trapezoids 4'433' and 3'322'. Area 1 is the sum of trapezoids 4'411' and 1'122'.

$$\text{Area } 2 = \tfrac{1}{2}(X_4 + X_3)(Y_4 - Y_3) + \tfrac{1}{2}(X_3 + X_2)(Y_3 - Y_2)$$

$$\text{Area } 2 = \tfrac{1}{2}(X_4 + X_1)(Y_4 - Y_1) + \tfrac{1}{2}(X_1 + X_2)(Y_1 - Y_2)$$

$$2A = [(X_4 + X_3)(Y_4 - Y_3) + (X_3 + X_2)(Y_3 - Y_2)] - [(X_4 + X_1)(Y_4 + X_1)(Y_4 - Y_1) + (X_1 + X_2)(Y_1 - Y_2)]$$

Expand this expression and collect the remaining terms:

$$2A = X_1(Y_2 - Y_4) + X_2(Y_3 - Y_1) + X_3(Y_4 - Y_2) + X_4(Y_1 - Y_3)$$

Stated simply, **the double area of a closed traverse is the algebraic sum of each $X$ coordinate multiplied by the difference between the $Y$ values of the adjacent stations**. The double area is divided by 2 to determine the final area. The final area can result in a positive or negative number, reflecting only the direction of computation approach (clockwise or counterclockwise). The area is, of course, positive; there is no such thing as a negative area.

■ **EXAMPLE 6.4**
*Area Computation by Coordinates*
Refer to the traverse example in Example 6.3, and the computed coordinates shown in Figure 6.18, which are summarized next:

| STATION | NORTH | EAST |
|---------|-----------|-----------|
| A | 1,089.981 | 935.049 |
| B | 1,000.000 | 1,000.000 |
| C | 1,078.754 | 1,068.139 |
| D | 1,046.635 | 1,205.498 |
| E | 1,154.366 | 1,030.252 |

$$2A = X_1(Y_2 - Y_4) + X_2(Y_3 - Y_1) + X_3(Y_4 - Y_2) + X_4(Y_1 - Y_3)$$

**Solution**
The **double area computation** (to the closest m²) is:

$$XA(YB - YE) = 935.049(1,000.000 - 1,154.366) \quad = -144,340$$

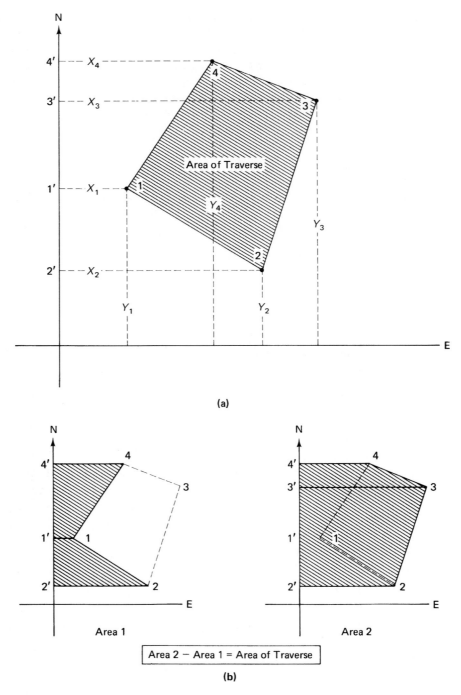

**(a)**

**(b)**

Area 2 − Area 1 = Area of Traverse

**FIGURE 6.19** Area by rectangular coordinates.

$$XB(YC - YA) = 1{,}000.000(1{,}078.754 - 1{,}089.981) = -11{,}227$$
$$XC(YD - YB) = 1{,}068.139(1{,}046.635 - 1{,}000.000) = +49{,}813$$
$$XD(YE - YC) = 1{,}205.498(1{,}154.366 - 1{,}078.754) = +91{,}150$$
$$XE(YA - YD) = 1{,}030.252(1{,}089.981 - 1{,}046.635) = \underline{+44{,}657}$$
$$2A = +30{,}053 \text{ m}^2$$

$$\text{Area} = 15{,}027 \text{ m}^2$$
$$= 1.503 \text{ hectares}$$

## ■ EXAMPLE 6.5

*Area Computation by Coordinates*

Refer to the traverse example in Section 6.6 and to Figures 6.15 and 6.22. The coordinates are summarized next:

| STATION | NORTH | EAST |
|---|---|---|
| A | 1,000.00 ft | 1,000.00 ft |
| B | 1,250.73 | 1,313.61 |
| C | 1,302.96 | 1,692.14 |
| D | 934.77 | 1,684.54 |
| E | 688.69 | 1,160.27 |

**Solution**

The double area computation (to the closest ft$^2$), using the relationships shown in Equation 6.7, is:

$$2A = X_1(Y_2 - Y_4) + X_2(Y_3 - Y_1) + X_3(Y_4 - Y_2) + X_4(Y_1 - Y_3)$$

$$
\begin{aligned}
XA(YB - YE) &= 1{,}000.00(1{,}250.73 - 688.69) &=& \quad +562{,}040 \\
XB(YC - YA) &= 1{,}313.61(1{,}302.96 - 1{,}000.00) &=& \quad +397{,}971 \\
XC(YD - YB) &= 1{,}692.14(934.77 - 1{,}250.73) &=& \quad -534{,}649 \\
XD(YE - YC) &= 1{,}684.54(688.69 - 1{,}302.96) &=& \quad -1{,}034{,}762 \\
XE(YA - YD) &= 1{,}160.27(1{,}000.00 - 934.77) &=& \quad \underline{+ 75{,}684} \\
& & & \quad -533{,}716 \text{ ft}^2 \\
& & 2A =& \quad 533{,}716 \text{ ft}^2
\end{aligned}
$$

$$\text{Area} = 266{,}858 \text{ ft}^2$$

Also:

$$\text{Area} = \frac{246{,}858}{43{,}560} = 6.126 \text{ acres} \qquad (1 \text{ acre} = 43{,}560 \text{ ft}^2)$$

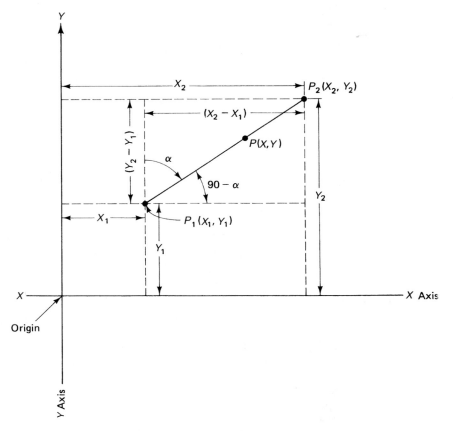

**FIGURE 6.20**  Geometry of rectangular coordinates.

## 6.15  Geometry of Rectangular Coordinates

Figure 6.20 shows two points $P_1(X_1, Y_1)$ and $P_2(X_2, Y_2)$ and their rectangular relationships to the $X$ and $Y$ axes.

$$\text{Length } P_1P_2 = \sqrt{(x_2 - x_1)^2 + (y_2 - y_1)^2} \tag{6.8}$$

$$\text{Tan } \alpha = \frac{X_2 - X_1}{Y_2 - Y_1} \tag{6.9}$$

where $\alpha$ is the bearing or azimuth of $P_1P_2$. Also:

$$\text{Length } P_1P_2 = \frac{X_2 - X_1}{\sin \alpha} \tag{6.10}$$

$$\text{Length } P_1P_2 = \frac{Y_2 - Y_1}{\cos \alpha} \tag{6.11}$$

Use the equation having the larger numerical value of $(X_2 - X_1)$ or $(Y_2 - Y_1)$.

It will be clear from Figure 6.20 that $(X_2 - X_1)$ is the departure of $P_1P_2$ and that $(Y_2 - Y_1)$ is the latitude of $P_1P_2$. In survey work, the $Y$ value (latitude) is usually known as the difference in northing, and the $X$ value (departure) is known as the difference in easting. From analytic geometry, the slope of a straight line is $M = \tan(90 - \alpha)$, where $(90 - \alpha)$ is the angle of the straight line with the $X$ axis (see Figure 6.20); that is:

$$M = \cot \alpha$$

From coordinate geometry, the equation of straight line $P_1P_2$, when the coordinates of $P_1$ and $P_2$ are known, is:

$$\frac{Y - Y_1}{Y_2 - Y_1} = \frac{X - X_1}{X_2 - X_1} \tag{6.12}$$

Equation 6.11 can be rewritten as:

$$Y_2 - Y_1 = \frac{Y_2 - Y_1}{X_2 - X_1}(X - X_1)$$

where $(Y_2 - Y_1)/(X_2 - X_1) = \cot \alpha = m$ (from analytic geometry) — the slope of the line. When the coordinates of one point $(P_1)$ and the bearing or azimuth of a line are known, the equation becomes:

$$Y - Y_1 = \cot \alpha \, (X - X_1) \tag{6.13}$$

where $\alpha$ is the azimuth or bearing of the line through $P_1$ $(X_1, Y_1)$. Also, from analytical geometry:

$$Y - Y_1 = \frac{-1}{\cot \alpha}(X - X_1) \tag{6.14}$$

which represents a line **perpendicular** to the line represented by Equation 6.13; that is, the slopes of perpendicular lines are negative reciprocals.

Equations for circular curves are quadratics in the following form:

$$(X - H)^2 + (Y - K)^2 = r^2 \tag{6.15}$$

where $r$ is the curve radius, $(H, K)$ are the coordinates of the center, and $(X, Y)$ are the coordinates of point $P$, which locates the circle (see Figure 6.21). When the circle center is at the origin, the equation becomes:

$$X^2 - Y^2 = r^2 \tag{6.16}$$

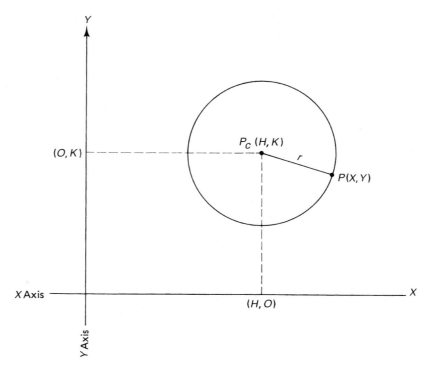

**FIGURE 6.21** Circular curve coordinates.

## 6.16 Illustrative Problems in Rectangular Coordinates

Several examples are provided in this section to give you practice in both writing line equations and solving for intersection coordinates.

■ **EXAMPLE 6.6**

From the information shown in Figure 6.22, calculate the coordinates of the point of intersection of lines $EC$ and $DB$ ($K_1$).

**Solution**

From Equation 6.12, the equation of $EC$ is:

$$Y - 688.69 = \frac{1{,}302.96 - 688.69}{1{,}692.14 - 1{,}160.27}(X - 1{,}160.27) \qquad (1)$$

The equation of $DB$ is:

$$Y - 934.77 = \frac{1{,}250.73 - 934.77}{1{,}313.61 - 1{,}684.54}(X - 1{,}684.54)$$

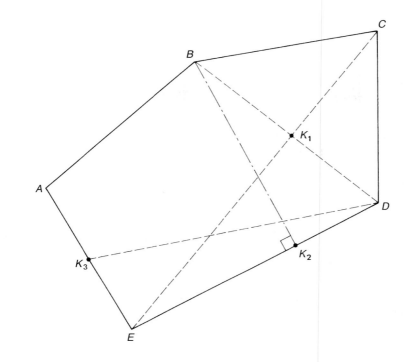

| Station | Coordinates North | Coordinates East |
|---------|-------------------|-------------------|
| A | 1,000.00 | 1,000.00 |
| B | 1,250.73 | 1,313.61 |
| C | 1,302.96 | 1,692.14 |
| D | 934.77 | 1,684.54 |
| E | 688.69 | 1,160.27 |

**FIGURE 6.22** Coordinates for traverse problem, Section 6.12.2 (see Table 6.10).

When simplified, these equations become:

$$EC: Y = 1.154925X - 651.3355 \qquad (1a)$$

$$DB: Y = -0.8518049X + 2369.669 \qquad (2a)$$

$$2.0067299X = 3021.004 \qquad (1a - 2a)$$

$$X = 1,505.436$$

Substitute the value of $X$ in Equation 2a and check the results in Equation 1a:

$$Y = 1,087.331$$

Therefore, the coordinates of point of intersection $K_1$ are (1,087.33 N, 1,505.44 E).

### ■ EXAMPLE 6.7

From the information shown in Figure 6.22, calculate (a) the coordinates $K_2$, the point of intersection of line $ED$, and a line **perpendicular** to $ED$ running through station $B$, and (b) distances $K_2D$ and $K_2E$.

**Solution**

(a) From Equation 6.12, the equation of $ED$ is:

$$\frac{Y - 688.69}{934.77 - 688.69} = \frac{X - 1,160.27}{1,684.54 - 1,160.27} \tag{1}$$

$$Y - 688.69 = \frac{242.08}{524.27}(X - 1,160.27) \tag{1a}$$

From Equation 6.13, the equation of $BK_2$ is:

$$Y - 1,250.73 = \frac{524.27}{246.08}(X - 1,313.61) \tag{2}$$

When simplified, these equations become:

$$ED: 0.46938X - Y = 144.09 \tag{1b}$$

$$BK_2: 2.13049X + Y = +4,049.36 \tag{2b}$$

$$2.59987X = 3,905.27 \tag{1b + 2b}$$

$$X = 1,502.102$$

Use five decimals to avoid rounding errors. Substitute the value of $x$ in Equation 1b and check the results in Equation 2:

$$Y = 849.15$$

Therefore, the coordinates of $K_2$ are (849.15 N, 1,502.10 E).

(b) Figure 6.23 shows the coordinates for stations $E$ and $D$ and intermediate point $K_2$ from Equation 6.8:

$$\text{Length } K_2D = \sqrt{85.62^2 + 182.44^2} = 201.53$$

$$\text{Length } K_2E = \sqrt{160.46^2 + 341.83^2} = 377.62$$

$$K_2D + K_2E = ED = 579.15$$

Check:

$$\text{Length } ED = \sqrt{246.08^2 + 524.27^2} = 579.15$$

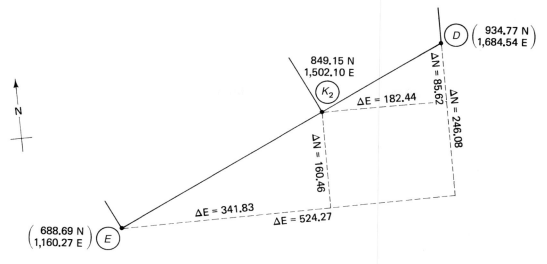

**FIGURE 6.23**  Sketch for Example 6.7.

The figure shows coordinates and dimensions:

- $D$ at $\begin{pmatrix} 934.77\ N \\ 1{,}684.54\ E \end{pmatrix}$
- $K_2$ at $849.15\ N$, $1{,}502.10\ E$
- $E$ at $\begin{pmatrix} 688.69\ N \\ 1{,}160.27\ E \end{pmatrix}$
- $\Delta E = 182.44$
- $\Delta N = 85.62$
- $\Delta N = 246.08$
- $\Delta N = 160.46$
- $\Delta E = 341.83$
- $\Delta E = 524.27$

## ■ EXAMPLE 6.8

From the information shown in Figure 6.22, calculate the coordinates of the point of intersection ($K_3$) of a line **parallel** to $CB$ running from station $D$ to line $EA$.

**Solution**

From Equation 6.12, the equation of $CB$ is:

$$\frac{Y - 1{,}302.96}{1.250.73 - 1{,}302.96} = \frac{X - 1{,}692.14}{1.313.61 - 1{,}692.14}$$

$$Y - 1{,}302.96 = \frac{-52.23}{-378.53} X - 1{,}692.14$$

$$\text{Slope (cot } \alpha) \text{ of } CB = \frac{-52.23}{-378.53}$$

Since $DK_3$ is parallel to $BC$:

$$\text{Slope (cot } \alpha) \text{ of } DK_3 = \frac{-52.23}{-378.53}$$

$$DK_3\text{: } Y - 934.77 = \frac{52.23}{378.53} (X - 1{,}684.54) \tag{1}$$

From Equation 6.12, the equation of EA is:

$$\frac{Y - 688.69}{1{,}000.00 - 688.69} = \frac{X - 1{,}160.27}{1000.00 - 1{,}160.27} \tag{2}$$

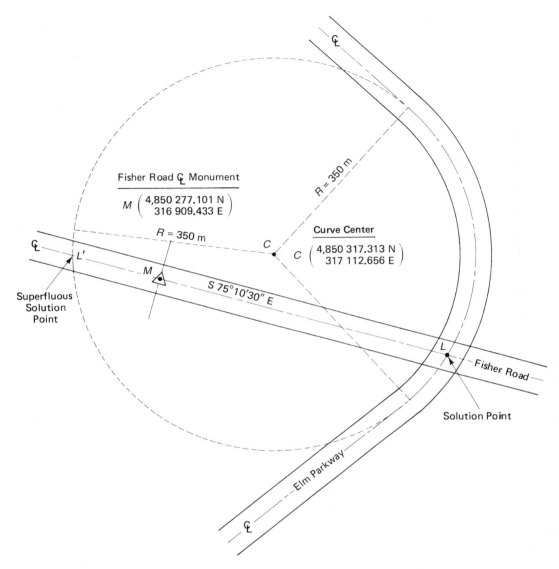

**FIGURE 6.24** Intersection of a straight line with a circular curve, Example 6.6.

$$DK_3: 0.13798X - Y = 702.34 \qquad (1a)$$

$$EA: 1.94241X\,1 - Y = -702.34 \qquad (2a)$$

$$2.08039X = +2,240.07 \qquad (1a + 2a)$$

$$X = 1,076.7547$$

**Table 6.15**  GRID COORDINATES REDUCED FOR COMPUTATIONS

| Station | Grid coordinates | | Reduced coordinates | |
|---|---|---|---|---|
| | $Y$ | $X$ | $Y'(Y - 4,850,000)$ | $X'(X - 316.500)$ |
| M | 4,850,277.101 | 316,909.433 | 277.101 | 409.433 |
| C | 4,850,317.313 | 317,112.656 | 317.313 | 612.656 |

Substitute the value of $X$ in Equation 1a and check the results in Equation 2a:

$$Y = 850.91$$

Therefore, the coordinates of $K_3$ are (850.91 N, 1,076.75 E).

■ **EXAMPLE 6.9**

From the information shown in Figure 6.24, calculate the coordinates of the point of intersection ($L$) of the ℄ of Fisher Road with the ℄ of Elm Parkway.

**Solution**

The coordinates of station $M$ on Fisher Road are (4,850,277.01 N, 316,909.433 E), and the bearing of the Fisher Road℄ ($ML$) is S 75°10′30″ E. The coordinates of the center of the 350 $M$ radius highway curve are (4,850,317.313 N, 317,112.656 E). The coordinates here are referred to a coordinate grid system having 0.000 m north at the equator, and 304,800.000 m east at longitude 70°30′ W.

The coordinate values are, of necessity, very large and would cause significant rounding errors if they were used in the computations by a calculator. Thus, an auxiliary set of coordinate axes will be used, allowing the values of the given coordinates to be greatly reduced for the computations. The amount reduced will later be added to give the final coordinates. The summary of coordinates is shown in Table 6.14.

From Equation 6.13, the equation of Fisher Road℄ ($ML$) is:

$$Y' - 277.101 = \cot 75°10′30″ (X' - 409.433) \tag{1}$$

From Equation 6.15, the equation of Elm Parkway℄ is:

$$(X' - 612.656)^2 + (Y' - 317.313)^2 = 350.000^2 \tag{2}$$

Simplify Equation 1 to:

$$Y' - 277.101 = -0.2646782X' + 108.368$$

$$Y' = -0.2646782X' + 385.469 \tag{1a}$$

Substitute the value of $Y'$ into Equation 2:

$$(X' - 612.656)^2 = (0.2646782X' + 385.469 - 317.313)^2 - 350.000^2 = 0$$
$$(X' - 612.656)^2 + (-0.2646782X' + 68.156)^2 - 350.000^2 = 0$$
$$1.0700545X'^2 - 1,261.391X' + 257,492.61 = 0$$

**Table 6.16**  REDUCED COORDINATES RESTORED TO GRID VALUES

|  | Reduced coordinates | | Grid coordinates | |
| --- | --- | --- | --- | --- |
| Station | $Y'$ | $X'$ | $Y(Y' + 4,850,000)$ | $X(X' + 316,500)$ |
| $L$ | 142.984 | 916.151 | 4,850,142.984 | 317,416.151 |
| $L'$ | 315.949 | 262.658 | 4,850,315.949 | 316,762.658 |

This quadratic of the form $aX^2 + bX + c = 0$ has the following roots:

$$X = \frac{-b \pm \sqrt{b^2 - 4ac}}{2a}$$

$$X' = \frac{1261.3908 \pm \sqrt{1,591,107.30 - 1,102,124.50}}{2.140109}$$

$$X' = \frac{1,261.3908 \pm 699.27305}{2.140109}$$

$$X' = 916.1514 \qquad \text{or} \qquad X' = 262.658$$

Solve for $Y'$ by substituting in Equation 1a:

$$Y' = 142.984 \qquad \text{or} \qquad Y' = 315.949$$

When these coordinates are now enlarged by the amount of the original axes reduction, the values shown in Table 6.16 are obtained.

   **Analysis of Figure 6.24 is required to determine which of the two solutions is the correct one.** The sketch shows that the desired intersection point $L$ is south and east of station $M$; that is, $L(4,850,142.984$ N, $317,416.151$ E) is the set of coordinates for the intersection of the centerlines of Elm Parkway and Fisher Road. The other intersection point ($L'$) is superfluous.

# Problems

**6.1**  A five-sided closed field traverse has the following angles: $A = 103°03'30''$, $B = 117°40'00''$, $C = 92°52'30''$, $D = 107°13'30''$, $E = 119°08'00''$. Determine the angular error of closure and balance the angles by applying equal corrections to each angle.

**6.2**  A four-sided closed field traverse has the following angles: $A = 81°53'30''$, $B = 70°28'30''$, $C = 86°09'30''$, $D = 121°30'30''$. The lengths of the sides are as follows: $AB = 636.45$ ft, $BC = 654.49$ ft, $CD = 382.65$ ft, $DA = 469.38$ ft. The bearing of $AB$ is S 13°56' W. $BC$ is in the SE quadrant.
   (a) Balance the field angles.
   (b) Compute the bearings or the azimuths.
   (c) Compute the latitudes and departures.
   (d) Determine the linear error of closure and the accuracy ratio.

**6.3**  Use the data from Problem 6.2 to:
   (a) Balance the latitudes and departures by use of the compass rule.

**(b)** Compute the coordinates of stations *A, C,* and *D* if the coordinates of station *B* are 1,000.00 N, 1,000.00 E.

**6.4** Use the data from Problems 6.2 and 6.3 to compute the area enclosed by the traverse using the coordinate method.

**6.5** A five-sided closed field traverse has the following distances in meters: *AB* = 51.766, *BC* = 26.947, *CD* = 37.070, *DE* = 35.292, *EA* = 19.192. The adjusted angles are as follows: *A* = 101°03′19″, *B* = 101°41′49″, *C* = 102°22′03″, *D* = 115°57′20″, *E* = 118°55′29″. The bearing of *AB* is N82°09′20″ E. *BC* is in the SE quadrant.
  **(a)** Compute the bearings or the azimuths.
  **(b)** Compute the latitudes and departures.
  **(c)** Determine the linear error of closure and the accuracy ratio.

**6.6** Use the data from Problem 6.5 to:
  **(a)** Balance the latitudes and departures by use of the compass rule.
  **(b)** Compute the coordinates of the traverse stations using the coordinates of station *A* as 1,000.000 N, 1,000.000 E.

**6.7** Use the data from Problems 6.5 and 6.6 to compute the area enclosed by the traverse. Use the coordinate method.

**6.8** The two frontage corners of a large tract of land were joined by the following open traverse:

| COURSE | DISTANCE (FT) | BEARING |
|---|---|---|
| *AB* | 80.32 | N 70°10′07″ E |
| *BC* | 953.83 | N 74°29′00″ E |
| *CD* | 818.49 | N 70°22′45″ E |

Compute the distance and bearing of the property frontage *AD*.

**6.9** Given the following data for a closed property traverse:

| COURSE | BEARING | DISTANCE (M) |
|---|---|---|
| *AB* | N 37°10′49″ E | 537.144 |
| *BC* | N 79°29′49″ E | 1,109.301 |
| *CD* | S 18°56′31″ W | |
| *DE* | | 953.829 |
| *EA* | N 26°58′31″ W | 483.669 |

  **(a)** Compute the missing data (i.e., distance *CD* and bearing *DE*).
  **(b)** Compute the area of the property bounded by the traverse.

**6.10** A six-sided traverse has the following station coordinates: *A* (559.319 N, 207.453 E), *B* (738.562 N, 666.737 E), *C* (541.742 N, 688.350 E), *D* (379.861 N, 839.008 E), *E* (296.099 N, 604.048 E), *F* (218.330 N, 323.936 E). Compute the distance and bearing of each side.

**6.11** Use the data from Problem 6.10 to compute the area (in hectares) enclosed by the traverse.

**6.12** Use the data from Problem 6.10 to solve the following: If the intersection point of lines *AD* and *BF* is *K,* and if the intersection point of lines *AC* and *BE* is *L,* compute the distance and bearing of line *KL.*

**6.13** A five-sided field traverse has the following balanced angles: *A* = 101°28′26″, *B* = 102°10′42″, *C* = 104°42′06″, *D* = 113°04′42″, *E* = 118°34′04″. The lengths of the sides are as follows: $AB$ = 50.276m, $BC$ = 26.947m, $CD$ = 37.090m, $DE$ = 35.292m, $EA$ = 20.845m. The bearing of $EA$ is N 20°20′20″ W, and $AB$ is oriented northeasterly.

(a) Compute the bearings.

(b) Compute the latitudes and departures.

(c) Compute the linear error of closure and the accuracy ratio.

**6.14** From the data in Problem 6.13, balance the latitudes and departures. Use employing the compass rule.

**6.15** Use the data in Problems 6.13 and 6.14. If the coordinates of station $A$ are (1,000.000 N, 1,000.000 E), compute the coordinates of the other stations.

**6.16** Use the data in Problems 6.14 and 6.15 and the coordinate method to compute the area of the enclosed figure.

**6.17** See Figure 6.25. A theodolite with EDM was set up at control station $K$, which is within the limits of a five-sided property. The coordinates of control station $K$ are 1,990.000 N, 2,033.000 E. Azimuth angles and distances to the five property corners were determined as follows:

| DIRECTION | AZIMUTH | HORIZONTAL DISTANCE (M) |
|---|---|---|
| $KA$ | 286°51′00″ | 34.482 |
| $KB$ | 37°35′28″ | 31.892 |
| $KC$ | 90°27′56″ | 38.286 |
| $KD$ | 166°26′49″ | 30.916 |
| $KE$ | 247°28′43″ | 32.585 |

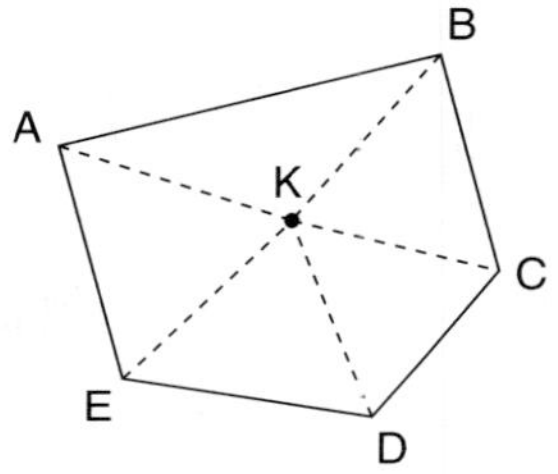

**FIGURE 6.25**

Compute the coordinates of the property corners $A, B, C, D,$ and $E$.

**6.18** Use the data from Problem 6.17 to compute the area of the property.

**6.19** Use the data from Problem 6.17 to compute the bearings and distances of the five sides of the property.

# Electronic Surveying Measurement

## 7.1 General Background

### 7.1.1 Electronic Distance Measurement

Electronic distance measurement (EDM), first introduced in the 1950s by Geodimeter Inc., has undergone continual refinement since those early days. The early instruments, which were capable of very precise measurements over long distances, were large, heavy, complicated, and expensive. Rapid advances in related technologies have provided lighter, simpler, and less expensive instruments. These EDM instruments are manufactured for use with theodolites and as modular components of *total station* instruments (see Section 7.9).

Technological advances in electronics continue at a rapid rate, as evidenced by recent market surveys indicating that most new electronic instruments have been on the market for less than two years. Current EDM instruments use infrared light, laser light, or microwaves. The microwave systems use a receiver/transmitter at both ends of the measured line, whereas infrared and laser systems utilize a transmitter at one end of the measured line and a reflecting prism at the other end. Some laser EDM instruments measure short distances (100 to 350 m) without a reflecting prism. They reflect the light directly off the feature (e.g., building wall) being measured. Microwave instruments are often used in hydrographic surveys and usually have an upper measuring range of 50 km. Although microwave systems can be used in poorer weather conditions (fog, rain, etc.), unlike infrared and laser systems, the uncertainties caused by varying humidity conditions over the length of the measured line may result in lower accuracy expectations. Hydrographic EDM measuring and positioning techniques have largely been replaced, in a few short years, by global positioning system (GPS) techniques (see Chapter 11).

Infrared and laser EDM instruments come in long range (10 to 20 km), medium range (3 to 10 km) and short range (0.5 to 3 km). EDM instruments can be mounted on the standards or the telescope of most theodolites. They can also be mounted directly in a tribrach (see Figure 7.1). When used with an electronic theodolite, the combined instruments can provide both the horizontal and the vertical position of one point relative to another.

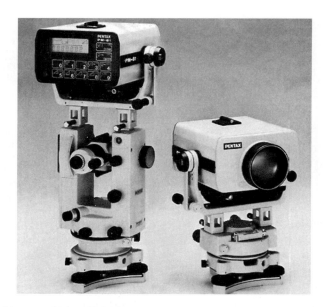

**FIGURE 7.1** Pentax PM 81 EDM mounted on a 6-second Pentax theodolite and also shown as tribrach-mounted. EDM has a triple-prism range of 2 km (6,600 ft) with SE = ±(5 mm + 5 ppm). (Courtesy of Pentax Corp., Colo.)

The slope distance provided by an add-on EDM instrument can be reduced to its horizontal and vertical equivalents by utilizing the slope angle provided by the theodolite. In total station instruments, this reduction is accomplished automatically.

### 7.1.2 Electronic Angle Measurement

The electronic digital theodolite, first introduced in the late 1960s by Carl Zeiss Inc., helped set the stage for modern field data collection and processing. (See Figure 5.7 for a typical electronic theodolite.) When the electronic theodolite is used with a built-in EDM (see the Zeiss Elta in Figure 7.2) or an add-on and interfaced EDM (the Wild T-1000 in Figure 7.3), the surveyor has a very powerful instrument. Add to that instrument an onboard microprocessor that automatically monitors the instrument's operating status and manages built-in surveying programs, and a data collector (built-in or interfaced) that stores and processes measurements and attribute data, and you have what is known as a *total station.*

## 7.2 Principles of Electronic Distance Measurement (EDM)

Figure 7.4 shows a wave of wavelength λ. The wave is traveling along the $X$ axis with a velocity of 299,792.5 ± 0.4 km/s (in vacuum). The frequency of the wave is the time taken for one complete wavelength.

$$\lambda = \frac{c}{f} \tag{7.1}$$

where   $\lambda$ = wavelength in meters

$c$ = velocity in km/s

$f$ = frequency in hertz (one cycle per second)

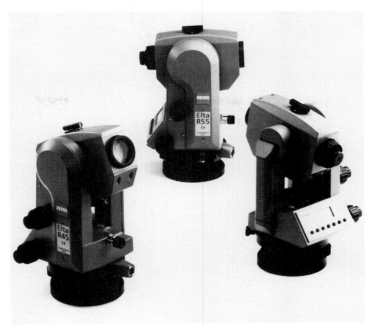

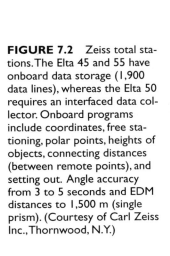

**FIGURE 7.2** Zeiss total stations. The Elta 45 and 55 have onboard data storage (1,900 data lines), whereas the Elta 50 requires an interfaced data collector. Onboard programs include coordinates, free stationing, polar points, heights of objects, connecting distances (between remote points), and setting out. Angle accuracy from 3 to 5 seconds and EDM distances to 1,500 m (single prism). (Courtesy of Carl Zeiss Inc., Thornwood, N.Y.)

**FIGURE 7.3** Wild T-1000 electronic theodolite, shown with D1 1000 Distomat EDM and the GRE 3 data collector. (Courtesy of Leica Co. Inc., Toronto)

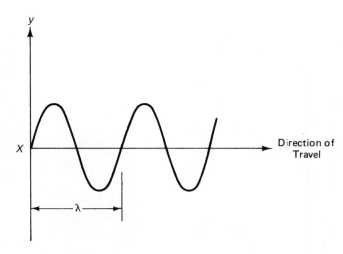

**FIGURE 7.4** Light wave.

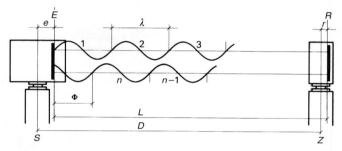

S   Station
Z   Target
E   Reference plane within the distance meter for phase comparison between transmitted and received wave
R   Reference plane for the reflection of the wave transmitted by the distance meter
a   Addition constant
e   Distance meter component of addition constant
r   Reflector component of addition constant
λ   Modulation wavelength
Φ   Fraction to be measured of a whole wavelength of modulation $(\triangle \lambda)$

The addition constant *a* applies to a measuring equipment consisting of a distance meter and reflector. The components *e* and *r* are only auxiliary quantities.

**FIGURE 7.5** Principles of EDM measurement. (Courtesy of Kern Instruments—Leica)

Figure 7.5 shows the modulated electromagnetic wave leaving the EDM instrument and being reflected (light waves) or retransmitted (microwaves) back to the EDM instrument. You can see that the double distance ($2L$) is equal to a whole number of wavelengths ($n\lambda$), plus the partial wavelength ($\varphi$) occurring at the EDM instrument.

$$L = \frac{n\lambda + \varphi}{2} \text{ meters} \qquad (7.2)$$

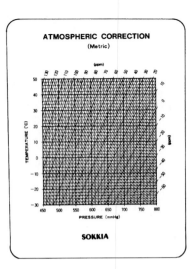

**FIGURE 7.6** Atmospheric correction graph. (Courtesy of Sokkia Co. Ltd.)

The partial wavelength ($\varphi$) is determined in the instrument by noting the phase delay required to match precisely the transmitted and the reflected or retransmitted waves. The instrument can send out a series of three or four modulated waves at different frequencies. By substituting the resulting values of $\lambda$ and $\varphi$ into Equation 7.2 for the three or four different frequencies, the value of $n$ can be found. The instruments are designed to carry out this procedure in a matter of seconds and then to display the value of $L$ in digital form. Other EDM instruments use pulsed laser emissions, which require those instruments to determine the distance by first measuring the time it takes for the sent pulsed signal to be returned to the instrument (see Section 7.8).

The velocity of light through the atmosphere can be affected by (1) temperature, (2) atmospheric pressure, and (3) water vapor content. In practice, the corrections for temperature and pressure can be determined manually by consulting nomographs similar to that shown in Figure 7.6, or the corrections can be performed automatically on some EDM instruments by their onboard processor/calculator after the values for temperature and pressure have been internally sensed or entered by the operator.

For short distances using light-wave EDM instruments, atmospheric corrections are relatively insignificant. For long distances using light-wave instruments and especially microwave instruments, atmospheric corrections can become quite important. Table 7.1 shows the comparative effects of atmospheric factors on both light waves and microwaves.

At this point, it is also worth noting that several studies of general EDM use show that more than 90 percent of all distance determinations involve distances of 1,000 m or less and that more than 95 percent of all layout measurements involve distances of 400 m or less. The values in Table 7.1 seem to indicate that, for the type of measurements normally encountered, instrumental errors and centering errors hold much more significance than do the atmosphere-related errors.

**Table 7.1** ATMOSPHERIC EFFECTS ON LIGHT WAVES AND MICROWAVES

| Parameter | Error | Error (parts per million) | |
| --- | --- | --- | --- |
| | | Light wave | Microwave |
| $T$, temperature | $+1°C$ | $-1.0$ | $-1.25$ |
| $P$, pressure | $+1$ mm Hg | $+0.4$ | $+0.4$ |
| $e$, partial water-vapor pressure | $1$ mm Hg | $-0.05$ | $+7$ at $20°C$ $+17$ at $45°C$ |

## 7.3 EDM Instrument Characteristics

The following list shows the characteristics of recent models of add-on EDM instruments. Generally the more expensive instruments have longer distance ranges and higher precision.

Distance range: 800 m to 1 km (single prism with average atmospheric conditions). Short-range EDM instrument distances can be extended to 1,300 m using 3 prisms. Long-range EDM instrument distances can be extended to 15 km using 11 prisms (Leica Co.).

Accuracy range: $\pm$ (15 mm + 5 ppm) for short-range EDM instruments, $\pm$ (3mm + 1 ppm) for long-range EDM instruments.

Measuring time: 1.5 seconds for short-range EDM instruments to 3.5 seconds for long-range EDM instruments. Both accuracy and time are considerably reduced in tracking mode measurements.

Slope reduction: manual or automatic, depending on the models.

Average of repeated measurements: available on some models.

Battery capability: 1,400 to 4,200 measurements, depending on the size of the battery and the temperature.

Temperature range: $-20°C$ to $+50°C$.

Nonprism measurements: available on some models; distances from 100 to 350 m (3 to 5 km with prisms). See Section 7.8.

## 7.4 Prisms

Prisms are used with electro-optical EDM instruments to reflect the transmitted signal (see Figure 7.7). A single reflector is a cube corner prism that has the characteristic of reflecting light rays precisely back to the emitting EDM instrument This retrodirect capability means that the prism can be somewhat misaligned with respect to the EDM instrument and still be effective. A cube corner prism is formed by cutting the corners off a solid glass cube. The quality of the prism is determined by the flatness of the surfaces and the perpendicularity of the 90° surfaces.

Prisms can be tribrach-mounted on a tripod, centered by optical plummet, or attached to a prism pole held vertical on a point with the aid of a bull's-eye level; however,

**FIGURE 7.7** Various target and reflector systems in tribrach mounts. (Courtesy of Topcon Instrument Corp., Paramus, N.J.)

prisms must be tribrach-mounted if a higher level of accuracy is required. In control surveys, tribrach-mounted prisms can be detached from their tribrachs and then interchanged with a theodolite (and EDM instrument) similarly mounted at the other end of the line being measured. This interchangeability of prism and theodolite (also targets) speeds up the work because the tribrach mounted on the tripod is centered and leveled only once. Equipment that can be interchanged and mounted on tribrachs already set up is known as *forced centering equipment.*

Prisms mounted on adjustable-length prism poles are very portable and, as such, are particularly well suited for stakeout surveys and topographic surveys. Figure 7.8 shows the prism pole being steadied with the aid of an additional target pole. The height of the prism is normally set to equal the height of the instrument; otherwise, consideration has to be given to the difference between the prism height and the instrument height. It is important that prisms mounted on poles or tribrachs be permitted to tilt up and down so that they can be made perpendicular to EDM signals that are being sent from much higher or lower positions. This characteristic is particularly important for short sights.

## 7.5   EDM Instrument Accuracies

EDM instrument accuracies are stated in terms of a constant instrumental error and a measuring error proportional to the distance being measured. Typically, accuracy is claimed as ±[5 mm + 5 parts per million (ppm)] or ±(0.02 ft + 5 ppm). The ±5 mm (0.02 ft) error is the instrument error that is independent of the length of the measurement, whereas the 5 ppm (5 mm/km) error denotes the distance-related error.

Most instruments now on the market have claimed accuracies in the range of ±(3 mm + 1 ppm) to ±(10 mm + 10 ppm). The proportional part error (ppm) is insignificant for most work, and the constant part of the error assumes less significance as the distance being measured lengthens. At 100 m, an error of ±5 mm represents 1/20,000 accuracy, whereas for 1,000 m, the same instrumental error represents 1/200,000 accuracy.

**FIGURE 7.8** Steadying the EDM reflector with the aid of a second target pole.

**FIGURE 7.9** Method of determining the instrument-reflector constant.

When dealing with accuracy, it should be noted that both the EDM instrument and the prism reflectors must be corrected for off-center characteristics. The measurement being recorded goes from the electrical center of the EDM instrument to the back of the prism (allowing for refraction through glass) and then back to the electrical center of the EDM instrument. The difference between the electrical center of the EDM instrument and the plumb line through the tribrach center is compensated for by the manufacturer at the factory. The prism constant (30 to 40 mm) is eliminated either by the EDM instrument manufacturer at the factory or in the field.

The instrument/prism constant value can be field-checked in the following manner. A long line (> 1 km) is laid out with end stations and an intermediate station (see Figure 7.9). The overall distance *AC* is measured, along with partial lengths *AB* and *BC*. The constant value will be present in all measurements; therefore:

$$AC - AB - BC = \text{instrument/prism constant} \tag{7.3}$$

The constant can also be determined by measuring a known baseline, if one can be conveniently accessed.

## 7.6 EDM Instrument Operation

Figures 7.1 and 7.10 show short- to medium-range EDM instruments. These instruments can be mounted on the theodolite telescope or standards, or they can be independently mounted in a tribrach. The operation of all EDM instruments involves the following basic steps: (1) set up, (2) aim, (3) measure, and (4) record.

### 7.6.1 Set Up

Tribrach-mounted EDM instruments are inserted into the tribrach (forced centering) after the tribrach has been set over the point by means of the optical plummet. Telescope or theodolite yoke-mounted EDM instruments are attached to the theodolite either before or after the theodolite has been set over the point. Prisms are set over the remote station point either by inserting the prism into an already setup tribrach (forced centering) or by holding the prism vertically over the point on a prism pole. The EDM instrument is turned on, and a quick check (for example, checks for battery, display, and the like) is made to ensure that it is in good working order. The height of the instrument (telescope axis) and the height of the prism (center) are measured and recorded. The prism is usually set to the height of the theodolite when it is mounted on an adjustable prism pole.

### 7.6.2 Aim

The EDM instrument is aimed at the prism by using either the built-in sighting devices on the EDM instrument or the theodolite telescope. Telescope or yoke-mount EDMs will have the optical line of sight a bit lower than the electronic signal. Most instrument manufacturers provide prism/target assemblies that permit fast optical sightings for both optical and electronic alignment (see Figure 7.7); that is, when the cross hair is sighted on target, the electronic signal will be maximized at the center of the prism. The surveyor can, if necessary, set the electronic signal precisely on the prism center (with some EDM instruments) by adjusting the appropriate horizontal and vertical slow-motion screws until a maximum signal intensity is indicated audibly or on a graphics display. Some older EDM instruments have an attenuator that must be adjusted for varying distances; the signal strength is reduced for short distances so that the receiving electronics are not overloaded. Newer instruments have automatic signal attenuation.

### 7.6.3 Measure

The slope distance measurement is accomplished by simply pressing the measure button and waiting a few seconds for the result to appear in the display. The displays are either liquid crystal display (LCD) or light emitting diode (LED). The measurement is shown to two decimals of a foot or three decimals of a meter; a foot/meter switch readily switches from one system to the other. If no measurement appears in the display, the surveyor should

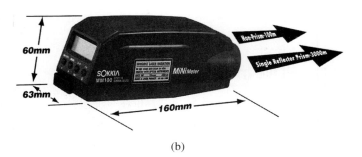

(b)

(c)

(a)

**Mounting on the "DT4F" is by convenient hot-shoe**

Connection via which power supply and data communication are provided.

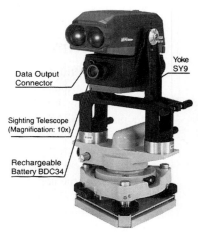

(d)

(e)

**FIGURE 7.10** Sokkia MiNi Meter MM100 laser add-on EDM. (a) EDM shown mounted on the telescope of Sokkia DT4F electronic 5″ theodolite. (b) MiNi Meter dimensions. (c) Display screen showing menu button, which provides access to programs permitting input for atmospheric corrections, height measurements, horizontal and vertical distances, self diagnostics, etc. (d) Illustration showing "hot shoe" electronics connection and counterweight. (e) MiNi Meter shown mounted directly into a tribrach—with attached sighting telescope, data output connector, and battery. (Courtesy of Sokkia Corporation, Overland Park, Kans.)

check on switch position, battery status, attenuation, and cross-hair location (sometimes a stadia hair is mistakenly centered on the target or prism).

EDM instruments with built-in calculators or microprocessors can now be used to compute horizontal and vertical distances; coordinates; and atmospheric, curvature, and prism constant corrections. The required input data (vertical angle, ppm-correction, prism constant, etc.) are entered via the keyboard. Most EDM instruments have a tracking mode, which is very useful in layout surveys and permits continuous distance updates as the prism is moved even closer to its final layout position. Handheld radios are useful for all EDM work because the long distances put a halt to normal voice communications. In layout work, clear communications are essential if the points are to be located properly. All microwave EDM instruments permit voice communication, which is carried right on the measuring signal.

### 7.6.4 Record

The measured data can be recorded conventionally in field note format, or they can be entered manually into an electronic data collector. The distance data must be accompanied by all relevant atmospheric and instrumental correction factors. Total station instruments, which have automatic data acquisition capabilities (see Section 7.9), automatically record the distance/angle information on either onboard or interfaced data collectors.

## 7.7 Geometry of EDM

Figure 7.11 illustrates the use of EDM when the optical target and the reflecting prism are at the same height (see the single prism assembly in Figure 7.7). The slope distance (S) is measured by the EDM instrument, and the slope angle ($\alpha$) is measured by the accompanying theodolite. The heights of the EDM instrument and theodolite (hi) are measured with a steel tape or by a graduated tripod centering rod (and sometimes with a leveling rod); the height of the reflector/target (HR) is measured in a similar fashion. As noted earlier, adjustable-length prism poles permit the surveyor to set the height of the prism (HR) equal to the height of the instrument (hi), thus simplifying the computations. If the elevation of station A from Figure 7.11 is known and the elevation of station B is required, then:

$$\text{Elevation of station B} = \text{elevation of station A} + \text{hi} \pm \text{V} - \text{HR} \qquad (7.4)$$

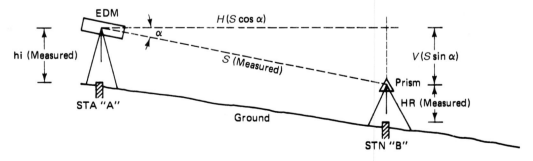

**FIGURE 7.11** Geometry of an EDM calculation, general case.

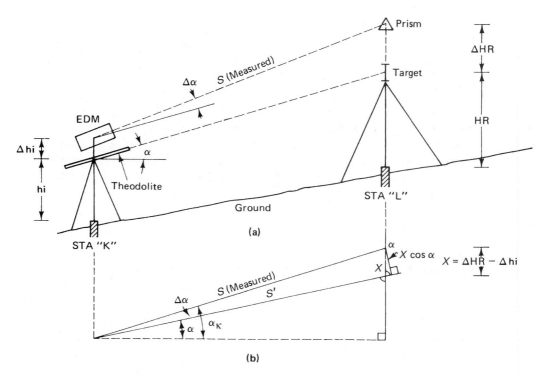

**FIGURE 7.12** Geometry of an EDM calculation, usual case.

When the EDM instrument is mounted on the theodolite and the target is located below the prism, the geometric relationship can be the same as that shown in Figure 7.12. The additional problem encountered in the situation depicted in Figure 7.12 is the computation of the correction to the vertical angle ($\Delta\alpha$) that occurs when $\Delta$hi and $\Delta$HR are different. The precise size of the vertical angle is important because it is used in conjunction with the measured slope distance to compute the horizontal and vertical distances. In Figure 7.12, the difference between $\Delta$HR and $\Delta$hi is X (i.e., $\Delta$HR $-$ $\Delta$hi $=$ X). The small triangle formed by extending S' [see Figure 7.12(b)] has the hypotenuse equal to X and an angle of $\alpha$. This permits computation of the side X cos $\alpha$, which can be used together with S to determine $\Delta\alpha$:

$$\frac{X \cos \alpha}{s} = \sin \Delta\alpha$$

## ■ EXAMPLE 7.1

An EDM slope distance $AB$ is determined to be 561.276 m. The EDM instrument is 1.820 m above station A, and the prism is 1.986 m above station B. The EDM instrument is mounted on a theodolite whose optical center is 1.720 m above the station. The theodolite was used to measure the vertical angle ($+6°21'38'$) to a target on the prism pole; the target is 1.810 m above station B. Compute both the horizontal distance $AB$ and the elevation of station B if the elevation of station A $=$ 186.275 m.

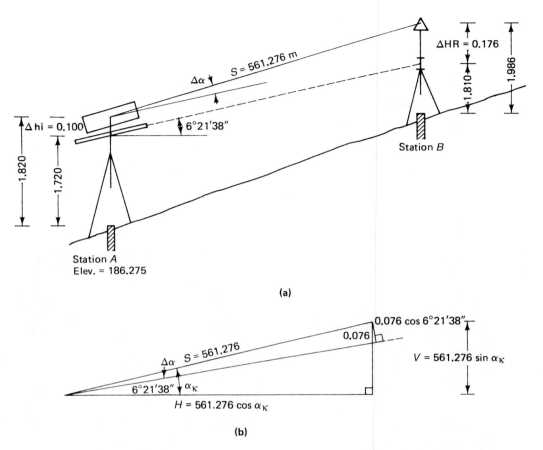

**(a)**

**(b)**

**FIGURE 7.13**  Illustration for Example 7.1. (a) Schematic of EDM measurement. (b) Deduced geometry for an EDM measurement.

**Solution**

The given data are shown in Figure 7.13(a), and the resultant figure is shown in Figure 7.13(b). The X value introduced in Figure 7.13(b) is, in this case, determined as follows:

$$X = (1.986 - 1.810) - (1.820 - 1.720)$$
$$= 0.176 - 0.100 = 0.076 \text{ m}$$

$$\sin \Delta\alpha = \frac{0.076 \cos 6°21'38''}{561.276}$$

$$\Delta\alpha = 28''$$

$$\alpha_k = 6°22'06''$$

$$H = 561.276 \cos 6°22'06'' = 557.813 \text{ m}$$

If H had been computed by using the field vertical angle of 6°21′38″, the result would have been 557.821 m, not a significant difference in this example.

$$\text{Elevation B} = \text{elevation A} + 1.820 + 561.276 \sin 6°22′06″ - 1.986$$
$$= 186.275 + 1.820 + 62.257 - 1.986 = 248.336 \text{ m}$$

If V had been computed by using 6°21′38″, the vertical distance result would have been 62.181 m instead of 62.257 m, a more significant discrepancy.

## 7.8 EDM without Reflecting Prisms

Some EDM instruments (see Figure 7.14) can measure distances without using reflecting prisms: the measuring surface itself is used as a reflector. Some manufacturers employ a

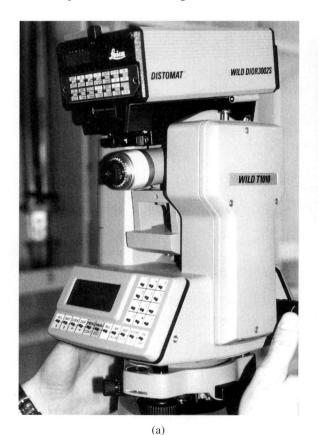

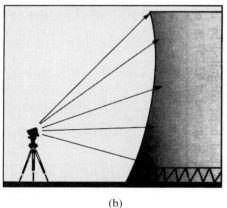

(a)                                                                                    (b)

**FIGURE 7.14** Distance measurement without reflectors. (a) Wild T1010 Electronic theodolite, together with an interfaced DIOR 3002S prismless EDM (angle accuracy is 3 seconds). (b) Illustrations of two possible uses for this technique. Upper: tunnel cross sections. Lower: profiling a difficult-access feature. (Courtesy of Leica Co., Toronto)

timed-pulse infrared signal, transmitted by a laser diode. These EDM instruments can be used conventionally with reflecting prisms for distances up to 4 km. When they are used without prisms, the range drops to 100 to 300 m, depending on the light conditions (cloudy days and night darkness provide better measuring distances). With prisms, the available accuracy is about $\pm(3$ mm $+ 1$ ppm); without prisms, the available accuracy drops to about $\pm 10$ mm. Targets with light-colored and flat surfaces perpendicular to the measuring beam (e.g., building walls) provide the best ranges and accuracies.

EDM instruments used without reflecting prisms provide quick results (0.8 seconds in rapid mode and 0.3 seconds in tracking mode), which means that applications for moving targets are possible. Applications in near-shore hydrographic surveying and in many areas of heavy construction are expected to be developed. This technique is already being used, with an interfaced data collector, to measure cross sections in mining applications automatically—with plotted cross sections and excavated volumes being generated automatically by digital plotter and computer.

Other applications will include cross-sectioning above-ground excavated works and material stockpiles; measuring to dangerous or difficult access points, for example, bridge components, cooling towers, and dam faces; and automatically measuring liquid surfaces, for example, municipal water reservoirs and catchment ponds. It is conceivable that these new techniques may have some potential in industrial surveying, where production line rates require this type of monitoring. These instruments are used with an attached visible laser, which helps to identify positively the feature being measured; that is, the visible laser beam is set on the desired feature so that the surveyor can be sure the correct surface, and not some feature just beside it or just behind it, is being measured. Since the measurement is so fast, care must be taken not to measure mistakenly to some object, for example, trucks or other traffic, that may temporarily intersect the measuring signal.

## 7.9 Total Stations

Total stations can read and record horizontal and vertical angles together with slope distances. The microprocessors in the total stations can perform various mathematical operations, for example, averaging multiple angle measurements; averaging multiple distance measurements; determining horizontal and vertical distances; determining X, Y, and Z coordinates, remote object elevations (that is, heights of sighted features), and distances between remote points; and making atmospheric and instrumental corrections. The data collector can be a handheld device connected by cable to the instrument (see Figures 7.3 and 7.15), but many instruments come with the data collector built into the instrument. Figures 7.16 to 7.18 illustrate some typical total stations currently in use.

Figure 7.16 shows a Sokkia total station, one of a series of instruments that have angle accuracies from 0.5 to 5 seconds, distance ranges (one prism) from 1,600 m to 2,400 m, dual axis compensation [Figure 7.16(d)], a wide variety of built-in programs, and a rapid battery charger, which can charge the battery in 70 minutes. Data are stored onboard in internal memory (about 1,300 points) and/or on memory cards (about 2,000 points per card). The data can be transferred directly to the computer from the total station via an RS-232 cable, or the data can be transferred from the data storage cards first to a card reader-writer, and from there to the computer.

SET-3

SDR2

Radio

**FIGURE 7.15** Sokkia total station Set 3 with cable-connected SDR2 electronic field book. Also shown is a two-way radio (2-mile range) with push-to-talk headset.

Figure 7.17 shows a Nikon total station with card readers for applications program cards (upper reader) and for data storage cards (lower reader). The data storage cards can be removed when they are full and read into a computer using standard PCMCIA card readers, now standard with most notebook computers. The operating system for this and some other total stations is MS-DOS compatible, which permits easy changes to user-defined applications software.

All the data collectors described here can do much more than just collect data. The capabilities vary a great deal from one manufacturer to another. The computational characteristics of the electronic theodolites themselves also vary widely. Some EDM/electronic theodolites (without the data collector) simply show the horizontal and vertical angles together with the slope distance, whereas others also show the resultant horizontal and vertical distances. Some total stations (without an attached data collector) can also compute remote elevations and distances between remote points, whereas others require the interfaced data collector to perform these functions.

Many data collectors are really very sophisticated and expensive handheld computers. If the total station is used alone, the capability of performing all survey computations, including closures and adjustments, is highly desirable. However, if the total station is used as part of a system (field data collection/data processing/digital plotting), then the computational capacity of the data collectors becomes less important. If the total station is used as part of a system, the data collector need collect only the basic information, that is, slope distance, horizontal angle, vertical angle, or coordinates and attribute data such as point number, point description, and perhaps operation code. Computations and adjustments are then performed by one of the many coordinate geometry programs now available for surveyors and engineers. See Figure 7.18 for a typical total station and interfaced data collector.

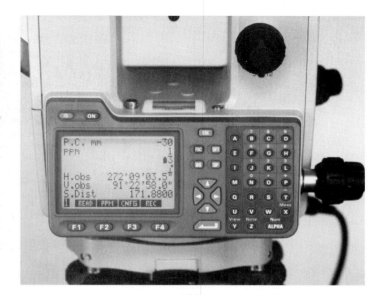

<table>
<tr><td>(a)</td><td>(b)</td></tr>
</table>

## ■ Graphic "Bull's-Eye" Level

A graphically displayed "bull's-eye" lets you quickly and efficiently
level the instrument.

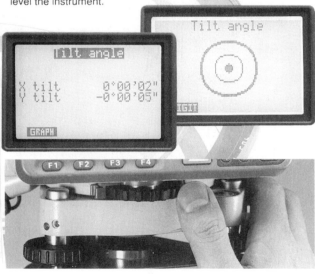

(c)

**FIGURE 7.16** (a) Sokkia SET1000 total station having angle display of 0.5 seconds (1″ accuracy) and a distance range to 2,400 m using one prism. The instrument comes with a complete complement of surveying programs, dual-axis compensation, and the ability to measure (to 120 m) to reflective sheet targets—a feature suited to industrial surveying measurements. (b) Keyboard and LCD display. (c) Graphics bull's-eye level allows you to level the instrument while observing the graphics display. (Courtesy of Sokkia Corp., Overland Park, Kans.)

*(continued)*

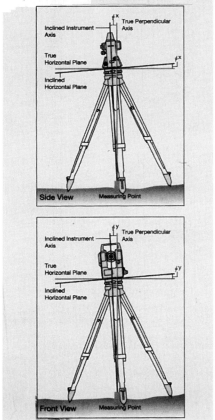

■ **Simultaneous Detection of Inclination in Two Directions And Automatic Compensation**

The built-in dual-axis tilt sensor constantly monitors the inclination of the vertical axis in two directions. It calculates the compensation value and automatically corrects the horizontal and vertical angles. (The compensation range is ±3'.)

**FIGURE 7.16** *(continued)*
(d) Dual-axis compensation illustration. (Courtesy of Sokkia Corp., Overland Park, Kans.)

(d)

Most early models and some current models use the absolute method for reading angles. These instruments are essentially optical coincidence instruments with photoelectronic sensors to scan and read the circles, which are divided into preassigned values from 0 to 360 degrees (or 0 to 400 grad or gon). Some later models employ an incremental method of angle measurement (see Figure 5.7). These instruments have a circle divided into many graduations, with both sides of the circle scanned simultaneously. A portion of the circle is magnified slightly and superimposed on the opposite side of the circle. The

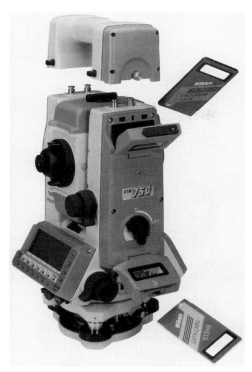

(a)

Upper Card Drive
Holds Program Cards

Lower Card Drive
Holds Data Memory
Cards

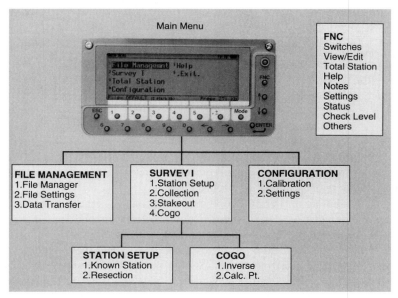

(b)

**FIGURE 7.17** (a) Nikon DTM 750 total station featuring: onboard storage on PCMCIA computer cards; applications software on PCMCIA cards (upper drive); guidelight for layout work (to 100 m); dual-axis tilt sensor; EDM range of 2,700 m (8,900 ft) to one prism; angle precision of 1 second to 5 seconds; distance precision of $\pm(2 + 2$ ppm) mm; operating system is MS-DOS compatible. (b) Menu schematic for the Nikon DTM 750. (Courtesy of Cansell Survey Equipment Co., Toronto)

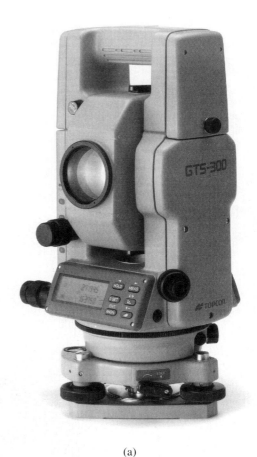

**FIGURE 7.18** (a) Topcon GTS 300 total station. The 300 series instruments have angle accuracies from 1 second to 10 seconds and single prism distances from 1,200 m (3,900 ft) to 2,400 m (7,900 ft) at 2 mm + 2 ppm accuracy.

(a)

result is a moiré pattern that can be analyzed (with the aid of photodiodes) to read the circles. Both systems enable the surveyor to assign zero degrees (or any other value) to an instrument setting after the instrument has been sighted in.

The total station has an onboard microprocessor that monitors the instrument status (e.g., level and plumb orientation, battery status, and return signal strength) and makes corrections to measured data for the first of these conditions, when warranted. In addition, the microprocessor controls the acquisition of angles and distances and then computes horizontal distances, vertical distances, coordinates, and the like. Many total stations are designed so that the data stored in the data collector can be downloaded automatically to a computer via an RS 232 interface. The download program is usually supplied by the manufacturer; a second program is required to translate the raw data into a format that is compatible with the surveyor's coordinate geometry (processing) programs.

Also, most total stations allow the surveyor to capture the slope distance and the horizontal and vertical angles to a point by simply pressing one button. The point number and

**FIGURE 7.18** *(continued)*
(b) Topcon FS2 Data Collector for use with GTS 300 series total stations. (Courtesy of Topcon Instrument Corp., Paramus, N.J.)

(b)

point description for that point can then be entered and recorded. In addition, the wise surveyor will prepare a sketch showing the overall detail and the individual point locations. This sketch will help keep track of the completeness of the work and will be invaluable later when the plot file is prepared.

## 7.10 Total Station Field Techniques

Total stations and/or their attached data collectors have been programmed to perform a wide variety of surveying functions. All total station programs require that the instrument station and at least one reference station be identified so that all subsequent tied-in stations can be defined ($X$, $Y$, and $Z$ coordinates). Some programs require that the proposed instrument station's coordinates and elevation, and at least the azimuth (sometimes the coordinates and elevations as well) to the proposed reference stations be first uploaded into the total station prior to the fieldwork. Other programs require the field surveyor to enter the point number, east and north coordinates, and elevation of the instrument station, as well as either the azimuth to the sighted reference station or the coordinates of the sighted reference station. After setup, and before the instrument has been oriented for surveying as described above, the hi and prism heights must be measured and recorded.

Typical total station programs include point location, missing line measurement, resection, azimuth calculations, remote object elevation calculations, offset measurements, layout or setting-out positions, and area computation. All these topics are discussed in the following sections.

## 7.10.1 Point Location

After the instrument has been properly oriented, the coordinates (northing, easting, and elevation) of any sighted point can be determined, displayed, and recorded in the following format: NEZ or ENZ; the format chosen reflects the format needs of the software program chosen to process the field data. At this time, the sighted point is numbered and coded for attribute data (point description)—all of which is recorded with the location data. This program is extensively used in topographic surveys.

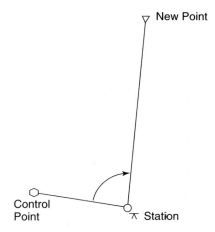

**POINT LOCATION PROGRAM
INPUTS AND SOLUTIONS**

*Known*: N, E, and Z coordinates of the instrument station ($\barπ$).

N, E, and Z coordinates of reference control point, or at least the azimuth of the line joining the instrument station and the control point.

*Measured*: Angles, or azimuths, from the control point and distances to the new point from the instrument station.

*Computed*: N, E, and Z coordinates of new points.

Azimuth of the line (and its distance) joining the instrument station to the new point.

## 7.10.2 Missing Line Measurement*

This program enables the surveyor to determine the horizontal and slope distances between any two sighted points, as well as the directions of the lines joining those sighted points. Onboard programs first determine the N, E, and Z coordinates of the sighted points and then compute (inverse) the joining distances and directions.

## 7.10.3 Resection

This technique permits the surveyor to set up the total station at any convenient position (sometimes referred to as a *free station*) and then to determine the coordinates and elevation of that instrument position by sighting previously coordinated reference stations.

*The illustrations in Sections 7.10.2, 7.10.3, and 7.10.5 through 7.10.8 courtesy of Sokkia Corp., Overland Park, Kans.

### *Missing line measurement program Inputs and solutions.*

*Known:*    - N, E and Z coordinates of the instrument station ($\pi$)
           - N, E and Z coordinates of a reference control
             point, or at least the azimuth of the line joining
             the instrument station and the control point

*Measured:*   - Angles, or azimuths, from the control point and
             distances to the new points from the instrument
             station.

*Computed:*   - N, E and Z coordinates of new points
             - Azimuths and horizontal, slope and vertical
             distances between the sighted points
             - Slopes of the lines joining any sighted points

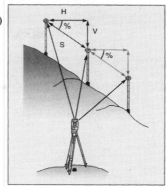

(Sketch courtesy of Sokkia Corporation, Overland Park, Kans.)

When sighting only two points of known position, it is necessary to measure and record both the distances and the angle between the reference points. When sighting several points (three or more) of known position, it is necessary to measure only the angles between the points. It is important to stress that most surveyors take more readings than are minimally necessary to obtain a solution; these redundant measurements give the surveyor increased precision and a check on the accuracy of the results. Once the instrument station's coordinates have been determined, the instrument is now oriented, and the surveyor can continue to survey using any of the other techniques described in this section.

### *Resection program inputs and solutions*

*Known:*      - N, E and Z coordinates of control point #1
           - N, E and Z coordinates of control point #2
           - N, E and Z coordinates of additional sighted control
            stations (up to a total of 10 control points). These can be
            entered manually or up-loaded from the computer
            depending on the instrument's capabilities.

*Measured:*   - Angles between the sighted control points.
            - Distances are also required from the instrument station to
            the control points, if only two control points are sighted.
            - the more measurements (angles and distances), the better
            the resection solution.

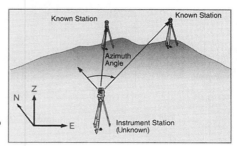

(Sketch courtesy of Sokkia Corporation, Overland Park, Kans.)

## 7.10.4   Azimuth Calculations

When the coordinates of the instrument station and a backsight reference station have been entered into the instrument processor, the azimuth of a line joining any sighted points can be readily displayed and recorded.

*Known*: N, E, and Z coordinates of the instrument station ($\pi$).
N, E, and Z coordinates of a reference control point,
or at least the azimuth of the line joining the instrument station and the control point.

*Measured*: Angles from the control point and distances to the
new points from the instrument station.

*Computed*: Azimuth of the lines joining the new points to the instrument station.
Slopes of the lines joining any sighted points.

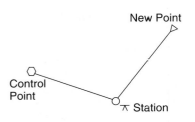

(Sketch courtesy of Sokkia Corporation, Overland Park, Kans.)

## 7.10.5 Remote Object Elevation Calculations

The surveyor can determine the heights of inaccessible points (for example, electricity conductors, bridge components, etc.) by simply sighting the pole-mounted prism as it is held directly under the object. When the object itself is then sighted, the object height can be promptly displayed. (the prism height must first be entered into the total station.)

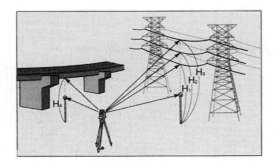

(Sketch courtesy of Sokkia Corporation, Overland Park, Kans.)

## 7.10.6 Offset Measurements

When an object is hidden from the total station, a measurement can be taken to the prism held out in view of the total station, and then the offset distance is measured. The angle (usually 90°) or direction to the hidden object, along with the measured distance, are entered into the total station, allowing it to compute the position of the hidden object.

## *Offset measurements (distance) programs solutions and inputs*

*Known:*   - N, E and Z coordinates of the instrument station ($\pi$)
           - N, E and Z coordinates (or the azimuth) for the reference
             control point

*Measured:*  - Distance from the instrument station to the offset point
            - Distance ($l$) from the offset point (at a right angle to the
              instrument line-of-sight) to the measuring point

*Computed:*  - N, E and Z coordinates of the "hidden" measuring points
            - Azimuths and distance from the instrument station to the
              "hidden" measuring point

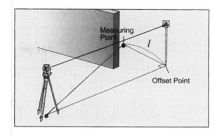

(Sketch courtesy of Sokkia Corporation, Overland Park, Kans.)


## *Offset measurements (angles) program inputs and solutions*

*Known:*   - N, E and Z coordinates of the instrument station ($\pi$)
           - N, E and Z coordinates (or the azimuth) of the reference
             control point

*Measured:*  - Angles from the prism being held on either side of the
             measuring point to the target center-point
             (The prism must be held such that both readings are the same
             distance from the instrument station - if both sides are
             measured)

*Computed:*  - N, E and Z coordinates of the "hidden" measuring points
            - Azimuths and distance from the instrument station to the
              "hidden" measuring point

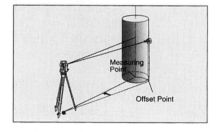

(Sketch courtesy of Sokkia Corporation, Overland Park, Kans.)


## 7.10.7   Layout or Setting-Out Positions

After the coordinates and elevations of the layout points have been uploaded into the total
station, the layout and setting-out software enables the surveyor to locate any layout point
by simply entering that point's number when prompted by the layout software. The instrument's display shows the left/right, forward/back, and up/down movements needed to
place the prism in each of the desired position locations. This capability is a great aid in
property and construction layouts.

## *Laying out, or setting out program inputs and solutions*

*Known:*    - N, E and Z coordinates of the instrument station (⊼)
- N, E and Z coordinates of a reference control point, or at least the azimuth of the line joining the instrument station and the control point
- N, E and Z coordinates of the proposed layout points (Entered manually, or previously up-loaded from the computer)

*Measured:* - Indicated angles (on the instrument display), or azimuths, from the control point and distances to each layout point
- The angles may be turned manually or automatically if a servo motor-driven instrument is being used.
- The distances (horizontal and vertical) are continually re-measured as the prism is eventually moved to the required layout position

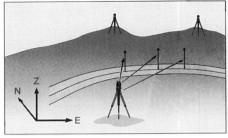

(Sketch courtesy of Sokkia Corporation, Overland Park, Kans.)

## 7.10.8    Area Computation

When this program has been selected, the processor will compute the area enclosed by a series of measured points. The processor first determines the coordinates of each station as described earlier and then, using those coordinates, computes the area in a manner similar to that described in Section 6.14.

### *Area computation program inputs and solutions*

*Known:*    - N, E and Z coordinates of the instrument station (⊼)
- N, E and Z coordinates of a reference control point, or at least the azimuth of the line joining the instrument station and the control point
- N, E and Z coordinates of the proposed layout points (Entered manually, or previously up-loaded from the computer)

*Measured:* - Angles, or azimuths, from the control point and distances to the new points, from the instrument station.

*Computed:* - N, E and Z coordinates of the area boundary points
- Area enclosed by the coordinated points

(Sketch courtesy of Sokkia Corporation, Overland Park, Kans.)

## 7.10.9    Summary of Typical Total Station Characteristics

**PARAMETER INPUT**

1. Angle units: degrees or gon
2. Distance units: feet or meters

3. Pressure units: in HG or mm HG*
4. Temperature units: °F or °C*
5. Prism constant (usually −0.03 m)
6. Offset distance (used when the prism cannot be held at the center of the object)
7. Face 1 or face 2 selection
8. Automatic point number incrementation
9. Height of instrument (hi)
10. Height of reflector (HR)
11. Point numbers and code numbers for occupied and sighted stations
12. Date and time settings—for total stations with onboard clocks

### CAPABILITIES (COMMON TO MANY TOTAL STATIONS)

1. Monitor: battery status, signal attenuation, horizontal and vertical axes status, collimation factors
2. Compute coordinates: northing, easting, elevation
3. Traverse closure and adjustment, and areas
4. Topography reductions
5. Remote object elevation, that is, object heights
6. Distances between remote points (missing line measurement)
7. Inversing
8. Resection
9. Layout (setting out)
10. Horizontal and vertical collimation corrections
11. Vertical circle indexing
12. Records search and review
13. Programmable features, that is, load external programs
14. Transfer of data to the computer (downloading)
15. Transfer of computer files to the data collector (uploading) for layout and reference purposes

# 7.11  Field Procedures for Total Stations in Topographic Surveys

Total stations can be used in any type of preliminary survey, control survey, or layout survey. They are particularly well suited for topographic surveys, in which the surveyor can capture the northings, eastings, and elevations of a large number of points—700 to 1,000 points per day. This significant increase in productivity means that in some

---

*Some newer instruments have built-in sensors that detect atmospheric effects and automatically correct readings for these natural errors.

medium-density areas, ground surveys are once again competitive in cost to aerial surveys. Although the increase in efficiency in the field survey is notable, an even more significant increase in efficiency can occur when the total station is part of a computerized surveying system—data collection, data processing (reductions and adjustments), and plotting.

One of the notable advantages of using electronic surveying techniques is that data are recorded in the electronic field book, which cuts down considerably on the time required to record data and on the opportunity of making transcription mistakes. Does this mean that manual field notes are a thing of the past? The answer is no; even in electronic surveys, there is a need for neat, comprehensive field notes. At the very least, such notes will contain the project title, names of field personnel, equipment description, date, weather conditions, instrument setup station identification, and backsight station(s) identification. In addition, for topographic surveys, many surveyors include in the manual notes a sketch showing the area's selected (in some cases, all) details—individual details such as trees, catch basins, and poles, and stringed detail such as water's edge, curbs, walks, and building outlines. As the survey proceeds, the surveyor will place all or selected point identification numbers directly on the sketch feature, thus showing clearly the type of detail being recorded. Later, after the data have been transferred to the computer and as the graphics features are edited, the presence of manual field notes will be invaluable in clearing up problems associated with any incorrect or ambiguous labeling and/or numbering of survey points.

## 7.11.1   Initial Data Entry

Most data collectors are designed to prompt for, or accept, some or all of the following initial configuration data:

- Project description
- Date and crew
- Temperature
- Pressure (some data collectors require a ppm correction input, which is read from a temperature/pressure graph—see Figure 7.6)
- Prism constant (0.03 m is a typical value; check the specifications)
- Curvature and refraction settings (see Chapter 3)
- Sea level corrections (see Chapter 10)
- Number of measurement repetitions—angle or distance (the average value is computed)
- Choice of face 1 and face 2 positions
- Choice of automatic point number incrementation
- Choice of Imperial units or SI units for all data

Many of these prompts can be bypassed, causing the microprocessor to use previously selected default values, or settings, in its computations. After the initial data have been entered and the operation mode has been selected, most data collectors will prompt the operator for all station and measurement entries. The following sections discuss typical topographic survey procedures.

## 7.11.2   Survey Station Descriptors

Each survey station or shot location (point) must be described with respect to surveying activity (for example, backsight, intermediate sight, foresight), station identification, and other attribute data. Total stations that come equipped with their own data collectors will, in many cases, prompt for the data entry [for example, occupied station, backsight reference station(s)] and then automatically assign appropriate labels, which will then show up on the survey printout. Point description data can be entered as alpha or numeric codes (see Figure 7.19). This

Point Identification Codes
(shown is part of Seneca dictionary)

#### Survey Points

| | | |
|---|---|---|
| 01 | BM | Bench Mark |
| 02 | CM | Concrete Monument |
| 03 | SIB | Standard Iron Bar |
| 04 | IB | Iron Bar |
| 05 | RIB | Round Iron Bar |
| 06 | IP | Iron Pipe |
| 07 | WS | Wooden Stake |
| 08 | MTR | Coordinate Monument |
| 09 | CC | Cut Cross |
| 10 | N&W | Nail and Washer |
| 11 | ROA | Roadway |
| 12 | SL | Street Line |
| 13 | EL | Easement Line |
| 14 | ROW | Right of Way |
| 15 | CL | Centerline |

#### Topography

| | | |
|---|---|---|
| 16 | EW | Edge Walk |
| 17 | ESHLD | Edge Shoulder |
| 18 | C&G | Curb and Gutter |
| 19 | EWAT | Edge of Water |
| 20 | EP | Edge of Pavement |
| 21 | RD | CL Road |
| 22 | TS | Top of Slope |
| 23 | BS | Bottom of Slope |
| 24 | CSW | Concrete Sidewalk |
| 25 | ASW | Asphalt Sidewalk |
| 26 | RW | Retaining Wall |
| 27 | DECT | Deciduous Tree |
| 28 | CONT | Coniferous Tree |
| 29 | HDGE | Hedge |
| 30 | GDR | Guide Rail |
| 31 | DW | Driveway |
| 32 | CLF | Chain Link Fence |
| 33 | PWF | Post and Wire Fence |
| 34 | WDF | Wooden Fence |

Code Sheet for Field Use

| 1 BM | 2 CM | 3 SIB | 4 IB | 5 RIB |
|---|---|---|---|---|
| 6 IP | 7 WS | 8 MTR | 9 CC | 10 N W |
| 11 ROA | 12 SL | 13 EL | 14 ROW | 15 CL |
| 16 EW | 17 ESHL | 18 C G | 19 EWAT | 20 EP |
| 21 RD | 22 TS | 23 BS | 24 CSW | 25 ASW |
| 26 RW | 27 DECT | 28 CONT | 29 HDGE | 30 GDR |
| 31 DW | 32 CLF | 33 PWF | 34 WDF | 35 SIGN |
| 36 MB | 37 STM | 38 HDW | 39 CULV | 40 SWLE |
| 41 PSTA | 42 SAN | 43 • BRTH | 44 CB | 45 DCB |
| 46 HYD | 47 V | 48 V CH | 49 M CH | 50 ARV |
| 51 WKEY | 52 HP | 53 UTV | 54 LS | 55 TP |
| 56 PED | 57 TMH | 58 TB | 59 BCM | 60 GUY |
| 61 TLG | 62 BLDG | 63 GAR | 64 FDN | 65 RWYX |
| 66 RAIL | 67 GASV | 68 GSMH | 69 G | 70 GMRK |
| 71 TL | 72 PKMR | 73 TSS | 74 SCT | 75 BR |
| 76 ABUT | 77 PIER | 78 FTG | 79 EDB | 80 POR |
| 81 SLS | 82 WTT | 83 STR | 84 BUS | 85 PLY |
| 86 TEN | 0 | 0 | 0 | 0 |
| 0 | 0 | 0 | 0 | 0 |
| 0 | 0 | 0 | 0 | 0 |

(a)                                                  (b)

**FIGURE 7.19**   Some (a) Alphanumeric codes for sighted point descriptions. (b) Code sheet for field use.

descriptive data will also show up on the printout and can (if desired) be tagged to show up on the plotted drawing. Some data collectors are now equipped with bar-code readers that, when used with prepared code sheets, permit instantaneous entry of descriptive data.

Some data collectors are designed to work only with specific total stations, whereas others are designed to work with all (or most) total stations. Figure 7.20 shows three data collectors designed to work with most total stations. Figure 7.20(a) shows a multitasking data collector that can be connected to a portable disk drive, thus permitting data to be downloaded in the field. This permits the surveyor to clear a full storage register and to continue with the survey. Other data collectors that store data on removable computer cards also permit the surveyor to continue when the full card is replaced with an empty card. Figure 7.20(b) shows a more modern data collector that can be used with total stations and/or GPS receivers; software can be purchased to perform various functions. (See Figure 11.22 for a full listing of the menu structure for this data collector.) Figure 7.20(c) shows a handheld computer outfitted with both data collection and data layout software. Although this type of data collector has fewer options than those shown in Figure 7.20(a) and (b), its functionality and much lower cost make it attractive to many surveyors.

Newer data collectors (and computer programs) permit the surveyor to enter not only the point code, but also various levels of attribute data for each coded point. A tie-in to a utility pole could also tag the pole number, the use (for example, electricity, telephone), the material (for example, wood, concrete, steel), connecting poles, year of installation, and so on. This type of expanded attribute data is typical of the data collected for a geographic information system (GIS). See Chapter 9.

### 7.11.2.1 AASHTO's survey data management system (SDMS)  The American Association of State Highway and Transportation Officials (AASHTO) developed in 1991 a survey data management system (SDMS) to aid in the nationwide standardization of field coding and computer-processing procedures used in highway surveys. The field data can be captured automatically by the data collector (electronic field book), as in the case of total stations, or the data can be entered manually in the data collector for a wide variety of theodolite and level surveys. AASHTO's software is compatible with most recently designed total stations and some third-party data collectors, and data processing can be accomplished using most MS-DOS based computers. For further information on these coding standards, contact AASHTO at 444 N. Capitol St. N.W., Suite 225, Washington, D.C. 20001(202-624-5800).

### 7.11.2.2 Occupied point (instrument station) entries

- Height of the instrument (the measured value is entered)
- Station number, for example, 111 (see the example in Figure 7.21)
- Station identification code (see the code sheet in Figure 7.19)
- Coordinates of occupied station. Coordinates can be assumed, state plane, or universal transverse Mercator (UTM). Such coordinates may have been uploaded previously from a computer
- Coordinates of backsight (BS) station, or reference azimuth to BS station

(a)

**FIGURE 7.20** (a) CMT MC V Total Station data collector interfaced with a portable disk drive. The collector, used with Surveyor's Assistant software, permits data collection with most popular Total Stations and provides a variety of coordinate geometry operations and plotting routines. The portable disk drive (3-1/2″ floppy disks) ensures unlimited memory storage for large, isolated projects. (Courtesy of Corvallis Micro Technology Inc., Corvallis, Ore.) (b) Trimble's TSCe data collector for use with robotic total stations and GPS receivers. When used with TDS Survey Pro Robotics software, this collector features real-time maps, 3-D design stakeout, and interactive DTM with real-time cut and fill computations. When used with TDS Survey pro GPS software, this collector can be used for general GPS work, as well as for RTK measurements at centimeter-level accuracy. (Portions © 2001 Trimble Navigation Limited. All rights reserved.)

(b)

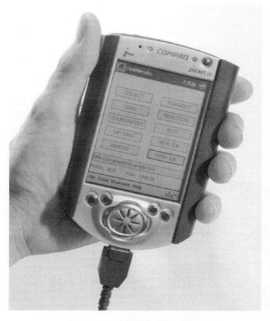

(i) Compaq Palm Computer.

(iii) Menu Selection.

(ii) Menu Default Settings.　　　(c)

**FIGURE 7.20** *(continued)*　　(c) Handheld computer and surveying software. (Courtesy of XYZ Works).

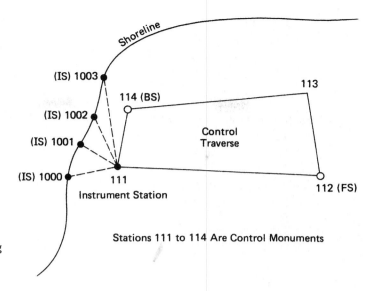

**FIGURE 7.21** Sketch showing intermediate shoreline ties to a control traverse.

With some data collectors, the coordinates of the above stations may instead be uploaded from computer files. Once the surveyor identifies specific points as being instrument station or backsight reference station(s), the coordinates of those stations then become active in the processor.

### 7.11.2.3 Sighted point entries

- Height of prism/reflector (HR) (the measured value is entered)
- Station number, for example, 114 (BS) (see Figure 7.21)
- Station identification code (see Figure 7.19)

## 7.11.3 Procedures for the Example Shown in Figure 7.21

1. Enter the initial data and instrument station data, as shown in Sections 7.11.1 to 7.11.2. Measure the height of the instrument, or adjust the height of the reflector to equal the height of the instrument.
2. Sight at station 114. Zero the horizontal circle (any other value can be set instead of zero, if desired). Most total stations have a zero-set button.
3. Enter the code (for example, BS), or respond to the data collector prompt.
4. Measure and enter the height of the prism/reflector (HR). If the height of the reflector has been adjusted to equal the height of the instrument, the value of 1,000 is often entered for both values because these hi and HR values usually cancel each other in computations.
5. Press the appropriate measure buttons, for example, slope distance, horizontal angle, vertical angle.

6. Press the record button after each measurement. Most instruments measure and record slope and horizontal and vertical data after the pressing of just one button (when they are in the automatic mode).

7. After the station measurements have been recorded, the data collector will prompt for the station point number (for example, 114 in Figure 7.21) and the station identification code (for example, 02 from Figure 7.19, which identifies "concrete monument").

8. If appropriate, as in traverse surveys, the next sight is to the FS station. Repeat steps 4, 5, 6, and 7 using correct data.

9. While at station 111, any number of intermediate sights (ISs) can be taken to define the topographic features being surveyed. Most instruments have the option of speeding up the work by employing "automatic point number incrementation." For example, if the topographic readings are to begin with point number 1,000, the surveyor will be prompted to accept the next number in sequence (for example, 1,001, 1,002, 1,003, etc.) at each new reading. If the prism is later held at a previously numbered point (for example, control point 107), the prompted value can easily be temporarily overridden with 107 being entered.

   The prism/reflector is usually mounted on an adjustable-length prism pole with the height of the prism (HR) set to the height of the total station (hi). The prism pole can be steadied with a brace pole, as shown in Figure 7.8, to improve the accuracy for more precise sightings.

   Some software permits the surveyor to identify, by attribute name or further code number, points that will be connected on the resultant plan (shoreline points in this example). This connect (on and off) feature permits the field surveyor to prepare the plan (for graphics terminal or plotter) while performing the actual field survey. Where necessary, the surveyor can later connect the points while in edit mode on the computer, depending on the software in use. Clear field notes are essential for this activity.

10. When all the topographic detail in the area of the occupied station (111) has been collected, the total station can be moved* to the next traverse station (112 in this example). The data collection can proceed in the same manner as that already described (that is, BS @ STA.111, FS @ STA. 113), and the surveyor can take all relevant IS readings.

## 7.11.4 Data Transfer and Data Processing

The collected data from the example in Figure 7.21, now must be downloaded to a computer. The download computer program is normally supplied by the total station manufacturer, and the actual transfer can be cabled through an RS 232 interface cable or a computer card reader. Once the data are in the computer, the data must be sorted into a format that is compatible with the computer program that will process the data. This translation program is usually written or purchased separately by the surveyor.

Many modern total stations have the data stored onboard, thus eliminating handheld data collectors. Some instruments store data on a module that can be transferred to a computer-connected reading device. Some manufacturers use PCMCIA cards, which can be read directly into a computer through a PCMCIA reader (see Figure 7.17). Other total

---

*When the total station is to be moved to another setup station, the instrument is always removed from the tripod and carried separately by its handle or in its case.

stations, including the geodimeter (see Figure 7.29), can be downloaded by connecting the instrument (or its keyboard) directly to the computer.

If the topographic data have been tied to a closed traverse, the traverse closure is calculated. Then all adjusted values for northings, eastings, and elevations ($Y$, $X$, and $Z$) are computed. Some total stations have sophisticated data collectors (which are actually small computers) that can perform preliminary analysis, adjustments, and coordinate computations, whereas others require the computer program to perform these functions. Once the field data have been stored in coordinate files, the data required for plotting by digital plotters can be assembled, and the survey can be plotted quickly at any desired scale. The survey can also be plotted at an interactive graphics terminal for graphics editing using one of the many available computer-aided design (CAD) programs.

## 7.12   Field-Generated Graphics

Many surveying software programs permit the field surveyor to identify field data shots so that subsequent processing will produce appropriate computer graphics. For example, MicroSurvey Software Inc. software has a typical description-to-graphics feature that enables the surveyor to join field shots, such as curb-line shots [see Figure 7.22(a)] by adding a Z prefix to all but the last "CURB" descriptor. When the program first encounters the Z prefix, it begins joining points with the same descriptors. Then, when the program encounters the first curb descriptor without the Z prefix, the joining of points is terminated. Rounding (e.g., curved curbs) can be introduced by substituting an X prefix for the Z prefix [see Figure 7.22(a)]. Other typical MicroSurvey graphic prefixes include the following:

- Y joins the last identical descriptor by drawing a line at a right angle to the established line [see the fence line in Figure 7.22(a)].
- A dash (-) causes a dot to be created in the drawing file, which is later transferred to the plan. The dot on the plan can be replaced by inserting a previously created symbol block, for example, a tree, a manhole, a hydrant [see MH in Figure 7.22(a)]. If a second dash follows the first prefix dash, the ground elevation will not be transferred to the graphics file [see HYD in Figure 7.22(a)] because some feature elevations may not be required.
- A period (.) instructs the system to close back on the first point of the string of descriptors with the same characters [see BLDG and BUS shelter in Figure 7.22(a) and POND in Figure 7.23].

Other software programs create graphic stringing by different techniques. For example, Sokkia software gives the code itself a stringing capability (for example, fence1, curb1, curb2, ℄), which the surveyor can easily turn on and off [see Figure 7.22(b)].

In some cases, it may be more efficient to assign the point descriptors from the computer keyboard after the survey has been completed. For example, the entry of descriptors is time consuming on some electronic field books (EFBs), particularly in automatic mode. In addition, some topographic features (for example, the edge of water in a pond or lake) can be captured in sequence, thus permitting the surveyor to add these descriptors efficiently from the computer in the processing stage instead of repeatedly entering dozens or even hundreds of identical attribute codes. (Some data collectors prompt for the last entry, thus allowing the surveyor to avoid rekeying identical attributes or descriptors.) If the point descriptors are to be added at the computer, clear field notes are indispensable.

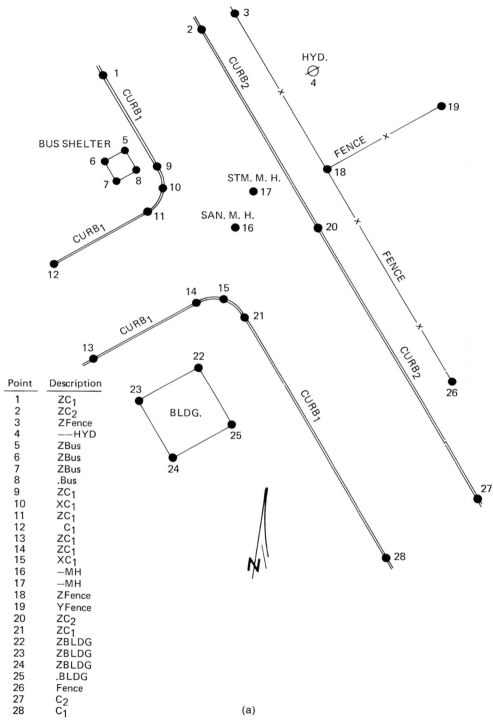

| Point | Description |
|-------|-------------|
| 1 | $ZC_1$ |
| 2 | $ZC_2$ |
| 3 | ZFence |
| 4 | ——HYD |
| 5 | ZBus |
| 6 | ZBus |
| 7 | ZBus |
| 8 | .Bus |
| 9 | $ZC_1$ |
| 10 | $XC_1$ |
| 11 | $ZC_1$ |
| 12 | $C_1$ |
| 13 | $ZC_1$ |
| 14 | $ZC_1$ |
| 15 | $XC_1$ |
| 16 | —MH |
| 17 | —MH |
| 18 | ZFence |
| 19 | YFence |
| 20 | $ZC_2$ |
| 21 | $ZC_1$ |
| 22 | ZBLDG |
| 23 | ZBLDG |
| 24 | ZBLDG |
| 25 | .BLDG |
| 26 | Fence |
| 27 | $C_2$ |
| 28 | $C_1$ |

(a)

**FIGURE 7.22** (a) Field notes for total station graphics descriptors—MicroSurvey Software Inc. codes.

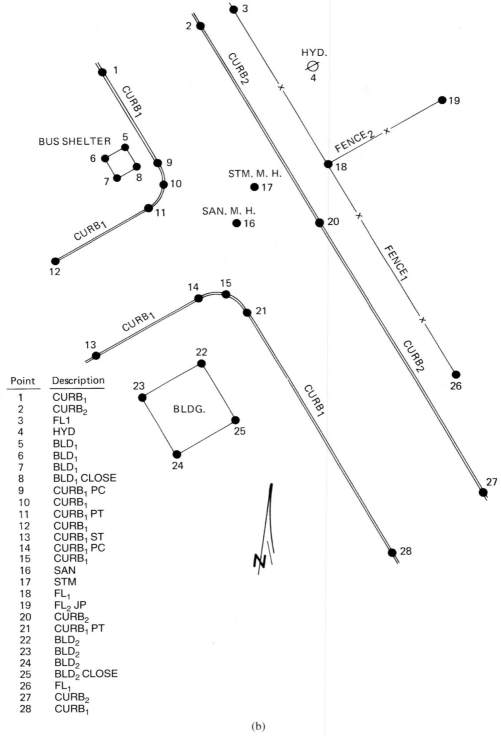

| Point | Description |
|---|---|
| 1 | $CURB_1$ |
| 2 | $CURB_2$ |
| 3 | FL1 |
| 4 | HYD |
| 5 | $BLD_1$ |
| 6 | $BLD_1$ |
| 7 | $BLD_1$ |
| 8 | $BLD_1$ CLOSE |
| 9 | $CURB_1$ PC |
| 10 | $CURB_1$ |
| 11 | $CURB_1$ PT |
| 12 | $CURB_1$ |
| 13 | $CURB_1$ ST |
| 14 | $CURB_1$ PC |
| 15 | $CURB_1$ |
| 16 | SAN |
| 17 | STM |
| 18 | $FL_1$ |
| 19 | $FL_2$ JP |
| 20 | $CURB_2$ |
| 21 | $CURB_1$ PT |
| 22 | $BLD_2$ |
| 23 | $BLD_2$ |
| 24 | $BLD_2$ |
| 25 | $BLD_2$ CLOSE |
| 26 | $FL_1$ |
| 27 | $CURB_2$ |
| 28 | $CURB_1$ |

(b)

**FIGURE 7.22 (continued)** (b) Field notes for total station graphics descriptors—Sokkia codes.

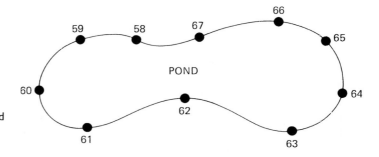

**FIGURE 7.23** In-sequence field shots defining a topographic feature.

See Figure 7.23 for an illustration of this stringing technique. The pond edge has been picked up (defined) by 10 shots, beginning with 58 and ending with 67. Using the MicroSurvey program introduced earlier, the point description edit feature is selected from the pull-down menu, and the following steps occur:

1. "Points to be described?" 58..66 [enter]
2. "Description?" ZPOND [enter]
3. "Points to be described?" 67 [enter]
4. "Description?" .POND [enter]

After the point descriptions have been suitably coded (either by direct field coding or by the editing technique shown here), a second command is accessed from another pull-down menu that simply (in one operation) converts the coded point description file so that the shape of the pond is produced in graphics. The four descriptor operations described here are less work than would be required to describe each point using field entries for the 10 points shown in this example. Larger features requiring many more field shots would be even more conducive to this type of postsurvey editing of descriptors.

It is safe to say that most projects requiring that graphics be developed from total station surveys will utilize a combination of point description field coding and postsurvey point description editing. Note that the success of some of these modern surveys still depends to a significant degree on old-fashioned, reliable survey field notes. It is becoming clear that the "drafting" of the plan of survey is increasingly becoming the responsibility of the surveyor, either through direct field coding techniques or through postsurvey data processing. All recently introduced surveying software programs enable the surveyor to produce a complete plan of survey.

## 7.13 Construction Layout Using Total Stations

We saw in the previous section that total stations are particularly well suited for collecting data in topographic surveys; we also noted that the collected data could be readily downloaded to a computer and processed into point coordinates—northing, easting, and elevation ($Y$, $X$, and $Z$)—along with point attribute data. The significant increases in efficiency made possible with total station topographic surveys can also be realized in layout surveys when the original point coordinates exist in computer memory or on floppy disk, together with the coordinates of all the key design points. To illustrate, consider the example of a road construction project. First, the topographic detail is collected using total stations set up at various control points (preliminary survey). The detail is then transferred to the computer; adjusted, if necessary; and converted into $Y$, $X$, and $Z$ coordinates. Various coordinate geometry and road design programs can then be used to design the proposed road. When the proposed horizontal, cross-section, and profile alignments have been established, the proposed coordinates ($Y$, $X$, and $Z$) for all key horizontal and vertical (elevation) features can be computed and stored in computer files. The points coordinated will include top-of-curb and centerline positions at regular stations, as well as all changes in direction or slope. Catch basins, traffic islands, and the like, will also be included, as will all curved or irregular road components.

Figure 7.24 illustrates a computer printout for a road construction project. The total station is set at control monument CX-80 with a reference backsight on RAP (reference azimuth point) 2 (point 957 on the printout). The surveyor has a choice of (1) setting the actual azimuth (213°57'01", line 957) on the backsight and then turning the horizontal circle to the printed azimuths of the desired layout points or (2) setting zero degrees for the backsight and then turning the clockwise angle listed for each desired layout point. As a safeguard, after sighting the reference backsight, the surveyor usually sights a second or third control monument (see the top 12 points on the printout) to check the azimuth or angle setting. The computer printout also lists the point coordinates and baseline offsets for each layout point.

Figure 7.25 shows data from a portion of the construction drawing that accompanies the computer printout in Figure 7.24. The drawing (usually drawn by digital plotter from computer files) helps the surveyor in the field in laying out the works correctly. All the layout points listed on the printout are also shown on the drawing, together with curve data and other explanatory notes.

More modern total stations offer an even more efficient technique. Instead of having the layout data only on a printout similar to that shown in Figure 7.24, the coordinates for all layout points can be uploaded into the total station microprocessor. The surveyor can then, in the field, identify the occupied control point and the reference backsight point(s), thus orienting the total station. The desired layout point number is then entered, with the required layout angle and distance inversed from the stored coordinates and displayed. The layout can proceed by turning the correct azimuth or angle (done automatically by motorized total stations), and then, by trial and error, the prism is moved to the layout distance (the total station is set to tracking mode for all but the final measurements). With some total stations, the prism is simply tracked with the remaining left/right ($\pm$) distance displayed alongside the remaining near/far ($\pm$) distance. When the correct location has been reached, both displays show 0.000 m (0.00 ft).

If the instrument is set up at an unknown position (free station), its coordinates can be determined by sighting control stations whose coordinates have been previously uploaded into the total station microprocessor. This technique, known as resection, is available on all modern total stations. Sightings on two control points can locate the instrument station, although additional sightings (up to a total of four) are recommended to provide a stronger solution and an indication of the accuracy level achieved. See Section 7.10.3.

Some theodolites and total stations come equipped with a guidelight, which can help move the prism holder on line very quickly. (See Figures 7.26 and 7.27.) The TC 800 is a total station that can be turned on and immediately used (no initialization procedure) and comes equipped with internal storage for 2,000 points and an EGL1® guidelight. The guidelight is very useful in layout surveys because prism holders can place themselves

THE MUNICIPALITY OF METROPOLITAN TORONTO - DEPARTMENT OF ROADS AND TRAFFIC

MIS # E152G

W.R. ALLEN ROAD FROM SHEPPARD AVENUE TO STANSTEAD DRIVE

ENGINEERING STAKEOUT

FROM STATION 269+80.00    TO STATION 271+30.00

BASE LINE

INSTRUMENT ON   CONST CONTROL MON CX-80
                AZIMUTH 213-57- 1
SIGHTING        RAP #2 - ANTENNA C.F.B.

| POINT NO. | STATION | DESCRIPTION | OFFSET FROM BASELINE | AZIMUTH DEG-MIN-SEC | DISTANCE | CLOCKWISE TURN ANGLE | ELEVATION | COORDINATES NORTH | EAST |
|---|---|---|---|---|---|---|---|---|---|
| 876 | 269+89.355 | CONST CONTROL MON CX-76 | 22.862 LEFT | 170-49-16 | 80.430 | 316-52-15 | 0.0 | 4845374.460 | 307710.370 |
| 885 | 271+29.785 | CONST CONTROL MON CX-85 | 22.857 LEFT | 350-49- 8 | 60.000 | 136-52- 7 | 0.0 | 4845513.091 | 307687.967 |
| 877 | 269+95.164 | CONST CONTROL MON CX-77 | 22.861 RIGHT | 139-19-24 | 87.513 | 285-22-24 | 0.0 | 4845387.490 | 307754.580 |
| 878 | 269+97.098 | CONST CONTROL MON CX-78 | 38.095 RIGHT | 130-50-11 | 94.861 | 276-53-11 | 0.0 | 4845391.830 | 307769.310 |
| 879 | 270+27.530 | CONST CONTROL MON CX-79 | 38.081 RIGHT | 115-33-22 | 74.155 | 261-36-21 | 0.0 | 4845421.870 | 307764.440 |
| 881 | 270+69.932 | CONST CONTROL MON CX-81 | 22.862 RIGHT | 80-38- 4 | 45.719 | 226-41- 3 | 0.0 | 4845461.300 | 307742.650 |
| 958 | 290+51.899 | RAP #3 - RADIO TOWER | 294.749 LEFT | 344-19-40 | 1990.850 | 130-22-40 | 0.0 | 4847370.697 | 307159.747 |
| 884 | 271+29.932 | CONST CONTROL MON CX-84 | 22.862 RIGHT | 28- 3-30 | 75.551 | 174- 6-29 | 0.0 | 4845520.531 | 307733.077 |
| 959 | 0+00.000 | CN TOWER | 0.0 | 152-46-14 | ******** | 298-49-14 | 0.0 | 4833410.793 | 313894.638 |
| 933 | 270+16.535 | CONST CONTROL MON CX-133 | 61.272 RIGHT | 113- 9- 1 | 99.566 | 259-12- 0 | 0.0 | 4845414.717 | 307789.088 |
| 956 | 271+72.134 | RAP #1 - BILLBOARD FRAME | 471.682 RIGHT | 69- 7-32 | 505.019 | 215-10-31 | 0.0 | 4845633.810 | 308169.411 |
| 960 | 269+67.759 | CONTROL MON MTR77-6119 | 9.329 RIGHT | 153-18-33 | 106.983 | 299-21-32 | 196.768 | 4845358.277 | 307745.594 |
| 957 | 268+98.575 | RAP #2 - ANTENNA C.F.B. | 183.253 LEFT | 213-57- 1 | 234.606 | 0- 0- 0 | 0.0 | 4845259.249 | 307566.519 |
| 483 | 269+83.555 | BC CORNER ROUND | 25.637 LEFT | 172-19-51 | 86.275 | 318-23-11 | 0.0 | 4845368.437 | 307708.556 |
| 753 | 269+83.622 | CATCH BASIN GUTTER | 25.142 LEFT | 172-20-12 | 86.193 | 318-23-11 | 0.0 | 4845368.291 | 307709.034 |
| 485 | 269+84.988 | PI CORNER ROUND | 13.500 LEFT | 164-31-15 | 85.312 | 310-34-15 | 0.0 | 4845371.643 | 307720.309 |
| 486 | 269+88.075 | MP CORNER ROUND | 16.973 LEFT | 166-41-56 | 81.922 | 312-44-55 | 0.0 | 4845374.136 | 307716.388 |
| 446 | 269+88.654 | PI CORNER ROUND | 13.500 LEFT | 146-40-47 | 88.906 | 292-43-46 | 196.352 | 4845379.569 | 307746.378 |
| 2103 | 269+90.000 | C/L OF CONSTRUCTION | 0.0 | 154-49-55 | 82.995 | 300-52-54 | 0.0 | 4845378.744 | 307732.836 |
| 444 | 269+90.625 | BC CORNER ROUND | 28.986 RIGHT | 137-35-48 | 94.626 | 283-38-47 | 0.0 | 4845383.986 | 307761.351 |
| 754 | 269+91.351 | CATCH BASIN GUTTER | 34.690 RIGHT | 133-33- 3 | 97.281 | 280-36- 2 | 0.0 | 4845385.613 | 307766.866 |
| 461 | 269+91.604 | BC CORNER ROUND | 36.674 RIGHT | 133-31-51 | 98.267 | 279-34-50 | 0.0 | 4845386.179 | 307768.784 |
| 434 | 269+92.355 | BC CORNER ROUND | 1.500 RIGHT | 153-21-22 | 81.172 | 299-24-17 | 0.0 | 4845381.308 | 307733.941 |
| 437 | 269+93.105 | BC BULLNOSE TOP OF CURB | 2.250 RIGHT | 152- 4-18 | 80.687 | 298-44-17 | 196.425 | 4845382.168 | 307734.562 |
| 435 | 269+93.105 | CP BULLNOSE TOP OF CURB ISLAND | 1.500 RIGHT | 153-11-45 | 80.456 | 299-14-44 | 196.395 | 4845382.048 | 307733.821 |
| 436 | 269+93.105 | EC BULLNOSE TOP OF CURB | 0.750 RIGHT | 153-42-23 | 80.233 | 299-45-22 | 196.410 | 4845381.929 | 307733.081 |
| 447 | 269+93.947 | MP CORNER ROUND | 18.162 LEFT | 142-24-37 | 86.221 | 288-27-36 | 196.425 | 4845385.538 | 307750.135 |
| 482 | 269+97.210 | CENTER PT CORNER ROUND | 27.250 LEFT | 174-16-54 | 72.708 | 320-19-53 | 0.0 | 4845381.513 | 307718.358 |
| 484 | 269+97.210 | EC CORNER ROUND-TOP CURB | 13.500 LEFT | 163-28-17 | 73.176 | 309-31-16 | 196.290 | 4845383.707 | 307718.232 |
| 755 | 269+98.000 | CATCH BASIN TOP OF CURB | 13.500 LEFT | 163-23-29 | 72.392 | 309-26-28 | 196.270 | 4845384.488 | 307717.913 |
| 2107 | 270+00.000 | TOP OF CURB | 13.500 LEFT | 163-10-51 | 70.410 | 309-13-51 | 196.036 | 4845386.462 | 307731.240 |
| 2106 | 270+00.000 | C/L OF CONSTRUCTION | 0.0 | 152-40-57 | 73.433 | 298-43-56 | 196.156 | 4845388.616 | 307757.460 |
| 443 | 270+04.265 | CENTER PT CORNER ROUND | 27.250 RIGHT | 133-24-39 | 82.485 | 279-27-38 | 0.0 | 4845397.175 | 307743.887 |
| 445 | 270+04.265 | EC CORNER ROUND-TOP CURB | 13.500 RIGHT | 141-47-32 | 74.932 | 287-50-31 | 196.050 | 4845394.981 | 307743.727 |
| 756 | 270+05.265 | CATCH BASIN TOP OF CURB | 13.500 RIGHT | 141-25- 0 | 74.059 | 287-28- 0 | 196.110 | 4845395.968 | 307742.971 |
| 2111 | 270+10.000 | TOP OF CURB | 13.500 RIGHT | 139-30-47 | 69.973 | 285-33-46 | 195.854 | 4845400.642 | 307716.317 |
| 2116 | 270+10.000 | TOP OF CURB | 13.500 LEFT | 161-55-21 | 60.513 | 307-58-20 | 195.854 | 4845396.334 | 307729.644 |
| 2109 | 270+10.000 | C/L OF CONSTRUCTION | 0.0 | 149-53-42 | 64.006 | 295-56-41 | 195.974 | 4845398.488 | 307714.722 |
| 2113 | 270+20.000 | TOP OF CURB | 13.500 LEFT | 160 10-24 | 50.857 | 308-13-23 | 195.686 | 4845406.206 | 30/714.722 |

**FIGURE 7.24**   Computer printout of layout data for a road construction project. (Courtesy of Department of Roads and Traffic, City of Toronto)

CITY OF TORONTO
MANAGEMENT SERVICES DEPARMENT DATA PROCESSING CENTRE

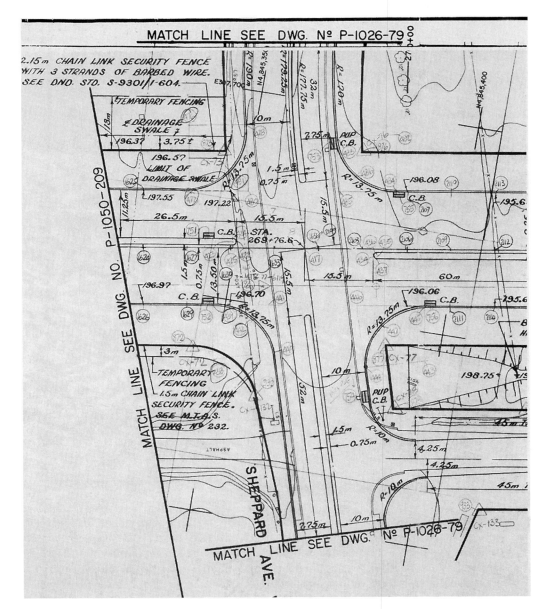

**FIGURE 7.25** Portion of a construction plan showing layout points. (Courtesy of Department of Roads and Traffic, City of Toronto)

(a)

**FIGURE 7.26** (a) Leica TC 800 total station with EGLI® guidelight. (Courtesy of Leica Geosystems, Norcross, Ga.) (b) Trimble's 3600 total station, featuring clamp-free operation (endless slow motion), can be upgraded to include reflectorless measurement, Tracklight™, laser plummet, and TDS onboard software. (Portions © 2001 Trimble Navigation Limited. All rights reserved.)

on-line quickly by noting the colored lights sent from the total station. The flashing lights (yellow on the left and red on the right, as viewed by the prism holder) are 12 m wide at a distance of 100 m and enable the prism holder to place the prism on-line, with final adjustments as given by the instrument operator. With automatic target recognition (ATR; see Section 7.14.1), the sighting-in process is completed automatically.

## 7.14   Motorized Total Stations

One adaptation of the total station has been the addition of servo motors to drive both the horizontal and the vertical motions of these instruments. Motorized instruments have been designed to search automatically for prism targets and then lock onto them precisely, to turn angles automatically to designated points using the uploaded coordinates of those points, and to repeat angles by automatically double-centering. These instruments, when combined with a remote controller held by the prism surveyor, enable the survey to proceed with a reduced need for field personnel.

## 7.14.1   Automatic Target Recognition (ATR)

Some manufacturers have designed an instrument with automatic target recognition, which utilizes an infrared light bundle sent co-axially through the telescope. First, the telescope must be pointed roughly at the target prism—either manually or under software control—and then the instrument does the rest. The ATR module is a digital camera that notes the

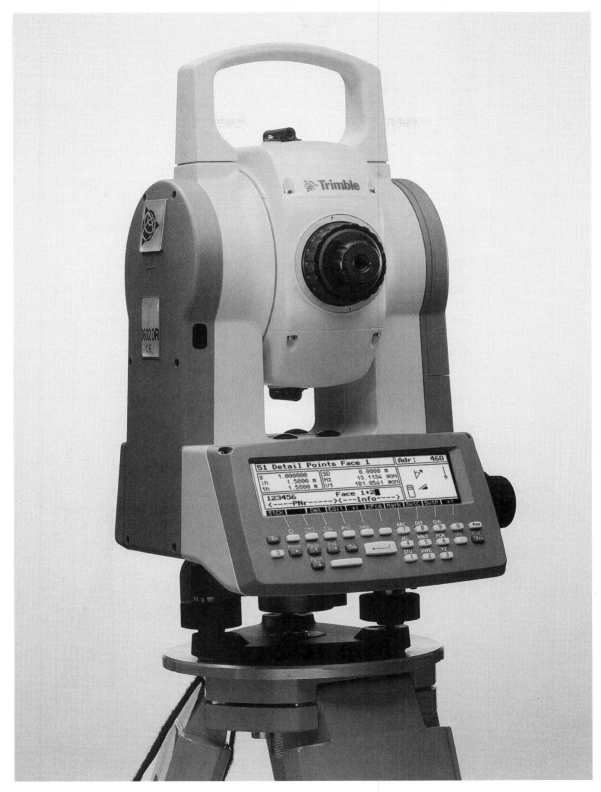

**FIGURE 7.26** *(continued)*      (b)

offset of the reflected laser beam, permitting the instrument then to move automatically until the cross hairs have been electronically set on the point precisely. After the point has been precisely "sighted," the instrument can then read and record the angle and distance. Reports indicate that the time required for this process is only one-third to one-half the time required to obtain the same results using conventional total station techniques.

ATR comes with a lock-on mode, where the instrument, once sighted at the prism, will continue to follow the prism as it is moved from station to station. To ensure that the prism is always pointed to the instrument, one manufacturer, Leica, designed a 360° prism (see Figure 7.28), which assists the surveyor in keeping the lock-on over a period of time. If lock-on is lost due to intervening obstacles, it is reestablished after manually pointing at the prism. ATR recognizes targets up to 1,000 m or 3,300 ft away, functions in darkness, requires no focusing or fine pointing, works with all types of prisms, and maintains a lock on prisms moving up to speeds of 11 mph or 5 mps (at a distance of 100 m).

## 7.14.2  Remote Controlled Surveying

Geodimeter, the company that first introduced EDM equipment in the early 1950s, introduced in the late 1980s a survey system in which the total station (Geodimeter 4000 Series; see Figure 7.29) has been equipped with motors to control both the horizontal and the vertical movements. This total station can be used as a conventional instrument, but when interfaced to a controller located with the prism, the station instrument can be remotely controlled by the surveyor at the prism station by means of radio telemetry.

When the remote control feature button on the total station is activated, control of the station instrument is transferred to the remote controller, called the remote positioning unit

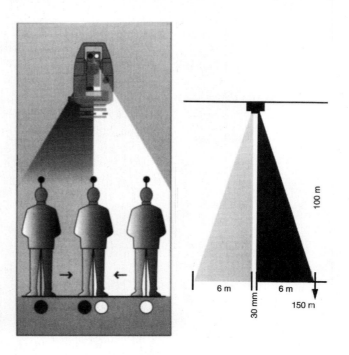

**FIGURE 7.27**  EGLI® guidelight.
(Courtesy of Leica Geosystems, Norcross, Ga.)

**FIGURE 7.28** Leica 360° prism—
used with remote-controlled total
stations and with automatic target
recognition (ATR) total stations. ATR
eliminates fine pointing and focusing.
The 360° feature means that the
prism is always facing the instrument.
(Courtesy of Leica Geosystems Inc.,
Norcross, Ga.)

(RPU; see Figure 7.30). The RPU consists of the pole (with circular bubble), the prism, a data collector (up to 10,000 points), telemetry equipment for communicating with the station instrument, and a sighting telescope that, when aimed back at the station instrument, permits a sensing of the angle of inclination, which is then transmitted to the station instrument via radio communication. As a result, the instrument can move its telescope automatically to the proper angle of inclination, thus enabling the instrument to commence an automatic horizontal sweeping that results in the station instrument being locked precisely onto the prism.

A typical operation requires that the station unit be placed over a control station or over a free station whose coordinates can be determined using resection techniques (see Section 7.10.3) and that a backsight be taken to another control point, thus fixing the location and orientation of the total station. The operation then begins with both units being activated at the RPU. The RPU sighting telescope is aimed at the station unit, and the sensed vertical angle is sent via telemetry to the station unit. The station unit then sets its telescope automatically at the correct angle in the vertical plane and begins a horizontal search for the RPU. The search area can be limited to a specific sector (for example, 70°), thus reducing search time. The limiting range of this instrument is about 700 m. When the measurements (angle and distance) have been completed, the point number and attribute data codes can be entered into the data collector attached to the prism pole.

When used for setting out, the desired point number is entered at the RPU. The total station instrument then automatically turns the required angle, which it computes from previously uploaded coordinates held in storage (both the total station and the RPU have the points in storage). The RPU operator can position the prism roughly on-line by noting

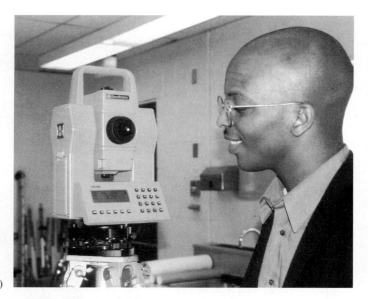

(a)

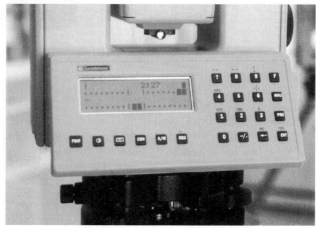

(b)

**FIGURE 7.29** (a) Geodimeter 4400 Base Station. A total station equipped with servo motors controlling both the horizontal and vertical circle movements. Can be used alone as a conventional total station or as a robotic base station controlled by the RPU operator. (b) Geodimeter keyboard showing in-process electronic leveling. Upper cursor can also be centered by finally adjusting the third leveling screw.

the Track-Light®, which shows as red or green (for this instrument), depending on whether the operator is left or right of the line, and as white when the operator is on the line (see also the EGL1® guidelight shown in Figure 7.27).

Distance and angle read-outs are then observed by the operator to position the prism pole precisely at the layout point location. The unit can fast-track (0.4 s) precise measurements and it can average multiple measurement readings, so very precise results can be obtained when using the prism pole by slightly "waving" the pole left and right and back and forth in a deliberate pattern. Since all but the backsight reference are obtained using infrared and telemetry, the system can be used effectively after dark, permitting nighttime layouts for next-day construction and for surveys in high-volume traffic areas that can be accomplished efficiently only in low-volume time periods. Figure 7.31(a) shows a

**FIGURE 7.30** Remote positioning unit (RPU)—a combination of prism, data collector, and radio communicator (with the base station) that permits the operator to engage in one-person surveys. (Courtesy of Geodimeter of Canada)

(a)

(b)

**FIGURE 7.31** (a) Leica TPS System 1000, used for roadway stakeout. Surveyor is controlling the remote-controlled total station (TCA 1100) at the prism pole using the RCS 1000 controller together with a radio modem. Assistant is placing steel bar marker at previous set-out point. (Courtesy of Leica Geosystems Inc., Norcross, Ga.) (b) Zeiss ELTA S 10 motorized total station. (Courtesy of Carl Zeiss Inc., Thornwood, N.Y.)

remotely controlled total station manufactured by Leica Geosystems Incorporated. This system utilizes ATR and the EGL1® to search for and then position the prism on the correct layout line, where the operator then notes the angle and distance read-outs to determine the precise layout location.

Figure 7.31(b) shows a motorized total station manufactured by Carl Zeiss, Inc. It has many features, including remote control through RecLink-S radio control, FineLock (a coaxial prism sensor that quickly locks precisely on the target prism), PositionLight (a multicolored beam that provides a fast technique of positioning the prism holder in setting-out jobs), a full complement of computational and setting-out software in the DOS-based system, and a large display screen, together with a QWERTY keyboard. These instruments come with a 1-second accuracy (ELTA S 10) or a 3-second accuracy (ELTA S 20).

## 7.15 Overview of Computerized Surveying Data Systems

Advances in computer science have had a tremendous impact on all aspects of modern technology. The effects on construction and engineering surveying have been significant. In the previous section, we saw how this new technology changed the way field data can be collected and processed. To appreciate the full impact of this new technology, one has to view the overall operation, that is, from field to computer, computer processing, and data portrayal in the form of maps and plans. Figure 7.32 gives a schematic overview of an integrated survey data system.

### 7.15.1 Data-Gathering Components

The upper portion of the Figure 7.32 schematic shows the various ways that data can be collected and transferred to the computer. In addition to the total station techniques already described, field surveys can be performed using conventional surveying instruments (theodolites, EDMs, and levels), with the field data entered into a data collector instead of conventional field books. This manual entry of field data lacks the speed associated with interfaced equipment, but after the data have been entered, all the advantages of electronic techniques are available to the surveyor. The raw field data, collected and stored by the total station, are transferred to the computer through a standard RS 232 interface connection. The raw data download program is supplied by the manufacturer, but the program required to translate the raw data into properly formatted field data is the responsibility of the surveyor.

At this stage, coordinate geometry programs can be used to calculate traverse closures and adjust all acceptable data into Y, X, and Z values. If only topography was taken, there may be no need for adjustments, and the program can compute the required coordinates directly. Also at this stage, additional data points (e.g., inaccessible ground points) can be computed and added to the data file. Figure 7.33(a) shows the translated field data and Figure 7.33(b) shows the computed point coordinates. The instrument location (OCC) coordinates and the backsight (BS) orientation can be entered into the data collector at the commencement of the survey, or they can be entered in a computer file, where they can be accessed directly for data processing. The data in Figure 7.33 are based on the survey shown in Figure 7.21.

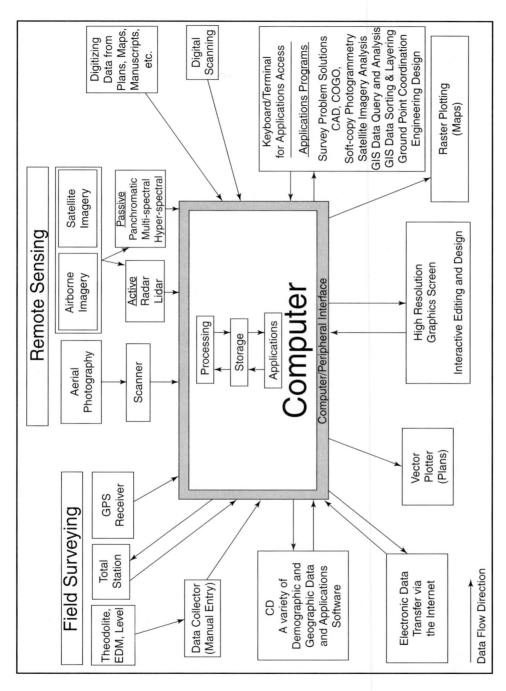

**FIGURE 7.32**  Geomatics data model, showing the collection, processing, analysis, design, and plotting of geodata.

| CODE | NUM | hi/HT | HCR | VCR | SDIST | OFFSET | LABEL |
|------|-----|-------|-----|-----|-------|--------|-------|
| OCC | 111 | 1.528 | | | | | *CM |
| BS | 114 | 1.222 | 0.0000 | 90.2025 | 211.723 | 0.000 | *CM |
| FS | 112 | 1.365 | 91.5532 | 88.1458 | 261.271 | 0.000 | *CM |
| IS | 1000 | 1.528 | 262.4514 | 92.1323 | 41.247 | 0.000 | *EDGE WATER |
| IS | 1001 | 1.528 | 277.1412 | 91.3404 | 58.478 | 0.550 | *EDGE WATER |
| IS | 1002 | 1.528 | 284.5856 | 90.2455 | 220.767 | 0.000 | *EDGE WATER |
| IS | 1003 | 1.528 | 341.5254 | 90.2225 | 245.444 | 0.000 | *EDGE WATER |
| IS | 1004 | 1.528 | 5.4526 | 90.1816 | 301.247 | 0.000 | *EDGE WATER |

(a)

| PTNUM | NORTHING | EASTING | ELEVATION | LABEL |
|-------|----------|---------|-----------|-------|
| 111 | 1000.000N | 1000.000E | 100.000 | CM |
| 112 | 991.225N | 1261.001E | 108.149 | CM |
| 114 | 1211.723N | 1000.000E | 98.743 | CM |
| 1000 | 994.801N | 959.113E | 98.400 | EDGE WATER |
| 1001 | 1007.433N | 941.464E | 98.400 | EDGE WATER |
| 1002 | 1057.071N | 786.743E | 98.403 | EDGE WATER |
| 1003 | 1233.269N | 923.673E | 98.404 | EDGE WATER |
| 1004 | 1299.723N | 1030.219E | 98.406 | EDGE WATER |

(b)

**FIGURE 7.33** Translated field data with computed coordinates. (a) Translated field data. (b) Northings, eastings, and elevations as computed by the coordinate geometry programs.

Existing maps and plans have a wealth of lower-precision data that may be relevant for an area survey. If such maps and plans are available, the data can be digitized on a digitizing table or by digital scanners and added to the Y, X, and Z coordinate files. In addition to distances and elevations, the digitizer can provide codes, identifications, and other attribute data for each digitized point. Two of the more important features of the digitizer are its abilities to digitize maps and plans at various scales and to store the distances and elevations in the computer at their ground (or grid) values. (See Chapter 8.)

The stereo analysis of aerial photos is a very effective method of collecting topographic ground data, particularly in high-density areas, where the costs for conventional surveys would be high. Many municipalities fly all major roads routinely and develop plans and profiles that can be used for design and construction (see Chapter 14). With the advent of computerized surveying systems, the stereoanalyzers can coordinate all horizontal and vertical features and transfer these Y, X, and Z coordinates to computer storage.

Satellite imagery is received from the U.S. (EOS and Landsat), French, European, Japanese, Canadian, Chinese, and South American satellites and can be processed by a digital image analysis system that classifies terrain into categories of soil, rock types, and vegetation cover. These and other data can be digitized and added to the computer storage. See Chapter 12. Finally, precise position location can be determined by satellite observations. The United States has established a system of positioning satellites called NAVSTAR, which was originally developed for military navigational purposes. The NAVSTAR system of positioning has revolutionized the way control surveys are performed (see Chapter 12).

In this section, several different ways of collecting topographic (and control) ground data have been outlined. The one element that they all have in common is that they are all computer-based. Thus, all the ground data for a specific area can be collected and stored in one computer but is available to many potential users. The collected data for an area are known as the data base for that area.

## 7.15.2 Data-Processing Components of the System

The central portion of the schematic in Figure 7.32 depicts the data-processing components of the system. Initially, as already described, the total station data can be closed and adjusted by means of various coordinate geometry programs. Missing data positions can also be computed by using various intersection, resection, and interpolation techniques, with the resultant coordinates added to the data base. If the data are to be plotted, a plot file may be created that contains point plot commands (including symbols) and join commands for straight and curved lines. Labels and other attribute data are also included (see Chapter 8).

Design programs are available for most construction endeavors. These programs can work with the stored coordinates to provide various possible designs, which can then be analyzed quickly with respect to costs and other factors. Some design programs incorporate interactive graphics, which permit a plot of the survey to be shown to scale on a high-resolution graphics screen. Points and lines can be moved, created, edited, and so forth, with the final positions coordinated right on the screen and the new coordinates added to the coordinate files. See Chapter 8 for information on digital plotting.

## Questions

1. How did the invention of electronic distance measurement (EDM) affect the field of surveying?
2. What impact did the creation of electronic angle measurement have on surveying procedures?
3. Explain the importance of electronic surveying in the field of surveying.

## Problems

7.1 To verify the constant of a particular prism, a straight line $EFG$ is laid out. The EDM instrument is first set up at $E$, with the following measurements recorded:

$$EG = 586.645 \text{ m} \qquad EF = 298.717 \text{ m}$$

The EDM instrument is then set up at $F$, where distance $FG$ is recorded as 287.958 m. Determine the prism constant.

7.2 The EDM slope distance between two points is 5,170.11 ft, and the vertical angle is $+2°45'30''$. The vertical angles were read at both ends of the line and then averaged using a co-axial theodolite/EDM combination. If the elevation of the instrument station is 630.15 ft and the heights of the theodolite/EDM and the target/reflector are all equal to 5.26 ft, compute the elevation of the target station and the horizontal distance to that station.

**7.3**  A line *AB* is measured at both ends as follows:

> ⊼ at *A*, slope distance = 1879.209 m, vertical angle = +1°26′50″
>
> ⊼ at *B*, slope distance = 1879.230 m, vertical angle = −1°26′38″

The heights of the instrument, reflector, and target are equal for each observation.
**(a)** Compute the horizontal distance *AB*.
**(b)** If the elevation at *A* is 181.302 m, what is the elevation at *B*?

**7.4**  A co-axial EDM instrument at station K (elevation = 241.69 ft) is used to sight stations *L, M,* and *N,* with the heights of the instrument, target, and reflector equal for each sighting. The results are as follows:

> ⊼ at STA. *L*, vertical angle = +3°30′, EDM distance = 2,000.00 ft
>
> ⊼ at STA. *M*, vertical angle = −1°30′, EDM distance = 2,000.00 ft
>
> ⊼ at STA. *N*, vertical angle = 0°00′, EDM distance = 3,000.00 ft

Compute the elevations of *L, M,* and *N,* correct for curvature and refraction.

**7.5**  Refer to Figure 7.12. A top-mounted EDM is set up at station A (elevation 110.222 m for this problem). Using the following values, compute the horizontal distance from *A* to *B* and the elevation of B. The optical center of the theodolite is 1.601 m (hi) above the station, and an angle of +4°18′30″ is measured to the target, which is 1.915 (HR) above station. The EDM instrument center is 0.100 m (Δhi) above the theodolite, and the reflecting prism is 0.150 m (ΔHR) above the target. The slope distance is measured to be 387.603 m.

**7.6**  Refer to Figure 7.12. A top-mounted EDM instrument is set up at station A (elevation 531.49 ft for this problem). Using the following values, compute the horizontal distance from *A* to *B* and the elevation of B. The optical center of the theodolite is 5.21 ft (hi) above the station, and an angle of +3°14′30″ is measured to the target, which is 5.78 ft (HR) above the station. The EDM instrument center is 0.31 ft (Δhi) above the theodolite, and the reflecting prism is 0.39 ft (ΔHR) above the target. The slope distance is recorded as 536.88 ft.

# Topographic Surveying and Mapping

## 8.1 General Background

**Mapping** and **drafting** are terms that cover a broad spectrum of scale graphics and related computations. With the rapid development of geographic information systems (GISs), which is discussed in Chapter 9, mapping has now become one of the products of the geodata collection, management, and analyses associated with GIS. Generally, **drafting** is a drawing term usually reserved for large- and intermediate-scale graphics (see Table 8.1) and is often encountered in surveying, engineering, and architectural applications in the preparation of plans. **Mapping** is a drawing term usually reserved for small-scale graphics, in the form of maps, often depicting topographic and boundary details of relatively large areas of the earth's surface. As noted in Chapter 7, when topographic surveys are undertaken using total stations, survey drafting is the responsibility of the field surveyor, who can prepare plot files using specific field codes that reflect the connecting or stringing characteristics of topographic features.

The essential difference between maps and plans is their use. As in an inventory, maps portray the detail (for example, topography, surface features, boundaries, etc.) for which they were designed. Maps can be of a general nature, such as the topographic maps compiled and published by the U.S. Geological Survey (scales normally ranging from 1:24,000 down to 1:1,000,000) or maps can be specific, showing only those data (for example, crop land inventory) for which they were designed (see also Chapter 9). Surveying plans, on the other hand, not only show existing terrain (or other) conditions, but they can also depict proposed alterations (i.e., designs) to the existing landscape. Most plans are drawn to a large scale, although comprehensive functional planning or route design plans for state and provincial highways can be drawn to a small scale (for example, 1:50,000) to give a bird's-eye view of a large study area.

**Table 8.1**   SUMMARY OF MAP AND PLAN SCALES AND CONTOUR INTERVALS

| | Metric scale | Foot/inch scale equivalents | | Contour interval for average terrain[a] | Typical uses |
|---|---|---|---|---|---|
| Large scale | 1:10<br>1:50<br>1:100<br>1:200<br>1:500<br>1:1,000 | $1'' = 1'$<br>$\frac{1}{4}'' = 1'$,<br>$\frac{1}{8}'' = 1'$,<br>$1'' = 20'$<br>$1'' = 40'$,<br>$1'' = 80'$, | $1'' = 5'$<br>$1'' = 10, 1'' = 8'$<br><br>$1'' = 50'$<br>$1'' = 100'$ | 0.5 m, 1 ft<br>1 m, 2 ft | Detail<br>Detail<br>Detail, profiles<br>Profiles<br>Municipal design plans<br>Municipal services and site engineering |
| Intermediate scale | 1:2,000<br>1:5,000<br>1:10,000 | $1'' = 200'$<br>$1'' = 400'$<br>$1'' = 800'$ | | 2 m, 5 ft<br>5 m, 10 ft<br>10 m, 20 ft | Engineering studies and planning (e.g., drainage areas, route planning) |
| Small scale | 1:20,000<br>1:25,000<br>1:50,000<br><br>1:100,000<br><br>1:200,000<br>1:250,000<br>1:500,000<br>1:1,000,000 | 1:25,000,<br><br>1:63,360,<br><br>1:126,720,<br><br><br>1:250,000,<br>1:625,000,<br>1:1,000,000, | $2\frac{1}{2}'' = 1$ mi<br><br>$1'' = 1$ mi<br><br>$\frac{1}{2}'' = 1$ mi<br><br><br>$\frac{1}{4}'' = 1$ mi<br>$\frac{1}{10}'' = 1$ mi<br>$\frac{1}{16}'' = 1$ mi | | Topographic maps, Canada and United States<br>Geological maps, Canada and United States<br>Special-purpose maps and atlases (e.g., climate, minerals) |

[a]The contour interval chosen must reflect the scale of the plan or map, but the terrain (flat or steeply inclined) and intended use of the plan are also factors in choosing the appropriate contour interval.

The techniques of plan and map preparation have now become digital based, with the maps and plans composed and edited on computers and the drawings produced on digital plotters. The mechanical techniques of mapping and quantity estimates are presented here to give you a foundation in the logic behind the computer programs now controlling this process. Table 8.1 summarizes typical scales and appropriate contour intervals; Table 8.2 shows standard drawing sizes.

## 8.2   Maps and Plans

The traditional techniques of producing maps and plans is included to show how survey data, obtained from either ground or aerial surveys, can be portrayed manually in scale drawings. The reproduction of maps traditionally involved photographing the finished inked or scribed map and preparing a printing plate from the negative. Lithographic offset printing was used to create the maps. Multicolor maps required a separate plate for each

**Table 8.2**  STANDARD DRAWING SIZES

| | International Standards Organization (ISO) | | | | | | ACSM[a] recommendations | |
| | Inch drawing sizes | | | Metric drawing sizes (mm) | | | | |
| Drawing size | Border size | Overall paper size | | Drawing size | Border size | Overall paper size | Drawing size | Paper size |
|---|---|---|---|---|---|---|---|---|
| A | 8.00 × 10.50 | 8.50 × 11.00 | | A4 | 195 × 282 | 210 × 297 | — | 150 × 200 |
| B | 10.50 × 16.50 | 11.00 × 17.00 | | A3 | 277 × 400 | 297 × 420 | A4 | 200 × 300 |
| C | 16.00 × 21.00 | 17.00 × 22.00 | | A2 | 400 × 574 | 420 × 594 | A3 | 300 × 400 |
| D | 21.00 × 33.00 | 22.00 × 34.00 | | A1 | 574 × 821 | 594 × 841 | A2 | 400 × 600 |
| E | 33.00 × 43.00 | 34.00 × 44.00 | | A0 | 811 × 1,159 | 841 × 1,189 | A1 | 600 × 800 |
| | | | | | | | A0 | 800 × 1,200 |

[a]American Congress on Surveying and Mapping Metric Workshop. March 14, 1975. Paper sizes rounded off for simplicity, still have cut-in-half characteristic.

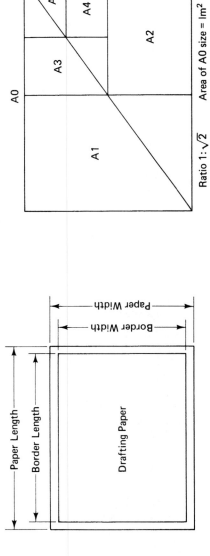

Ratio $1:\sqrt{2}$     Area of A0 size = $1\text{m}^2$

Metric Drawing Paper

245

color, although shading can be accomplished with screens. Modern techniques use digital plotters to convert computer data (vector or raster formats) to produce the desired graphics.

**Scribing** is a cartographic mapping technique in which the map details are cut directly onto drafting film that has a soft, opaque coating. This scribed film takes the place of a photographic negative in the photolithography printing process. Scribing was preferred by many because of the sharp definition made possible by this cutting technique. Plans, on the other hand, are reproduced in an entirely different manner. The completed plan, in ink or pencil, can simply be run through a direct-contact negative printing machine (blueprint) or a direct-contact positive printing machine (whiteprint). The whiteprint machine now in use in most drafting and design offices uses paper sensitized with diazo compounds that, when exposed to light and ammonia vapor, produce prints. The quality of whiteprints cannot be compared to map-quality reproductions; however, the relatively inexpensive whiteprints are widely used in surveying and engineering offices where they function as working plans, customer copies, and contract plans. Although reproduction techniques are vastly different for maps and plans, the basic plotting procedures are quite similar.

## 8.3 Scales and Precision

Maps and plans are drawn so that a distance on the map or plan conforms to a set distance on the ground. The ratio (called scale) between plan distance and ground distance is consistent throughout the plan. Scales can be stated as equivalencies, for example, $1'' = 50'$ or $1'' = 1,000'$, or the same scales can be stated as representative fractions: 1:600 (1:50 $\times$ 12″) or 1:12,000 (1:1,000 $\times$ 12″). When representative fractions are used, all units are valid; that is, 1:500 is the same scale for inches, feet, meters, and so on. Only representative fractions are used in the metric (SI) system. Table 8.1 shows recommended map and plan scales and the equivalent scales in the foot-inch system. Almost all surveying work required for the production of intermediate and small-scale maps is done by aerial imaging, with the maps produced photogrammetrically (see Chapter 12).

Even in municipal areas, where services (roads, sewers, water) plans for housing developments can be drawn at 1:1,000 and plans for municipal streets are drawn at 1:500, it is not uncommon to have the surveys flown and the maps produced photogrammetrically. For street surveys, the surveying manager will have a good idea of the cost per kilometer or mile for various orders of urban density and will arrange for field or aerial surveys, depending on which method is deemed cost effective.

Before a field survey is undertaken, a clear understanding of the reason for the survey is necessary so that appropriately precise techniques can be employed. If the survey is required to locate points that will later be shown on a small-scale map, the precision of the survey will be of a very low order. Generally, points are located in the field with a precision that will at least be compatible with the plotting precision possible at the designated plan (map) scale. For example, if points can be plotted to the closest 0.5 mm (1/50 in.) at a scale of 1:500, this represents a plotting capability to the closest ground distance of 0.25 m (i.e., 0.0005 $\times$ 500), whereas at a scale of 1:20,000, the plotting capability is (20,000 $\times$ 0.0005) = 10 m of ground distance. In the former example, plotting capabilities indicate that a point should be tied into the closest 0.25 m. In reality, however, the point probably would be tied into a higher level of precision (for example, 0.1 m).

The following points should be kept in mind:

1. Some detail (for example, building corners, railway tracks, bridge beam seats, or other structural components) can be defined and located precisely.
2. Some detail (for example, stream banks, edges of a gravel road, ₵ of ditches, limits of a wooded area, rock outcrops, etc.) cannot be defined or located precisely.
3. Some detail (for example, large single trees, culverts, docks, etc.) can be located with only moderate precision using normal techniques.

Usually, the detail that is fairly well defined is located with more precision than is required just for plotting. The reasons are as follows:

1. As in the preceding example, it takes little (if any) extra effort to locate detail to 0.1 m than it would to locate it to 0.25 m.
2. By using the same techniques to locate all detail, as if all detail were precisely defined, the survey crew can develop uniform practices, which will reduce mistakes and increase efficiency.
3. Some location measurements taken in the field, and design parameters that may be based on those field measurements, are also shown on the plan as layout dimensions (that is, levels of precision are required that greatly supersede the precision required simply for plotting).

Most natural features are themselves not precisely defined. If a topographic survey is required in an area having only natural features (for example, stream or water-course surveys, site development surveys, large-scale mapping surveys), a relatively imprecise survey method such as aerial or satellite imaging can be employed.

All topographic surveys are tied into both horizontal and vertical (benchmarks) control. The horizontal control for topographic surveys can be comprised of closed-loop traverses, traverses from a coordinate grid monument closed to another coordinate grid monument, route centerline (₵), or some assumed baseline. The survey measurements used to establish the horizontal and vertical control are always taken more precisely than are the location ties.

Surveyors are conscious of the need for accurate and well-referenced survey control. If the control is inaccurate, the survey and resulting design will also be inaccurate; if the control is not well referenced, it will be costly (perhaps impossible) to relocate the control precisely in the field once it is lost. In addition to providing control for the original survey, the same survey control should be used if additional survey work is required to supplement the original survey, and of course the same survey control should be used for any construction layout resulting from designs based on the original survey.

# 8.4  Plan Plotting

## 8.4.1  General Background

The size of drafting paper required can be determined by knowing the scale to be used and the area or length of the survey. Standard paper sizes are shown in Table 8.2. The title

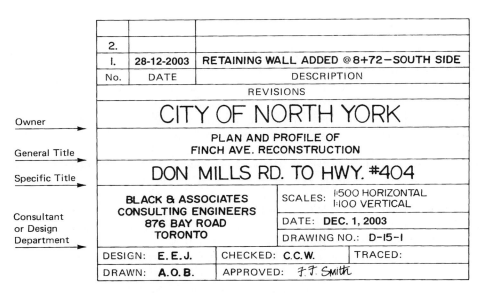

| 2. | | |
|---|---|---|
| I. | 28-12-2003 | RETAINING WALL ADDED @ 8+72—SOUTH SIDE |
| No. | DATE | DESCRIPTION |
| | | REVISIONS |

Owner →

## CITY OF NORTH YORK

General Title →

PLAN AND PROFILE OF
FINCH AVE. RECONSTRUCTION

Specific Title →

## DON MILLS RD. TO HWY. #404

Consultant
or Design
Department →

| BLACK & ASSOCIATES CONSULTING ENGINEERS 876 BAY ROAD TORONTO | SCALES: 1:500 HORIZONTAL 1:100 VERTICAL |
| | DATE: DEC. 1, 2003 |
| | DRAWING NO.: D-15-1 |

| DESIGN: E.E.J. | CHECKED: C.C.W. | TRACED: |
| DRAWN: A.O.B. | APPROVED: F.J. Smith | |

**FIGURE 8.1** Typical title block.

block is often a standard size and has a format similar to that shown in Figure 8.1. The block is often placed in the lower right corner of the plan, but placement often depends on the filing system. Revisions to the plan are usually referenced immediately above the title block, showing the date and a brief description of the revision. Many consulting firms and engineering departments attempt to limit the variety of their drawing sizes so that plan filing can be standardized. Some vertical-hold filing cabinets are designed so that title blocks in the upper right corner can be seen more easily.

Manual plotting begins by first plotting the survey control (for example, the ℄, traverse line, coordinate grid, etc.) on the drawing. The control is plotted so that the data plot will be centered suitably on the available paper. Sometimes the data outline is plotted roughly first on tracing paper so that the plan's overall dimension requirements can be oriented properly on the available drafting paper. It is customary to orient the data plot so that north is toward the top of the plan; a north arrow is included on all property survey plans (plats) and many engineering drawings. The north direction on maps is indicated clearly by lines of longitude or by NS, EW grid lines. The plan portion of the plan and profile does not usually have a north indication. Instead, local practice often dictates the direction of increasing stationing (e.g., stationing increasing left to right for west to east and south to north directions).

Chapter 7 described how field drafting is begun using connecting or "stringing" field coding as the data is recorded in the total station. Graphical data can then be edited and even created (from auxiliary data files) on an interactive graphics screen before being transferred to a CAD program for final presentation work and before being plotted on a digital plotter (see Section 8.4.2). Next, we will describe how the field data can be plotted manually.

Once the control has been plotted and checked, the features can be plotted with either rectangular ($X, Y$ coordinates) or polar (radial: $r$; $\theta$ coordinates) methods. Rectangular plots (*X*, *Y* coordinates) can be laid out with a T-square and set square, although the parallel rule has now largely replaced the T-square. When using either the parallel rule or the T-square, the paper is first set square and then secured with masking tape to the drawing board. Once the paper is square and secure, the parallel rule, together with a set square and scale, can be used to lay out and measure rectangular dimensions.

Polar plots are accomplished with a protractor and a scale. The protractor can be a plastic graduated circle or half-circle with various diameters (the larger the circle or half-circle, the more precise it will be), a paper full-circle protractor for use under or on the drafting paper, or a flexible-arm drafting machine complete with right-angle-mounted graduated scales. Field data that have been collected with polar techniques (e.g., theodolite/EDM or total station) can be plotted efficiently with polar techniques. See Figure 8.2 for standard map and plan symbols.

The techniques described here are still used in surveying and engineering applications; however, computer-based techniques, as described in Chapter 7, are quickly replacing manual techniques in most applications.

## 8.4.2 Digital Plotting

Once the plotting files have been established by working with CAD programs, data can be plotted in various ways. Data can be plotted onto a high-resolution graphics screen. The plot can be checked for completeness and accuracy. If interactive graphics are available, the plotted features can be deleted, enhanced, corrected, crosshatched, labeled, dimensioned, and so on. At this stage, a hard copy of the screen display can be printed either on a simple printer or on an ink-jet color printer. Plot files can be plotted directly on a digital plotter similar to the one shown in Figure 8.3. The resulting plan can be plotted to any desired scale, limited only by the paper size. Some plotters have only one or two pens, although plotters are available with four to eight pens; a variety of pens permits colored plotting or plotting using various line weights. Plans, and plan and profiles, drawn on digital plotters are becoming more common on construction sites. Automatic plotting (with a digital plotter) can be used when the field data have been coordinated and stored in computer memory. Coordinated field data are by-products of data collection by total stations, airborne imagery, satellite imagery, and digitized (or scanned) data from existing plans and maps (see Figure 7.32).

You can create a plot file that includes the following:

- Title
- Scale
- Limits (for example, the plot can be defined by the southwesterly coordinates, northerly range, and easterly range)
- Plot all points
- Connect specific points (through feature coding or CAD commands)
- Pen number (various pens can have different line weights or colors; two to four pens are common)
- Symbol (symbols are predesigned and stored by identification number in a symbol library)
- Height of characters (the heights of labels, text, coordinates, and symbols can be defined)

| | | | |
|---|---|---|---|
| Primary highway, hard surface | | Boundaries: National | |
| Secondary highway, hard surface | | State | |
| Light-duty road, hard or improved surface | | County, parish, municipio | |
| Unimproved road | | Civil township, precinct, town, barrio | |
| Road under construction, alignment known | | Incorporated city, village, town, hamlet | |
| Proposed road | | Reservation, National or State | |
| Dual highway, dividing strip 25 feet or less | | Small park, cemetery, airport, etc. | |
| Dual highway, dividing strip exceeding 25 feet | | Land grant | |
| Trail | | Township or range line, United States land survey | |

Township or range line, approximate location

| | | |
|---|---|---|
| Railroad: single track and multiple track | | Section line, United States land survey |
| Railroads in juxtaposition | | Section line, approximate location |
| Narrow gage: single track and multiple track | | Township line, not United States land survey |
| Railroad in street and carline | | Section line, not United States land survey |
| Bridge: road and railroad | | Found corner: section and closing |
| Drawbridge: road and railroad | | Boundary monument: land grant and other |
| Footbridge | | Fence or field line |
| Tunnel: road and railroad | | |
| Overpass and underpass | | |

| | |
|---|---|
| Small masonry or concrete dam | Index contour · · · · · Intermediate contour |
| Dam with lock | Supplementary contour · · · Depression contours |
| Dam with road | Fill · · · · · · Cut |
| Canal with lock | Levee · · · · · Levee with road |
| | Mine dump · · · · · Wash |
| Buildings (dwelling, place of employment, etc.) | Tailings · · · · · Tailings pond |
| School, church, and cemetery | Shifting sand or dunes · · · Intricate surface |
| Buildings (barn, warehouse, etc.) | Sand area · · · · · Gravel beach |

| | |
|---|---|
| Power transmission line with located metal tower | Perennial streams · · · Intermittent streams |
| Telephone line, pipeline, etc. (labeled as to type) | Elevated aqueduct · · · Aqueduct tunnel |
| Wells other than water (labeled as to type) · · · oOil · · oGas | Water well and spring · · Glacier |
| Tanks: oil, water, etc. (labeled only if water) · · · Water | Small rapids · · · · Small falls |
| Located or landmark object; windmill | Large rapids · · · · Large falls |
| Open pit, mine, or quarry; prospect · · · · × · · · · x | Intermittent lake · · · Dry lake bed |
| Shaft and tunnel entrance | Foreshore flat · · · · Rock or coral reef |
| | Sounding, depth curve · · · Piling or dolphin |
| Horizontal and vertical control station: | Exposed wreck · · · · Sunken wreck |
| | Rock, bare or awash; dangerous to navigation |

| | |
|---|---|
| Tablet, spirit level elevation · · · · · BM △ 5653 | |
| Other recoverable mark, spirit level elevation · · · △ 5455 | |
| Horizontal control station: tablet, vertical angle elevation VABM △ 95/9 | Marsh (swamp) · · · · Submerged marsh |
| Any recoverable mark, vertical angle or checked elevation △3775 | Wooded marsh · · · · Mangrove |
| Vertical control station: tablet, spirit level elevation · · · · BM × 957 | Woods or brushwood · · · Orchard |
| Other recoverable mark, spirit level elevation · · · · · · × 954 | Vineyard · · · · · Scrub |
| Spot elevation · · · · · × 7369 × 7369 | Land subject to |
| Water elevation · · · · · 670 670 | controlled inundation · · · Urban area |

(a)

**FIGURE 8.2** (a) Topographic map symbols. (Courtesy of U.S. Department of Interior, Geological Survey).

250

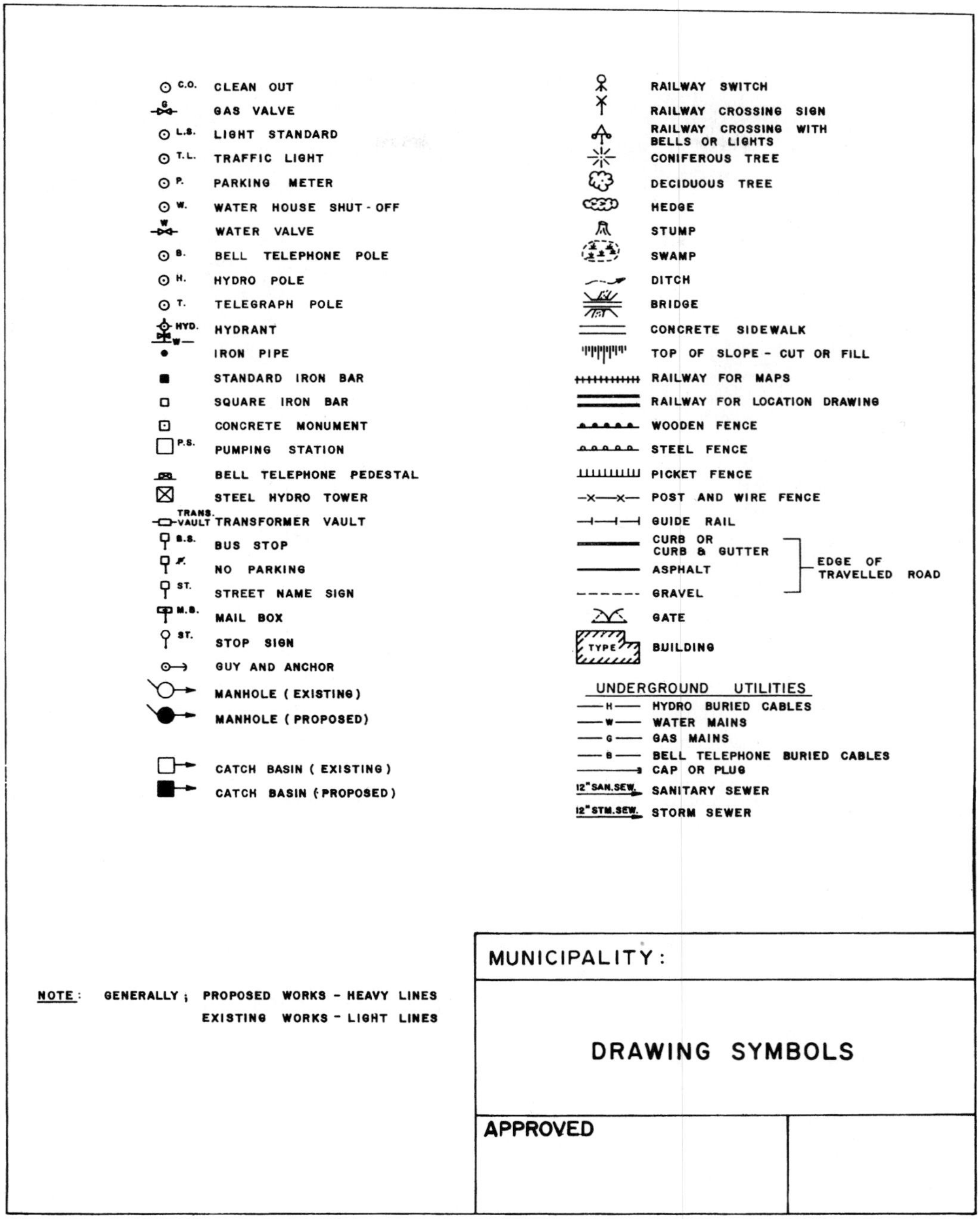

| | | | |
|---|---|---|---|
| ⊙ C.O. | CLEAN OUT | ⊼ | RAILWAY SWITCH |
| GAS VALVE | | RAILWAY CROSSING SIGN | |
| ⊙ L.S. | LIGHT STANDARD | | RAILWAY CROSSING WITH BELLS OR LIGHTS |
| ⊙ T.L. | TRAFFIC LIGHT | | CONIFEROUS TREE |
| ⊙ P. | PARKING METER | | DECIDUOUS TREE |
| ⊙ W. | WATER HOUSE SHUT-OFF | | HEDGE |
| WATER VALVE | | STUMP | |
| ⊙ B. | BELL TELEPHONE POLE | | SWAMP |
| ⊙ H. | HYDRO POLE | | DITCH |
| ⊙ T. | TELEGRAPH POLE | | BRIDGE |
| HYD. | HYDRANT | | CONCRETE SIDEWALK |
| • | IRON PIPE | | TOP OF SLOPE - CUT OR FILL |
| ■ | STANDARD IRON BAR | | RAILWAY FOR MAPS |
| □ | SQUARE IRON BAR | | RAILWAY FOR LOCATION DRAWING |
| □ | CONCRETE MONUMENT | | WOODEN FENCE |
| □ P.S. | PUMPING STATION | | STEEL FENCE |
| | BELL TELEPHONE PEDESTAL | | PICKET FENCE |
| ⊠ | STEEL HYDRO TOWER | | POST AND WIRE FENCE |
| TRANS. VAULT | TRANSFORMER VAULT | | GUIDE RAIL |
| B.S. | BUS STOP | | CURB OR CURB & GUTTER |
| | NO PARKING | | ASPHALT |
| ST. | STREET NAME SIGN | | GRAVEL |
| M.B. | MAIL BOX | | GATE |
| ST. | STOP SIGN | | BUILDING |
| | GUY AND ANCHOR | | |
| | MANHOLE (EXISTING) | | UNDERGROUND UTILITIES |
| | MANHOLE (PROPOSED) | — H — | HYDRO BURIED CABLES |
| | | — W — | WATER MAINS |
| | | — G — | GAS MAINS |
| | | — B — | BELL TELEPHONE BURIED CABLES |
| □ | CATCH BASIN (EXISTING) | | CAP OR PLUG |
| ■ | CATCH BASIN (PROPOSED) | 12" SAN.SEW. | SANITARY SEWER |
| | | 12" STM.SEW. | STORM SEWER |

NOTE: GENERALLY ; PROPOSED WORKS – HEAVY LINES
EXISTING WORKS – LIGHT LINES

MUNICIPALITY:

DRAWING SYMBOLS

APPROVED

(b)

**FIGURE 8.2 (continued)** (b) Municipal works plan symbols, including typical title block. (Courtesy of Municipal Engineers Association, Ontario)

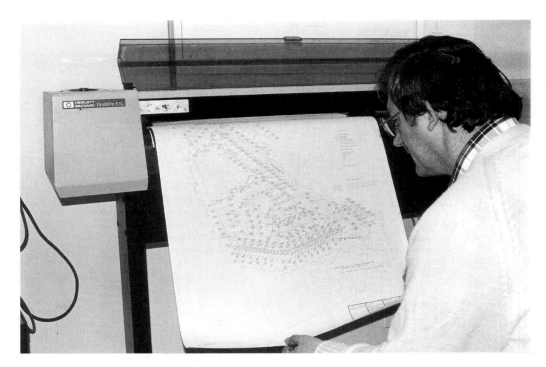

**FIGURE 8.3**  Land division plot on a Hewlett-Packard 8-pen digital plotter.

The actual plotting can be performed by simply keying in the plot command required by the specific computer program and then by keying in (or selecting) the name of the plot file to be plotted.

The coordinated field point files can also be transferred to an interactive graphics terminal (see Figure 8.4), with the survey plot created and edited graphically right on the high-resolution graphics screen. Some surveying software programs have this graphics capability, whereas others permit coordinate files to be transferred easily to an independent graphics program (i.e., CAD) using a dxf-type format for later editing and plotting. Once the plot has been completed on the graphics screen (and all the point coordinates have been stored in the computer), the plot can be transferred to a digital plotter for final presentation.

This latter technique is now being used successfully in a wide variety of applications. In the not-too-distant future (as costs continue to decrease), most survey data processing will be handled in this or a similar manner. The savings in time and money are too great to be overlooked, especially when the actual engineering or construction design can be accomplished on the same graphics terminal, with all design elements also stored in the computer files and all construction drawings produced on the digital plotter.

## 8.5  Contours

Contours are lines drawn on a plan that connect points having similar elevations. Contour lines represent an even elevation value (see Table 8.1), with the contour interval selected

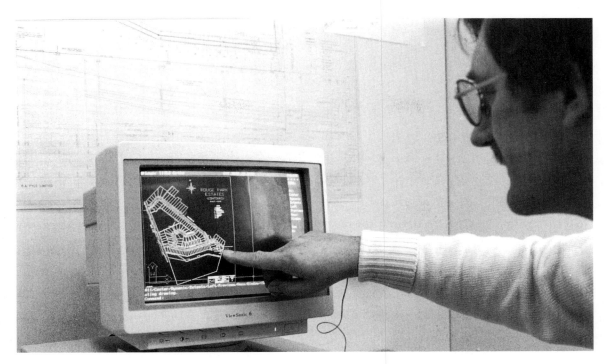

**FIGURE 8.4**  Land division design and editing on a desktop computer.

for terrain, scale, and intended use of the plan. It is common for elevations to be determined to half the contour interval; this convention permits, for example, a 10-ft contour interval on a plan where it is required to know elevations to the closest 5 ft.

Contours are manually plotted by scaling between two adjacent points of known elevation (assuming that a uniform slope exists between these points). In Figure 8.5(a), the scaled distance (any scale can be used) between points 1 and 2 is 0.75 units, and the difference in elevation is 5.4 ft. The difference in elevation between point 1 and contour line 565 is 2.7 ft; therefore, the distance from point 1 to contour line 565 is:

$$\frac{2.7}{5.4} \times 0.75 = 0.38 \text{ units}$$

To verify this computation, the distance from contour line 565 to point 2 is:

$$\frac{2.7}{5.4} \times 0.75 = 0.38 \text{ units} \qquad 0.38 + 0.38 \approx 0.75 \qquad \text{Check}$$

The scaled distance between points 3 and 4 is 0.86 units, and their difference in elevation is 5.2 ft. The difference in elevation between point 3 and contour line 565 is 1.7 ft; therefore, the distance from point 3 to contour line 565 is:

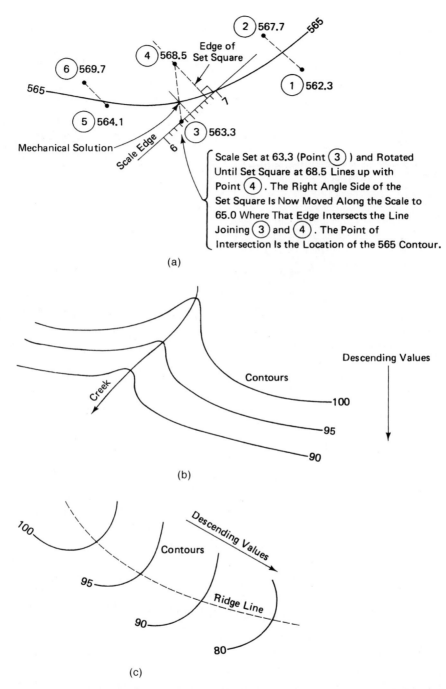

(a)

(b)

(c)

**FIGURE 8.5** Contours. (a) Plotting contours by interpolation. (b) Valley line. (c) Ridge line.

$$\frac{1.7}{5.2} \times 0.86 = 0.28 \text{ units}$$

This result can be verified by computing the distance from contour line 565 to point 4:

$$\frac{3.5}{5.2} \times 0.86 = 0.58 \text{ units} \qquad 0.58 + 0.28 = 0.86 \qquad \text{Check}$$

The scaled distance between points 5 and 6 is 0.49 units, and the difference in elevation is 5.6 ft. The difference in elevation between point 5 and contour line 565 is 0.9 ft; therefore, the distance from point 5 to contour line 565 is:

$$\frac{0.9}{5.6} \times 0.49 = 0.08 \text{ units}$$

and from line 565 to point 6, the distance is:

$$\frac{4.7}{5.6} \times 0.49 = 0.41 \text{ units}$$

In addition to the foregoing arithmetic solution, contours can be interpolated with mechanical techniques. It is possible to scale off units on a barely taut elastic band and then stretch the elastic so that the marked-off units fit the interval being analyzed. The contour elevation problem can also be solved by rotating a scale while using a set square to line up the appropriate divisions with the field points. In Figure 8.5(a), a scale is set at 63.3 on point 3 and then rotated until the 68.5 mark lines up with point 4 using a set square on the scale. The set square is then slid along the scale until it lines up with 65.0; the intersection of the set square edge (90° to the scale) with the straight line joining points 3 and 4 yields the solution (that is, the location of elevation at 565 ft). This technique is faster than the arithmetic technique.

Because contours are plotted by analyzing adjacent field points, it is essential that the ground slope be uniform between those points. An experienced survey crew will ensure that enough rod readings are taken to define the ground surface suitably. The survey crew can further define the terrain if care is taken in identifying and tying in valley lines, ridge lines, ditch lines, top/bottom of slope lines, etc. These are often referred to as *break lines*.

Figure 8.5(b) shows how contour lines bend uphill as they cross a valley; the steeper the valley, the more the line diverges uphill. Figure 8.5(c) shows how contour lines bend downhill as they cross ridge lines. Figure 8.6 shows the plot of control, elevations, and valley and ridge lines. Figure 8.7 shows contours interpolated from the data in Figure 8.6. Figure 8.8(b) shows the completed plan, with additional detail (roads and buildings) also shown. Figure 8.8(a) shows typical field notes for a stadia survey. Figure 8.8(c) shows a contour plan and a derived profile line (*AB*).

Contours are now almost exclusively produced using any of the current software programs. Most software programs generate a triangulated irregular network (TIN); the sides of the triangles are analyzed so that contour crossings can be interpolated. The field surveyor must also note and mark *break lines* that define significant changes in topography (for example, the tops and bottoms of hills, channels, depressions, creeks, etc.) so that the

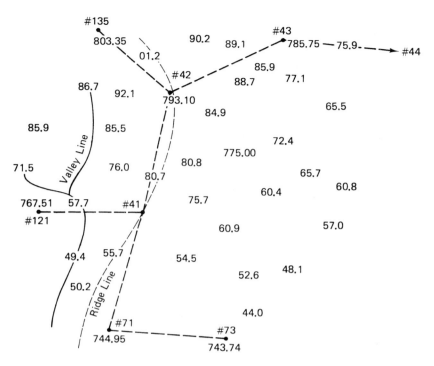

**FIGURE 8.6** Plot of survey control, ridge and valley lines, and spot elevations.

software program can generate contours that reflect actual field conditions accurately. Break lines will show up as TIN edges in TIN surface models [see Figure 8.9(a)].

Figure 8.9 shows the steps in a typical contour production process. Two basic methods have been used: the uniform grid approach and the more popular TIN approach (used here). First, the triangulated irregular network (TIN) is created from the plotted points and defined break lines [Figure 8.9(a)] and then the raw contours [Figure 8.9(b)] are computer-generated from that data. To make the contours pleasing to the eye, as well as representative of the ground surface, some form of ground-true smoothing technique must be used to soften the sharp angles occurring when contours are generated from TINs (as opposed to the less angular lines resulting in contours derived from a uniform grid approach). For more on this topic, refer to Christensen, A. H. J., "Contour Smoothing by an Eclectic Procedure," *Photogrammetric Engineering and Remote Sensing (RE&RS)*, April 2001: 516.

# 8.6 Summary of Contour Characteristics

The following list summarizes the characteristics of contours:

1. Closely spaced contours indicate steep slopes.

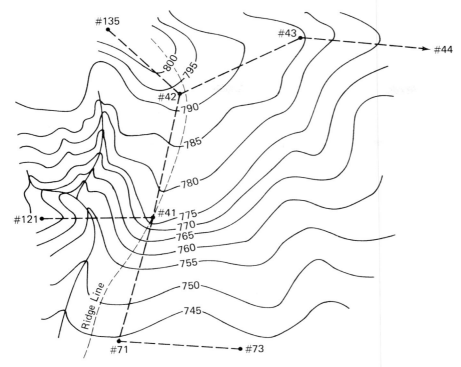

**FIGURE 8.7** Contours plotted by interpolating between spot elevations, with additional plotting information given when the locations of ridge and valley lines are known.

2. Widely spaced contours indicate moderate slopes (spacing here is a relative relationship).

3. Contours must be labeled to give the elevation value. Either each line is labeled, or every fifth line is drawn darker (wider) and it is labeled.

4. Contours are not shown going through buildings.

5. Contours crossing a human-made horizontal surface (roads, railroads) will be straight parallel lines as they cross the facility.

6. Because contours join points of equal elevation, contour lines cannot cross (caves present an exception).

7. Contour lines cannot begin or end on the plan.

8. Depressions and hills look the same; you must note the contour value to distinguish the terrain. (Some agencies use hachures or shading to identify depressions.)

9. Contours deflect uphill at valley lines and downhill at ridge lines. Line crossings are perpendicular: U-shaped for ridge crossings; V-shaped for valley crossings.

10. Contour lines must close on themselves, either on the plan or in locations off the plan.

**Example:** Station 42   Elevation 793.10 m   Instr. Theodolite/EDM

| Point | Horizontal Angle | Horizontal Distance | Difference in Elevation | Elevation |
|-------|------------------|---------------------|-------------------------|-----------|
| 42    |                  |                     |                         | 793.10    |
| 41    | 00.0             | 197.80              | − 17.30                 | 775.80    |
| 43    | 232 25.2         | 199.10              | − 7.35                  | 785.75    |
| 135   | 120 05.2         | 145.20              | + 10.25                 | 803.35    |
| a     | 234 50           | 76.10               | − 2.60                  | 790.50    |
| b     | 247 10           | 76.30               |                         | 793.10    |
| c     | 277 22           | 85.30               | − 8.20                  | 784.90    |
| d     | 322 10           | 100.50              | − 7.60                  | 785.50    |
| etc.  |                  |                     |                         |           |

(a)

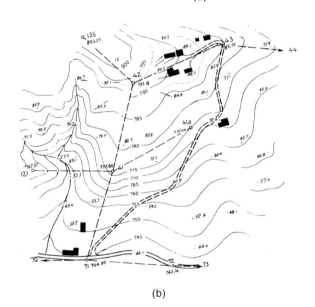

**FIGURE 8.8** (a) Survey field notes. (b) Plan plotted from notes shown in Figures 8.6, 8.7, and 8.8(a). (Courtesy of Leica Co. Ltd.)

(b)

11. The ground slope between contour lines is uniform. Had the ground slope not been uniform between the points, additional elevation readings would have been taken at the time of the survey.

12. Important points can be further defined by including a "spot" elevation (height elevation).

13. Contour lines tend to parallel each other on uniform slopes.

In addition to contours, some software programs provide three-dimensional perspective plots to portray the landscape as viewed from any azimuth position and from various altitudes. See Figure 8.10.

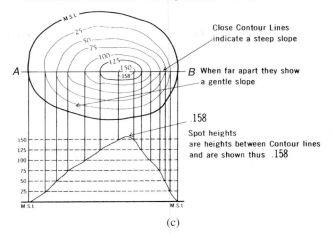

## CONTOUR LINES

These are drawn through points having the same elevation. They show the height of ground above sea level (M.S.L.) in either feet or metres and can be drawn at any desired interval.

Close Contour Lines indicate a steep slope

When far apart they show a gentle slope

.158
Spot heights are heights between Contour lines and are shown thus .158

**FIGURE 8.8 *(continued)*** (c) Contour plan with derived profile (line *AB*). (Courtesy of Department of Energy, Mines, and Resources, Canada)

(c)

# 8.7 Topographic Surveys

## 8.7.1 General Background

**Topographic surveys** determine the position of natural and human-made features, for example, trees, shorelines, roads, sewers, buildings, etc. These features can then be drawn to scale on a plan or map. In addition, topographic surveys include the determination of ground elevations, which can later be drawn on plans or maps for the construction of contours, or plotted in the form of cross sections and profiles.

The vast majority of topographic surveys are now performed using aerial surveying techniques, with the plans and digital elevation models (DEMs) constructed using modern computerized photogrammetric, or laser imaging, techniques as described in Chapter 12. Smaller surveys are often performed using electronic equipment, such as total stations. The horizontal location (*X* and *Y*) and the vertical (elevation) location (*Z*) can be captured easily with one sighting, with point descriptions and other attribute data entered into electronic storage for later transfer to the computer. Electronic surveying techniques were discussed in detail in Chapter 7.

The focus here will be on the rectangular and polar surveying techniques, first introduced in Section 1.12, employing pre-electronic field techniques. The rectangular technique discussed here utilizes right-angle offsets for detail location and cross sections for elevations and profiles. The polar technique discussed here utilizes theodolite/EDM techniques for both horizontal location and elevation capture and contours for elevation depiction.

## 8.7.2 Feature Locations by Right-Angle Offsets

Many traditional topographic surveys, excluding mapping surveys but including many pre-engineering surveys, use the right-angle offset technique to locate detail. This technique

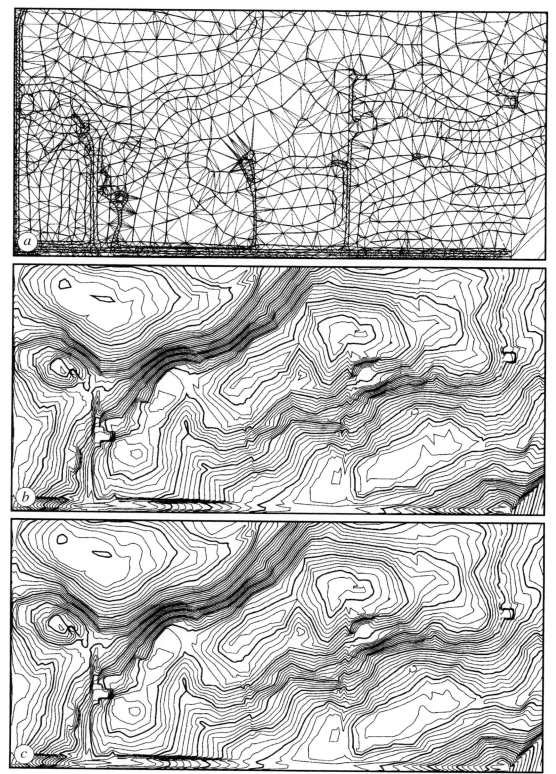

**FIGURE 8.9** Contouring (a) Break lines and TIN. (b) Raw contours. (c) Contours smoothing with the eclectic procedure. (Reproduced with permission, the American Society for Photogrammetry and Remote Sensing. A. H. J. Christensen, "Contour Smoothing by an Eclectic Procedure." *Photogrammetric Engineering and Remote Sensing [RE&RS]*. April 2001:516.)

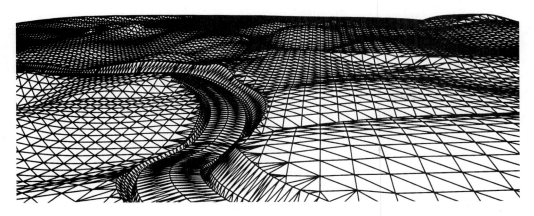

**FIGURE 8.10**  QuickSurfTGRID showing smoothed, rolling terrain coupled with road definition. (Courtesy of MicroSurvey Software Inc., Westbank, B.C., Canada)

**FIGURE 8.11**  Double right-angle prism. (Courtesy of Keuffel & Esser Co.)

not only provides the location of plan detail but also provides location for area elevations taken by cross sections. Plan detail is located by measuring the distance perpendicularly from the baseline to the object and, in addition, measuring along the baseline to the point of perpendicularity (see Figure 1.11). The baseline is laid out in the field with stakes (nails in pavement) placed at appropriate intervals, usually 100 ft or 20 to 30 m. A sketch is entered in the field book before the measuring commences. If the terrain is smooth, a tape can be laid on the ground between the station marks. This will permit the surveyor to move along the tape (toward the forward station), noting and booking the stations of the already sketched detail on both sides of the baseline. The right angle for each location tie can be established using a pentaprism (see Figure 8.11), or a right angle can be established approximately in the following manner (swung-arm technique). The surveyor stands on the baseline facing the detail to be tied in and then points one arm down the baseline in one direction and then the other arm down the baseline in the opposite direction. After checking both arms (pointed index fingers) for proper alignment, the surveyor closes his or her eyes while swinging his or her arms together in front, pointing (presumably) at the detail. If the surveyor is not pointing at the detail, the surveyor moves slightly along the baseline and repeats the procedure until the detail has been sighted in correctly. The station is then read off the tape and booked in the field notes. This approximate method is used a great deal in manual route surveys and municipal surveys. This technique provides good results over short offset distances (50 ft or 15 m). For longer offset distances or for very important detail, a pentaprism or even a theodolite can be used to determine the stationing.

Once all the stations have been booked for the interval (100 ft or 20 to 30 m), only the offsets left and right of the baseline are left to measure. If the steel tape has been left lying on the ground during the determination of the stations, it is usually left in place to mark the baseline while the offsets are measured with another tape (for example, a fiberglass tape).

Figure 8.12(a) illustrates topographic field notes that have been booked using a single baseline and, in Figure 8.12(b), using a split baseline. In Figure 8.12(a), the offset distances are shown on the dimension lines, and the baseline stations are shown opposite the dimension line or as close as possible to the actual tie point on the baseline. In Figure 8.12(b), the baseline has been "split"; that is, two lines are drawn representing the baseline, leaving a space of zero dimension between them for the inclusion of the stations. The split-baseline technique is particularly valuable in densely detailed areas where single-baseline notes would tend to become crowded and difficult to decipher. The earliest topographic surveyors in North America used the split-baseline method of note keeping (see Figure 15.11).

## 8.7.3 Feature Locations by Polar (Radial) Measurement

Planimetric and topographic measurements can be captured efficiently using theodolites with attached EDMs (or total stations). In this technique, survey control is first established on the survey site, for example, by using a verified traverse (open or closed). The theodolite/EDM or total station is set on a control station with a reference backsight to another control point. The horizontal angle can be set to zero or any azimuth value. Once the theodolite/EDM has been field-oriented in this manner, the survey can commence with the HCR (horizontal angle), vertical distance, and horizontal distance recorded in the field book (or in onboard storage). Elevations are determined later by adding or subtracting the vertical distances to the elevation of the instrument station. If, for some reason, the height of the prism (HR) was not made equal to the height of the instrument (hi), then (+hi − HR) must be factored into the computations for elevations. Total station techniques give the elevations directly.

The party chief usually prepares a sketch of the area to be surveyed and places the reading number directly on the sketch as the captured data is field recorded. Complete field notes are invaluable when questions later arise concerning wrongly numbered or wrongly identified field data. See Appendix G for sample field notes for this type of survey.

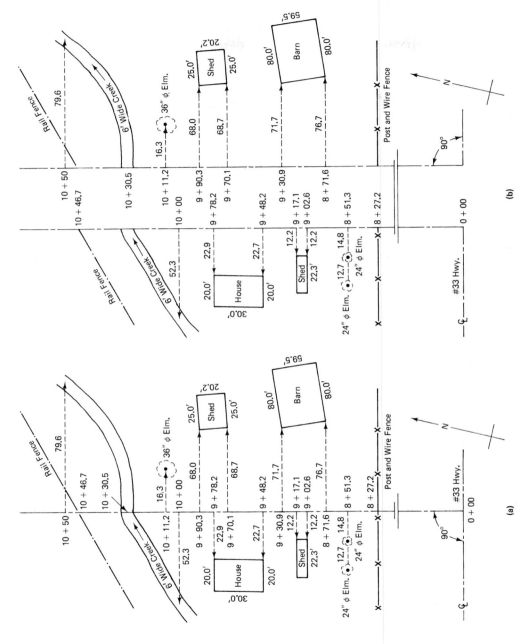

**FIGURE 8.12** Topographic field notes. (a) Single baseline. (b) Split baseline.

# 8.8 Cross Sections and Profiles

## 8.8.1 Cross Sections

*Cross sections* are a series of elevations taken at **right angles to a baseline** at specific stations, whereas *profiles* are series of elevations taken **along a baseline** at some specified repetitive station interval. The elevations thus determined can be plotted on maps and plans either as spot elevations or as contours, or they can be plotted as end areas for construction quantity estimating. As in offset ties, the baseline interval is usually 100 ft (20 to 30 m), although in rapidly changing terrain the interval is usually smaller (for example, 50 ft or 10 to 15 m). In addition to the regular intervals, cross sections are also taken at each abrupt change in the terrain (top and bottom of slopes, etc.).

Figure 8.13 illustrates how the rod readings are used to define the ground surface. In Figure 8.13(a), the uniform slope permits a minimum (ℂ and both limits of the survey) number of rod readings. In Figure 8.13(b), the varied slope requires several more (than the minimum) rod readings to define the ground surface adequately. Figure 8.13(c) illustrates how cross sections are taken before and after construction.

The profile consists of a series of elevations along the ℂ, or other required line. If cross sections have been taken, the necessary data for plotting a ℂ profile will also have been taken. If cross sections are not planned for an area for which a profile is required, the profile elevations can be determined simply by taking rod readings along the required line at regular station intervals and at all points where the ground slope changes (see Figure 3.20). Typical field notes for profile leveling were shown in Figure 3.21. Cross sections are booked in two different formats. Figure 3.24 showed cross sections booked in standard level note format. All the rod readings for one station (that can be "seen" from the HI) are booked together. In Figure 3.25, the same data were entered in a format popular with highway agencies. The latter format is more compact and thus takes less space in the field book; the former format takes more space in the field book but allows for a description for each rod reading, an important consideration for municipal surveyors.

The assumption in this and the previous section is that the data are being collected by conventional offset ties and cross-section methods (i.e., steel and cloth tapes for the tie-ins and a level and rod for the cross sections). In past municipal work, a crew of four surveyors could have been used efficiently. While the party chief was making sketches for the detail tie-ins, the instrument operator (rod readings and bookings) and two surveyors (one on the tape, the other on the rod) could perform the cross sections. (In theory, with the robotic total station described in Section 7.14, it is possible that this crew of four surveyors could be replaced by just one surveyor.)

Chapter 7 described total stations. These instruments use polar techniques and can measure distances and differences in elevation very quickly, as with theodolite/EDM surveys, the total station surveyor holds a reflecting prism mounted on a range pole instead of holding a rod. Many of these instruments have the distance and elevation data recorded automatically for future computer processing, while others require that the data be entered manually into the data recorder. Either method can be used to advantage on a multitude of other surveying projects, including right-angle offset tie-ins and cross sections.

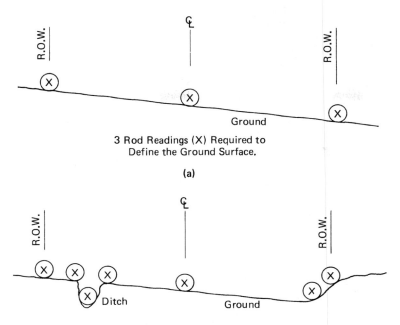

3 Rod Readings (X) Required to
Define the Ground Surface.

(a)

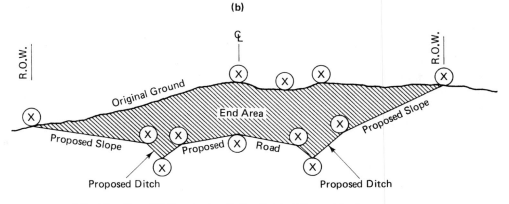

7 Rod Readings (X) Required to
Define this Ground Surface.

(b)

5 Rod Readings (X) Required to Define Original Ground Surface.
9 Rod Readings (X) Required to Define the Constructed Ground Surface.

(c)

**FIGURE 8.13** Cross sections used to define ground surface. (a) Uniform slope. (b) Varied slope. (c) Ground surface before and after construction.

## 8.8.2 Profiles Derived from Contours

Profiles establish ground elevations along a defined route (see Figures 8.8c and 8.14). Profile data can be surveyed directly, as when a road ₵ has rod readings taken at specific intervals (for example, 100 ft), as well as at all significant changes in slope, or profile data can be taken from contour drawings. For example, in Figure 8.8, the profile of line 71-41-42 can be determined as follows. The original scale was given as 1 in. = 150 ft, and this is used to scale the distance 71 to 41 (198 ft) and 41 to 42 (198 ft). The distances to the various contour crossings are as follows:

| | |
|---|---|
| 71 to 745 = 16′ | 71 to 775 = 188′ |
| 71 to 750 = 63′ | 41 to 780 = 51′ |
| 71 to 755 = 115′ | 41 to 785 = 118′ |
| 71 to 760 = 138′ | 41 to 790 = 165′ |
| 71 to 765 = 155′ | 41 to 795 = 225′ |
| 71 to 770 = 172′ | |

Figure 8.14 shows line 71-41-42 and the contour crossings replotted at 1″ = 100′ (for clarity). Directly below, the elevations are plotted vertically at 1″ = 30′. The horizontal scale for both plan and profile is always identical; the vertical scale of the profile is usually exaggerated to display the terrain line properly. In Figure 8.14, a convenient elevation datum line (740) was suitably placed on the available paper so that the profile would be centered.

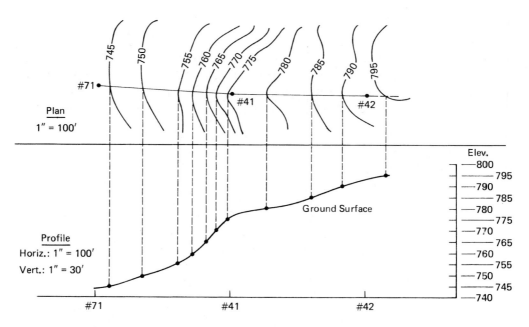

**FIGURE 8.14** Plan and profile [from Figure 8.8(b)].

# 8.9 Cross Sections, End Areas, and Volumes

Cross sections establish ground elevations at right angles to a proposed route. Cross sections can be developed from a contour plan, as profiles were in Section 8.8.2, although it is common to have cross sections taken by field surveys (see Chapter 3). Cross sections are useful in determining quantities of cut and fill in construction design. If the original ground cross section is plotted, and then the as-constructed cross section is also plotted, the *end area* at that particular station can be computed. In Figure 8.15(a), the proposed road at station 7 + 00 is at an elevation below existing ground. This indicates a *cut* situation; that is, the contractor will cut out that amount of soil shown between the proposed section and the original section. In Figure 8.15(b), the proposed road elevation at station 3 + 00 is above the existing ground, indicating a *fill* situation: the contractor will bring in or fill in that amount of material shown. Figure 8.15(c), shows a transition section between cut and fill sections.

When the end areas of cut or fill have been computed for adjacent stations, the volume of cut or fill between those stations can be computed by simply averaging the end areas and multiplying the average end area by the distance between the end area stations. Figure 8.16 illustrates this concept. Equation 8.1 shows the mathematical relationship:

$$V = \frac{(A_1 + A_2)L}{2} \tag{8.1}$$

Equation 8.1 gives the general case for volume computation, where $A_1$ and $A_2$ are the end areas of two adjacent stations, and $L$ is the distance (in feet or meters) between the stations. The answer in cubic feet is divided by 27 to give the answer in cubic yards; when metric units are used, the answer is left in cubic meters.

The average end-area method of computing volumes is valid only when the area of the midsection is, in fact, the average of the two end areas. This is seldom the case in actual earthwork computations; however, the error in volume resulting from this assumption is insignificant for the usual earthwork quantities of cut and fill. For special earthwork quantities (for example, expensive structures excavation) or for higher-priced materials (for example, concrete in place), a more precise method of volume computation, the **prismoidal formula,** should be used.

■ **EXAMPLE 8.1** *Volume by End Areas*
Figure 8.17(a) shows a pavement cross section for a proposed four-lane curbed road. As shown, the total pavement depth is 605 mm, the total width is 16.30 m, the subgrade is sloping to the side at 2%, and the top of the curb is 20 mm below the elevation of the ℄. The proposed cross section is shown in Figure 8.17(b) along with the existing ground cross section at station 0 + 340. You can see that all subgrade elevations were derived from the proposed cross section, together with the ℄ design elevation of 221.43. The desired end area is the area shown below the original ground plot and above the subgrade plot.

**Solution**
At this point, an elevation datum line is arbitrarily chosen (220.00). The datum line chosen can be any elevation value rounded to the closest foot, meter, or 5-ft value

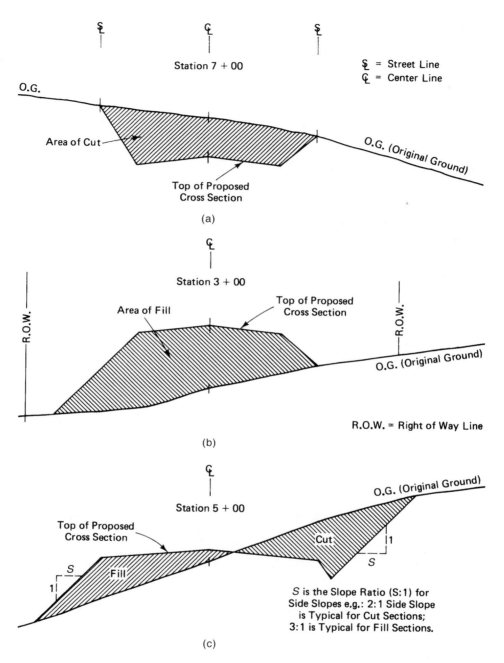

**FIGURE 8.15**   End areas. (a) Cut section. (b) Fill section. (c) Transition section (that is, both cut and fill).

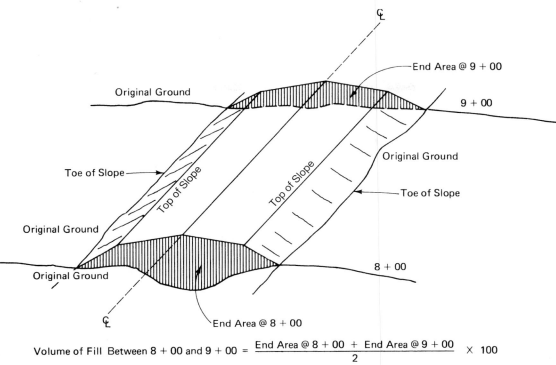

Original Ground

End Area @ 9 + 00

9 + 00

Original Ground

Toe of Slope

Top of Slope

Top of Slope

Toe of Slope

Original Ground

Original Ground

8 + 00

End Area @ 8 + 00

$$\text{Volume of Fill Between } 8 + 00 \text{ and } 9 + 00 = \frac{\text{End Area @ } 8 + 00 \ + \ \text{End Area @ } 9 + 00}{2} \times 100$$

**FIGURE 8.16**  Fill volume computations using end areas.

that is lower than the lowest elevation in the plotted cross section. Figure 8.18 illustrates that end-area computations involve the computation of two areas:

1. Area between the ground cross section and the datum line
2. Area between the subgrade cross section and the datum line

The desired end area (cut) is area 1 minus area 2. For fill situations, the desired end area would be area 2 minus area 1. The end-area computation can be determined as shown in Table 8.3. Assuming that the end area at $0 + 300$ has been computed to be 18.05 m², the volume of cut between $0 + 300$ and $0 + 340$ can now be computed using Equation 8.1:

$$V = \frac{(18.05 + 15.95)}{2} \times 40 = 680 \text{ m}^3$$

# 8.10   Prismoidal Formula

If values more precise than those given by end-area volumes are required, or if the sections are changing from cut to fill and converge to a prism shape, the prismoidal formula can be

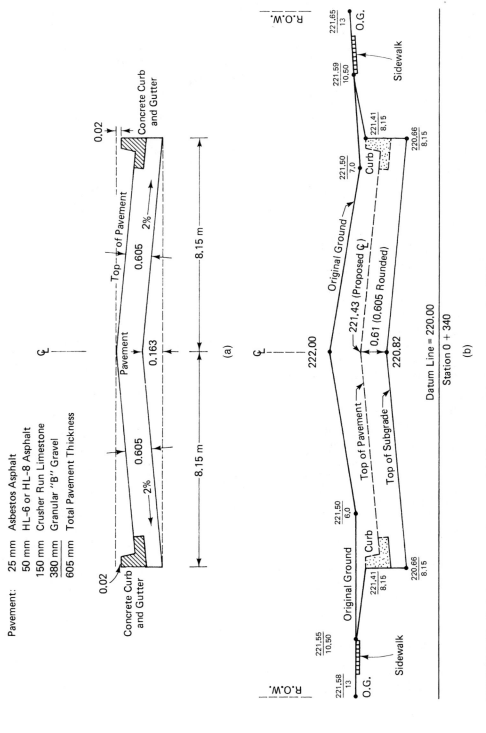

Pavement:
25 mm   Asbestos Asphalt
50 mm   HL-6 or HL-8 Asphalt
150 mm  Crusher Run Limestone
380 mm  Granular "B" Gravel
605 mm  Total Pavement Thickness

(a)

Datum Line = 220.00

Station 0 + 340

(b)

**FIGURE 8.17** End-area computation, general. (a) Typical arterial street cross section. (b) Survey and design data plotted to show both the original ground and the design cross sections.

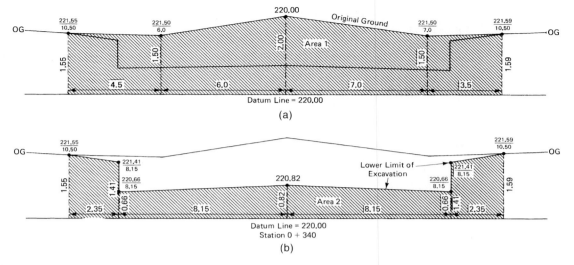

**FIGURE 8.18** End-area computations for cut areas. (a) Area between ground cross section and datum line. (b) Area between subgrade cross section and datum line.

**Table 8.3** END AREA COMPUTATIONS

| Station | Plus | Area 1 | Minus | Area 2 |
|---------|------|--------|-------|--------|
| 0 + 340 | $\dfrac{1.55 + 1.50}{2} \times 4.5 =$ | 6.86 | $\dfrac{1.55 + 1.41}{2} \times 2.35 =$ | 3.48 |
| | $\dfrac{1.50 + 2.00}{2} \times 6.0 =$ | 10.50 | $\dfrac{0.66 + 0.82}{2} \times 8.15 =$ | 6.03 |
| | $\dfrac{2.00 + 1.50}{2} \times 7.0 =$ | 12.25 | $\dfrac{0.82 + 0.66}{2} \times 8.15 =$ | 6.03 |
| | $\dfrac{1.50 + 1.59}{2} \times 3.5 =$ | 5.41 | $\dfrac{1.41 + 1.59}{2} \times 2.35 =$ | 3.53 |
| | Check: $\overline{21}$ m | $\overline{35.02}$ m$^2$ | Check: $\overline{21}$ m | $\overline{19.07}$ m$^2$ |
| | End area $= 35.02 - 19.07 = 15.95$ m$^2$ | | | |

used. A **prismoid** is a solid with parallel ends joined by plane or continuously warped surfaces. The prismoidal formula is:

$$V = L \frac{(A_1 + 4A_m + A_2)}{6} \qquad \text{ft}^3 \text{ or m}^3 \qquad (8.2)$$

where $A_1$ and $A_2$ are the two end areas, $A_m$ is the area of a section midway between $A_1$ and $A_2$, and $L$ is the distance from $A_1$ to $A_2$. $A_m$ is not the average of $A_1$ and $A_2$, but is derived from distances that are the average of corresponding distances required for $A_1$ and $A_2$ computations.

Sec. 8.10   Prismoidal Formula

The formula in Equation 8.2 is also used for other geometric solids (for example, truncated prisms, cylinders, and cones). To justify its use, the surveyor must refine the field measurements to reflect the increase in precision sought. A typical application of the prismoidal formula is the computation of in-place volumes of concrete. The difference in cost between a cubic yard or meter of concrete and a cubic yard or meter of earth cut or fill is sufficient reason for the increased precision.

## 8.11  Construction Volumes

In highway construction, for economic reasons, the designers try to balance cut and fill volumes optimally. Cut and fill cannot be balanced precisely because of geometric and esthetic design considerations, and because of the unpredictable effects of shrinkage and swell. **Shrinkage** occurs when a cubic yard (meter) is excavated and then placed while being compacted. The same material that formerly occupied 1 yd$^3$ (m$^3$) volume now occupies a smaller volume. Shrinkage reflects an increase in density of the material and is obviously greater for silts, clays, and loams than it is for granular materials such as sand and gravel. **Swell** is a term used to describe the change in volume of shattered (blasted) rock. Obviously, 1 yd$^3$ (m$^3$) of solid rock will expand significantly when shattered. Swell is usually in the range of 15% to 20%, whereas shrinkage is in the range of 10% to 15%, although values as high as 40% are possible with organic material in wet areas.

To keep track of cumulative cuts and fills as the profile design proceeds, the cumulative cuts (plus) and fills (minus) are shown graphically in a mass diagram. The total cut-minus-fill is plotted at each station directly below the profile plot. The mass diagram is an excellent method of determining waste or borrow volumes and can be adapted to show haul (transportation) considerations (Figure 8.19.)

Large fills require *borrow* material, usually taken from a nearby *borrow pit.* Borrow pit leveling procedures are described in Section 3.9 and Figure 3.26. The borrow pit in Figure 3.26 was laid out on a 50-ft grid. The volume of a grid square is the average height $(a + b + c + d)/4$ times the area of the base ($50^2$). The partial grid volumes (along the perimeter of the borrow pit) can be computed by forcing the perimeter volumes into regular geometric shapes (wedge shapes or quarter-cones).

When high precision is less important, volumes can be determined by analysis of contour plans; the smaller the contour interval, the more precise the result. The areas enclosed by a contour line can be taken off by planimeter; electronic planimeters are very useful for this purpose. Modern earthwork software programs will also compute quantities from digital terrain models (DTMs) before and after construction.

$$V = I\frac{(C_1 + C_2)}{2} \tag{8.3}$$

$V$ is the volume (ft$^3$ or m$^3$) of earth or water, $C_1$ and $C_2$ are areas of adjacent contours, and $I$ is the contour interval. The prismoidal formula can be used if $m$ is an intervening contour ($C_2$) between $C_1$ and $C_3$. This method is well suited for many water-storage volume computations.

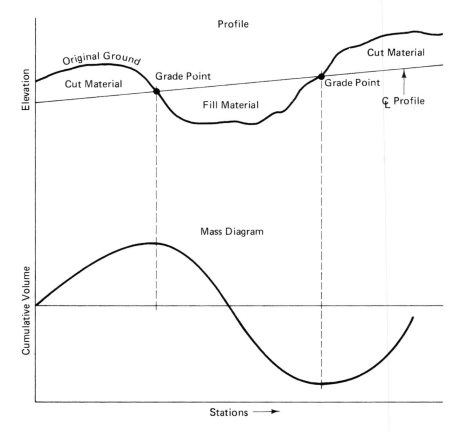

**FIGURE 8.19** Mass diagram.

Finally, perhaps the most popular current volume-computation technique involves the use of computers with any one of a large number of available earthwork software programs. The computer programmer uses techniques similar to those described here, but the surveyor's duties may end with proper data entry into the computer.

## 8.12 Area Computations

Areas enclosed by closed traverses can be computed using the coordinate method (see Section 6.15). Figure 8.20 will illustrate two additional area computation techniques.

### 8.12.1 Trapezoidal Technique

The area in Figure 8.20 was measured using a cloth or fiberglass tape for the offset distances. A common interval of 15 ft was chosen to delineate the riverbank suitably. Had the riverbank been more uniform, a larger interval could have been used, and had the riverbank been even more irregular, a smaller interval would have been appropriate. The **trapezoidal**

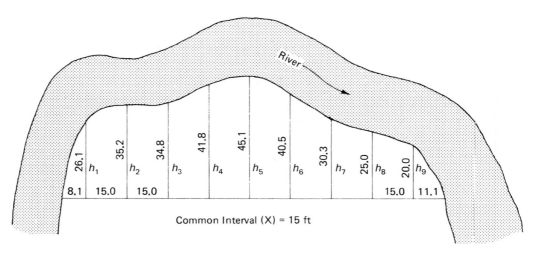

**FIGURE 8.20** Irregular area computation.

**technique** assumes that the lines joining the ends of each offset line are straight lines (the smaller the common interval, the more valid this assumption).

The end sections can be treated as triangles:

$$A = \frac{8.1 \times 26.1}{2} = 106 \text{ ft}^2$$

and

$$A = \frac{11.1 \times 20.0}{2} = 111 \text{ ft}^2$$

$$= 217 \text{ ft}^2 \qquad \text{Subtotal}$$

The remaining areas can be treated as trapezoids. The trapezoidal rule is stated as follows:

$$\text{Area} = X\left(\frac{h_1 + h_n}{2} + h_2 + \ldots + h_{n-1}\right) \tag{8.4}$$

where $X$ = common interval between the offset lines
$\quad h$ = offset measurement
$\quad n$ = number of offset measurements

$$A = 15\left(\frac{26.1 + 20.0}{2} + 35.2 + 34.8 + 41.8 + 45.1 + 40.5 + 30.3 + 25.0\right)$$
$$= 4,136 \text{ ft}^2$$

$$\text{Total area} = 4,136 + 217 = 4,353 \text{ ft}^2$$

## 8.12.2   Simpson's One-Third Rule

This technique gives more precise results than the trapezoidal technique and is used where one boundary is irregular, like the one shown in Figure 8.20. The rule assumes that an odd number of offsets is involved and that the lines joining the ends of three successive offset lines are parabolic in configuration. Simpson's **one-third rule** is stated as follows:

$$A = \frac{\text{interval}}{3} (h_1 + h_n + 2\Sigma h \text{ odd} + 4\Sigma h \text{ even}) \qquad (8.5)$$

That is, one-third of the common interval times the sum of the first and last offsets ($h_1 + h_n$) plus twice the sum of the other odd offsets ($\Sigma h$ odd) plus four times the sum of the even-numbered offsets ($\Sigma h$ even).

From Figure 8.20:

$$A = \frac{15}{3} [26.1 + 20.0 + 2(34.8 + 45.1 + 30.3) + 4(35.2 + 41.8 + 40.5 + 25.0)]$$

$$= 4,183 \text{ ft}^2$$

$$\text{Total area} = 4,183 + 217 \text{ (from preceding example)}$$
$$= 4,400 \text{ ft}^2$$

If a problem is encountered with an even number of offsets, the area between the odd number of offsets is determined by Simpson's one-third rule, with the remaining area determined with the trapezoidal technique. The discrepancy between the trapezoidal technique and Simpson's one-third rule here is 47 ft$^2$ in a total of 4,400 ft$^2$ (about 1% in this case).

# 8.13   Area by Graphical Analysis

We have seen that areas can be determined by using coordinates (Chapter 6) and, less precisely, by using the somewhat approximate methods illustrated by the trapezoidal rule and Simpson's one-third rule. Areas can also be determined by analyzing plotted data on plans and maps. For example, if a transparent sheet is marked off in grid squares to some known scale, an area outlined on a map can be determined by placing the squared paper over (sometimes under) the map and counting the number of squares and partial squares within the boundary limits shown on the map. The smaller the squares, the more precise will be the result.

Another method of graphic analysis involves the use of a planimeter (see Figures 8.21, 8.22, and 8.23). A *planimeter* consists of a graduated measuring drum attached to an adjustable or fixed tracing arm (which itself is attached to a pole arm), one end of which is anchored to the working surface by a needle. The graduated measuring drum gives partial revolution readings, while a disc keeps count of the number of full revolutions. Areas are determined by placing the pole-arm needle in a convenient location, setting the measuring drum and revolution counter to zero (some planimeters require recording an initial

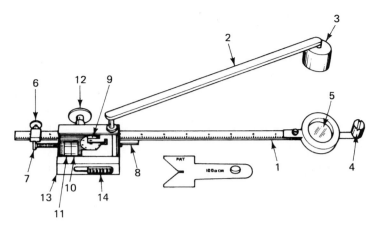

Part 1 Tracer Arm
Part 2 Pole Arm
Part 3 Pole Weight
Part 4 Hand Grip
Part 5 Tracing Magnifier
Part 6 Clamp Screw
Part 7 Fine Movement Screw

Part 8 Tracer Arm Vernier
Part 9 Revolution Recording Dial
Part 10 Measuring Wheel
Part 11 Measuring Wheel Vernier
Part 12 Idler Wheel
Part 13 Carriage
Part 14 Zero Setting Slide Bar

**FIGURE 8.21** Polar planimeter.

**FIGURE 8.22** Area takeoff by polar planimeter.

**FIGURE 8.23** Area takeoff by an electronic planimeter.

reading), and then tracing (using the tracing pin) the outline of the area to be measured. As the tracing proceeds, the drum (which is also in contact with the working surface) revolves, thus measuring a value that is proportional to the area being measured.

Some planimeters measure directly in square inches, while others can be set to map scales. When in doubt, or as a check on planimeter operation, the surveyor can measure out a scale figure (for example, 4 in. [100 mm] square) and then measure the area (16 in.$^2$) with a planimeter so that the planimeter area can be compared with the actual area laid off by scale. If the planimeter gives a result in square inches, say, 51.2 in.$^2$, and the map is at a scale of 1 in. = 100 ft, the actual ground area portrayed by 51.2 in.$^2$ would be 51.2 $\times$ 100$^2$ = 512,000 ft$^2$ = 11.8 acres.

The planimeter is normally used with the pole-arm anchor point outside the area to be traced. If it is necessary to locate the pole-arm anchor point inside the area to be measured, as in the case of a relatively large area, the area of the zero circle of the planimeter must be added to the planimeter readings. This constant is supplied by the manufacturer or can be deduced by simply measuring a large area twice, once with the anchor point outside the area and once with the anchor point inside the area.

Planimeters are particularly useful in measuring end areas (Section 8.9) used in volume computations. Planimeters are also used effectively in measuring watershed areas, as a check on various construction quantities (for example, areas of sod, asphalt), and as a check on areas determined by coordinates. Electronic planimeters (see Figure 8.23) measure larger areas in less time than do traditional polar planimeters. Computer software is available for highways and other earthwork applications (e.g., cross sections) and for drainage basin areas. The planimeter shown in Figure 8.23 has a 36 $\times$ 30 in. working area capability, with a measuring resolution of 0.01 in.$^3$ (0.02 in.$^2$ accuracy).

Computer programs are now used to compute and display profiles, cross sections, and areas. Once the coordinates (N, E, and elevation) of field points are in the database, quantity determinations and engineering design can be readily accomplished. Digitizing tablets or tables can also be used to digitize (i.e., determine X and Y positions) the location of many features on maps, plans, and cross sections, thus permitting the computation of areas.

# Problems

A topographic survey was performed on a tract of land using theodolite/EDM techniques to locate the topographic detail. The sketch in Figure 8.24 shows the traverse (A to G) and the grid baseline (0 + 00 at A) used to control the survey. Also given are bearings and distances of the traverse sides (Table 8.4), grid elevations (Table 8.5), and angle and distance ties for the topographic detail (Table 8.6). Problems 8.1 through 8.8 combine to form a comprehensive engineering project; the project can be covered completely by solving all the problems of this section, or individual problems can be selected to illustrate specific topics. Numerical values can be chosen as meters or feet. All field and design data for these problems are shown on this page and on the following pages.

**8.1** Establish the grid, plot the elevations (the decimal point is the plot point from Table 8.4), and interpolate the data to establish contours at 1-m (1-ft) intervals. Scale at 1:500 for metric units, or $1'' = 10$ ft or 15 ft for foot units. Use pencil and Table 8.5.

**8.2** Compute the interior angles of the traverse and check for geometric closure, that is, $n - 2(180°)$. (See Table 8.4.)

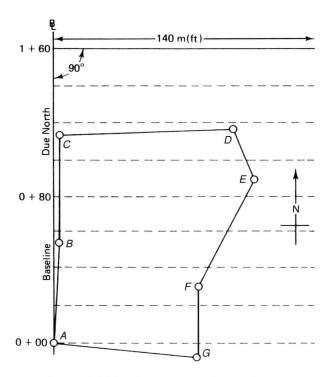

**FIGURE 8.24**   Grid traverse and control.

**Table 8.4** BALANCED TRAVERSE DATA

| Course | Bearing | Distance [m (ft)] |
|--------|---------|-------------------|
| AB | N  3°30′ E | 56.05 |
| BC | N  0°30′ W | 61.92 |
| CD | N 88°40′ E | 100.02 |
| DE | S 23°30′ E | 31.78 |
| EF | S 28°53′ W | 69.11 |
| FG | South | 39.73 |
| GA | N 83° 37′ W | 82.67 |

**Table 8.5** ELEVATION DATA: SURVEYING GRID ELEVATIONS (PROBLEM 8.1)

| Station | Baseline | 20 m (ft) E | 40 m (ft) E | 60 m (ft) E | 80 m (ft) E | 100 m (ft) E | 120 m (ft) E | 140 m (ft) E |
|---------|----------|------|------|------|------|------|------|------|
| 1 + 60 | 68.97 | 69.51 | 70.05 | 70.53 | 70.32 | | | |
| 1 + 40 | 69.34 | 69.82 | 71.12 | 71.00 | 71.26 | 71.99 | | |
| 1 + 20 | 69.29 | 70.75 | 69.98 | 71.24 | 72.07 | 72.53 | 72.61 | |
| 1 + 00 | 69.05 | 71.02 | 70.51 | 69.91 | 72.02 | 73.85 | 74.00 | 75.18 |
| 0 + 80 | 69.09 | 71.90 | 74.13 | 71.81 | 69.87 | 71.21 | 74.37 | 74.69 |
| 0 + 60 | 69.12 | 70.82 | 72.79 | 72.81 | 71.33 | 70.97 | 72.51 | 73.40 |
| 0 + 40 | 68.90 | 69.66 | 70.75 | 72.00 | 72.05 | 69.80 | 71.33 | 72.42 |
| 0 + 20 | 68.02 | 68.98 | 69.53 | 70.09 | 71.11 | 70.48 | 69.93 | 71.51 |
| 0 + 00 | 67.15 | 68.11 | 68.55 | 69.55 | 69.92 | 71.02 | | |
| @ Sta. A | | | | | | | | |

**8.3** Plot the traverse, using the interior angles and the given distances. Scale as in Problem 8.1.

**8.4** Plot the detail using the plotted traverse as control. Scale as in Problem 8.1. See Table 8.6.

**8.5** Determine the area enclosed by the traverse in m² (ft²) by using one or more of the following methods.

   **(a)** Use grid paper as an overlay or underlay. Count the squares and partial squares enclosed by the traverse, and determine the area represented by one square at the chosen scale. From that relationship, determine the area enclosed by the traverse.

   **(b)** Use a planimeter to determine the area.

   **(c)** Divide the traverse into regular-shaped figures (squares, rectangles, trapezoids, triangles) and use a scale to determine the figure dimensions. Calculate the areas of the individual figures and add them to produce the overall traverse area.

   **(d)** Use the balanced traverse data in Table 8.6 and the technique of coordinates to compute the area enclosed by the traverse.

**8.6** Draw profile A to E showing both the existing ground and the proposed ℄ of highway. Use the following scales: metric—horizontal is 1:500, vertical is 1:100; foot—horizontal is 1 in. = 10 ft or 15 ft, vertical is 1 in. = 2 ft or 3 ft.

**8.7** A highway is to be constructed to pass through points A and E of the traverse. The proposed highway ℄ grade is +2.30% rising from A to E (℄ elevation at A = 68.95). The

**Table 8.6** SURVEY NOTES (PROBLEM 8.4)

|  | Horizontal angle | Distance [m (ft)] | Description |
|---|---|---|---|
| | | Sta. ⊼ @ Station B (sight C, 0°00′) | |
| 1 | 8°15′ | 45.5 | S. limit of treed area |
| 2 | 17°00′ | 57.5 | S. limit of treed area |
| 3 | 33°30′ | 66.0 | S. limit of treed area |
| 4 | 37°20′ | 93.5 | S. limit of treed area |
| 5 | 45°35′ | 93.0 | S. limit of treed area |
| 6 | 49°30′ | 114.0 | S. limit of treed area |
| | | ⊼ @ Station A (sight B, 0°00′) | |
| 7 | 50°10′ | 73.5 | ₵ gravel road (8 m ± width) |
| 8 | 50°10′ | 86.0 | ₵ gravel road (8 m ± width) |
| 9 | 51°30′ | 97.5 | ₵ gravel road (8 m ± width) |
| 10 | 53°50′ | 94.5 | N. limit of treed area |
| 11 | 53°50′ | 109.0 | N. limit of treed area |
| 12 | 55°00′ | 58.0 | ₵ gravel road |
| 13 | 66°15′ | 32.0 | N. limit of treed area |
| 14 | 86°30′ | 19.0 | N. limit of treed area |
| | | ⊼ @ Station D (sight E, 0°00′) | |
| 15 | 0°00′ | 69.5 | ₵ gravel road |
| 16 | 7°30′ | 90.0 | N. limit of treed area |
| 17 | 64°45′ | 38.8 | N.E. corner of building |
| 18 | 13°30′ | 75.0 | N. limit of treed area |
| 19 | 88°00′ | 39.4 | N.W. corner of building |
| 20 | 46°00′ | 85.0 | N. limit of treed area |

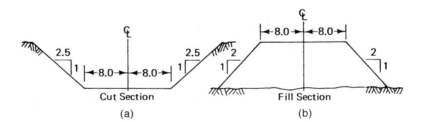

**FIGURE 8.25** Proposed cross sections (Problem 8.7). (a) Cut section. (b) Fill section.

proposed cut and fill sections are shown in Figure 8.25(a) and (b). Plot the highway ₵ and 16 m (ft) width on the plan (see Problems 8.1, 8.3, and 8.4). Show the limits of cut and fill on the plan.

**8.8** Combine Problems 8.1, 8.3, 8.4, 8.6, and 8.7 on one sheet of drafting paper Arrange the plan and profile together with the balanced traverse data and an appropriate title block. Use size A2 paper or the equivalent.

# 9 Geographic Information Systems

## 9.A General Background

## 9.1 The Evolution from Mapping to Geographic Information Systems (GISs)

Since the earliest days of mapping, topographic features have routinely been portrayed on scaled maps and plans. These maps and plans provided an inventory of selected or general features that were found in a given geographic area. With the emergence of large data bases, which were collected primarily for mapping, attention was given to new techniques for analyzing and querying the computer-stored data. In the 1960s, the term *geographic information system (GIS)* appeared in works by Dr. Roger Tomlinson, a Canadian geographer, who was a major contributor in the vast Canada-wide mapping undertaking—the Canada Land Inventory (CLI).

The introduction of topological techniques permitted the data to be connected in a relational sense, in addition to their spatial connections. Thus, it became possible not only to determine where a *point* (for example, a hydrant) or a *line* (for example, a road) or an *area* (park, neighborhood, etc.) was located, but also to analyze those features with respect to the **adjacency** of other spatial features, **connectivity** (network analysis), and **direction** of vectors. Adjacency, connectivity, and direction opened the data base to a wider variety of analyzing and querying techniques. For example, it is possible in a GIS real-estate application to display, in map form, all the industrially zoned parcels of land with rail-spur possibilities, within 1.5 miles of freeway access, in the range of 1.2 to 3.1 acres in size. Relational characteristics also permit the data base to be used for the routing of travelers like emergency personnel and vacationers.

GIS data can be assembled from existing data bases, digitized or scanned from existing maps and plans, or collected using conventional surveying techniques, including global positioning system (GPS) surveying techniques. One GPS method that has recently

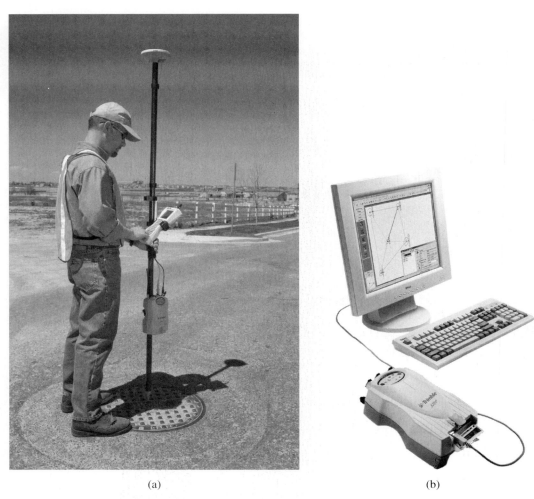

(a)                                                    (b)

**FIGURE 9.1**  (a) Trimble's 5700 GPS receiver with the pole-mounted antenna and data collector shown being used to capture municipal asset data location for a GIS data base. (b) Trimble's 5700 GPS receiver shown connected to a computer directly down-loading to Trimble's Geomatics Office software.

become very popular for GIS data collection is that of differential GPS (see Section 11.11.3.3). This technique utilizes a less expensive GPS receiver and radio signal corrections from a base station receiver to provide submeter accuracies that are acceptable for mapping and GIS data base inventories. See Figure 9.1 for typical differential GPS equipment.

The ability to store in computer memory a wide variety of data on feature-unique layers permits the simple production of special-feature maps. For example, it is possible to produce maps that show only the registered parcel outlines of an area, or only drainage and

(c)

**FIGURE 9.1 (continued)**   (c) Trimble's 5600 Robotic total station together with their GPS 5700 receiver and the interchangeable TSCe data collector. The basic 5600 total station is upgradable from Servo to Autolock to Robotic capabilities. (Portions © 2001 Trimble Navigation Limited. All rights reserved.)

contour information, or any other feature-specific data. In fact, any selected layer or combination of selected layers can be depicted on a computer screen or on a hard-copy map at any desired scale (see Figure 9.2).

In a GIS, spatial entities have two key characteristics: location and attributes. Location can be given by coordinates, street addresses, etc., and attributes describe some characteristic(s) of the feature being analyzed. GIS has now blossomed into a huge and diverse field of activity. Most activity can be identified as being in one of two broad fields: (1) geographic feature-specific activities such as mapping, engineering, environment, resources, and agriculture; and (2) cultural/social activities such as marketing research, census, demographics, and social/economic studies. Since GIS is a tool used by engineers, planners, geographers, and other social scientists, it is not surprising that there seems to be as many definitions for GIS as there are fields in which GIS is employed. My choice for a definition comes from the University of Edinborough's GIS faculty, which states that a *geographic information system (GIS)* is a computerized system for capturing, storing,

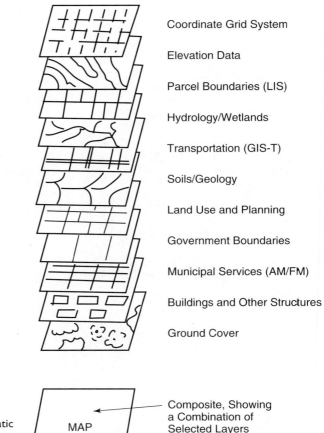

Coordinate Grid System

Elevation Data

Parcel Boundaries (LIS)

Hydrology/Wetlands

Transportation (GIS-T)

Soils/Geology

Land Use and Planning

Government Boundaries

Municipal Services (AM/FM)

Buildings and Other Structures

Ground Cover

MAP

Composite, Showing a Combination of Selected Layers

**FIGURE 9.2**   Illustration of thematic layers.

checking, integrating, manipulating, analyzing, and displaying data related to positions on the earth's surface.

The switch from hard-copy maps to computerized GIS has provided many benefits. For example now we can:

1. Store and easily update large amounts of data.
2. Sort and store spatial features, called entities, into thematic layers. Data are stored in layers so that complex spatial data can be manipulated and analyzed efficiently by layer rather than trying to deal with the entire data base at the same time.
3. Zoom into sections of the displayed data to generate additional graphics, which may be hidden at default scales. We can also query items of interest to obtain tables of attribute information that may have been tagged to specific points of interest.
4. Analyze both entities and their attribute data using sophisticated computer programs.

5. Prepare maps showing only selected thematic layers of interest (and thus reduce "clutter"). We can also update maps quickly as new data are assembled.

6. Use the stored data to prepare maps at different scales, for a wide range of purposes.

7. Import stored data (both spatial and nonspatial) electronically from different agencies and thus save the costs of collecting the data.

8. Build and augment a data base by combining digital data from all the data-gathering techniques illustrated in Figure 7.32: field surveying, remote sensing, map digitization, scanning, and Internet transfer/CD-ROM imports.

9. Create new maps by modeling or re-interpreting existing data.

Some ask, How do GIS and CAD (computer-assisted drafting/design) compare? Both systems are computer-based, but CAD is often associated with higher precision engineering design and surveying applications, and GIS is more often associated with mapping and planning—activities requiring lower levels of precision. CAD is similar to mapping because it is essentially an inventory of entered data and computed data that can provide answers to the question, Where is it located? GIS can model data and provide answers to the spatial and temporal questions like, What occurred? What if? Topology gives GIS the ability to determine spatial relationships, such as adjacency and connectivity, between physical features or entities.

Typical subsets of geographic feature-specific GIS include land information systems (LISs), which deal exclusively with parcel title description and registration; automated mapping and facility management (AM/FM), which models the location of all utility/plant facilities; and transportation design and management (GIS-T).

## 9.1.1 LIS

LIS is a computerized, parcel-based land cadastre anchored in the original township fabric of lots and ranges (concessions), including the ongoing subdivision of lots into real-estate developments. The U.S. Bureau of Land Management (BLM) has begun in the western states during the late 1990s to assemble a data base of coordinates (latitude/longitude) of corner positions and other monuments recorded in the Public Land Surveys System (PLSS). Since most land plats and descriptions are referenced to the PLSS, these coordinates help form the basis for georeferencing ownership details on a parcel GIS layer.

## 9.1.2 AM/FM

AM/FM is an important field of GIS activity with macro-applications in the management of municipal utilities. City engineers can map and inventory roadways, pipelines, cables, and other municipal infrastructure utilities using AM/FM software programs. These programs also record all relevant characteristics of the utility; for example, sewers may have the following data recorded: pipe diameter, pipe type, length of run between manholes, inverts and pipe slopes, date of installation, record of maintenance, etc. The programs can be designed to issue work orders for scheduled maintenance automatically and to prepare plans and profiles that show the locations of all services.

AM/FM micro-applications manage the physical plant and services of large office and industrial complexes. All services, including electrical, heating, air conditioning, elevators, fire protection, communications, as well as building design and layout, are stored on three-dimensional, layer-specific sections of the computer storage. Computer assisted drawing (CAD) drawings can be produced for specific floors of the facility and can show any desired combination of layered entities.

## 9.1.3 GIS-T

This subset of GIS came into being because transportation represents a large and unique sphere of GIS activity. State and provincial transportation agencies have long collected data based on various linear reference systems (LRSs). Traditionally, points on a specific highway route were directionally referenced to mileage posts or other reference posts, survey stations (chainages), state plane or UTM coordinates, latitude and longitude, and street or highway intersections (called **nodes** in GIS). GIS programs have been designed to adapt to the linear referencing systems to which large amounts of highway data have already been referenced. Highway data are usually modeled in vector fashion by digitizing the centerline (₵) as lines or arcs, and nodes. Lines or arcs join two coordinated points, and nodes are points of intersection with other highway centerlines or other linear features. Divided highways may be captured by digitizing the median ₵ or by digitizing the ₵ of each side of the highway. Each technique permits the drawing of pavement edges through the use of a parallel-line graphics function. Highway reference methods are based on the presence and/or absence of specific attributes to be analyzed or displayed, for example, the number of traffic lanes or the width of traffic lanes; that is attributes are stored in separate data bases categorized by their attribute characteristics.

## 9.1.4 Proceeding to a New Information Utility

Some of the early by-products of the computer revolution were the simple procedures developed for computing and storing the coordinates of any number of ground points. Surveyors, long accustomed to working with coordinates, quickly adapted their field and computation techniques for computer use. Computations for adjustments, areas, etc., were made quickly and with fewer mistakes. When total stations came into wide use in the early 1980s, the surveyor could locate field items with a single pointing and store the location data—coordinates, or slope distance, and horizontal and vertical angles—along with labels and other attribute data in the data collector. When the data collector was downloaded to the computer, all the field data were transferred, free of transcription errors. Once the data were in the computer, it was possible to process (coordinate) the data and plot them in the form of a plan. This information constituted the start of a data base for the area surveyed. Additional data could be retrieved from existing maps and plans (drawn to a wide variety of scales) covering the same area by using digitizing tables and scanners. The data base could be further augmented by the addition of digitized data from a wide variety of additional sources (see Figure 7.32). The total data in the data base (regardless of the capture technique) could be accessed for query and analysis using GIS programs or for plotting by digital plotters; in addition, the data could be manipulated, sorted, and delivered in various report formats.

A word of caution: as data is imported from various sources and as data bases are combined, you should not lose sight of the relative precision used in various forms of data capture. For example, data captured by digitizing existing maps and plans cannot be indiscriminately mixed with data captured using GPS or total station techniques unless the objectives of the exercise require only the lower-order precision normally expected in mapping applications. (See Section 9.6, Metadata.)

When municipalities first considered GIS purchases many years ago, the engineering or public works departments often provided the impetus for the acquisition of the technology. In a few years, it became obvious that the data in the data base could be used for many other purposes; that is, in addition to streets and street hardware inventories, municipalities could use coordinated data for land registration, street numbering, assessment data, and a wide variety of other municipal managerial and planning functions. For example, the unique coordinates $(X, Y)$ that identified a specific property could also include attribute data describing the type of dwelling, area of lot, building floor area, number of occupants, taxes paid, zoning, and any other data relating to the property or to the owner. Three-dimensional coordinates $(X, Y,$ and $Z)$ could be used to identify or register high-rise condominium commercial and residential ownership precisely. Regional and federal census data (for example, TIGER) are now available from government agencies for the low costs of reproduction, and private market-research companies provide spatial data for a fee. When all this data, available on CD-ROM or by electronic transfer via the Internet, are added to a local data base, the potential for applications increases dramatically. Add to all this static information the link to a dynamic positioning system, such as GPS (see Chapter 11), and you have what could be identified as a new information utility.

Just as the electric and the telephone utilities transformed society, so this new information utility will have a great impact on modern society. Land locations identified uniquely by their three-dimensional coordinates will in the future be thought of as addresses instead of targets. Moving vehicles—planes, trains, automobiles, and ships—will have their "addresses" updated as they move, with direction and time vectors, to any other point in the data base. Applications are limited only by one's imagination.

## 9.2    Components of a GIS

GIS can be divided into four major activities:

1. Data collection and input.
2. Data storage and retrieval.
3. Data analysis.
4. Data output and display.

GIS may be further described by listing its typical components:

- The computer—which, along with the GIS software, is the heart of GIS and typically uses Windows, NT, or Unix operating systems.
- Data collection—which can be divided into the geomatics components shown in Figure 7.32: field surveying, remote sensing, digitization of existing maps and plans, digital data transfer via the Internet or CD-ROM.

- Computer storage: hard drives, optical disks, etc.
- Software designed to download, edit, sort, and analyze data, for example, database software, relational database software, GIS software, geometric and drawing software (COGO, CAD, etc.), soft-copy photogrammetry, and satellite imagery analysis software.
- Software designed to process and present data in the form of graphics and maps and/or plans.
- Hardware components, including the computer, surveying and remote sensing equipment, CD-ROM, CD-RW, digitizers, scanners, interactive graphics terminals, and plotters and printers.

The growth in GIS is assured because it has been estimated that as much as 80% of all information used by local governments is referenced geographically. GIS is a tool that encourages planners, designers, and other decision makers to study and analyze spatial data along with an enormous amount of attribute data (cultural, social, geographic, economic, resources, environmental, infrastructure, etc.): data that can be tagged to specific spatial entities.

## 9.B    Data Capture

## 9.3    Sources for GIS Data

It is often remarked that the most expensive part of any GIS is the collection of data. Obviously, if you can obtain suitable data already collected from other sources, the efficiency of the process increases. When importing data from other sources, it is imperative that the accuracy level of the collected data be certified as being appropriate for its intended use. For example, if you are building a data base to be used in high-accuracy design applications, it would not be suitable to import data digitized from the U.S. Geological Survey (USGS) 1:100,000 topographic maps (as is much of the U.S. census TIGER data), where accuracy can be restricted to ±170 feet. For small-scale projects (e.g., planning, resources/environmental studies), however, the nationwide TIGER file has become one of the prime sources of easy-to-obtain data in the United States. Government data sources like USGS, TIGER, and others provide data, for the cost of reproduction, to the general public. Traditional sources for data collection include:

- Field surveying.
- Remotely sensed images—rectified and digitized aerial photographs (orthophotos) and processed aerial and satellite imagery.
- Existing topographic maps, plans, and photos via digitizing and/or scanning.
- Census data.
- Electronic transfer of previously digitized data from government agencies or commercial firms.

## 9.4    Georeferencing

Like the map-makers of the past, GIS specialists must find some way to relate geospatial data to the surface of the earth, and eventually to relate spatial data to the surfaces of other planets. If all or most geographic data users employ the same (or well-recognized) earth-reference techniques, data can be shared economically among agencies using various computer systems.

To begin with, the most widely accepted shape of the earth has been geometrically modeled as an ellipsoid of revolution, with a semimajor axis of 6,378,135 m, called the GRS80 ellipsoid (see Section 10.1 and Figure 11.23). Once the shape of the earth has been modeled and a geodetic datum defined, some method must be used to show the earth's curved surface accurately, with minimal distortion, on plane-surface map sheets. Several map projections have been developed. In North America, the projections used most are the Lambert projection and the transverse Mercator projection (in the United States) and the universal transverse Mercator projection (primarily used in Canada). Along with a specific projection, it is possible to define a coordinate grid that can be used to minimize distortion as we move from a spherical surface to a plane surface. (See Chapter 10 for more on this topic.) Measurements on the grid can be in feet, U.S. feet, or meters (see Table 1.1).

### 9.4.1    Coordinate Grids

The United States has adopted either the Lambert conical projection or the transverse Mercator cylindrical projection and has created coordinate grid systems (false northing and easting) defined for each state. The state plane coordinate system 1983 (SPCS83), which superseded the SPCS27, has been applied to all states, and the universal transverse Mercator grid has been applied to Canada. Software programs will readily convert coordinates based on one projection to any other commonly used projection. Coordinate grids are discussed in Chapter 10.

### 9.4.2    Transformation

When data is imported from various sources, it is likely that different earth-reference models may have been used. If a GIS is tied to a specific coordinate grid and specific orientation, new data may have to be transformed to fit the working model. Transformations can be made in grid reference, scale, and orientation, and GIS programs, are designed to translate from one grid reference to another, to convert from one scale to another, and to rotate to achieve appropriate orientation (see Figure 9.3).

### 9.4.3    Geocoding

Spatial data describes spatial location (for example, geographic coordinates, map coordinates, street addresses, postal codes, etc.) of an entity, whereas attribute data (often shown in related tables) describes the different aspects of the entity being collected. Examples of attribute data include population of towns, ground cover (including crop types), number of occupants of a dwelling, etc. The linking of entity and attribute data to a specific geographic location is known as *geocoding*. GIS programs should be able to recognize the defining characteristics of imported data in the geocodes from the metadata (see Section

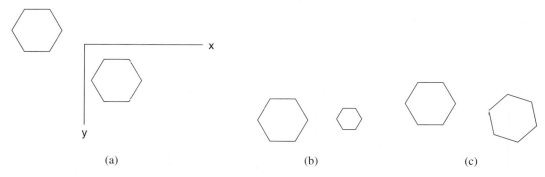

**FIGURE 9.3**    Transformation techniques. (a) Translation. (b) Scale. (c) Rotation.

9.6) information supplied and then make the necessary conversions so that the imported data are tied to the same reference datum as are the working data.

## 9.5    Database Management

A GIS is concerned with large amounts of both spatial data and nonspatial (attribute) data. Data must be organized so that information about entities and their attributes can be accessed by rapid computerized search and retrieval techniques. When data in a specific category is organized in such a fashion, that data collection is known as a data base. Data collections can range in complexity from simple unstructured lists and tables to ordered lists and tables (for example, alphabetical, numerical, etc.), to indexes (see the index at the back of this text), and finally to sets of more complex categorized tables.

The computerized tabular data structure used by many GIS programs is called a **relational database.** A relational database is a set theory–based data structure comprised of ordered sets of attribute data (entered in rows known as "tuples") grouped in two-dimensional tables called **relations.** When searching the columns of one or more data bases for specific information, a key, called a **primary key,** or some other unique identifier must be used. A primary key is an unambiguous descriptor(s) such as a place name, coordinates of a point, postal code address, etc. The data in one table is related to similar data in another table by a GIS technique of **relational join.** Any number of tables can be related if they all share a common column.

For example, using a postal code address or even state plane coordinates, a wide variety of descriptive tables can be accessed containing information relevant to that specific location. One table may contain parcel data, including current and former ownership, assessment, etc., while other tables may contain municipal services available at that location, rainfall/snowfall statistics, pedestrian and vehicular traffic counts at different periods of the day, etc.

Queries of a relational data base are governed by a standard query language (SQL), developed by IBM in the 1970s, to access data in a logically structured manner. Traditional SQL continues to be modified by software designers (with assistance from the Open GIS Consortium—see Section 9.6) for specific applications in GIS, for example, with the inclusion of spatial operators and tools such as adjacency, overlap, buffering, area, etc. See Sections 9.15 and 9.16 at the end of this chapter for more information on this topic.

## 9.6 Metadata

Metadata are "data about data." They describe the content, quality, condition, and other characteristics of data. In 1994, the Federal Geographic Data Committee (FGDC) of the National Spatial Data Infrastructure (NSDI) approved standards for "*Coordinating Geographic Data Acquisition and Access*" (updated in 1998) and in 2000 published a "*Content Standard for Geospatial Metadata Workbook*," available on-line at http://www.fgdc. gov/publications/documents/metadata/workbook_0501_bmk.pdf.

As we noted earlier in this chapter, the cost of obtaining data is one of the chief expenses in developing a data base. Many agencies and commercial firms cannot afford to create all the data that may be needed for various GIS analyses, thus the need for standards in the collection, dissemination, and cataloging of data sets (a data set is a collection of related data).

FGDC lists the different aspects of data described by metadata:

- Identification: What is the name of the data set? Who developed the data set? What geographic area does it cover? What themes of information does it include? How current are the data? Are there restrictions on accessing or using the data?
- Data quality: How good are the data? Is information available that allows the user to decide if the data are suitable for the intended purpose? What is the positional and attribute accuracy? Are the data complete? What data were used to create the data set and what processes were applied to these sources?
- Spatial data organization: What spatial data model was used to code the spatial data? How many spatial objects are there? Are methods other than coordinates, such as street addresses, used to encode locations?
- Spatial reference: Are coordinate locations encoded using longitude and latitude? Is a map projection or grid system such as the state plane coordinate system used? What horizontal and vertical datums are used? What parameters should be used to convert the data to another coordinate grid system?
- Entity and attribute information: What geographic information (roads, houses, elevation, temperature, etc.) is included? How is this information encoded? Were codes used? What do the codes mean?
- Distribution: From whom can you obtain the data? What formats are available? What media are available? Are the data available on-line? What is the price of the data?
- Metadata reference: When were the metadata compiled? By whom?

## 9.7 Spatial Data Transfer Standard (SDTS)

Since the cost of data is one of the largest expenses in GIS endeavors, it is imperative that some standards be created so that people using data processed in one GIS system may import data processed on another GIS system. The national spatial data infrastructure (NSDI), established in 1994, identified a basic framework of seven thematic layers that are often used in the creation of maps and the analysis of geographic spatial data: (1) horizontal control (geodetic control monuments), (2) digital orthoimagery, (3) elevation,

(4) hydrography (surface water features), (5) government boundaries (federal, state, county, municipal), (6) cadastre (property ownership), and (7) transportation.

SDTS is a comprehensive standard for earth-referenced data and is designed for the transfer of all types of spatial data between dissimilar computer systems. By 1992, SDTS issued base standards in three parts: Part 1, Logical Specifications; Part 2, Spatial Features; and Part 3, ISO 8211 Encoding. To implement SDTS, profiles are designed to address the unique issues in each field. SDTS supports United States Geodetic Survey (USGS) digital line graphs (DLGs) such as large-scale DLF data at 7.5 minute quadrangles and a scale of 1:25,000 or 1: 24,000. This data is sold in nine layers—public land survey system (PLSS), boundaries, transportation, hydrography, hypsography, surface cover, nonvegetative surface features, survey control and markers, and human-made or cultural features. Other smaller scale USGS DLG data are also available such as 1:100,000, which provides data on hydrography and transportation layers, and the 1:2,000,000 DLG, which provides data layered as hydrography, transportation, boundaries, public land survey system, and human-made features.

- Topological vector profile (TVP) was the first profile approved and is regarded as Part 4 of the SDTS. This profile was designed to support geographic vector data with geometry and topology. It includes SDTS-defined spatial objects representing vector data with full topology. The Census Bureau will also use this TVP to distribute its topologically integrated geographic encoding and referencing (TIGER) data files.
- Raster profile and extensions (RPE) is Part 5 of SDTS and was developed to support two-dimensional spatial data sets in which features or images are represented in raster or grid form.
- The transportation network profile (TNP) will provide specifications for use with geographic vector data and network topology.
- The point profile, which is referred to as SDTS Part 6, is designed to support a major release of geodetic control point data from NOAA's National Geodetic Survey (NGS), as well as point-only data from other agencies.

For additional information on SDTS profile development, see the FGDC Standards Working Group website at http://www.fgdc.gov/SWG/swg.html.

It appears that most readily available data is in raster format, derived from small-scale (for example, 1:100,000, 1:2,000,000) U.S. Geological Survey (USGS) digital line graph (DLG) data and from the larger scale (1:24,000 and 1:25,000) DLGs. More information on this ongoing development of the data standard can be found at the SDTS home page at http://mcmcweb.er.usgs.gov/sdts/index.html.

It should be noted here that some GIS development firms are also actively addressing the need for standards and interoperability by sharing their data routines so that most programs can read the routines of the programs of the other major GIS vendors. An open GIS consortium (OGC), made up of more than 100 agencies representing GIS software development, computer hardware design, educational research, etc., has been established to develop an open geodata interoperability specification (OGIS) so that GIS users can, in the future, work more easily with data from different sources and with different brands of software. Visit the consortium's website at www.opengis.org/techno/specs.htm.

## 9.C   Data Analysis

## 9.8   Spatial Entities or Features

Spatial data have two characteristics: location and descriptive attributes. In GIS, entities are modeled as either points, lines, or areas (polygons). When a polygon is given the dimension of height, an additional model, surface, is created. Surface models include contoured drawing, rainfall runoff, etc. Each entity can have various attributes assigned to it. Attributes describe something about that entity, and their values can be kept in relational tables, as in the vector model, or attached to the layer grid cells themselves, as in the raster model.

Spatial data describe the geographic location of a feature or entity and its location, with respect to other area features, is given either by rectangular coordinates (vector model) or by grid cells (raster model) described by grid column and row. Other locators, such as postal codes, route mileage posts, etc., can also be used.

Point is the simplest spatial entity, having zero dimension, and usually specifies geometric location. In vector representation [see Figure 9.4(a)], a point is described by a set of $X/Y$ or east/north coordinates. In raster representation [see Figure 9.4(b)], a point is described by a single grid cell. Points have attributes that describe the entity; for example, a utility pole entity may have an attribute such as a traffic signal or traffic sign or electrical distribution. In Figure 9.4, for example, the entity described by the code number 6 could be industrially zoned property.

Line (arc) is a spatial entity having one dimension and joins two points; a string is comprised of a sequence of connected lines or arc segments. The line or arc can be defined by an ordered series of coordinated points (vector representation) or by a series of grid cells (raster representation). Lines or arcs have attributes that describe those particular entities. For example, a line entity may represent a ℄ (centerline) section of a municipal pipeline, and attributes for that entity can include use, pipe type, slope, diameter, inverts, date of installation, date of last maintenance, etc. In vector models, this attribute data would be stored in a table in a relational data base.

Polygon is a spatial entity having two dimensions and is described by an enclosed area defined by an arc or a series of arcs closing back to the starting point. Polygons have attributes that describe the whole area, such as tree cover, land zoning, etc. In the case of vector models, the polygon has a single number representing the attribute of the enclosed area; and in the case of raster models, the code number representing the attribute for an area is displayed in each grid cell within that enclosed area. See Figure 9.4.

## 9.9   Typical Data Representation

Typical data representation depends on the defined scale or resolution. The following lists show the categories typically used:

| POINT | LINE OR STRING | POLYGON (AREA) |
|---|---|---|
| Well | River or shoreline | Pond or lake |
| Utility pole or tower | Distribution line | Transmission station |
| Hydrant or valve | Water line | Water line grid |

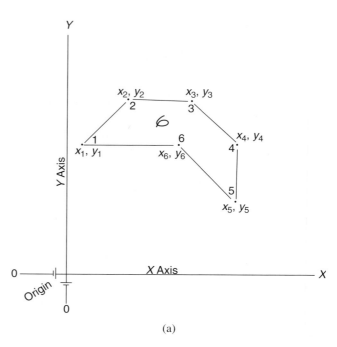

(a)

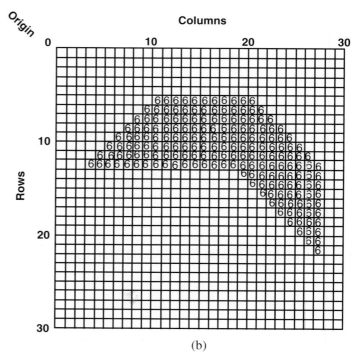

**FIGURE 9.4** Data models used in GIS. (a) Vector model. (b) Raster model. 6 is a numeric attribute code that describes a function or description of the ground area being modeled. For example, 6 can be land zoned for industrial development.

(b)

294

| | | |
|---|---|---|
| Bus shelter | Sidewalk or road | Parking lot |
| Storm water manhole | Storm water pipeline | Catchment/runoff area |
| Property monument | Lot line/fence line | Land parcel |
| Land parcel | Neighborhood | Town/city or political boundary |
| Deciduous tree | Row of trees | Tree stand |
| Roads ℄ intersection | Road ℄ | Section of road, right of way (ROW) |
| Farmhouse | Irrigation channel | Crop field |
| Refreshment booth | Path | Park |

1. On larger-scale maps, large rivers, expressways, and so on, will be shown as having width and can then be classified as polygons (when section end lines are drawn).

2. Before entities can be modeled as points, lines, polygons, or surfaces, scale must be taken into consideration. For example, on small-scale maps, towns may show up as dots (points), whereas on larger-scale maps, towns will probably show up as polygons or areas.

3. Scale also affects the way entities are shown on a map. On small-scale maps, meandering rivers will be shown with fewer and smoother bends, and small crop fields may not show up at all.

## 9.10    Spatial Data Models

In GIS, real-world physical features are called entities and are modeled using one or both of the following techniques: vector model or raster model. Both are discussed in the following sections.

### 9.10.1    Vector Model

Surveying and engineering students are already familiar with the concept of vectors, where collected data are described and defined by their discrete Cartesian coordinates ($X, Y$) or (easting, northing) and the origin (0, 0) of a rectangular grid is at the lower left corner of the grid. Points are identified by their coordinates, whereas lines, or a series of lines, are identified by the coordinates of their endpoints. Areas or polygons are described by a series of lines (arcs) that loop back to the coordinated point of beginning. See Figure 9.4(a). Points are described as having zero dimension, lines have one dimension, and areas or polygons have two dimensions.

In addition to treating points, lines, and polygons, vector GIS, also recognizes line/polygon intersections as well as the topological aspects of network analysis (connectivity) and adjacency (see Section 9.12). These capabilities give GIS its unique capabilities of querying and routing. Attribute data, which describe or classify entities, are located in a data base or in tables, linked to the coordinated vector model. Attributes can be numbers, characters, images, or even CAD drawings.

Data captured using field data techniques usually come with acceptably accurate coordinates. When data are captured by digitizing (using a digitizing table or digitizing tablet) from existing maps and plans, some additional factors must be considered. First, the scale of the map or plan being digitized will be a limiting factor in the accuracy of the resulting coordinates; second, when irregular features are captured by sampling with the digitizing cursor or puck, some errors will be introduced, depending on the sampling interval. For example, it is generally agreed that feature sample points should be digitized at each beginning and end point and change in direction, but how often do you sample curving lines? If the curved lines are geometrically defined (for example, circular, spiral), a few sampling points may be sufficient, but if the curve is irregular, the sampling rate will have to depend on the relative importance of the feature and perhaps the scale of any proposed output graphics.

## 9.10.2 Raster Model

Raster modeling was a logical consequence of the collection of data through remote sensing and scanning techniques. Here, topographic images are represented by pixels (picture elements) that have the structure of a multi-celled grid. A raster is a GIS data structure comprised of a matrix of rectangular (usually square) grid cells. Each cell represents a specific area on the ground; the resolution of the raster is defined by the ground area represented by the raster grid cell. A cell could represent a 10 $ft^2/m^2$, 100 $ft^2/m^2$, or even 1,000 $ft^2/m^2$ ground area—all depending on the resolution or scale of the grid cell. The higher the resolution of the grid, the more cells are required to portray a given area of the ground surface; the larger the ground area represented by a grid cell, the less precise is the cell's ability to define position. Thus, we see in the raster model that the considerations of scale enter the picture at the beginning of a project. The resolution of the raster is often a function of the scale of the map from which the spatial data may have been scanned or digitized [see Figure 9.4(b)]. Be careful when first using GIS programs to identify the resolution of the raster grid with which you may be working because some GIS programs display cursor coordinates to two or three decimal places (that change as the cursor is moved over the screen), even when the grid resolution is only ten to twenty (or more) feet/meters.

Raster grid cells are identified as being in rows and columns, with the location of any raster cell given by the column and row numbers. The zero row and column (the origin) is often located at the upper left of the raster grid (the location of the origin is defined differently by various software agencies). Features defined by their raster cell are thus not only geographically located but are also located relative to all other features in the raster. Since raster grid cells represent areas (not points) on the earth, they cannot be used for precise measurements. Each cell contains an attribute value (often a number) that describes the entity represented by that layer-specific cell. In multispectral imagery, the cell is identified by its grey-scale number, for example, a number in the range of 0 to 255 for eight-bit imagery.

Pixels (a term employed in the field of remote sensing), like grid cells, portray an area subdivided into very small square (usually) cells. Pixels (short for "picture elements") are the result of capturing data through the digitization of aerial/satellite imagery. The distribution of an image's colors and tones is established by assigning digital number (DN) values to each pixel; much of this can now be accomplished using automated soft-copy (digital) photogrammetry techniques and digital image analysis (see Chapter 12). Image resolution is stated by defining the ground area represented by one pixel. The concept of dots per inch (dpi) is used in some applications, where each dot is a pixel. If an image has a dpi of 100, each dot or pixel would have a grid cell side length of 1/100 of an inch.

Pixels are identified by unique numerical codes called a digital number (DN). Each cell has only one DN; much GIS software now uses eight-bit ($2^8$) data, which allows for 256 numbers, from 0 to 255. (See also Section 12.5 for a discussion of digital numbers.) Early in the GIS design, the attributes to be displayed in which feature layers are determined, and as the GIS construction proceeds, each cell in each layer can be given a unique code number or letter identifying the predominant (or average) attribute for that cell. For example, a grid cell code of 16 can be defined to represent areas zoned as residential, for housing. Each cell has more than one attribute code assigned and stored on separate feature layers.

# 9.11   GIS Data Structures

## 9.11.1   General Background

GIS software programs usually support both raster and vector models, and some programs readily convert from one to the other. The type of model selected is usually determined by the source of the data and the intended use of the data. For example, the vector model is used when there is access to coordinated data consistent with fieldwork, and the raster model is used when the data flows from scanned map data or remotely sensed imagery, where the smallest identifiable area, a pixel, is the raster equivalent of a grid cell. When the project objectives concern large-scale engineering design or analysis, a vector model GIS will almost certainly be employed. If the objective concerns small-scale land zoning, planning analysis, or some types of cultural or social studies, a raster model GIS may be the best choice. An additional consideration deals with the nature of the data. For example, features that vary continuously, such as elevation or temperature, lend themselves to raster depiction, whereas discrete features, such as roads and pipelines, lend themselves to vector depiction.

Both vector and raster models permit storage of thematic data on separate layers. Typical thematic layers include (see Figure 9.2):

- Spatial reference system, for example, coordinate grid system, etc. (see Chapter 10). The control data on this layer is used to correlate the placement of spatial data on all related layers.
- Elevation data (including contours).
- Parcel (property) boundaries.
- Hydrology/wetlands (runoff and catchment areas, drainage, streams, and rivers).
- Transportation.
- Soil types.
- Geology.
- Land use and zoning.
- Municipal services.
- Government boundaries.
- Buildings and other structures.

• Ground cover (including crop types and tree stands).

Individual layers, or any combination of layers, can be overlaid and analyzed together or plotted together using digital plotters. Although vector models provide for a higher level of accuracy than do raster models, GIS vector analyses require a much higher level of processing and computer storage.

If large-scale graphics are to be an important consideration, it should be reiterated that, in raster plots, lines may have a stepped appearance that detracts from the overall presentation. The lower the resolution of the grid cell, the more pronounced is the appearance of stepping. [See Figure 9.6(c) and (d).] When performing overlay analysis, raster data is more efficient because all the cells from each layer match. With network analysis, vector depiction is preferred because here we are dealing with attributes of discrete linear features (for example, a road's speed limit, the number of stop signs, etc.).

## 9.11.2 Model Data Conversion

At times, data in vector format must be converted to raster format, and vice versa. To understand the working of the various software programs designed to perform those functions, it helps to analyze different data models that represent the same planimetric features. Figure 9.5 shows features as depicted on a topographic map, along with both vector and raster models, of a simplified area.

Figure 9.5(a) is a map representation of collected field data. The stream looks more "natural" here because it has been cartographically smoothed for the sake of appearances. In Figure 9.5(b), the data is shown in vectors, and the stream, although perhaps more geometrically correct, is less pleasing to the eye. Here, the lines joining coordinated ground points define part of a stream chain, with each segment directionally defined.

To convert the vector model to a raster format, a raster of specified resolution is overlaid the vector model. The more grid cells, the higher the resolution and the more realistic the portrayal of the area features. Note in Figure 9.5(c) that the length of the sides of each grid cell is half the length of the grid cells in Figure 9.5(d), resulting in four times as many cells. If GIS users were to define very high resolution raster grids in an attempt to improve the model's accuracy, appearance, etc., they may soon run into problems resulting from exponential increases in the quantity of data, which has serious implications for computer memory requirements and program analysis run-times. Another factor that weighs heavily here is the level of accuracy of the original data and the use to which the GIS will be put.

Since vectors represent discrete coordinated locations, and raster grids represent grid cells having areas of some defined size, precise conversions are not possible. As model data is converted, some choices will have to be made. For example, since each grid cell can have only one attribute, what happens when more than one feature on a vector model is at least partially captured in a raster grid cell? Which of the possible feature attributes will be designated for that specific grid cell?

Figure 9.5 shows seven identified attributes: road, stream, grass, orchard, drive, well, and house. Many grid cells have at least two possible attributes. Which is more important, stream or grass? If we pick grass, the stream feature will not show up at all, and the same for the well, the road, and the drive. If we want to portray these features, we have to find some consistent technique for ranking their importance in the raster display. What happens

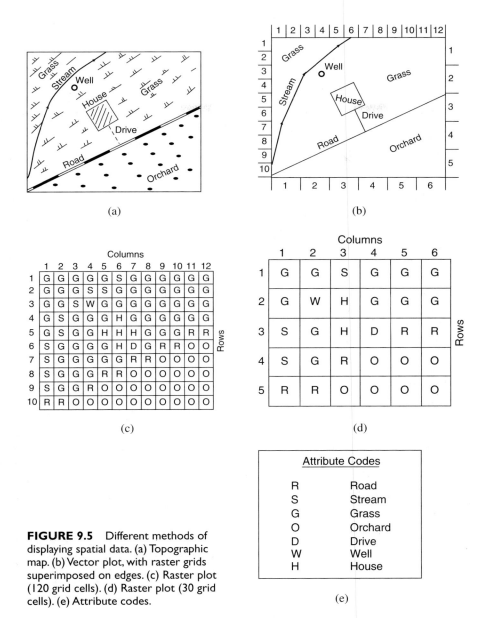

**FIGURE 9.5** Different methods of displaying spatial data. (a) Topographic map. (b) Vector plot, with raster grids superimposed on edges. (c) Raster plot (120 grid cells). (d) Raster plot (30 grid cells). (e) Attribute codes.

| Attribute Codes | |
|---|---|
| R | Road |
| S | Stream |
| G | Grass |
| O | Orchard |
| D | Drive |
| W | Well |
| H | House |

(e)

when same-cell features are equally important? Generally, there are four methods of assigning cell attributes:

1.  Presence or absence: first, we have to determine whether or not a specific feature is present within the area of the cell; a simple boolean operator can be used in the software to implement this yes/no operation. This technique permits a quick search for specific features.

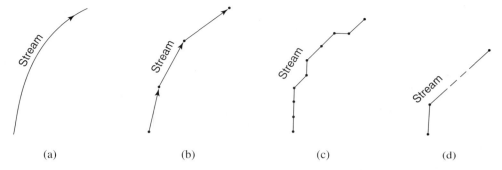

(a)                              (b)                              (c)                              (d)

**FIGURE 9.6**   Stream feature depictions, using four models. (a) Topographic map plot: smoothed plot of data capture. (b) Vector model plot: coordinated tie-points are plotted. (c) Moderate resolution: raster model plot. (d) Coarse resolution: raster model plot. Raster plots are the result of joining the stream feature grid cell's midpoints. Illustrations (a)–(d) are derived from the illustrations (a)–(d) of Figure 10.5.

2. Centerpoint: which feature is closest to the cell centerpoint?

3. Dominant feature: which feature, if any, is more dominant, that is, occupies more than 50% of the grid cell?

4. Precedence: the rank of a feature within a cell is considered; that is, which of the captured features are more important? In Figure 9.5, the road, stream, drive, house, and well are more important features than the surrounding grass and orchard, features that may be more dominant in the cells and closer to many of the cell's center.

To convert from raster to vector, the cell centerpoints are often identified and then joined, resulting in the stepped appearances displayed in Figure 9.6(c) and (d). As noted earlier, the lower the resolution, the more stepped is the appearance and the less realistic the portrayal of that specific feature. If line smoothing techniques are used to improve the stepped display appearance in raster models, errors are introduced that may be quite significant. Figure 9.6(a) and (b) shows the stream in topographic and vector modeling, respectively, a much smoother presentation.

## 9.12   Topology

Topology describes the relationships that geographic entities (polygons, lines, and points) have with each other. The relationships may be spatial in nature (proximity, adjacency, connectivity), or the relationships may be based on entity attributes (for example, tree species planted or harvested within a certain time period). Topology gives GIS its ability to analyze geospatial data. Topology gives a vector GIS its ability to permit querying of a data base and thus differentiates GIS from simple CAD systems, which merely show spatial location of entities and their attributes, not their relationships with each other.

Topological structure is comprised of arcs and nodes. Arcs are one or more line segments that begin and end at a node. Nodes are the points of intersection of arcs, or terminal points of arcs. Polygons are closed figures consisting of a series of three or more connected chains.

Topology does not define geometric relationships, only relational relationships. The example often used for this distinction is the use of rubber sheeting, a technique used to join surfaces originally tied to different projections or coordinate grids, where surfaces are stretched to fit with other surfaces. This stretching process may affect distances and angles between entities but will not affect the relational (adjacency, networking, etc.) characteristics of the features. Topological relationships include:

- Connectivity: determines where (for example, at which node) chains are connected and gives a sense of direction among connected chains by specifying **to nodes** and **from nodes.**
- Adjacency: determines what spatial features (points, lines, and areas) are adjacent to chains and polygons. The descriptions "left" and "right" can be applied once direction has been established by defining to and from nodes.
- Containment: determines which spatial features (points, lines, and smaller polygons) are enclosed within a specified polygon.

Entities such as polygons, chains, and nodes can have a wide variety of relational characteristics. For example, a polygon defining the location of a stand of spruce trees can overlap or be adjacent to a polygon defining a stand of pine trees (see Figure 9.7). This simple two-attribute data set can be queried to identify six possibilities: those areas (polygons) that contain pine trees, spruce trees, only pine trees, or only spruce trees, or coniferous (spruce and pine) trees, or that area of overlap containing both pine and spruce trees. Figure 9.7 also shows the Boolean operators that can be used to implement the same type of analysis. If the appropriate data have been collected and input, the data base can be further queried to ascertain attribute data, such as the age of various parts of each tree stand, tree diameters, and a potential selected harvest (for example, board feet of lumber).

Line entities can be similarly analyzed. Figure 9.8 shows a network of chains with nodes that act as points of intersection of chains or where a feature (like a roadway) begins, ends, or intersects (connects) with other roadways. The expressway ℄ can be analyzed with respect to the lengths between off/on interchanges. Crosstown Blvd. and Crosstown Expressway can also be analyzed to show the location and extent of their combined roadway. Note that Second Ave., Third Ave., and Fourth Ave., as well as Oak St. and Elm St., cross but do not connect to the Crosstown Expressway; nodes are shown only at connection points. With a network of roads in the database and given sufficient data (including one-way streets, detours, etc.), analysis can be done for routing. For example, you can find the shortest route from one point to another or one address to another, the most scenic route, the quickest access to a particular location, etc. Line features can also be analyzed with respect to polygons, such as when train tracks or roads intersect or abut properties that may be land-use zoned for various development purposes.

Point entities can be analyzed with respect to each other or with respect to line and polygon features. A pumping station, for example, may be shown as a node in a water distribution system, which itself can be shown as chains or a network of chains, all of which can be shown within a polygon representing a town or a neighborhood. The pumping station can be one of many on the network. Each pumping station may contain pumps of

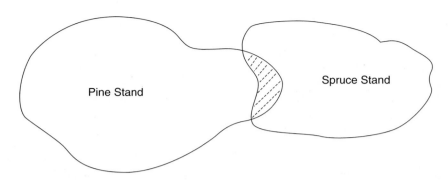

Pine Stand

Spruce Stand

Choices

1. Pine
2. Spruce
3. Pine, Without Spruce
4. Spruce, Without Pine
5. Coniferous (Spruce and Pine)
6. Only Spruce and Pine Together

Boolean Operators

| 1. | Union | | Pine and Spruce |
| 2. | Minus | | Pine But Not Spruce |
| 3. | Intersect | | Only Spruce and Pine Together |
| 4. | Difference | | |

**FIGURE 9.7**   Polygon analysis.

various capacities, with and without emergency power capability, employee washrooms, etc. All of this related tabular data can be accessed and shown on a computer screen with the click of the cursor.

If all of the above overlaying techniques are combined, it would be possible, for example, to search for a piece of available real estate that is between 1 and 3 acres in area, has access to an adequate water supply, is zoned for industrial development, is adjacent to a rail spur, is within 600 ft of fire hydrants, and is within 1 mile from a crosstown expressway access. The GIS process of establishing areas or zones of limiting distance around an entity is accomplished by buffering or by defining "geographic extent." With this type of GIS search technique, a project formerly taking days or even weeks to accomplish can now be completed in a few hours.

Before data can be analyzed, a great deal of time may be spent "cleaning up" the data. There may have been errors in spatial data, such as line overshoot, which may be detected by checking topological integrity, or there may be errors in attribute data, such as mistaken identity, a misplaced decimal, etc. All of these may be checked using map overlays, that is, by comparing the geographic position of data points stored on one layer with

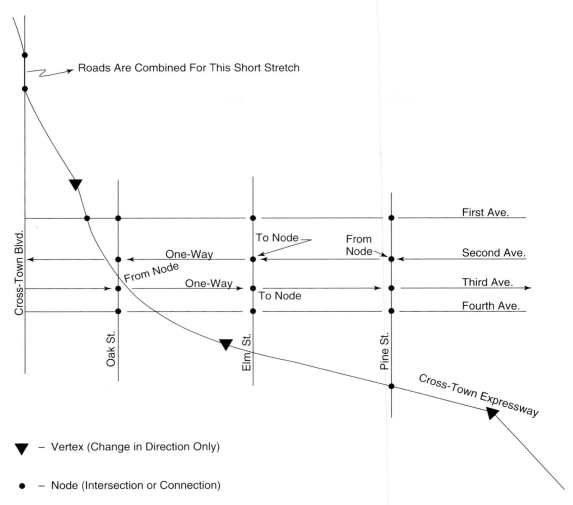

Roads Are Combined For This Short Stretch

First Ave.

To Node From Node

Second Ave.

One-Way

From Node

One-Way

Third Ave.

To Node

Fourth Ave.

Cross-Town Blvd.

Oak St.

Elm St.

Pine St.

Cross-Town Expressway

▼ — Vertex (Change in Direction Only)

● — Node (Intersection or Connection)

**FIGURE 9.8**  Line and chain analysis for connectivity.

the position of data points stored on other layers within the same data base. When collecting digitized data from a map, it is possible that the original map projection was unknown. Perhaps a rubber-sheeting process was used in which some specified known points were kept fixed while other points were stretched to fit in. You can refer to texts specializing in GIS for more information on these topics.

## 9.13  Data Analysis Summary

GIS software programs have been designed to permit a wide variety of data analyses. Measurements can be made of lengths, areas, slopes, direction of slopes, and these processes differ in the raster and vector models. Cells can be summed in the raster model; in the vector model, coordinates can be used in length and area calculations (see Chapter 6). The results of feature measurements then become additional attributes of those features. Detailed analyses can also be performed, and they will be described next.

## 9.13.1  Reclassification

The reclassification of data is often used in GIS analysis. For example, the number of categories of tree cover can be simplified by reducing the number of classes; many different individual species of deciduous and coniferous trees in a specific geographic area can be reclassified (and thus simplified) by being described just as deciduous or coniferous. Reclassification is also useful in creating a mask layer to isolate specific feature properties. In Figure 9.9, land areas are assigned zeros for wet or cool or ones for dry or warm. By using only zeros and ones, a multiply overlay identifies the areas that are both dry and warm.

## 9.13.2  Overlay Analysis

Overlay is an analysis often used to compare and contrast geographic data stored on separate feature layers by superimposing only those layers holding data of interest into a new composite layer. In the mapping age, such comparisons could be made only by visually comparing maps drawn (perhaps at different scales) to portray specific features, for example, soil maps compared with hydrographic maps.

With a GIS, siting searches for, let's say, a suitable crop selection for a given area may result in a new layer that includes soil types, moisture conditions, sunlight hours, etc. All of this information is stored on separate data layers within the GIS. Siting searches for suitable retail locations may result in a new layer that which includes information on proximity to arterial roads, available municipal services, pedestrian traffic counts, vehicular

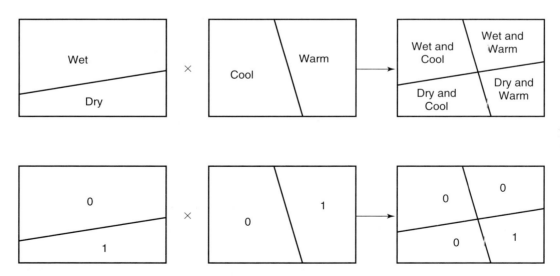

**FIGURE 9.9**   Multiplying overlay reclassification.

traffic counts, median income of locality, land costs, taxes, bylaw restrictions, etc. Each type of information is stored directly on a separate layer or in layer-related tables within the GIS.

## 9.13.3   Location

The location of features near or adjacent to other specified features can be ascertained in two ways: (1) by creating (with the cursor) a box that defines the geographic locational extent of an area to be examined and queried, and (2) by buffering. The box created with the cursor can be queried with respect to the presence or absence of certain defined features, or queried about the closeness of defined features to a specific location. For example, within the defined area, how many schools, churches, and malls exist? Which schools are within 1,500 feet of a specific property? Buffering can be used to define a set space around points, lines, and polygons to ask queries. For example, which industrially zoned properties of a certain size range are for sale within a half mile of an existing expressway?

## 9.13.4   Connectivity

This type of line linkage analysis permits routing design and analysis. Road networks can be analyzed to determine the shortest route, the fastest route, the most scenic route, etc. Pipeline networks can be analyzed to determine which land parcels will be affected by a pipeline break, and which valves should be turned off to isolate the broken section so that repairs can be made. See also Figure 9.8, where you can see that, although the Crosstown Expressway crosses many streets, only with Pine St., First Ave., and Crosstown Blvd. are there connections for vehicle access. The stream/river network of a watershed, in conjunction with modeled rain intensities, can be analyzed to predict flooding and thus provide warnings to affected residents.

## 9.13.5   Adjacency

The strength of GIS as an analytical tool is the wealth of information that can be attached to a specific feature (point, line, or polygon). In addition to information on the feature itself (see Figure 9.10), GIS data can be accessed directly for all its adjacent features. For example, the line-feature road shown in Figure 9.5 can be queried not only with respect to its location, its direction (bearing), and its surface materials, but also about the features adjacent to that road. After defining the direction for the road, left and right properties (parcel polygons) can be queried for property owners' names, street addresses, assessment, square footage of buildings, ground cover, etc.

## 9.13.6   Coordinate Transformation

Additional data can be added to the GIS data base and made compatible by transforming projections, scales, and coordinate systems, as needed, to agree with the specifications of the operating GIS. Additional data can also be added or modified by using the keyboard and cursor.

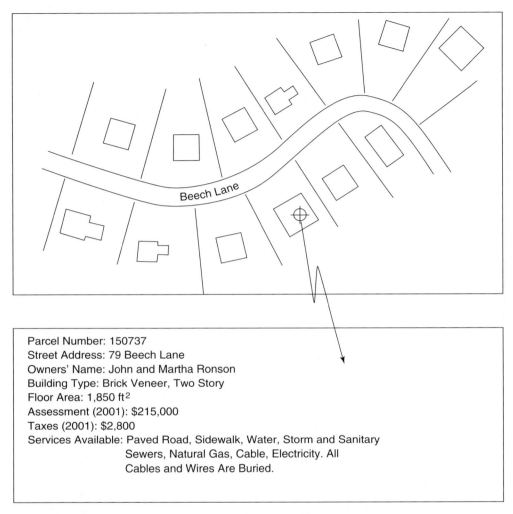

Parcel Number: 150737
Street Address: 79 Beech Lane
Owners' Name: John and Martha Ronson
Building Type: Brick Veneer, Two Story
Floor Area: 1,850 ft$^2$
Assessment (2001): $215,000
Taxes (2001): $2,800
Services Available: Paved Road, Sidewalk, Water, Storm and Sanitary
                    Sewers, Natural Gas, Cable, Electricity. All
                    Cables and Wires Are Buried.

**FIGURE 9.10**   Zoomed-in portion of a GIS layer showing the type of feature data available with a specific cursor selection.

## 9.13.7   Multicriteria Analysis

Boolean operators (used in symbolic logic) can be used to analyze data layers to produce new features and attributes. For example, the conditions can be set so that the software identifies only those residentially zoned properties above a certain elevation. This yes/no approach excludes all features and areas that do not meet the search specifications, regardless of extenuating conditions that may exist.

A more liberal approach permits ranked results. Attribute data can be ranked with respect to importance. For example, if a site search is made for a resort hotel, waterfront or waterfront access can be assigned a high rank, and cost ranges for land acquisition can be assigned an even higher rank. Perhaps highway access would be ranked, as would hours of sunlight in the location, presence of existing structures, proximity to competing resources, proximity to the entertainment district(s), etc. The results of this type of GIS analysis would yield several solutions, each with a mix of ranked outcomes. Then a committee can determine trade-off preferences, for example, lower costs for land versus poorer highway accessibility, or choicer location versus higher acquisition costs. With this type of analysis, no choices are automatically excluded.

## 9.14  GIS Glossary

**address matching** GIS geocoding software that can identify street addresses (such as are compiled in the U.S. Census Bureau's TIGER data) by conversion from grid coordinates.

**arc** An arc is a line entity, used in topology. *See* link.

**attribute** A nongraphical descriptor of a geographic feature or entity. It can be qualitative or quantitative, such as numerical codes tied to qualitative descriptors (the number 8 representing "commercial development" on a land-use layer).

**buffer** A specified zone around an entity that can be used to query a data base.

**cell** The basic rectangular element of a raster grid. It is called a pixel in digital images.

**centroid** The centerpoint (or other identified point) of a polygon at which attribute information for that polygon may be tagged. For example, for a polygon representing a specific neighborhood, population, assessment, voting preferences, etc., all may be stored at the designated centroid coordinates or grid cell.

**chain** Directional and nonintersecting arcs or strings with nodes at each end.

**digitizing** The conversion of analog data from existing map sheets into digital (coordinated) data by using a cursor on a digitizing table.

**entity** Also called *feature*; a real-world object that can be positioned or located geographically.

**geocoding** The linking of entity and attribute data to a specific geographic location.

**layer** In a GIS, a collection of similar (thematic) data for a given geographic area, stored in a specific location in computer memory.

**line** A one-dimensional entity that links two coordinated endpoints directly.

**link** A one-dimensional topological entity that connects two nodes directly. A directed link defines direction from a *from node* to a *to node*. *See* arc.

**network** An entity of interconnected lines that permits the analysis of route flow.

**node** A zero-dimensional topological point entity that represents a beginning or ending of chains (representing arcs or lines), including intersections.

**overlay** The GIS technique of selectively comparing and combining layers (categories) of entities and their variable attributes, which have been stored on separate thematic layers, for a specified ground area.

**pixel** Like a raster grid cell, a pixel (picture element) is the basic element of a digital image (for example, a satellite image or scanned image) whose resolution represents a defined amount of geographic space. See Chapter 12.

**point** A zero-dimensional entity that specifies geometric location (for example, by coordinates).

**relational database** A data base that stores attribute and spatial data in the form of tables that can all be linked through a common identifier (for example, with a primary key), such as a coordinated spatial locator.

**routing** Analysis of networks to determine optimal travel paths or flow from one point to another.

**rubber sheeting** A process of arbitrarily reconciling (stretching) data from different sources that may not fit perfectly together because of problems arising from differing scales, orientations, and projections.

**scale** In GIS and mapping, the size ratio between a ground distance or area and the depiction of that ground distance or area on a map or raster grid.

**scanner** A raster input device that scans a document one line at a time and records the location of scanned objects in a raster matrix.

**segmentation** The creation of new lines or arcs as changes occur to the original line or arc, such as occurs when there is a change in attributes (a two-lane road becomes a four-lane road, or a valve is inserted into a water distribution line) or the creation of new segments caused by intersecting lines or polygons.

**string** A sequence of line segments.

**thematic layer or map** Computer storage layers or maps that display the geographic locations of spatial entities with one or more common attributes.

**TIGER** Topologically Integrated Geographic Encoding and Referencing System; a topological data model designed by the U.S. Bureau of the Census. Much data digitized for this model has come from small-scale USGS maps.

**vertex** Similar to a node, a vertex point entity signals a simple change in direction of a line or arc (but not an intersection).

## 9.15   Internet Websites

The websites listed here include web links to various related sites. Although the websites shown here were verified at the time of publication, some changes are inevitable. Corrected site locations and new sites may be accessed by searching the web links found at sites listed here.

American Association of Geographers (AAG): www.aag.org

American Association of State Highway and Transportation Officials (AASHTO): www.aashto.org

American Congress on Surveying and Mapping ACSM: www.survmap.com

American Society for Photogrammetry and Remote Sensing (ASPRS): www.asprs.org

ARCINFO tutorial home page: http://boris.qub.ac.uk/shane/arc/ARChome.html

Association for Geographic Information: www.agi.org.uk/

Blue Marble Geographics: www.bluemarblegeo.com

Brody's home page—Internet index: www.index-site.com/gis.html

BYU's distributed geographic information links data base: www.geog.byu.edu/gisonline/links/main.htm

Canadian Geodetic Survey: http://www.geod.nrcan.gc.ca
Clark Labs (Idrisi): www.clarklabs.org
CORS information: www.ngs.noaa.gov/CORS/cors-data.html
ERDAS (mapping) tutorial: www.erdas.com
ESRI: ftp://esri.com
ESRI glossary: ftp://esri.com/pub/marketing/misc/glossary.pdf
GeoWorld magazine: www.geoplace.com/gw
GIS—Kingston University Center (UK): http://www.kingston.ac.uk/geog/gis
Intergraph Corporation: http://www.intergraph.com/software/photogrammetry
MAPINFO (mapping): www.mapinfo.com
Map Maker, Ltd.: www.mapmaker.com
National Center for Geographic Information and Analysis:www.ncgia.ucsb.edu/
National Imagery and Mapping agency (NIMA): www.nima.mil/
National Wetlands Inventory: www.nwi.fws.gov/
NGS home page: http://.www.ngs.noaa.gov/
Open GIS Consortium (OGC): www.opengis.org/techno/specs.htm
Penn State Geographic Visualization Science Technology: www.geovista.psu.edu/
POB Point of Beginning magazine: http://www.pobonline.com
Professional Surveyor magazine: http://www.profsurv.com
Trimble—GIS: www.trimble.com/gis/index.htm
U.S. Bureau of Land Management—GIS Data and Metadata: www.blm. gov/gis/nsdi.html
U.S. Bureau of the Census: www.census.com
United States Coast Guard (USCG) Navigation Center: http://www.navcen.uscg.mil
U.S. Geological Survey: http://www.usgs.gov/
U.S. Spatial Data Transfer Standard (SDTS) information: www.mcmcweb.er. usgs.gov/sdts/
University of Maine: http://www.spatial.maine.edu/
Urban and Regional Information Systems Association (URISA): www.urisa.org

## 9.16 Publications

Chrisman, N., *Exploring Geographic Information Systems* (John Wiley and Sons, New York, 1997).

DeMers, M., *Fundamentals of Geographic Information Systems* (John Wiley and Sons, New York, 1997).

Easa, S., and Chan, Y., *Urban Planning and Development Applications of GIS* (American Society of Civil Engineers [ASCE], Reston, Va., 2000).

Foresman, Timothy, *The History of Geographic Information Systems* (Prentice Hall Inc., Upper Saddle River, N.J., 1998).

Heywood, I., Cornelius, S., Carver, C., *An Introduction to Geographical Information Systems* (Prentice Hall Inc., Upper Saddle River, N.J., 1998).

Korte, G. B., *The GIS Book,* Fifth Edition (Thompson Learning, Albany, N.Y., 2001).

Worboys, Michael, F., *GIS, A Computing Perspective* (Taylor and Francis Inc., Bristol, Pa., 1995).

# Questions

1. How do scale and resolution affect the creation and operation of a GIS?
2. What are the various ways that scale can be shown on a map?
3. When is it advantageous to use cylindrical projections? To use conical projections? (See also Chapter 10.)
4. Which features are best modeled using vector techniques? Using raster techniques?
5. List and describe as many GIS applications as you can.
6. GIS is difficult to define. Describe GIS in your own words.
7. What are the similarities and differences between mapping and GIS?
8. What are the similarities and differences between GIS and CAD?
9. What modern developments enabled the creation of GIS?
10. Why is it important to tie spatial data to a recognized reference system?
11. Why does the conversion of raster data to vector data have the potential for locational errors?
12. How do you measure polygon areas in a vector model? In a raster model?

# 10 Control Surveys

## 10.1 General Background

The highest order of control surveys are national or continental in scope. Control surveys covering such enormous areas of the earth's surface must take into account the spherical shape of the earth and are thus called *geodetic surveys*. The early control net of the United States was tied into the control nets of both Canada and Mexico, giving a consistent continental net. The first major adjustment in control data was made in 1927, resulting in the North American Datum (NAD 27). Since that time, a great deal more has been learned about the shape and mass of the earth; these new and expanded data come to us from releveling surveys, precise traverses, satellite positioning surveys, earth movement studies, and gravity surveys. The mass of data thus accumulated has been utilized to update and expand existing control data, and the new geodetic data have provided scientists with the means to define more precisely the actual geometric shape of the earth.

The reference ellipsoid previously used for this purpose (the Clarke spheroid of 1866) was modified to reflect current knowledge of the earth's dimensions. Accordingly, a World Geodetic System, first proposed in 1972 (WGS 1972) and later endorsed in 1979 by the International Association of Geodesy (IAG), included proposals for an earth-mass-centered ellipsoid (GRS 80 ellipsoid) that would represent more closely the planet on which we live. Model defining parameters are shown below:

|                | CLARKE SPHEROID OF 1866 | GRS 80 ELLIPSOID |
|----------------|-------------------------|------------------|
| Semimajor axis | 6,378,206.4 m           | 6,378,137.0 m    |
| Semiminor axis | 6,356,583.8 m           | 6,356,752.3 m    |

GRS 80 is used to define the North American Datum of 1983 (NAD 83), which covers the North American continent, including Greenland and parts of Central America. All individual control nets are included in a weighted simultaneous computation. A good tie to the global system is given by satellite positioning.

The geographic coordinates of points in this system are latitude ($\varphi$) and longitude ($\lambda$). Although this system is widely used in geodetic surveying and mapping, it has been found too cumbersome for use in everyday surveying; for example, the latitude and

**311**

**Table 10.1**  POSITIONING ACCURACY STANDARDS

| Survey Categories | Order | Base error e (cm) | Line-length dependent error p (ppm) | Line-length dependent error a (1:a) |
|---|---|---|---|---|
| HARN | | | | |
| Global-regional geodynamics | AA | 0.3 | 0.01 | 1:100,000,000 |
| National Geodetic Reference System, "primary" network | A | 0.5 | 0.1 | 1:10,000,000 |
| National Geodetic Reference System, "secondary" networks | B | 0.8 | 1 | 1:1,000,000 |
| National Geodetic Reference System (terrestrial based) | C | | | |
| | 1 | 1.0 | 10 | 1:100,000 |
| | 2-I | 2.0 | 20 | 1:50,000 |
| | 2-II | 3.0 | 50 | 1:20,000 |
| | 3 | 5.0 | 100 | 1:10,000 |

The "Minimum geometric accuracy standard[a]" spans the Base error and Line-length dependent error columns.

[a]95 percent confidence level.

*Source:* From Geometric Geodetic Accuracy Standards Using GPS Relative Positioning Techniques. [Federal Geodetic Control Subcommittee (FGCS) 1988]. Publications available through the National Geodetic Survey (NGS), (301) 443-8631.

longitude angles must be expressed to three or four decimals of a second (01.0000″) to give position to the closest 0.01 ft. (At latitude 44°, 1 in. latitude = 101 ft and 1 in. longitude = 73 ft.) Conventional field surveying (as opposed to control surveying) is usually referenced to a plane grid (see Section 10.2). In most cases, the accuracies between NAD 83 first-order stations are better than 1:200,000, which would have been unquestioned in the pre–global positioning system (GPS) era. However, the increased use of very precise GPS surveys and the tremendous potential for new applications using this new technology created a demand for high-precision upgrades to the control net, using GPS techniques.

A cooperative network upgrading program, including federal and state agencies, began in 1986 in Tennessee and was completed in Indiana in 1997. About 16,000 horizontal control survey stations were upgraded to either A-order or B-order status. Horizontal A-order stations have a relative accuracy of 5 mm ± 1:10,000,000 relative to other A-order stations. Horizontal B-order stations have a relative accuracy of 8 mm ± 1:1,000,000 relative to other A-order and B-order stations. Of the 16,000 survey stations, the National Geodetic Survey (NGS) has committed to the maintenance of about 1,400 survey stations (AA-and A-order stations) called the federal base network, (FBN) and individual states will maintain the remainder of the survey stations (B-order stations) called the cooperative base network. See Table 10.1 for accuracy standards for the new high accuracy reference network (HARN) using GPS techniques, and accuracy standards for traditional terrestrial techniques.

Work was also completed on an improved vertical control net with revised values for about 600,000 benchmarks in the United States and Canada. This work was largely com-

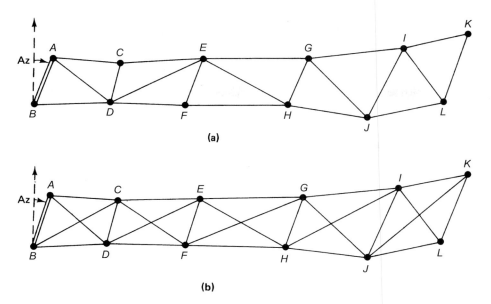

**FIGURE 10.1** Control survey configurations. *AB* is the measured baseline, with known (or measured) azimuth. (a) Chain of single triangles. (b) Chain of double triangles (quadrilaterals).

pleted in 1988 and resulted in a new North American Datum (NAVD 88); the original adjustment of continental vertical values was performed in 1929.

First-order horizontal control accuracy using terrestrial (pre-electronics) techniques were originally established using triangulation methods. This technique involved (1) a precisely measured baseline as a starting side for a series of triangles or chains of triangles; (2) the determination of each angle in the triangle; using a precise theodolite, which permitted the computation of the lengths of each side; and (3) a check on the work made possible by measuring precisely a side of a subsequent triangle (the spacing of check lines depended on the desired accuracy level). See Figure 10.1.

Triangulation was originally favored because the basic measurement of angles (and only a few sides) could be taken more quickly and precisely than could the measurement of all the distances (the surveying solution technique of measuring only the sides of a triangle is called trilateration). The advent of EDM instruments in the 1960s changed the approach to terrestrial control surveys. It became possible to measure precisely the length of a triangle side in about the same length of time as was required for angle determination.

Figure 10.1 shows two control survey configurations. Figure 10.1(a) depicts a simple chain of single triangles. In triangulation (angles only), this configuration suffers from the weakness that essentially only one route (sine law) can be followed to solve for side *KL*. Figure 10.1(b) shows a chain of double triangles or quadrilaterals. This configuration is preferred for triangulation because side *KL* can be solved using different routes (many more redundant measurements). Modern terrestrial control survey practice favors a combination of triangulation and trilateration (that is, measure both the angles and the distances), thus ensuring many redundant measurements even for the simple chain of triangles shown in Figure 10.1(a).

**Table 10.2** TRAVERSE SPECIFICATIONS—UNITED STATES

| Classification | First order | Second order | | Third order | |
|---|---|---|---|---|---|
| | | Class I | Class II | Class I | Class II |
| Recommended spacing of principal stations | Network stations 10–15 km; other surveys seldom less than 3 km | Principal stations seldom less than 4 km, except in metropolitan area surveys, where the limitation is 0.3 km | Principal stations seldom less than 2 km, except in metropolitan area surveys, where the limitation is 0.2 km | Seldom less than 0.1 km in tertiary surveys in metropolitan area surveys; as required for other surveys | |
| *Position closure* After azimuth adjustment | 0.04 m $\sqrt{K}$ or 1:100,000 | 0.08 m $\sqrt{K}$ or 1:50,000 | 0.2 m $\sqrt{K}$ or 1:20,000 | 0.4 m $\sqrt{K}$ or 1:10,000 | 0.8 m $\sqrt{K}$ or 1:5,000 |

*Source:* From Federal Control Committee, United States, 1974.

Whereas triangular control surveys were originally used for basic state or provincial controls, precise traverses and GPS surveys are now used to densify the basic control net. The advent of reliable and precise EDM instruments has elevated the traverse to a valuable role, both in strengthening a triangulation net and in providing its own stand-alone control figure. To provide reliability, traverses must close on themselves or on previously coordinated points. Table 10.2 gives a summary of characteristics and specifications for traverses. Tables 10.3 and 10.4 show summaries of characteristics and specifications for vertical control for the United States and Canada.

More recently, with the advent of the programmed total station, the process called *resection* is used much more often. This process permits the surveyor to set up the total station at any convenient location and then, by sighting (measuring just angles or both angles and distances) to two or more coordinated control stations, the coordinates of the set-up station can be computed. See Section 7.10.3.

In traditional (pre-GPS) surveying, to obtain high accuracy for conventional field control surveys, the surveyor must use high-precision equipment and high-precision techniques. High-precision equipment, used to measure angles and vertical and horizontal slope distances, is illustrated in Figures 10.2, 10.3, and 10.4. Specifications for horizontal high-precision techniques stipulate the least angular count of the theodolite, the number of observations, the rejection of observations exceeding specified limits from the mean, the spacing of major stations, and the angular and positional closures.

Higher-order specifications are seldom required for engineering or mapping surveys. An extensive interstate highway control survey could be one example where higher-order specifications are used in engineering work. Control for large-scale projects (for example, interchanges, large housing projects) that are to be laid out using polar ties (angle/distance) by total stations may require accuracies in the range of 1/10,000 to 1/20,000, depending on the project, and would fall between second- and third-order accuracy specifications (Table 10.1). Control stations established using GPS techniques will inherently have the potential for higher orders of accuracy. The lowest requirements are reserved for small engineering

**Table 10.3** AMERICAN CONGRESS ON SURVEYING AND MAPPING—MINIMUM ANGLE, DISTANCE, AND CLOSURE REQUIREMENTS FOR SURVEY MEASUREMENTS THAT CONTROL LAND BOUNDARIES FOR ALTA-ACSM LAND TITLE SURVEYS[a]

| Direct reading of instrument[b] | Instrument reading, estimated[c] | Number of observations per station[d] | Spread from mean of D&R not to exceed[e] | Angle closure where $N$ = number of stations not to exceed | Linear closure[f] | Distance measurement[g] | Minimum length of measurements |
|---|---|---|---|---|---|---|---|
| 20″<1′> 10″ | 5″<0.1′>N.A. | 2 D&R | 5″<0.1′> 5″ | $10''\sqrt{N}$ | 1:15,000 | EDM or doubletape with steel tape | 81 m[h], 153 m[L], 20 m[j] |

[a]All requirements of each class must be satisfied to qualify for that particular class of survey. The use of a more precise instrument does not change the other requirements, such as number of angles turned, etc.

[b]Instrument must have a direct reading of at least the amount specified (not an estimated reading), that is, 20″ = micrometer reading theodolite, <1′> = scale reading theodolite, 10″ = Electronic reading theodolite.

[c]Instrument must have the capability of allowing an estimated reading below the direct reading to the specified reading.

[d]D&R means the direct and reverse positions of the instrument telescope: for example, urban surveys require that two angles in the direct and two angles in the reverse position be measured and meaned.

[e]Any angle measured that exceeds the specified amount from the mean must be rejected and the set of angles remeasured.

[f]Ratio of closure after angles are balanced and closure calculated.

[g]All distance measurements must be made with a properly calibrated EDM or steel tape, applying atmospheric, temperature, sag, tension, slope, scale factor, and sea level corrections as necessary.

[h]EDM having an error of 5 mm, independent of distance measured (manufacturer's specifications).

[i]EDM having an error of 10 mm, independent of distance measured (manufacturer's specifications).

[j]Calibrated steel tape.

315

**Table 10.4**  STANDARDS FOR LAND TITLE SURVEYS

| Class of survey | Positional tolerances |
| --- | --- |
| Urban surveys | 0.07 feet (or 20 mm) + 50 ppm |
| Suburban surveys | 0.13 feet (or 40 mm) + 100 ppm |
| Rural surveys | 0.26 feet (or 80 mm) + 200 ppm |
| Mountain/marshland surveys | 0.66 feet (or 200 mm) + 200 ppm |

*Source:* From Classifications of ALTA-ACSM Land Title Surveys, as adopted by American Land Title Association and ACSM, 1997

(a)

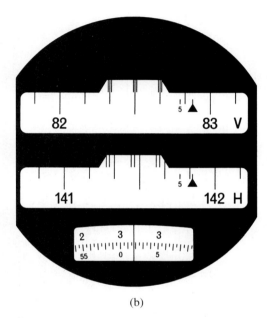

(b)

**FIGURE 10.2**  (a) Kern DKM 3 precise theodolite; angles directly read to 0.5 seconds; used in first-order surveys. (b) Kern DKM 3 scale reading (vertical angle = 82°53′01.8″). (Courtesy of Leica Co.)

or mapping projects that are limited in scope, for example, traffic studies, drainage studies, borrow pit volume surveys, etc. To enable the surveyor to perform reasonably precise surveys and still use plane geometry and trigonometry for related computations, several forms of plane coordinate grids have been introduced.

The American Congress on Surveying and Mapping (ACSM) and the American Land Title Association (ALTA) collaborated to produce classifications for cadastral surveys based on present and proposed land use. These 1992 classifications (subject to state regulations) are shown in Table 10.3. Recognizing the impact of GPS techniques on all branches of surveying, ACSM and ALTA published in 1997 positional tolerances for different classes of surveys (see Table 10.4).

**FIGURE 10.3** Zeiss Ni 1 precise automatic level featuring 40× magnification with a nominal accuracy of ±0.2 mm distance in kilometers. (Courtesy of Carl Zeiss-Oberkochen)

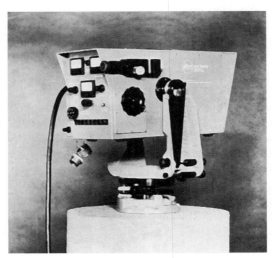

**FIGURE 10.4** Kern Mekometer ME 3000, a high-precision EDM [SE = ± (0.2 mm ± 1 ppm)] with a triple-prism distance range of 2.5 km. Used wherever first-order results are required, for example, deformation studies, network surveys, plant engineering, and baseline calibration. (Courtesy of Kern Instruments—Leica)

## 10.2  Plane Coordinate Grids

### 10.2.1  General Background

The United States uses the State Plane Coordinate Grid System (SPCS), which utilizes both the transverse Mercator projection and the Lambert conformal conic projection. In Canada, both the universal transverse Mercator projection (6° zones) and the modified transverse Mercator projection (3° zones) are used.

As already noted, geodetic control surveys are based on the best estimates of the actual shape of the earth. For many years, geodesists used the Clarke 1866 spheroid as a

**Table 10.5** STATE PLANE COORDINATE GRID SYSTEMS

| Transverse Mercator system | | Lambert system | | Both systems |
|---|---|---|---|---|
| Alabama | Mississippi | Arkansas | North Dakota | Alaska |
| Arizona | Missouri | California | Ohio | Florida |
| Delaware | Nevada | Colorado | Oklahoma | New York |
| Georgia | New Hampshire | Connecticut | Oregon | |
| Hawaii | New Jersey | Iowa | Pennsylvania | |
| Idaho | New Mexico | Kansas | Puerto Rico | |
| Illinois | Rhode Island | Kentucky | South Carolina | |
| Indiana | Vermont | Louisiana | South Dakota | |
| Maine | Wyoming | Maryland | Tennessee | |
| | | Massachusetts | Texas | |
| | | Michigan | Utah | |
| | | Minnesota | Virginia | |
| | | Montana | Virgin Islands | |
| | | Nebraska | Washington | |
| | | North Carolina | West Virginia | |
| | | | Wisconsin | |

base for their work, including the development of the first North American Datum in 1927 (NAD 27). The National Geodetic Survey (NGS) created the State Plane Coordinate System (SPCS 27) based on the NAD 27 datum. In this system, map projections that best suit the geographic needs of individual states are used; the Lambert conformal conical projection is used in states with a larger east/west dimension and the transverse Mercator cylindrical projection is used in states with a larger north/south dimension. See Table 10.5.

To minimize the distortion that always occurs when a spherical surface is converted to a plane surface, the Lambert projection grid was limited to a relatively narrow strip of about 158 miles in a north/south direction, and the transverse Mercator projection grid was limited to about 158 miles in an east/west direction. At the maximum distance of 158 miles, or 254 km, a maximum scale factor of 1:10,000 exists at the zone boundaries. As noted earlier, modernization in both instrumentation and technology permitted the establishment of a more representative datum based on the Geodetic Reference System 1980 (GRS 80), which was used to define the new NAD 83 datum. A new State Plane Coordinate System of 1983 (SPCS 83) was developed based on the NAD 83 datum.

Surveyors using both old and new SPCSs can compute positions using tables and computer programs made available from the NGS. The SPCS 83, which enables the surveyor to work in a more precisely defined datum than did SPCS 27, uses similar mathematical approaches with some new nomenclature. For example, in the SPCS 27, the Lambert coordinates were expressed as $X$ and $Y$, with values given in feet (U.S. survey foot, see Table 1.1), and the convergence angle (mapping angle) was displayed as $\theta$. In the transverse Mercator grid, the convergence angle (in seconds) was designated by $\Delta\lambda''$. The SPCS 83 uses metric values for coordinates (designated as eastings and northings), as well as foot units (U.S. survey foot or international foot). The convergence angle is now shown in both the Lambert and transverse Mercator projections as $\gamma$.

In North America, the grids used most often are the state plane coordinate grids. These grids are used in each of the states within the United States; the universal transverse Mercator grid is used in much of Canada. The Federal Communications Commission has mandated that, by 2005, all cell phones must be able to provide the spatial location of 911 callers. By 2002, half the telephone carriers opted for network-assisted GPS (A-GPS) for 911 caller location. The other carriers proposed to implement caller location using enhanced observed time difference of arrival (E-OTD); this technique utilizes the cellular network itself to pinpoint caller location.

With such a major initiative in the use of GPS to help provide caller location, some believe that to provide seamless service, proprietary map data bases should be referenced to a common grid, that is, a U.S. national grid (USNG) for spatial addressing. One such grid being considered is the military grid reference system (MGRS), which is based on the universal transverse Mercator (UTM) grid. In addition to the need for a national grid for 911 purposes, the Federal Geographic Data Committee (FGDC) recognizes the benefits of such a national grid for the many applications now developed for the GIS field. The ability to share data from one proprietary software program to another depends on a common grid, such as that proposed in the U.S National grid (USNG). (See http://www.fgdc. gov/standards/documents/proposals/usngprop.html.)

In addition to supplying tables for computations in SPCS 83, the NGS provides both interactive computations on the Internet and PC software available for downloading at www.ngs.noaa.gov. Many surveyors prefer computer-based computations to working with cumbersome tables. A manual that describes SPCS 83 in detail, NOAA Manual NOS NGS 5: *State Plane Coordinate System of 1983,* is available from NGS.* This manual contains an introduction to SPCS; a map index showing all state plane coordinate zone numbers (zones are tied to state counties), which are required for converting state plane coordinates to geodetic positions; a table showing the SPCS legislative status of all states (1988); a discussion of the (*t-T*) convergence "second-term" correction, which is needed for precise surveys of considerable extent; the methodology required to convert NAD 83 latitude/longitude to SPCS 83 northing/easting; plus the reverse process. The manual also introduces the four equations needed to convert from latitude/longitude to northing/easting (that is, for northing, easting, convergence, and the grid scale factor) and the four equations needed to convert from northing/easting to latitude/longitude (latitude, longitude, convergence factor, and grid scale factor). Refer to the NGS manual for these conversion equation techniques. NGS uses the term **conversion** to describe these techniques and reserves the term **transformation** to describe the process of converting coordinates from one datum or grid to another, for example, from NAD 27 to NAD 83, or from SPCS 27 to SPCS 83 to UTM, etc.

The National Geodetic Survey (NGS) also has a range of software programs designed to assist the surveyor in several areas of geodetic inquiry. You can find the NGS Tool Kit at www.ngs.noaa.gov/TOOLS/. This site has on-line calculation capability for

---

*To obtain NGS publications, contact NOAA, National Geodetic Survey, N/NGS12, 1315 East-West Highway, Station 9202, Silver Springs, MD 20910-3282. Publications can also be ordered by phoning (301) 713-3242.

many of the geodetic activities listed below. To download PC software programs, go to www.ngs.noaa.gov and click on the PC software icon.

- DEFLEC99 computes deflections of the vertical at the surface of the earth for the conterminous United States, Alaska, Puerto Rico, Virgin Islands, and Hawaii.
- G99SSS computes the gravimetric height values for the conterminous United States.
- GEOID99 computes geoid height values for the conterminous United States.
- HTDP is a time-dependent horizontal positioning software that allows users to predict horizontal displacements and/or velocities at locations throughout the United States.
- NADCON transforms geographic coordinates between the NAD 27, Old Hawaiian, Puerto Rico, or Alaska Island data and NAD 83 values.
- State Plane Coordinate GPPCGP converts NAD 27 state plane coordinates to NAD 27 geographic coordinates (latitudes and longitudes) and back.
- SPCS83 converts NAD 83 state plane coordinates to NAD 83 geographic positions and back.
- Surface Gravity Prediction predicts surface gravity at specified geographic positions and topographic heights.
- The tidal information and orthometric elevations of a specific survey control mark can be viewed graphically. This data can be referenced to the NAVD 88, NGVD 29, or the mean lower low water (MLLW) data.
- VERTCON computes the modeled difference in orthometric height between the North American Vertical Datum of 1988 (NAVD 88) and the National Geodetic Vertical Datum of 1929 (NGVD 29) for any given location specified by latitude and longitude.

In Canada, software programs designed to assist the surveyor in various geodetic applications are available on the Internet from the Canadian Geodetic Survey at www.geod.nrcan.gc.ca. The following list is a selection of available services, including on-line applications and programs that can be downloaded:

- Precise GPS satellite ephemerides.
- GPS satellite clock corrections.
- GPS constellation information.
- GPS calendar.
- National gravity program.
- Universal transverse Mercator (UTM) to and from geographic coordinate conversion (UTM is in 6° zones, with a scale factor of 0.9996).
- Transverse Mercator (TM) to and from geographic coordinate conversion (TM is in 3° zones, with a scale factor of 0.9999, similar to U.S. state plane grids).
- GPS height transformation (based on GSD99; see Section 11.13).

## 10.2.2 Use of the NGS TOOLS to Convert Coordinates

a. NGS state plane coordinate zones (bold type indicates entries, selections, or program outputs): *Find an SPC zone* (http://www.ngs.noaa.gov/cgi-bin/spc_zones.prl). When this program has been selected, the user is prompted to choose either

O By County
**O By Position** (latitude/longitude)

After a position is chosen (in this example, By Position) by selecting that circle mark with the cursor, the user is prompted to enter the latitude and longitude and select either NAD 27 or NAD 83 datum. In this example,

| | | |
|---|---|---|
| Latitude | **N 421423** | (42° 14′ 23″) |
| Longitude | **W0792035** | (79°20′25″) |
| **O NAD 83** | | |
| 0 NAD 27 | | |

The program response is:

| **INPUT = Latitude** | **Longitude** | **Datum** |
|---|---|---|
| **N421423** | **W0792036** | **NAD 83** |

**NY013 (Chautauqua C0.)          NAD 83 Zone = 3103 (Transverse Mercator W)**

In addition to the Zone number (3103), the program also shows the county (Chautauqua, N.Y.), the datum (NAD 83), and the projection type (transverse Mercator W). The details for this example are shown in parentheses.

b. Convert geodetic positions to state plane coordinates: When the user selects http://www.ngs.noaa.gov/cgi-bin/spc_getpc.prl, he or she is asked to choose NAD 83 or NAD 27, enter the geodetic coordinates, and enter the zone number. (The zone number is not really required here because the program automatically generates the zone number directly from the geodetic coordinates of latitude and longitude.) The longitude degree entry must always be three digits, 079 in this example.

**O NAD 83**
O NAD 27
| | |
|---|---|
| Latitude | **N421423.0000** |
| Longitude | **W0792035.0000** |
| Zone[    ] (This can be left blank) | |

The program response is:

| **INPUT = Latitude** | **Longitude** | **Datum** | **Zone** |
|---|---|---|---|
| **N421423.0000** | **W0792035.0000** | **NAD 83** | **3103** |

| North (Y) Meters | East (X) Meters | Area | Convergence DD MM SS.ss | Scale |
|---|---|---|---|---|
| 248999.059 | 287296.971 | NY W | −0 30 38.62 | 0.99998586 |

c. Convert state plane coordinates to geodetic positions: When the user selects http://www.ngs.noaa.gov/cgi-bin/spc_getgp.prl, he or she must select either NAD 83 or NAD 27, enter the state plane coordinates, and enter the SPCS zone number.

**O NAD 83**
O NAD 27

Northing = **248999.059**
Easting = **287296.971**

Zone = **3103**

The program response is:

| INPUT = North (meters) | East (meters) | Datum | Zone |
|---|---|---|---|
| 248999.059 | 287296.971 | NAD 83 | 3103 |

| Latitude DD MM SS.sssss | Longitude DD MM SS.sssss | Area | Convergence | Scale Factor |
|---|---|---|---|---|
| 42 14 23.00000 | 079 20 35.00001 | NY W | −0° 30 38.62 | 0.9999859 |

## 10.2.3 Use of the Canadian Geodetic Survey On-Line Sample Programs

The programs can be downloaded free.

Use the same geographic position as in Section 10.2.2.

a. Geographic position to universal transverse Mercator: Go to http://www.geod. NRCan.gc.ca/products/html-public/GSDapps/English/gsrug-gtou.html. Enter the geographic coordinates of the point you want to compute. For this example, enter the following:

Latitude:    **42** degrees **14** minutes **23.0000** seconds **north**
Longitude:  **079** degrees **20** minutes **35.0000** seconds **west**

Ellipsoid: **GRS 80 (NAD 83, WGS84)**        Zone width **6° UTM**

The desired ellipsoid and zone width, 6° or 3°, are selected by highlighting the appropriate entry while scrolling through the list. The program response is

**Input Geographic Coordinates**

**Latitude: 42 degrees 14 minutes 23.0000 seconds North**

**Longitude: 079 degrees 20 minutes 35.0000 seconds West**

Ellipsoid: NAD 83 (WGS84)

Zone Width: 6 UTM

Output: UTM Coordinates:

UTM Zone: 17
Northing: 4677721.911 meters North
Easting: 636709.822 meters

b. Universal transverse Mercator (UTM) to geographic: Go to http://www.geod. NRCan.gc.ca/products/html-public/GSDapps/English/gsrug-utog.html. Enter the UTM coordinates of the point you want to compute. For this example, enter the following:

Zone: **17**
Northing: **4677721.911** meters **North**
Easting: **636709.822** meters
Ellipsoid: **GRS 80 (NAD83, WGS84)** Zone Width **6° UTM**

The program's response is:

Input geographic coordinates
**UTM Zone 17**
**Northing: 4677721.911 meters North**
**Easting: 636709.822 meters**
**Ellipsoid: NAD83 (WGS84)**
**Zone Width: 6° UTM**

Output geographic coordinates

**Latitude: 42 degrees 14 minutes 23.000015 seconds North**
**Longitude: 79 degrees 20 minutes 34.999989 seconds West**

# 10.3  Lambert Projection

The Lambert projection is a conical conformal projection. The imaginary cone is placed around the earth so that the apex of the cone is on the earth's axis of rotation above the north pole, for northern hemisphere projections, and below the south pole, for southern hemisphere projections. The location of the apex depends on the area of the ellipsoid that is being projected. Figures 10.5 and 10.6 confirm that, although the east-west direction is relatively free from distortion, the north-south coverage must be restrained (to 158 miles) to maintain the integrity of the projection. Therefore, the Lambert projection is used for states having a greater east-west dimension, such as Pennsylvania and Tennessee. Table 10.5 gives a list of all the states and indicates the type of projection used. New York, Florida, and Alaska utilize both the transverse Mercator and the Lambert projections. The NGS publication *State Plane Coordinate Grid system of 1983* gives a more detailed listing of each state's projection data.

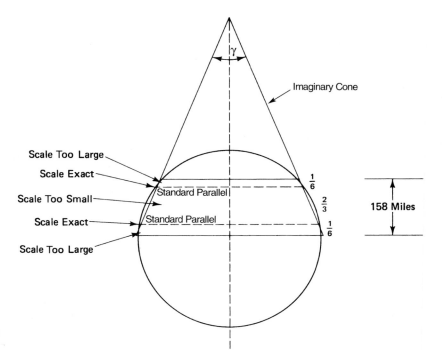

Scale Too Large
Scale Exact
Scale Too Small
Scale Exact
Scale Too Large

Standard Parallel
Standard Parallel

Imaginary Cone

$\frac{1}{6}$
$\frac{2}{3}$
$\frac{1}{6}$

158 Miles

**FIGURE 10.5**
Lambert secant
projection.

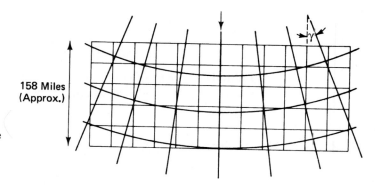

158 Miles
(Approx.)

**FIGURE 10.6** Lines of latitude
(parallels) and lines of longitude
(meridians) on the Lambert projection grid.

## 10.4 Transverse Mercator Projection

The transverse Mercator projection is created by placing an imaginary cylinder around the
earth, with its circumference tangent to the earth along a meridian (central meridian; see
Figure 10.7). When the cylinder is flattened, a plane is developed that can be used for grid
purposes. At the central meridian, the scale is exact [Figures 10.7 and 10.8(a)], and the
scale becomes progressively more distorted as the distance east and west of the central
meridian increases. This projection is used in states with a more predominant north/south

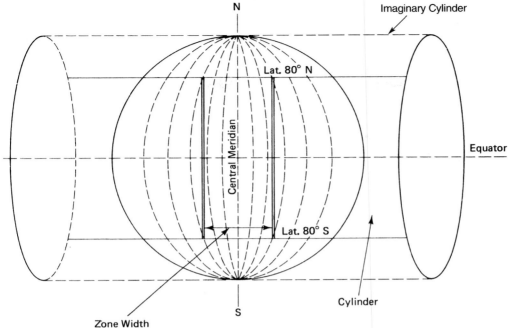

N

Imaginary Cylinder

Lat. 80° N

Central Meridian

Equator

Lat. 80° S

Cylinder

S

Zone Width

1. 6° for UTM

2. 3° for MTM (Some Regions in Canada)

3. About 158 Miles for State Plane Coordinate Grid (United States)

**FIGURE 10.7** Transverse Mercator projection cylinder *tangent* to the earth's surface at the central meridian (CM) (see Figure 10.11 for zone number).

dimension, such as Illinois and New Hampshire. The distortion (which is always present when a spherical surface is projected onto a plane) can be minimized in two ways. First, the distortion can be minimized by keeping the zone width relatively narrow (158 miles in SPCS); second, the distortion can be lessened by reducing the radius of the projection cylinder (secant projection) so that, instead of being tangent to the earth's surface, the cylinder cuts through the earth's surface at an optimal distance on either side of the central meridian [see Figures 10.8(b) and 10.9]. The scale factor at the central meridian is less than unity (0.9999); it is unity at the line of intersection at the earth's surface and more than unity between the lines of intersection and the zone limit meridians. Figure 10.10 shows a cross section of an SPCS transverse Mercator zone. For both the Lambert and transverse Mercator grids, the scale factor of 0.9999 at the central meridian (this value is much improved for some states in the SPCS 83 ) gives surveyors the ability to work within a specification of 1:10,000 while neglecting the impact of scale distortion.

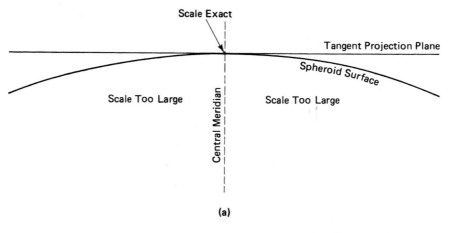

**(a)**

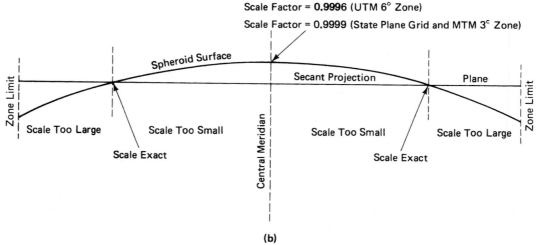

**(b)**

**FIGURE 10.8**  (a) Section view of the projection plane and earth's surface (*tangent projection*). (b) Section view of the projection plane and the earth's surface (*secant projection*).

## 10.5  Universal Transverse Mercator (UTM) Grid System

### 10.5.1  General Background

The UTM grid is as described above except that the zones are wider: set at a width 6° of longitude. This grid is used worldwide for both military and mapping purposes. UTM coordinates are now published (in addition to SPCS and geodetic coordinates) for all NAD 83 control stations. With a wider zone width than the SPCS zones, the UTM has a scale factor at the central meridian of only 0.9996. Surveyors working at specifications better than 1:2,500 must apply scale factors in their computations.

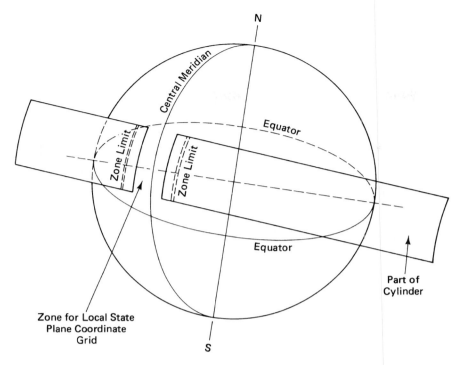

**FIGURE 10.9**   Transverse Mercator projection. *Secant* cylinder for state plane coordinate grids.

UTM zones are numbered beginning at longitude 180°W from 1 to 60. Figure 10.11 shows that United States territories range from zone 1 to zone 20 and that Canada's territory ranges from zone 7 to zone 22. The central meridian of each zone is assigned a false easting of 500,000 m, and the northerly is based on a value of zero at the equator.

### CHARACTERISTICS OF THE UNIVERSAL TRANSVERSE MERCATOR (UTM) GRID SYSTEM

1. A zone is 6° wide. There is a zone overlap of 0°30′ (see also Table 10.6).
2. The latitude of the origin is the equator, 0°.
3. The easting value of each central meridian = 500,000.000 m.
4. The northing value of the equator = 0.000 m (10,000,000.000 m in the southern hemisphere).
5. The scale factor at the central meridian is 0.9996 (that is, 1/2, 500).
6. Zone numbering commences with 1 in the zone 180°W to 174°W and increases eastward to zone 60 at the zone 174°E to 180°E (see Figure 10.8).
7. Projection limits of latitude 80°S to 80°N.

See Figure 10.12 for a cross section of a 6° zone (UTM).

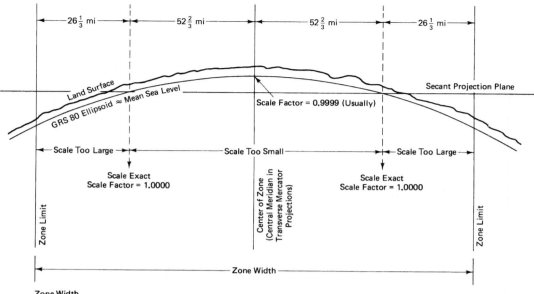

Zone Width

About 158 Miles for State Plane Coordinate Systems:
— East-West Orientation for Transverse Mercator Projections.
— North-South Orientation for Lambert Projections.

**FIGURE 10.10** Section of the projection plane and the earth's surface for state plane grids (secant projection).

## 10.5.2 Modified Transverse Mercator (MTM) Grid System

Some regions and agencies outside the United States have adopted a modified transverse Mercator system. The modified projection is based on 3° wide zones instead of 6° wide zones. By narrowing the zone width, the scale factor at the central meridian is improved from 0.9996 (1/2,500) to 0.9999 (1/10,000), the same as for the SPCS grids. The improved scale factor permits surveyors to work at moderate levels of accuracy without having to account for projection corrections. The zone width of 3° (about 152 miles wide at latitude 43°) compares closely with the 158-mile-wide zones used in the United States for transverse Mercator and Lambert projections in the state plane coordinate system.

### CHARACTERISTICS OF THE 3° ZONE

1. A zone is 3° wide.
2. The latitude of origin is the equator, 0°.
3. The easting value of the central meridian, for example, 1,000,000.000 ft or 304,800.000 m, is set by the agency.
4. The northing value of the equator is 0.000 ft or m.
5. The scale factor at the central meridian is 0.9999 (that is, 1/10,000).

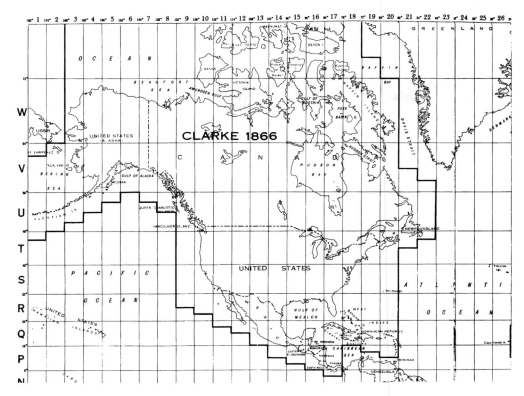

**FIGURE 10.11** Universal transverse Mercator grid zone numbering system.

**Table 10.6** UTM ZONE WIDTH

| North latitude | Width (km) |
|---|---|
| 42°00′ | 497.11827 |
| 43°00′ | 489.25961 |
| 44°00′ | 481.25105 |
| 45°00′ | 473.09497 |
| 46°00′ | 464.79382 |
| 47°00′ | 456.35005 |
| 48°00′ | 447.76621 |
| 49°00′ | 439.04485 |
| 50°00′ | 430.18862 |

*Source:* Ontario Geographical Referencing Grid, Ministry of Natural Resources, Ontario, Canada.

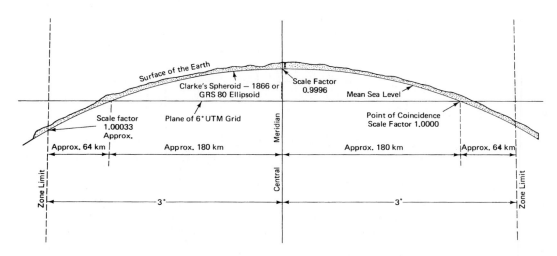

**FIGURE 10.12**  Cross section of a 6° zone (UTM).

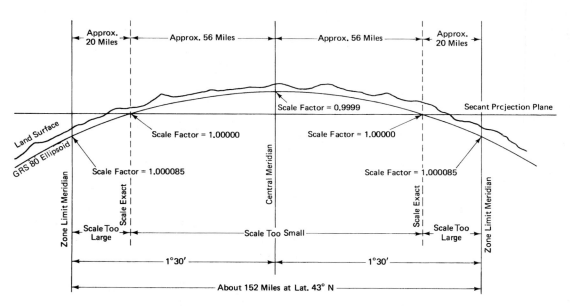

**FIGURE 10.13**  Section of the projection plane for the modified transverse Mercator (3°) grid and the earth's surface (secant projection).

Keep in mind that narrow grid zones (1:10,000) permit the surveyor to ignore only corrections for scale, and that other corrections to field measurements, such as those for elevation, temperature, etc., and the balancing of errors are still routinely required. See Figures 10.12 and 10.13 for cross sections of the UTM and modified transverse Mercator projection planes.

# 10.6 Use of Grid Coordinates

## 10.6.1 Grid/Ground Distance Relationships: Elevation and Scale Factors

When local surveys (traverse or trilateration) are tied into coordinate grids, corrections must be provided so that:

1. Grid and ground distances can be reconciled by applying elevation and scale factors.
2. Grid and geodetic directions can be reconciled by applying convergence corrections.

**10.6.1.1 Elevation factor** Figures 10.13 and 10.14 show the relationship among ground distances, sea level distances, and grid distances. A distance measured on the earth's surface must first be reduced for equivalency at sea level, and then it must be further reduced (in this illustration) for equivalency on the projection plane. The first reduction involves multiplication by an *elevation factor* (sea-level factor); the second reduction (adjustment) involves multiplication by the *scale factor.*

The elevation (sea-level) factor can be determined by establishing a ratio, as illustrated in Figures 10.14(a) and 10.15.

$$\text{Elevation factor} = \frac{\text{sea-level distance}}{\text{ground distance}} = \frac{R}{R + H} \tag{10.1}$$

where $R$ is the average radius of the earth (average radius of sea-level surface = 20,906,000 ft or 6,372,000 m), and $H$ is the elevation above mean sea level. For example, at 500 ft, the elevation factor would be

$$\frac{20,906,000}{20,906,500} = 0.999976$$

and a ground distance of 800.00 ft at an average elevation of 500 ft would become 800 × 0.999976 = 799.98 at sea level.

Figure 10.14(b) shows the case (encountered in very precise surveys) where the geoid separation (N) must also be considered. Geoid separation is the height difference between the sea-level surface and the ellipsoid surface. NOAA Manual NOS NGS 5, *State Plane Coordinate System of 1983,* notes, for example, that a geoid height of −30 m (in the conterminous United States, the ellipsoid is above the geoid) systematically affects reduced distances by −4.8 ppm (1:208,000), which is certainly not a factor in any but the most precise surveys. (See also Section 11.13.)

**10.6.1.2 Scale factor** For state plane projections, the computer solution gives scale factors for positions of latitude difference (Lambert projection) or for distances east or west of the central meridian (transverse Mercator projections). By way of illustration, scale factors for the transverse Mercator projections may also be computed by the following equation:

$$M_p = M_o \left( 1 + \frac{x^2}{2R^2} \right) \tag{10.2}$$

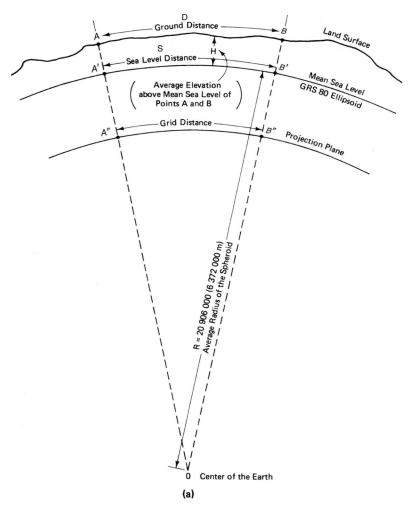

**FIGURE 10.14** (a) General case: relationship of ground distances to sea-level distances and grid distances.

where $M_p$ = the scale factor at the survey station, $M_o$ = the scale factor at the central meridian (CM), $x$ = the east/west distance of the survey station from the central meridian, and $R$ = the average radius of the spheroid ($x^2/2R^2$ can be expressed in feet, meters, miles, or kilometers). For example, survey stations 12,000 ft from a central meridian with a scale factor of 0.9999 would have a scale factor determined as follows:

$$M_p = 0.9999 \left( 1 + \frac{12{,}000^2}{2 \times 20{,}906{,}000^2} \right) = 0.9999002$$

**10.6.1.3 Combined factor** When the elevation factor is multiplied by the scale factor, the result is known as the *combined factor*.

## Elevation Factor

$$\frac{S}{D} = \frac{R}{R + h}$$

$$S = D \left( \frac{R}{R + h} \right)$$

$$h = N + H$$

$$S = D \left( \frac{R}{R + N + H} \right)$$

Where  $S$ = Geodetic Distance
$D$ = Horizontal Distance
$H$ = Mean Elevation
$N$ = Mean Geoid Height
$R$ = Mean Radius of Earth
or ( 6,372,000 m)
    (20,906,000 ft)

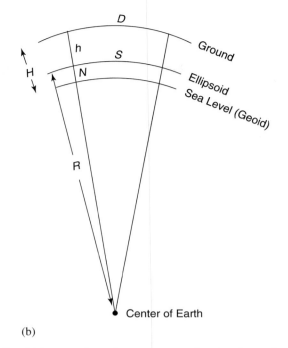

(b)

**FIGURE 10.14 (continued)**  (b) Impact of geoid separation on elevation factor determination. Used only on very precise surveys.

$$\text{Ground distance} \times \text{combined factor} = \text{grid distance} \qquad (10.3)$$

Stated another way, the equation becomes:

$$\frac{\text{grid distance}}{\text{combined factor}} = \text{ground distance}$$

In practice, it is seldom necessary to use Equations 10.1 and 10.2 because computer programs are now routinely used for computations in all state plane grids and the universal transverse Mercator grid. Previously, computations were based on data from tables and graphs (see Figure 10.16 and Table 10.7).

### ■ EXAMPLE 10.1

Using Table 10.7 (MTM projection), determine the combined scale and elevation factor (grid factor) of a point 125,000 ft from the central meridian (scale factor = 0.9999) and at an elevation of 600 ft above mean sea level. See Table 10.8 for an interpolation technique.

**Solution**

To determine the combined factor for a point 125,000 ft from the central meridian and at an elevation of 600 ft, a solution involving double interpolation must be used

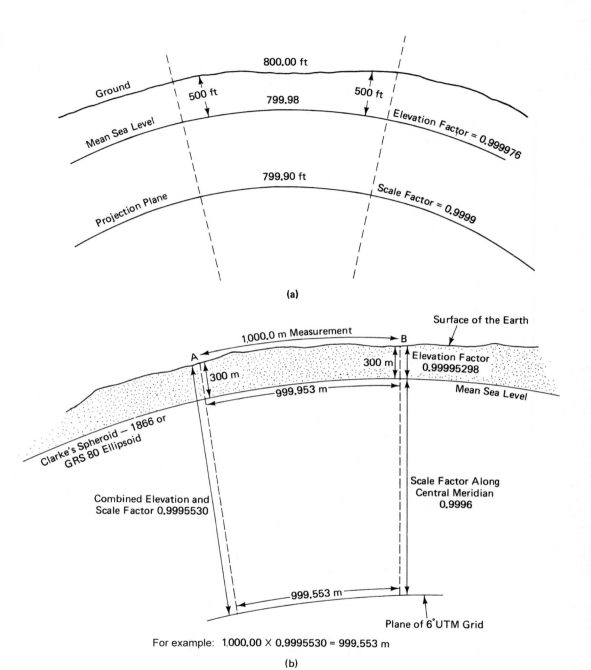

For example: 1,000.00 × 0.9995530 = 999.553 m

(b)

**FIGURE 10.15** Conversion of a ground distance to a grid distance using the elevation factor and the scale factor. (a) SPCS 83 grid. (b) Universal transverse Mercator (UTM) grid, 6° zone.

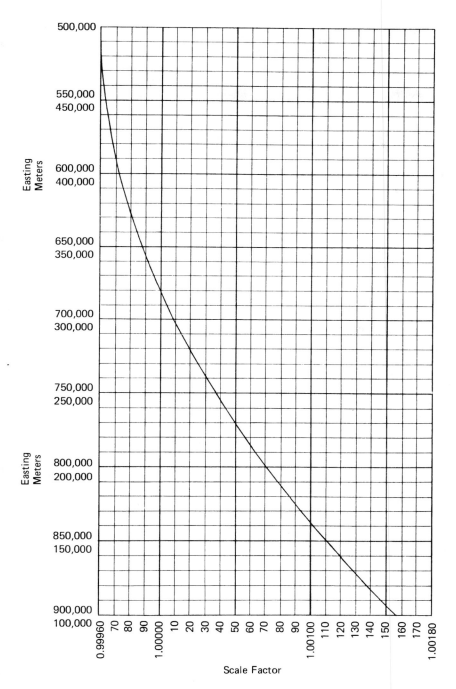

**FIGURE 10.16** Universal transverse Mercator grid scale factors. (Courtesy of U.S. Department of the Army, TM5-241-4/1)

**Table 10.7** 3° MTM COMBINED GRID FACTOR BASED ON CENTRAL SCALE FACTOR OF 0.9999 FOR THE MODIFIED TRANSVERSE MERCATOR PROJECTION[A]

| Elevation (ft) | Distance from central meridian (thousands of feet) | | | | | | | | | | | | |
|---|---|---|---|---|---|---|---|---|---|---|---|---|---|
| | 0 | 50 | 100 | 150 | 200 | 250 | 300 | 350 | 400 | 450 | 500 | 550 | 600 |
| 0 | 0.999900 | 0.999903 | 0.999911 | 0.999926 | 0.999946 | 0.999971 | 1.000003 | 1.000040 | 1.000083 | 1.000131 | 1.000186 | 1.000245 | 1.000311 |
| 250 | 0.999888 | 0.999891 | 0.999899 | 0.999914 | 0.999934 | 0.999959 | 0.999991 | 1.000028 | 1.000071 | 1.000119 | 1.000174 | 1.000234 | 1.000299 |
| 500 | 0.999876 | 0.999879 | 0.999888 | 0.999902 | 0.999922 | 0.999947 | 0.999979 | 1.000016 | 1.000059 | 1.000107 | 1.000162 | 1.000222 | 1.000287 |
| 750 | 0.999864 | 0.999867 | 0.999876 | 0.999890 | 0.999910 | 0.999936 | 0.999967 | 1.000004 | 1.000047 | 1.000095 | 1.000150 | 1.000210 | 1.000275 |
| 1000 | 0.999852 | 0.999855 | 0.999864 | 0.999878 | 0.999898 | 0.999924 | 0.999955 | 0.999992 | 1.000035 | 1.000083 | 1.000138 | 1.000198 | 1.000263 |
| 1250 | 0.999840 | 0.999843 | 0.999852 | 0.999864 | 0.999886 | 0.999912 | 0.999943 | 0.999980 | 1.000023 | 1.000072 | 1.000126 | 1.000186 | 1.000251 |
| 1500 | 0.999828 | 0.999831 | 0.999840 | 0.999854 | 0.999874 | 0.999900 | 0.999931 | 0.999968 | 1.000011 | 1.000060 | 1.000114 | 1.000174 | 1.000239 |
| 1750 | 0.999816 | 0.999819 | 0.999828 | 0.999842 | 0.999862 | 0.999888 | 0.999919 | 0.999956 | 0.999999 | 1.000048 | 1.000102 | 1.000162 | 1.000227 |
| 2000 | 0.999804 | 0.999807 | 0.999816 | 0.999830 | 0.999850 | 0.999876 | 0.999907 | 0.999944 | 0.999987 | 1.000036 | 1.000090 | 1.000150 | 1.000216 |
| 2250 | 0.999792 | 0.999795 | 0.999804 | 0.999818 | 0.999838 | 0.999864 | 0.999895 | 0.999932 | 0.999975 | 1.000024 | 1.000078 | 1.000138 | 1.000204 |
| 2500 | 0.999781 | 0.999784 | 0.999792 | 0.999806 | 0.999626 | 0.999852 | 0.999883 | 0.999920 | 0.999963 | 1.000012 | 1.000066 | 1.000126 | 1.000192 |
| 2750 | 0.999796 | 0.999771 | 0.999780 | 0.999794 | 0.999814 | 0.999840 | 0.999871 | 0.999908 | 0.999951 | 1.000000 | 1.000054 | 1.000114 | 1.000180 |

[a]Ground distance × grid factor = grid distance.

Source: Adapted from the "Horizontal Control Survey Precis," Ministry of Transportation and Communications, Ottawa, Canada, 1974.

**Table 10.8**

| Elevation | Distance from central meridian (thousands of feet)[a] | | |
|---|---|---|---|
| | 100 | 150 | 125 (interpolated) |
| 500 | 0.999888 | 0.999902 | 0.999895 |
| 750 | 0.999876 | 0.999890 | 0.999883 |
| | | | 0.000012 |

[a]Data taken from Table 10.7.

(see Table 10.8). We must interpolate between combined values for 500 ft and for 750 ft elevation, and between combined values for 100,000 and for 150,000 ft from the central meridian. First, the combined value for 125,000 ft from the central meridian can be interpolated simply by averaging the values for 100,000 and 150,000. Second, the value for 600 ft can be determined as follows. From Table 10.8 for 600 ft:

$$\frac{100}{250} \times 12 = 5$$

$$\text{Grid factor} = 0.999895 - 0.000005 = 0.999890$$

For important survey lines, grid factors can be determined for both ends and then averaged. For lines longer than 5 miles, intermediate computations are required to maintain high precision.

## 10.6.2 Grid/Geodetic Azimuth Relationships

**10.6.2.1 Convergence** In plane grids, the difference between grid north and geodetic north is called convergence (also called the mapping angle). In the SPCS 27 transverse Mercator grid, convergence was denoted by $\Delta\alpha''$, and in the Lambert grid, it was denoted by $\theta$. In the SPCS 83, convergence (in both projections) is denoted by $\gamma$ (gamma). On a plane grid, grid north and geodetic north coincide only at the central meridian. As you work farther east or west of the central meridian, convergence becomes more pronounced.

Using SPCS 83 symbols, approximate methods can be determined as follows:

$$\gamma'' = \Delta\lambda'' \sin \varphi \, P \tag{10.4}$$

where $\Delta\lambda''$ is the difference in longitude, in seconds, between the central meridian and point $P$, and $\varphi P$ is the latitude of point $P$. When long sights (>5 miles) are taken, a second term (present in the interactive Internet programs used in Sections 10.2.2 and 10.2.3 and in all precise computations) is required to maintain directional accuracy (see also Section 10.6.2.2).

When the direction of a line from $P_1$ to $P_2$ is considered, the expression becomes:

$$\gamma'' = \Delta\lambda'' \sin \frac{(\varphi P_1 + \varphi P_2)}{2}$$

If the distance from the central meridian is known, the expression becomes:

$$\gamma'' = 32.370 dk \tan \varphi \qquad (10.5)$$

or

$$\gamma'' = 52.09 d \tan \varphi \qquad (10.6)$$

where $\gamma$ = convergence angle, in seconds

$d$ = departure distance from the central meridian, in miles ($dk$ is the same distance, in kilometres)

$\varphi$ = average latitude of the line

See Section 15.2 for additional discussion of convergence.

**10.6.2.2 Corrections to Convergence** When high precision and/or long distances are involved, a "second term" correction is required for convergence. This term $\delta$ refers to $t$-$T$ (the grid azimuth − the projected geodetic azimuth) and results from the fact that the projection of the geodetic azimuth $\alpha$ onto the grid is not the grid azimuth but the projected geodetic azimuth, symbolized as $T$. Figure 10.17 shows the relationships between geodetic and grid azimuths.

# 10.7 Illustrative Examples

These approximate methods are included only to broaden your comprehension in this area. For current precise solution techniques, see NOAA Manual NOS NGS 5, *State Plane Coordinate System of 1983,* or the Geodetic Tool Kit discussed in Section 10.2.

■ **EXAMPLE 10.2**

Given the transverse Mercator coordinate grid of two horizontal control monuments and their elevations (see Figure 10.18 for additional given data), compute the ground distance and geodetic direction between them.

**Solution**

Table 10.9 lists the two monuments and their coordinates. By subtraction. coordinate distances, $\Delta N$ = 255.161 ft, $\Delta E$ = 919.048 ft. The solution is obtained as follows:

1. Grid distance 870 to 854:

$$\text{Distance} = \sqrt{255.161^2 + 919.048^2} = 953.811 \text{ ft}$$

2. Grid bearing:

$$\text{Tan bearing} = \Delta E / \Delta N = 919.048/255.161 = 3.6018357$$

$$\text{Grid bearing} = 74.48\ 342°$$
$$= \text{N } 74°29'00'' \text{ E}$$

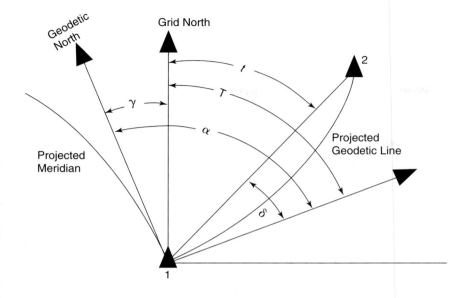

Grid North

Geodetic North

t

T

γ

α

2

Projected Geodetic Line

Projected Meridian

δ

1

$$t = \alpha - \gamma + \delta$$

α = Geodetic Azimuth Reckoned From North

T = Projected Geodetic Azimuth

t = Grid Azimuth Reckoned From North

γ = Convergence Angle (Mapping Angle)

δ = t-T = Second Term Correction = Arc-to-Chord Correction

**FIGURE 10.17**  Relationships among geodetic and grid azimuths. (From the NOAA Manual NOS NGS 5 State Plane Coordinate System of 1983, Section 2.5)

3. Convergence: use method (a) or (b). Average latitude = 43°47′31″; average longitude = 79°20′54″ (Figure 10.18). The slight difference (0.5″) in the results for (a) and (b) reflects the approximate approach.

(a)  $\gamma'' = 52.09d \tan \varphi$

$$= 52.09 \times \frac{(40{,}367.657 + 39{,}448.609)}{2 \times 5280} \tan 43°47′31″$$

$$= 377.45″$$

$$\gamma'' = 0°06′17.5″$$

(b)  $\gamma'' = \Delta\lambda'' \sin \varphi \, P$

$$= (79°30′ = 79°20′54″) \sin 43°47′31″$$

$$= 546″ \times \sin 43°47′31″$$

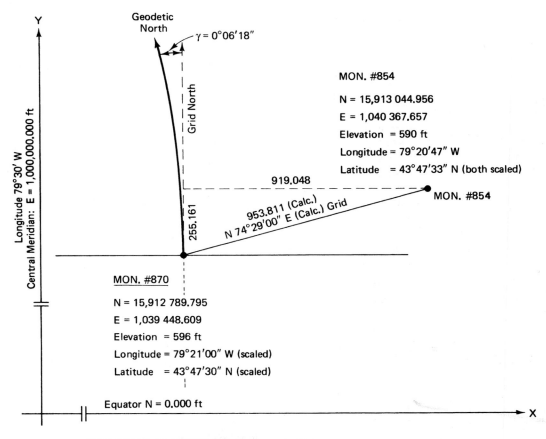

**FIGURE 10.18** Illustration for Example 10.2.

**Table 10.9**[a]

| Station | Elevation | Northing | Easting |
|---|---|---|---|
| Monument 870 | 595 ft | 15,912,789.795 ft | 1,039,448.609 ft |
| Monument 854 | 590 ft | 15,913,044.956 ft | 1,040,367.657 ft |

[a]Scale factor at CM = 0.9999.

$$= 377.85''$$
$$\gamma'' = 0°06'17.9''$$

*Use a convergence of 0°0618'*. Convergence, in this case, neglects the second term correction and is computed only to the closest second of arc. (*Note:* The average latitude need not have been computed because the latitude range, 03″, was insignificant in this case.)

For Figure 10.19, the geodetic bearing is equal to the grid bearing plus convergence:

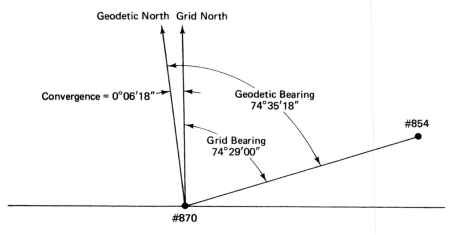

**FIGURE 10.19** Illustration for Example 10.2.

$$\text{Grid bearing} = \text{N } 74°29'00'' \text{ E} + \text{convergence} = 0°06'18''$$

$$\text{Geodetic bearing} = \text{N } 74°35'18'' \text{ E}$$

4. Scale factor: The scale factor at CM is $M_o = 0.9999$.

$$\text{Distance } (x) \text{ from CM} = \frac{40{,}368 + 39{,}449}{2} = 39{,}908 \text{ ft}$$

The scale factor at the midpoint between 870 and 854 can be found by using Equation 10.2:

$$M_p = M_o\left(\frac{1 + x^2}{2R^2}\right)$$

$$= 0.9999\left(1 + \frac{39{,}908^2}{2 \times 20{,}906{,}000^2}\right)$$

$$= 9999018$$

5. The elevation factor can be found by using Equation 10.1:

$$\text{Elevation factor} = \frac{\text{sea-level distance}}{\text{ground distance}} = \frac{R}{R + H}$$

$$= \frac{20{,}906{,}000}{20{,}906{,}000 + 593} = 0.999716$$

The value of 593 is the midpoint (average) elevation in feet.

6. Use method (a) or (b) to find the combined factor.

**Table 10.10**

| Elevation, ft | Distance from central meridian (thousands of ft) | | |
| --- | --- | --- | --- |
| | 0 | 50 | 39.9 (interpolated) |
| 500 | 0.999876 | 0.999879 | 0.999878 |
| 593 | | | |
| 750 | 0.999864 | 0.999867 | 0.999866 |

(a) Combined factor = scale factor × elevation factor

$$= 0.9999018 \times 0.9999716$$

$$= 0.9998734$$

(b) The combined factor can also be determined through double interpolation of Table 10.8, as follows. The values in Table 10.10 are taken from Table 10.8; required elevation is 593 ft at 39,900 ft from the CM. After first interpolating the values at 0 and 50 for 39,900 feet from the CM, it is a simple matter to interpolate for the elevation of 593 ft.

$$0.999878 - (0.000012) \times \frac{93}{250} = 0.999873$$

Thus, the combined factor at 39,900 ft from the CM at an elevation of 593 ft is 0.999873.

7. Rearrange Equation 10.3 to determine the ground distance:

$$\text{Ground distance} = \frac{\text{grid distance}}{\text{grid factor}}$$

$$\text{Ground distance (870 to 854)} = \frac{953.811}{0.9998734} = 953.93 \text{ ft}$$

### ■ EXAMPLE 10.3

Given the coordinates on the UTM 6° coordinate grid (based on the Clarke 1866 ellipsoid) of two horizontal control monuments, Mon. 113 and Mon. 115, and their elevations, compute the ground distance and geodetic direction between them [see Figure 10.20(a)]. The following information is also provided:

| STATION | ELEVATION | NORTHING | EASTING |
| --- | --- | --- | --- |
| 113 | 181.926 m | 4,849,872.066 m | 632,885.760 |
| 115 | 178.444 m | 4,849,988.216 m | 632,971.593 |

Zone 17 UTM; CM at 81° longitude west (see Figure 10.20)
Scale factor at CM = 0.9996

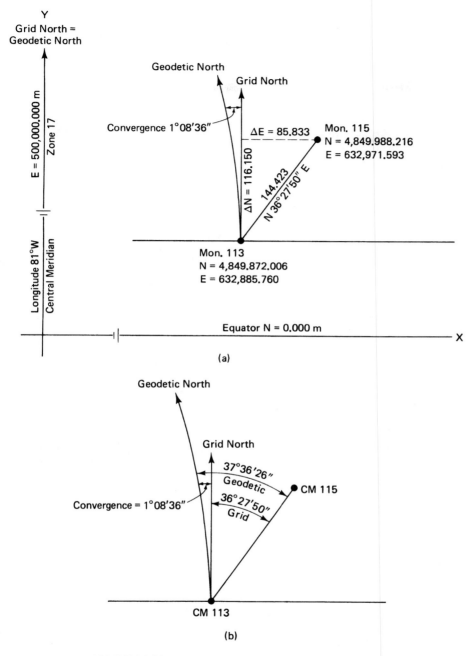

FIGURE 10.20 Illustration for Example 10.3. (a) Grid. (b) Application of convergence.

$$\varphi \text{ (latitude)} = 43°47'33''$$

Scaled from topographic map for midpoint of line joining Mon. 113 and Mon. 115.

$$\lambda \text{ (longitude)} = 79°20'52''$$

**Solution**

By subtraction, coordinate distances are $\Delta N = 116.150$ m, $\Delta E = 85.833$ m.

1. Grid distance from Mon. 113 to Mon. 115:

$$\text{Distance} = \sqrt{116.150^2 + 85.833^2} = 144.423 \text{ m}$$

2. Grid bearing:

$$\text{Tan bearing} = \frac{\Delta E}{\Delta N} = \frac{85.833}{116.150}$$

$$\text{Bearing} = 36.463811°$$

$$\text{Grid bearing} = \text{N } 36°27'50'' \text{ E}$$

3. Convergence:

$$\gamma'' = \Delta\lambda'' \sin \varphi P$$
$$= (81° - 79°20'52'') \sin 43°47'33''$$
$$= 4116.3''$$
$$= 1°08'36''$$

[See Figure 10.20(b) for an application of convergence. As in the previous example, this technique yields convergence only to the closest second of an arc. For more precise techniques, including second-term correction for convergence, see the NGS Tool Kit.]

4. Scale factor:

$$\text{Scale factor at CM} = 0.9996$$

$$\text{Distance from CM} = \frac{132{,}885.760 + 132{,}971.593}{2} = 132{,}928.677 \text{ m or } 132.929 \text{ km}$$

The scale factor at the midpoint on the line between Mon. 113 and Mon. 115 can be found by using Equation 10.2 and 20,906,000 ft or 6,372,000 m as the average radius of sea-level surface:

$$M_p = M_o\left(1 + \frac{x^2}{2R^2}\right)$$

**Table 10.11**

| Elevation | Distance from CM (km) | | |
|---|---|---|---|
| | 130 | 140 | 132.9 (interpolated) |
| 100 | 0.999792 | 0.999825 | 0.999802 |
| 200 | 0.999777 | 0.999810 | 0.999787 |

$$M_p = 0.9996 \left( 1 + \frac{132.929^2}{2 \times 6372^2} \right) = 0.999818$$

5. The elevation factor can be found by using Equation 10.1:

$$\text{Elevation factor} = \frac{\text{sea-level distance}}{\text{ground distance}} = \frac{R}{R + H}$$

$$= \frac{6372}{6372.00 + 0.180} = 0.999972$$

The value of 0.180 is the midpoint elevation divided by 1,000.

6. Use method (a) or (b) to find the combined factor.

   (a) Combined factor = elevation factor $\times$ scale factor

   $$= 0.999972 \times 0.999818 = 0.999790$$

   (b) The values in Table 10.11 come from Table 10.12. All that remains is to interpolate for the elevation value of 180 m; that is:

   $$0.999802 - \left( \frac{80}{100} \times 0.000015 \right) = 0.999790$$

7. To calculate the ground distance, use the following equation:

$$\text{Ground distance} = \frac{\text{grid distance}}{\text{combined factor}}$$

In this example:

$$\text{Ground distance Mon. 113 to Mon. 115} = \frac{144.423}{0.999790} = 144.453 \text{ m}$$

## 10.8 Horizontal Control Techniques

Typically, the highest-order control is established by federal agencies, secondary control is established by state or provincial agencies, and the lower-order control is established by municipal agencies or large-scale engineering works' surveyors. Sometimes the federal

**Table 10.12** COMBINED SCALE AND ELEVATION FACTORS (GRID FACTORS): UTM

| Distance from CM (km) | Elevation above mean sea level (m) | | | | | | | | | | |
|---|---|---|---|---|---|---|---|---|---|---|---|
| | 0 | 100 | 200 | 300 | 400 | 500 | 600 | 700 | 800 | 900 | 1,000 |
| 0 | 0.999600 | 0.999584 | 0.999569 | 0.999553 | 0.999537 | 0.999522 | 0.999506 | 0.999490 | 0.999475 | 0.999459 | 0.999443 |
| 10 | 0.999601 | 0.999586 | 0.999570 | 0.999554 | 0.999539 | 0.999523 | 0.999507 | 0.999492 | 0.999476 | 0.999460 | 0.999445 |
| 20 | 0.999605 | 0.999589 | 0.999574 | 0.999558 | 0.999542 | 0.999527 | 0.999511 | 0.999495 | 0.999480 | 0.999464 | 0.999448 |
| 30 | 0.999611 | 0.999595 | 0.999580 | 0.999564 | 0.999548 | 0.999533 | 0.999517 | 0.999501 | 0.999486 | 0.999470 | 0.999454 |
| 40 | 0.999620 | 0.999604 | 0.999588 | 0.999573 | 0.999557 | 0.999541 | 0.999526 | 0.999510 | 0.999494 | 0.999479 | 0.999463 |
| 50 | 0.999631 | 0.999615 | 0.999599 | 0.999584 | 0.999568 | 0.999552 | 0.999537 | 0.999521 | 0.999505 | 0.999490 | 0.999474 |
| 60 | 0.999644 | 0.999629 | 0.999613 | 0.999597 | 0.999582 | 0.999566 | 0.999550 | 0.999535 | 0.999519 | 0.999503 | 0.999488 |
| 70 | 0.999660 | 0.999645 | 0.999629 | 0.999613 | 0.999598 | 0.999582 | 0.999566 | 0.999551 | 0.999535 | 0.999519 | 0.999504 |
| 80 | 0.999679 | 0.999663 | 0.999647 | 0.999632 | 0.999616 | 0.999600 | 0.999585 | 0.999569 | 0.999553 | 0.999538 | 0.999522 |
| 90 | 0.999700 | 0.999684 | 0.999668 | 0.999653 | 0.999637 | 0.999621 | 0.999606 | 0.999590 | 0.999574 | 0.999559 | 0.999543 |
| 100 | 0.999723 | 0.999707 | 0.999692 | 0.999676 | 0.999660 | 0.999645 | 0.999629 | 0.999613 | 0.999598 | 0.999582 | 0.999566 |
| 110 | 0.999749 | 0.999733 | 0.999717 | 0.999702 | 0.999686 | 0.999670 | 0.999655 | 0.999639 | 0.999623 | 0.999608 | 0.999592 |
| 120 | 0.999777 | 0.999761 | 0.999746 | 0.999730 | 0.999714 | 0.999699 | 0.999683 | 0.999667 | 0.999652 | 0.999636 | 0.999620 |
| 130 | 0.999808 | 0.999792 | 0.999777 | 0.999761 | 0.999745 | 0.999730 | 0.999714 | 0.999698 | 0.999683 | 0.999667 | 0.999651 |
| 140 | 0.999841 | 0.999825 | 0.999810 | 0.999794 | 0.999778 | 0.999763 | 0.999747 | 0.999731 | 0.999716 | 0.999700 | 0.999684 |
| 150 | 0.999877 | 0.999861 | 0.999845 | 0.999830 | 0.999814 | 0.999798 | 0.999783 | 0.999767 | 0.999751 | 0.999736 | 0.999720 |
| 160 | 0.999915 | 0.999899 | 0.999884 | 0.999868 | 0.999852 | 0.999837 | 0.999821 | 0.999805 | 0.999790 | 0.999774 | 0.999758 |
| 170 | 0.999955 | 0.999940 | 0.999924 | 0.999908 | 0.999893 | 0.999877 | 0.999861 | 0.999846 | 0.999830 | 0.999814 | 0.999799 |
| 180 | 0.999999 | 0.999983 | 0.999967 | 0.999952 | 0.999936 | 0.999920 | 0.999905 | 0.999889 | 0.999873 | 0.999858 | 0.999842 |
| 190 | 1.000044 | 1.000028 | 1.000013 | 0.999997 | 0.999981 | 0.999966 | 0.999950 | 0.999934 | 0.999919 | 0.999903 | 0.999887 |
| 200 | 1.000092 | 1.000076 | 1.000061 | 1.000045 | 1.000029 | 1.000014 | 0.999998 | 0.999982 | 0.999967 | 0.999951 | 0.999935 |
| 210 | 1.000142 | 1.000127 | 1.000111 | 1.000095 | 1.000080 | 1.000064 | 1.000048 | 1.000033 | 1.000017 | 1.000001 | 0.999986 |
| 220 | 1.000195 | 1.000180 | 1.000164 | 1.000148 | 1.000133 | 1.000117 | 1.000101 | 1.000086 | 1.000070 | 1.000054 | 1.000039 |
| 230 | 1.000251 | 1.000235 | 1.000219 | 1.000204 | 1.000188 | 1.000172 | 1.000157 | 1.000141 | 1.000125 | 1.000110 | 1.000094 |
| 240 | 1.000309 | 1.000293 | 1.000277 | 1.000262 | 1.000246 | 1.000230 | 1.000215 | 1.000199 | 1.000183 | 1.000168 | 1.000152 |
| 250 | 1.000369 | 1.000353 | 1.000338 | 1.000322 | 1.000306 | 1.000290 | 1.000275 | 1.000259 | 1.000243 | 1.000228 | 1.000212 |

In triangulation surveys, a great deal of attention is paid to the geometric **strength of figure** of each control configuration. Generally, an equilateral triangle is considered strong, whereas triangles with small (less than 10°) angles are considered relatively weak. Trigonometric functions vary in precision as the angle varies in magnitude. The sines of small angles (near 0°), the cosines of large angles (near 90°), and the tangents of both small (0°) and large (90°) angles are all relatively imprecise. That is, relatively large changes in the values of the trigonometric functions result from relatively small changes in angular values. For example, the angular error of 5 seconds in the sine of 10° could result in an accuracy ratio of 1/7,300, whereas the angular error of 5 seconds in the sine of 20° could give 1/15,000, and the angular error of 5 seconds in the sine of 80° could give 1/234,000 (see Example 10.4). You can see that if sine or cosine functions are used in triangulation to calculate the triangle side distances, you must ensure that the trigonometric function itself is **not** contributing to the solution errors more significantly than the specified surveying error limits.

When all angles and distances are measured for each triangle, the redundant measurements ensure an accurate solution, and the configuration strength of the figure becomes somewhat less important. Given the opportunity, however, most surveyors still prefer to use well-balanced triangles, and to avoid using the sine and tangent of small angles and the cosine and tangent of large angles, to compute control distances. This concept of strength of figure helps to explain why GPS measurements are more precise when the observed satellites are spread right across the visible sky instead of bunched together in just one portion of the sky.

■ **EXAMPLE 10.4**  *Effect of the Angle Magnitude on the Precision and Accuracy of Computed Distances*

(a) Consider a right-angle triangle with a hypotenuse 1,000.00 ft long.

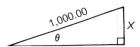

(b) Consider a right triangle with the adjacent side 1,000.00 ft long.

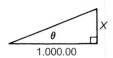

**Solution**

(a) Use various values for $\theta$ investigate the effect of 05″ angular errors.

    1. $\theta = 10°$              $X = 173.64818$ ft
       $\theta = 10°00'05''$      $X = 173.67205$ ft
                           Difference $= 0.02387$ in 173.65 ft, a possible accuracy of 1/7,300
    2. $\theta = 20°$              $X = 342.02014$ ft
       $\theta = 20°00'05''$      $X = 342.04292$ ft
                           Difference $= 0.022782$ in 342.02 ft, a possible accuracy of 1/15,000
    3. $\theta = 80°$              $X = 984.80775$ ft

$$\theta = 80°00'05''  \qquad  X = 984.81196 \text{ ft}$$

Difference $= 0.00421$ in 984.81 ft, a possible accuracy of 1/234,000

(b) Use various values for $\theta$ to investigate the effect of 05″ angular errors.

1. $\theta = 10°$      $X = 176.32698$ ft

    $\theta = 10°00'05''$      $X = 176.35198$ ft

       Difference $= 0.025$, a possible accuracy of 1/7,100

2. $\theta = 45°$      $X = 1,000.00$ ft

    $\theta = 45°00'05''$      $X = 1,000.0485$ ft

       Difference $= 0.0485$, a possible accuracy of 1/20,600

3. $\theta = 80°$      $X = 5,671.2818$ ft

    $\theta = 80°00'05''$      $X = 5,672.0858$ ft

       Difference $= 0.804$, a possible accuracy of 1/7,100

4. If the angle can be determined to the closest second, the accuracy would be as follows:

    $\theta = 80°$      $X = 5,671.2818$ ft

    $\theta = 80°00'01''$      $X = 5,671.4426$ ft

       Difference $= 0.1608$, a precision of 1/35,270

Example 10.4 illustrates that the surveyor should avoid using weak (relatively small) angles in distance computations. If weak angles must be used, they should be measured more precisely than would normally be required. Also illustrated here is the need for the surveyor to pre-analyze the proposed control survey configuration to determine optimal field techniques and attendant precisions.

## 10.9 Project Control

### 10.9.1 General Background

Project control begins with either a boundary survey (for example, in large housing projects or subdivisions) or an all-inclusive peripheral survey (for example, in construction sites). The boundary or site peripheral survey will, if possible, be tied into state or provincial grid control monuments so that references can be made to the state or provincial coordinate grid system. The peripheral survey is densified with judiciously placed control stations over the entire site. The survey data for all control points are entered into the computer for accuracy verification and error adjustment and finally for coordinate determination of all control points. All key layout points (for example, lot corners, radius points, ℄ stations, curve points, construction points) are also coordinated using coordinate geometry computer programs. Printout sheets are used by the surveyor to lay out the proposed facility from coordinated control stations. The computer results will give the surveyor the azimuth and distance from one, two, or perhaps three different control points to one layout point.

Positioning a layout point from more than one control station provides the opportunity for an exceptional check on the accuracy of the work. Generally, a layout point can be positioned by simultaneous angle sightings from two control points, with the distance being established by EDM from one of those stations, or a layout point can be positioned by simultaneous angle sightings from three control points. Both techniques provide the vital redundancy in measurement that permits positional accuracy determination.

To ensure that the layout points have been located accurately (for example, with an accuracy level of between 1/5,000 and 1/10,000), the control points themselves must be located to an even higher level of accuracy (typically better than 1/15,000). These accuracies can be achieved using GPS techniques and/or EDMs used for distances and one- or two-second dual axis–compensated theodolites used for angle measurement. As noted earlier, in addition to quality instrumentation, the surveyor must use "quality" geometrics in designing the shape of the control net; a series of interconnected equilateral triangles provides the strongest control net.

When positioning control points keep the following in mind:

1. Good visibility to other control points and an optimal number of layout points is important.
2. The visibility factor is considered not only for existing ground conditions but also for potential visibility lines during all stages of construction.
3. A minimum of two reference ties (three is preferred) is required for each control point so that it can be reestablished if it is destroyed. Consideration must be given to the availability of features suitable for referencing (that is, features into which nails can be driven or cut-crosses chiseled, etc.). Ideally, the three ties should be 120° apart.
4. Control points should be placed in locations that will not be affected by primary or secondary construction activity. In addition to keeping clear of the actual construction site positions, the surveyor must anticipate temporary disruptions to the terrain resulting from access roads, materials stockpiling, and so on. If possible, control points are safely located adjacent to features that will **not** be moved (e.g., electrical or communication towers, concrete walls, large valuable trees).
5. Control points must be established on solid ground (or rock). Swampy area or loose fill areas must be avoided. (See Section 10.10 for various types of markers.)

Once the control point locations have been tentatively chosen, they are plotted so that the quality of the control net geometrics can be considered. At this stage, it may be necessary to go back into the field and locate additional control points to strengthen weak geometric figures. When the locations have been finalized on paper, each station is given a unique identification code number, and then the control points are set in the field. Field notes, showing reference ties to each point, are carefully taken and then filed. Now the actual measurements of the distances and angles of the control net are taken. When all the field data have been collected, the closures and adjustments are computed. The coordinates of any layout points can then be computed, with polar ties being generated for each layout point, from two or possibly three control stations.

Figure 10.21(a) shows a single layout point being positioned by angle only from three control sights. The three control sights can simply be referenced to the farthest of the control points themselves (for example, angles A, B, and C). If a reference azimuth point (RAP) has been identified and coordinated in the locality, it would be preferred because it no doubt would be farther away and thus capable of providing more precise sightings (for example, angles 1, 2, and 3). RAPs are typically communication towers, church spires, or other identifiable points that can be seen from widely scattered control stations. Coordinates of RAPs are computed by turning angles to

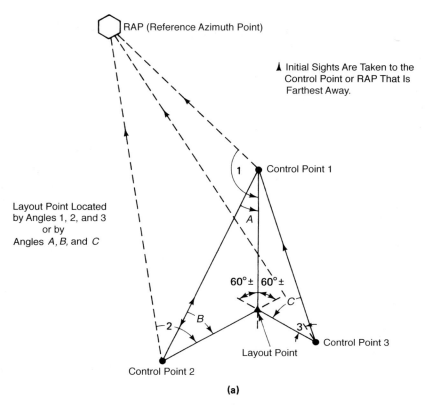

**(a)**

**FIGURE 10.21**   Examples of coordinate control for polar layout. (a) Single point layout, located by three angles.

the RAP from project control monuments or preferably from state or provincial control grid monuments. Figure 10.21(b) shows a bridge layout involving azimuth and distance ties for abutment and pier locations. Note that, although the perfect case of equilateral triangles is not always present, the figures are quite strong, with redundant measurements providing accuracy verification.

Figure 10.22 illustrates a method of recording angle directions and distances to control stations with a list of derived azimuths. Station 17 can be found quickly by the surveyor from the distance and alignment ties to the hydrant, cut cross on the curb, and the nail in the pole. Had station 17 been destroyed, it could have been reestablished from these and other reference ties. The row marked "check" indicates that the surveyor has "closed the horizon" by continuing to revolve the theodolite back to the initial target point (100 in this example) and then reading the horizontal circle. An angle difference of more than 5″ between the initial reading and the check reading usually means that the series of angles in that column must be repeated.

After the design of a facility has been coordinated, polar layout coordinates can be generated for points to be laid out from selected stations. The surveyor can copy the computer data directly into the field book (see Figure 10.23) for use later in the field. On large projects (expressways, dams, etc.), it is common practice to have printed and bound vol-

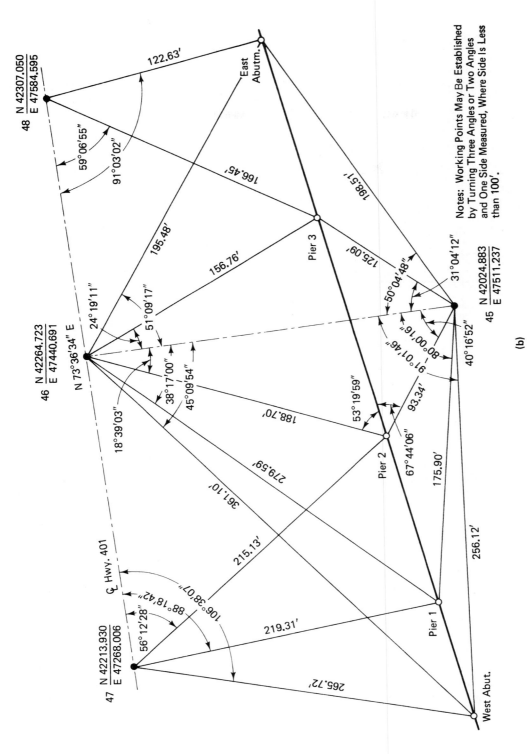

**FIGURE 10.21 (continued)** (b) Bridge layout, located by angle and distance. (Adapted from the *Construction Manual*, Ministry of Transportation, Ontario)

351

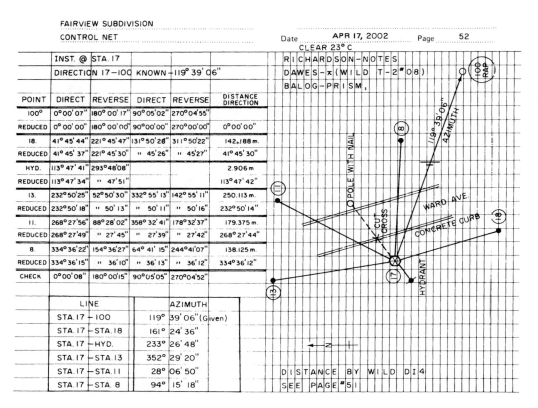

**FIGURE 10.22** Field notes for control point directions and distances.

umes that include polar coordinate data for all control stations and all layout points. Modern total station practice permits the direct uploading of the coordinates of control points and layout points to be used in layout surveys (see Chapter 7).

Figure 10.24 shows a primary control net established to provide control for a construction site. The primary control stations are tied into a national, state, or provincial coordinate grid by a series of precise traverses or triangular networks. Points on baselines (secondary points) can be tied into the primary control net by polar ties, intersection, or resection. The actual layout points of the structure (columns, walls, footings, etc.) are established from these secondary points. International standard ISO 4463 (from the International Organization for Standardization) points out that the accuracy of key building or structural layout points should not be influenced by possible discrepancies in the state or provincial coordinate grid. For that reason, the primary project control net is analyzed and adjusted independently of the state or provincial coordinate grid. This "free net" is tied to the state or provincial coordinate grid without becoming an integrated adjusted component of that grid. The relative positional accuracy of project layout points to each other is more important than the positional accuracy of these layout points relative to a state or provincial coordinate grid.

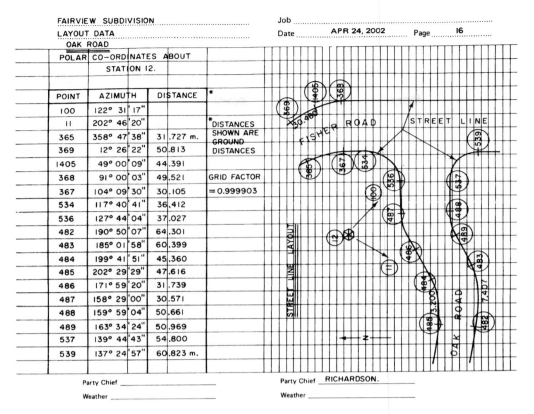

| FAIRVIEW SUBDIVISION | | | Job | |
|---|---|---|---|---|
| LAYOUT DATA | | | Date APR 24, 2002 Page 16 | |

**OAK ROAD**

**POLAR CO-ORDINATES ABOUT STATION 12.**

| POINT | AZIMUTH | DISTANCE | * |
|---|---|---|---|
| 100 | 122° 31′ 17″ | | |
| 11 | 202° 46′ 20″ | | *DISTANCES SHOWN ARE ~~GROUND~~ DISTANCES |
| 365 | 358° 47′ 38″ | 31.727 m. | |
| 369 | 12° 26′ 22″ | 50.813 | |
| 1405 | 49° 00′ 09″ | 44.391 | |
| 368 | 91° 00′ 03″ | 49.521 | GRID FACTOR |
| 367 | 104° 09′ 30″ | 30.105 | = 0.999903 |
| 534 | 117° 40′ 41″ | 36.412 | |
| 536 | 127° 44′ 04″ | 37.027 | |
| 482 | 190° 50′ 07″ | 64.301 | |
| 483 | 185° 01′ 58″ | 60.399 | |
| 484 | 199° 41′ 51″ | 45.360 | |
| 485 | 202° 29′ 29″ | 47.616 | |
| 486 | 171° 59′ 20″ | 31.739 | |
| 487 | 158° 29′ 00″ | 30.571 | |
| 488 | 159° 59′ 04″ | 50.661 | |
| 489 | 163° 34′ 24″ | 50.969 | |
| 537 | 139° 44′ 43″ | 54.800 | |
| 539 | 137° 24′ 57″ | 60.823 m. | |

Party Chief _____

Weather _____

Party Chief RICHARDSON.

Weather _____

**FIGURE 10.23**  Prepared polar coordinate layout notes.

## 10.9.2  Positional Accuracies (ISO 4463)

### 10.9.2.1 Primary system control stations

1. Permissible deviations of the distances and angles obtained when measuring the positions of primary points, and those calculated from the adjusted coordinates of these points, shall not exceed:

$$\text{Distances: } \pm\ 0.75\ \sqrt{L}\ \text{mm}$$

$$\text{Angles: } \pm\ 0.045\ \text{degrees}\ \sqrt{L}$$

or

$$\pm\ \frac{0.05}{\sqrt{L}}\ \text{gon}$$

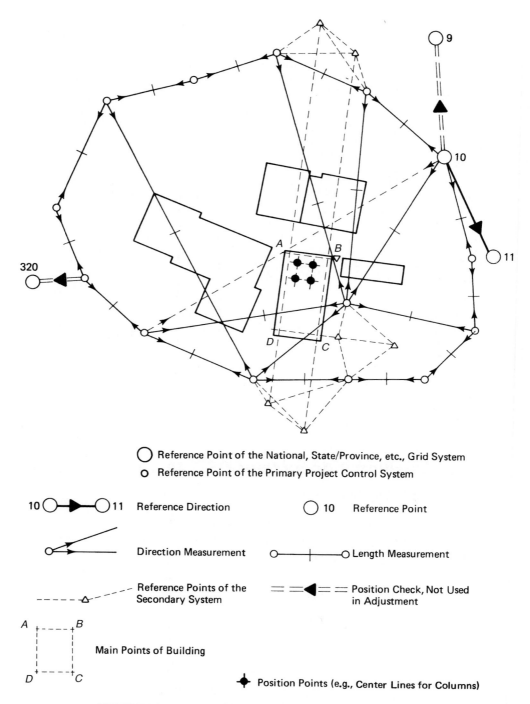

○ Reference Point of the National, State/Province, etc., Grid System

o Reference Point of the Primary Project Control System

10 ○━━▶━○ 11　Reference Direction　　　　　○ 10　　Reference Point

Direction Measurement　　　　○━━┼━━○ Length Measurement

Reference Points of the
Secondary System　　　　　═ ═◀ ═ ═ Position Check, Not Used
in Adjustment

A B
D C
Main Points of Building

✦ Position Points (e.g., Center Lines for Columns)

**FIGURE 10.24** Project control net. (Adapted from International Organization for Standardization [ISO], Standard 4463)

where $L$ is the distance in meters between primary stations (in the case of angles, $L$ is the shorter side of the angle); 1 revolution $= 360° = 400$ gon (also grad—a European angular unit); 1 gon $= 0.9$ degrees (exactly).

2. Permissible deviations of the distances and angles obtained when checking the positions of primary points shall not exceed:

$$\text{Distances: } \pm 2\sqrt{L} \text{ mm}$$

$$\text{Angles: } \pm \frac{0.135}{\sqrt{L}} \text{ degrees}$$

or

$$\pm \frac{0.15}{\sqrt{L}} \text{ gon}$$

where $L$ is the distance (in meters between primary stations (in the case of angles, $L$ is the shorter side of the angle).

Angles are measured with a 1-second theodolite, with the measurements made in two sets (each set is formed by two observations, one on each face of the instrument. Distances can be measured with steel tapes or EDMs, and they should be measured at least twice by either method. Steel tape measurements should be corrected for temperature, sag, slope, and tension. A tension device should be used while taping. EDM instruments should be checked regularly against a range of known distances.

## 10.9.2.2 Secondary system control stations

1. Secondary control stations and main layout points (for example, *ABCD,* Figure 10.24) constitute the secondary system. The permissible deviations for a checked distance from a given or calculated distance between a primary control station and a secondary point shall not exceed:

$$\text{Distances: } \pm 2\sqrt{L} \text{ mm}$$

2. The permissible deviations for a checked distance from the given or calculated distance between two secondary points in the same system shall not exceed:

$$\text{Distances: } \pm 2\sqrt{L} \text{ mm}$$

where $L$ is the distance in meters. For $L$ less than 10 m, permissible deviations are $\pm 6$ mm.

$$\text{Angles: } \pm \frac{0.135}{\sqrt{L}} \text{ degrees}$$

or

**Table 10.13**   ACCURACY REQUIREMENT CONSTANTS FOR LAYOUT SURVEYS

| K | Application |
|---|---|
| 10 | Earthwork without any particular accuracy requirement (for example, rough excavation, embankments) |
| 5 | Earthwork subject to accuracy requirements (for example, roads, pipelines, structures) |
| 2 | Poured concrete structures (for example, curbs, abutments) |
| 1 | Precast concrete structures, steel structures (for example, bridges, buildings) |

*Source:* Adapted from Table 8-1, ISO 4463.

$$\pm\frac{0.15}{\sqrt{L}}\text{ gon}$$

where $L$ is the length in meters of the shorter side of the angle.

Angles are measured with a transit or theodolite reading to at least one minute. The measurement should be made in at least one set (i.e., two observations, one on each face of the instrument). Distances can be measured using steel tapes or EDMs and should be measured at least twice by either method. Taped distances should be corrected for temperature, sag, slope, and tension. A tension device should be used with the tape. EDM instruments should be checked against a range of known distances regularly.

**10.9.2.3 Layout points**   The permissible deviations of a checked distance between a secondary point and a layout point, or between two layout points, are:

$$\pm K\sqrt{L}\text{ mm}$$

where $L$ is the specified distance in meters, and $K$ is a constant taken from Table 10.13. For $L$ less than 5 m, permissible deviation is $\pm 2K$ mm.

The permissible deviations for a checked angle between two lines, dependent on each other, through adjacent layout points are:

$$\pm\frac{0.0675}{\sqrt{L}}K\text{ degrees or }\pm\frac{0.075}{\sqrt{L}}K\text{ gon}$$

where $L$ is the length in meters of the shorter side of the angle and $K$ is a constant from Table 10.13.

Figure 10.25 illustrates the above specifications for the case involving a stakeout for a curved concrete curb. The layout point on the curve has a permissible area of uncertainty generated by $\pm 0.015$/m due to angle uncertainties and by $\pm 0.013$/m due to distance uncertainties.

## 10.10   Control Survey Markers

Generally, **horizontal control survey markers** are used for (1) state or provincial coordinate grids, (2) property and boundary delineation, and (3) project control. The type of marker used varies with the following factors:

- Type of soil or material at the marker site.

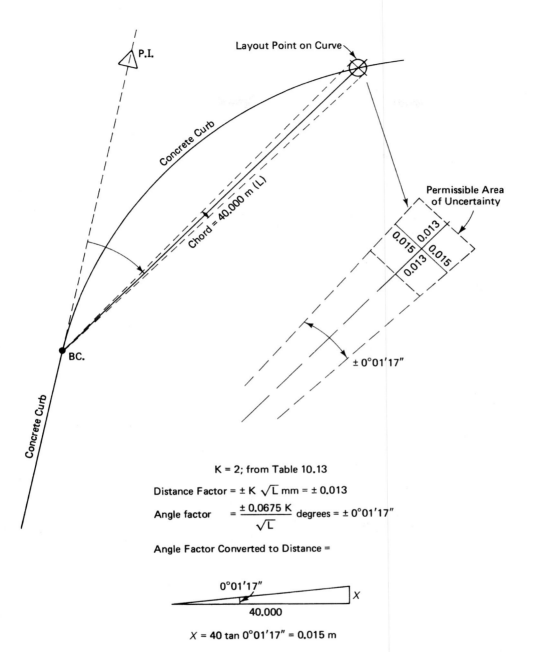

K = 2; from Table 10.13

Distance Factor = $\pm K \sqrt{L}$ mm = $\pm 0.013$

Angle factor $= \dfrac{\pm 0.0675 K}{\sqrt{L}}$ degrees = $\pm 0°01'17''$

Angle Factor Converted to Distance =

$X = 40 \tan 0°01'17'' = 0.015$ m

**FIGURE 10.25** Accuracy analysis for a concrete curb layout point. (See ISO Standard 4463.)

- Degree of permanence required.
- Cost of replacement.
- Precision requirements.

Early North American surveyors marked important points with suitably inscribed 4 in. × 4 in. cedar posts, sometimes embedded in rock cairns. Adjacent trees were used for reference ties, with the initials BT (bearing tree) carved into a blazed portion of the trunk. As time went on, surveyors used a wide assortment of markers (for example, glass bottles, gun barrels, iron tubes, iron bars, concrete monuments with brass top plates, tablet and bolt markers for embedding into rock and concrete drill holes, and aluminum break-off markers with built-in magnets to facilitate relocation).

Common markers in use today are:

1. For property markers: iron tubes, square iron bars (1″ or ½″ square), and round iron bars.
2. For construction control: reinforcing steel bars (with and without aluminum caps) and concrete monuments with brass caps.
3. For control surveys: bronze tablet markers, bronze bolt markers, post markers, sleeve-type survey markers, and aluminum break-off markers.

The latter type of aluminum marker (see Figure 10.26) has become quite popular for both control and construction monuments. The chief features of these markers are their light weight (compared to concrete or steel) and the break-off, which ensures that, if disturbed, the monument will not bend (as iron bars will) and thus give an erroneous location point. Instead, these monuments will break off cleanly, leaving the lower portion (including the base) in its correct location. The base can be used as a monument, or it can be used in the location of its replacement. The base of these monuments is equipped with a magnet (as is the top portion) to facilitate relocation when magnetic locating instruments are used by the surveyor.

Whichever type of monument is considered for use, the key characteristic must be that of horizontal directional stability. Some municipalities establish secondary and tertiary coordinate grid monuments (survey tablet markers, Figure 10.27) in concrete curbs and sidewalks. In areas that experience frost penetration, vertical movement will take place as the frost enters and then leaves the soil supporting the curb or walk. Normally, the movement is restricted to the vertical direction, leaving the monument's horizontal coordinates valid.

Vertical control survey markers (benchmarks) are established on structures that restrict vertical movement. The same survey marker is seldom used for both horizontal and vertical control. Markers such as those illustrated in Figure 10.27 can be unreliable for elevation reference unless they have been installed on concrete structures that are not affected by frost or loading movement. The marker shown in Figure 10.28 was designed specifically for use as both a horizontal and vertical marker.

Most agencies prefer to place vertical control markers on vertical structural members (for example, masonry building walls, concrete piers, abutments, walls), that is, on any structural component whose footing is well below the level of frost penetration. Tablet markers used for benchmarks are sometimes manufactured with a protruding ledge so that the rod can be supported easily on the mark.

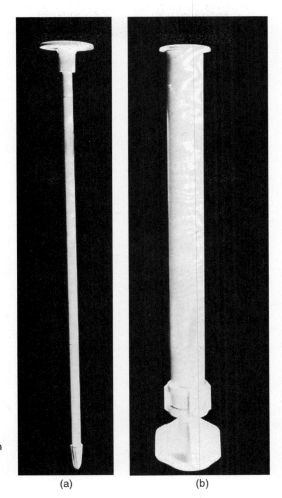

**FIGURE 10.26** Lightweight aluminum monuments. (a) Rod with aluminum cap. (b) Break-off pipe monument. (Courtesy of Berntsen, Inc.)

(a)                    (b)

Temporary benchmarks (TBMs) can be chiseled marks on concrete, rock, or steel or spikes in utility poles, tree roots, and the like. The unambiguous description of TBM locations, along with their elevations, are not published (as are regular benchmarks) but are kept on file for same-agency use.

## 10.11 Direction of a Line by Observation on Polaris

Polaris, also called the North Star, has been used for centuries by sailors navigating in the northern hemisphere of our globe. Polaris is particularly useful because its apparent path of rotation keeps the star very close to the extension of the earth's polar axis through the North Pole. The actual position of Polaris, along with the position of the sun and many other stars, is computed (and published annually) in a nautical almanac or ephemeris and in computer programs.

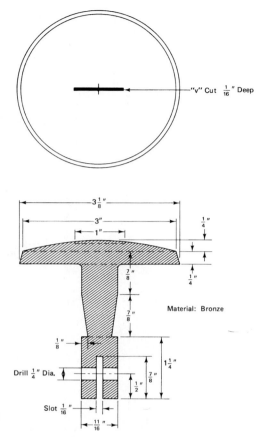

**FIGURE 10.27** Survey tablet marker for use in concrete, masonry, or rock.

Although positions and directions are now routinely determined using GPS techniques, sightings on Polaris and the sun are still used by surveyors to establish astronomical directions on survey control lines. In built-up areas, surveyors can establish control-line directions by tying into existing surveys having known azimuths or bearings, or they can tie into horizontal control monuments whose grid coordinates are known. In more remote areas, often the easiest method of establishing direction is to take GPS observations or observations on the sun or the North Star.

Observations based on the position of the sun are usually more convenient to take than are observations based on the positions of the stars (they can be accomplished during normal working hours); however, due to the size of the sun and the speed at which it appears to move, directions based on solar observations are generally less precise than those based on the stars (to the closest 1 to 2 min for solar observations and to the closest 0.1 min for observations on Polaris, using normal procedures). Using more precise techniques and repetitive observations with modern theodolites with dual-axis compensators, accuracies of 10 to 15 seconds (arc) for solar observations and 2 to 5 seconds (arc) for Polaris observations are now possible. Accuracies for conventional theodolites can be improved through increased repetitions and by leveling the instrument with two screws

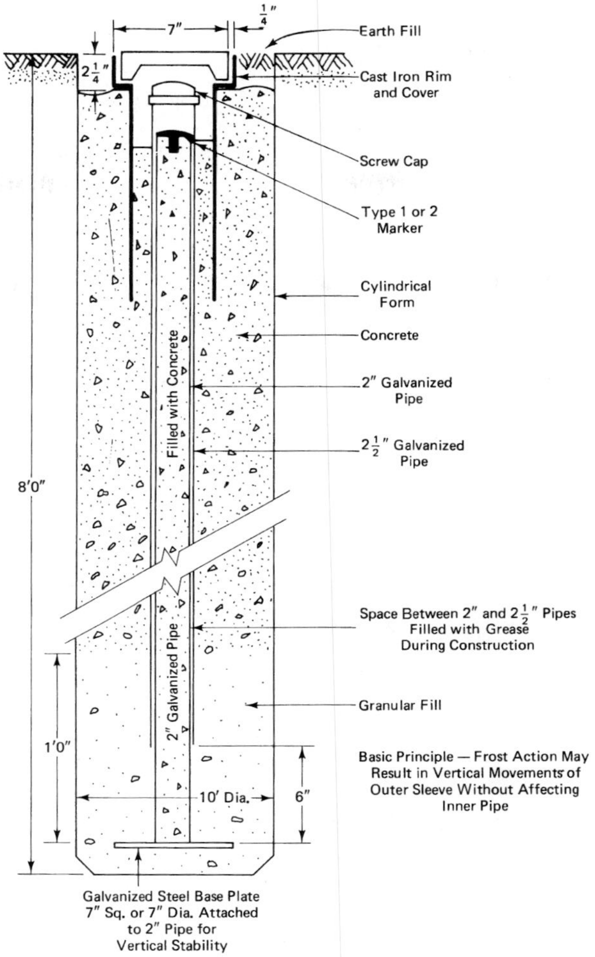

7″
$\frac{1}{4}$″
Earth Fill
$2\frac{1}{4}$″
Cast Iron Rim and Cover
Screw Cap
Type 1 or 2 Marker
Cylindrical Form
Concrete
2″ Galvanized Pipe
$2\frac{1}{2}$″ Galvanized Pipe
Filled with Concrete
8′0″
Space Between 2″ and $2\frac{1}{2}$″ Pipes Filled with Grease During Construction
2″ Galvanized Pipe
Granular Fill
1′0″
Basic Principle — Frost Action May Result in Vertical Movements of Outer Sleeve Without Affecting Inner Pipe
10′ Dia.
6″
Galvanized Steel Base Plate 7″ Sq. or 7″ Dia. Attached to 2″ Pipe for Vertical Stability


**FIGURE 10.28** Sleeve-type survey marker; can be used as a horizontal or a vertical control monument. (Courtesy of Department of Energy, Mines, and Resources, Surveys and Mapping Branch, Ottawa)

(three-screw instrument) perpendicular to the direction of the sun or star. It seems likely that in the near future, directions (and positions) will result chiefly from GPS observations.

Because many astronomical concepts are abstract, it simplifies overall comprehension and positional computations to consider the earth as stationary at the center of a celestial sphere of infinitely large radius. The stars then appear to be fixed on the surface of this infinitely large sphere, which itself appears to be rotating from east to west (see Figure 10.29). To determine the bearing of Polaris at any time, the position of Polaris on the celestial sphere must first be determined. As you can see in Figure 10.29, the position of Polaris (*S*) is given by the declination (*d*), which is equivalent to the latitude on earth, and by the Greenwich hour angle (GHA), which is measured westward from the Greenwich meridian (0°). The GHA, for the first 180°, is equivalent to west longitude on earth. (Longitudes are measured east and west from the Greenwich meridian for 180°, whereas the GHA is simply measured west a full 360°.)

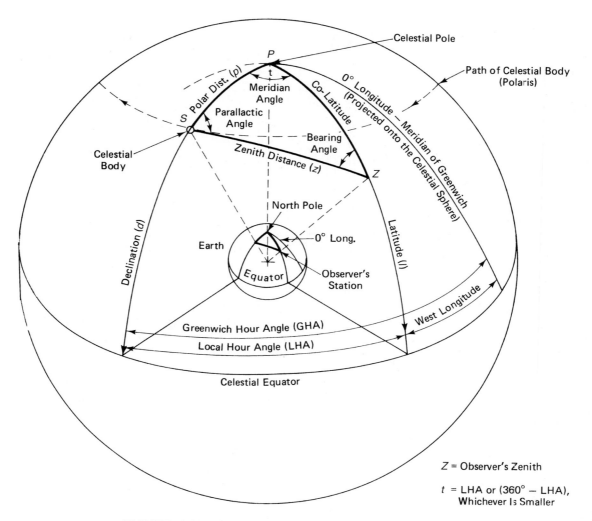

**FIGURE 10.29** Celestial sphere.

Figure 10.29 also shows the spherical triangle *PZS*, which can be solved to provide the bearing of Polaris. Point *Z* is the zenith of the observer (that is, a point made on the celestial sphere when a vertical line through the theodolite is produced straight upward). *S* is the location of the celestial body (Polaris, in this case), and *P* is the celestial pole (the extension of the earth's polar axis upward through the North Pole).

Angle *t,* the meridian angle, is given by the local hour angle (LHA) or by 360° − LHA, whichever is smaller. As you can see in Figure 10.29, the LHA is an angle measured westward from the meridian through the observer's station to the meridian occupied by Polaris. If the LHA is less than 180°, Polaris is west of the North Pole; if the LHA is more than 180°, Polaris is east of the North Pole.

Figure 10.29 also shows that the LHA is determined by subtracting the west longitude from the GHA (western hemisphere):

$$LHA = GHA - \text{west longitude} \tag{10.7}$$

In the eastern hemisphere:

$$LHA = GHA + \text{east longitude} \tag{10.8}$$

The following formula can be used to compute the azimuth ($Z$) of Polaris:

$$Z = \tan^{-1} \frac{\sin LHA}{\sin \varphi \cos LHA - \cos \varphi \tan d} \tag{10.9}$$

where $\varphi$ = latitude of the observer

$d$ = declination of Polaris

$Z$ = azimuth of Polaris (a negative value indicates that the star is west of north)

## 10.12 Time

We usually consider one day to be one complete revolution of the earth on its axis. We can see from Figure 10.30 that the earth, while rotating on its axis, is also traveling in an elliptical orbit around the sun. If we reference the earth to a point (a star) that is an infinite distance away, one complete revolution of the earth, which is called a *sidereal day* (star day) is exactly 360°. You can see in Figure 10.30 that the earth, while in position 2, has turned 360° to describe a sidereal day, but that the earth now has to revolve an additional angle ($K$)

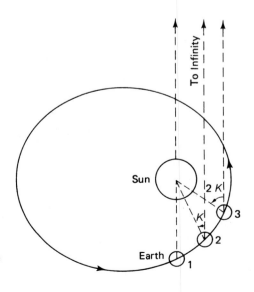

**FIGURE 10.30** Elliptical path of the earth around the sun (scale distorted).

**Table 10.14**

|       |                            | At          | Add hours to convert to GCT |
|-------|----------------------------|-------------|-----------------------------|
| GCT   | Greenwich Civil Time       | 0° long W   | —                           |
| AST   | Atlantic Standard Time     | 60° long W  | 4                           |
| EST   | Eastern Standard Time      | 75° long W  | 5                           |
| CST   | Central Standard Time      | 90° long W  | 6                           |
| MST   | Mountain Standard Time     | 105°long W  | 7                           |
| PST   | Pacific Standard Time      | 120°long W  | 8                           |
| YST   | Yukon Standard Time        | 135°long W  | 9                           |
| AHST  | Alaska/Hawaii Standard Time| 150°long W  | 10                          |

DST, Daylight Saving Time. DST in a zone is equal to standard time in the next zone to the east.

to complete its revolution with respect to the sun. A solar day is, therefore, 360° plus the partial revolution of angle $K$. Because the earth travels around the sun once in one year, the addition of all the partial revolutions of angle $K$ must equal one complete revolution of the earth.

The earth makes 366.2422 revolutions on its axis (that is, 366.2422 sidereal days) while completing the annual solar orbit. Since a solar day is longer than a sidereal day by the partial revolution angle $K$ and since all partial revolutions equal one day, there must therefore be 365.2422 solar days in one year.

The additional partial revolutions (angle $K$) are not all equal because the earth's orbit around the sun is not uniform; the average partial revolution is 0°59.15'. Since it is not possible to have days of different lengths, we keep time on a 24-hour basis and call that mean solar or civil time. The difference between mean solar time and the time required for a complete solar revolution on any one given day of the year is called the equation of time. Values for this time equation, and for solar day–sidereal day relationships, are given in the ephemeris.

In 24 hours, the earth revolves through 360° of longitude, and in 1 hour the earth revolves through 15° of longitude. To facilitate timekeeping, local time zones are established at 15° intervals as shown in Table 10.14. The relationship between time and longitude is summarized as follows:

| TIME/LONGITUDE | LONGITUDE/TIME |
|----------------|----------------|
| 24 hours = 360° | 360° = 24 hours |
| 1 hour = 15° | 1° = 4 minutes |
| 1 minute = 15' | 1' = 4 seconds |
| 1 second = 15" | 1" = 0.067 seconds |

From these relationships, you can see that the solar day, which included an additional partial revolution averaging 0°59.15', is an average 3 minutes, 56.6 seconds longer than a sidereal day. This relationship is used in ephemeris conversions from Greenwich civil time to Greenwich sidereal time.

*Universal time* (UT) is the mean solar time of the meridian at Greenwich, England. UT is kept precisely by atomic clocks. Surveyors can obtain UTC (coordinated universal time—general use) or UT (precise universal time) from various radio stations, for example:

United States: Station WWV, 2.5, 5, 10, 15, and 20 MHz.
Canada:       Station CHU, 3.33, 7.335, and 14.667 MHz. This signal gives EST, which can be converted to UT by adding 5 hours.

Accurate time signals can also be obtained by phoning 303-499-7111; less accurate time can be obtained by simply turning on a GPS receiver.

## 10.13   Polaris

Figure 10.31 shows that because of the direction of the earth's revolution, Polaris appears to trace a counterclockwise path around the north celestial pole. The star makes one complete revolution in one sidereal day. The star is at upper culmination at 2 hours sidereal every day, at western elongation at 8 hours sidereal every day, at lower culmination at 14 hours sidereal every day, and at eastern elongation at 20 hours sidereal every day.

At the equator, the star appears to describe a circular orbit about the pole, with a horizontal elongation angle of about $\pm 0°48'$ and a vertical culmination angle also of about $\pm 0°48'$. As the observer moves northward, the orbit becomes elliptical in appearance, with the horizontal elongation angle varying with latitude. The range in elongation angles varies from about $0°48'$ at the equator to about $2°20'$ at latitude $70°$.

Figure 10.32 demonstrates that the altitude of Polaris is directly related to the latitude of the observer's station. A correction in altitude ($\Delta h$) is required to account for the culmination movement of the star. It follows that at eastern and western elongation, the altitude of Polaris is, in fact, the latitude of the observer, and at all other points in the star's orbit, the altitude is equal to latitude $\pm \Delta h$.

$$\text{Altitude of Polaris} = \text{latitude } (\varphi) \pm \Delta h$$

## 10.14   Procedure for Observing Polaris

The success of a star observation depends a great deal on being prepared well in advance of the actual sighting. The ideal time for observations is just before nightfall. At that time, although Polaris is visible only through a telescope, it is the only star in the telescopic field of view. Later, after nightfall, Polaris is seen easily with the naked eye. But when a sight on Polaris is taken, confusion can result from the large number of stars now visible in the magnified field of view. An additional advantage to taking the observation prior to nightfall is that illumination is not required for targets, scales, or note keeping, and the work can proceed quickly. The wise surveyor will be prepared, however, with well-charged batteries and illuminators in case the observation cannot be completed before nightfall.

To sight Polaris at dusk, north must be approximated. A compass reading corrected for magnetic declination (see Section 4.12) is used by many surveyors. The following describes a procedure for observation of Polaris (see Figure 10.33 and Section 10.15):

1. Prepare note forms in advance.
2. Check to see that equipment is working properly and that a good supply of batteries (including spares) is available.
3. Determine the latitude (can be scaled from a topographic map).

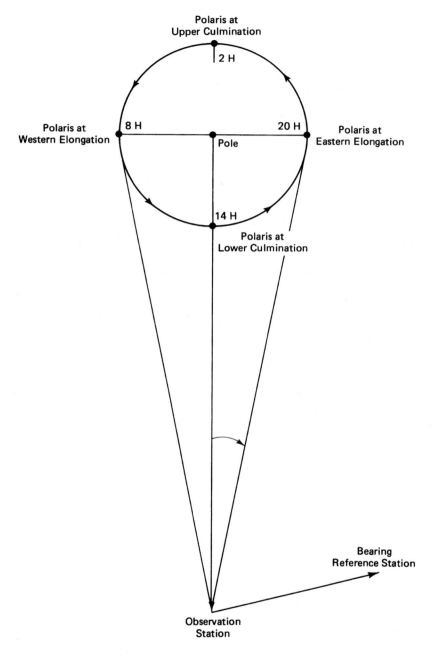

**FIGURE 10.31** Apparent path taken by Polaris, along with the four major positions.

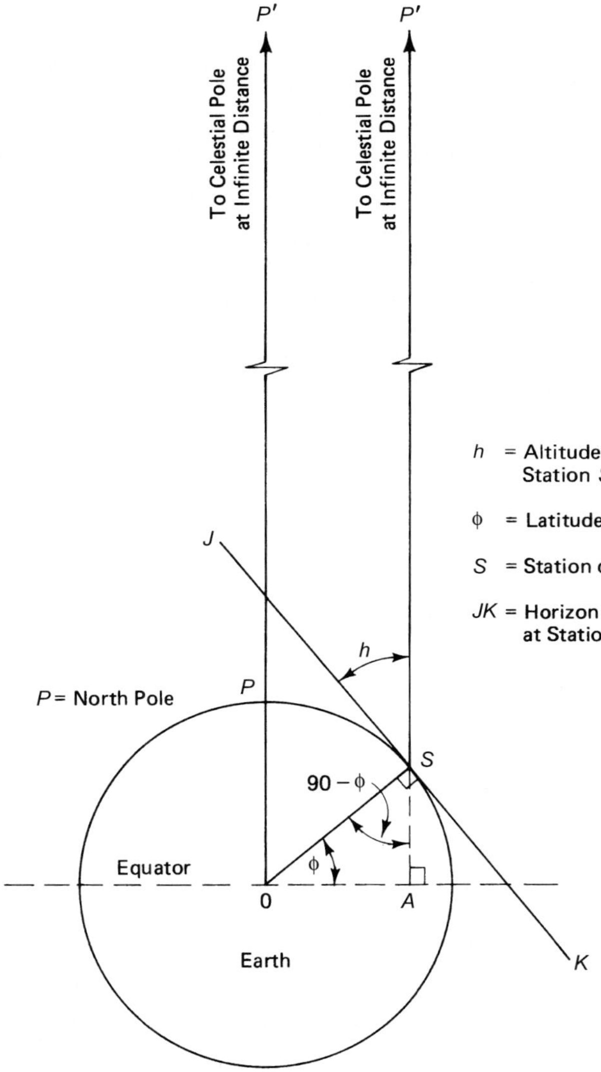
P'
P'
To Celestial Pole at Infinite Distance
To Celestial Pole at Infinite Distance
h = Altitude of Polaris at Station S
ϕ = Latitude of Station S
S = Station of Observer
JK = Horizon of Observer at Station S
J
h
P
P = North Pole
S
90 − ϕ
Equator
ϕ
0
A
Earth
K

Relationship

1. $h$ = angle $ASK$
2. $ASK + (90 - \phi) = 90°$
3. $ASK = \phi$
4. $h = \phi$

**FIGURE 10.32** Relationship between the latitude of the observer station and the altitude of Polaris when viewed at that station.

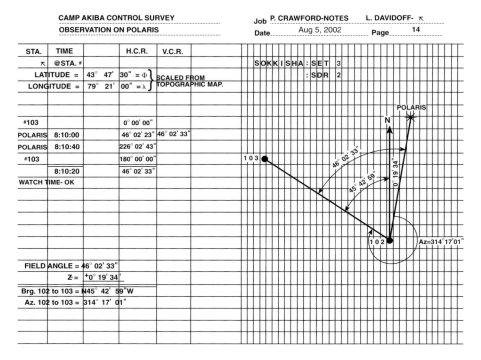

**FIGURE 10.33** Field notes for Polaris observation.

4. After carefully setting up the instrument (station 102), determine approximately the direction of north and establish a target.

5. With the horizontal scales zeroed, sight at the reference station (station 103).

6. Sight an object about 250 m (800 ft) away and focus carefully; this is the instrument's infinite focus, which must be set when sighting the star. Some surveyors mark this point on the focus ring so that the infinite focus can be reestablished after dark when there may be no suitable long-range sight available. Proper identification of the infinite focus position on the focusing ring is emphasized because if the telescope is only slightly off focus, the star will not even appear in the telescopic field of view and much time will be wasted.

7. If the telescope has been directed properly toward north, if the correct approximate altitude has been set on the vertical circle, and if the focus adjustment has been set properly (infinite focus), Polaris should appear in the telescopic field of view at least 15 minutes before nightfall. It may be necessary to move the telescope through slight horizontal and vertical arcs to find the star.

8. At the instant the star has been centered carefully on the cross hairs, record the time, and read and book the horizontal angle.

9. Transit (plunge) the telescope, and resight the star. Once again, record the time and horizontal angle.

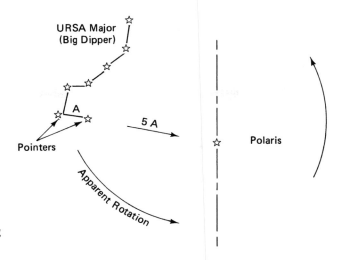

**FIGURE 10.34** Aid for locating Polaris.

10. Finally, sight the telescope back on the original reference station (103), and note the angle (it should be 180°00′). This procedure may be repeated if higher accuracies are required.

11. Use the average time for the bearing calculation for Polaris (see Section 10.15), and use the average angle to determine the bearing of line 102–103 (see Figure 10.33).

When Polaris is to be observed during darkness, it can be located by using the two Big Dipper (Ursa Major) stars as pointers. See Figure 10.34. In addition to tabular solutions, surveyors can purchase various computer programs that will compute the azimuth of Polaris and the azimuth of the field line. Required input is the date, year, universal times, latitude, longitude, and field angle to star.

## 10.15 Computation Technique for Azimuth Determination—Tabular Solution

Location (see the sketch in Figure 10.33):

$$\text{Latitude} = 43°47′30″ = \varphi$$
$$\text{Longitude} = 79°21′00″ = \lambda$$

Determine GCT or UT (universal time):
August 5, 2002: 8:10:20 P.M. DST, EST

$+12$  conversion to P.M.
20:10:20 LMT
$+\ 4$  conversion to Greenwich
24:10:20
**0:10:20 GCT Aug. 6, 2002**  [≈ **UT (Universal Time)**]

Determine GHA:
GHA (from Table 10.15)

| | |
|---|---|
| Aug. 7, 2002 | 0 hours: 276°45′03.9″ |
| Aug. 6, 2002 | 0 hours: 275°46′23.9″ |
| Difference | 0°58′40.0″ |
| + | 360° |
| Change in 24 hours | 360°58′40.0″ |

275°46′23.9″
+ 2°35′25.3″*

**GHA**     **278°21′49.2″ at 0$^h$ 10$^m$ 20$^s$ GCT Aug. 6, 2002**

*Change in GHA for 0$^h$ 10$^m$ 20$^s$

$$= \frac{0^h \ 10^m \ 20^s}{24^h} \times 360°58′40.0″$$

$$= \frac{0.1722222}{24} \times 360.9777777$$

$$= 2.590349° = 2°35′25.3″$$

Determine LHA:

LHA = GHA − WEST LONGITUDE (see Figure 10.29)
i.e.:           278°21′49.2″

                 79°21′

**LHA =**       **199°00′49.2″**

Determine declination:
DECLINATION (*d*) (from Table 10.15)

Aug. 6, 2002
89°16′08.98″ Aug. 7
89°16′08.83″ Aug. 6
Difference = 0°00′00.15″†

**DECLINATION (*d*) = 89°16′08.83″ Aug. 6, 2002 @ 0$^h$ 10$^m$ 20$^s$ GCT**

†Change in declination for 0$^h$ 10$^m$ 20$^s$

$$= 0.17222/24 \times 0.15″ = 0.00″$$

[No correction required for this short time period.]

Determine the azimuth of Polaris:

**Table 10.15**  SUN AND POLARIS EMPHEMERIS, AUGUST 2002. TABLE COURTESY OF JERRY L. WAHL, BUREAU OF LAND MANAGEMENT. COMPLETE EMHEMERIS IS AVAILABLE AT HIS INTERNET SITE: http://www.cadastral.com.

| 2002 Date | SUN Declination | For 0 hrs Universal Time | | | Polaris Declination | 0 hrs UT GHA | |
|---|---|---|---|---|---|---|---|
| | | GHA | Eq of Tm | Semi-Di | | | |
| | d m s | d m s | m s | m s | d m s | d m s | h |
| Aug 1 TH | +18 06 52.8 | 178 24 51.1 | −06 20.59 | 15 45.5 | 89 16 08.42 | 270 53 10.4 | 5 |
| Aug 2 FR | +17 51 45.1 | 178 25 46.1 | −06 16.93 | 15 45.6 | 89 16 08.46 | 271 51 50.2 | 5 |
| Aug 3 SA | +17 36 19.8 | 178 26 49.8 | −06 12.68 | 15 45.7 | 89 16 08.52 | 272 50 29.0 | 5 |
| Aug 4 SU | +17 20 37.2 | 178 28 02.4 | −06 07.84 | 15 45.8 | 89 16 08.59 | 273 49 07.1 | 5 |
| Aug 5 MO | +17 04 37.7 | 178 29 23.8 | −06 02.41 | 15 45.9 | 89 16 08.70 | 274 47 45.2 | 5 |
| Aug 6 TU | +16 48 21.6 | 178 30 54.0 | −05 56.40 | 15 46.1 | 89 16 08.83 | 275 46 23.9 | 5 |
| Aug 7 WE | +16 31 49.1 | 178 32 33.0 | −05 49.80 | 15 46.2 | 89 16 08.98 | 276 45 03.9 | 5 |
| Aug 8 TH | +16 15 00.6 | 178 34 20.7 | −05 42.62 | 15 46.3 | 89 16 09.14 | 277 43 45.9 | 5 |
| Aug 9 FR | +15 57 56.4 | 178 36 17.3 | −05 34.85 | 15 46.5 | 89 16 09.31 | 278 42 29.7 | 5 |
| Aug 10 SA | +15 40 36.8 | 178 38 22.6 | −05 26.49 | 15 46.6 | 89 16 09.46 | 279 41 15.1 | 5 |
| Aug 11 SU | +15 23 02.2 | 178 40 36.7 | −05 17.56 | 15 46.8 | 89 16 09.59 | 280 40 00.8 | 5 |
| Aug 12 MO | +15 05 12.8 | 178 42 59.5 | −05 08.04 | 15 47.0 | 89 16 09.71 | 281 38 45.9 | 5 |
| Aug 13 TU | +14 47 08.9 | 178 45 30.9 | −04 57.94 | 15 47.1 | 89 16 09.80 | 282 37 29.4 | 5 |
| Aug 14 WE | +14 28 51.0 | 178 48 11.0 | −04 47.27 | 15 47.3 | 89 16 09.90 | 283 36 10.9 | 5 |
| Aug 15 TH | +14 10 19.3 | 178 50 59.6 | −04 36.03 | 15 47.5 | 89 16 10.01 | 284 34 50.5 | 5 |
| Aug 16 FR | +13 51 34.1 | 178 53 56.5 | −04 24.24 | 15 47.6 | 89 16 10.14 | 285 33 29.1 | 4 |
| Aug 17 SA | +13 32 35.8 | 178 57 01.6 | −04 11.90 | 15 47.8 | 89 16 10.29 | 286 32 07.5 | 4 |
| Aug 18 SU | +13 13 24.8 | 179 00 14.6 | −03 59.02 | 15 48.0 | 89 16 10.47 | 287 30 46.5 | 4 |
| Aug 19 MO | +12 54 01.2 | 179 03 35.5 | −03 45.63 | 15 48.2 | 89 16 10.67 | 288 29 26.8 | 4 |
| Aug 20 TU | +12 34 25.6 | 179 07 04.0 | −03 31.73 | 15 48.4 | 89 16 10.88 | 289 28 08.8 | 4 |
| Aug 21 WE | +12 14 38.1 | 179 10 39.8 | −03 17.34 | 15 48.6 | 89 16 11.09 | 290 26 52.5 | 4 |
| Aug 22 TH | +11 54 39.0 | 179 14 22.8 | −03 02.48 | 15 48.8 | 89 16 11.30 | 291 25 37.7 | 4 |
| Aug 23 FR | +11 34 28.7 | 179 18 12.6 | −02 47.16 | 15 49.0 | 89 16 11.50 | 292 24 23.9 | 4 |
| Aug 24 SA | +11 14 07.5 | 179 22 09.1 | −02 31.39 | 15 49.2 | 89 16 11.69 | 293 23 10.5 | 4 |
| Aug 25 SU | +10 53 35.6 | 179 26 11.9 | −02 15.20 | 15 49.4 | 89 16 11.86 | 294 21 57.0 | 4 |
| Aug 26 MO | +10 32 53.3 | 179 30 20.9 | −01 58.61 | 15 49.6 | 89 16 12.03 | 295 20 42.9 | 4 |
| Aug 27 TU | +10 12 01.0 | 179 34 35.7 | −01 41.62 | 15 49.8 | 89 16 12.19 | 296 19 27.8 | 4 |
| Aug 28 WE | + 9 50 59.0 | 179 38 56.1 | −01 24.26 | 15 50.0 | 89 16 12.35 | 297 18 11.5 | 4 |
| Aug 29 TH | + 9 29 47.5 | 179 43 21.8 | −01 06.54 | 15 50.2 | 89 16 12.52 | 298 16 54.2 | 4 |
| Aug 30 FR | + 9 08 26.8 | 179 47 52.6 | −00 48.49 | 15 50.4 | 89 16 12.70 | 299 15 35.8 | 4 |
| Aug 31 SA | + 8 46 57.3 | 179 52 28.3 | −00 30.11 | 15 50.6 | 89 16 12.90 | 300 14 16.8 | 3 |

$$\text{Az (Z)} = \tan^{-1} \frac{\sin 199°00'49.2''}{\sin 43°47'30'' \cos 199°00'49.2'' - \cos 43°47'30'' \tan 89°16'08.83''}$$

(10.8)

$$Z = \tan^{-1}(+0.0056917)$$
$$\mathbf{Z = 0°19'33.98''}$$

$$
\begin{array}{rl}
\text{Field angle} = & 46°02'33'' \\
-Z & \underline{\phantom{4}0°19'34''} \\
\text{Field angle (corr.)} = & 45°42'59''
\end{array}
$$

**Azimuth 102 to 103 = 314°17'01''**
See Figure 10.33.

## 10.16   Direction of a Line by Gyro-Theodolite

In Chapters 11 and 12, gyroscopes are described as the platform-stabilizing agents used with accelerometers in the inertial survey system technique of position determination. Several surveying equipment manufacturers produce gyro attachments for use with repeating theodolites (usually 6- or 20-second theodolites). Figure 10.35 shows a gyro attachment mounted on a 20-second theodolite.

The gyro attachment (gyrocompass) consists of a wire-hung pendulum supporting a high-speed, perfectly balanced gyromotor capable of attaining the required speed (for the illustrated instrument) of 12,000 rpm in 1 min. Basically, the rotation of the earth affects the orientation of the spin axis of the gyroscope so that the gyroscope spin axis orients itself toward the pole in an oscillating motion that is observed and measured in a plane perpendicular to the pendulum. This north-seeking oscillation, which is known as preces-

**FIGURE 10.35** Gyro attachment, mounted on a 20-second theodolite. Shown with battery charger and control unit. (Courtesy of Sokkia Co. Ltd.)

sion, is measured on the horizontal circle of the theodolite; extreme left (west) and right (east) readings are averaged to arrive at the meridian direction.

The gyro-equipped theodolite is set up and oriented approximately to north, using a compass; the gyromotor is engaged until the proper angular velocity has been reached (about 12,000 rpm for the instrument shown in Figure 10.35), and then the gyroscope is released. The precession oscillations are observed through the gyro-attachment viewing eyepiece, and the theodolite is adjusted closer to the northerly direction if necessary. When the theodolite is pointed to within a few minutes of north, the extreme precession positions (west and east) are noted in the viewing eyepiece and then recorded on the horizontal circle. As noted earlier, the position of the meridian is the value of the averaged precession readings. This technique, which takes about a half-hour to complete, is accurate to within 20 seconds of azimuth.

These instruments can be used to full advantage in mining and tunneling surveys for azimuth determination. More precise (3- to 5-seconds) gyrotheodolites can be used in the extension of surface control surveys.

# Questions

1. What are the advantages of referencing a survey to a recognized plane grid?
2. Describe why the use of a plane grid distorts spatial relationships.
3. How can the distortions in spatial relationships be minimized?
4. Describe the factors you would consider in establishing a net of control survey monuments to facilitate the design and construction of a large engineering works, for example, an airport.
5. Some have said that, with the advent of the global positioning system (GPS), the need for extensive ground control survey monumentation has been much reduced. Explain.

# Problems

Problems 10.1 through 10.5 use the control point data given in Table 10.16.

**Table 10.16** SMALL-AREA URBAN CONTROL MONUMENT DATA FOR PROBLEMS 10.1 TO 12.05[a]

| Monument | Elevation | Northing | Easting | Latitude | Longitude |
|---|---|---|---|---|---|
| A | 179.832 | 4,850,296.103 | 317,104.062 | 43°47'33" N | 079°20'50" W |
| B | 181.356 | 4,480,218.330 | 316,823.936 | 43°47'30" N | 079°21'02" W |
| C | 188.976 | 4,850,182.348 | 316,600.889 | 43°47'29" N | 079°21'12" W |
| D | 187.452 | 4,850,184.986 | 316,806.910 | 43°47'29" N | 079°21'03" W |

Average longitude = 079°21'02" (Mon. B)   Easting at CM = 304,800.000 m
Average latitude = 43°47'30" N (Mon. B)   Northing at equator = 0.000 m
Central meridian (CM) at longitude = 079°30' W   Scale factor at CM = 0.9999

[a]Data is consistent with the 3° transverse Mercator projection, related to NAD 83.

**10.1** Draw a representative sketch of the four control points and then determine the grid distances and grid bearings of sides *AB, BC, CD,* and *DA.*

**10.2** From the grid bearings computed in Problem 10.1, compute the interior angles (and their sum) of the traverse *ABCDA,* thus verifying the correctness of the grid bearing computations.

**10.3** Determine the ground distances for the four traverse sides by applying the scale and elevation factors (the grid factors). Use average latitude and longitude.

**10.4** Determine the convergence correction for each traverse side, and determine the geodetic bearings for each traverse side. Use average latitude and longitude.

**10.5** From the geodetic bearings computed in Problem 10.4, compute the interior angles (and their sum) of the traverse *ABCDA,* thus verifying the correctness of the geodetic bearing computations.

**10.6** A star observation was taken on August 10, 2002, at 7:20:13 P.M. EST (mean) in the Toronto, Ontario, area; latitude = 43°47′30″N, longitude = 79°21′00″W. An angle of 43°43′38″ (mean) was measured right from Polaris to station 17 while occupying station 16. Compute the azimuth of line 16–7.

**10.7** A star observation was taken on August 4, 2002, at 9:27:30 P.M. PST (mean) in the Santa Barbara, California, area; latitude = 34°29′30″N; longitude = 119°40′00″W. An angle of 61°32′20″ (mean) was turned left from Polaris to monument 331 while occupying monument 332. Compute the azimuth of line 332–331.

# 11 Global Positioning Systems (GPSs)

## 11.1 General Background

By the mid-1980s, the second-generation guidance system of the U.S. Department of Defense (DoD)—the Navigation Satellite Timing and Ranging (NAVSTAR) Global Positioning System (GPS)—had evolved to many of its present capabilities. In December 1993, the U.S. government officially declared that the system had reached its initial operational capability (IOC), with 26 satellites (23 Block II satellites) then potentially available for tracking. Additional Block II satellites (their life span is thought to be about seven years) continue to be launched. Current GPS satellite status and the constellation configuration can be accessed via the Internet at http://www.ngs.noaa.gov/ (see Table 11.1). Table 11.2 shows a satellite status report for the Russian GLONASS system. Some GPS receivers can track both GPS and GLONASS satellite signals, thus providing the potential for improved positioning.

Prior to NAVSTAR, precise positioning was often determined by using low-altitude satellites or inertial guidance systems. The first-generation satellite positioning system, called TRANSIT, consisted of six satellites in polar orbit at an altitude of only 1,100 km. Precise surveys, with positioning from 0.2 to 0.3 m, were accomplished using translocation techniques—that is, one receiver occupies a position of known coordinates while another occupies an unknown position. Data received at the known position were used to model signal transmission and to determine orbital errors, thus permitting more precise results.

The positioning analysis techniques in the TRANSIT system utilize a ground receiver capable of noting the change in satellite frequency transmission as the satellite first approaches and then recedes from the observer. The change in frequency is affected by the velocity of the satellite itself. The change in velocity of transmissions from the approaching and then receding satellite, known as the Doppler effect, is directly proportional to the shift in frequency of the transmitted signals and is thus proportional to the change of distance between the satellite and the receiver over a given time interval. When

**Table 11.1** GPS SATELLITE STATUS REPORT[a]

SUBJ: GPS STATUS  24 Jan 2002

1. SATELLITES, PLANES, AND CLOCKS (CS = CESIUM RB = RUBIDIUM):

A. BLOCK I : NONE

| B. BLOCK II: PRNS | 1, | 2, | 3, | 4, | 5, | 6, | 7, | 8, | 9, | 10, | 11, | 13, | 14, | 15 |
|---|---|---|---|---|---|---|---|---|---|---|---|---|---|---|
| PLANE : SLOT | F4, | B3, | C2, | D4, | B4, | C1, | C4, | A3, | A1, | E3, | D2, | F3, | F1, | D5 |
| CLOCK : | CS, | CS, | CS, | RB, | CS, | CS, | RB, | RB, | CS, | CS, | RB, | RB, | RB, | CS |
| BLOCK II: PRNS | 17, | 18, | 20, | 21, | 22, | 23, | 24, | 25, | 26, | 27, | 28, | 29, | 30, | 31 |
| PLANE : SLOT | D3, | E4, | E1, | E2, | B1, | E5, | D1, | A2, | F2, | A4, | B5, | F5, | B2, | C3 |
| CLOCK : | RB, | RB, | RB, | CS, | RB, | CS, | CS, | CS, | RB, | CS, | RB, | RB, | RB, | CS |

[a]Daily updates are available on the Internet at http://www.navcen.uscg.gov/ftp/GPS/status.txt

**Table 11.2** GLONASS CONSTELLATION STATUS REPORT (JANUARY 28, 2002)[a]

| GLONASS number | Cosmos number | Plane/ slot | Frequency channel | Launch date | Intro. date | Status | Outage date |
|---|---|---|---|---|---|---|---|
| 778 | 2324 | 2/15 | 11 | 14.12.95 | 26.04.99 | Withdrawn | 30.12.01 |
| 779 | 2364 | 1/1 | 2 | 30.12.98 | 18.02.99 | Operating | |
| 784 | 2363 | 1/8 | 8 | 30.12.98 | 29.01.99 | Operating | |
| 786 | 2362 | 1/7 | 7 | 30.12.98 | 29.01.99 | Operating | |
| 783 | 2374 | 3/18 | 10 | 13.10.00 | 05.01.01 | Operating | |
| 787 | 2375 | 3/17 | 5 | 13.10.00 | 04.11.00 | Operating | |
| 788 | 2376 | 3/24 | 3 | 13.10.00 | 21.11.00 | Operating | |
| 789 | 2381 | 1/03 | 12 | 01.12.01 | 04.01.02 | Operating | |
| 790 | 2380 | 1/06 | 9 | 01.12.01 | 04.01.02 | Operating | |
| 711 | 2382 | 1/05 | | 01.12.01 | | | |

[a]All the dates (DD.MM.YY) are given at Moscow Time (UTC + 0300). Daily updates are available on the Internet at http://www.rssi.ru/SFCSIC/english.html.

the satellite's orbit was known precisely and the position of the satellite in that orbit was also known precisely through ephemeris data and universal time (UT), the position of the receiving station could be computed.

Another, quite different positioning system utilizes inertial measurements and requires a vehicle (truck, airplane, or helicopter) to occupy a point of known coordinates (northing, easting, and elevation) and to remain stationary for a zero velocity update. As the vehicle moves, its location is updated constantly by the use of three computer-controlled accelerometers, each aligned to the north-south, east-west, or vertical axis. The accelerometer platform is oriented north-south, east-west, and plumb by means of three computer-controlled gyroscopes, each of which is aligned to one of three axes (see Figure 11.1). Analysis of acceleration data gives rectangular (latitude and longitude) displacement factors for horizontal movement, in addition to vertical displacement. Inertial technology is currently used, in conjunction with GPS, to control data collection while collecting airborne imagery including *lidar* (**l**ight **d**etection **a**nd **r**anging) images.

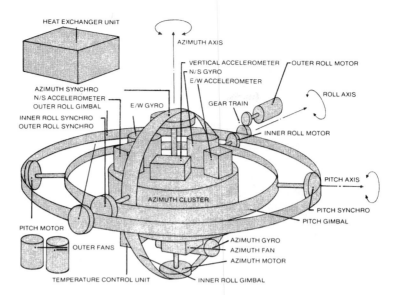

**FIGURE 11.1** Inertial platform schematic. (Courtesy of Nortech, Canada)

# 11.2 Global Positioning

Satellite positioning is based on accurate ephemeris data for the real-time location of each satellite and on time that is kept very precisely. It uses satellite signals, accurate time, and sophisticated algorithms to generate distances to ground receivers and thus provide "resectioned" positions anywhere on earth. GPS can also provide navigation data, such as the speed and direction of a mobile receiver, as well as estimated arrival times at specific locations.

Satellite orbits have been designed so that ground positioning can usually be determined at any location on earth at any time of the day or night. A minimum of four satellites must be tracked to solve the positioning intersection equations dealing with position ($X$, $Y$, and $Z$ coordinates, which later can be translated to easting, northing, and elevation) and with clock differences between the satellites and ground receivers. In reality, five or more satellites are tracked, if possible, to introduce additional redundancies and to strengthen the geometry of the satellite array. Additional satellites (more than the required minimum) can provide more accurate positioning and can also reduce the receiver occupation time at each survey station.

In addition to the satellites arrayed in space, the GPS includes tracking stations evenly spaced around the earth. Stations are located at Colorado Springs, Colorado (the master control station), and on the islands of Ascension, Diego Garcia, Kwajalein, and Hawaii. All satellites' signals are observed at each station, with all the clock and ephemeris data transmitted to the control station at Colorado Springs. The system is kept at peak efficiency because corrective data are transmitted back to the satellites from Colorado Springs (and a few other ground stations) every few hours. More recently, satellites have also been given the ability to communicate with each other.

This system, originally designed for military guidance and positioning, has quickly attracted a wide variety of civilian users in the positioning and navigation applications fields. Additional applications have already been developed in commercial aviation navigation, boating and shipping navigation, trucking and railcar positioning, emergency routing, automobile dashboard electronic charts, and orienteering navigation (see Section 11.12). Also, in 2002, manufacturers have begun to install GPS chips in cell phones to help satisfy the 911 service requirement for precise caller locations.

## 11.3 Receivers

GPS receivers range in ability (and cost) from survey-level receivers capable of use in surveys requiring high accuracy and costing more than $20,000, to mapping and geographic information system (GIS) receivers (submeter accuracy) costing about $3,000 each, to marine navigation receivers (accuracy 1 to 5 m) costing about $1,000, and finally to orienteering (hiking) and low-precision mapping/GIS receivers costing only a few hundred dollars. See Figures 11.2 to 11.6 and Figure F.8. The major differences in the receivers are the number of channels available (the number of satellites that can be tracked at one time) and whether or not the receiver can observe both L1 and L2 frequencies (code phase and carrier phase may also be measured). Generally speaking the higher-cost, dual-frequency receivers require much shorter observation times for positioning measurements than do the less expensive single-frequency receivers, and they can be used for real-time positioning. Some low-end, general-purpose GPS receivers track only one channel at a time (sequencing from satellite to satellite as tracking progresses); an improved low-end, general-purpose receiver tracks on two channels but must sequence the tracking to other satellites to achieve positioning. Some low-end surveying receivers can observe continuously on five channels (sequencing not required), whereas some high-end surveying receivers can observe on 12 channels. Some receivers can control photogrammetric camera operation, and some receivers can datalog every second, while others datalog every 15 seconds. The more expensive receivers can be used in all GPS survey modes with shorter observation times, whereas less expensive receivers can be restricted to a certain type of survey and will require longer observation times and perhaps longer processing times as well. At the time of publication, new software and hardware are continually being developed that will increase capabilities while reducing costs.

The cost for three precise surveying receivers, together with appropriate software, ranges up from $50,000, with expectations of lower costs as production increases and technology improves. In contrast, two lower-order receivers can be used in differential positioning to determine position to within a few meters, a precision that might be acceptable for selected mapping and GIS data bases. The total cost (including software) of this system can be as low as $7,000. As noted in Section 11.6, surveys can be performed while using only one receiver if access is available to radio-transmitted corrections from a permanent receiver, as is the case with the U.S. Coast Guard's differential global positioning system (DGPS).

## 11.4 Satellites

GPS satellites (an example is shown in Figure 11.7) are manufactured by Rockwell International, weigh about 1,900 pounds, span 17 feet (with solar panels deployed), and orbit

**FIGURE 11.2** Ashtech Dimension GPS Receiver with Corvalis CMT-CV5 Data Collector. Featuring 12 channels, C/A code and carrier, 2 MB internal memory, two RS-232 I/O ports, and an internal microstrip antenna. (Courtesy of Ashtech, California)

the earth at 10,900 nautical miles (20,000 km) in a period of 11 hours, 58 minutes. The satellites' constellation (see Figure 11.8) consists of 24 satellites (including three spares) placed in six orbital planes. This configuration ensures that at least four satellites (the minimum number needed for precise measurements) are always potentially visible anywhere on earth. Russia has also created a satellite constellation, called GLONASS, which consists of 24 satellites, placed in three orbital planes at 19,100 km, with an orbit time of 11 hours, 15 minutes. As with GPS, GLONASS satellites continuously broadcast their own precise positions along with less precise positions for all other same-constellation satellites. Tables 11.1 and 11.2 show the status for both GPS and GLONASS satellites. Daily updates of satellite status are available on the Internet at the addresses shown in the tables. Note that only 8 satellites are listed as operational (for the date shown) on the GLONASS home page. Knowing the "health" of the satellites is critical to mission planning.

Some GPS receivers are now capable of tracking both GPS and GLONASS satellite signals. The advantages of using both constellations are: (1) the increased number of visible satellites results in the potential for shorter observation times and increased accuracy,

**FIGURE 11.3** Leica SYS 300. System includes SR9400 GPS receiver (single frequency) with AT201 antenna, CR333 GPS controller (electronic field book) that collects data and provides software for real-time GPS surveying, and a radio modem. It can provide the following accuracies: 10 mm to 20 mm + 2 ppm using differential carrier techniques; and .30 m to .50 m using differential code measurements. (Courtesy of Leica Geosystems Inc., Norcross, Georgia)

and (2) the increased number of satellites available to a receiver could mean that surveys interrupted by poor satellite geometry (in one constellation) or by local obstructions caused by buildings, tree canopy, etc., could continue uninterrupted by tracking satellites from the second constellation.

## 11.5 Satellite Signals

GPS satellites transmit at two L-band frequencies with the characteristics shown in Table 11.3. The coarse acquisition (C/A) code is available to the public, whereas the P code is designed for military use exclusively. Only the P code is modulated on the L2 band. Originally, the DoD implemented selective availability (SA), which was designed to degrade signal accuracy in times of national emergency. Selective availability resulted in errors in the range of 100 m and occurred on both L1 and L2. SA has been permanently de-activated as of May 2000. This policy change improved GPS accuracies in basic point positioning by a five-fold factor (down from 100 m to about 10 m to 20 m). Another method designed to deny accuracy to the user is called antispoofing (AS). Antispoofing occurs as the P code is encrypted to prevent tinkering by hostile forces. At present, AS, along with most natural

**Table 11.3** L-BAND FREQUENCY CHARACTERISTICS

| L1 frequency | L1 frequency |
|---|---|
| L1 at 1575.42 MHz | •C/A code |
| $\lambda = c/f$ | |
| where $\lambda$ is the wavelength, $c$ is the speed of light, and $f$ is the frequency. | •P code |
| $\lambda = \dfrac{300,000,000 \text{ m/s}}{1,575,420,000 \text{ Hz}} = 0.190 \text{ m}$ | •Navigation message (clock corrections and orbital data) |
| The wavelength is about 19 cm. | •Y code (antispoofing code) |
| L2 frequency | L2 frequency |
| L2 at 1227.60 MHz | •P code |
| $\lambda = c/f$ | |
| $\lambda = \dfrac{300,000,000 \text{ m/s}}{1,227,600,000 \text{ Hz}} = 0.244 \text{ m}$ | •Navigation message (clock corrections and orbital data) |
| The wavelength is about 24 cm. | •Y code (antispoofing code) |

and other errors associated with the GPS measurements, can be eliminated by using *differential positioning (DGPS)*.

The more types of data that are collected, the faster and more accurate the solutions. For example, some GPS suppliers have computer programs designed to deal with some or all of the following collected data: C/A code pseudorange on L1, both L1 and L2 P code pseudoranges, both carrier phases, both Doppler observations, and a measurement of the cross-correlation of the encrypted P code (Y code) on the L1 and L2 frequencies. All of this data can be used to produce real-time or postprocessing solutions.

The White House announced in early 1999 that two additional civilian signals will be added on the next generation of satellites, by 2005. The new C/A code will be added to the L2 signal of Block IIR satellites scheduled for launch in 2003. A new civil signal, called L5, will also be included on the new Block IIF satellites scheduled for launch in 2005; this new civil signal will transmit on a frequency of 1176.45 MHz. These new civil signals will make positioning faster and more accurate under many measuring conditions.

Finally, there are plans to establish another satellite constellation (called Galileo) in Europe. When this occurs, surveyors and other users will have a much expanded global positioning system. The combination of GPS, GLONASS, and the proposed Galileo system is referred to as the global navigation satellite system (GNSS).

One key dimension in positioning is the parameter of time. Time is kept onboard the satellites by so-called atomic clocks with a precision of 1 nanosecond (.0000000001 s). The ground receivers are equipped with less precise quartz clocks. Uncertainties caused by these less precise clocks are resolved when observing the signals from four satellites, instead of the basic three-satellite configuration required for *X/Y/Z* positioning.

Microstrip Antenna

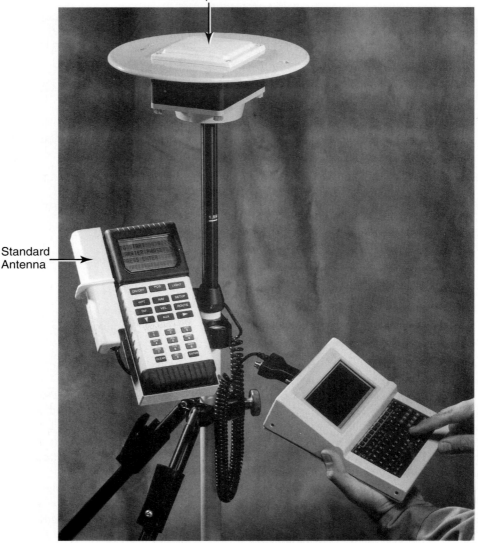

Standard Antenna

**FIGURE 11.4** Magellan 5-channel GPS NAVPRO 5000 receiver shown with multipath resistant microstrip antenna and data collector (I meg HP 95LXGPS). When used with the large antenna in differential mode, submeter accuracy can be achieved with 10 minutes of observations. (Courtesy of Magellan Systems Corp., San Dimas, California)

## 11.6 Position Measurements

Position measurements generally fall into one of two categories: code measurement and carrier phase measurement. Civilian code measurement is restricted to the C/A code, which can provide accuracies only in the range of 10 m to 15 m when used in point positioning,

**FIGURE 11.5** Trimble navigation total station GPS. Real-time positioning for a wide variety of applications. Features include GPS antenna and electronic field book at the adjustable pole; receiver, radio, and radio antenna in the backpack. The receiver has been equipped with GPS processing software and the electronic field book has been equipped with the applications software (for example, layout), thus permitting real-time data capture or layout. (Courtesy of Trimble Navigation, Sunnyvale, Calif.)

and accuracies in the "submeter" to 5 m range when used in various differential positioning techniques. P code measurements can apparently provide the military with much better accuracies. Point positioning is the technique that employs one GPS receiver to track satellite code signals so that it can determine the coordinates of the receiver station directly.

## 11.6.1 Relative Positioning

Relative positioning is a technique that employs two GPS receivers to track satellite code signals and/or satellite carrier phases to determine the baseline vector ($\Delta X$, $\Delta Y$, and $\Delta Z$) between the two receiver stations. The two receivers must collect data from the same satellites simultaneously (same epoch) and their observations then are combined to produce results that are superior to those achieved with just a single point positioning. Using this technique, computed (postprocessed) baseline accuracies can be in the meter range for C/A code measurements, and in the millimeter range for carrier phase measurements.

**FIGURE 11.6**  Garmin eMap handheld GPS used in navigation and GIS-type data location. It can be used with a DGPS radio beacon receiver to improve accuracy to within a few meters or less.

## 11.6.2   Differential Global Positioning System (DGPS)

The theory behind DGPS is based on the use of two or more GPS receivers to track the same satellites simultaneously. At least one of the GPS receivers must be set up at a station of known coordinates; as this base station receives satellites' signals, it can compare its computed position to its known position and derive a "difference" value. Since this difference will reflect all the measurement errors (except for multipath), this difference can be included in the nearby (<15 km) roving GPS receivers' computations to remove the common errors in their measurements. There are several ways to incorporate differential corrections in positioning computations:

- Postprocessing computations, using data collected manually from the base station and rovers.
- A commercial service like OmniSTAR (www.omnistar.com), which collects GPS data at several sites and weighs them to produce an optimized set of corrections that

**FIGURE 11.7** GPS satellite. (Courtesy of Leica Geosystems Inc., Norcross, Georgia)

**FIGURE 11.8** GPS satellites in orbit around the earth.

are uplinked to geostationary satellites. These satellites then broadcast the corrections to subscribers, who pay an annual fee for this service. This service provides for real-time measurements because the corrections are applied automatically to data collected by the subscribers' GPS roving receivers.

• A radio-equipped GPS receiver at the base station (known coordinates) that can compute errors and broadcast corrections to any number of radio-equipped roving receivers in the area. This technique also provides for real-time measurements.

- Postprocessing computations using code range and carrier phase data available from the National Geodetic Survey's Continuously Operating Reference System (CORS), a nationwide network of stations (including links to the Canadian Active Control System). This data can be downloaded from the Internet at www.ngs.noaa.gov/CORS. (See also Section 11.8.)
- Real-time mapping-level measurements can also be made by accessing DGPS radio corrections that are broadcast from permanent GPS receiver locations established by the U.S. Coast Guard. The roving receiver must be equipped with an ancillary or built-in radio beacon receiver.

Some GPS receivers are now manufactured with built-in radio receivers for use with each of the above real-time techniques. Roving receivers equipped with appropriate software can then determine the coordinates of their stations in real time.

The types of surveying applications where code pseudorange measurements or carrier measurements are made at a base station and then used to correct measurements made at another survey station are called differential positioning. Although the code measurement accuracies (submeter to 10 m) may not be sufficient for traditional control and layout surveys, they are ideal for most navigation needs and for many GIS and mapping surveys. The U.S. Coast Guard Maritime Differential GPS Service has created a code measurement differential system (DGPS) consisting of 50 remote broadcast sites and two control centers, originally designed to provide navigation data in coastal areas, the Great Lakes, and major river sites. The system includes continuously operating GPS receivers, at locations of known coordinates, that determine pseudorange values and then radio transmit the code error corrections to working navigators and surveyors at distances ranging from 100 to 400 km. The system uses international standards for its broadcasts—the Radio Technical Commission for Maritime (RTCM) services. The surveyor or navigator using the DGPS broadcasts, along with his or her own receiver, has the advantages normally found when using two receivers, and since the corrections for many of the errors (orbital and atmospheric) will be very similar for nearby receivers, the accuracies thus become much improved.

Information on DGPS and on individual broadcast sites can be obtained on the Internet at the U.S. Coast Guard Navigation Center website at www.navcen.uscg.gov/. Figure 11.9 shows typical data available for site number 839, Youngstown, New York. See also Section 11.8 on the continuously operating reference station (CORS) network.

Since the late 1990s, work has been underway at the Jet Propulsion Laboratory (JPL), California Institute of Technology, in the design of a global differential GPS system capable of providing decimeter-level accuracy in real time for NASA. This system is presently comprised of 60 dual-frequency receivers spread around the globe and all connected via the Internet. Control for this system is provided by a dozen or so stations utilizing atomic clocks and providing GPS ephemeris and clock corrections, also downloaded via the Internet.

## 11.6.3 Code Measurements

As previously noted, military personnel can utilize both the P code and the C/A code. The C/A code is used by the military to access the P code quickly. The civilian user must, at present, be content with using only the C/A code.

**DGPS BROADCAST SITE STATUS and OPERATING SPECIFICATIONS**
**STATUS AS OF 1/28/02**

USERS SHOULD NOTIFY THE NIS WATCHSTANDER AT (703)313-5900 OF ANY
OBSERVED OUTAGES, PROBLEMS, OR REQUESTS. ALL CURRENT OUTAGE
INFORMATION WILL BE LISTED FOLLOWING EACH SITE.

THE COAST GUARD DGPS SERVICE IS AVAILABLE FOR POSITIONING AND
NAVIGATION. USERS MAY EXPERIENCE SERVICE INTERRUPTIONS WITHOUT
ADVANCE NOTICE. COAST GUARD DGPS BROADCASTS SHOULD NOT BE
USED UNDER ANY CIRCUMSTANCES WHERE A SUDDEN SYSTEM FAILURE
OR INACCURACY COULD CONSTITUTE A SAFETY HAZARD.

**NOTE: Differential corrections are based on the NAD 83 position**
**of the reference station (REFSTA) antenna. Positions**
**obtained using DGPS should be referenced to NAD 83**
**coordinate system only. All sites are broadcasting**
**RTCM Type 9-3 correction messages.**

## The Latest Status for YOUNGSTOWN, NY

**YOUNGSTOWN, N.Y.**

```
Status:                      Operational

RBn Antenna Location:        43,13.8N;78, 58.2W

REFSTA Ant Location (A):     43,13.8748N;78, 58.20992W

REFSTA Ant Location (B):     43, 13.87466N;78, 58.18778W

REFSTA RTCM SC-104 ID (A):   118

REFSTA RTCM SC-104 ID (B):   119

REFSTA FIRMWARE VERSION:     RD00-1C19

Broadcast Site ID:           839

Transmission Frequency:      322 KHZ

Transmission Rate:           100 BPS

Signal Strength:             75uVm at 150 SM


Outages:

No current Outages.
```

**FIGURE 11.9** Status report for a DGPS station. See http://www.navcen.uscg.gov. Select
**Most Requested Information,** then select **DGPS sites,** finally select
**status** for specific scrolled sites. (Courtesy of the U.S. Coast Guard)

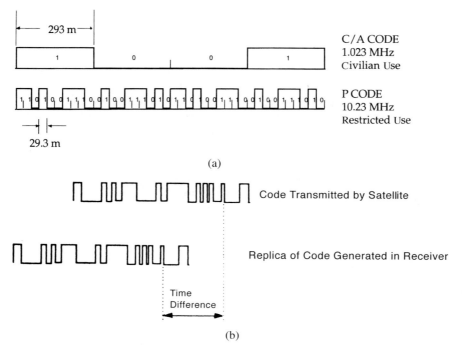

**FIGURE 11.10** (a) C/A code and P code. (b) Time determination.

Both codes are digital codes comprised of 0s and 1s (see Figure 11.10), and each satellite transmits codes unique to that satellite. Although both codes are carefully structured, they have been given the name pseudo random noise (PRN) because the codes sound like random electronic "noise." The PRN code number (see Table 11.1) indicates which of the 37 seven-day segments of the P code PRN signal is presently being used by each satellite (it takes the P code PRN signal 267 days to transmit). Each one-week segment of the P code is unique to each satellite and is reassigned each week (see Table 11.1). Receivers have replicas of all satellite codes in the onboard memory, which they use to identify the satellite and then to measure the time difference between the signals from the satellite to the receiver. Time is measured as the receiver moves the replica code (retrieved from memory) until a match between the transmitted code and the replica code is achieved. See Figure 11.10(b). Errors caused by the slowing effects of the atmosphere on the transmission of satellite radio waves can be corrected by simultaneously performing position measurements utilizing two different wavelengths—such as L1 and L2.

The distance, called pseudorange, is determined by multiplying the time factor by the speed of light.

$$\rho = t(300,000,000)$$

where $\rho$ (lowercase Greek letter rho) is the pseudorange

$t$ = travel time of the satellite signal in seconds

$300,000,000$ = the velocity of light in meters per second (actually 299,792,458 m/s)

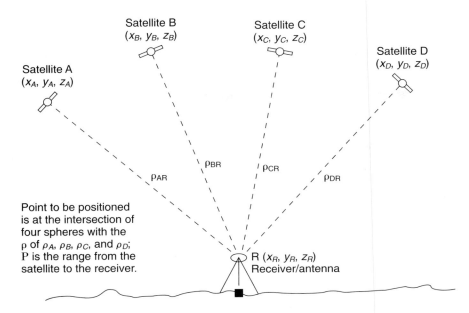

Satellite B
$(x_B, y_B, z_B)$

Satellite C
$(x_C, y_C, z_C)$

Satellite D
$(x_D, y_D, z_D)$

Satellite A
$(x_A, y_A, z_A)$

$\rho_{BR}$

$\rho_{CR}$

$\rho_{AR}$

$\rho_{DR}$

Point to be positioned
is at the intersection of
four spheres with the
$\rho$ of $\rho_A$, $\rho_B$, $\rho_C$, and $\rho_D$;
P is the range from the
satellite to the receiver.

R $(x_R, y_R, z_R)$
Receiver/antenna

**FIGURE 11.11**    Geometry of point positioning.

When the pseudorange ($\rho$) is corrected for clock errors, atmospheric delay errors, multipath errors, and the like, it is then called the range and is abbreviated by the uppercase Greek letter rho, P; that is, $P = (\rho + \text{error corrections})$.

Figure 11.11 shows the geometry involved in point positioning. Computing three pseudoranges ($\rho_{AR}, \rho_{BR}, \rho_{CR}$) is enough to solve the intersection of three developed spheres—although this computation gives two points of intersection. One point (a superfluous point) will obviously be irrelevant; that is, it probably will not even fall on the surface of the earth. The fourth pseudorange ($\rho_{DR}$) is required to remove the fourth unknown—the receiver clock error.

## 11.6.4   Carrier Phase Measurement

GPS codes, which are modulations of the carrier frequencies, are comparatively lengthy. Compare the C/A code at 293 m and the P code at 29.3 m (Figure 11.10) with the wavelengths of L1 and L2 at 0.19 m and 0.24 m, respectively. It follows that carrier phase measurements have the potential for much higher accuracies than do code measurements.

We first encountered phase measurements in Chapter 7, when we observed how EDM equipment measured distances (see Figure 7.3). Essentially EDM distances are determined by measuring the phase delay required to match the transmitted carrier wave signal with the return signal (two-way signaling). Equation 7.2 (repeated below) calculated this distance:

$$L = \frac{n\lambda + \varphi}{2} \tag{7.2}$$

where $\varphi$ is the partial wavelength determined by measuring the phase delay (through comparison with an onboard reference), $n$ is the number of complete wavelengths (from the electronic distance measurement instrument [EDM] to the prism and back to the EDM instrument), and $\lambda$ is the wavelength. The integer number of wavelengths is determined as the EDM instrument successively sends out (and receives back) signals at different frequencies.

Since GPS ranging involves only one-way signaling, other techniques must be used to determine the number of full wavelengths. GPS receivers can measure the phase delay (through comparison with onboard carrier replicas) and count the full wavelengths after lock-on to the satellite has occurred, but more complex treatment is required to determine $N$, the initial cycle ambiguity; that is, $N$ is the number of full wavelengths sent by the satellite prior to lock-on. Since a carrier signal is comprised of a continuous transmission of sinelike waves with no distinguishing features, the wave count cannot be accomplished directly.

$$P = \varphi + N\lambda + \text{errors}$$

where $P$ = satellite-receiver range

$\varphi$ = measured carrier phase

$\lambda$ = wavelength

$N$ = initial ambiguity (the number of full wavelengths at lock-on)

Once the cycle ambiguity between a receiver and a satellite has been resolved, it does not have to be addressed further unless a loss of lock occurs between the receiver and the satellite. When loss of lock occurs, the ambiguity must be resolved again. Loss of lock results in a loss of the integer number of cycles and is called a cycle slip. The surveyor is alerted to loss of lock when the receiver commences a beeping sequence. As an example, loss of lock can occur when a roving receiver passes under a bridge, a tree canopy, or any other obstruction that blocks all or some of the satellite signals.

Cycle ambiguity can be determined through the process of differencing. GPS measurements can be differenced between two satellites, between two receivers, and between two epochs. An *epoch* is an event in time, a short observation interval in a longer series of observations. After the initial epoch has been observed, later epochs will reflect the fact that the constellation has moved relative to the ground station and, as such, presents a new geometrical pattern and thus new intersection solutions.

## 11.6.5 Differencing

*Relative positioning* occurs when two receivers are used to observe satellite signals simultaneously and to compute the vectors (known as a baseline) joining the two receivers. Relative positioning can provide better accuracies because of the correlation possible between measurements made simultaneously over time by two or more different satellite receivers. Differencing is the technique of simultaneous baseline measurements and falls into the categories of single difference, double difference, and triple difference.

- Single difference: When two receivers observe the same satellite simultaneously, it is possible to correct for most of the effects of satellite clock errors, orbit errors, and atmospheric delay. See Figure 11.12(a).

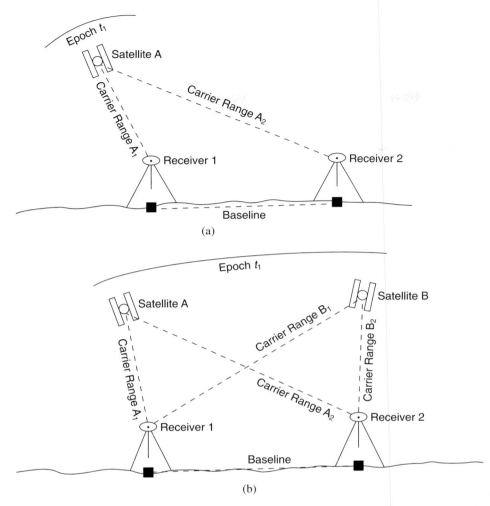

**FIGURE 11.12** Differencing. (a) Single difference: two receivers observing the same satellite simultaneously (i.e., difference between receivers). (b) Double difference: two receivers observing the same satellite(s) simultaneously (i.e., difference between receivers and between satellites).

*(continued)*

- Double difference: When one receiver observes two (or more) satellites, the measurements can be freed of receiver clock error, and atmospheric delay errors can also be eliminated. When using both differences (between the satellites and between the receivers), a double difference occurs. Clock errors, atmospheric delay errors, and orbit errors can all be eliminated. See Figure 11.12(b).

- Triple difference: The difference between two double differences is the triple difference; that is, the double differences are compared over two (or more) successive epochs. This procedure is also effective in detecting and correcting cycle slips and

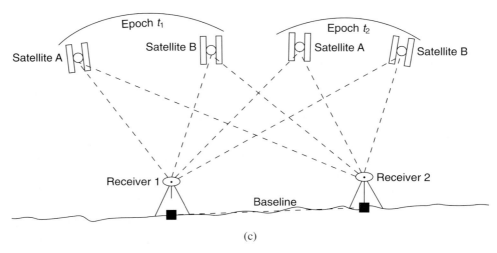

Epoch $t_1$

Satellite A

Satellite B

Epoch $t_2$

Satellite A

Satellite B

Receiver 1

Receiver 2

Baseline

(c)

**FIGURE 11.12 (continued)** (c) Triple difference: The difference between two double differences (i.e., differences between receivers, satellites, and epochs).

for computing first-step approximate solutions that are used in double difference techniques. See Figure 11.12(c).

Cycle ambiguities can also be resolved by utilizing algorithms dealing with double differences; triple differences; both code and carrier phase measurements and the methods of kinematic surveying that utilize startups of antenna swap, known location occupation, and on-the-fly (OTF) initialization—a technique that can be used while the roving receiver is in motion (see Section 11.11.3). The references at the end of this chapter provide more information on the theory of signal observations and ambiguity resolution.

## 11.7 Errors

The chief sources of error in GPS are listed below:

1. Clock errors of the receivers.
2. Ionospheric (50 to 1,000 km above the earth) and tropospheric (earth's surface to 80 km above the earth) refraction. Signals are slowed as they travel through these earth-centered layers. The errors worsen as satellite signals move from directly overhead to down near the horizon. These errors can be reduced by scheduling nighttime observations, by gathering sufficient redundant data and using reduced baseline lengths (1 to 5 km), or by collecting data on both frequencies over long (20 km or more) distances. Most surveying agencies do not record observations from satellites below 10° to 15° of elevation above the horizon.
3. Multipath interference, which is similar to the ghosting effect seen on televisions. Some signals are received directly and others are received after they have been reflected from adjacent features. Recent improvements in antenna design have reduced these errors significantly.

4. A weak geometric figure that results from poorly located four-satellite signal intersections. This consideration is called the dilution of precision (DOP). (See also Section 10.8.) DOP can be optimized if many satellites (beyond the minimum of four) are tracked, the additional data will strengthen the position solution. Most survey-level receivers are now capable of tracking 5 to 12 satellites simultaneously. GDOP refers to the general dilution of precision—the geometric effect of satellite vector measurement errors together with receiver clock errors. Elevation solutions require strong GDOP, and these solutions are strengthened when satellite elevations in excess of 70° are available for the observed satellite orbits. It used to be that observations were discontinued if the GDOP was above 7; now, some receiver manufacturers suggest that a GDOP of 8 is acceptable.

5. Errors associated with the satellite orbital data.

6. Setup errors. Centering errors can be reduced if the equipment is checked to ensure that the optical plummet is true, and hi measuring errors can be reduced by utilizing equipment that provides a built-in (or accessory) measuring capability to measure precisely (either directly or indirectly) the hi or by using fixed-length tripods and bipods.

7. Selected availability (SA), which is a denial of accuracy that was turned off permanently in May 2000.

Many of the effects of the above errors, including denial of accuracy by the DoD (if it were to be reintroduced), can be surmounted by using differential positioning surveying techniques.

# 11.8 Continuously Operating Reference Station (CORS)

The DGPS differential code measurement system developed by the U.S. Coast Guard (Section 11.6) has been adapted so it is now a nationwide differential positioning system known as CORS. See Figure 11.13. Differential positioning requires at least two receivers, with one (called the base station) occupying a point of known position. The observed satellite signals are used to compute the base station position, which is then compared to the correct position coordinates. The difference (thus differential) between the correct position and computed position is then made available over the Internet for use in the postprocessing of the field observations collected by the roving receivers.

The continuously operating reference station (CORS) network includes stations set up by the National Geodetic Survey (NGS), the U.S. Coast Guard, the U.S. Army Corps of Engineers (USACE), and more recently, stations set up by other federal and local agencies. The network (which in 2002 comprised more than 253 stations is expected to increase to 250 stations by 2005) is managed by the NGS, part of the National Oceanic and Atmospheric Administration. In addition to the CORS installations initiated by the U.S. Coast Guard, several states' departments of transportation (DOTs) are now also adding to the densification of CORS coverage by establishing their own CORS active control. Soon, surveyors working in any region will be able to take advantage of this technology.

The coordinates at each site are computed from 24-hour data sets collected over a 10- to 15-day period. These highly accurate coordinates are then transformed into the

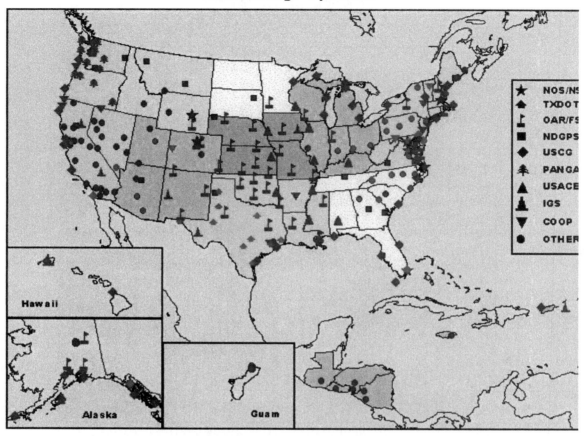

**FIGURE 11.13** CORS coverage as of April 2001, available (and continuously updated) at http://www.ngs.noaa.gov/CORS.

North American Datum (NAD) 1983 horizontal datum for use by local surveyors. Each CORS tracks GPS satellite signals continuously and creates files of both carrier measurements and code range measurements to assist in positioning surveys. NGS converts all receiver data and individual site meteorological data to Receiver Independent Exchange (RINEX) format, version 2. The files can be accessed via the Internet at http://www.ngs.noaa.gov. Once in the website, the new user should select "Products and Services" and then select "GPS Continuously Operating Reference Station (CORS)." The user is urged to download and read the "readme" files and the "frequently asked questions" file on the first visit. The NGS stores data from all sites for 31 days, and then the data are normally transferred to CD-ROMs, which are available for a fee. The data are usually collected at a 30-s epoch rate, although some sites collect data at 5-s and 15-s epoch rates. The local surveyor, armed with data sets in his or her locality at the time of an ongoing survey and having entered these data into his or her GPS program, has the equivalent of an additional dual-frequency GPS receiver. A surveyor with just one receiver can proceed as if two receivers were being used in the relative positioning mode.

## 11.9   Canadian Active Control System (ACS)

The Geodetic Survey Division (GSD) of Geomatics Canada has combined with the Geological Survey of Canada to establish a network of active control points (ACPs) in the Canadian Active Control System. The system includes 10 unattended dual-frequency tracking stations (ACPs) that continuously measure and record carrier phase and pseudorange measurements for all satellites in view at a 30-s sampling interval. A master ACP in Ottawa coordinates and controls the system. The data are archived in RINEX format and are available on-line 4 hours after the end of the day (11:59:59) Eastern Standard Time. Precise ephemeris data, computed with input from 24 globally distributed core GPS tracking stations of the International GPS Service for Geodynamics (IGS), are available on-line within 2 to 5 days after the observations; precise clock corrections are also available in the 2- to 5-day time frame. The Canadian Active Control System is complemented by the Canadian Base Network, which provides 200-km coverage in Canada's southern latitudes for high-accuracy control (centimeter accuracy). These control stations are used to evaluate and to complement a wide variety of control stations established by various government agencies over the years. These products, which are available for a subscription fee, enable a surveyor to position any point in the country with a precision ranging from a centimeter to a few meters. Code observation positioning at the meter level, without the use of a base station, is possible using precise satellite corrections. Real-time service at the meter level is also available. The data can be accessed on the Internet at http://www.geod.nrcan.gc.ca.

## 11.10   Survey Planning

Planning is important for GPS surveys so that almanac data can be analyzed to obtain optimal time sets when a geometrically strong array of satellites is available above 15° of elevation (above the horizon) and to identify topographic obstructions that may hinder signal reception. Planning software can graphically display geometric dilution of precision (GDOP) at each time of the day (GDOP of 7 or below is usually considered suitable for positioning—a value of 5 or lower is ideal). See Figures 11.14 to 11.18 for various computer screen plots that the surveyor can use to help the mission-planning process and select not only the optimal days for the survey, but also the hours of the day that will result in the best data.

### 11.10.1   Static Surveys

For static surveys (see Section 11.11.2 for a definition), survey planning includes a visit to the field to inspect existing stations and to place monuments for new stations. A compass and clinometer (Figure 2.7) are handy in sketching the location and elevation of potential obstructions at each station on a visibility (obstruction) diagram (see Figure 11.19). These obstructions are entered into the software for later display. The coordinates (latitude and longitude) of stations should be scaled from a topographic map. Scaled coordinates can help some receivers to lock onto the satellites more quickly.

**FIGURE 11.14** GPS planning software. Graphical depiction of satellite availability, elevation, and GDOP almanac data, which are processed by SKI software for a specific day and location. (Courtesy of Leica, Canada)

Computer graphics displays include the number of satellites available (Figure 11.15); satellite orbits and obstructions, showing orbits of satellites as viewed at a specific station on a specific day (Figure 11.16); a visibility plot of all satellites over one day (Figure 11.17); and a polar plot of all visible satellites at a moment in time (Figure 11.18). For the location shown in Figure 11.16 (latitude and longitude), most satellite orbits are in the south sky; accordingly, survey stations at that location should be located south of high obstructions, where possible, to minimize topographic interference. Almanac data, used in survey planning, can be updated regularly through satellite observations. Most software suppliers provide almanac updates via their computer bulletin boards.

Static surveys work best with receivers of the same type; that is, they should have the same number of channels and signal-processing techniques. Also, the sampling rate must be set; faster rates require more storage but can be helpful in detecting cycle slips, particularly on longer lines ($> 50$ km). And the time (hours) of observation must be determined—given the available GDOP and the need for accuracy—as well as the start/stop times for each session. All this information is entered into the software, with the results uploaded into the receivers.

## 11.10.2 Kinematic Surveys

Much of the discussion above for planning static surveys also applies to kinematic surveys (see Section 11.11.3 for definitions). For kinematic surveys, the route must also be planned

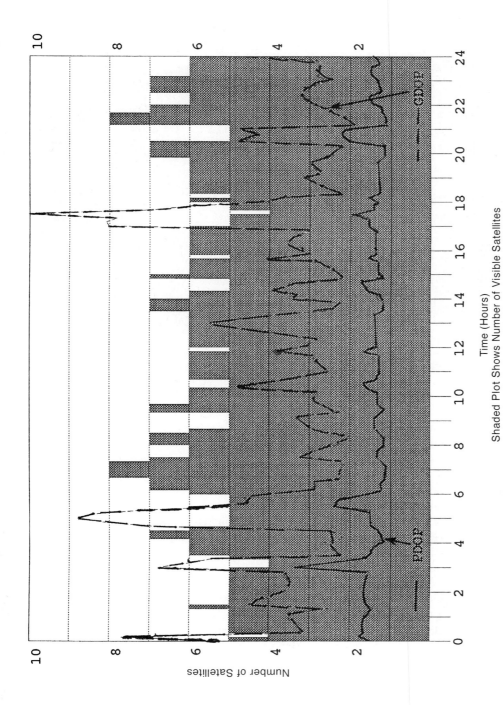

**FIGURE 11.15** GPS planning software. GDOP and position dilution of precision (PDOP) during a specific day. (Courtesy of Leica, Canada)

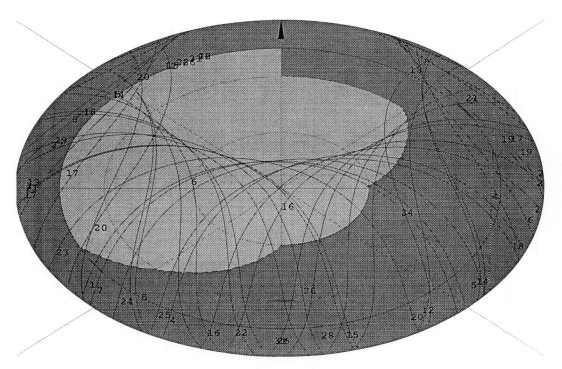

**FIGURE 11.16** GPS planning software. Computer "sky plot" display showing satellite orbits and obstructions for a particular station (darker shading). (Courtesy of Leica, Canada)

for each roving receiver so that best use is made of control points, crews, and equipment. The type of receiver chosen will depend, to some degree, on the accuracy required. For topographic or GIS surveys, low-order (submeter) survey roving receivers (see, for example, Figures 11.4 and 11.5) may be a good choice. For construction layout in real time, high-end roving receivers capable of centimeter or millimeter accuracy (see, for example, Figure 11.6) may be selected. The base station receiver must be compatible with the survey mission and the roving receivers; one base station can support any number of roving receivers. The technique to be used for initial ambiguity resolution must be determined; that is, will it be antenna swap, known station occupation, or on-the-fly (OTF)? And at which stations will this resolution take place?

If the survey is designed to locate topographic and built features, then the codes for the features should be defined or accessed from a symbols library, the same as for EDM surveys (see Chapter 7). If required, additional asset data (attribute data) should be tied to each symbol; the GPS software should permit the entry of several layers of asset data. For example, if the feature to be located is a pole, the pole symbol can be backed up with pole use (illumination, electric wire, telephone, etc.), the type of pole can be booked (concrete, wood, metal, etc.), and the year of installation can be entered (municipal computers can automatically generate work orders for any facility's maintenance based on the original date of installation). Planning will ensure that when the roving surveyor is at the feature

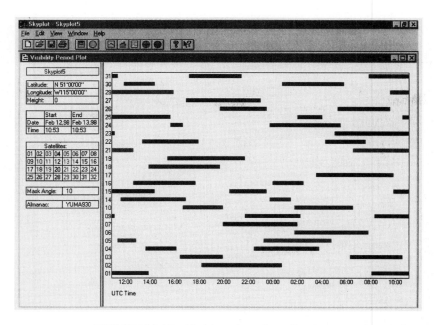

**FIGURE 11.17** Visibility plot—from Skyplot series (it is color-coded in its original format). (Courtesy of Position Inc., Calgary, Alberta)

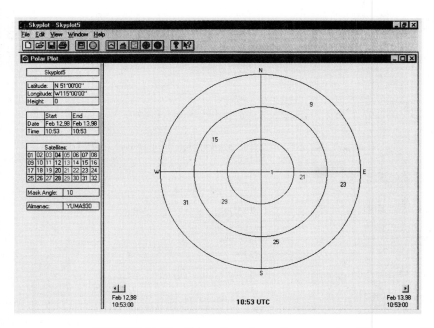

**FIGURE 11.18** Polar plot—from Skyplot series. (Courtesy of Position Inc., Calgary, Alberta)

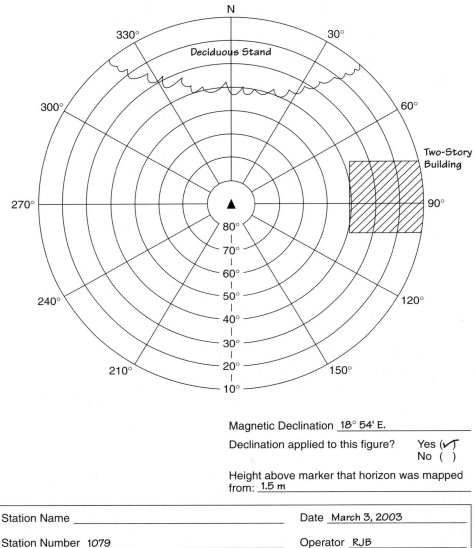

GPS Station Obstruction Diagram

Magnetic Declination  18° 54' E.

Declination applied to this figure?    Yes (✓)
                                        No  ( )

Height above marker that horizon was mapped
from:  1.5 m

| | |
|---|---|
| Station Name _____ | Date  March 3, 2003 |
| Station Number  1079 | Operator  RJB |
| Latitude  46° 36' 30" N. | Longitude  122° 18' 00" W. |

**FIGURE 11.19**   Station visibility diagram.

point, all possible prompts will be displayed to capture the data completely for each way point. The success of any kinematic survey depends a great deal on the thoroughness of the presurvey reconnoiter, on the preparation of the job file, and on using the GPS software.

## 11.11 GPS Field Procedures

### 11.11.1 Tripod- and Pole-Mounted Antenna Considerations

GPS antennas can be mounted directly to tripods via optical plummet-equipped tribrachs. All static survey occupations and base station occupations for all other types of GPS surveys require the use of a tripod. Care is taken to center the antenna precisely and to measure the hi precisely. All antennas have a direction mark (often an N or arrow, or a series of numbered notches along the outside perimeter of the antenna), which enables the surveyor to align the roving antenna in the same direction (usually north) as the base station antenna. This helps to eliminate any bias in the antennas. The measured hi (corrected or uncorrected) is entered into the receiver. When a lock has been established to the satellites, a message is displayed on the receiver display, and observations begin. If the hi cannot be measured directly, then slant heights are measured. Some agencies measure in two or three slant locations and average the results. The vertical height can be computed using the Pythagorean theorem: hi $= \sqrt{\text{slant height}^2 - \text{antenna radius}^2}$. See Figure 11.20.

GPS receiver antennas can also be mounted on adjustable-length poles (similar to prism poles) or bipods. These poles and fixed-length bipods may have built-in power supply conduits, a built-in circular bubble, and the ability to display the hi. When using poles, the GPS receiver program automatically prompts the surveyor to accept the last-used hi; if there has been no change in the antenna height, the surveyor simply accepts the prompted value. As with most surveys, field notes are important, both as backup and as confirmation of entered data. The hi at each station is booked along with equipment numbers, session times, crew, file (job) number, and any other pertinent data (see Figure 11.20).

### 11.11.2 Static Surveys

**11.11.2.1 Traditional static** This technique of relative GPS positioning places one base receiver antenna (single- or dual-frequency) over a point of known coordinates $(X, Y, Z)$ on a tripod, while other antennas are placed, also on tripods, over permanent stations to be positioned. Observation times are 1 hour or more (perhaps days), depending on the receiver, accuracy requirements, the satellites' geometric configuration, the length of line, and atmospheric conditions. This technique is used for long lines ($> 20$ km) in geodetic control, control densification, and photogrammetric control for aerial surveys and precise engineering surveys. It is also used as a fallback technique when the available geometric array of satellites is not compatible with other GPS techniques. The preplanning of station locations takes into consideration potential obstructions presented by trees and buildings, which must be considered and minimized.

**11.11.2.2 Rapid static** This technique, which was developed in the early 1990s, can be employed where dual-frequency receivers are used over short (up to 15 km) lines. As

Project Name _____          Project Number _____

Receiver Model/No. _____          Station Name _____

Receiver Software Version _____          Station Number _____

Data Logger Type/No. _____          4-Character ID _____

Antenna Model/No. _____          Date _____

Cable Length _____          Obs. Session _____

Ground Plane Extensions  Yes ( )  No ( )          Operator _____

*Data Collection*          *Receiver Position*

Collection Rate _____          Latitude _____

Start Day/Time _____          Longitude _____

End Day/Time _____          Height _____

Obstruction or possible interference sources _____

_____

General weather conditions _____

_____

Detailed meteorological observations recorded:  Yes ( )  No ( )

*Antenna Height Measurement*

Show on sketch measurements taken to derive the antenna height. If slant measurements are taken, make measurement on two opposite sides of the antenna. Make measurements before and after observing session.

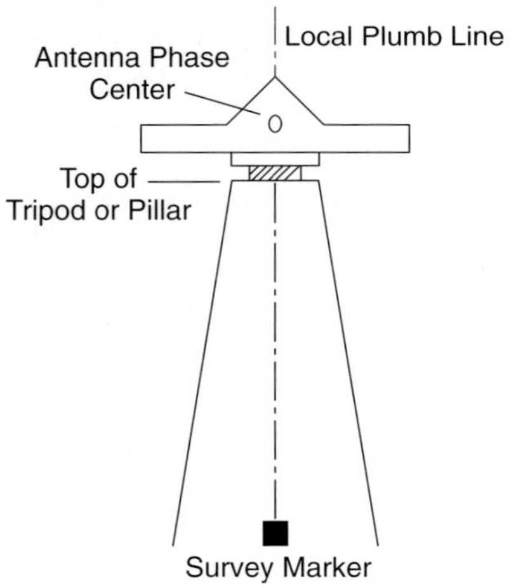

Vertical measurements  ( )

Slant measurements  ( ) : radius _____ m

|  | BEFORE | AFTER |
|---|---|---|
| | _____ m _____ in. | _____ m _____ in. |
| | _____ m _____ in. | _____ m _____ in. |
| Mean | _____ | |
| Corrected to vertical if slant measurement | _____ | |
| Vertical offset to phase center | _____ | |
| Other offset (indicate on sketch) | _____ | |
| TOTAL HEIGHT | _____ | |

Verified by: _____

**FIGURE 11.20**   GPS field log. (Courtesy of Geomatics Canada)

with static surveys, this technique requires one receiver antenna to be positioned (on a tripod) at a known base station, and the roving surveyor moves from station to station with the antenna pole-mounted. With good geometry, initial phase ambiguities can be resolved within a minute (3 to 5 minutes for single-frequency receivers). With this technique, there is no need to maintain lock on the satellites while moving rover receivers—the roving receivers can even be turned off to preserve their batteries. Accuracies of a few millimeters are possible using this technique. Observation times of 5 to 10 minutes are typical.

**11.11.2.3 Reoccupation** This technique (also called pseudokinematic and pseudostatic) can be used when fewer than four satellites are available or when GDOP is weak (above a value of 7 or 8). Survey stations are occupied on at least two different occasions at least 1 hour apart. The solution may be strengthened if the base station receiver has been moved to another control station for the second set of observations. The data are processed as for a static survey. The processing software will combine the satellite observations to provide a solution; that is, if there are only three satellites available on the first occupation and another three available on the second occupation, the software will process the data as if six satellites are available at once. Observation times of 10 minutes are typical. Roving receivers have their antennas pole-mounted.

## 11.11.3   Kinematic Surveys

**11.11.3.1 STOP and GO** This technique is an efficient way to survey detail points for engineering and topographic surveys. It begins with both the base unit and the roving unit occupying a 10-km (or shorter) baseline (two known positions) until ambiguities are resolved. Alternatively, short baselines with one known position can be used where the distance between the stations is short enough to permit antenna swapping. Here, the base station and a nearby (within reach of the antenna cable) undefined station are occupied for a short period of time (say, 2 minutes) in the static mode, after which the antennas are swapped (while still receiving the satellite signals—but now in the roving mode) for an additional few minutes of readings in the static mode (techniques may vary with different manufacturers).

After the antennas have been returned to their original tripods and after an additional short period of observations in the static mode, the roving receiver—in roving mode—then moves (on a pole, backpack, truck, boat, etc.) to position all required detail points while keeping a lock on the satellite signals. If the lock is lost, the receiver is held stationary until the ambiguities are once again resolved so that the survey can continue. Observation times of 2 or 3 seconds are all that is required to compute accurate positions. The base station stays in the static mode unless it is planned to leapfrog the base and roving stations.

**11.11.3.2 Traditional kinematic** This technique computes a relative differential position at preset time intervals instead of at operator-selected points. Lock must be maintained to a minimum of four satellites, or it must be reestablished if it is lost. This technique is used for road profiling, ship positioning in sounding surveys, and aircraft positioning in aerial surveys. As an example of this technique, Leica (Canada) reported in 1994 that a road profile survey was conducted using one of their antennas mounted on a 4-m

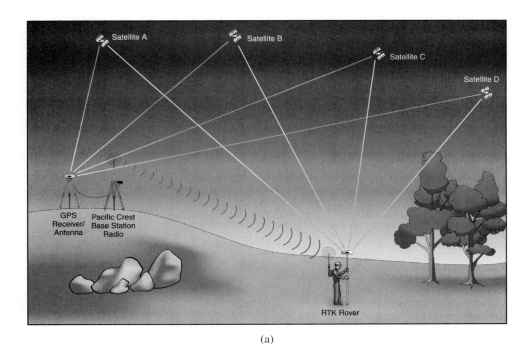

(a)

**FIGURE 11.21** (a) A base station GPS receiver and a base station radio, as well as the roving GPS receiver equipped with a radio receiver that allows for real-time positioning. (Sketch courtesy of Pacific Crest Corporation, Santa Clara, Calif.)

adjustable arm attached to a highway truck capable of following the edge of the pavement to within 0.05 m. Measurements were taken every second, with the truck traveling at 15 km/hr (4 m/s). The nearly 10,000 points collected were processed in about 8 hours. Control was provided by two master GPS stations, and the vehicle stopped over 22 control stations en route. The results showed, at the 95 percent confidence level, that there was a maximum spread of error ranging to 0.050 m in horizontal and to 0.070 m in vertical. Continuous surveying can be interrupted to take observations (a few epochs) at any required way points.

### 11.11.3.3 Real-time differential
This technique is also known as real-time kinematic (RTK). The real-time combination of GPS receivers, mobile data communications, onboard data processing, and onboard applications software contributes to an exciting new era in surveying. As with the motorized total stations described in Section 7.14, real-time positioning offers the potential of a one-person capability in mapping and quantity surveys (the base station receiver can be unattended). Layout surveys need two surveyors, one to operate the receiver and one to mark the stations in the field. RTK requires a base station to measure the satellite signals, to process baseline corrections, and then to broadcast the corrections to any number of roving receivers via radio transmission. See Figure 11.21 for a typical radio and amplifier used in code and carrier differential surveys. By 2001, cell phones were also being introduced as the base station to field rover communication devices.

**FIGURE 11.21 (continued)** (b)
Base station radio. (Courtesy of Pacific
Crest Corporation, Santa Clara, Calif.)

(b)

This technique can commence without the rover first occupying a known baseline. The base station transmits code and carrier phase data to the roving receiver, which can use this data to help resolve ambiguities and to solve for changes in coordinate differences between the reference and the roving receivers. The range of the radio transmission of the carrier phase data from the base to the rover can be extended by booster radios to a distance of about 10 km; longer ranges require commercially licensed radios, as do even shorter ranges in some countries. This technique can utilize either single-frequency or dual-frequency receivers. Loss of signal lock can be regained by single-frequency receivers by reoccupying a point of known position, and by dual-frequency receivers either by remaining stationary for a few minutes or by using on-the-fly resolution—while proceeding to the next survey position. With software being developed and upgraded constantly in this field, it seems that there is now a software solution to all surveying applications. When a second civilian frequency is provided, solutions will be enhanced even more.

One example of extended applications, first popularized by Trimble Navigation, is discussed here (see Figure 11.6). This system works generally as described above for base station and rovers, except that the field system has been expanded to include processing software and applications software for topographic and layout surveys. The GPS total station includes the antenna and data collector mounted on an adjustable-length pole, with the receiver, radio, and radio antenna mounted in the backpack. More recent models have all equipment mounted on the pole. This receiver (model 4800) can track nine satellites, store 50 hours of L1/L2 data, and track six satellites continuously at 15-s epochs. The pole kit weighs only 8.5 pounds. This system is available with both single-frequency and dual-frequency receivers. The more expensive dual-frequency receiver has better potential for surveys in areas where satellite visibility may be reduced by topographic obstructions. The radio range on this system is 1 to 3 km, with a range of 10 km possible with booster radios (a range more than adequate for most engineering surveys).

## 11.12   GPS Applications

Although GPS was originally devised to assist in military navigation, guidance, and positioning, civilian applications continue to evolve rapidly. From its earliest days, GPS was welcomed by the surveying community and recognized as an important tool in precise positioning. Prior to GPS, published surveying accuracy standards (then tied to terrestrial techniques like triangulation, trilateration, and precise traversing) had an upper limit of 1:100,000. With GPS, accuracy standards have risen as follows: AA (global), 1:100,000,000; A (national, primary network), 1:10,000,000; and B (national, secondary network), 1:1,000,000. In addition to continental control, GPS has now become a widely used technique for establishing and verifying state/provincial and municipal horizontal control, as well as horizontal control for large-scale engineering and mapping projects.

### 11.12.1   General Techniques

When in the field, the surveyor first sets the receiver over the point and then measures, records (in the field log), and enters the hi into the receiver. The session programming is verified, and the mode of operation is selected. Satellite lock and position computation are then verified. As the observations proceed, the process is monitored, and finally, when the session is complete, the receiver is turned off (base station) or moved to the next way point (roving receiver). The survey controller (data collector) has application programs for topography, radial and linear stakeout, cut/fill, and intersections by bearing-bearing, bearing-distance, and distance-distance. In addition, the controller can perform inverse, sea level, curvature and refraction, datum transformations [universal transverse mercator (UTM), state plane, Lambert, etc.], and geoid corrections. See Figure 11.22 for typical operations capability for data collectors used for both EDM total station and GPS total station surveys.

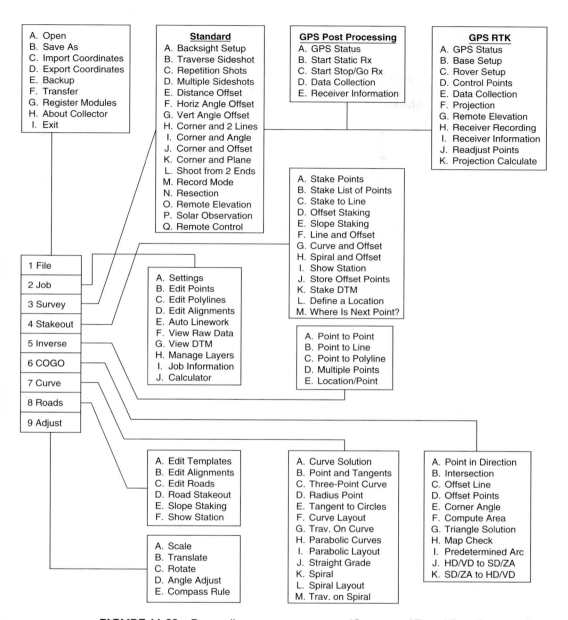

**FIGURE 11.22** Data collector menu structure. (Courtesy of Tripod Data Systems, Corvallis, Ore.)

## 11.12.2 Topographic Surveys

When GPS is used for topographic surveys, detail is located by short occupation times and described with the input of appropriate coding. Input may be accomplished by keying in, by using bar-code readers, or by keying in prepared library codes. Line work may require no special coding (see Z codes, Section 7.12) because entities (curbs, fences, etc.) can be joined by their specific codes (curb2, fence3, etc.). Some software displays the accuracy of each observation for horizontal and vertical position, giving the surveyor the opportunity to take additional observations if the displayed accuracy does not meet job specifications. In addition to positioning random detail, this GPS technique permits the data collection on specified profile, cross-section, and boundary locations with the navigation functions. Contours may be plotted readily from the collected data. At the start of the survey, GPS is also useful in locating boundary and control markers that may be covered with snow or other ground cover. If the marker's coordinates are in the receiver, the navigation mode will take the surveyor directly to the location of the marker. Data captured using these techniques can be added to a mapping or GIS data base or plotted directly to scale using a digital plotter (see Chapter 8).

## 11.12.3 Layout Surveys

For layout work, the coordinates of all relevant control points and layout points are uploaded from computer files before going out to the field. After the base station receiver has been set up over a control point and the roving receiver appropriately referenced, the layout can begin. As each layout point number is keyed into the collector, the azimuth and distance to the required position are displayed on the screen. The surveyor, guided by these directions, eventually moves to the desired point, which is then staked. One base receiver will support any number of rover receivers, thus permitting the instantaneous layout of large-project boundaries, pipelines, roads, and building locations by several surveyors, each working only on a specific type of facility, or by all roving surveyors working on all proposed facilities but on selected geographic sections of the project.

As with topographic applications, the precision of the proposed location is displayed on the receiver as the antenna pole is held on the grade stake or other marker to confirm that layout specifications have been met. If the displayed precision is below specifications, the surveyor simply waits at the location until the processing of data from additional epochs provides him or her with the necessary precision. On road layouts, both line and grade can be given directly to the builder (by marking grade stakes), and progress in cut/fill can be monitored. Slope stakes can be located without any need for intervisibility. The next logical stage, which is to mount GPS antennas directly on various construction excavating equipment to provide line and grade control directly, has already been taken by some GPS receiver manufacturers.

As with the accuracy/precision display previously mentioned, not only are cut/fill, grades, and the like, displayed at each step along the way, a permanent record is also kept on all of these data in case a review is required. Accuracy can also be confirmed by reoccupying selected layout stations and noting and recording the displayed measurements—an inexpensive yet effective method of quality control.

When used for material inventory measurements, GPS techniques are particularly useful in open-pit mining, where original, in-progress, and final surveys can be performed easily for quantity and payment purposes. Material stockpiles can also be surveyed quickly and volumes computed using appropriate onboard software.

For both GPS topographic and layout work, there is no way to get around the fact that existing and proposed stations must be occupied by the antenna. If some of these specific locations are such that satellite visibility is impossible, perhaps because obstructions are blocking the satellites' signals (even when using receivers capable of tracking both constellations), then ancillary surveying techniques (for example, total stations, Chapter 7; handheld total stations, Figures 16.14 and 16.15) must be used. We may soon see total stations (with prismless measuring ability) equipped with GPS chips and antennas so that all needed measurements can be performed by one instrument.

## 11.12.4 Additional Applications

GPS is ideal for the precise type of measurements needed in deformation studies, whether they are for geological events (for example, plate slippage) or for structure stability studies such as bridges and dams monitoring. In both cases, measurements from permanently established remote sites can be transmitted to more central control offices for immediate analysis.

In addition to the static survey control described above, GPS can also be utilized in dynamic applications of aerial surveying and hydrographic surveying, where onboard GPS receivers can be used to supplement existing ground or shore control or where they can now be used in conjunction with inertial guidance equipment (inertial navigation system, INS) for control purposes, without the need for external (shore or ground) GPS receivers. Navigation has always been one of the chief uses of GPS. Civilian use in this area has really taken off. Commercial and pleasure boating now have an accurate and relatively inexpensive navigation device. With the cessation of SA, the precision of low-cost receivers has improved to the <10-meter range, and that range can be further improved to the submeter level using differential (for example, radio beacon) techniques. Using low-cost GPS receivers, we can now navigate to the correct harbor, and we can also navigate to the correct mooring within that harbor. GPS, together with onboard inertial systems (INSs), are rapidly becoming the norm for aircraft navigation.

GPS navigation has now become a familiar tool for backpackers, where the inexpensive GPS receiver (often less than $300) has become a superior adjunct to the compass (see Figure 11.6). Using GPS, the backpacker can determine geographic position at selected points (waypoints) such as trail intersections, river crossings, campsites, and other points of interest. Inexpensive software (for less than $100) can be used to transfer collected waypoints to the computer, make corrections for DGPS input, and to display data on previously loaded maps and plans. The software can also be utilized to identify waypoints on a displayed map, which can be coordinated and then downloaded to a GPS receiver so that the backpacker can go to the field and navigate to the selected waypoints. Many backpackers continue to use a compass while navigating from waypoint to waypoint to maneuver under tree canopy cover, for example, where GPS signals are blocked, and to conserve GPS receiver battery life.

# 11.13　Vertical Positioning

Most surveyors have, until recently, been able to ignore the implications of geodesy for normal engineering plane surveys. The distances encountered are so relatively short that global implications are negligible. However, the elevation coordinate ($h$) given by GPS solutions refers to the height from the surface of the reference ellipsoid (GRS80) (see Figure 11.23) to the ground station, whereas the surveyor needs the orthometric height ($H$). The ellipsoid is referenced to a spatial Cartesian coordinate system (Figure 11.24) called the international terrestrial reference framework (ITRF94). The center (0, 0, 0) of the framework is the center of the mass of the earth, and the $X$ axis is a line drawn from the origin through the equatorial plane to the Greenwich meridian. The $Y$ axis is in the equatorial plane perpendicular to the $X$ axis, and the $Z$ axis is drawn from the origin perpendicular to the equatorial plane, as shown in Figure 11.25.

Essentially, GPS observations permit the computation of $X$, $Y$, and $Z$ Cartesian coordinates of a geocentric ellipsoid; these Cartesian coordinates can then be transformed to geodetic coordinates: latitude ($\varphi$), longitude ($\lambda$), and ellipsoidal height ($h$). Finally, the geodetic coordinates can be transferred to UTM, state plane, or other grids—together with geoid corrections (see Figure 11.25 and Section 11.13.1)—to provide working coordinates (northing, easting, and elevation) for the field surveyor.

The ellipsoid presently used by many to portray the earth is the World Geodetic System (WGS84), which is generally agreed to represent the earth more accurately than previous versions. Ongoing satellite observations permitted scientists to improve their estimates of the size and mass of the earth. An earlier reference ellipsoid—the Geodetic Reference System (GRS80) of the International Union of Geodesy and Geophysics (IUGG), which was adopted in 1979 by that group as the model then best representing the earth—is the ellipsoid on which the horizontal datum, the North American datum of 1983 (NAD 1983) is based (see Figure 11.23). In this system, the geographic coordinates are given by the ellipsoidal latitude ($\varphi$), longitude ($\lambda$), and height (h) above the ellipsoidal surface to the ground station. The GEOID99 model (see Section 11.13.1) is based on known relationships between NAD 1983 and the ITRF spatial reference frame, together with GPS height measurements on the North American vertical datum of 1988 (NAVD 1988) benchmarks.

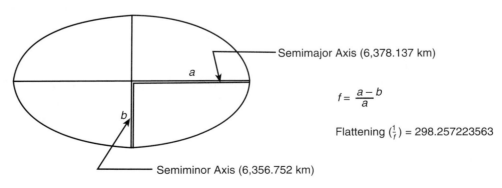

$$f = \frac{a - b}{a}$$

Flattening ($\frac{1}{f}$) = 298.257223563

Semimajor Axis (6,378.137 km)

Semiminor Axis (6,356.752 km)

**FIGURE 11.23**　Ellipse parameters of the GRS80 ellipsoid (flattening is exaggerated).

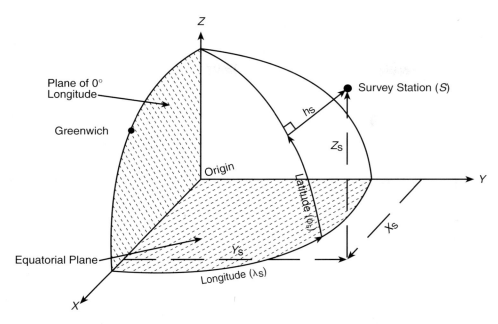

**FIGURE 11.24** Cartesian $(X, Y, Z)$ and geodetic $(\phi_s, \lambda_s, h_s)$ coordinates.

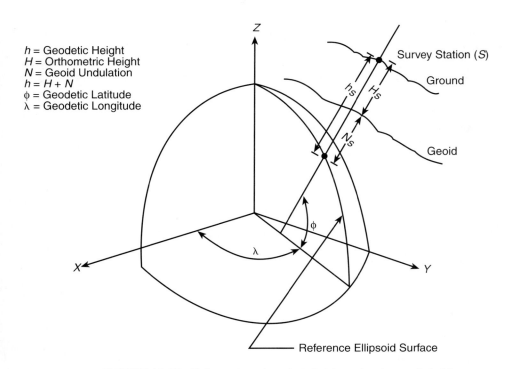

$h$ = Geodetic Height
$H$ = Orthometric Height
$N$ = Geoid Undulation
$h = H + N$
$\phi$ = Geodetic Latitude
$\lambda$ = Geodetic Longitude

**FIGURE 11.25** Relationship of geodetic height and orthometric height.

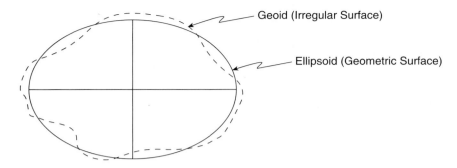

**FIGURE 11.26**   GRS 80 ellipsoid and the geoid.

Traditionally surveyors are used to working with spirit levels and reference orthometric heights (*H*) to the "average" surface of the earth, as depicted by MSL. The surface of mean sea level can be approximated by the equipotential surface of the earth's gravity field, called the *geoid*. The geoid, which is an irregular surface, is influenced by the density of adjacent land masses at any particular survey station. Its surface does not follow the surface of the ellipsoid; sometimes it is below the ellipsoid, and other times it is above it. For most of the North American continent, the geoid is above the ellipsoid. Wherever the mass of the earth's crust changes, the geoid's gravitational potential also changes, resulting in a nonuniform and unpredictable geoid surface. Since the geoid does not lend itself to mathematical expression, as does the ellipsoid, geoid undulation (the difference between the geoid surface and the ellipsoid surface) must be measured at specific sites to determine the local geoid undulation value (see Figures 11.26 and 11.27).

## 11.13.1   Geoid Modeling

Geoid undulations can be determined both by gravimetric surveys and by the inclusion of points of known elevation in GPS surveys. When the average undulation of an area has been determined, only the residual undulations over the surveyed area must be determined. While residual undulations are usually less than 0.020 m over areas of 50 km$^2$, the undulation itself ranges from +75 m at New Guinea to −104 m at the south tip of India.

After all the known geoid separations have been plotted, the geoid undulations (*N*) at any given survey station can be interpolated. The orthometric height (*H*) can be determined from the relationship $H = h - N$, where *h* is the ellipsoid height (*N* is positive when the geoid is above the ellipsoid and negative when it is below the ellipsoid; see Figures 11.24 and 11.25). Geoid modeling data can be obtained from government agencies, and in many cases, GPS suppliers provide this data as part of their software. Because of the uncertainties still inherent in geoid modeling, it is generally thought that accuracies in elevation are only about half the accuracies achievable in horizontal positioning; that is, if a horizontal accuracy is defined to be ± (5 mm + 1 ppm), the vertical accuracy is probably close to ± (10 mm + 2 ppm).

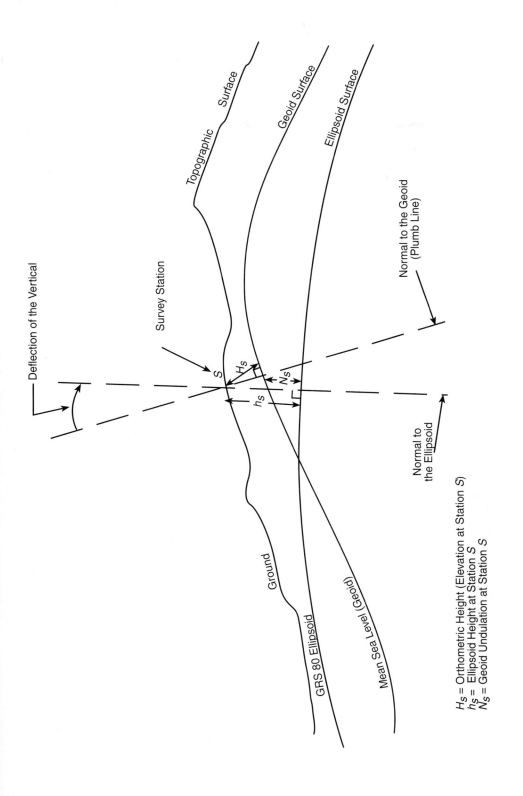

$H_S$ = Orthometric Height (Elevation at Station $S$)
$h_S$ = Ellipsoid Height at Station $S$
$N_S$ = Geoid Undulation at Station $S$

($N$ Is Positive When Geoid Is Above the Ellipsoid)

$$h_S = H_S + N_S$$

**FIGURE 11.27** The three surfaces of geodesy (undulations greatly exaggerated).

### 11.13.1.1 GSD95 geoid (Canada)
The Ministry of Energy, Mines, and Resources in Canada has developed a geoid model, GSD95 (a refinement of GSD91), which takes into account more than 700,000 surface gravity observations in Canada, with additional observations taken in the United States, Greenland, and Denmark. These data are available from the ministry, which is located in Ottawa. The Canadian geoid separation program uses a quadratic interpolation algorithm to determine undulations within a relative accuracy of about 0.010 m over a 10-km separation.

### 11.13.1.2 GEOID99 (United States)
GEOID99 (a refinement of GEOID96, GEOID93, and GEOID 90) is a geoid-elevation estimation model referenced to the GRS80 ellipsoid. It consists of computer software containing geoid undulation data, together with contour maps showing the undulations. These data, which have been developed by the National Geodetic Survey, cover the country in 2-ft by 2-ft grids (latitude and longitude); GEOID93 was in 3-ft grids. GEOID99 has incorporated more than 2,900 new GPS heights on known benchmarks; it also reflects the advances made in the new gravimetric geoid model (G99SSS), which incorporated almost 2 million gravity observations. Together, these advancements provide much better accuracies in converting directly from GPS heights to orthometric heights. When values developed from GEOID99 are compared to values determined by spirit leveling, local orthometric datums can be established.

GEOID99 height grids are available in three overlapping files:

Eastern United States: 24°–50°N,  66°– 90°W
Central United States: 24°–50°N,  83°–107°W
Western United States: 24°–50°N, 101°–125°W

These files, together with the interpolation program (GEOID), are available from the National Geodetic Information Center, (301) 713-3242. Additional information is available from the NGS website: http://www.ngs.noaa.gov/GEOID/GEOID99/. See also Section 10.1.

## 11.14   Conclusion

Table 11.4 provides a summary of the GPS positioning techniques described in this chapter. GPS techniques hold such promise that most future horizontal and vertical control will likely be coordinated using these techniques. It is also likely that many engineering, mapping, and GIS surveying applications will be developed using emerging advances in real-time GPS data collection. In the future, the collection of GPS data will be enhanced as more and more North American local and federal agencies install continuously operating receivers and transmitters, which provide positioning solutions for a wide variety of private and government agencies involved in surveying, mapping, planning, GIS-related surveying, and navigation.

## 11.15   GPS Glossary

**absolute positioning** The direct determination of a station's coordinates by receiving positioning signals from a minimum of four GPS satellites. Also known as *(point positioning)*.

**Table 11.4** GPS MEASUREMENTS SUMMARY[a]

*Two basic modes:*

**Code-based measurements:** Satellite-to-receiver pseudorange is measured and then corrected to provide the range; four satellite ranges are required to determine position—by removing the uncertainties in $X$, $Y$, $Z$, and receiver clocks. The military can access both P code and C/A code; civilians can access only the C/A code—where the accuracy is degraded to the 100 m level.

**Carrier-based measurements:** The carrier waves themselves are used to compute the satellite(s)-to-receiver range; similar to EDM. Most carrier receivers utilize both code measurements and carrier measurements to compute positions.

*Two basic techniques:*

**Point positioning:** Code measurements are used to compute the position of the receiver directly. Only one receiver required.

**Relative positioning:** Code and/or carrier measurements are used to compute the baseline vector ($\Delta X$, $\Delta Y$, and $\Delta Z$) from a point of known position to a point of unknown position, thus enabling the computation of the coordinates of the new position.

*Relative positioning:* Two receivers required—one occupying a point of known position.

*Static:* Accuracy—5 mm + 1 ppm. Observation times—1 hour to many hours. Use—control surveys; standard method when lines longer than 20 km. Uses dual- or single-frequency receivers.

*Rapid static:* Accuracy—5 to 10 mm + 1 ppm. Observation times—5 to 10 minutes. Initialization time of 1 minute for dual-frequency and about 3 to 5 minutes for single-frequency receivers. Receiver must have specialized rapid static observation capability. The roving receiver does not have to maintain lock on satellites (useful feature in areas with many obstructions). Used for control surveys, including photogrammetric control for lines 10 km or less. The receiver program determines the total length of the sessions, and the receiver screen displays "time remaining" at each station session.

*Reoccupation* (also known as pseudostatic and pseudo-kinematic): Accuracy—5 to 10 mm + 1 ppm. Observation times about 10 minutes, but each point must be reoccupied after at least 1 hour, for another 10 minutes. No initialization time required. Useful when GDOP is poor. No need to maintain satellite lock. Same rover receivers must reoccupy the points they initially occupied. Moving the base station for the second occupation sessions may improve accuracy. Voice communications are needed to ensure simultaneous observations between base receiver and rover(s).

*Kinematic:* Accuracy—10 mm + 2 ppm. Observation times—1 to 4 epochs, (1 to 2 minutes on control points); the faster the rover speed, the quicker must be the observation (shorter epochs). Sampling rate is usually between 0.5 and 5 seconds. Initialization by occupying two known points—2 to 5 minutes, or by antenna swap—5 to 15 minutes. Lock must be maintained on 4 satellites (5 satellites are better in case one of them moves close to the horizon). Good technique for open areas (especially hydrographic surveys) and where large amounts of data are required quickly.

*Stop and go:* Accuracy—10 to 20 mm + 2 ppm. Observation times—a few seconds to a minute. Lock must be maintained to 4 satellites and if loss of lock occurs, it must be reinitialized [that is, occupy known point, rapid static techniques, or on-the-fly (OTF) resolution—OTF requires dual-frequency receivers]. This technique is one of the more effective ways of locating topographic and built features, as for engineering surveys.

*DGPS:* The U.S. Coast Guard's system of providing differential code measurement surveys. Accuracy—submeter to 10 m. Roving receivers are equipped with radio receivers capable of receiving base station broadcasts of pseudorange corrections, using RTCM standards. For use by individual surveyors working within range of the transmitters (100 km to 400 km). Positions can be determined in real time. Surveyors using just one receiver have the equivalent of two receivers.

*Real-time differential surveys:* Also known as real-time kinematic (RTK). Accuracies—1 to 2 cm. Requires a base receiver occupying a known station, which then radio transmits error corrections to any number of roving receivers, thus permitting them to perform data gathering and layout surveys in real time. All required software is onboard the roving receivers. Dual-frequency receivers permit OTF reinitialization after loss of lock. Baselines are restricted to about 10 km. Five satellites are required. This, or similar techniques, is without doubt the future for many engineering surveys.

*CORS:* Nationwide differential positioning system—using code and/or carrier observations. When fully implemented (by about the year 2005) this system of approximately 250 continuously operating reference stations will enable surveyors working with one GPS receiver to obtain the same results as if working with two. The CORS receiver is a highly accurate dual-frequency receiver. Surveyors can access station data for the appropriate location, date and time via the Internet—data is then input to the software to combine with the surveyor's own data to produce accurate (postprocessed) positioning. Canada's nationwide system, active control system (ACS), provides base station data for a fee.

---

[a]Observation times and accuracies are affected by the quality and capability of the GPS receivers, by signal errors, and by the geometric strength of the visible satellite array (GDOP). Vertical accuracies are about half the horizontal accuracies.

**active control station (ACS)** *See* CORS.

**ambiguity** The integer number of carrier cycles between the GPS receiver and a satellite.

**CORS** Continuously operating reference station (GPS). CORS transmitted data can be used by single-receiver surveyors or navigators to permit higher precision differential positioning through postprocessing computations.

**cycle slip** A temporary loss of lock on satellite carrier signals, causing a miscount in carrier cycles; lock must be reestablished to continue positioning solutions.

**differential positioning** Obtaining satellite measurements at a known base station to correct simultaneous same-satellite measurements made at rover receiving stations. Corrections can be postprocessed, or corrections can be real time (RTK), as when they are broadcast directly to the roving receiver.

**epoch** An observational event in time that forms part of a series of GPS observations.

**GDOP (general dilution of precision)** A value that indicates the relative uncertainty in position, using GPS observations, caused by errors in time (GPS receivers) and satellite vector measurements. A minimum of four widely spaced satellites at high elevations usually produce good results (that is, lower GDOP values).

**geodetic height** ($h$) The distance from the ellipsoid surface to the ground surface.

**geoid surface** A surface that is approximately represented by mean sea level (MSL) and is, in fact, the equipotential surface of the earth's gravity field.

**geoid undulation** ($N$) The difference between the geoid surface and the ellipsoid surface. $N$ is negative if the geoid surface is below the ellipsoid surface. Also known as *geoid height.*

**global positioning system (GPS)** A ground positioning ($Y$, $X$, and $Z$) technique based on the reception and analysis of NAVSTAR satellite signals.

**ionosphere** The section of the earth's atmosphere that is about 50 km to 1,000 km above the earth's surface.

**ionospheric refraction** The impedance in the velocity of signals (GPS) as they pass through the ionosphere.

**NAVSTAR** A set of orbiting satellites used in navigation and positioning.

**orthometric height** ($H$) The distance from the geoid surface to the ground surface. Also known as *elevation.*

**pseudorange** The uncorrected distance from a GPS satellite to a GPS ground receiver determined by comparing the code transmitted from the satellite to the replica code residing in the GPS receiver. When corrections are made for clock and other errors, the pseudorange becomes the range.

**real-time positioning (real-time Kinematic, RTK)** RTK requires a base station to measure the satellites' signals, process the baseline corrections, and then broadcast the corrections (differences) to any number of roving receivers that are simultaneously tracking the same satellites.

**relative positioning** The determination of position through the combined computations of two or more receivers simultaneously tracking the same satellites, resulting in the determination of the baseline vector ($X$, $Y$, $Z$) joining two receivers.

**troposphere** The part of the earth's atmosphere that stretches from the surface to about 80 km upward (includes the stratosphere as its upper portion).

# 11.16 Recommended Readings and Related Websites

Books and articles:

Geomatics Canada, *GPS Positioning Guide*. Ottawa: Natural Resources Canada, 1993.

Hofman-Wellenhof et al., *GPS Theory and Practice*. fourth ed. New York: Springer-Verlag Wien, 1997.

Hurn, Jeff, *Differential GPS Explained*. Sunnyvale, Calif.: Trimble Navigation Co., 1993.

Leick, Alfred, *GPS Satellite Surveying*. second ed. New York: John Wiley & Sons, 1995.

Muellerschoen, Ronald J., Bar-Sever, Yoaz E., Bertiger, William I., and Stowers, David A. "NASA's Global DGPS for High Precision Users." GPS World, January.

Reilly, James P., "The GPS Observer" (ongoing column), *Point of Beginning (POB)*.

Spofford, Paul, and Neil Weston, "CORS—The National Geodetic Survey's Continuously Operating Reference Station Project." *ACSM Bulletin*. March/April 1998.

Trimble Navigation Co., GPS, *A Guide to the Next Utility*. Sunnyvale, Calif., 1989 (Information on these and other Trimble publications is available at the Trimble website listed below.)

Trimble Navigation Co., GPS, *Surveyor's Field Guide*. Sunnyvale, Calif., 1992.

Van Sickle, Jan, *GPS for Land Surveyors*. Chelsea, Mich.: Ann Arbor Press Inc., 1996.

Wells, David, et al., *Guide to GPS Positioning*. Fredericton, N.B.: Canadian GPS Associates, 1986.

Magazines for general information (including archived articles):

*ACSM Bulletin,* American Congress on Surveying and Mapping, http://www.ascm.net

*GPS World,* http://www.gpsworld.com/

*Point of Beginning (POB),* http://www.pobonline.com/

*Professional Surveyor,* http://www.profsurv.com

Websites for general information, reference, and web links, and GPS receiver manufacturers (see the list of additional Internet references in Appendix E):

Ashtech, http://www.ashtech.com/

Carl Zeiss, http://www.zeiss.com/survey/

DGPS, http://www.navcen.uscg.mil/ (U.S. Coast Guard Navigation Center)

GLONASS, http://www.rssi.ru/SFCSIC/english.html

GPS Overview, Peter H. Dana, Department of Geography, University of Texas, http://www.utexas.edu/depts/grg/gcraft/notes/gps/gps.html

Land Surveying and Geomatics, Maynard H. Riley, PLS, Illinois, http://homepage.interaccess.com/maynard/

Land Surveyors' reference page, Stan Thompson, PLS, Huntington Technology Group, http://www.lsrp.com/

Leica, http://www.leica.com/
National Geodetic Survey (NGS), http://www.ngs.noaa.gov/
Natural Resources Canada, http://www.nrcan.gc.ca/
Nikon, http://www.nikonusa.com/
Sokkia, http://www.sokkia.com/
Topcon Positioning, http://topconps.com (Javad GPS tutorial)
Trimble, http://www.trimble.com/
U.S. Coast Guard and Navigation Center: http//www.navcen.uscg.gov

# Questions

1. Why is it necessary to observe a minimum of four GPS satellites to solve for position?
2. How does the GPS constellation compare with the GLONASS constellation?
3. How does differential positioning work?
4. What is the difference between range and pseudorange?
5. What are the chief sources of error in GPS measurements? How can you minimize or eliminate each of these errors?
6. What are the factors that must be analyzed in GPS survey planning?
7. Describe RTK techniques used for a layout survey.
8. What effect has GPS had on national control surveys?
9. Explain why station visibility diagrams are used in survey planning. Why is it better to locate a survey station on the south side of a tall building rather than on the north side?
10. Explain the difference between orthometric heights and ellipsoid heights.
11. Explain the CORS system.

# PART
# II
# Remote Sensing

# CHAPTER 12 Remote Sensing

## 12.A Satellite Imagery

## 12.1 General Background

*Remote sensing* is a term used to describe geodata collection and interpretive analysis for both airborne and satellite imagery. Satellite platforms collect geodata using various digital sensors, for example, multispectral scanners, lidar and radar. Imaging advances in 2000 have resulted in multispectral scanning techniques, now also available on airborne platforms, in addition to the traditional aerial photography techniques. Both airborne digital imagery and satellite imagery have some advantages over airborne film-based photography:

- Large data-capture areas can be processed more quickly using computer-based analyses.
- Satellite imagery can be recaptured every few days or weeks, which permits the tracking of rapidly changing conditions, for example, disaster response for forest fires, flooding, etc.
- Feature identification can be much more effective when combining multispectral scanners with panchromatic imagery. For example, with the analysis of spectral reflectance variations, even tree foliage differentiation is possible. (In near-IR, coniferous trees are distinctly darker in tone than are deciduous trees.)
- Ongoing measurements track slowly changing conditions, for example, crop diseases, etc.
- Imaging is relatively inexpensive. The consumer need purchase only that level of image processing needed for a specific project.
- In digital format, data is ready for computer processing.
- With the use of radar, which has the ability to penetrate cloud cover, remotely sensed data can be collected under an expanded variety of weather conditions, night and day.

- With the use of lidar measurements, ground surface measurements (DEMs) can be taken relatively inexpensively, day or night, from aircraft or from satellites [for example, NASA's vegetation canopy lidar mission (VCL) scheduled for launch in the early 2000s].
- Imaging results are a good source for the data needed to build GIS layers.

As with all measurement techniques, satellite imagery is susceptible to errors and other problems requiring analysis:

- Although individual ground features typically reflect light from unique portions of the spectrum, reflectance can vary for the same type of features.
- Sensors are sensitive only to specified wavelengths. There is a limit to the number of sensors that can be deployed on a satellite or on an aircraft.
- The sun's energy, the source of reflected and emitted signals, can vary over time and location.
- Atmospheric scattering and absorption of the sun's radiation can vary unpredictably over time and location.
- Depending on the resolution of the images, some detail may be missed or mistakenly identified.
- Although vast amounts of data can be collected very quickly, processing the data takes considerable time. The space shuttle Endeavor's ten-day radar topography of the earth mission in 2000 collected about 1 trillion images, and it will take about two years to process the data into map form.
- Scale, or resolution, may be a limiting factor on some projects.
- The effect of ground moisture on longer wavelengths, microwaves in particular, make some analyses complex.

Since aerial imaging is usually at a much larger scale than is satellite imaging, aerial images are presently more suitable for projects requiring maximum detail and precision, for example, engineering works. However, the functional planning of corridor works such as highways, railways, canals, electrical transmission lines, etc., have been greatly assisted with the advances in satellite imagery.

Remote sensing data do not necessarily have their absolute geographic positions recorded at the time of data acquisition. Each point within an image (pixel, or picture element) is located with respect to other pixels within a single image, but the image must be geocorrected before it can be inserted accurately into a GIS or a design document. In addition to the geocorrections needed to establish spatial location (GPS and inertial techniques are now relied upon for much of this work), the identification of remotely sensed image features must be verified using ground-truth techniques, that is, analyzing aerial photos, on-site reconnaissance with visual confirmations, map analysis (for example, soils maps), etc. Ground-truth techniques are required not only to verify or classify surface features but also to calibrate sensors (see Section 12.6). "A chief use of remote sensing is the classification of the myriad of features in a scene—usually presented as an image—into meaningful categories or classes. The image then becomes a thematic map (the theme is selectable, e.g., land use, geology, vegetation types, rainfall)" (NASA). A major advantage of remote sensing information is the ability to provide a basis for updates on GIS information on a repetitive and inexpensive basis.

## 12.2 Techniques of Remote Sensing

There are two main categories of remote sensing: active and passive. Active remote sensing instruments (for example, radar and lidar) transmit their own electromagnetic waves and then develop images of the earth's surface as the electromagnetic pulses (known as backscatter) are reflected back from the target surface. Passive remote sensing instruments develop images of the ground surface as they detect the natural energy that is either reflected (if the sun is the signal source) or emitted from the observed target area.

## 12.3 Electromagnetic Spectrum

The fundamental unit of electromagnetic radiation is the photon. The photon, which has energy but no mass, moves at the speed of light. The wave theory of light has light traveling in wavelike patterns, with its energy characterized by its wavelength or frequency. The speed of light is generally considered to be 300,000 km/sec or 186, 000 miles/s, as we saw in Equation 7.1:

$$c = f\lambda$$

where $c$ is the velocity of light in m/s; $f$ is the frequency of the light energy in hertz* (frequency is the number of cycles of a wave passing a fixed point in a given time period); and $\lambda$ is the wavelength, in m, as measured between successive wave crests (see Figure 7.2).

Figure 12.1 shows the electromagnetic spectrum, with wavelengths ranging in size from the very small (cosmic, gamma, and x-rays) to the very large (radio and television).

*Hertz (Hz) is a frequency of one cycle per second; kilohertz (KHz) is $10^3$ Hz, megahertz (MHz) is $10^6$ Hz, and gigahertz (GHz) is $10^9$ Hz.

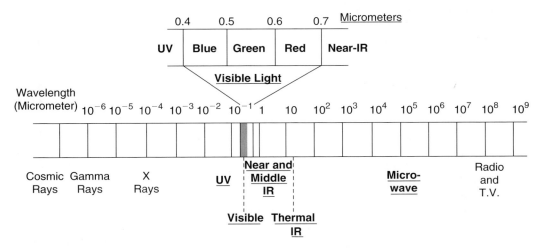

**FIGURE 12.1** Electromagnetic spectrum.

**Table 12.1** VISIBLE SPECTRUM

| Color | Bandwidth |
|-------|-----------|
| Violet | 0.4–0.446 μm |
| Blue | 0.446–0.500 μm |
| Green | 0.500–0.578 μm |
| Yellow | 0.578–0.592 μm |
| Orange | 0.593–0.620 μm |
| Red | 0.620–0.7 μm |

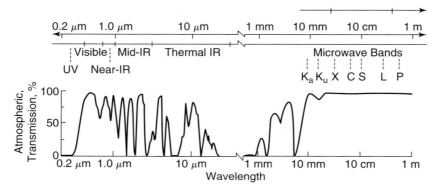

**FIGURE 12.2** Electromagnetic spectrum showing atmospheric transmission windows in the visible, near, middle, and thermal infrared and microwave regions. Notice the excellent atmospheric transmission capabilities in the entire range of the microwave (Courtesy NASA).

In most remote sensing applications, radiation is described by its wavelength, although those using microwave (radar) sensing have traditionally used frequency instead to describe these much longer wavelength signals.

Visible light is generally agreed to be on that very small part of the electromagnetic spectrum ranging from about 0.4 μm to 0.7 μm (μm is the symbol for micrometer or micron, a unit that is one millionth of a meter;—see Table 12.1). Infrared radiation (IR) ranges from about 0.7 μm to 100 μm, and that range can be further subdivided into reflected IR (ranging from about 0.7 μm to about 3.0 μm) and the thermal region (ranging from about 3.0 μm to about 100 μm). The other commonly used region of the spectrum is that of microwaves (for example, radar), which ranges from about 1 mm to 1 m.

Radiation having different wavelengths travels through the atmosphere with varying degrees of success. Radiation is scattered unpredictably by particles in the atmosphere, and radiation is absorbed by atmospheric constituents such as water vapor, carbon dioxide, and ozone. Radiation scattering and absorption rates vary with the radiation wavelengths and the atmospheric particle size. Only radiation in the visible, infrared (IR), and microwave sections of the spectrum travel through the atmosphere relatively free of blockage. These atmospheric transmission anomalies, known as atmospheric windows, are utilized for most common remote sensing activities (see Figure 12.2). Note that the relatively short wavelengths of blue light suffer from atmospheric scattering to the extent that it is

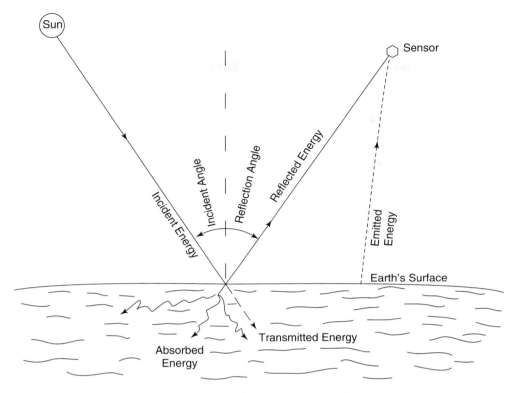

**FIGURE 12.3** Interaction of electromagnetic radiation with the earth.

often difficult to distinguish features on the resulting blue band image. This scattering is known as the Raleigh effect and is the reason why the sky appears to be blue.

Radiation that is not absorbed or scattered in the atmosphere (incident energy) will reach the surface of the earth where three types of interaction can occur (see Figure 12.3):

- Transmitted energy passes through an object surface with a change in velocity.
- Absorbed energy is transferred through surface features by way of electron or molecular reactions.
- Reflected energy is reflected back to a sensor, with the incident angle equal to the angle of reflection (those wavelengths that are reflected determine the color of the surface).

Incident energy = transmitted energy + absorbed energy + reflected energy    (12.1)

To illustrate, chlorophyll (a constituent of leaves) absorbs radiation in the red and blue wavelengths but reflects the green wavelengths. Thus, at the height of the growing season, when chlorophyll is present in large amounts, leaves appear greener. Water absorbs the longer wavelengths in the visible and near IR portions of the spectrum and reflects the shorter wavelengths in the blue/green part of the spectrum. This situation results in the often seen blue/green hues of water. In addition, energy emitted from an object can be detected in the thermal infrared section of the spectrum and recorded. Emitted energy can be the result of the previous absorption of energy—a process that creates heat. Remote-sensing instruments can be designed to detect reflected and/or emitted energy.

## 12.3.1 Reflected Energy

Different types of feature surfaces reflect radiation differently. Smooth surfaces act like mirrors and reflect most light in a single direction; this is called specular reflection. At the other extreme, rough surfaces reflect radiation equally in all directions; this is called diffuse reflection. Between these two extremes are an infinite number of reflection possibilities that are often a characteristic of a specific material or surface condition (see Figure 12.4).

## 12.4 Selection of Radiation Sensors

Satellite sensors are designed to meet various considerations, for example:

- To use those parts of the electromagnetic spectrum that are less affected by scatter and absorption.
- To sense data effectively from different sources (active or passive sensing).
- To select the spectral ranges of energy that react most favorably with specified target surfaces. Because various types of ground cover, rocks and soils, water, and built features react differently with radiation from different parts of the spectrum, it is common to install sensors (for example, multispectral scanners) on spacecraft that can detect radiation from several appropriate wavelength ranges.

Most remote-sensing instruments use scanners to evaluate successfully small portions of the earth at instants in time. At each instant, the sensor quantizes the earth's surface into pixels (picture elements) or bands, as when side-looking airborne radar (SLAR) is used. Pixel resolution can range from 1 m (IKONOS satellite) to greater than 1 km, depending on the instrumentation and altitude of the sensing platform. As in aerial photography, spec-

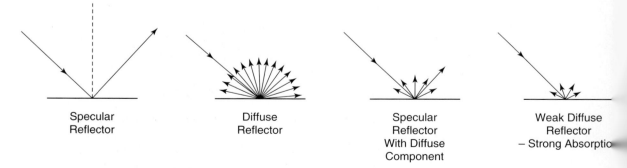

Specular
Reflector

Diffuse
Reflector

Specular
Reflector
With Diffuse
Component

Weak Diffuse
Reflector
– Strong Absorptio

**FIGURE 12.4** Specular and diffuse reflection.

tral scanning utilizes lenses and, like aerial photography, stereo-paired images can be captured and digital elevation models (DEMs) can be created. Stereo (three-dimensional) viewing is a great aid in visual imaging. There are two main types of scanners: across-track and along-track.

Across-track scanners, also called whisk-broom scanners, scan lines perpendicular to the forward motion of the spacecraft using rotating mirrors. As the spacecraft moves across the earth, a series of scanned lines are collected, producing a two-dimensional image of the earth. Each onboard sensor in the vehicle collects reflected or emitted energy in a specific range of wavelengths. These electrical signals are converted to digital data and stored until they are transmitted to earth.

Along-track scanners, also called push-broom scanners, utilize the forward motion of the spacecraft itself to record successive scan lines. Instead of rotating mirrors, these scanners are equipped with linear array charged couple devices (CCDs) that build the image as the satellite moves forward.

Once the data have been captured and downloaded to earth, much more work has to be done to convert the data into a usable format. Details on these processes, which include image enhancement and image classification, are beyond the scope of this text. Please see the references at the end of the chapter for additional information on these topics, or look for digital imaging processing (DIP) techniques in your library or on the Internet.

## 12.5    An Introduction to Image Analysis

### 12.5.1    General Background

Analysis of remotely sensed images is a highly specialized field. Because environmental characteristics include most of the physical sciences, the image interpreter should have an understanding of the basic concepts of geography, climatology, geomorphology, geology, soil science, ecology, hydrology, and civil engineering. For this reason, multidisciplinary teams of scientists, geographers, and engineers trained in image interpretation are frequently used to help develop the software utilized in this largely automated process.

Just as photogrammetry/air photo interpretation helps the analyst to identify objects in an aerial photograph, digital image analysis helps the analyst to identify objects depicted in satellite and airborne images. With the blossoming of computerized image analyses that employ automated digital imagery processing, the relative numbers of trained analysts needed to process data has sharply declined. Satellite imagery has always been processed in digital format, and aerial photos (films) can be scanned easily to convert from analog to digital format. The interpretation of aerial photography has been largely automated using soft-copy photogrammetric techniques on the digitized photos (see Section 12.22), and satellite and airborne imagery analysis is also largely automated. As with aerial photography, satellite images must have ground control and must be corrected for geometric distortion and relief displacement, and also for distortions caused by the atmosphere, radiometric errors, and the earth's rotation. Satellite imagery can be purchased with some or many of these distortions removed—the price of the imagery is directly related to the degree of processing requested. Some of the "1 meter resolution" satellites can, with good ground control, produce a planimetric accuracy of 2 meters. They can produce a vertical accuracy of 3 meters when geometric and radiometric corrections are made.

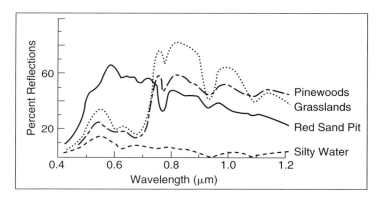

**FIGURE 12.5** Spectral reflectance curves of four different targets. (Adapted from NASA's *Landsat 7 Image Assessment System Handbook,* 2000; courtesy NASA)

Unlike aerial photographic images, different satellite images of the same spatial area taken by two or more different sensors can be fused together to produce a new image with distinct characteristics and thus provide even more data. A digital image target may be a point, line, or area (polygon) feature that is distinguishable from other surrounding features. Digital images are comprised of many pixels, each of which has been assigned a digital number (DN). The digital number represents the brightness level for that specific pixel. For example, in eight-bit ($2^8$) imagery, the 256 brightness levels range from 0 (black) to 255 (white).

Each satellite has the capability of capturing images and then transmitting the images, in digital format, to ground receiving stations that are located around the globe. Modern remote-sensing satellites are equipped with sensors collecting data from selected bands of the electromagnetic spectrum; for example, Landsat 7's sensors collect data from eight bands (channels): seven bands of reflected energy and one band of emitted energy. Since radiation from various portions of the electromagnetic spectrum reacts in a unique fashion with different materials found on the surface of the earth, it is possible to develop a signature of the reflected and emitted signal responses and, from those signatures, identify the object or class of objects.

When the interactions of reflected, emitted, scattered, and absorbed energy (at the various wavelengths collected by onboard sensors) with the ground surface are plotted, the resultant unique curve, called a spectral signature, can be used to help identify that material. Figure 12.5 shows four signatures of different ground surfaces, with the reflection as a function of wavelength used for plotting purposes. The curves were plotted from data received from the eight sensors onboard Landsat 7. When the results are plotted as percentage reflectance for two or more bands (see Figure 12.6) in multidimensional space, the ability to identify the surface materials precisely increases markedly. This spectral separation permits the effective analysis of satellite imagery, most of which can be performed through computer applications. Image analysis can be applied productively to a broad range of scientific inquiry (see Table 12.2).

## 12.5.2   Image Resolution

Image resolution defines the ability of a sensor to distinguish between spatial characteristics of objects on the earth's surface. Resolution can change due to sensor design, detector size, focal length, satellite altitude, and time.

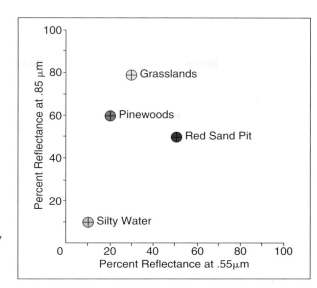

**FIGURE 12.6** Spectral separability using just two bands. (Adapted from NASA's *Landsat 7 Image Assessment Handbook,* 2000; courtesy NASA)

**Table 12.2** APPLICATIONS OF REMOTELY SENSED IMAGES

| Field | Applications |
|---|---|
| Forestry/agriculture | Inventory of crop and timber acreage, estimating crop yields, crop disease tracking, determination of soil conditions, assessment of fire damage, precision farming, and global food analysis. |
| Land Use/mapping | Classification of land use, mapping and map updating, categorization of land use capability, monitoring urban growth, local and regional planning, functional planning for transportation corridors, mapping land/water boundaries, and flood plain management. |
| Geology | Mapping of major geologic units; revising geologic maps; recognition of rock types; mapping recent volcanic surface deposits; mapping landforms; mineral, gas, and oil exploration; and estimating slope failures. |
| Natural resources | Natural resources exploration and management. |
| Water resources | Mapping of floods and flood plains, determining extent of area snow and ice, measurement of glacial features, measurement of sediment and turbidity patterns, delineation of irrigated fields, inventory of lakes, and estimating snow melt runoff. |
| Coastal resources | Mapping shoreline changes; mapping shoals and shallow areas; and tracing oil spills, pollutants, and erosion. |
| Environment | Monitoring the effect of human activity (lake eutrophication, defoliation,), measuring the effects of natural disasters, monitoring surface mining and reclamation, assessing drought impact, siting for solid waste disposal, siting for power plants and other industries, regulatory compliance studies, development impact analysis. |

**12.5.2.1 Spatial Resolution**   Generally, the farther away (the greater the altitude) is the sensor, the larger is the area that can be seen, but the ability to distinguish some detail may be lost. Some sensors have greater ability to "see" detail—that is, they have greater spatial resolution. Spatial resolution refers to the smallest possible feature that can be detected. If a sensor has a spatial resolution of, say, 30 m, and if the image is displayed at full resolution, each pixel (picture element) will represent an area of 30 m by 30 m. The finer the resolution of the image, usually the smaller will be the ground area in that image.

Two terms are presently used to describe the spatial resolution of satellite imagery: ground sample distance (GSD), expressed in meters or kilometers, and instantaneous field of view (IFOV), expressed in milliradians (mrad). The IFOV defines the pixel size and, with the altitude, determines the area of terrain or ocean covered by the field of view of a single detector. The general equation for calculating spatial resolution is:

$$GSD \text{ (meters)} = IFOV \text{ (radians)} \times altitude \text{ (meters)} \qquad (12.2)$$

For example, a 2.5 mrad (0.0025 rad) IFOV at 1,000 m altitude results in a GSD of 2.5 m.

The Landsat 7 satellite senses the earth's surface at three different resolutions (see Table 12.3): 30 m for bands 1–5 and 7, 60 m for band 6, and 15 m for band 8. IKONOS, which carries the space imaging sensor, has a resolution of 1 m. The French SPOT panchromatic sensor has a resolution of 10 m, whereas the SPOT multispectral (XS) sensor has a resolution of 20 m. Indian remote-sensing satellites (IRS) have a resolution of about 36 m.

### 12.5.2.2 Spectral Resolution
Surface features can be identified by analyzing the spectral responses over distinct wavelength changes. Common surfaces, such as vegetation and water, can be identified using a broad range of the electromagnetic spectrum, whereas a more detailed study, for example, different tree types and different rock types, require analysis over much finer wavelength ranges. Thus, the higher the spectral resolution of the sensor, the more distinctions that can be made of surface materials. Newer satellites record spectral responses over several wavelength ranges at different spectral resolutions—these are called multispectral sensors. More recent advances in multispectral sensing (for example, hyperspectral sensing) can involve the application of hundreds of very narrow spectral bands, which greatly extends the ability to distinguish between very similar surface features under various seasonal conditions. Hyperspectral remote sensing is becoming popular in exploration geology, where certain minerals cannot be detected using broadband scanners. Spectral responses from identical ground surface features may vary for several reasons:

- Atmospheric constituents.
- Angle of the sun (for reflected emissions).
- Shadow.
- Smoke.
- Soil moisture.
- Temporal changes (when comparing images collected on different dates).
- Altitude.
- Topographic surface (whether flat or steeply graded).
- Feature height (heights can be determined using lidar, radar, or stereo image analysis).

### 12.5.2.3 Radiometric Resolution
Radiometric resolution refers to the sensors' ability to detect small changes in energy and reflects the number of bits available for each pixel. Imagery data are represented by positive digital numbers that range from 0 to a

**Table 12.3** BANDWIDTH CHARACTERISTICS—LANDSAT 7

| Sensor | Band 1 | Band 2 | Band 3 | Band 4 | Spectral Bandwidths (μm) Band 5 | Band 6 | Band 7 | Band 8 |
|---|---|---|---|---|---|---|---|---|
| TM | .45–.52 | .52–.60 | .63–.69 | .76–.90 | 1.55–1.75 | 10.4–12.5 | 2.08–2.35 | [Not applicable] |
| ETM+ | .45–.52 | .53–.61 | .63–.69 | .78–.90 | 1.55–1.75 | 10.4–12.5 | 2.09–2.35 | .52–.90 |
| | Blue | Green | Red | Near IR | Shortwave IR | Thermal IR | Shortwave IR | Panchromatic |
| Resolution (pixel size) | 30 m | 30 m | 30 m | 30 m | 30 m | 60 m | 30 m | 15 m |

| Band | Use |
|---|---|
| 1 | Soil/vegetation discrimination; bathymetry/coastal mapping; cultural/urban feature identification. |
| 2 | Green vegetation mapping; cultural/urban feature identification. |
| 3 | Vegetated versus non-vegetated and plant species discrimination. |
| 4 | Identification of plant/vegetation types, health and biomass content, water body delineation, soil moisture. |
| 5 | Sensitive to moisture in soil and vegetation; discrimination of snow and cloud-covered areas. |
| 6 | Vegetation stress and soil moisture discrimination related to thermal radiation; thermal mapping (urban, water). |
| 7 | Discrimination of mineral and rock types; sensitive to vegetation moisture content. |
| 8 | Panchromatic: mapping, planning, design. |

Landsat 7 is operated under the direction of NOAA. Data can be obtained from: USGS—EROS Data Center, Sioux Falls, SD 57198.

Courtesy of NOAA.

selected exponent of 2. This range is the same as that used for coding numbers in binary format. Each bit records an exponent of 2, that is, 2-bit is $2^2 = 4$, 4-bit is $2^4 = 16$, 8-bit is $2^8 = 256$, 9-bit is $2^9 = 512$, and 10-bit is $2^{10} = 1,024$. The number of bits used to represent the recorded data determines the number of brightness levels available. To illustrate, if you were to compare images of the same ground area at both 2-bit and 8-bit resolution, you would notice the finer detail available in the 8-bit image. Many images are now recorded in 8-, 9- and 10-bit (and higher) resolutions. This permits a range of 256, 512, or 1,024 digital numbers (DNs) of gray tone ranging from black at a value of zero to white at a value of 255, 511, or 1,023. Whereas the human eye may be able to differentiate between only 20 to 30 steps of gray tone, some sensors can detect all levels of gray tone. A further advantage to using digital images is that analysis can be almost completely automated using computer algorithms, thus greatly reducing the need for continual human intervention, with its attendant potential drawbacks in the areas of human error, inconsistent analysis, and higher costs.

### 12.5.2.4 Temporal Resolution
The surface of the earth is always changing. Changes may occur very slowly, as with geologic processes, or changes may occur somewhat more rapidly, as with urban development, shoreline erosion, etc. Changes may occur at a catastrophic rate, as with crop diseases, large fires, flooding, and even troop movements during wartime. As satellites orbit the earth, the earth is also revolving on its axis so that each subsequent swath of the satellite covers a slightly different portion of the earth's surface. Eventually, the satellites' orbits begin to repeat the surface coverage. The time period required to achieve repeat coverage of the same surface is called the revisit time, which varies from a few days to a month (see Table 12.4). Revisit times can be greatly shortened for those satellites that have motorized direction-controlled detectors, which can be sent coded instructions from ground stations to "look" toward specified areas as the orbit proceeds. Revisit time is also a function of swath overlap, which is considerable at the higher latitudes.

Temporal variations in surface features can be used to identify some features positively and to track systematically the changes in other features. Additionally, repeat revisiting of all surface features helps to overcome the significant problems that cloud cover poses for passive optical remote sensors.

## 12.6   Classification

Satellite imagery contains a wealth of information, all of which may not be relevant for specific projects. A decision must be made about which feature classifications are most relevant. Once the types of features to be classified have been determined, a code library, with a unique code for each included feature, is constructed. The identification can then be represented by a unique code (for example, R for residential) rather than a digital number (DN) giving the gray scale designation. For example, a typical GIS project (see Chapter 9) may require that the following features be classified:

- Pervious/impervious surfaces (needed for rainfall runoff calculations).
- Water.
- Wetland.

**Table 12.4** SELECTED SATELLITES SUMMARY[a]

| Satellite | Launch Date | Sensor Data | Altitude | Swath | Orbit Type | Orbit Period | Revisit Time |
|---|---|---|---|---|---|---|---|
| ERS-2 | 05/20/95 | SAR C band | 785 km | 105.5 km | Near polar; sun synchronous[b] | 100 min | 35 days |
| IKONUS-2 | 09/24/99 | MSS/panchromatic | 681 km | 20 km | Near polar; sun synchronous | 98 min | 2.9 days |
| IRS | 2000 | Panchromatic/ hyperspectral | | 146 km | | | 22 days |
| Landsat 5 | 03/01/84 | TM and MSS | 705 km | 185 km | Near polar; sun synchronous | 99 min | 16 days |
| Landsat 7 | 05/15/99 | ETM MSS | 830 km | 185 km | Near polar; sun synchronous | 99 min | 16 days |
| RADARSAT-1 | 12/20/95 | SAR C band | 798 km | 50–500 km | Circular; sun synchronous | 100.7 min | 24 days |
| QUICKBIRD | 2000 | MSS/panchromatic | 470 km | | Not sun synchronous | | Less than 5 days |
| SPOT 1 | 02/22/86 | MSS/panchromatic | 830 km | 60–120 km | Near polar; sun synchronous | 101 min | 26 days |
| SPOT 2 | 01/21/90 | MSS/Panchromatic | 830 km | 60–120 km | Near polar; sun synchronous | 101 min | 26 days (4–5 days possible) |
| SPOT 4 | 03/24/98 | MSS/Panchromatic | 822 km | 60–120 km | Near polar; sun synchronous | 101 min | 26 days (4–5 days possible) |
| SPOT 5 | 2001 | | | | | | |
| TERRA (EOS-1)[c] | 12/18/99 | MODIS ASTER[d] | 705 km | 2,100 km | Near polar; sun synchronous | 96.5 min | 16 days |

[a]Many space agencies have planned additional (improved) satellite launches throughout the new millennium's first decade.
[b]Sun synchronous orbits permit the satellite to visit each part of the earth at the same local time each day, thus ensuring constant sun position and illumination.
[c]EOS (earth observing system) is a series of small to intermediate size spacecraft that is the centerpiece of NASA's Earth Science Enterprise program.
[d]MODIS 36 channel, 250 m to 1 km resolution; used to study land, ocean, and cloud properties.
ASTER: 3 scanners covering the visible and IR bands with 15 m to 90 m resolution; used to study rock and vegetation and to produce DEMs.

- Pavement.
- Bare ground.
- Residential.
- Commercial.
- Industrial.
- Grass.
- Tree stands.
- Transportation corridors.

## 12.7 Feature Extraction

Feature extraction (image interpretation) can be accomplished using manual methods or automated methods. When using automated methods, which employ computer algorithms to classify images in relation to surface features, four techniques are presently in use.

- Unsupervised: this technique relies on color and tone as well as statistical clustering to identify features.
- Supervised: this technique requires comparative examples of imaging for each ground feature category.
- Hybrid: this technique is a combination of the first two.
- Classification and regression tree (CART): this technique uses binary partitioning software to analyze and arrive eventually at a best estimate about the ground feature identification.

## 12.8 Ground-Truth or Accuracy Assessment

How do we know if the sophisticated image analysis techniques in use are giving us accurate identifications? We have to establish a level of reliability to give credibility to the interpretation process. With aerial photo interpretation, we begin with a somewhat intuitive visual model of the ground feature; with satellite imagery, we begin with pixels identified by their gray-scale digital number (DN)—characteristics that are not intuitive.

What we need is a process whereby we can determine the accuracy and reliability of interpretation results. In addition to providing reliability, such a process will enable the operator to correct errors, and to compare the successes of the various types of feature extraction that may have been used in the project. This process will also be invaluable in the calibration of imaging sensors.

Ground-truth or accuracy assessment can be accomplished by comparing the automated feature extraction identifications with feature identifications given by other methods for a given sample size. Alternative interpretation or extraction techniques may include air photo interpretation, analyses of existing thematic maps of the same area, and fieldwork involving same-area ground sampling.

Since it is not practical to check the accuracy of each pixel identification, a representative sample is chosen for accuracy assessment. The sample is representative with respect

Reference Data (Sampling Data)

| Diagonal | Water | Agricultural | Urban | Row Totals |
|---|---|---|---|---|
| Water | 17 Correct | 5 | 1 | 23 |
| Agricultural | 10 | 22 Correct | 10 | 42 |
| Urban | 2 | 5 | 28 Correct | 35 |
| Column Total | 29 | 32 | 39 | 100 |

*Interpreted Data*

**FIGURE 12.7** Error matrix example.

to both the size and locale of the sampled geographic area. Factors to be considered when defining the sample include the following:

- Is the land privately owned and/or restricted to access?
- How will the data be collected?
- How much money can you afford to dedicate to this process?
- Which geographic areas should be sampled—areas that consist of homogeneous features together with areas consisting of a wide mix of features, even overlapping features?
- How can the randomness of the sample points be assured, given practical constraints (for example, restricted access to specified ground areas, lack of current air photos and thematic maps, etc.)?
- If verification data is to be taken from existing maps and plans, what effect will their dates of data collection have on the analysis (the more current the data, the better the correlation)?

The answers to many of the above questions come only with experience. Much of this type of work is based on trial and error decisions. For example, when the results of small samples compare favorably with the results of large samples, it may be assumed that, given similar conditions, such small samples may be appropriate in subsequent investigations. On the other hand, if large samples give significantly different (better) results than do small sample sizes, it may be assumed that such small sample sizes should not be used again under similar circumstances.

Figure 12.7 shows an error matrix consisting of ground point identifications that have been extracted using automated techniques and ground point identifications determined using other techniques (including field sampling). With the example shown here, 17 out of 23 sampling sites for "water" were verified, 22 out of 42 sampling sites for "agri-cultural" were verified, and 28 out of 35 sampling points for "urban" were verified. These verified points, shown along the diagonal, total 67 out of a total of 100; that is, the verified accuracy was, 67% in this example.

Is accuracy of 67% acceptable? The answer depends on the intended use of the data and, once again, experience is the determining factor. You may decide that this method of data collection (for example, satellite imagery) is inappropriate because it is not accurate enough or it is too expensive for the intended purposes of the project. On the other hand, 67% accuracy may be more than enough for the types of analyses to be made using the presented data.

## 12.9  Remote-Sensing Satellites

### 12.9.1  Landsat 7 Satellite

Landsat 7 was launched April 15, 1999, from Vandenburg Air Force Base, in California, on a Delta-11 launch vehicle. The spacecraft weighs 4,800 lbs, measures about 14 ft long by 9 ft in diameter, and flies at an altitude of 705 km. Landsat 7 employs an extended thematic mapper (ETM+ is a scan mirror spectrometer), an eight-band multispectral scanner capa-ble of providing high-resolution image information of the earth's surface as it collects 7 bands or channels of reflected energy and one band of emitted energy. Its panchromatic band (0.52–0.90 μm) has a resolution of 15 m (see Table 12.3). The Landsat program was designed to monitor seasonal small-scale processes on a global scale, for example, cycles of vegetation growth, deforestation, agricultural land use, erosion, etc.

Another NASA satellite, the experimental TERRA (EO-1), launched December 18, 1999, employs a push-broom spectrometer/radiometer—Advanced Land Imager (ALI)—with many more spectral ranges (hyperspectral scanning) and flies the same orbits with the same altitude as does Landsat 7. It is designed to sample similar surface features at roughly the same time (only minutes apart) for comparative analysis. TERRA's panchromatic band (0.48–0.68 μm) has a resolution of 10 m. This is an experimental satellite designed to obtain much more data at reduced cost and will influence the design of the next stage (2000–2015) of U.S. exploration satellites.

### 12.9.2  Other Multispectral Scanning Satellites

Since the 1960s, there have been more than 100 satellites launched by the scientific and intel-ligence agencies of many of the earth's leading countries—the United States, France, Russia, China, India, Japan, Europe, Canada, Australia, Israel, and Brazil. By 2000, there were twelve satellites similar to Landsat 7, they include the French SPOT satellites, (SPOT 4, 1997) India's IRS satellites (IRS-1 C, 1995; IRS-1 D, 1997; IRS-P5, 1998; and IRS-2A, 1999); the Chinese and Brazilian satellites (CBERS 1, 1998, CBERS 2, 1999); the U.S./Japanese satel-lite (EOS AM-1, 1998), and the U.S. commercial resource 21 satellites (R-21, A–D). By 2010, it is anticipated that there will be dozens more orbiting satellites with ever improving spatial and radiometric resolutions. See Table 12.4 for a selected summary of current satellites.

### 12.9.3 High-Resolution Satellites

In the late 1990s, several high-resolution satellites were launched by commercial and intelligence agencies. These satellites, which have resolutions as fine as 1 m, include IKONOS-2, Quickbird, OrbImage (all from the United States), EROS A and B (from Israel and the United States), and IRS-P6 (from India). The IKONOS satellite provides 1-m resolution in panchromatic (black and white) and 4-m resolution for multispectral (true color and infrared) images.

### 12.9.4 Hyperspectral Satellites

Hyperspectral scanners can have sensors that detect over a spectral range of 32 to 256 bands, and beyond. Hyperspectral satellites from the United States include TRW Lewis, 1997; EO-1, 1999; and HRST, 2000. Another hyperspectral satellite, from Australia, is ARIES, 2000.

## 12.10  Imaging Radar Satellites

Radar (radio detection and ranging) instruments are active scanners that operate in the 1-cm to 1-m microwave range of the electromagnetic spectrum. Because microwaves have a longer wavelength, they are not as prone to scattering as they travel through the atmosphere. Radar waves can penetrate clouds, haze, dust, and all but the heaviest of rainfalls, depending on the channels used. Unlike the passive spectral scanners that record reflected and emitted signals, imaging Radar records the signals that are sent from the satellite and then returned (bounced or echoed) from the surface of the earth back to the satellite. As satellites orbit the earth, half the mission is flown in sunlight and the other half in darkness. Passive sensors rely on sunlight for their reflected signals and thus collect only those data on the bright side of the orbit. Radar satellites can record reflected data throughout the entire orbit (ascending or descending).

Unlike aerial photography and most other remote-sensing techniques, synthetic aperture radar (SAR) can scan an area below and off to the side of the aircraft or space vehicle. As you can see in Figures 12.8, 12.9, and 12.10, the scanned swath is some distance off to the side of the nadir track, which itself is directly below the vehicle flight track. Synthetic aperture radar (SAR) is a high-resolution, ground-mapping technique that effectively synthesizes a large receiving antenna by processing the phase of the reflected radar return. Radar beamwidth is inversely proportional to the antenna length (also referred to as the aperture), which means that a longer antenna (or aperture) will produce a narrower beam and a finer resolution. Since there is a limit to the size of the antenna that can be carried on aircraft or spacecraft, the forward motion of the craft and the sophisticated processing of backscatter echos are used to simulate or synthesize a very long antenna and thus increase azimuth resolution.

Radar imaging resolution depends on the effective length of the pulse in the slant (across-track) direction and on the width of the beam in the azimuth (along-track) direction. In Figure 12.8, you can see that the length of the pulse, in the slant direction, determines which objects can be "seen." For example, when two objects are closer together than half the length of the pulse (P/2)—see targets 1 and 2 in (Figure 12.10)—they cannot be

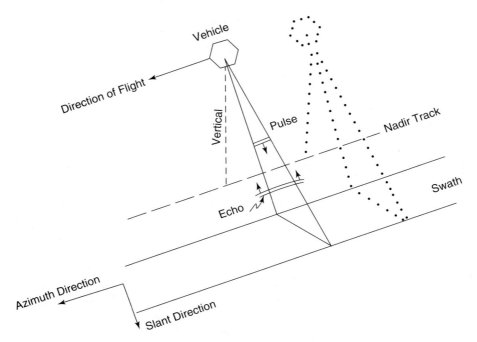

**FIGURE 12.8** Imaging radar geometry: swath track.

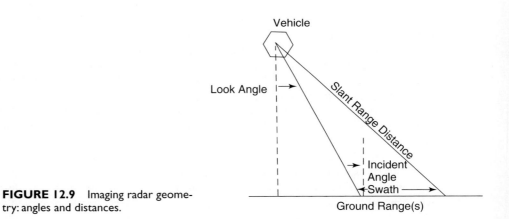

**FIGURE 12.9** Imaging radar geometry: angles and distances.

separated, but when the targets are farther apart than half the pulse length, they are separable (targets 3 and 4). The beamwidth (a measure of the illumination pattern) itself must also be considered, as well as the fact that as the slant range increases, the beamwidth increases—thus decreasing resolution. In Figure 12.10, targets 1 and 2 (in the near range) are separable, while targets 3 and 4 (at a farther range) are not.

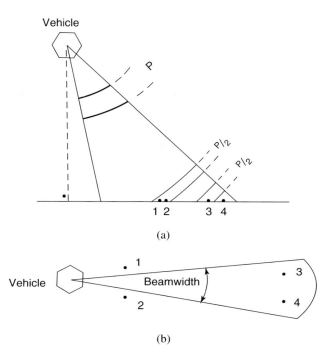

**FIGURE 12.10** Radar imagery resolution factors. (a) Range, or across-track resolution. (b) Azimuth, or along-track resolution.

Interest in radar imaging grew when it became clear that, even with the successes of the early Landsat satellites, many regions of the earth remained almost continuously under cloud cover and thus hidden from view. Polar regions too were almost beyond the capability of existing MSS-type satellites because of extended periods of darkness. Radar became a way of obtaining constant data for polar regions for climate studies and navigation. Radar also provides a unique look at the earth's surface that complements reflected data and adds a great deal to the store of knowledge about the earth's surface.

Satellite radar imaging began in 1978 with the launch of the U.S. SEASAT (L-band). By the 1990s, Japan, the USSR (as it was called then), Europe, and Canada have entered this area of exploration. Several enterprises are also involved in aircraft SAR systems that operate in the C, L, P, and X bands and cover much smaller swaths, for example, 3 to 60 km (slant distance). See Table 12.5. Resolution of radar imaging ranges from submeter for defense satellites to 10–30 m for most civilian satellites.

## 12.10.1 RADARSAT-1

RADARSAT-1 is the first of a series of SAR satellites planned by the Canadian Space Agency (CSA). (RADARSAT-2 has a launch date in 2003.) This satellite was launched by NASA at Vandenburg Air Force Base in November 1995. RADARSAT is a right-looking (facing east during the ascending orbit and west during the descending orbit) radar satellite that flies at an altitude of 798 km, with an orbit period of 100.7 minutes and a revisit period of 24 days. Since the sensor can be redirected by ground commands, swath widths and

**Table 12.5** MICROWAVE BANDS[a]

| Wavelength | Band |
|---|---|
| 0.1 cm–2.4 cm | Ka band, Ku band, K Band: shortwave bands, used in early airborne radar, uncommon today. |
| 2.4 cm–3.75 cm | X-band: used extensively for military airborne and terrain mapping. |
| 3.75 cm–7.5 cm | C-band, common on many airborne systems; ERS 1, 2 (5.7); RADARSAT (5.7); NASA (various). |
| 7.5 cm–15 cm | S-band: used on Russian satellite (10). |
| 15 cm–30 cm | L-band: used on U.S. SEASAT (23.5), Japan's JERS (23.5), and NASA satellites. |
| 30 cm–100 cm | P-band: longest radar wavelengths; used on NASA experimental systems. |

[a]Numbers in parentheses refer to the specific wavelength (cm) used within a band category.

look angles can be adjusted so that the revisit period can be reduced to just 3–6 days for specific geographic regions, depending on the latitude. RADARSAT instrumentation permits a choice of three transmit pulses and a selection of beams for a wide range of swath widths, incident angles, and image resolutions (see Figure 12.11).

## 12.10.2   Space Shuttle Endeavor

In February 2000, NASA launched the Endeavor, whose shuttle radar topography mission (SRTM) was to map the earth using the C band (225-km swath) and the X band (56-km swath) of imaging radar. In just eleven days, the Endeavor captured images of almost the entire earth (56°S to 60°N latitudes) in 1 trillion measurements. Traveling at 7.7 km per second, it mapped an area equivalent in size to the state of Florida every 97.5 seconds. The mission lasted ten days and used a deployed mast of 200 ft in length with two separated antennas mounted on the mast. Resolution of the imaging is 20 m. NASA plans to publish maps of the earth based on this mission by 2003. Many of the SRTM images are available free on the Internet.

## 12.11   Satellite Imagery Versus Airborne Imagery

Prior to 2000, the chief differences between aerial imagery and satellite imagery were characterized by scale and by the additional data that could be gathered using spectral scanning from satellite platforms. Now that spectral scanning is available for both airborne and satellite platforms, the chief difference (all other things being equal) is now one of scale. As the resolution of satellite images improves (NASA predicts image resolutions of 0.5 m by 2005), many of the differences between airborne imagery and satellite imagery will disappear.

Figures 12.12 and 12.13 show the types of images generally available using either method of remote sensing. Both images show part of the Niagara frontier. The satellite image (Figure 12.12) shows the Niagara peninsula and northwestern New York state, whereas the aerial image (Figure 12.13—an aerial photograph) shows, in much greater detail, a small part of the area shown in the satellite image: the mouth of the Niagara River (the river flows north into Lake Ontario) and the towns of Youngstown, New York, and

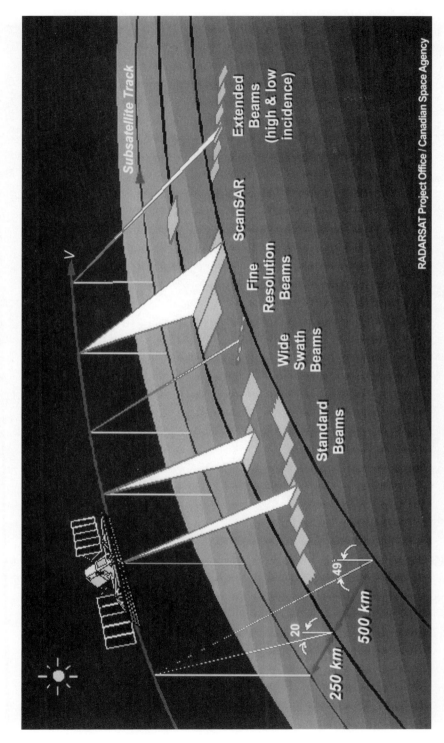

**FIGURE 12.11** RADARSAT operating modes. (Image provided by the Canadian Space Agency [CSA].)

441

**FIGURE 12.12**   Landsat image showing western New York and the Niagara region. (Courtesy of U.S. Geological Survey, Sioux Falls, S.Dak.)

**FIGURE 12.13** Aerial photograph, at 20,000 ft, showing the mouth of the Niagara River. (Courtesy of U.S. Geological Survey, Sioux Falls, S.Dak.)

Niagara-on-the-Lake, Ontario. See also Figure F.1 for a comparison of the level of detail provided by ground techniques versus aerial and satellite techniques.

## 12.B Airborne Imagery

## 12.12 General Background

Airborne imagery introduces the topics of aerial photography and the more recent (2000) topic of airborne digital imagery. Aerial photography has a history dating back to the mid-1800s, when balloons and even kites were used as camera platforms from which photos could be taken. About fifty years later, in 1908, photographs were taken from early aircraft. During World Wars I and II, the use of aerial photography mushroomed in the support of military reconnaissance. Aerial photography became (from the 1930s to the present) an accepted technique for collecting mapping and other ground data in North America.

This chapter deals with the utilization of aerial imagery in the acquisition of planimetric and elevation ground data. Most airborne imagery is still collected using aerial photographs, although it has been predicted that in the future, much of data capture and analysis will be accomplished using digital imagery techniques described in Section 12.2.2.

Under the proper conditions, the cost savings for survey projects using aerial surveys rather than ground surveys can be enormous. Consequently, it is critical that the surveyor be capable of identifying the situations in which the use of aerial imagery may be beneficial. First, we discuss the basic principles required to use aerial photographs intelligently, the terminology involved, the limitations of their use, and specific applications to various projects.

*Photogrammetry* is the science of making measurements from aerial photographs. Measurements of horizontal distances and elevations form the backbone of this science. These capabilities result in the compilation of planimetric maps or orthophoto maps showing the horizontal locations of both natural and cultural features, and topographic maps showing spot elevations and contour lines. Both black and white panchromatic and color film are used in aerial photography. Color film has three emulsions—blue, green, and red light sensitive. In color infrared (IR), the three emulsion layers are sensitive to green, red, and the photographic portion of near IR, which are processed, in false color, to appear as blue, green, and red, respectively.

## 12.13 Aerial Camera Systems

### 12.13.1 General Background

The recent introduction of digital cameras has revolutionized photography. Digital and film-based cameras both use optical lenses. Whereas film-based cameras use photographic film to record an image, digital cameras record image data with electronic sensors: charge-coupled devices (CCDs) or complementary metal-oxide-semiconductor (CMOS) devices. One chief advantage to digital cameras is that the image data can be stored, transmitted, and analyzed electronically. Cameras on board satellites can capture photographic data and then have this data, along with other sensed data, transmitted back to earth for further electronic processing.

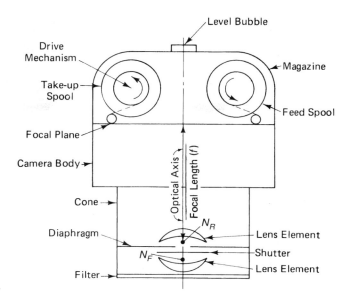

**FIGURE 12.14** Components of aerial survey camera (large format).

Although airborne digital imagery is already making a significant impact in the remote-sensing field, we will first discuss film-based photography, a technology that still accounts for the majority of aerial imaging. The 9 in. by 9 in. format used for most film-based photographic cameras captures a wealth of topographic detail, and the photos, or the film itself, can be scanned efficiently (see Figure 12.25), thus preparing the image data for electronic processing.

Two main types of camera systems are commonly used for acquiring aerial photographs. The first is the single camera illustrated in Figure 12.14, which uses a fixed focal length, large-format negative, usually 9 in. (230 mm) by 9 in. (230 mm). This camera is used strictly for aerial photography and is equipped with a highly corrected lens and vacuum pressure against the film to minimize distortion. This sophisticated system is required to obtain aerial photographs for photogrammetric purposes due to the stringent accuracy requirements. The second camera system consists of one or more cameras using a smaller photographic format (negative size), such as the common 35 mm used for ground photographs. These smaller-format systems do not have the high-quality lens that is required to meet the normal measurement accuracies for the production of standard maps using photogrammetry. Smaller-format camera systems are very useful and inexpensive for updating land-use changes and for the acquisition of special types of photography to enhance particular terrain aspects, such as vegetative health and algae blooms on lakes.

## 12.13.2 Large-Format Aerial Camera

The aerial camera illustrated in Figure 12.14 is distinguished by the complexity and accuracy of its lens assembly. Although the lens is shown in simplified form in Figure 12.14, it is actually composed of several elements involving different types of glass with different optical characteristics. This setup is necessary to satisfy the requirements of high resolution and minimal distortion of the image created on the film by the passage of the light rays

**FIGURE 12.15** Comparison of large-format aerial camera lens and 35-mm camera lens. (Courtesy of Leica Canada.)

through the lens. The quality of the lens is the most important consideration and hence represents the greatest cost factor for this type of camera. The complexity and size of the lens are illustrated by the comparison of this lens with the 35-mm camera lens in Figure 12.15.

The drive mechanism is housed in the camera body, as shown in Figure 12.14. This mechanism is motor driven, and the time between exposures to achieve the required overlap is set based on the photographic scale and the ground speed of the aircraft. The film is thus advanced from the feed spool to the take-up spool at automatic intervals. The focal plane is equipped with a vacuum device to hold the film flat at the instant of exposure. The camera also has four fiducial marks built in so that each exposure can be oriented properly to the camera calibration. Most cameras also record the frame number, time of exposure, and height of the aircraft on each exposure. This is necessary to achieve sharp focusing. The lower air pressures outside the aircraft tend to pull the film away from the focal plane toward the lens, resulting in incorrect focusing.

The camera mount permits flexible movement of the camera for leveling purposes. The operator uses the level bubble mounted on the top of the camera body as the indicator, and every attempt is made to have the camera as level as possible at the instant of exposure. This requires constant attention by the operator because the aircraft is subject to pitching and rolling, resulting in a tilt when the photographs are taken. The viewfinder is mounted vertically to show the area being photographed at any time.

Two points, $N_F$ and $N_R$, are shown on the optical axis in Figure 12.14. These are the front and rear nodal points of the lens system, respectively. When light rays strike the front nodal point ($N_F$), they are refracted by the lens so that they emerge from the rear nodal point ($N_R$) parallel with their original direction. The focal length ($f$) of the lens is the distance between the rear nodal point and the focal plane along the optical axis, as shown in Figure 12.14. The value of the focal length is determined accurately through calibration for each camera. The most common focal length for aerial cameras is 6 in. (152 mm).

Because atmospheric haze contains an excessive amount of blue light, a filter is used in front of the lens to absorb some of the blue light, thus reducing the haze on the actual photograph. A yellow, orange, or red filter is used, depending on atmospheric conditions and the flying height of the aircraft above mean ground level. The shutter of a modern aerial camera is capable of speeds ranging from 1/50 s to 1/2,000 s. The range is commonly between 1/100 s and 1/1,000 s. A fast shutter speed minimizes blurring of the photograph, known as image motion, which is caused by the ground speed of the aircraft.

## 12.14 Photographic Scale

The scale of a photograph is the ratio between a distance measured on the photograph and the ground distance between the same two points. The features, both natural and cultural, shown on a photograph are similar to those on a planimetric map, but with one important difference. The planimetric map has been rectified through ground control, so that the horizontal scale is consistent among any points on the map. The air photo will contain scale variations unless the camera was perfectly level at the instant of exposure and the terrain being photographed was also level. Because the aircraft is subject to tip, tilt, and changes in altitude due to updrafts and downdrafts, the chances of the focal plane being level at the instant of exposure are minimal. In addition, the terrain is seldom flat. As illustrated in Figure 12.16, any change in elevation will cause scale variations. The basic problem is transferring an uneven surface like the ground to the flat focal plane of the camera.

In Figure 12.16(a), points $A$, $O$, and $B$ are at the same elevation and the focal plane is level. Therefore, all scales are true on the photograph because the distance $AO = A'O'$ and $OB = O'B'$. $A$, $O$, and $B$ are points on a level reference datum that would be comparable to the surface of a planimetric map. Therefore, under these unusual circumstances, the scale of the photograph is uniform because the ratio $ao{:}AO$ is the same as the ratio $ob{:}OB$.

Figure 12.16(b) illustrates a more realistic situation: the focal plane is tilted and the topographic relief is variable. Points $A$, $B$, $O$, $D$, $E$, and $F$ are at different elevations. You can see visually that, although $A'B'$ equals $B'O'$, the ratio $ab{:}bo$ is far from equal. Therefore, the photographic scale for points between $a$ and $b$ will be significantly different than that for points between $b$ and $o$. The same variations in scale can also be seen for the points between $d$ and $e$ and between $e$ and $f$.

The overall average scale of the photograph is based partially on the elevations of the mean datum shown in Figure 12.16(b). The mean datum elevation is intended to be the average ground elevation. This is determined by examining the most accurate available contour maps of the area and selecting the apparent average elevation. Distances between points on the photograph that are situated at the elevations of the mean datum will be at the intended scale. Distances between points having elevations above or below the mean datum will be at a different photographic scale, depending on the magnitude of the local relief.

The scale of a vertical photograph can be calculated from the focal length of the camera and the flying height above the mean datum. Note that the flying height and the altitude are different elevations having the following relationships:

$$\text{Altitude} = \text{flying height} + \text{mean datum}$$

By similar triangles, as shown in Figure 12.16(a):

$$\frac{ao}{AO} = \frac{Co}{CO} = \frac{f}{h}$$

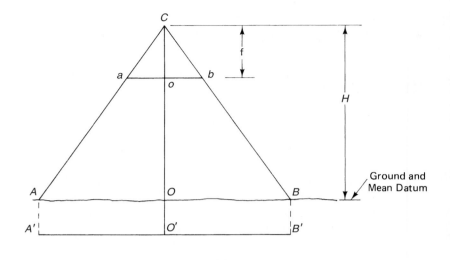

(a)

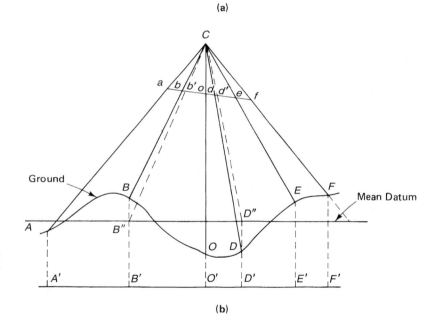

**FIGURE 12.16**
Scale differences caused by tilt and topography. (a) Level focal plane and level ground. (b) Tilted focal plane and hilly topography.

(b)

where $AO/ao$ = the scale ratio between the ground and the photograph

$f$ = the focal length

$H$ = the flying height above the mean datum

Therefore, the scale ratio is:

$$SR = \frac{H}{f} \qquad (12.3)$$

For example, if $H = 1,500$ m and $f = 150$ mm:

$$SR = 1,500/0.150 = 10,000$$

Therefore, the average scale of the photograph is 1:10,000. In the foot system, the scale would be stated as 1 in. = 10,000/12, or 1 in. = 833 ft. The conversion factor of 12 is required to convert both sides of the equation to the same unit.

## 12.15   Flying Heights and Altitude

When planning an air photo acquisition mission, the flying height and altitude must be determined. This is particularly true if the surveyor is acquiring supplementary aerial photography using a small-format camera.

The flying height is determined using the same relationships discussed in Section 12.14 and illustrated in Figure 12.15, and using the relationship in Equation 12.3, $H = SR \times f$.

■ **EXAMPLE 12.1**
If the desired scale ratio ($SR$) is 1:10,000 and the focal length of the lens ($f$) is 150 mm, then $H = 10,000 \times 0.150 = 1,500$ m ($\pm 4,920$ ft).

■ **EXAMPLE 12.2**
If the desired scale ratio ($SR$) is 1:5,000 and the focal length of the lens is 50 mm, then $H = 5,000 \times 0.050 = 250$ m ($\pm 820$ ft).

The flying heights calculated in Examples 12.1 and 12.2 are the vertical distances that the aircraft must fly above the mean datum, illustrated in Figure 12.16. Therefore, the altitude at which the plane must fly is calculated by adding the elevation of the mean datum to the flying height. If the elevation of the mean datum had been 330 ft (100 m), the altitudes for Examples 12.1 and 12.2 would be 1,600 m ($\pm 5,250$ ft) and 350 m ($\pm 1,150$ ft), respectively. These are the readings for the aircraft altimeter throughout the flight to achieve the desired average photographic scale.

If the scale of existing photographs is unknown, it can be determined by comparing a distance measured on the photograph with the corresponding distance measured on the ground or on a map of known scale. The points used for this comparison must be easily identifiable on both the photograph and the map, such as road intersections, building corners, and river or stream intersections. The photographic scale is found using the following relationship:

$$\frac{\text{photo scale}}{\text{map scale}} = \frac{\text{photo distance}}{\text{map distance}}$$

Because this relationship is based on ratios, the scales on the left side must be expressed in the same units. The same applies to the measured distances on the right side of the equation. For example, if the distance between two identifiable points on the photograph is

5.75 in. (14.38 cm) and on the map it is 1.42 in. (3.55 cm), and the map scale is 1:50,000, the photo scale is:

$$\frac{\text{photo scale}}{1:50,000} = \frac{5.75 \text{ in.}}{1.42 \text{ in.}}$$

$$\text{photo scale} = \frac{5.75}{50,000 \times 1.42}$$

$$= 1:12,349$$

If the scale is required in inches and feet, it is calculated by dividing the 12,349 by 12 (number of inches per foot), which yields 1,029. Therefore, the photo scale is 1 in. = 1,029 ft between these points only. The scale will be different in areas that have different ground elevations.

## 12.16   Relief (Radial) Displacement

Relief displacement occurs when the point being photographed is not at the elevation of the mean datum. As previously explained, and as illustrated in Figure 12.16(a), when all ground points are at the same elevation, no relief displacement occurs. However, the displacement of point $b$ on the focal plane (photograph) in Figure 12.16(b) is illustrated. Because point $B$ is above the mean datum, it appears at point $b$ on the photograph rather than at point $b'$, the location on the photograph for point $B'$, which is on the mean datum.

Fiducial marks are placed precisely on the camera back plate so that they reproduce in exactly the same position on each air photo negative. These marks are located either in the corners, as illustrated in Figure 12.17, or in the middle of each side, as illustrated in Figure 12.21. Their primary function is the location of the principal point, which is located at the intersection of straight lines drawn between each set of opposite fiducial marks, as illustrated in Figure 12.21.

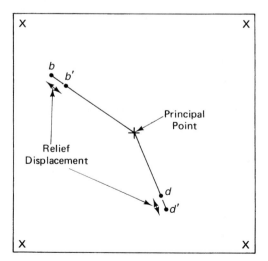

**FIGURE 12.17**   Direction of relief displacement (compare with Figure 12.16(b); X denotes fiducial marks.

Relief displacement depends on the position of the point on the photograph and the elevation of the ground point above or below the mean datum. Note the following in Figure 12.16(b):

- The displacement at the center, or principal point, represented by $O$ on the photograph, is zero.
- The farther that the ground point is located from the principal point, the greater is the relief displacement. The displacement $dd'$ is less than $bb'$, even though the ground point $D$ is farther below the mean datum than point $B$ is above it.
- The greater the elevation of the ground point above or below the mean datum, the greater is the displacement. If the ground elevation of point $B$ were increased so that it was farther above the mean datum, the displacement $bb'$ would increase correspondingly.

Relief displacement is radial to the principal point of the photograph, as illustrated in Figure 12.17. The direction of the relief distortion on the photograph is shown for photo points $b$ and $d$ in Figure 12.16(b).

The practical aspects of relief displacement relate primarily to the proper horizontal location of all points and secondarily to the assemblage of mosaics. A mosaic is a series of overlapping aerial photographs that form one continuous picture (see Section 12.19). This technique involves matching the terrain features on adjacent photographs as closely as possible. Because the relief displacement of the same ground point will vary substantially—both in direction and magnitude—for the reasons discussed previously, this presents a real difficulty in matching identical features on adjacent photographs when assembling a mosaic. A partial solution to this problem involves using only the central portion of each photograph in assembling the mosaic because relief displacement is greatest near the photograph edges.

## 12.17 Flight Lines and Photograph Overlap

It is important to understand the techniques by which aerial photographs are taken. Once the photograph scale, flying height, and altitude have been calculated, the details of implementing the mission are carefully planned. Although the planning process is beyond the scope of this text, the most significant factors include the following:

- A suitable aircraft and technical personnel must be arranged, including their availability if the time period for acquiring the photography is critical to the project. The costs of having the aircraft and personnel available, known as mobilization, are extremely high.
- The study area must be outlined carefully and the means of navigating the aircraft along each flight line, using either ground features or magnetic bearings, must be determined. GPS is used more often now in aircraft to maintain proper flight line alignment.
- The photographs must be taken under cloudless skies. The presence of high clouds above the aircraft altitude is unacceptable because of the shadows they cast on the

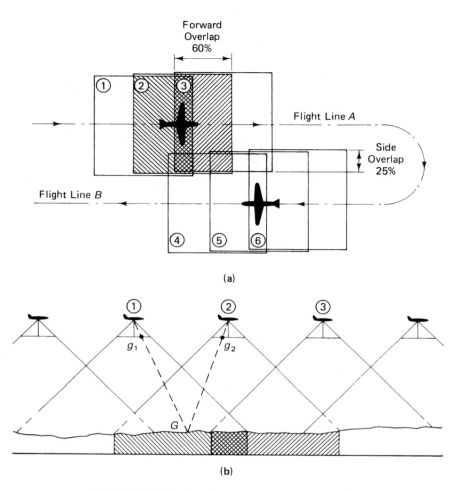

**FIGURE 12.18** Flight lines and photograph overlap. (a) Photographic overlap. (b) Overlap along flight line.

ground. Therefore, the aircraft personnel are often required to wait for suitable weather conditions. This downtime can be very expensive. Most aerial photographs are taken between 10 A.M. and 2 P.M. to minimize the effect of long shadows obscuring terrain features. Consequently, the weather has to be suitable at the right time.

To achieve photogrammetric mapping and to examine the terrain for air photo interpretation purposes, it is essential that each point on the ground appear in two adjacent photographs along a flight line so that all points can be viewed stereoscopically. Figure 12.18 illustrates the relative locations of flight lines and photograph overlaps, both along the flight line and between adjacent flight lines. An area over which it has been decided to acquire air photo coverage is called a block. The block is outlined on the most accurate available topographic map. The locations of the flight lines required to cover the area properly are then plotted, such as flight lines *A* and *B* in Figure 12.18(a). The aircraft proceeds along flight line *A*, and air photos are taken at time intervals calculated to provide 60% forward overlap between adjacent photographs. As illustrated in Figure 12.18(a), the format of each photograph is square. Therefore, the hatched area represents the forward overlap between air photos 2 and 3 in flight line *A*. The minimum overlap to ensure that all ground points show on two adjacent photographs is 50%. However, at least 60% forward overlap is standard because the aircraft is subject to altitude variations, tip, and tilt as the flight proceeds. The extra 10% forward overlap allows for these contingencies. The air photo coverage of flight line *B* overlaps that of *A* by 25%, as illustrated in Figure 12.18(a). This ensures that the photographs will not have gaps of unphotographed ground, and it also extends control between flight lines for photogrammetric methods, often called sidelap.

The flight line is illustrated in Figure 12.18(b) in profile view. The single-hatched areas represent the forward overlap between air photos 1 and 2 and photos 2 and 3. Due to the forward overlap of 60%, the ground points in the double-hatched area will appear on each of the three photographs, thus permitting full photogrammetric treatment. (See also Section 12.22, where the airborne digital sensor records ground point in three separate images.)

The problems of mosaic assemblage caused by relief displacement (discussed in Section 12.16) are solved partially by increasing the forward overlap to as high as 80%. Although this results in roughly twice the total number of air photos at a similar scale, a smaller portion of the central portion of each photo, which is least affected by relief displacement, can be used to assemble the mosaic. Consequently, the surveyor should consider increasing the forward overlap in areas of high topographic relief or performing mosaic assemblage using orthophotos (Section 12.22).

The number of air photos required to cover a block or study area is a very important consideration. Keep in mind that each air photo has to be cataloged and stored, or scanned into a digital file. Most important, these photographs have to be used individually and collectively and/or examined for photogrammetric mapping and/or air photo interpretation purposes. All other factors being equal, such as focal length and format size, the photographic scale is the controlling factor regarding the number of air photos required. The approximate number of air photos required to cover a given area stereoscopically (every ground point is shown on at least two adjacent photos along the flight line) can be calculated easily. The basic relationships required for this computation are set out next for a forward overlap of 60% and a side overlap of 25%.

For a photographic scale of 1:10,000, the area covered by one photograph, accounting for loss of effective area through overlaps, is 0.4 square miles, or 1 $km^2$. Therefore, the number of air photos required to cover a 200-square-mile (500-$km^2$) area is 200/0.4 = 500, or 500/1 = 500.

The approximate number of photographs varies as the **square** of the photographic scale. For example, if the scale is 1:5,000 versus 1:10,000 in Figure 12.18, the aircraft would be flying at one-half the altitude. Consequently, the ground area covered by each air photo would be reduced in half in **both** directions. Twice the number of air photos would be required along each flight line and the number of flight lines required to cover the same area would be doubled. The following examples illustrate the effect on the total number of air photos required, based on the coverage required for a 200-square-mile (500-km$^2$) area.

1. For a scale of 1:5,000, the number of photographs is $500 \times (10,000/5,000)^2 = 2,000$.
2. For a scale of 1:2,000, the number of photographs is $500 \times (10,000/2,000)^2 = 12,500$.
3. For a scale of 1:20,000, the number of photographs is $500 \times (10,000/20,000)^2 = 125$.

Thus, you can see that the proper selection of scale for mapping or the air photo interpretation purposes intended is critical. The scale requirements for photogrammetric mapping depend on the accuracies of the analytical equipment to be used in producing the planimetric maps. For general air photo interpretation purposes, including survey boundary line evidence (cut lines, land-use changes), photographic scales of between 1:10,000 and 1:20,000 are optimal.

## 12.18   Ground Control for Mapping

As stated previously, the aerial photograph is not perfectly level at the instant of exposure and the ground surface is seldom flat. As a result, ground control points are required to manipulate the air photos physically or mathematically before mapping can be done. Two situations require ground control. One involves the establishment of control points where **existing** photography is to be used for the mapping. The other requires the establishment of ground control points **prior** to the acquisition of the air photos. Although the principles for both are similar, each technique is described below.

Ground control is required for each data point positioning. The accuracy with which the measurements must be made varies in each case, depending on the following final product requirements:

- Measurements of distances and elevations, such as building dimensions, highway or road locations, and cross-sectional information for quantity payments for cut and fill in construction projects.
- Preparation of topographic maps, usually including contour lines at a fixed interval.
- Construction of controlled mosaics.
- Construction of orthophotos and rectified photographs (see Section 12.22).

Acquisition of ground control data can be a costly aspect of map preparation using air photos. The surveyor should therefore give considerable thought and planning to every detail of ground control requirements.

Recent advances in kinematic GPS techniques have resulted in the development of GPS receivers, which are designed both to compute position and to control the rate of photographic exposures. Two or more receivers, both on the ground (base station) and on the aircraft, can locate each photo precisely with respect to the ground, and onboard inertial measuring units (IMUs) can assist in the determination of altitude variations, tip, and tilt for each exposure, thus greatly reducing processing needs. (See also Section 12.22.)

## 12.18.1  Existing Photographs

When mapping of an area is required and air photos with a suitable scale are available, by far the most economical procedure involves using the existing photographs. The minimum ground control for one pair of overlapping air photos is three points. Because leveling of the stereoscopic model (area within the overlap) is the objective, you can equate the requirements with the minimum number of legs required by an ordinary table to stand by itself. Vertical control (elevations) is required for all three points, and at least one horizontal distance between two points is also required. Normally, because all three control points must be accessed on the ground, the normal procedure involves the acquisition of north and east coordinates as well as the elevation of each point.

The selection of ground control points must be based on the following criteria:

1. The ground control points must be separated in the overlap area. If the points are clearly separated, the model will be more stable and therefore the results will be more accurate. Using the table analogy, the table will be supported better if its legs are near the corners rather than grouped in the center.

2. The control points must be easily identifiable on both adjacent air photos. If the ground control points are not easy to identify, the control point will be useless. Because the photographs are taken at an angle that varies directly with the distance from the principal point or air photo center, features such as trees or shadows from adjacent buildings can obscure the control point on one of the air photos. This difficulty can be identified by closing one eye and then the other while viewing the overlaps stereoscopically. If the potential control point disappears on either photograph, it is not acceptable.

3. Permanent significant changes may have taken place in the overlap area since the existing photographs were taken. The ground points should be selected on the assumption that they will still exist when the ground survey is carried out. Points such as building corners, main road intersections, angles or corners of year-round docking facilities, and fence intersections clear of overhanging trees are suitable. Natural features generally do not provide good control points because they are subject to erosion, landslides, and cultural activities such as timbering. A clearly defined intersection of rock fracture lines would be satisfactory because permanency is almost guaranteed.

4. The surveyor should consider ease of access to all control points to minimize open-ended traverse lines, particularly over heavily wooded terrain with high topographic relief. GPS stations should be in relatively accessible areas, free from obstructions that may block satellite signals.

The selected identifiable points on the photograph are termed either **photo points** or **picture points.** The horizontal control between these points is usually obtained by electronic distance measurement (EDM) between the control points, if clear lines of sight exist, by a closed traverse connecting the points, or by GPS positioning. Vertical control is obtained using GPS positioning trigonometric leveling (total station) or differential leveling. The field method chosen depends on field costs and the required accuracy, which depends on the scale of the map or mosaic and the contour interval to be mapped. While a minimum of three control points is required for controlling a single overlap or "model" between two adjacent photographs, each model along a flight line or within a block does not require three ground control points. This saving in ground surveying is achieved through a process termed **bridging,** which is discussed in Section 12.21.

## 12.18.2 New Photography

While several situations can arise in which new photography is required, the three listed here are common, and assume that a high degree of accuracy is required for the photogrammetric mapping:

1. Areas containing few identifiable ground control points. Because natural features do not make good ground control points (for reasons previously discussed), premarked points, or targets, must be used.
2. Legal surveys of densely developed areas. If the property lines in a municipality require resurveying as a group, considerable savings can be achieved by placing targets over or close to all known boundary corners and subsequently obtaining the horizontal coordinates of each, using photogrammetric methods.
3. Municipal surveys of roads and services. As discussed in Chapter 14, municipalities often require accurate maps showing the location of both aboveground and underground services. Targets are easily set by painting the appropriate symbol on existing roads and/or sidewalks. This ground control network can be surveyed at convenient times of low-traffic volumes. Aerial photography is obtained under low-traffic conditions, and features such as manhole covers, hydro lines, roads, and sidewalks can be recognized on the photographs and mapped accurately.

The targets for each of these surveys must be placed prior to the acquisition of the air photos. This should be done as close to the anticipated flight time as possible, particularly in populated areas. The targets are an attraction of sorts, and people remove them readily for whatever purpose. For example, I performed a property boundary survey for a small town and used photogrammetric methods. A total of 650 targets were placed during the early morning of the day of the flight, which was to be carried out that afternoon. By the time of the flight, however, about 50 targets did not show on the air photos.

The targets come in several shape configurations. For the preceding example, small (1 ft or 0.3 m) square plywood targets were centered over the monuments. In other situations, such as higher-altitude photography, a target in the form of a cross is common. Painted targets on roads and sidewalks for municipal surveys are more flexible with regard to shape. In addition, they cannot be easily removed and are often used for more than one flight.

The photographic tone of the terrain on which the target is placed is a critical consideration. The camera records only **reflected** light. For example, a black or dark gray asphalt highway will commonly appear light gray to white on the photograph because of its smooth reflective surface. Therefore, a white target on what appears to be a dark background will disappear on the air photos. Too much contrast between the target and the background will result in lateral image spread, which is caused by a gradient in the film density from the light object to the dark. This condition is caused primarily by scattering of light in the film emulsion at the edge of the target. The effect of this phenomenon can render the target unidentifiable, at worst, or cause difficulties in locating the center point, at best. The surveyor is well advised to consider the following:

1. Examine previous air photos of the area, usually available from the appropriate government agency or a private aerial survey company, to determine the relative gray tones of various backgrounds, such as asphalt roads, gravel roads, grass, and cultivated fields.

2. Determine the best gray tone of the targets for each type of background to achieve the delicate balance of contrast. For example, a medium to dark gray target on a white background (gravel road) would be logical. Also, a white target on a medium gray background (grass) would be suitable.

3. Bare or recently disturbed soils, a situation created by digging to uncover an existing monument, usually photograph as a light tone, even though they may appear medium to dark gray from ground observation. Therefore, a medium to dark gray target is required for identification on the air photo.

4. Ground control points are normally targeted using a configuration that is different from the property corners for ease of recognition during the photogrammetric mapping process.

Differential GPS techniques are becoming more common; they use GPS ground base stations and GPS receivers mounted in the aircraft. The need for the traditional ground control techniques described here are becoming less significant.

## 12.19 Mosaics

A mosaic is an assembly of two or more air photos to form one continuous picture of the terrain. Mosaics are extremely useful for one or more of the following applications because of the wealth of detail portrayed:

1. Plotting of ground control points at the optimum locations to ensure the required distribution and **strength of figure** (see Section 10.8).

2. A map substitute for field checkpoint locations and approximate locations of natural and cultural features. A mosaic is not an accurate map because of relief displacement (see Section 12.16) and minor variations in scale due to flying height differences during the flight.

3. A medium for presenting ground data. Using standard photographic procedures, a copy negative is produced. It is then common practice to produce a transparency with an air photo background. Economical whiteprints can be produced easily from this transparency, using standard blue or white printing equipment. If the contrast in the air photo background is reduced through a photographic process called screening, sufficient terrain detail will still show on the print. The advantage of screening is that valuable information can be drafted onto the transparency and still be clearly read because it is not obscured by the darker-toned areas of the air photo background.

After photograph film has been processed, each negative of a flight line is numbered consecutively. The flight line number is also shown. Other information that may also be shown is the roll number and the year that the photographs were taken. Because these numbers are always shown in one corner of the photograph prints, it is useful to construct a mosaic by arranging the photographs in order and matching the terrain features shown on each so that all numbered information is visible. These mosaics, termed index mosaics, are useful to determine the photograph numbers required to cover a particular area. These mosaics are often reproduced photographically in a smaller size for ease of storage.

For projects in which having photo numbers on the finished product is not a concern, every second photograph is set out. For example, in Figure 12.18, photos 1 and 3 from flight line *A,* and photos 4 and 6 from flight line *B* would form the mosaic. Photo 2 from flight line *A,* and photo 5 from flight line *B* are then available to permit stereoscopic viewing of the mosaic by simply placing the single photos properly on top of the mosaic. Information can then be transferred directly onto the mosaic during the stereoscopic viewing process.

This type of mosaic and the index mosaic are uncontrolled. The only practical way to adjust the overall mosaic scale involves photographing it and producing a positive print to the desired scale. If the mosaic is constructed using alternative prints and is to be used for stereoscopic viewing (see Section 12.20), the scale **cannot** be adjusted because this will render stereoscopic viewing impossible using the single photos that are not part of the mosaic.

It is often illogical to take the original mosaic to the field for on-site investigations because of possible damage or loss. Instead, a positive print at the same scale can be made on photographic paper at a nominal cost. The single photos not used in the mosaic, but necessary for stereoscopic viewing, can be taken to the field with the positive print of the mosaic, thus permitting stereo viewing in the field.

If an uncontrolled mosaic is to be used for graphical presentation purposes and/or as a base for mapping terrain information, it is necessary to feather the photograph to avoid shadows along the edges of the overlapping air photos, as well as to improve the appearance of the mosaic. Feathering is accomplished by cutting through the emulsion with a razor-edge knife and pulling the outside of the photograph toward the photo center, thus leaving only the thin emulsion where the photographs join. The overlapping photograph edges are matched to the terrain features on both adjoining photos as accurately as possible. The best means of permanently attaching the adjacent photos is using a hot roller to apply a special adhesive wax to the underside of the overlapping photograph. Forms of rubber cement are satisfactory for this work, but the photo edges tend to curl. The joins between the photos are then taped securely on the back of the mosaic using masking tape. The mosaics may be constructed by pasting the photographs to a mounting board such as masonite. Two facts should be kept in mind if you use mounting boards: (1) portability for field use is limited, and (2) requirements for storage space increase substantially.

The advantages and disadvantages of mosaics versus maps prepared by ground survey methods are listed below:

**ADVANTAGES**

1. The mosaic can be produced more rapidly because the time requirements to carry out the ground surveys and to plot the related information on a map are extensive.

2. The mosaic is less expensive, even if the cost of acquiring the air photos is included.

3. The mosaic shows more terrain detail because all natural and cultural features on the ground surface show clearly on the air photo. Ground surveys are carried out to locate only the features specified by the contract and/or features that can be shown by standard symbols in the legend.

4. For air photo interpretation purposes, subtle terrain characteristics such as tone, texture, and vegetation must be visible. Therefore, the use of mosaics for these purposes is essential.

### DISADVANTAGES

1. Horizontal scale measurements between any two points on a mosaic, regardless of the degree of ground and photo control employed, are limited in accuracy primarily due to relief displacement.

2. Mosaics are not topographic maps and therefore do not show elevations.

## 12.20  Stereoscopic Viewing and Parallax

Stereoscopic viewing is defined as observing an object in three dimensions (see also Section 12.26). To achieve stereoscopic vision, it is essential to have two images of the same object taken from different points in space. The eyes thus meet this requirement. A person with vision in only one eye cannot see stereoscopically.

See Figure 12.19(a) for a simple pocket stereoscope being used on stereo-pair air photos. Use of the stereoscope on the stereo-pair photos in this section will assist you in learning the basics about this type of image analysis. The following list offers some suggestions on the use of a stereoscope:

- Adjust the width between the lenses to accommodate each individual.
- Adjust the two photos so that identical features are directly below each of the lenses. Features will then appear to be superimposed.
- Relax and let your eyes find their own focus. After a few seconds, the three-dimensional (stereo) image will appear.
- If the three-dimensional image does not readily appear, try shifting the photos slightly, adjusting the lens width, or rotating the stereoscope slightly.

On two adjacent air photos, over half the ground points on both photos are imaged from two different points in space because of forward overlap. For example, the image of ground point $G$ in Figure 12.18(b) is located at $g_1$ and $g_2$ on photos 1 and 2, respectively. If the observer looks at point $g_1$ on photo 1 with the left eye and at point $g_2$ on photo 2 with the right eye, point $G$ can be seen stereoscopically.

The eyes are used to converge on an object and therefore resist diverging. Divergence is necessary if each eye is to focus on the images of the same point on two adjacent photographs because the air photos have to be separated by between 2 in. (5 cm) and 3 in. (7.5 cm). This is illustrated in Figure 12.19, where a pocket or lens stereoscope with two-power magnification is placed over two adjacent air photos. The stereoscope assists in allowing the eyes to diverge. Pocket stereoscopes are easily portable for fieldwork and are

(a)

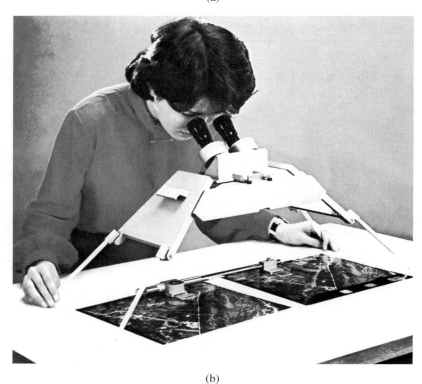

(b)

**FIGURE 12.19** Lens and mirror stereoscopes. (a) Lens (pocket) stereoscope. (b) Mirror stereoscope. (Courtesy of Cansell Survey Equipment Limited, Canada)

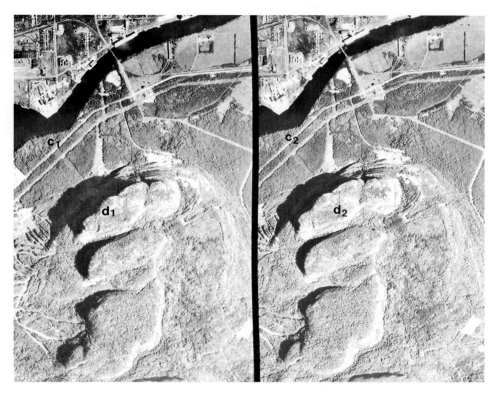

**FIGURE 12.20** Stereopair illustrating high topographic relief. (Courtesy of Bird & Hale Ltd., Toronto)

also inexpensive. A mirror stereoscope is often used for office work because the internal mirror system allows the adjacent air photos to be placed a greater distance apart, as illustrated in Figure 12.19(b). As a result, the observer can view the total area covered by the overlap of the two photos. This permits the stereoscopic examination to take place more rapidly. Also, the degree of magnification can be varied easily by substituting the removable binoculars shown in Figure 12.19(b). The eye base for both types of stereoscopes is adjustable to suit the observer. Also, the adjacent air photos must be adjusted slightly until the images coincide to provide stereoscopic viewing.

Figure 12.20 provides an excellent example of an area of high topographic relief. The mountain labeled $d_1$ and $d_2$ is approximately 800 ft (270 m) high. The two images ($d_1$, $d_2$) of the same area on these adjacent air photos are set at an average spacing between identical points of 2.4 in. (6 cm). A pocket or lens stereoscope can be placed over this stereopair, and the high relief will be seen clearly. The distance between the lenses, known as the interpupillary range, is adjustable from 2.2 in. (55 mm) to 3.0 in. (75 mm). This adjustment will assist the observer in viewing any stereopair stereoscopically without eye strain.

The ratio between the distance between the principal points, $PP1$ and $PP2$ on Figure 12.21, to the flying height is much greater than the ratio of the interpupillary distance to the distance from the stereoscope lens to the photo. This fact combined with long-range focusing when using a stereoscope thus creates the phenomenon of vertical exaggeration.

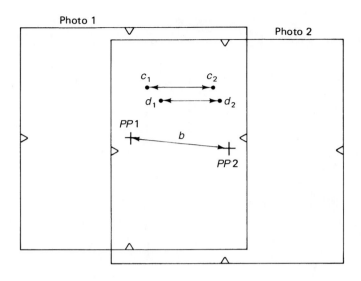

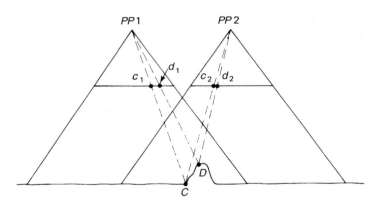

**FIGURE 12.21** X parallax along the flight line.

The height of a feature appears higher through stereoscopic viewing of air photos than the actual height. This discrepancy is usually exaggerated by a factor of between 2:1 and 2.5:1, depending on the interpupillary distance of the individual. This also applies to the examination and estimation of terrain slopes, an important factor in air photo interpretation. Vertical exaggeration is useful for both photogrammetry and air photo interpretation because it emphasizes ground elevation differences, thus rendering them easier to observe and measure. However, this exaggeration must be kept in mind when estimating slopes for terrain analysis purposes.

In Figure 12.21, the mountain shown on the stereopair in Figure 12.20 has been photographed from two consecutive camera stations, $PP1$ and $PP2$. The images for both the bottom and top of the mountain are designated $c_1$ and $d_1$ for the left photo (photo 1) and $c_2$ and $d_2$ for the right photo (photo 2). The same designations are shown on both Figures 12.20 and 12.21.

Parallax is the displacement along the flight line of the same point on adjacent aerial photographs. For example, the difference between the distances $c_1c_2$ and $d_1d_2$ in Figure 12.21 is the displacement in the $X$ direction (the direction along the flight line), or the difference in parallax between the image points $c$ and $d$. This difference in parallax is a direct indication of the elevation difference of the height of an object. If points $c$ and $d$ were at the same elevation (not true in this example), the difference in parallax would be zero.

$$dh = \frac{dp \times H}{dp + b}$$

where $dh$ = difference in elevation

$dp$ = difference in parallax

$H$ = flying height

$b$ = photo base (distance between the two adjacent principal points, $PP1$ to $PP2$, in this example)

Examples 12.3 and 12.4 illustrate the calculation of $dh$ using both measurement systems. All pertinent data are illustrated in Figures 12.20 and 12.21, and the calculations determine the $dh$ between points $c$ and $d$ (the height of the mountain). The data supplied or measured are:

$$H = 18,000 \text{ ft } (5,472 \text{ m})$$
$$b = 3.00 \text{ in. } (76.2 \text{ mm})$$
$$dp = 0.17 \text{ in. } (4.32 \text{ mm})$$

Note that $dp$ is determined in this example by measuring $c_1c_2$ and $d_1d_2$ and taking the difference: $2.41 - 2.24 = 0.17$ in. (4.32 mm). See Figure 12.21.

### ■ EXAMPLE 12.3
Calculate the difference in elevation using Imperial units.

**Solution**

$$dh = \frac{0.17\,(18,000)}{0.17 + 3.00} = 965 \text{ ft}$$

### ■ EXAMPLE 12.4
Calculate the difference in elevation using metric units.

**Solution**

$$dh = \frac{4.32\,(5472)}{4.32 + 76.2} = 293 \text{ m}$$

The following procedure is used to determine $b$ and $dp$:

1. The air photos are aligned so that (a) the principal points shown in Figure 12.22 form a straight line, as illustrated, and (b) the air photos are the proper distance apart for stereoscopic viewing by a mirror stereoscope, as shown in Figure 12.19(b).

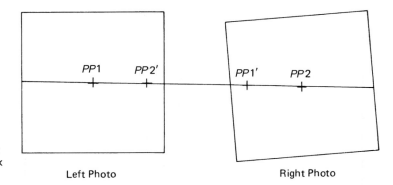

**FIGURE 12.22** Positioning of adjacent photos for parallax measurements.

Left Photo                  Right Photo

2. The air photos are taped in position, and an instrument known as a parallax bar is used to measure the distances along the flight line between the identical image points for which differences in elevation are required. As illustrated in Examples 12.3 and 12.4, $dp$ is obtained by calculating the difference between these two measurements.

3. The principal points of each air photo are determined by the intersection of lines between opposite fiducial marks (see Figure 12.21). These marks show the midpoint of each side of the air photo and are set permanently in the focal plane of each aerial camera. As shown in Figure 12.22, the principal points of each adjacent air photo are plotted on the other photograph by transferring the ground point through stereoscopic viewing. The value of $b$ is determined by averaging the distances $PP1$ to $PP2'$ and $PP1'$ to $PP2$, thus canceling the effects of relief displacement.

The parallax bar is designed so that a small dot is placed on the bottom side of the plastic plates at each end, as illustrated in Figure 12.19(b). The adjustment dial at the left end of the bar on this figure allows the distances between the dots to be adjusted. When viewed stereoscopically with two adjacent air photos, the dots at each end of the bar appear as one floating mark. The bar is adjusted until the floating mark appears to be at the same elevation as the point being examined, and the distance is read from the bar scale. This process is repeated for the other point involved in the difference of elevation calculation. The two measurements are then subtracted to calculate $dp$.

The parallax bar is a useful piece of equipment, and the theory of parallax is one of the keys of photogrammetric measurement. The use of the parallax bar to measure difference of parallax is reliable, only when carried out by an experienced person. Initially, it is difficult to determine when the floating mark is directly on top of a terrain feature.

## 12.21  Photogrammetric Stereoscopic Plotting Techniques

Stereoplotters have traditionally been used for image rectification, that is, to extract planimetric and elevation data from stereopaired aerial photographs for the preparation of topographic maps. The photogrammetric process includes the following steps:

1. Establish ground control for aerial photos.
2. Obtain aerial photographs.

3. Orient adjacent photos so that the ground control matches.

4. Use aerotriangulation to reduce the number of ground points needed.

5. Generate a digital elevation model (DEM).

6. Produce an orthophoto.

7. Collect data using photogrammetric techniques.

Steps 3 to 7 are accomplished using stereoplotting equipment and techniques. Essentially, stereoplotters incorporate two adjustable projectors that are used to duplicate the attitude of the camera at the time the film was exposed. Camera tilt and differences in flying height and flying speed can be noted and rectified. A floating mark can be made to rest on the ground surface when the operator is viewing stereoscopically, thus enabling the skilled operator to trace planimetric detail and deduce both elevations and contours.

In the past fifty years, aerial photo stereoplotting has undergone four distinct evolutions. The original stereoplotter (Kelsh Plotter) was a heavy and delicate mechanical device. Then came the analog stereoplotter, and after that the analytical stereoplotter: an efficient technique that utilizes computer-driven mathematical models of the terrain. The latest technique (developed in the 1990s) is soft-copy (digital) stereoplotting. Each new generation of stereoplotting reflects revolutionary improvements in the mechanical, optical, and computer components of the system. Common features of the first three techniques were size, complexity, high capital costs, high operating costs of the equipment—and the degree of skill required by the operator. Soft-copy photogrammetry utilizes (1) high-resolution scanners to digitize the aerial photos and (2) sophisticated algorithms to process the digital images on workstations (for example, Sun, Unix, etc.) and on personal computers with the Windows NT operating system. The following three subsections cover the analytical stereoplotter, stereoplotting using photo prints, and soft-copy (digital) stereoplotting.

## 12.21.1 Analytical Stereoplotter

The operation of the stereoplotter has been discussed previously. It is important to realize that this equipment is capable of bridging or aerotriangulation, a process that reduces the number of ground control points required. Because the acquisition of ground control coordinates is a costly part of any photogrammetric mapping operation, a reduction in the total number of points has cost benefits.

The process of aerotriangulation can be visualized using the following example. Mapping is required for a flight line or strip consisting of 10 photographs and therefore 9 stereoscopic models. The photographs are numbered consecutively from 1 to 10. Ground control points are available for stereoscopic models for photos 1 and 2 and photos 9 and 10. Assume, for simplicity, that all adjustments required for absolute orientation of the stereoscopic models are made by mechanically adjusting the positions of the diapositives. Also, a computer forms part of the system, thus permitting reading and storage of $X, Y,$ and $Z$ coordinates. The following procedure is used to bridge from model 1, 2 (stereoscopic model for photos 1 and 2) to model 9, 10 (stereoscopic model for photos 9 and 10):

1. Model 1, 2 is oriented absolutely in the plotter. Both photos are in the identical position regarding tip, tilt, and flying height at the instant they were taken in the aircraft.

2. Photo 1 is removed and photo 3 is substituted for it in the plotter. Photo 3 is oriented to photo 2. Because photo 2 is absolutely oriented, the same is now true of photo 3. Therefore, model 2, 3 is absolutely oriented.

3. The operator selects three or more photo control points for model 2, 3 using the same criteria discussed in Section 12.18. The coordinates of each of these points are entered into the computer. The physical location of each point is carefully marked and numbered on a paper print of either photo 2 or photo 3.

4. Photo 2 is removed and photo 4 is substituted for it. The process described in step 2 is carried out to achieve absolute orientation for model 3, 4. Photo control points are selected, coordinated, and plotted on the photo print.

5. The preceding steps are continued for the remainder of the flight line. Because model 9, 10 has established ground control points, the photo coordinates for these same points are obtained using the plotter. If the photo coordinates agree with the ground coordinates within the specified tolerances, the bridging process is complete. If the number of air photos in the flight lines is large, factors such as earth curvature must be considered. Therefore, an adjustment is required by which each of the photo coordinates for models 2, 3 to 8, 9 (inclusive) are corrected by a computer having the necessary program or software.

This procedure means that any portion of the flight line can be mapped because either photo or ground control points exist for each stereoscopic model. Using a similar process, it is possible to bridge between adjacent flight lines because of the 25%; overlap discussed in Section 12.17. Some reduction in the accuracy of measurements occurs because of the bridging process. However, because the ground coordinates are determined to a high degree of accuracy and the stereoplotter used for this process is a high-precision instrument, the reductions in accuracy are not critical, provided that the bridging is not carried across an excessive number of air photos and/or flight lines. (See Figure 12.23.)

**FIGURE 12.23**  Computer-assisted plotting system. (Courtesy of Leica Canada Ltd.)

## 12.21.2 Stereoplotting Using Photo Prints

Plotters that use photographic prints rather than stable-base diapositives as the basis for photogrammetric measurements are available. These measurements are not as accurate because the photo prints do not have the dimensional stability of the diapositives. Several instruments that have the capabilities of measuring from photo prints are available. Some provide for mechanical adjustment of the prints for tip and tilt corrections for orientation, although the solutions are approximate. Other instruments, such as the Zeiss Stereocord (shown in Figure 12.24), use digital computers to carry out the orientation. These computers correct for model deformation, relief displacements, and tip and tilt. Elevations are measured using the parallax bar concept, and the resulting data are provided to very close approximations. The stage on which the photographs are mounted is moved manually under the stereoscope and parallax bar. The digitizer coordinates the points along the travel path, and these locations are plotted digitally.

## 12.21.3 Soft-Copy Photogrammetry (Digital Photogrammetry)

This latest generation of stereoplotting technique (the successor to analytical stereoplotting) uses digital raster images (soft-copy medium) rather than aerial photographs (hard-copy medium) to perform the photogrammetric process. Aerial photographs, in the form of 23-cm (9-in.) photographs or continuous-roll films, are processed through high-resolution scanners to provide the digital images used in the process. The scanner (see Figure 12.25) converts light transmitted through the photographic image into picture elements (called pixels) of fixed size, shape, spacing, and brightness. The size of the pixel is important, with manufacturers claiming that

**FIGURE 12.24**  Computer-assisted plotter for use with photo prints. From left to right: plotter, computer, digitizer, and binocular system for viewing stereoscopic model.

**FIGURE 12.25** DSW300 scanner with Sun Ultra 60® host computer. This high-precision photogrammetric photo and film scanner has four elements: (1) movable *xy* cross carriage stage with flat film platen; (2) fixed array charge-coupled device (CCD) camera and image optics; (3) Xenon light source and color scanning software; and (4) computer hardware, including storage. (Courtesy of LH Systems, San Diego, CA).

a size of 7 μm to 10 μm (μm is a micrometer—a millionth of a meter) is needed for this type of image processing. This scanning process could be bypassed if aerial digital cameras (introduced in 2000) were used in the first place (see Section 12.22).

Once the digital image files have been created, stereopaired images can be observed in three dimensions on a computer monitor (21-inch is recommended) by an operator wearing stereoglasses. The operator can, at this stage, perform the same functions available with the highly efficient analytical plotters. But because of the digital nature of the image files, much more of the process can be accomplished automatically. The five steps in aerial photography digital processing are:

1. Scanning of aerial photos (if film-based cameras are used).
2. Aerotriangulation.
3. Elevation mapping (DEM/DTM).

**FIGURE 12.26**   SOCET SET® Windows NT workstation. This shot shows a human operator using the passive polarized viewing system, in this case the Stereo-Graphics® Corporation ZScreen® system: A polarizing bezel is placed and secured in front of an off-the-shelf, high-performance monitor. The operator wears passive, polarized spectacles. In this case the workstation is a very recent model with dual 450 MHz Pentium II processors. (Courtesy of LH Systems, San Diego, California)

4. Orthophoto (and mosaics) production.
5. Planimetric features mapping.

DEM refers to digital elevation model, and DTM refers to digital terrain model. Some would say that a DTM is a DEM with the breaklines included, which are needed to define the elevation surface properly (as in contouring).

Software will divide the huge data file into subfiles (called tiles) that can be manipulated more easily by the computers, at the appropriate time. Computer processors should have large storage and fast speed. High refresh-rate monitors and various graphics accelerator boards will permit efficient processing of the huge data files. With the development of software compatible with Windows NT systems, users no longer have to invest huge sums in stereoplotters or workstation computers; instead, the principal part of the hardware process is a readily available, off-the-shelf computer that is also capable of performing a host of other functions—ranging from the use of CAD and GIS programs to the use of business software. The only photogrammetry-specific hardware needed are the scanner, stereoglasses, floating mark controller, three-dimensional mouse or pointer, and appropriate hard-copy plotters (see Figure 12.26.)

Soft-copy photogrammetry has several advantages over earlier generations of stereoplotting:

1. It produces perspective views.

2. It handles all types of remote-sensing data, not just digitized photos.

3. It prepares data for use in GIS and CAD software.

4. It can import external files such as GIS, CAD, TIGER, etc.

5. The smaller size and stability of computers that are unaffected by vibration (versus conventional stereoplotters) means that the system can be placed in any desired location. Some report that required rental space has been reduced by half. (Stereoplotters require a large floor area that is well supported to take the substantial weight.)

6. The computer base provides a direct link among photogrammetry, remote sensing, GIS, CAD, and GPS control point surveys (see Figure 7.32).

7. It provides a large advancement in automation (with some operator editing), with potential for even more automation.

8. It reduces the number of highly trained operators needed.

9. Equipment calibration time and costs (mostly limited to the scanner) are much reduced.

10. All data file formats can be in TIFF (raster files) and PostScript (raster and vector files), which are used industrywide in most related processing operations.

11. Hard-copy output can be achieved by any of the available printers and plotters, or high-resolution techniques can be contracted to various agencies in the printing industry.

## 12.22  Airborne Digital Imagery

In Section 12.21.3, we noted that photogrammetric analysis had become almost completely automated through the techniques of soft-copy (digital) photogrammetry. In that process, the only step not digitized was that of image capture. The traditional 9″ by 9″ aerial photograph held such a wealth of detail that the incentive to change to digital techniques was a bit weaker than it was for the other steps in the process. Once the traditional (film-based) photos or the film itself was digitized using high-speed scanners (Figure 12.25), the remainder of the digital processing and analysis could proceed mostly using automated techniques.

In 2000, however, several companies introduced airborne digital cameras or panchromatic sensors combined with interfaced or modular multispectral scanners. For example, one company, L H Systems, introduced an airborne digital sensor, ADS40 (a pushbroom scanner; see Figure 12.27), which collects scanned data on the following bands:

| SPECTRAL BANDS FOR THE ADS40* | |
|---|---|
| BAND | $\lambda$ ($\mu$m) |
| Panchromatic (trapezoidal) | 465–680 (at $\lambda \cong 50\%$) |
| Red (rectangular) | 610–660 |
| Green (rectangular) | 535–585 |
| Blue (rectangular) | 430–490 |
| Near infrared (rectangular) | 835–885 |

*See Section 12.3, Table 12.1, and Figure 12.1.

(a)

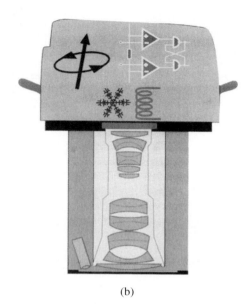

(b)

**FIGURE 12.27**  (a) LH System's airborne digital sensor (ADS40). (b) An iconic view of the ADS40 showing sensor head, electronics, the internal IMU, and the heating/cooling system. (Courtesy of LH Systems, Calif.)

The ADS40 three-line panchromatic scanner has forward, nadir, and backward looking arrays. Every ground point thus appears in three images, producing an effect similar to that given by the 60% overlap in aerial photography. Thus, it provides full stereoscopic viewing. The single lens has a focal length of 63 mm, a cross-track angular coverage of 64°, and a beam-splitter that breaks the incident light into red, green, and blue bands. The red, green, and blue band sensors are positioned for forward pointing, whereas the near infrared band sensor is mounted for near-nadir pointing. Each of the sensing linear arrays comprises two 12,000 pixel lines of charged coupling devices (CCDs). See also Section 12.4 for a discussion of image scanners.

At normal flying speeds of 200 knots (370 km/hr), the minimum ground sampling distance (GSD) is 15 cm. An integral component of this system is an inertial measuring unit (IMU). This device uses its position and attitude data to rectify the scanned images. (See Figure 11.1 for an example of an inertial measuring unit.) Figure 12.28 shows the area spread for data collection using the various ADS40 bands.

Airborne digital imagery is in its infancy. It has been predicted that its development will usher in a new era in airborne sensing.

## 12.23  Orthophotos

Relief, tip, and tilt affect the positions of points on air photos, as previously discussed in this chapter. The most direct effect of these displacements relates to the construction of mosaics. Even for a controlled mosaic (see Section 12.19), the overall accuracy for scaling horizontal measurements will be good. This is not true for scaling the distance between

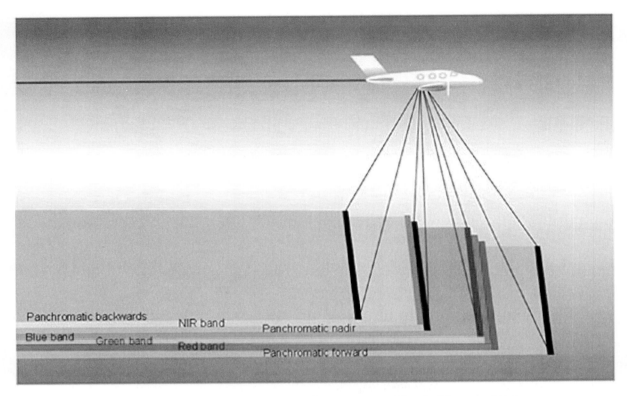

**FIGURE 12.28**   ADS40 airborne digital sensor spectral bands. (Courtesy LH Systems, Calif.)

two points relatively close together, particularly if their ground elevations are significantly different.

Horizontal measurements made from an absolutely oriented stereoscopic model are very accurate because they are made from orthogonal projections to form a map beneath the model, as illustrated in Figure 12.29. An orthophoto combines the accuracy of scaling, such as from a map, with the detailed photographic representation of the mosaic. The orthophoto is produced by manipulating the images on the photograph using mechanical, electronic, or computer techniques (see Section 12.21) to eliminate the adverse effects of tip, tilt, and relief displacement on scale. Although there are several methods for preparing orthophotos, the simplest to understand is the fixed-line-element rectification method. The principles of this method are described next.

The stereoscopic model is absolutely oriented, as illustrated by the terrain model in Figure 12.29. The film stage shown in the figure is covered by a layer of orthochromatic film, which is not sensitive to red light. The terrain model is divided into strips for purposes of the process; six strips are shown in Figure 12.29. A slit through the viewing platen is moved at constant speed in the direction shown in strip 1. The film stage is moved up and down vertically as the slit scans the strip, so that the film on top of the stage is in constant contact with the

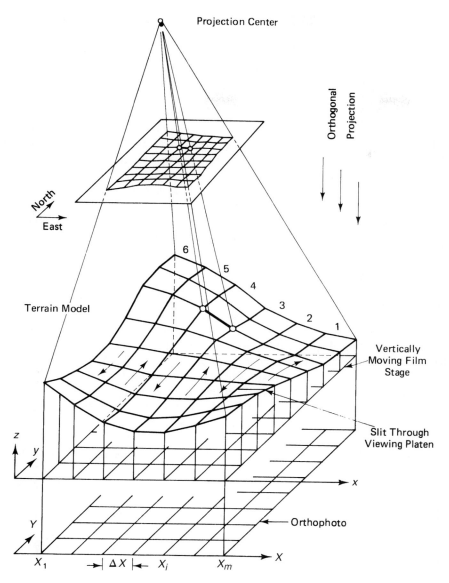

**FIGURE 12.29** Relationships of photograph, terrain model, and orthophoto. (Courtesy of Leica Canada Ltd.)

surface of the terrain model. The only light projected onto the film is the light passing through the slit. This is achieved by keeping the rest of the film covered by movable curtains. The slit scans along strip 1 and then returns along strip 2 in the opposite direction, as illustrated. The remaining strips are then scanned until the model is completed. This process produces the same effect as if the aircraft were flying at exactly the same height above each terrain feature.

The net result is an orthographic projection, which is developed as an orthophoto, shown graphically below the film stage in Figure 12.29. You can see that the distortions due to relief displacement, tip, and tilt have been largely removed. Minimal distortions still occur within each strip because the film stage is moved to match the average terrain elevation across the strip. Therefore, the number of strips can be increased and the width of each can be subsequently decreased to reduce these minor distortions; however, this would increase the cost of the production process.

Figure 12.30 shows the strip boundaries on the terrain model superimposed on the original air photo in the upper right corner. The effect of relief displacement is particularly obvious in the hilly area in the upper left portion of this air photo. The rest of the figure is the orthophoto, with distortions largely removed.

Strips of adjacent orthophotos are matched easily to each other, thus resulting in a true scale mosaic. Also, contour lines obtained from the stereoplotting process can be superimposed on the orthophotos (creating an orthophoto topographic map) with reliability because their horizontal location on the photos will be correct, at least from strip to strip.

## 12.24   Lidar Mapping

Light detection and ranging (Lidar) is a laser mapping technique that has recently become popular in both topographic and hydrographic surveying. Over land, laser pulses can be transmitted and then returned from ground surfaces. The time required to send and then receive the laser pulses is used to create a digital elevation model (DEM) of the earth surface. Processing software can separate rooftops from ground surfaces and also treetops and other vegetation from the bare ground surface beneath the trees. Although the laser pulses cannot penetrate very heavily foliaged trees, they can penetrate tree cover and other lower-growth vegetation at a much more efficient rate than does either aerial photography or digital imaging because of the huge number of measurements—thousands of terrain measurements every second. "Bare-earth" DEMs are particularly useful for design and estimating purposes.

One of the important advantages to using this technique is the rapid processing time. One supplier claims that 1,000 km² of hilly, forested terrain can be surveyed by laser in less than 12 hours, and that the DEM data are available within 24 hours of the flight. Thus, data processing doesn't take much longer than does data collection. Because each laser pulse is individually georeferenced, there is no need for the orthorectification steps needed in aerial photo processing. Additional advantages include the following:

- Laser mapping can be flown during the day or at night when there are fewer clouds and calmer air.
- Vertical accuracies of 15 cm (or better) can be achieved.
- There are no shadow or parallax problems, as with aerial photos.
- Laser data is digital and is thus ready for digital processing.
- It is less expensive than aerial imaging for the creation of DEMs.

Lidar can be mounted in a helicopter or fixed-wing aircraft, and the lower the altitude, the better the resulting ground resolution. Typically, lidar can be combined with a

**FIGURE 12.30** Comparison of orthophoto and original air photo (upper right corner). (Courtesy of Leica Canada Ltd.)

**FIGURE 12.31**  "Earth features," such as signs and ramps, can be displayed using visualization software based on data extracted from lidar imaging. (Courtesy of TxDOT, Texas)

digital imaging sensor (panchromatic and multispectral) as described in Section 12.24; an IMU to provide data to correct pitch, yaw, and roll; and GPS receivers to provide precise positioning. When the data-gathering package also includes a digital camera to collect panchromatic imagery, then it is possible, with appropriate processing software, to produce high-quality orthorectified aerial imagery so that each pixel can be assigned $X$, $Y$, and $Z$ values.

Ground lidar operates in the near-IR portion of the spectrum; this part of the spectrum produces wavelengths that tend to be absorbed by water (including rain and fog) and asphalt surfaces (such as roofing and highways). These surfaces produce "holes" in the coverage that can be recognized as such and then edited during data processing. Even rolling traffic on a highway at the time of data capture can be removed through editing. See Figures 12.31, 12.32, and 12.33 for examples of lidar instruments and use. The growing number of applications for Lidar include:

- Highway design and redesign.
- Flood plain mapping.
- Forest inventory, including canopy coverage, tree density and heights, and timber output.
- Line-of-sight modeling using Lidar-generated three-dimensional building renderings—used in telecommunications and airport facilities design.

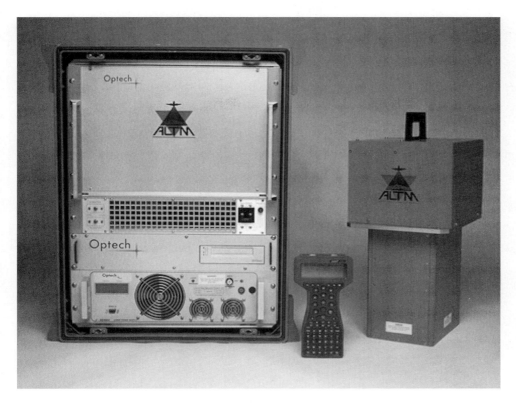

**FIGURE 12.32**    Optech's lidar instrumentation. (Courtesy of Optech Ltd., Toronto)

- Generation of lower-cost DEMs.

See Section 16.10 for airborne laser bathymetry (ALB).

# 12.25   Aerial Surveying and Photogrammetric Mapping

## 12.25.1   Advantages

The advantages of using aerial surveying and photogrammetric mapping over traditional ground surveying methods are listed below:

1. Cost savings: This is related to the size of the area to be mapped, assuming that the ground is not obscured from view by certain dense vegetation types such as coniferous trees. The surveyor is advised to cost the mapping using all methods and to select the most economical. As the size of the mapping area increases, aerial and photogrammetric methods become rapidly cheaper on a per-acre or per-hectare basis. *Note:* The development and use of total stations, with their wide variety of programmed functions, together with the error-free transfer of data to the computer, has greatly speeded up the fieldwork portion of a survey project (see Chapter 7). The

**FIGURE 12.33**   Three-dimensional lidar image of Buttonville Airport. (Courtesy of Optech Ltd., Toronto)

creation of sophisticated data processing and plotting software programs has also provided additional efficiencies to this aspect of the survey project.

2. Reduction in fieldwork required: It is generally recognized that fieldwork is a very high cost component of any surveying project. It also depends on access and weather. The relatively few control points required for photogrammetric mapping

thus reduce the field problems and reduce the time of data acquisition substantially.

3. Speed of compilation: The time required to prepare maps using digital methods is minimal compared to the time required to carry out the ground survey and process the data.

4. Freedom from inaccessible terrain conditions.

5. Provision of a temporal record: The air photos and images provide an accurate record of the terrain features at one instant in time. This is useful for direct comparisons with imagery taken at other times to record either subtle or major changes in the landscape.

6. Flexibility: Photogrammetric mapping can be designed for any map scale, provided that the proper flying heights, focal lengths, ground control point placement, and plotting instruments are selected. Scales vary from 1:200 upward to 1:250,000. Contour intervals as small as 0.5 ft (0.15 m) can be determined.

7. New technology: The recent development of new technology in GPS airborne control, soft-copy photogrammetry, airborne digital imagery, and lidar mapping will make the first six advantages all the more relevant.

## 12.25.2 Disadvantages

Aerial surveying and photogrammetric mapping also have some disadvantages, which are explained below:

1. Viewing terrain through dense vegetation cover: If the aerial images have been acquired under full-leaf cover and/or if the vegetative cover is coniferous, the ground may not be visible in the stereo model. This problem can be overcome only by obtaining leaf-free air photos in the spring or fall if the tree cover is deciduous, or by supplementing the mapping with field measurements if the vegetation is coniferous, or possibly by using lidar measurements.

2. Contour line locations in flat terrain: It is more difficult to place the floating mark accurately in the plotter on areas of flat terrain. Consequently, it is sometimes necessary to carry out additional field measurements in such areas.

3. Going to the site: A visit to the site is necessary to determine the type of roads and surfacing, locations of certain utility lines not easily visible on the air photos, and roads and place names. This can usually be achieved effectively and is usually combined with spot checks of the mapping to ensure that the relief is represented properly.

## 12.26 Aerial Photography Interpretation

Image interpretation is achieved by a combination of direct human analysis and by automated soft-copy processes. With the introduction in 2000 of airborne multispectral sensors, the ability to interpret the images has greatly increased. Image interpretation techniques are based on three fundamental assumptions:

1. The remotely sensed images are records of the results of long- and short-term natural and human processes.

2. The surface features seen on the image can be grouped together to form patterns that are characteristic of particular environmental conditions.

3. The environmental conditions and their reflected image patterns are repetitive within major climatic zones; that is, similar environments will produce similar image patterns, whereas different environments will usually produce different image patterns.

The terrain elements that collectively produce patterns on remotely sensed images include the topography (geometry of the surface), regional drainage, local erosion, vegetation, and cultural features.

The three-dimensional viewing of stereo-pair images was discussed earlier in this chapter. Use of this technique greatly assists the photo analyst in interpreting photo detail. When using soft-copy techniques, the operator wears stereo glasses while viewing the computer monitor (see Figure 12.26), whereas when using aerial photos, the operator must use a stereoscope (see Figure 12.19).

Before attempting to interpret terrain, the interpreter must know something of the properties inherent in the photographs themselves. The conventional black and white aerial photo, used as a record of surface conditions, is created by the reflection of certain spectra of electromagnetic energy from the surface of objects. A panchromatic photo records the surface only as tones of gray, and not, as does the human eye, in tones of gray and variations of color. Thus, two widely different colors that would be readily differentiated by the human eye may have the same gray tone on a black-and-white photograph. In addition, the photo is a much reduced image of the actual situation; that is, it is a **scaled** representation. Familiar pattern elements may become so reduced in size that they present an unfamiliar appearance on an aerial photograph; for example, the familiar linear pattern of a plowed field becomes an even gray tone without perceptible pattern when the scale of the photo is very small. In general, photographs have two basic properties: (1) photo tone, which is the variation in tones of gray on a photograph, and (2) photo texture, which is the combination of tones of gray on an exceedingly small scale so that individual features are close to the limit of resolution but in which an overall pattern of variation can still be detected.

Air photo interpretation has, in the past, required professionals highly skilled in the interpretive process; however with the advent of combining photographs supplemented by multi-spectral scannings, the computerized interpretive process has become much more automated.

## 12.27   Applications of Air Photo Interpretation for the Engineer and the Surveyor

Air photo interpretation of physical terrain characteristics is used for a wide variety of projects. The main advantages of this technique are as follows:

1. The identification of land forms and consequently site conditions, such as soil type, soil depth, average topographic slopes, and soil and site drainage characteristics, is made before going to the field to carry out either engineering or surveying fieldwork.

When the fieldwork begins, you should have a strong feeling of having been at the site before because of the familiarity achieved through careful examination of the air photos.

2. The surveyor can examine the topographic slopes, areas of wet or unstable ground, and the density and type of vegetation cover. Therefore, he or she can become familiar with the ease or difficulty to be expected in carrying out the field survey. From the air photos, the surveyor can also determine the location of property or section boundaries some of which are extremely difficult to see on the ground.

3. Air photos provide an excellent overview of the site and the surrounding area, which cannot be achieved through groundwork alone. For example, if evidence of soil movement such as landslides is indicated on the air photos, the surveyor can avoid placing monuments in such an area because they would be subject to movement with the soils. The engineer would avoid using this area for any heavy structures because of the potential for gradual or sudden soil failure.

4. Soil test holes should always be used to verify the results of the air photo interpretation, and these can be preselected carefully on the air photo prior to doing the fieldwork. Existing road or stream bank cuts can be pre-identified for use as field checkpoints, thus saving on drilling costs.

## 12.28   Remote Sensing Internet Websites

### 12.28.1   Satellite Websites

ALOS: http://eos-p71b.hq.nasda.go.jp/alos.html
ENVISAT: http://envisat.estec.esa.nl/
Ikonus, IRS, Landsat 5: www.spaceimage.com
IRS: www.isro.org/programmes.htm
JERS, Remote Sensing Technology Center of Japan: www.restec.or.jp/restec_e.html
Landsat 7: http://geo.arc.nasa.gov/sge/landsat/landsat.html
OrbView: www.orbital.com/, www.orbimage.com
Quickbird: www.digitalglobe.com/, http://satellites.satellus.se/quickbird.asp
Radarsat: www.space.gc.ca/csa_sectors/earth_environmental/radarsat/default.asp
Space imaging: http://spaceimaging.com
Space shuttle Endeavor: http://www.jpl.nasa.gov/srtm
SPIN-2: www.spin-2.com/
SPOT: www.spot.com/spot/spot-us.htm
Terra (EO-1): http://asterweb.jpl.nasa.gov/asterhome/, http://terra.nasa.gov

### 12.28.2   Airborne Imagery Websites

EagleScan Remote Sensing Services: http://www.3dillc.com/rem-lidar.html
L H Systems (digital imagery and digital photogrammetry): http://www.lhsystemsgroup.com/

Optech [airborne laser terrain mapper (ALTM)]: www.optech.on.ca

Scanning Hydrographic Operational Airborne Lidar Survey (**SHOALS**) system, U.S Army Corps of Engineers (USACE): http://sam.usae.army.mil/op/shoals/pages/airborne.htm

Vegetation canopy lidar (VCL) mission, NASA: http://essp.gsfc.nasa/vcl/

### 12.28.3   General Reference Websites

American Society for Photogrammetry and Remote Sensing (ASPRS): www.asprs. org

Australian Surveying and Land Information Group: http://www.auslig.gov.au/acres/facts.htm

Earth Science Information Center: http://mapping.usgs.gov/esic/esic.html

ERS, European Space Agency: www.ese.int

Landsat 7 Science Data Users Handbook: http://ltpwww.gsfc.nasa.gov/IAS/handbook

NASA, EROS Data Center: http://edcwww.cr.usgs.gov

Natural Resources, Canada: www.ccrs.nrcan

Natural Resources Canada tutorial: http://www.ccrs.nrcan.gc.ca/ccrs/eduref/tutorial

Remote Sensing Tutorial (NASA): http://rst.gsfc.nasa.gov

## 12.29   Additional Reading

American Society for Photogrammetry and Remote Sensing, *Digital Photogrammetry: An Addendum to the Manual of Photogrammetry* (Bethesda, Maryland, 1996).

Anderson, Floyd M., and Lewis, Anthony J, Editors, "*Principles and Applications of Imaging Radar, Manual of Remote Sensing,* Third Edition, Volume 2 (New York: Wiley, 1998).

Jensen, John R., *Remote Sensing of the Environment,* An Earth Resource Perspective (Upper Saddle River: N.J.: Prentice Hall Series in Geographic Information Science, 2000).

Lillesand, Thomas M., and Ralph W. Kiefer, *Remote Sensing and Image Interpretation,* Fourth Edition (New York: John Wiley and Sons, 2000).

Wolf, Paul R., and Bon A Dewitt: *Elements of Photogrammetry,* Third Edition (New York: McGraw Hill, 2000).

## Questions

1. What are the chief differences between maps based on satellite imagery and maps based on airborne imagery?
2. What are the advantages inherent in the use of hyperspectral sensors over multispectral sensors?
3. Describe all the types of data collection that could be used to plan the location of a highway/utility corridor spanning several counties.
4. How does the use of lidar imaging enhance digital imaging?

5. Why is radar imaging preferred over passive sensors for Arctic and Antarctic data collection?

6. Compare and contrast the two techniques of remote sensing—aerial and satellite imagery—by listing the appropriate uses for each technique. Use the comparative examples shown in Figures 12.12 and 12.13.

7. Why can't aerial photographs be used for scaled measurements?

8. What is the chief advantage of digital cameras over film-based cameras?

9. What effects does aircraft altitude have on aerial imagery?

10. Why are overlaps and sidelaps designed into aerial photography acquisition?

11. Describe the adjustments that can be made when the use of a stereoscope fails to produce three-dimensional images.

12. Discuss the fundamental components of a landscape with respect to aerial image interpretation.

# Problems

12.1 Calculate the flying heights and altitudes, given the following information.
   (a) Photographic scale = 1:20,000, lens focal length = 153 mm, elevation of mean datum = 180 m.
   (b) Photographic scale is 1 in. = 20,000 ft, lens focal length = 6.022 in., elevation of mean datum = 520 ft.

12.2 Calculate the photo scales, given the following data.
   (a) Distance between points A and B on a topographic map (scale 1:50,000) = 4.75 cm, distance between the same points on an air photo = 23.07 cm.
   (b) Distance between points C and D on a topographic map (scale 1:100,000) = 1.85 in., distance between the same points on an air photo = 6.20 in.

12.3 Calculate the approximate numbers of photographs required for stereoscopic coverage (60% forward overlap and 25% sidelap) for each of the following conditions.
   (a) Photographic scale = 1:30,000, ground area to be covered is 30 km by 45 km.
   (b) Photographic scale = 1:15,000, ground area to be covered is 15 miles by 33 miles.
   (c) Photographic scale is 1 in. = 500 ft, ground area to be covered is 10 miles by 47 miles.

12.4 Calculate the dimensions of the area covered on the ground in a single stereo model having a 60% forward overlap if the scale of the photograph ( 9″ by 9″ format) is:
   (a) 1: 10,000.
   (b) 1 in. = 400 ft.

12.5 (a) Calculate how far the camera would move during the exposure time for each of the following conditions:
      1. Ground speed of aircraft = 350 km/h, exposure time = 1/100 s.
      2. Ground speed of aircraft = 350 km/h, exposure time = 1/1,000 s.
      3. Ground speed of aircraft = 200 miles/h, exposure time = 1/500 s.
   (b) Compare the effects on the photograph of all three situations in part (a).

12.6 Does a longer focal-length camera increase or decrease the relief displacement? Briefly explain the reason for your answer.

12.7 Would a wide-angle lens increase or decrease relief displacement? Briefly explain the reason for your answer.

**12.8** Choose the best alternative from the following list for the assemblage of an uncontrolled mosaic, using alternative photographs, over rolling terrain having vertical relief differences of up to 50 ft (15 m). Give the main reasons for your choice.

(a) Focal length = 150 mm, scale = 1:20,000.

(b) Focal length = 150 mm, scale = 1:5,000.

(c) Focal length = 12 in. (300 mm), scale 1 in. = 1,000 ft.

(d) Focal length = 12 in. (300 mm), scale 1 in. = 2,000 ft.

**12.9** Calculate the time interval between air photo exposures if the ground speed of the aircraft is 100 miles/h (160 km/h), the focal length is 50 mm (2 in.), the format is 70 mm (2.8 in.), the photographic scale is 1:500 (approximately 1 in. = 40 ft), and the forward overlap = 60%.

# PART

# III

# Surveying Applications

Highway Curves

## 13.1 Route Surveys

Highway and railroad routes are chosen only after a complete and detailed study of all possible locations has been completed. Functional planning and route selection usually involves the use of aerial imagery, satellite imagery, and ground surveys as well as the analysis of existing plans and maps. One route is chosen over others because it satisfies all design requirements with minimal social, environmental, and financial impact.

The proposed centerline (℄) is laid out in a series of straight lines (tangents) beginning at $0 + 00$ ($0 + 000$, metric) and continuing to the route terminal point. Each time the route changes direction, the deflection angle between the back tangent and forward tangent is measured and recorded. Existing detail that could have an effect on the highway design is tied in either by conventional ground surveys, aerial surveys, or a combination of the two methods. Typical details include lakes, streams, trees, structures, existing roads and railroads, and so on.

In addition to the detail location, the surveyor will determine elevations along the proposed route, with elevations also determined across the route width at right angles to the ℄ at regular intervals (full stations, half stations, etc.) and at locations dictated by changes in the topography. The elevations thus determined will be used to aid in the design of horizontal and vertical alignments. These elevations will also form the basis for the calculation of construction cut and fill quantities (see Chapter 8). Advances in aerial imaging, including lidar and radar imaging (Chapter 12), have resulted in ground surface measuring techniques that can eliminate much of the time-consuming field surveying techniques traditionally employed.

The location of detail and the determination of elevations are normally confined to that relatively narrow strip of land representing the highway right of way (ROW). Exceptions include potential river, highway, and railroad crossings, where approach profiles and sight lines (railroads) may have to be established.

## 13.2 Circular Curves: General Background

We noted in the previous section that a highway route survey was initially laid out as a series of straight lines (tangents). Once the ℄ location alignment has been confirmed, the

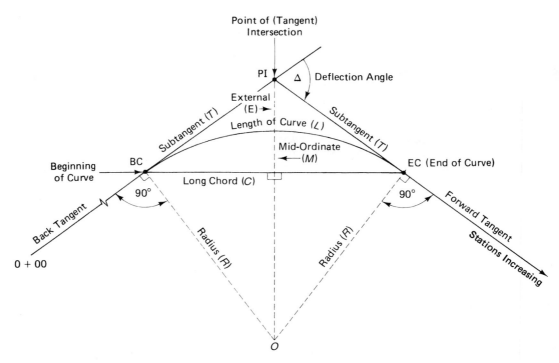

**FIGURE 13.1** Circular curve terminology.

tangents are joined by circular curves that allow for smooth vehicle operation at the speeds for which the highway was designed. Figure 13.1 illustrates how two tangents are joined by a circular curve and shows some related circular curve terminology. The point at which the alignment changes from straight to circular is known as the beginning of curve (BC). The BC is located distance $T$ (subtangent) from the point of tangent intersection (PI). The length of circular curve ($L$) depends on the central angle and the value of $R$ (radius). The point at which the alignment changes from circular back to tangent is known as the end of curve (EC). Since the curve is symmetrical about the PI, the EC is also located distance $T$ from the PI. From geometry, we know that the radius of a circle is perpendicular to the tangent at the point of tangency. Therefore, the radius is perpendicular to the back tangent at the BC and to the forward tangent at the EC. The terms BC and EC are also referred to by some agencies as point of curve (PC) and point of tangency (PT), and by others as tangent to curve (TC) and curve to tangent (CT).

## 13.3  Circular Curve Geometry

Most curve problems are calculated from field measurements ($\Delta$ and the chainage or stationing of the PI) and from design parameters ($R$). Given $R$ (which depends on the design speed) and $\Delta$, all other curve components can be computed.

Analysis of Figure 13.2 shows that the curve deflection angle at the BC (PI-BC-EC) is $\Delta/2$, and that the central angle at O is equal to $\Delta$, the tangent deflection angle. The line

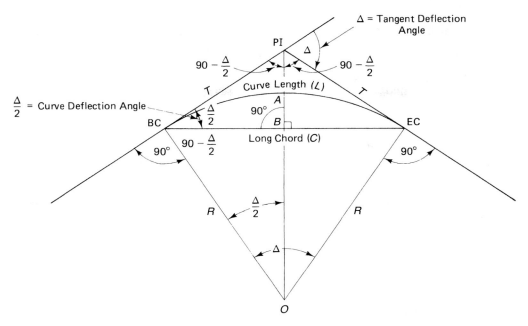

**FIGURE 13.2** Geometry of the circle.

(O-PI), joining the center of the curve to the PI, effectively bisects all related lines and angles.

Tangent: In triangle BC-O-PI
$$\frac{T}{R} = \tan\frac{\Delta}{2}$$

$$T = R\tan\frac{\Delta}{2} \tag{13.1}$$

Chord: In triangle BC-O-B
$$\tfrac{1}{2}\frac{C}{R} = \sin\frac{\Delta}{2}$$

$$C = 2R\sin\frac{\Delta}{2} \tag{13.2}$$

Midordinate:
$$\frac{OB}{R} = \cos\frac{\Delta}{2}$$

$$OB = R\cos\frac{\Delta}{2}$$

But
$$OB = R - M$$

$$R - M = R\cos\frac{\Delta}{2}$$

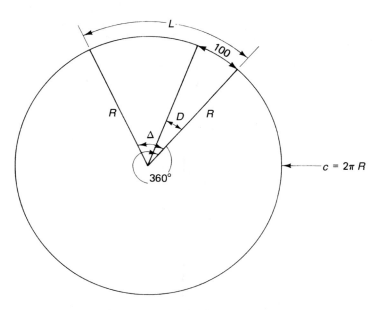

**FIGURE 13.3** Relationship between the degree of curve (*D*) and the circle.

$$M = R\left(1 - \cos\frac{\Delta}{2}\right) \tag{13.3}$$

External: In triangle BC-O-PI $\qquad$ O to PI = $R$ + E

$$\frac{R}{(R + E)} = \cos\frac{\Delta}{2}$$

$$E = R\left(\frac{1}{\cos\Delta/2} - 1\right) \tag{13.4}$$

$$= R\left(\sec\frac{\Delta}{2} - 1\right) \qquad \text{(alternate)}$$

From Figure 13.3, we can develop the following relationships:

$$\text{Arc: } \frac{L}{2\pi R} = \frac{\Delta}{360} \qquad L = \frac{2\pi R\Delta}{360} \tag{13.5}$$

where $\Delta$ is expressed in degrees and decimals of a degree.

The sharpness of the curve is determined by the choice of the radius (*R*); large radius curves are relatively flat, whereas small radius curves are relatively sharp. Some highway agencies use the concept of degree of curve (*D*) to define the sharpness of the curve. Degree of curve *D* is defined as that central angle subtended by 100 ft of arc. (In railway design, *D* is defined as the central angle subtended by 100 ft of chord.) From Figure 13.3:

$$D \text{ and } R: \quad \frac{D}{360} = \frac{100}{2\pi R}$$

$$D = \frac{5{,}729.58}{R} \tag{13.6}$$

$$\text{Arc:} \quad \frac{L}{100} = \frac{\Delta}{D}$$

$$L = 100\left(\frac{\Delta}{D}\right) \tag{13.7}$$

### ■ EXAMPLE 13.1

Refer to Figure 13.4. Given the following relationships:

$$\Delta = 16°38'$$
$$R = 1{,}000 \text{ ft}$$
$$\text{PI at } 6 + 26.57$$

calculate the station of the BC and EC; also calculate lengths C, M, and E.

**Solution**

$$T = R \tan\left(\frac{\Delta}{2}\right) \qquad\qquad L = 2R\left(\frac{\Delta}{360}\right)$$

$$= 1{,}000 \tan 8°19' \qquad\qquad = 2\pi \times 1000 \times \frac{16.6333}{360}$$

$$= 146.18 \text{ ft} \qquad\qquad = 290.31 \text{ ft}$$

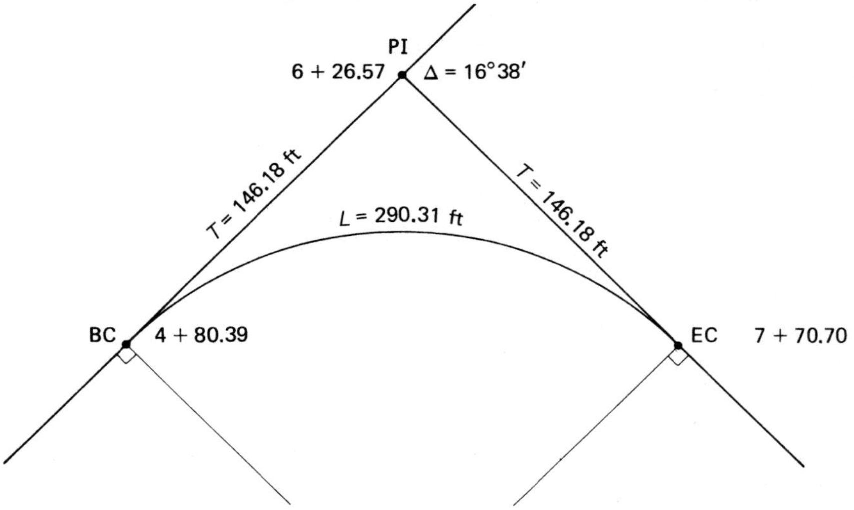

**FIGURE 13.4** Sketch for Example 13.1. *Note:* To aid in comprehension, the magnitude of the Δ angle has been exaggerated in this section.

$$PI \text{ at} \quad 6 + 26.57$$
$$+T \quad \underline{1 \quad 46.18}$$
$$BC = 4 + 80.39$$
$$+L \quad \underline{2 \quad 90.31}$$
$$EC = 7 + 70.70$$

$$C = 2R \sin\left(\frac{\Delta}{2}\right)$$
$$= 2 \times 1{,}000 \times \sin 8°19'$$
$$= 289.29 \text{ ft}$$

$$M = R\left(1 - \cos\frac{\Delta}{2}\right)$$
$$= 1{,}000(1 - \cos 8°19')$$
$$= 10.52 \text{ ft}$$

$$E = R\left(\sec\frac{\Delta}{2 - 1}\right)$$
$$= 1{,}000(\sec 8°19' - 1)$$
$$= 10.63 \text{ ft}$$

A common mistake made by students first studying circular curves is to determine the station of the EC by adding the $T$ distance to the PI. Although the EC is physically a distance of $T$ from the PI, the stationing (chainage) must reflect the fact that the centerline (℄) no longer goes through the PI. The ℄ now takes the shorter distance ($L$) from the BC to the EC.

### ■ EXAMPLE 13.2

Refer to Figure 13.5. Given the following information:

$$\Delta = 12°51'$$
$$R = 400 \text{ m}$$
$$PI \text{ at } 0 + 241.782$$

calculate the station of the BC and EC.

**Solution**

$$T = R \tan\frac{\Delta}{2} \qquad\qquad L = 2\pi R\left(\frac{\Delta}{360}\right)$$

$$= 400 \tan 6°25'30'' \qquad\qquad = 2\pi \times 400 \times \frac{12.850}{360}$$

$$= 45.044 \text{ m} \qquad\qquad = 89.710 \text{ m}$$

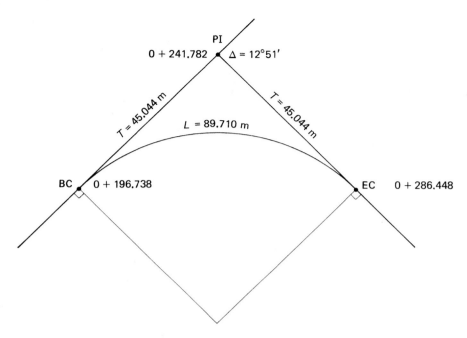

**FIGURE 13.5** Sketch for Example 13.2.

$$
\begin{aligned}
\text{PI at} \quad & 0 + 241.782 \\
-T \quad & \underline{\phantom{0000}45.044} \\
\text{BC} = \; & 0 + 196.738 \\
+L \quad & \underline{\phantom{0000}89.710} \\
\text{EC} = \; & 0 + 286.448
\end{aligned}
$$

## ■ EXAMPLE 13.3
Refer to Figure 13.6. Given the following information:

$$
\Delta = 11°21'35''
$$
$$
\text{PI at } 14 + 87.33
$$
$$
D = 6°
$$

calculate the station of the BC and EC.

**Solution**

$$
R = 5729.58/D = 954.93 \text{ ft}
$$
$$
T = R \tan \Delta/2 = 954.93 \tan 5.679861° = 94.98 \text{ ft}
$$
$$
L = 100 \, \Delta/D = 100 \times 11.359722/6 = 189.33 \text{ ft}
$$

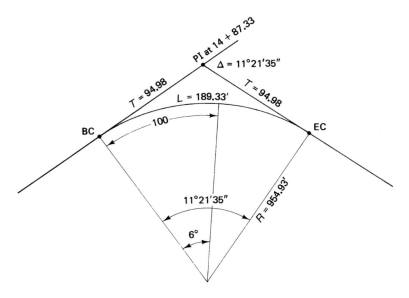

**FIGURE 13.6**   Sketch for Example 13.3.

or

$$L = 2\pi R\ \Delta/360 = 2\pi \times 954.93 \times 11.359722/360 = 189.33 \text{ ft}$$

$$
\begin{array}{ll}
\text{PI at} & 14 + 87.33 \\
-T & \underline{\phantom{1}\ \ 94.98} \\
\text{BC} = & 13 + 92.35 \\
+L & \underline{1\ \ \ 89.33} \\
\text{EC} = & 15 + 81.68
\end{array}
$$

## 13.4   Circular Curve Deflections

A common method of locating a curve in the field uses deflection angles. Typically, the theodolite is set up at the BC, and the deflection angles are turned from the tangent line (see Figure 13.7). If we use the data from Example 13.2:

$$\text{BC at } 0 + 196.738$$

$$\text{EC at } 0 + 286.448$$

$$\frac{\Delta}{2} = 6°25'30'' = 6.4250°$$

$$L = 89.710 \text{ m}$$

$$T = 45.044 \text{ m}$$

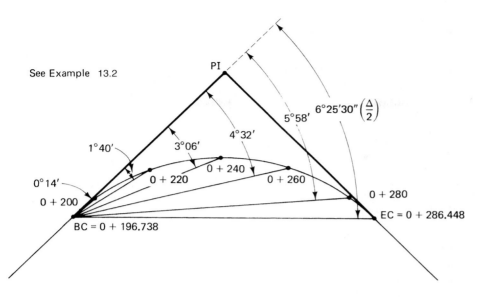

See Example 13.2

**FIGURE 13.7** Field location for deflection angles. See Example 13.2.

And if the layout is to proceed at 20-m intervals, the procedure would be as follows:

1. Compute the deflection angles for the three required arc distances (deflection angle = arc/L × Δ/2):
   a. BC to first even station (0 + 200): (0 + 200) − (0 + 196.738) = 3.262
      6.4250/89.710 × 3.262 = 0.2336° = 0°14′01″
   b. Even station interval: 6.4250/89.710 × 20 = 1.4324° = 1°25′57″
   c. Last even station (0 + 280) to EC: 6.4259.89.710 × 6.448 = 0.4618° = 0°27′42″
2. Prepare a list of appropriate stations together with **cumulative** deflection angles.

$$
\begin{array}{lll}
\text{BC} & 0 + 196.738 & 0°00′00″ \\
& 0 + 200 & 0°14′01″ \,(+1°25′57″) \\
& 0 + 220 & 1°39′58″ \,(+1°25′57″) \\
& 0 + 240 & 3°05′55″ \,(+1°25′57″) \\
& 0 + 260 & 4°31′52″ \,(+1°25′57″) \\
& 0 + 280 & 5°57′49″ \,(+1°25′57″) \\
\text{EC} & 0 + 286.448 & 6°25′31″ \approx 6°25′30″ = Δ/2
\end{array}
$$

For many engineering layouts, the deflection angles are rounded to the closest minute or half-minute.

Another common method of locating a curve in the field uses the "setting out" feature of total stations (see Chapter 7). The coordinates of each station on the curve are first uploaded into the total station, permitting its processor to compute the angle and distance from the instrument.

## 13.5 Chord Calculations

In the previous example, the deflection angle for station 0 + 200 was determined to be 0°14'01". It follows that 0 + 200 can be located by placing a stake on the transit line at 0°14' and at a distance of 3.262 m (200 = 196.738) from the BC. Furthermore, station 0 + 220 can be located by placing a stake on the transit line at 1°40' (rounded) and at a distance of 20 m along the arc from the stake locating 0 + 200. The remaining stations can be located in a similar manner. Note, however, that this technique will contain some error because the distances measured with a steel tape are not arc distances; they are straight lines known as subchords.

To calculate the subchord, Equation 13.2 can be used. This equation, derived from Figure 13.2, is the special case of the long chord and the total deflection angle. The general case can be stated as follows:

$$C = 2R \text{ sin deflection angle} \tag{13.8}$$

Any subchord can be calculated if its deflection angle is known.

Relevant chords for the previous example can be calculated as follows (see Figure 13.8):

First chord: $C = 2 \times 400 \sin 0°14'01" = 3.2618$ m $= 3.262$ m (at three decimals, chord = arc)
Even station chord: $C = 2 \times 400 \sin 1°25'57" = 19.998$ m
Last chord: $C = 2 \times 400 \sin 0°27'42" = 6.448$ m

If these chord distances are used, the curve layout can proceed without error.

Although the calculation of the first and last subchord shows the chord and arc to be equal (that is, 3.262 m and 6.448 m), the chords are always marginally shorter than the arcs. In the cases of short distances (above) and in the case of flat (large radius) curves, the arcs and chords can often appear to be equal. If more decimal places are introduced into the calculation, the marginal difference between the arc and chord will become evident.

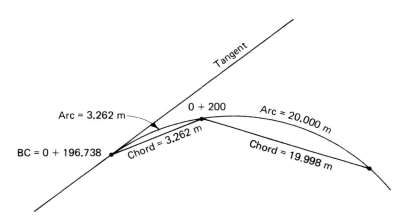

**FIGURE 13.8** Curve arcs and chords.

Chap. 13    Highway Curves

## 13.6  Metric Considerations

Countries, like Canada, that have switched from foot to metric (SI) units have adopted for highway use a reference station of 1 km (for example, $1 + 000$); cross sections at 50 m, 20 m, and 10 m intervals; and a curvature design parameter based on a rational (even meter) value radius, as opposed to a rational value degree (even degree) of curve ($D$). The degree of curve originally found favor with most highway agencies because of the somewhat simpler calculations associated with its use, a factor that was significant in the pre-electronics age when most calculations were performed by using logarithms. A comparison of techniques involving both $D$ and $R$ (radius) shows that the only computation in which the rational aspect of $D$ is carried through is that for the arc length—that is, $L = 100\Delta/D$ (Equation 13.7)—and even in that one case, the ease of calculation depends on delta ($\Delta$) also being a rational number. In all other formulas, the inclusion of trigonometric functions or pi ($\pi$) ensures a more complex computation requiring the use of a calculator or a computer.

In fieldwork, the use of $D$ (as opposed to $R$) permits quick determination of the deflection angle for even stations. For example, in foot units, if the degree of curve were $2°$, the deflection angle for a full station (100 ft) would be $D/2$ or $1°$; for 50 ft, the deflection angle would be $0°30'$; and so on. In metric units, the degree of curve would be the central angle subtended by 100 m of arc, and the deflections would be computed similarly. For a metric $D$ of $6°$, the deflections would be as follows: for 100 m, $3°$ for 50 m, $1°30'$; for 20 m, $0°36'$; and for 10 m, $0°18'$. The metric curve deflections here are not quite as simple as in the foot system, but they are still uncomplicated and rational. However, curve stake-outs require more stations than just those on the even stations. For example, the BC and EC, catch basins or culverts, vertical curve stations, and the like, usually occur on odd stations, and the deflection angles for those odd stations involve irrational number calculations requiring the use of a calculator or computer.

The widespread use of handheld calculators and office computers has greatly reduced the importance of techniques that permit only marginal reductions in computations. Surveyors now routinely solve their problems with calculators and computers rather than the seemingly endless array of tables that once characterized the back section of survey texts. An additional reason for the lessening importance of $D$ in computing deflection angles is that many curves (particularly at interchanges) are now being laid out by control point–based polar or intersection techniques (i.e., angle/distance or angle/angle) instead of deflection angles (see Chapter 7).

Those countries using the metric system, almost without exception, use a rational value for the radius ($R$) as a design parameter.

## 13.7  Field Procedure

With the PI location and $\Delta$ angle measured in the field, and with the radius or degree of curve ($D$) chosen consistent with the design speed, all curve computations can be completed. The surveyor then goes back to the field and measures the tangent ($T$) distance from the PI to locate the BC and EC on the appropriate tangent lines. The theodolite is then set up at the BC and zeroed and sighted on the PI. The $\Delta/2$

angle (6°25′30″ in Example 13.2) is then turned off in the direction of the EC mark (wood stake, nail, etc.). If the computations for $T$ and the field measurements of $T$ have been performed correctly, the line of sight of the $\Delta/2$ angle will fall over the EC mark. If this does not occur, the $T$ computations and then the field measurements are repeated.

The $\Delta/2$ line of sight over the EC mark will, of necessity, contain some error. In each case, the surveyor will have to decide if the resultant alignment error is acceptable for the type of survey in question. For example, if the $\Delta/2$ line of sight misses the EC mark by 0.10 ft (30 mm) in a ditched highway ℄ survey, the surveyor would probably find the error acceptable and then proceed with the deflections. However, a similar error in the $\Delta/2$ line of sight in a survey to lay out an elevated portion of urban freeway would not be acceptable; in that case, an acceptable error would be roughly one-third of the preceding error (0.03 ft or 10 mm).

After the $\Delta/2$ check has been completed satisfactorily, the curve stakes are set by turning off the deflection angle and measuring the chord distance for the appropriate stations. If possible, the theodolite is left at the BC (see next section) for the entire curve stakeout, whereas the distance measuring moves continually forward from station to station. The rear taping surveyor keeps his or her body to the outside of the curve to avoid blocking the line of sight from the instrument. If total stations or EDMs are used for the deflections, there is no rear surveyor to obstruct the line of sight.

A final verification of the work is available after the last even station has been set, as the chord distance from the last even station to the EC stake is measured and compared to the theoretical value. If the check indicates an unacceptable discrepancy, the work is checked and the discrepancy is removed.

After the curve has been deflected in, the party chief usually walks the curve, looking for any abnormalities. If a mistake has been made (putting in two stations at the same deflection angle is a common mistake), it will probably be evident. The circular curve's symmetry is such that even minor mistakes are obvious in a visual check. Note that many highway agencies use polar layout for interchanges and other complex features. If the coordinates of centerline alignment stations are determined, they can be used to locate the facility. In this application, the total station is placed at a known (or resection) station and aligned with another known station so that the instrument's processor can compute and display the angle and distance needed for layout (see also Chapters 7 and 14).

## 13.8   Moving up on the Curve

The curve deflections shown in Section 13.4 are presented in a form suitable for deflecting in while set up at the BC, with a zero setting at the PI. However, the entire curve often cannot be deflected in from the BC, and two or more instrument setups may be required before the entire curve has been located. The reasons for this situation include a loss of line of sight due to intervening obstacles (for example, detail or elevation rises).

In Figure 13.9, the data from Example 13.2 are used to illustrate the geometric considerations in moving up on the curve. In this case, station 0 + 260 cannot be established with the theodolite at the BC (as were the previous stations). The line of sight from the BC to 0 + 260 is obscured by a large tree. To establish station 0 + 260, the instrument is moved forward to the last station (0 + 240) established from the BC. The horizontal circle

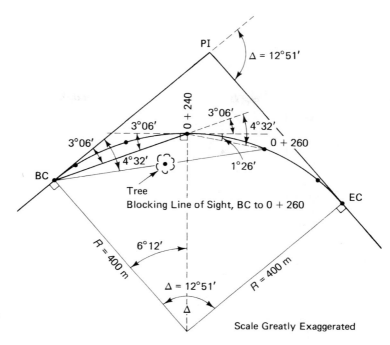

**FIGURE 13.9** Moving up on the curve.

Scale Greatly Exaggerated

is zeroed, and the BC is then sighted with the telescope in its inverted position. When the telescope is transited, the theodolite is once again oriented to the curve; that is, to set off the next (0 + 260) deflection, the surveyor refers to the previously prepared list of deflections and sets the appropriate deflection (4°32′—rounded) for the desired station location and then for all subsequent stations.

Figure 13.9 shows the geometry involved in this technique. A tangent to the curve is shown by a dashed line through station 0 + 240 (the proposed setup location). The angle from that tangent line to a line joining 0 + 240 to the BC is the deflection angle 3°06′. When the line from the BC is produced through station 0 + 240, the same angle (3°06′) occurs between that line and the tangent line through 0 + 240 (opposite angles). The deflection angle for 20 m was determined to be 1°26′ (Section 13.4). When 1°26′ is added to 3°06′, the angle of 4°32′ for station 0 + 260 results, the same angle previously calculated for that station.

This discussion has limited the move up to one station; in fact, the move up can be repeated as often as necessary to complete the curve layout. The technique can generally be stated as follows: **when the instrument is moved up on the curve and the instrument is backsighted with the telescope inverted at any other station, the theodolite will be oriented to the curve if the horizontal circle is first set to the value of the deflection angle for the sighted station.** In the case of a BC sight, the deflection angle to be set is obviously zero; if the instrument were set on 0 + 260 and sighted at 0 + 240, a deflection angle of 3°06′ would first be set on the scale.

When the inverted telescope is transited to its normal position, all subsequent stations can then be sighted by using the original list of deflections. This is the meaning of the phrase "theodolite oriented to the curve," and this is why the list of deflections can be made first, before the instrument setup stations have been determined and (as we shall see in the next section) even before it has been decided whether to run in the curve centerline (℄) or whether it would be more appropriate to run in the curve on some offset line.

## 13.9   Offset Curves

Curves laid out for construction purposes must be established on offsets so that the survey stakes are not disturbed by construction activities. Some highway agencies prefer to lay out the curve on ℄ (centerline) and then offset each ℄ stake a set distance left and right (left and right are oriented by facing toward a forward station). The stakes can be offset to one side by using the arm-swing technique described in Section 8.7.2, with the hands pointing to the two adjacent stations. If this procedure is done carefully, the offsets on that one side can be established on radial lines without too much error. After one side has been offset in this manner, the other side is then offset by lining up the established offset stake with the ℄ stake and measuring the offset distance, ensuring that all three stakes are visually in a straight line. Keeping the three stakes in a straight line will ensure that any alignment error existing at the offset stakes will steadily diminish as one moves toward the ℄ and the construction works.

In the construction of most municipal roads, particularly curbed roads, the centerline may not be established. Instead, the road alignment will be established directly on offset lines that are located a safe distance from the construction works. To illustrate, consider the curve in Example 13.2 used to construct the curbed road shown in Figure 13.10. The face

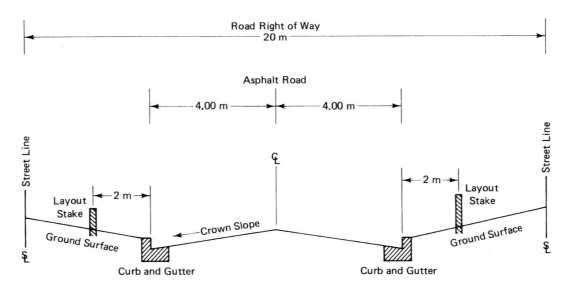

**FIGURE 13.10**   Municipal road cross section.

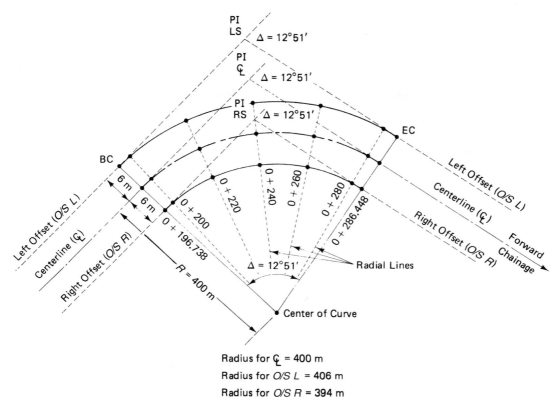

**FIGURE 13.11** Offset curves.

of the curb is to be 4.00 m left and right of the centerline. Assume that the curb layout can be offset 2 m (each side) without interfering with construction (generally, the less cut or fill required, the smaller can be the offset distance).

Figure 13.11 shows that if the layout is to be kept on radial lines through the ₵ stations, the station arc distances on the left-side (outside) curve will be longer than the corresponding ₵ arc distances, whereas the station arc distances on the right-side (inside) curve will be shorter than the corresponding ₵ arc distances. The figure also clearly shows that the ratio of the outside arc to the ₵ arc is identical to the ratio of the ₵ arc to the inside arc. (See the arc computations in the next section.) **By keeping the offset stations on radial lines, the surveyor can use the ₵ deflections previously computed.**

When using setting-out programs in total stations to locate offset stations in the field, the surveyor can simply identify the offset value (when prompted by the program) so that the processor can compute the offset stations' coordinates and then inverse to determine (and display) the required angle and distance from the instrument station. Civil COGO-type software can also be used to compute the coordinates of all offset stations, and the layout angles and distances from selected proposed instrument stations.

■ **EXAMPLE 13.4**  *Illustrative Problem for Offset Curves (Metric Units)*
Consider the problem of a construction offset layout using the data of Example 13.2, the deflections developed in Section 13.4, and the offset of 2 m introduced in the previous section.

$$\text{Given data: } \Delta = 12°51'$$

$$R = 400 \text{ m}$$

$$\text{PI at } 0 + 241.782$$

$$\text{Calculated data: } T = 45.044 \text{ m}$$

$$L = 89.710 \text{ m}$$

$$\text{BC at } 0 + 196.738$$

$$\text{EC at } 0 + 286.448$$

Required: Curbs to be laid out on 2-m offsets at 20-m stations.

**Solution**
Refer to Table 13.1.

**Table 13.1**

| Station | Computed deflection | Field deflection |
|---------|---------------------|------------------|
| BC 0 + 196.738 | 0°00′00″ | 0°00′ |
| 0 + 200 | 0°14′01″ | 0°14′ |
| 0 + 220 | 1°39′58″ | 1°40′ |
| 0 + 240 | 3°05′55″ | 3°06′ |
| 0 + 260 | 4°31′52″ | 4°32′ |
| 0 + 280 | 5°57′49″ | 5°58′ |
| EC 0 + 286.448 | 6°25′31″ | $6°25'30'' = \dfrac{\Delta}{2}$; Check |

Calculated deflections: Figures 13.10 and 13.11 show that the left-side (outside) curb face will have a radius of 404 m. A 2-m offset for that curb will result in an offset radius of 406 m. The offset radius for the right-side (inside) curb will be $400 - 6 = 394$ m.

Because we will use the deflections already computed, it remains only to calculate the corresponding left-side arc or chord distances and the corresponding right-side arc or chord distances. Although layout procedure (angle and distance) indicates that chord distances will be required, for illustrative purposes we will compute both the arc and chord distances on offset.

Arc distance computations: Figure 13.12 shows that the offset (o/s) arcs can be computed by direct ratio:

$$\frac{\text{o/s arc}}{\text{\textcentoldstyle arc}} = \frac{\text{o/s radius}}{\text{\textcentoldstyle radius}}$$

For the first arc (BC to 0 + 200):

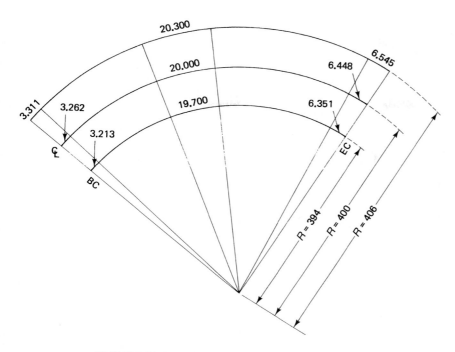

**FIGURE 13.12** Offset arc lengths calculated by ratios.

$$\text{Left side: o/s arc} = 3.262 \times \frac{406}{400} = 3.311 \text{ m}$$

$$\text{Right side: o/s arc} = 3.262 \times \frac{394}{400} = 3.213 \text{ m}$$

For the even station arcs:

$$\text{Left side: o/s arc} = 20 \times \frac{406}{400} = 20.300 \text{ m}$$

$$\text{Right side: o/s arc} = 20 \times \frac{394}{400} = 19.700 \text{ m}$$

For the last arc (0 + 280 to EC):

$$\text{Left side: o/s arc} = 6.448 \times \frac{406}{400} = 6.545 \text{ m}$$

$$\text{Right side: o/s arc} = 6.448 \times \frac{394}{400} = 6.351 \text{ m}$$

Arithmetic check:

$$\text{LS} - \math‌{C} = \math‌{C} - \text{RS}$$

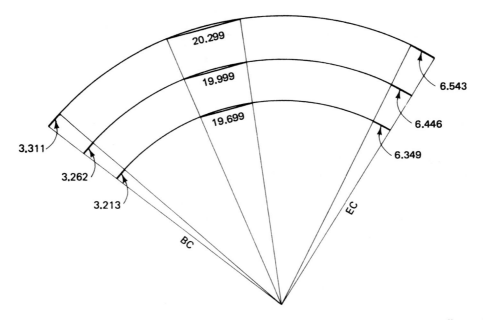

**FIGURE 13.13** Offset chords calculated from deflection angles and offset radii.

Chord distance computations: Refer to Figure 13.13. For any deflection angle, the equation for chord length (see Section 13.5 and Equation 13.8) is:

$$C = 2R \sin \text{deflection angle}$$

In this problem, the deflection angles have been calculated previously, and it is the radius ($R$) that is the variable. For the first chord (BC to $0 + 200$):

Left side: $C = 2 \times 406 \times \sin 0°14'01'' = 3.311$ m

Right side: $C = 2 \times 394 \times \sin 0°14'01'' = 3.213$ m

For the even station chords:

Left side: $C = 2 \times 406 \times \sin 1°25'57'' = 20.299$ m

Right side: $C = 2 \times 394 \times \sin 1°25'57'' = 19.699$ m

See Section 13.4. For the last chord:

Left side: $C = 2 \times 406 \times \sin 0°27'42'' = 6.543$ m

Right side: $C = 2 \times 394 \times \sin 0°27'42'' = 6.349$ m

Arithmetic check:

$$\text{LS chord} - \text{\textcentoldstyle\,chord} = \text{\textcentoldstyle\,chord} - \text{RS chord}$$

■ **EXAMPLE 13.5** *Curve Problem (Foot Units)*

Given the following ₵ data:

$$D = 5°$$

$$\Delta = 16°28'30''$$

$$PI \text{ at } 31 + 30.62$$

You must furnish stakeout information for the curve on 50-ft offsets left and right of ₵ at 50-ft stations.

**Solution**

$$R = \frac{5,729.58}{D} = 1145.92 \text{ ft}$$

$$T = R \tan \frac{\Delta}{2} = 1,145.92 \tan 8°14'15'' = 165.90 \text{ ft}$$

$$L = 100 \frac{\Delta}{D} = \frac{(100 \times 16.475)}{5} = 329.50 \text{ ft}$$

or

$$L = 2\pi R \frac{\Delta}{360} = 329.50 \text{ ft}$$

$$
\begin{array}{rl}
PI \text{ at} & 31 + 30.62 \\
-T & 1 \quad 65.90 \\
\hline
BC = & 29 + 64.72 \\
+L & 3 \quad 29.50 \\
\hline
EC = & 32 + 94.22
\end{array}
$$

Refer to Table 13.2.

Computation of deflections:

$$\text{Total deflection for curve} = \frac{\Delta}{2} = 8°14'15'' = 494.25'$$

$$\text{Deflection per foot} = \frac{494.25}{329.50} = 1.5' \text{ per ft}$$

Because $D = 5°$, the deflection for 100 ft is $D/2$ or $2°30' = 150'$. The deflection, therefore, for 1 ft is 150/100 or 1.5'.

Deflection for first station: $35.28 \times 1.5 = 52.92' = 0°52.9'$

Deflection for even 50-ft stations: $50 \times 1.5 = 75' = 1°15'$

Deflection for last station: $44.22 \times 1.5 = 66.33' = 1°06.3'$

**Table 13.2**

|  | Deflections (cumulative) | |
| Stations | Office | Field (closest minute) |
| --- | --- | --- |
| BC 29 + 64.72 | 0°00.0′ | 0°00′ |
| 30 + 00 | 0°52.9′ | 0°53′ |
| 30 + 50 | 2°07.9′ | 2°08′ |
| 31 + 00 | 3°22.9′ | 3°23′ |
| 31 + 50 | 4°37.9′ | 4°38′ |
| 32 + 00 | 5°52.9′ | 5°53′ |
| 32 + 50 | 7°07.9′ | 7°08′ |
| EC 32 + 94.22 | 8°14.2′ | 8°14′ |
|  | $\approx 8°14.25′$ |  |
|  | $= \dfrac{\Delta}{2}$, Check |  |

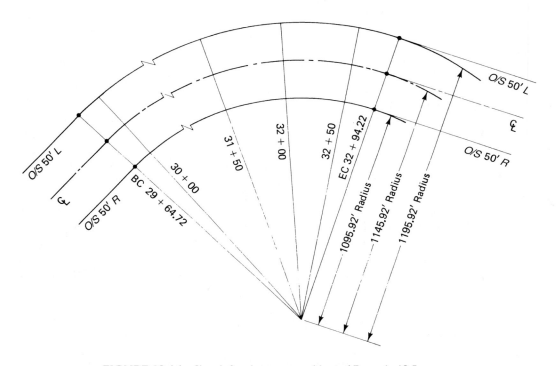

**FIGURE 13.14**   Sketch for the curve problem of Example 13.5.

Chord calculations for left- and right-side curves on 50-ft (from ℄) offsets (see Table 13.3 and Figure 13.14) are as follows:

$$\text{Radius for } ℄ = 1{,}145.92 \text{ ft}$$
$$\text{Radius for LS} = 1{,}195.92 \text{ ft}$$
$$\text{Radius for RS} = 1{,}095.92 \text{ ft}$$

**Table 13.3** CHORD CALCULATIONS FOR EXAMPLE 13.5

| Interval | Left side | $\mathcal{C}$ | Right side |
|---|---|---|---|
| BC to 30 + 00 | $C = 2 \times 1,195.92$ <br> $\times \sin 0°52.9'$ <br> $= 36.80$ ft | $C = 2 \times 1,145.92$ <br> $\times \sin 0°52.9'$ <br> $= 35.27$ ft | $C = 2 \times 1,095.92$ <br> $\times \sin 0°52.9'$ <br> $= 33.73$ ft |
| | | Diff. = 1.53 ↗  ↖ Diff. = 1.54 ↗ | |
| 50-ft stations | $C = 2 \times 1,195.92$ <br> $\times \sin 1°15'$ <br> $= 52.18$ ft | $C = 2 \times 1,145.92$ <br> $\times \sin 1°15'$ <br> $= 50.00$ (to 2 decimals) | $C = 2 \times 1,095.92$ <br> $\times \sin 1°15'$ <br> $= 47.81$ ft |
| | | Diff. = 2.18 ↗  ↖ Diff. = 2.19 ↗ | |
| 32 + 50 EC | $C = 2 \times 1,195.92$ <br> $\times \sin 1°06.3'$ <br> $= 46.13$ ft | $C = 2 \times 1,145.92$ <br> $\times \sin 1°06.3'$ <br> $= 44.20$ ft | $C = 2 \times 1,095.92$ <br> $\times \sin 1°06.3'$ <br> $= 42.27$ ft |
| | | Diff. = 1.93 ↗  ↖ Diff. = 1.93 ↗ | |

## 13.10 Compound Circular Curves

A compound curve consists of two (usually) or more circular arcs between two main tangents turning in the same direction and joining at common tangent points Figure 13.15 shows a compound curve consisting of two circular arcs joined at a point of compound curve (PCC). The lower station (chainage) curve is number 1, whereas the higher station curve is number 2. The parameters are $R_1, R_2, \Delta_1, \Delta_2$ ($\Delta_1 + \Delta_2 = \Delta$), $T_1$, and $T_2$. If four of these seven parameters are known, the others can be solved. Under normal circumstances, $\Delta_1$ and $\Delta_2$, or $\Delta$, are measured in the field, and $R_1$ and $R_2$ are given by design considerations, with minimum values governed by design speed.

Although compound curves can be manipulated to provide practically any vehicle path desired by the designer, they are not employed where simple curves or spiral curves can be used to achieve the same desired effect. Compound curves are reserved for those applications where design constraints (topographic or cost of land) preclude the use of simple or spiral curves, and they are now usually found chiefly in the design of interchange loops and ramps. Smooth driving characteristics require that the larger radius be no more than 1⅓ times larger than the smaller radius (this ratio increases to 1½ when dealing with interchange curves).

Solutions to compound curve problems vary, depending on which of the data are known in any one problem. All problems can be solved by use of the sine law or cosine law or by the omitted measurement traverse technique illustrated in Example 6.3. If the omitted measurement traverse technique is used, the problem becomes a five-sided traverse (see Figure 13.15) with sides $R_1, T_1, T_2, R_2$, and $(R_1 - R_2)$, and with angles 90°, 180 − Δ°, 90°, 180 + Δ°$_2$, and Δ°$_1$. An assumed azimuth can be chosen that will simplify the computations; that is, set the direction of $R_1$ to be 0°00'00″.

## 13.11 Reverse Curves

Reverse curves [see Figure 13.16(a) and (b)] are seldom used in highway or railway alignment. The instantaneous change in direction occurring at the point of reverse curve (PRC)

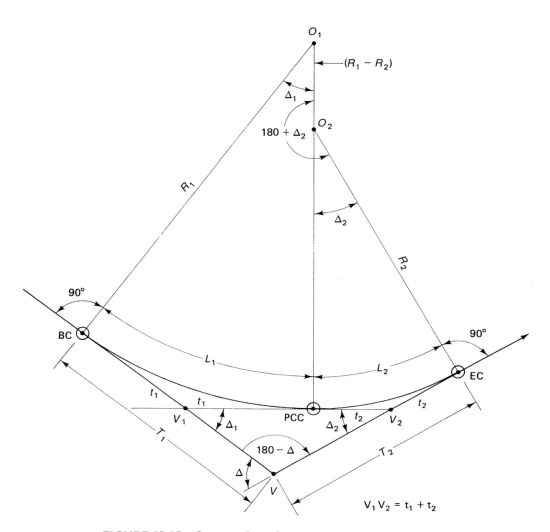

**FIGURE 13.15** Compound circular curve.

would cause discomfort and safety problems for all but the slowest of speeds. Additionally, since the change in curvature is instantaneous, there is no room to provide superelevation transition from cross-slope right to cross-slope left. However, reverse curves can be used to advantage where the instantaneous change in direction poses no threat to safety or comfort.

The reverse curve is particularly pleasing to the eye and is used with great success on park roads, formal paths, waterway channels, and the like. This curve can be encountered in both situations illustrated in Figure 13.16(a) and (b); the parallel tangent application is particularly common ($R_1$ is often equal to $R_2$). As with compound curves, reverse curves have six independent parameters ($R_1, \Delta_1, T_1, R_2, \Delta_2, T_2$). The solution technique depends on which parameters are unknown, and the techniques noted for compound curves will also provide the solution to reverse curve problems.

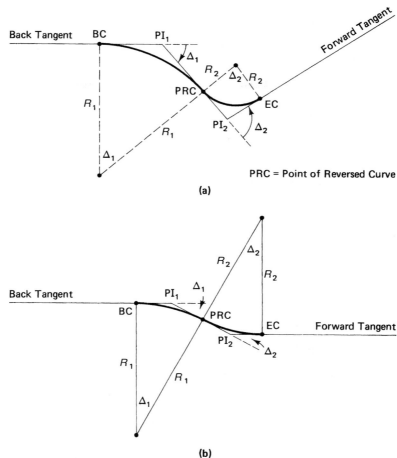

**FIGURE 13.16**
Reverse curves.
(a) Nonparallel tangents.
(b) Parallel tangents.

## 13.12 Vertical Curves: General Background

Vertical curves are used in highway and street vertical alignment to provide a gradual change between two adjacent grade lines. Some highway and municipal agencies introduce vertical curves at every change in grade-line slope, whereas other agencies introduce vertical curves into the alignment only when the net change in slope direction exceeds a specific value (for example, 1.5% or 2%).

In Figure 13.17, vertical curve terminology is introduced: $g_1$ is the slope (percentage) of the lower chainage grade line, $g_2$ is the slope of the higher chainage grade line, BVC is the beginning of the vertical curve, EVC is the end of the vertical curve, and PVI is the point of intersection of the two adjacent grade lines. The length of vertical curve ($L$) is the projection of the curve onto a horizontal surface and, as such, corresponds to plan distance. The algebraic change in slope direction is $A$, where $A = g_2 - g_1$. For example, if $g_1 = +1.5\%$ and $g_2 = -3.2\%$, $A$ would be equal to $(-3.2 - 1.5) = -4.7$.

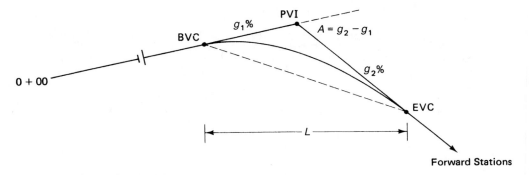

**FIGURE 13.17** Vertical curve terminology (profile view shown).

The geometric curve used in vertical alignment design is the vertical axis parabola. The parabola has the desirable characteristics of (1) a constant rate of change of slope, which contributes to smooth alignment transition, and (2) ease of computation of vertical offsets, which permits easily computed curve elevations. The general equation of the parabola is:

$$y = ax^2 + bx + c \tag{13.9}$$

The slope of this curve at any point is given by the first derivative:

$$\frac{dy}{dx} = 2ax + b \tag{13.10}$$

and the rate of change of slope is given by the second derivative:

$$\frac{d^2y}{dx} = 2a \tag{13.11}$$

which is a constant, as was previously noted. The rate of change of slope ($2a$) can also be written as $A/L$.

If, for convenience, the origin of the axes is placed at the BVC (see Figure 13.18), the general equation becomes:

$$y = ax^2 + bx$$

and because the slope at the origin is $g_1$, the expression for the slope of the curve at any point becomes:

$$\frac{dy}{dx} = \text{slope} = 2ax + g_1 \tag{13.12}$$

The general equation can finally be written as:

$$y = ax^2 + g_1x \tag{13.13}$$

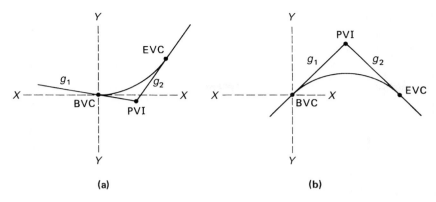

**FIGURE 13.18** Types of vertical curves. (a) Sag curve. (b) Crest curve.

## 13.13 Geometric Properties of the Parabola

Figure 13.19 illustrates the following relationships:

- The difference in elevation between the BVC and a point on the $g_1$ grade line at a distance $x$ units (feet or meters) is $g_1 x$ ($g_1$ is expressed as a decimal).

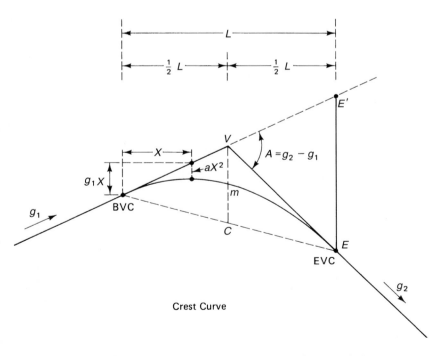

Crest Curve

**FIGURE 13.19** Geometric properties of the parabola.

- The tangent offset between the grade line and the curve is given by $ax^2$, where $x$ is the horizontal distance from the BVC; that is, tangent offsets are proportional to the squares of the horizontal distances.
- The elevation of the curve at distance $x$ from the BVC is given by $\text{BVC} + g_1 x - ax^2 =$ curve elevation (the signs would be reversed in a sag curve).
- The grade lines ($g_1$ and $g_2$) intersect midway between the BVC and the EVC; that is, BVC to $V = \frac{1}{2} L = V$ to EVC.
- Offsets from the two grade lines are symmetrical with respect to the PVI ($V$).
- The curve lies midway between the PVI and the midpoint of the chord; that is, $Cm = mV$.

## 13.14 Computation of the High or Low Point on a Vertical Curve

The locations of curve high and low points (if applicable) are important for drainage considerations; for example, on curbed streets, catch basins must be installed precisely at the drainage low point.

We noted earlier in Equation 13.12 that the slope was given by the equation:

$$\text{Slope} = 2ax + g_1$$

Figure 13.20 shows a sag vertical curve with a tangent drawn through the low point. It is obvious that the tangent line is horizontal with a slope of zero; that is:

$$2ax + g_1 = 0 \tag{13.14}$$

Had a crest curve been drawn, the tangent through the high point would have exhibited the same characteristics. Because $2a = A/L$, Equation 13.14 can be rewritten as:

$$x = -g_1\left(\frac{L}{A}\right) \tag{13.15}$$

where $x$ is the distance from the BVC to the high or low point.

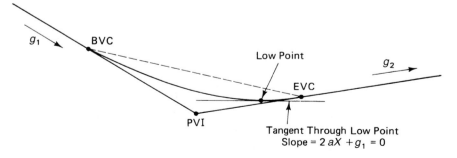

**FIGURE 13.20** Tangent at curve low point.

# 13.15 Procedure for Computing a Vertical Curve

1. Compute the algebraic difference in grades: $A = g_2 - g_1$.
2. Compute the chainage of the BVC and EVC. If the chainage of the PVI is known, ½ L is simply subtracted and added to the PVI chainage.
3. Compute the distance from the BVC to the high or low point (if applicable) using Equation 13.15 and determine the station of the high or low point.
4. Compute the tangent grade-line elevation of the BVC and the EVC.
5. Compute the tangent grade-line elevation for each required station.
6. Compute the midpoint of the chord elevation:

$$\frac{\text{Elevation of BVC + elevation of EVC}}{2}$$

7. Compute the tangent offset ($d$) at the PVI (that is, the distance Vm in Figure 13.19):

$$d = \frac{\text{difference in elevation of PVI and midpoint of chord}}{2}$$

8. Compute the tangent offset for each individual station (see line $ax^2$ in Figure 13.19):

$$\text{Tangent offset} = \frac{d(x)^2}{(L/2)^2} \text{ or } \frac{(4d)}{L^2} x^2 \tag{13.16}$$

where $x$ is the distance from the BVC or EVC (whichever is closer) to the required station.

9. Compute the elevation on the curve at each required station by combining the tangent offsets with the appropriate tangent grade-line elevations (add for sag curves and subtract for crest curves).

The techniques used in vertical curve computations are illustrated in the following example.

### ■ EXAMPLE 13.6
Given that $L = 300$ ft, $g_1 = -3.2\%$, $g_2 = +1.8\%$, and PVI at 30 + 30 with elevation $= 465.92$, determine the location of the low point and elevations on the curve at even stations, as well as at the low point.

**Solution**

1. $A = 1.8 - (-3.2) = 5.0$
2. PVI − ½ L = BVC; BVC at (30 + 30) − 150 = 28 + 80.00
   PVI + ½ L = EVC; EVC at (30 + 30) + 150 = 31 + 80.00
   EVC − BVC = L; (31 + 80) − (28 + 80) = 300      Check
3. Elevation of PVI = 465.92
   150 ft at 3.2% = 4.80 (see Figure 13.21)

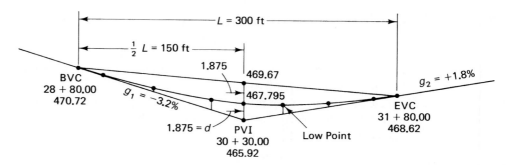

**FIGURE 13.21** Sketch for Example 13.6.

**Table 13.4** PARABOLIC CURVE ELEVATIONS BY TANGENT OFFSETS

| Station | tangent elevation | + tangent offset $\left(\dfrac{x}{1/2\,L}\right)^2 d^*$ | = curve elevation |
|---|---|---|---|
| BVC 28 + 80 | 470.72 | $(0/150)^2 \times 1.875 = 0$ | 470.72 |
| 29 + 00 | 470.08 | $(20/150)^2 \times 1.875 = .03$ | 470.11 |
| 30 + 00 | 466.88 | $(120/150)^2 \times 1.875 = 1.20$ | 468.08 |
| PVI  30 + 30 | 465.92 | $(150/150)^2 \times 1.875 = 1.875$ | 467.80 |
| Low | | | |
| Point 30 + 72 | 466.68 | $(108/150)^2 \times 1.875 = .97$ | 467.65 |
| 31 + 00 | 467.18 | $(80/150)^2 \times 1.875 = .53$ | 467.71 |
| EVC 31 + 80 | 468.62 | $(0/150)^2 \times 1.875 = 0$ | 468.62 |
| See Section 13.16 | | | |
| ⎰ 30 + 62 | 466.50 | $(118/150)^2 \times 1.875 = 1.16$ | 467.66 ⎱ |
| ⎨ 30 + 72 | 466.68 | $(108/150)^2 \times 1.875 = 0.97$ | 467.65 ⎬ |
| ⎰ 30 + 82 | 466.86 | $(98/150)^2 \times 1.875 = 0.80$ | 467.66 ⎱ |

*Where $x$ is the distance from BVC or EVC, whichever is closer.

Elevation BVC = 470.72

Elevation PVI = 465.92

150 ft at 1.8% = 2.70

Elevation EVC = 468.62

4. Location of low point is calculated using Equation 13.15:

$$x = \frac{(3.2 \times 300)}{5} = 192.00 \text{ ft} \qquad \text{(from the BVC)}$$

5. Tangent grade-line computations are entered in Table 13.4. For example:

Elevation at 29 + 00 = 470.72 − (0.032 × 20) = 470.72 − 0.64 = 470.08

6. Mid-chord elevation:

$$\frac{470.72 \text{ (BVC)} + 468.62 \text{ (EVC)}}{2} = 469.67 \text{ ft}$$

7. Tangent offset at PVI $(d)$:

$$d = \frac{\text{difference in elevation of PVI and midchord}}{2}$$

$$= \frac{469.67 - 465.92}{2} = 1.875 \text{ ft}$$

8. Tangent offsets are computed by multiplying the distance ratio squared, $(x/L/2)^2$, by the maximum tangent offset $(d)$. See Table 13.4.

9. The computed tangent offsets are added (in this example) to the tangent elevation to determine the curve elevation.

## 13.15.1 Parabolic Curve Elevations Computed Directly from the Equation

In addition to the tangent offset method shown earlier, vertical curve elevations can also be computed directly from the general equation:

$$y = ax^2 + bx + c$$

where $a = (g_2 - g_1)/2L$

$\quad L$ = horizontal length of vertical curve

$\quad b = g_1$

$\quad c$ = elevation at BVC

$\quad x$ = horizontal distance from BVC

$\quad y$ = elevation on the curve at distance $x$ from the BVC

This technique is illustrated in Table 13.5 using the data from Example 13.6.

**Table 13.5** PARABOLIC CURVE ELEVATIONS FROM THE EQUATION $y = ax^2 + bx + c$

| Station | Distance from BVC | $ax^2$ | $bx$ | $c$ | $y$ (elevation on the curve) |
|---------|---------|---------|---------|---------|---------|
| BVC 28 + 80 | 0 | | | | 470.72 |
| 29 + 00 | 20 | 0.03 | −0.64 | 470.72 | 470.11 |
| 30 + 00 | 120 | 1.20 | −3.84 | 470.72 | 468.08 |
| PVI 30 + 30 | 150 | 1.88 | −4.80 | 470.72 | 467.80 |
| Low 30 + 72 | 192 | 3.07 | −6.14 | 470.72 | 467.65 |
| 31 + 00 | 220 | 4.03 | −7.04 | 470.72 | 467.71 |
| EVC 31 + 80 | 300 | 7.50 | −9.60 | 470.72 | 468.62 |

## 13.16 Design Considerations

From Section 13.14, $2a = A/L$ is an expression giving the constant rate of change of slope for the parabola. Another useful relationship is the inverse, or:

$$K = \frac{L}{A}$$

(13.17)

where $K$ is the horizontal distance required to effect a 1% change in slope on the vertical curve. Substituting for $L/A$ in Equation 13.15 yields:

$$x = -g_1 K$$

(13.18)

where $x$ is the distance to the low point from the BVC (the result is always positive), or

$$x = +g_2 K$$

(13.19)

where $x$ is the distance to the low point from the EVC.

You can see in Figure 13.19 that $EE'$ is the distance generated by the divergence of $g_1$ and $g_2$ over the distance $L/2$:

$$EE' = \frac{(g_2 - g_1)}{100} \times \frac{L}{2}$$

You can also see in Figure 13.19 that $VC = \frac{1}{2} EE'$ (similar triangles) and that $Vm = d = \frac{1}{4} EE'$; thus:

$$d = \left(\frac{1}{4}\right)\frac{(g_2 - g_1)}{100} \times \frac{L}{2} = \frac{AL}{800}$$

(13.20)

or from Equation 13.17:

$$d = \frac{KA^2}{800}$$

(13.21)

Equations 13.18, 13.19, and 13.21 are useful when design criteria are defined in terms of $K$.

Table 13.6 shows values of $K$ for minimum stopping sight distances. On crest curves, it is assumed that the driver's eye height is at 1.05 m and the object that the driver must see is at least 0.38 m. The defining conditions for sag curves would be night-time restrictions, and they would relate to the field of view given by headlights with an angular beam divergence of 1°.

In practice, the length of the vertical curve is rounded to the nearest even meter and, if possible, the PVI is located at an even station so that the symmetrical characteristics of the curve can be fully used. To avoid the aesthetically unpleasing appearance of very short vertical curves, some agencies insist that the length of the vertical curve ($L$) be at least as long in meters as the design velocity is in kilometers per hour.

Closer analysis of the data shown in Table 13.4 indicates a possible concern. The vertical curve at the low or high point has a relatively small change of slope. This is not a

| Design speed, $v$ (km/h) | Minimum stopping sight distance, $s$ (m) | K factor Crest (m) | K factor Sag (m) |
|---|---|---|---|
| 40 | 45 | 4 | 8 |
| 50 | 65 | 8 | 12 |
| 60 | 85 | 15 | 18 |
| 70 | 110 | 25 | 25 |
| 80 | 135 | 35 | 30 |
| 90 | 160 | 50 | 40 |
| 100 | 185 | 70 | 45 |
| 110 | 215 | 90 | 50 |
| 120 | 245 | 120 | 60 |
| 130 | 275 | 150 | 70 |
| 140 | 300 | 180 | 80 |

*Source:* "Vertical Curve Tables," Ministry of Transportation, Ontario.

problem for crest curves or for sag curves for ditched roads and highways (ditches can have grade lines independent of the ₵ grade line). However, when sag curves are used for curbed municipal street design, a drainage problem is introduced. The curve elevations in parentheses in Table 13.4 cover 10 ft on either side of the low point. These data illustrate that for a distance of 20 ft, there is almost no change in elevation (that is, only 0.01 ft). If the road were built according to the design, chances are that the low-point catch basin would not drain the extended low-point area completely. The solution to this problem is for the surveyor to lower the catch-basin grate arbitrarily (1 in. is often used) to ensure proper drainage, or to install additional catch basins in the extended low area.

# 13.17 Spiral Curves: General Background

A spiral is a curve with a uniformly changing radius. Spirals are used in highway and railroad alignment to overcome the abrupt change in direction that occurs when the alignment changes from a tangent to a circular curve, and vice versa. The length of the spiral curve is also used for the transition from normally crowned pavement to fully superelevated (banked) pavement.

Figure 13.22 illustrates how the spiral curve is inserted between tangent and circular curve alignment. At the beginning of the spiral (T.S. = tangent to spiral), the radius of the spiral is the radius of the tangent line (infinitely large). The radius of the spiral curve decreases at a uniform rate until, at the point where the circular curve begins (S.C. = spiral to curve), the radius of the spiral equals the radius of the circular curve. In the previous section, we noted that the parabola, which is used in vertical alignment, had the important property of having a uniform rate of change of slope. Here, we find that the spiral, used in horizontal alignment, has a uniform rate of change of radius (curvature). This property

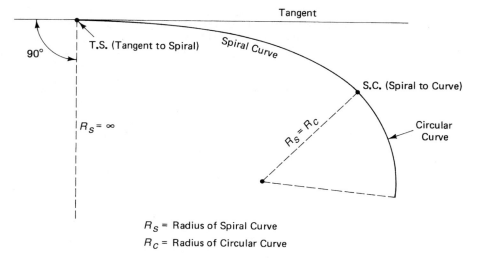

$R_S$ = Radius of Spiral Curve
$R_C$ = Radius of Circular Curve

**FIGURE 13.22** Spiral curves.

permits the driver to leave a tangent section of highway at relatively high rates of speed without experiencing problems in safety or comfort.

Figure 13.23 illustrates how the circular curve is moved inward (toward the center of the curve), leaving room for the insertion of a spiral at either end of the shortened circular curve. The amount that the circular curve is shifted in from the main tangent line is known as $P$. This shift results in the curve center ($O$) being at the distance ($R + P$) from the main tangent lines.

The spirals illustrated in this text reflect the common practice of using equal spirals to join the ends of a circular or compound curve to the main tangents. For more complex spiral applications, such as unequal spirals and spirals joining circular arcs, refer to a text on route surveying. This text shows excerpts from spiral tables (see Tables 13.7 through 13.10). Each state and province prepares and publishes similar tables for use by their personnel. A wide variety of spirals, both geometric and empirical, have been used to develop spiral tables. Geometric spirals include the cubic parabola and the clothoid curve, and empirical spirals include the A.R.E.A. 10-chord spiral used by many railroads. Generally, the use of tables is giving way to computer programs for spiral solutions. All spirals give essentially the same appearance when staked out in the field.

## 13.18  Spiral Curve Computations

Usually, data for a spiral computation are obtained as follows (refer to Figure 13.24):

1. $\Delta$ is determined in the field.
2. $R$ or $D$ (degree of curve) is given by design considerations (usually defined by design speed but sometimes by property constraints).
3. Stationing (chainage) of PI is determined in the field.
4. $L_s$ is chosen with respect to design speed and the number of traffic lanes.

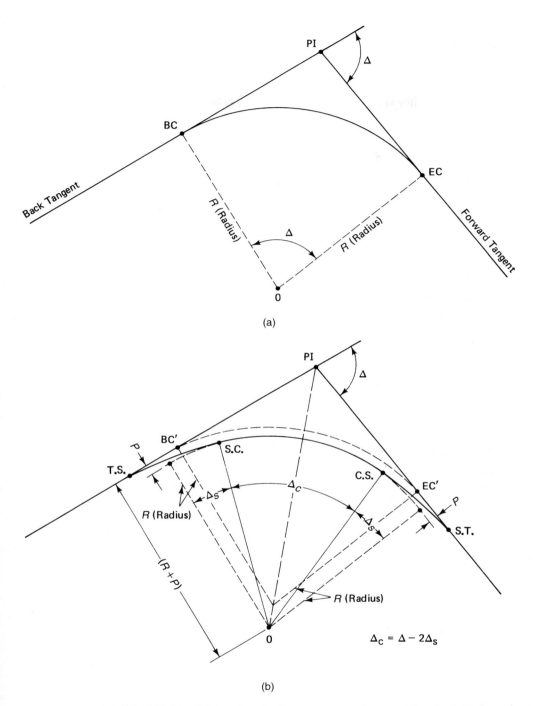

(a)

(b)

**FIGURE 13.23** Shifting the circular curve to make room for the insertion of spirals. (a) Circular curve joining two tangents. (b) Circular curve shifted inward (toward curve center) to make room for the insertion of spiral curves at either end of the circular curve.

**Table 13.7** SPIRAL TABLES FOR $L_s$ = 150 FEET

| $D$ | $\Delta_s$ | $R$ | $p$ | $R+p$ | $q$ | $LT$ | $ST$ | $D$ | $\Delta_s$ | $X_c$ | $Y_c$ | $\dfrac{D}{10L_s}$ |
|---|---|---|---|---|---|---|---|---|---|---|---|---|
| 7°30' | 5°37'30" | 763.9437 | 1.2268 | 765.1705 | 74.9759 | 100.0305 | 50.0459 | 7°30' | 5.62500° | 149.86 | 4.91 | 0.00500 |
| 8°00' | 6°00'00" | 716.1972 | 1.3085 | 717.5057 | 74.9726 | 100.0575 | 50.0523 | 8°00' | 6.00000° | 149.84 | 5.23 | 0.00533 |
| 30' | 6°22'30" | 674.0680 | 1.3902 | 675.4582 | 74.9691 | 100.0649 | 50.0590 | 30' | 6.37500° | 149.81 | 5.56 | 0.00567 |
| 9°00' | 6°45'00" | 636.6198 | 1.4719 | 638.0917 | 74.9653 | 100.0728 | 50.0662 | 9°00' | 6.75000° | 149.79 | 5.88 | 0.00600 |
| 30' | 7°07'30" | 603.1135 | 1.5536 | 604.6671 | 74.9614 | 100.0811 | 50.0738 | 30' | 7.12500° | 149.77 | 6.21 | 0.00633 |
| 10°00' | 7°30'00" | 572.9578 | 1.6352 | 574.5930 | 74.9572 | 100.0899 | 50.0817 | 10°00' | 7.50000° | 149.74 | 6.54 | 0.00667 |
| 30' | 7°52'30" | 545.6741 | 1.7169 | 547.3910 | 74.9528 | 100.0991 | 50.0901 | 30' | 7.87500° | 149.72 | 6.86 | 0.00700 |
| 11°00' | 8°15'00" | 520.8707 | 1.7985 | 522.6692 | 74.9482 | 100.1088 | 50.0989 | 11°00' | 8.25000° | 149.69 | 7.19 | 0.00733 |
| 30' | 8°37'30" | 498.2242 | 1.8802 | 500.1044 | 74.9434 | 100.1190 | 50.1082 | 30' | 8.62500° | 149.66 | 7.51 | 0.00767 |
| 12°00' | 9°00'00" | 477.4648 | 1.9618 | 479.4266 | 74.9384 | 100.1295 | 50.1178 | 12°00' | 9.00000° | 149.63 | 7.84 | 0.00800 |
| 13°00' | 9°45'00" | 440.7368 | 2.1249 | 442.8617 | 74.9277 | 100.1521 | 50.1383 | 13°00' | 9.75000° | 149.57 | 8.49 | 0.00867 |
| 14°00' | 10°30'00" | 409.2556 | 2.2880 | 411.5436 | 74.9161 | 100.1765 | 50.1605 | 14°00' | 10.50000° | 149.50 | 9.14 | 0.00933 |
| 15°00' | 11°15'00" | 381.9719 | 2.4510 | 384.4229 | 74.9037 | 100.2027 | 50.1843 | 15°00' | 11.25000° | 149.42 | 9.79 | 0.01000 |
| 16°00' | 12°00'00" | 358.0986 | 2.6139 | 360.7125 | 74.8905 | 100.2307 | 50.2098 | 16°00' | 12.00000° | 149.34 | 10.44 | 0.01067 |
| 17°00' | 12°45'00" | 337.0340 | 2.7767 | 339.8107 | 74.8764 | 100.2606 | 50.2370 | 17°00' | 12.75000° | 149.26 | 11.09 | 0.01133 |
| 18°00' | 13°30'00" | 318.3099 | 2.9394 | 321.2493 | 74.8614 | 100.2924 | 50.2659 | 18°00' | 13.50000° | 149.17 | 11.73 | 0.01200 |
| 19°00' | 14°15'00" | 301.5567 | 3.1020 | 304.6587 | 74.8456 | 100.3259 | 50.2964 | 19°00' | 14.25000° | 149.07 | 12.38 | 0.01267 |
| 20°00' | 15°00'00" | 286.4789 | 3.2645 | 289.7434 | 74.8290 | 100.3614 | 50.3287 | 20°00' | 15.00000° | 148.98 | 13.03 | 0.01333 |
| 21°00' | 15°45'00" | 272.8370 | 3.4269 | 276.2639 | 74.8115 | 100.3987 | 50.3627 | 21°00' | 15.75000° | 148.87 | 13.67 | 0.01400 |
| 22°00' | 16°30'00" | 260.4354 | 3.5891 | 264.0245 | 74.7932 | 100.4379 | 50.3983 | 22°00' | 16.50000° | 148.76 | 14.31 | 0.01467 |
| 23°00' | 17°15'00" | 249.1121 | 3.7512 | 252.8633 | 74.7740 | 100.4790 | 50.4357 | 23°00' | 17.25000° | 148.65 | 14.96 | 0.01533 |
| 24°00' | 18°00'00" | 238.7324 | 3.9132 | 242.6456 | 74.7539 | 100.5219 | 50.4748 | 24°00' | 18.00000° | 148.53 | 15.60 | 0.01600 |
| 25°00' | 18°45'00" | 229.1831 | 4.0750 | 233.2581 | 74.7331 | 100.5668 | 50.5157 | 25°00' | 18.75000° | 148.40 | 16.26 | 0.01667 |
| 26°00' | 19°30'00" | 220.3684 | 4.2367 | 224.6051 | 74.7114 | 100.6135 | 50.5582 | 26°00' | 19.50000° | 148.27 | 16.88 | 0.01733 |

*Source:* "Spiral Tables," foot units, courtesy Ministry of Transportation, Ontario, $L_s$ = 150.

All other spiral parameters can be determined by computation and/or by use of spiral tables.

$$\text{Tangent to spiral (see Figure 13.24): } T_s = (R + P) \tan \frac{\Delta}{2} + q \qquad (13.22)$$

$$\text{Spiral tangent deflection: } \Delta_s = \frac{L_s D}{200} \qquad (13.23)$$

In circular curves, $\Delta = LD/100$ (see Equation 13.7). Since the spiral has a uniformly changing $D$, the spiral angle ($\Delta_s$) equals the length of spiral ($L_s$) in stations times the average degree of curve ($D/2$):

$$\text{Total length: } L = L_c + 2L_s \qquad (13.24)$$

See Figure 13.24, where $L$ is the **total length of the curve system.**

$$\text{Total deflection (see Figure 13.24): } \Delta = \Delta_c + 2\Delta_s \qquad (13.25)$$

$$\text{Spiral deflection: } \theta_s = \frac{\Delta_s}{3} \qquad \text{(approximate)} \qquad (13.26)$$

where $\theta_s$ is the total spiral deflection angle; compare to circular curves, where the deflection angle is $\Delta/2$. This approximate formula gives realistic results for the vast majority of spiral problems. When, for example, $\Delta_s$ is as large as 21°—which is seldom the case—the correction to $\Delta_s$ is approximately $+30''$.

$$L_c = \frac{2\pi R \Delta_c}{360} \qquad \text{(foot or meter units)} \qquad (13.27)$$

$$L_c = \frac{100\Delta_c}{D} \qquad \text{(foot units)} \qquad (13.28)$$

$$\Delta_s = \frac{90}{\pi} \times \frac{L_s}{R} \qquad (13.29)$$

$$\varphi = \left(\frac{1}{L_s}\right)^2 \theta_s \qquad (13.30)$$

Equation 13.30 comes from the spiral definition, where $\varphi$ is the deflection angle for any distance $l$, and $\varphi$ and $\theta_s$ are in the same units. Practically:

$$\varphi' = \frac{l^2 (\theta_s \times 60)}{L_s^2}$$

where $\varphi'$ is the deflection angle in minutes for any distance $l$ measured from the T.S. or the S.T.

**Table 13.8** SPIRAL CURVE LENGTHS AND SUPERELEVATION RATES: SUPERELEVATION (e) MAXIMUM OF 0.06, TYPICAL FOR **NORTHERN CLIMATES**

| D | V = 30 e | L (ft) 2 lane | L (ft) 4 lane | V = 40 e | L (ft) 2 lane | L (ft) 4 lane | V = 50 e | L (ft) 2 lane | L (ft) 4 lane | V = 60 e | L (ft) 2 lane | L (ft) 4 lane | V = 70 e | L (ft) 2 lane | L (ft) 4 lane | V = 80 e | L (ft) 2 lane | L (ft) 4 lane |
|---|---|---|---|---|---|---|---|---|---|---|---|---|---|---|---|---|---|---|
| 0°15′ | NC | 0 | 0 | NC | 0 | 0 | NC | 0 | 0 | NC | 0 | 0 | NC | 0 | 0 | RC | 250 | 250 |
| 0°30′ | NC | 0 | 0 | NC | 0 | 0 | NC | 0 | 0 | RC | 200 | 200 | RC | 200 | 200 | .023 | 250 | 250 |
| 0°45′ | NC | 0 | 0 | NC | 0 | 0 | RC | 150 | 150 | .021 | 200 | 200 | .026 | 200 | 200 | .033 | 250 | 250 |
| 1°00′ | NC | 0 | 0 | RC | 150 | 150 | .020 | 150 | 150 | .027 | 200 | 200 | .033 | 200 | 200 | .041 | 250 | 250 |
| 1°30′ | RC | 100 | 100 | .020 | 150 | 150 | .028 | 150 | 150 | .036 | 200 | 200 | .044 | 200 | 200 | .053 | 250 | 300 |
| 2°00′ | RC | 100 | 100 | .026 | 150 | 150 | .035 | 150 | 150 | .044 | 200 | 200 | .052 | 200 | 250 | .059 | 250 | 300 |
| 2°30′ | .020 | 100 | 100 | .031 | 150 | 150 | .040 | 150 | 150 | .050 | 200 | 200 | .057 | 200 | 300 | .060 | 250 | 300 |
| 3°00′ | .023 | 100 | 100 | .035 | 150 | 150 | .044 | 150 | 200 | .054 | 200 | 250 | .060 | 200 | 300 | $D_{max}$ = 2°30′ | | |
| 3°30′ | .026 | 100 | 100 | .038 | 150 | 150 | .048 | 150 | 200 | .057 | 200 | 250 | $D_{max}$ = 3°00′ | | | | | |
| 4°00′ | .029 | 100 | 100 | .041 | 150 | 150 | .051 | 150 | 200 | .059 | 200 | 250 | | | | | | |
| 5°00′ | .034 | 100 | 100 | .046 | 150 | 150 | .056 | 150 | 200 | .060 | 200 | 250 | | | | | | |
| 6°00′ | .038 | 100 | 100 | .050 | 150 | 200 | .059 | 150 | 250 | $D_{max}$ = 4°30′ | | | | | | | | |
| 7°00′ | .041 | 100 | 150 | .054 | 150 | 200 | .060 | 150 | 250 | | | | | | | | | |
| 8°00′ | .043 | 100 | 150 | .056 | 150 | 200 | $D_{max}$ = 7°00′ | | | | | | | | | | | |
| 9°00′ | .046 | 100 | 150 | .058 | 150 | 200 | | | | | | | | | | | | |
| 10°00′ | .048 | 100 | 150 | .059 | 150 | 200 | | | | | | | | | | | | |
| 11°00′ | .050 | 100 | 150 | .060 | 150 | 200 | | | | | | | | | | | | |
| 12°00′ | .052 | 100 | 150 | $D_{max}$ = 11°00′ | | | | | | | | | | | | | | |
| 13°00′ | .053 | 100 | 150 | | | | | | | | | | | | | | | |
| 14°00′ | .055 | 100 | 150 | | | | | | | | | | | | | | | |
| 16°00′ | .058 | 100 | 200 | | | | | | | | | | | | | | | |
| 18°00′ | .059 | 150 | 200 | | | | | | | | | | | | | | | |
| 20°00′ | .060 | 150 | 200 | | | | | | | | | | | | | | | |
| 21°00′ | .060 | 150 | 200 | | | | | | | | | | | | | | | |
| $D_{max}$ = 21°00′ | | | | | | | | | | | | | | | | | | |

Legend:

$V$, design speed, mph

$e$, rate of superelevation, feet per foot of pavement width

$L$, length of superelevation runoff or spiral curve

NC, normal crown section

RC, remove adverse crown, superelevate at normal crown slope

$D$, degree of circular curve

Above the heavy line, spirals are not required, but superelevation is to be run off in distances shown.

*Source:* Ministry of Transportation and Communications, Ontario.

**Table 13.9** SPIRAL CURVE LENGTHS AND SUPERELEVATION RATES: SUPERELEVATION (e) MAXIMUM OF 0.100, TYPICAL FOR **SOUTHERN CLIMATES**

| | | V = 30 | | | V = 40 | | | V = 50 | | | V = 60 | | | V = 70 | | |
|---|---|---|---|---|---|---|---|---|---|---|---|---|---|---|---|---|
| | | | L | | | L | | | L | | | L | | | L | |
| D | R | e | 2 lane | 4 lane | e | 2 lane | 4 lane | e | 2 lane | 4 lane | e | 2 lane | 4 lane | e | 2 lane | 4 lane |
| 0°15′ | 22918′ | NC | 0 | 0 | NC | 0 | 0 | NC | 0 | 0 | NC | 0 | 0 | RC | 200 | 200 |
| 0°30′ | 11459′ | NC | 0 | 0 | NC | 0 | 0 | RC | 150 | 150 | RC | 175 | 175 | RC | 200 | 200 |
| 0°45′ | 7639′ | NC | 0 | 0 | RC | 125 | 125 | RC | 150 | 150 | 0.018 | 175 | 175 | 0.020 | 200 | 200 |
| 1°00′ | 5730′ | NC | 0 | 0 | RC | 125 | 125 | 0.018 | 150 | 150 | 0.022 | 175 | 175 | 0.028 | 200 | 200 |
| 1°30′ | 3820′ | RC | 100 | 100 | 0.020 | 125 | 125 | 0.027 | 150 | 150 | 0.034 | 175 | 175 | 0.042 | 200 | 200 |
| 2°00′ | 2865′ | RC | 100 | 100 | 0.027 | 125 | 125 | 0.036 | 150 | 150 | 0.046 | 175 | 190 | 0.055 | 200 | 250 |
| 2°30′ | 2292′ | 0.020 | 100 | 100 | 0.033 | 125 | 125 | 0.045 | 150 | 160 | 0.059 | 175 | 240 | 0.069 | 210 | 310 |
| 3°00′ | 1910′ | 0.024 | 100 | 100 | 0.038 | 125 | 125 | 0.054 | 150 | 190 | 0.070 | 190 | 280 | 0.083 | 250 | 370 |
| 3°30′ | 1637′ | 0.027 | 100 | 100 | 0.045 | 125 | 140 | 0.063 | 150 | 230 | 0.081 | 220 | 330 | 0.096 | 290 | 430 |
| 4°00′ | 1432′ | 0.030 | 100 | 100 | 0.050 | 125 | 160 | 0.070 | 170 | 250 | 0.090 | 240 | 360 | 0.100 | 300 | 450 |
| 5°00′ | 1146′ | 0.038 | 100 | 100 | 0.060 | 130 | 190 | 0.083 | 200 | 300 | 0.099 | 270 | 400 | $D_{max}$ = 3.9° | | |
| 6°00′ | 955′ | 0.044 | 100 | 120 | 0.068 | 140 | 210 | 0.093 | 220 | 330 | 0.100 | 270 | 400 | | | |
| 7°00′ | 819′ | 0.050 | 100 | 140 | 0.076 | 160 | 240 | 0.097 | 230 | 350 | $D_{max}$ = 5.5° | | | | | |
| 8°00′ | 716′ | 0.055 | 100 | 150 | 0.084 | 180 | 260 | 0.100 | 240 | 360 | | | | | | |
| 9°00′ | 637′ | 0.061 | 110 | 160 | 0.089 | 190 | 280 | 0.100 | 240 | 360 | | | | | | |
| 10°00′ | 573′ | 0.065 | 120 | 180 | 0.093 | 200 | 290 | $D_{max}$ = 8.3° | | | | | | | | |
| 11°00′ | 521′ | 0.070 | 130 | 190 | 0.096 | 200 | 300 | | | | | | | | | |
| 12°00′ | 477′ | 0.074 | 130 | 200 | 0.098 | 210 | 310 | | | | | | | | | |
| 13°00′ | 441′ | 0.078 | 140 | 210 | 0.099 | 210 | 310 | | | | | | | | | |
| 14°00′ | 409′ | 0.082 | 150 | 220 | 0.100 | 210 | 320 | | | | | | | | | |
| 16°00′ | 358′ | 0.087 | 160 | 240 | $D_{max}$ = 13.4° | | | | | | | | | | | |
| 18°00′ | 318′ | 0.093 | 170 | 250 | | | | | | | | | | | | |
| 20°00′ | 286′ | 0.096 | 170 | 260 | | | | | | | | | | | | |
| 22°00′ | 260′ | 0.099 | 180 | 270 | | | | | | | | | | | | |
| 24.8° | 231′ | 0.100 | 180 | 270 | | | | | | | | | | | | |
| | | $D_{max}$ = 24.8° | | | | | | | | | | | | | | |

NOTES. NC = normal crown section. RC = remove adverse crown, superelevate at normal crown slope. Spirals are desirable but not as essential above heavy line. Lengths rounded in multiples of 25 or 50 ft permit simpler calculations. The higher e value (0.100) in this table permits a sharper maximum curvature.
*Source:* American Association of State Highway and Transportation Officials (AASHTO).

**Table 13.10** SPIRAL CURVE LENGTHS AND SUPERELEVATION RATES (METRIC)

| Radius (m) | 40 *e* | 40 *A* 2 lane | 40 *A* 3 and 4 lane | 50 *e* | 50 *A* 2 lane | 50 *A* 3 and 4 lane | 60 *e* | 60 *A* 2 lane | 60 *A* 3 and 4 lane | 70 *e* | 70 *A* 2 lane | 70 *A* 3 and 4 lane | 80 *e* | 80 *A* 2 lane | 80 *A* 3 and 4 lane |
|---|---|---|---|---|---|---|---|---|---|---|---|---|---|---|---|
| 7000 | NC | | | NC | | | NC | | | NC | | | NC | | |
| 5000 | NC | | | NC | | | NC | | | NC | | | NC | | |
| 4000 | NC | | | NC | | | NC | | | NC | | | NC | | |
| 3000 | NC | | | NC | | | NC | | | NC | | | NC | | |
| 2000 | NC | | | NC | | | NC | | | RC | 275 | 275 | RC | 300 | 300 |
| 1500 | NC | | | NC | | | RC | 225 | 225 | RC | 250 | 250 | 0.024 | 250 | 250 |
| 1200 | NC | | | NC | | | RC | 200 | 200 | 0.023 | 225 | 225 | 0.028 | 225 | 225 |
| 1000 | NC | | | RC | 170 | 170 | 0.021 | 175 | 175 | 0.027 | 200 | 200 | 0.032 | 200 | 200 |
| 900 | NC | | | RC | 150 | 150 | 0.023 | 175 | 175 | 0.029 | 180 | 180 | 0.034 | 200 | 200 |
| 800 | NC | | | RC | 150 | 150 | 0.025 | 160 | 160 | 0.031 | 175 | 175 | 0.036 | 175 | 175 |
| 700 | NC | | | 0.021 | 140 | 140 | 0.027 | 150 | 150 | 0.034 | 175 | 175 | 0.039 | 175 | 175 |
| 600 | NC | 120 | 120 | 0.024 | 125 | 125 | 0.030 | 140 | 140 | 0.037 | 150 | 150 | 0.042 | 175 | 175 |
| 500 | RC | 100 | 100 | 0.027 | 120 | 120 | 0.034 | 125 | 125 | 0.041 | 140 | 150 | 0.046 | 150 | 160 |
| 400 | 0.023 | 90 | 90 | 0.031 | 100 | 100 | 0.038 | 115 | 120 | 0.045 | 125 | 135 | 0.051 | 135 | 150 |
| 350 | 0.025 | 90 | 90 | 0.034 | 100 | 100 | 0.041 | 110 | 115 | 0.048 | 120 | 125 | 0.054 | 125 | 140 |
| 300 | 0.028 | 80 | 80 | 0.037 | 90 | 100 | 0.044 | 100 | 110 | 0.051 | 120 | 125 | 0.057 | 125 | 135 |
| 250 | 0.031 | 75 | 80 | 0.040 | 85 | 90 | 0.048 | 90 | 100 | 0.055 | 110 | 120 | 0.060 | 125 | 125 |
| 220 | 0.034 | 70 | 80 | 0.043 | 80 | 90 | 0.050 | 90 | 100 | 0.057 | 110 | 110 | 0.060 | 125 | 125 |
| 200 | 0.036 | 70 | 75 | 0.045 | 75 | 90 | 0.052 | 85 | 100 | 0.059 | 110 | 110 | Minimum *R* = 250 | | |
| 180 | 0.038 | 60 | 75 | 0.047 | 70 | 90 | 0.054 | 85 | 95 | 0.060 | 110 | 110 | | | |
| 160 | 0.040 | 60 | 75 | 0.049 | 70 | 85 | 0.056 | 85 | 90 | Minimum *R* = 190 | | | | | |
| 140 | 0.043 | 60 | 70 | 0.052 | 65 | 80 | 0.059 | 85 | 90 | | | | | | |
| 120 | 0.046 | 60 | 65 | 0.055 | 65 | 75 | 0.060 | 85 | 90 | | | | | | |
| 100 | 0.049 | 50 | 65 | 0.058 | 65 | 70 | Minimum *R* = 130 | | | | | | | | |
| 90 | 0.051 | 50 | 60 | 0.060 | 65 | 70 | | | | | | | | | |
| 80 | 0.054 | 50 | 60 | 0.060 | 65 | 70 | | | | | | | | | |
| 70 | 0.058 | 50 | 60 | Minimum *R* = 90 | | | | | | | | | | | |
| 60 | 0.059 | 50 | 60 | | | | | | | | | | | | |
| | 0.059 | 50 | 60 | | | | | | | | | | | | |
| | Minimum *R* = 55 | | | | | | | | | | | | | | |

**Table 13.10** (*continued*)

| 90 e | 90 A 2 lane | 90 A 3 and 4 lane | 100 e | 100 A 2 lane | 100 A 3 and 4 lane | 110 e | 110 A 2 lane | 110 A 3 and 4 lane | 120 e | 120 A 2 lane | 120 A 3 and 4 lane | 130 e | 130 A 2 lane | 130 A 3 and 4 lane | 140 e | 140 A 2 lane | 140 A 3 and 4 lane |
|---|---|---|---|---|---|---|---|---|---|---|---|---|---|---|---|---|---|
| NC | | | NC | | | NC | | | NC | | | NC | 700 | 700 | RC | 700 | 700 |
| NC | | | NC | | | NC | 500 | 500 | RC | 600 | 600 | 0.021 | 600 | 600 | 0.024 | 625 | 625 |
| NC | | | RC | 480 | 480 | RC | 500 | 500 | 0.022 | 500 | 500 | 0.025 | 500 | 500 | 0.028 | 560 | 560 |
| RC | 390 | 400 | 0.025 | 400 | 400 | 0.023 | 450 | 450 | 0.027 | 450 | 450 | 0.030 | 450 | 450 | 0.034 | 495 | 495 |
| 0.023 | 300 | 350 | 0.027 | 340 | 340 | 0.031 | 350 | 350 | 0.035 | 350 | 350 | 0.039 | 400 | 400 | 0.043 | 400 | 400 |
| 0.029 | 270 | 275 | 0.033 | 300 | 300 | 0.037 | 300 | 300 | 0.041 | 300 | 300 | 0.046 | 330 | 330 | 0.050 | 345 | 340 |
| 0.033 | 249 | 240 | 0.038 | 250 | 250 | 0.042 | 275 | 275 | 0.047 | 285 | 285 | 0.051 | 300 | 300 | 0.056 | 330 | 330 |
| 0.037 | 225 | 225 | 0.042 | 240 | 240 | 0.046 | 250 | 260 | 0.051 | 250 | 275 | 0.055 | 300 | 300 | 0.060 | 325 | 325 |
| 0.039 | 200 | 200 | 0.044 | 225 | 225 | 0.049 | 230 | 250 | 0.053 | 250 | 270 | 0.057 | 300 | 300 | 0.060 | 325 | 325 |
| 0.042 | 200 | 200 | 0.047 | 200 | 225 | 0.051 | 225 | 250 | 0.056 | 250 | 260 | 0.060 | 275 | 275 | Minimum *R* = 1000 | | |
| 0.045 | 185 | 195 | 0.049 | 200 | 220 | 0.054 | 225 | 235 | 0.059 | 250 | 250 | 0.060 | 275 | 275 | | | |
| 0.048 | 175 | 185 | 0.053 | 200 | 200 | 0.057 | 220 | 220 | 0.060 | 250 | 250 | Minimum *R* = 800 | | | | | |
| 0.052 | 160 | 175 | 0.057 | 200 | 200 | 0.060 | 220 | 220 | Minimum *R* = 650 | | | | | | | | |
| 0.057 | 160 | 165 | 0.060 | 200 | 200 | Minimum *R* = 525 | | | | | | | | | | | |
| 0.059 | 160 | 160 | Minimum *R* = 420 | | | | | | | | | | | | | | |
| 0.060 | 160 | 160 | | | | | | | | | | | | | | | |
| Minimum *R* = 340 | | | | | | | | | | | | | | | | | |

NOTES:

$e_{max} = 0.06$

*e* is superelevation.

*A* is spiral parameter in meters.

NC is normal cross section.

RC is remove adverse crown and superelevate at normal rate.

Spiral length, $L = A^2 \div$ radius.

Spiral parameters are minimum and higher values should be used where possible.

Spirals are desirable but not essential above the heavy line.

For 6-lane pavement: above the dashed line used 4-lane values, below the dashed line use 4-lane values $\times$ 1.15.

A divided road having a median less than 7 m may be treated as a single pavement.

*Source:* Roads and Transportation Association of Canada (RTAC).

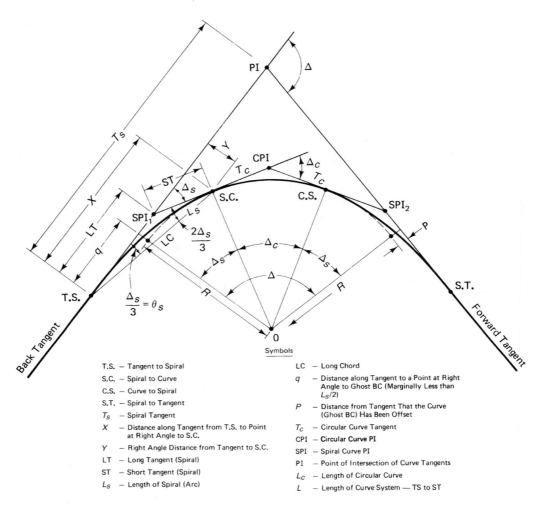

Symbols

| | | | |
|---|---|---|---|
| T.S. | – Tangent to Spiral | LC | – Long Chord |
| S.C. | – Spiral to Curve | q | – Distance along Tangent to a Point at Right Angle to Ghost BC (Marginally Less than $L_S/2$) |
| C.S. | – Curve to Spiral | | |
| S.T. | – Spiral to Tangent | P | – Distance from Tangent That the Curve (Ghost BC) Has Been Offset |
| $T_S$ | – Spiral Tangent | | |
| X | – Distance along Tangent from T.S. to Point at Right Angle to S.C. | $T_C$ | – Circular Curve Tangent |
| | | CPI | – Circular Curve PI |
| Y | – Right Angle Distance from Tangent to S.C. | SPI | – Spiral Curve PI |
| LT | – Long Tangent (Spiral) | PI | – Point of Intersection of Curve Tangents |
| ST | – Short Tangent (Spiral) | $L_C$ | – Length of Circular Curve |
| $L_S$ | – Length of Spiral (Arc) | L | – Length of Curve System — TS to ST |

**FIGURE 13.24** Summary of spiral geometry and spiral symbols.

Other values such as *x, y, P, q, ST,* and *LT* are routinely found in spiral tables issued by state and provincial highway agencies and can also be found in route surveying texts. For the past few years, solutions to these problems have been achieved almost exclusively by the use of computers and appropriate coordinate geometry computer software.

With the switch to metric that took place in the 1970s in Canada, a decision was reached to work exclusively with the radius in defining horizontal curves. It was decided that new spiral tables based solely on the *R* definition would be appropriate. The Roads and Transportation Association of Canada (RTAC) prepared spiral tables based on the spiral property defined as follows. The product of any instantaneous radius *r* and the corresponding spiral length λ (that is, l) from the beginning of the spiral to that point is equal to the product of the spiral end radius $R$ and the entire length $(L_s)$ of that spiral, which means it is a constant. Thus:

$$r\lambda = RL_s = A^2 \qquad (13.31)$$

The constant is denoted as $A^2$ to retain dimensional consistency because it represents a product of two lengths. It follows that:

$$\frac{A}{R} = \frac{L_s}{A} \qquad (13.32)$$

The RTAC tables are based on design speed and the number of traffic lanes, together with a design radius. The constant value $A$ is taken from the table and used in conjunction with $R$ to find all the spiral table curve parameters noted earlier.

Concurrent with the changeover to metric units, a major study in Ontario of highway geometrics resulted in spiral curve lengths that reflected design speed, attainment of super-elevation, driver comfort, and aesthetics. Accordingly, the spiral lengths vary somewhat from the foot unit system to the metric system.

## 13.19 Spiral Layout Procedure Summary

Refer to Figure 13.24 when following the procedure for a spiral layout:

1. Select $L_s$ (foot units) or $A$ (metric units) in conjunction with the design speed, number of traffic lanes, and sharpness of the circular curve (radius or $D$).
2. From the spiral tables, determine $P$, $q$, $x$, $y$, and so on.
3. Compute the spiral tangent ($T_s$; Equation 13.22) and the circular tangent ($T_c$; Equation 13.1).
4. Compute the spiral angle $\Delta_s$. Use Equation 13.23 for foot units or Equation 13.29 for metric units (or use tables).
5. Prepare a list of relevant layout stations. This list will include all horizontal alignment key points (for example, T.S., S.C., C.S., and S.T.), as well as all vertical alignment key points, such as grade points, BVC, low point, and EVC.
6. Calculate the deflection angles. See Equation 13.30.
7. From the established PI, measure the $T_s$ distance to locate the T.S. and S.T.
8. a. From the T.S., turn off the spiral deflection ($\theta_s = \frac{1}{3} \Delta_s$ approximately), measure the long chord (LC), and thus locate the S.C.

    **or**

    b. From the T.S., measure the $LT$ distance along the main tangent and locate the spiral PI (SPI); the spiral angle ($\Delta_s$) can now be turned, and the ST distance measured to locate the S.C.
9. From the S.C., measure the circular tangent ($T_c$) along the line $SPI_1$–SC to establish the CPI.
10. The procedure to this point is repeated, starting at the S.T.

11. The key points are verified by checking all angles and redundant distances. Some surveyors prefer to locate the CPI by intersecting the two tangent lines (that is, lines through SPI$_1$ and S.C. and through SPI$_2$ and C.S.). The locations can be verified by checking the angle $\Delta_c$ and by checking the two tangents ($T_c$).

12. Only after all key control points have been verified can the deflection angle stakeout commence. The lower chainage spiral is run in from the T.S., whereas the higher chainage spiral is run in from the S.T. The circular curve can be run in from the S.C., although it is common practice to run half the curve from the S.C. and the other half from the C.S. so that any acceptable errors that accumulate can be isolated in the middle of the circular arc where, relatively speaking, they will be less troublesome.

■ **EXAMPLE 13.7**   *Illustrative Spiral Problem (Foot Units)*
You are given the following data:

$$\Delta = 25°45' \text{ RT}$$
$$V = 40 \text{ mph}$$
$$D = 9°$$
$$\text{PI at } 36 + 17.42$$
$$\text{Two-lane highway, 24 ft wide}$$

Compute all key stations and curve deflections for 50-ft stations.

**Solution**

1. From Table 13.8:

$$L_s = 150 \text{ ft}$$
$$e = 0.058 \text{ (superelevation rate)}$$

2. From Table 13.7:

$\Delta_s = 6.75000°$ (or from Equation 13.23,
$$\Delta_s = L_s D/200 = 150/200 \times 9 = 6.75000°)$$

$R = 636.6198$ ft

$P = 1.4719$ ft

$R + P = 638.0917$ ft

$q = 74.9653$ ft

$LT = 100.0728$ ft

$ST = 50.0662$ ft

$X = 149.79$ ft

$Y = 5.88$ ft

3. $T_s = (R + p) \tan \Delta/2 + q = 638.0917 \tan 12°52.5' + 74.9653 = 220.82$ ft
4. $\Delta_c = \Delta - 2\Delta_s = 25°45' - 2(6°45') = 12°15'$
5. $L_c = 100\Delta_c = (100 \times 12.25)/9 = 136.11$ ft

6. Key station computation:

$$
\begin{array}{lrr}
\text{PI at} & 36 \,+ & 17.42 \\
-T_s & 2 & 20.82 \\
\hline
\text{T.S.} = & 33 \,+ & 96.60 \\
+L_s & 1 & 50.00 \\
\hline
\text{S.C.} = & 35 \,+ & 46.60 \\
+L_c & 1 & 36.11 \\
\hline
\text{C.S.} = & 36 \,+ & 82.71 \\
+L_s & 1 & 50.00 \\
\hline
\text{S.T.} = & 38 \,+ & 32.71 \\
\end{array}
$$

7. $\theta_s = \Delta_s/3 = 6.753000°/3 = 2.25° = 2°15'00''$

Circular curve deflections (see Table 13.11):

$$\Delta_c = 12°15'$$

$$\frac{\Delta_c}{2} = 6°07.5' = 367.5'$$

**Table 13.11**  CURVE SYSTEM DEFLECTION ANGLES

| Station | Distance from T.S. (or S.T.) $l$ (ft) | $l^2$ | $\dfrac{\theta_s° \times 60}{L_s^2}$ | $\dfrac{l^2(\theta_s \times 60)}{L_s^2}$ Deflection angle (minutes) | Deflection |
|---|---|---|---|---|---|
| T.S. 33 + 96.60 | 0 | 0 | 0.006 | 0 | 0°00'00'' |
| 34 + 00 | 3.4 | 11.6 | 0.006 | 0.070 | 0°00'04'' |
| 34 + 50 | 53.4 | 2851.4 | 0.006 | 17.108 | 0°17'06'' |
| 35 + 00 | 103.4 | 10691.6 | 0.006 | 64.149 | 1°04'09'' |
| S.C. 35 + 46.60 | 150 | 22500 | 0.006 | 135 | $\theta_s = 2°15'00''$ |

| Station | Circular curve data | | | Deflection angle | Deflection |
|---|---|---|---|---|---|
| S.C. 35 + 46.60 | $\Delta_c = 12°15', \dfrac{\Delta_c}{2} = 6°07'30''$ | | | 0°00.0 | 0°00'00'' |
| 35 + 50 | Deflection for 3.40' = 9.18' | | | 0°09.18 | 0°09'11'' |
| 36 + 00 | Deflection for 50' = 135' | | | 2°24.18 | 2°24'11'' |
| 36 + 50 | Deflection for 32.71' = 88.32' | | | 4°39.18 | 4°39'11'' |
| C.S. 36 + 82.71 | | | | 6°07.50 | 6°07'30'' |

| Station | $l$ (ft) | $l^2$ | $\dfrac{\theta_s° \times 60}{L_s^2}$ | Deflection angle (minutes) | Deflection |
|---|---|---|---|---|---|
| C.S. 36 + 82.71 | 150* | 22500 | 0.006 | 135 | $\theta_s = 2°15'00''$ |
| 37 + 00 | 132.71 | 17611.9 | 0.006 | 105.672 | 1°45'40'' |
| 37 + 50 | 87.71 | 6840.9 | 0.006 | 41.046 | 0°41'03'' |
| 38 + 00 | 32.71 | 1069.9 | 0.006 | 6.420 | 0°06'25'' |
| S.T. 38 + 32.71 | 0 | 0 | 0.006 | 0 | 0°00'00'' |

* Note that $l$ is measured from the S.T.

From Section 13.4, the deflection angle for one unit of distance is $(\Delta/2)/L$. Here, the deflection angle for one foot of arc (minutes) is:

$$\frac{\Delta_c/2}{L_c} = \frac{367.5}{136.11} = 2.700'$$

Alternatively, since $D = 9°$, then the deflection for 100 ft is $D/2$, or $4°30'$, which is $270'$. The deflection angle for 1 ft $= 270/100 = 2.700'$ (as previously noted).

The required distances (from Table 13.11) are:

$$(35 + 50) - (35 + 46.60) = 3.4'; \text{ deflection angle} = 3.4 \times 2.7 = 9.18'$$

$$\text{Even interval} = 50'; \text{ deflection angle} = 50 \times 2.7 = 135'$$

$$(36 + 82.71) - (36 + 50) = 32.71; \text{ deflection angle} = 32.71 \times 2.7 = 88.32'$$

These values are now entered cumulatively in Table 13.11.

■ **EXAMPLE 13.8**  *Illustrative Spiral Problem (Metric Units)*
You are given the following data:

$$\text{PI at } 1 + 086.271$$
$$V = 80 \text{ kmh}$$
$$R = 300 \text{ m}$$
$$\Delta = 16°00' \text{ } RT$$
$$\text{Two-lane road (7.5 m wide)}$$

Compute the spiral and circular curve deflections for layout on even 20-meter stations.

**Solution**
From Table 13.10, $A = 125$ and $e = 0.057$. (See Section 13.21 for a discussion of superelevation.) From Table 13.12, we obtain the following:

| Steps 1 and 2: | For A = 125 | and R = 300 |
|---|---|---|
| | $L_s = 52.083$ m | LT = 34.736 m |
| | $P = 0.377$ m | ST = 17.374 m |
| | $X = 52.044$ m | $\Delta_s = 4°58'24.9''$ |
| | $Y = 1.506$ m | $\theta_s = 1/3 \, \Delta_s = 1°39'27.9''$ |
| | $q = 26.035$ m | LC = 52.066 m long chord |

From Equation 13.29, we have:

$$\Delta_s = \frac{90}{\pi} \times L_s/R$$

$$= \frac{90}{\pi} \times \frac{52.083}{300} = 4.9735601° = 4°58'24.8''$$

**Table 13.12  FUNCTIONS OF THE STANDARD SPIRAL FOR A = 125 M**

| R (m) | A/R | $L_s$ | X | Y | q | P | LT | ST | LC | $\Delta_s$ | $\theta_s$* Degrees | Minutes | Seconds |
|---|---|---|---|---|---|---|---|---|---|---|---|---|---|
| | | | | | Meters | | | | | | | | |
| 115 | 1.0870 | 135.870 | 131.204 | 26.095 | 67.152 | 6.606 | 92.293 | 46.851 | 133.774 | 33 50 48.3 | 11 | 14 | 55.1 |
| 120 | 1.0417 | 130.208 | 126.428 | 23.057 | 64.471 | 5.825 | 88.183 | 44.658 | 128.513 | 31 05 05.8 | 10 | 20 | 08.3 |
| 125 | 1.0000 | 125.000 | 121.911 | 20.464 | 61.983 | 5.162 | 84.451 | 42.685 | 123.617 | 28 38 52.4 | 9 | 31 | 44.3 |
| 130 | 0.9615 | 120.192 | 117.649 | 18.240 | 59.671 | 4.595 | 81.044 | 40.898 | 119.055 | 26 29 11.7 | 8 | 48 | 46.1 |
| 140 | 0.8929 | 111.607 | 109.847 | 14.661 | 55.509 | 3.686 | 75.034 | 37.755 | 110.821 | 22 50 16.5 | 7 | 36 | 08.5 |
| 150 | 0.8333 | 104.167 | 102.918 | 11.953 | 51.875 | 3.001 | 69.888 | 35.126 | 103.610 | 19 53 39.7 | 6 | 37 | 28.8 |
| 160 | 0.7813 | 97.656 | 96.751 | 9.868 | 48.677 | 2.475 | 65.425 | 32.844 | 97.253 | 17 29 07.0 | 5 | 49 | 25.8 |
| 170 | 0.7353 | 91.912 | 91.242 | 8.239 | 45.844 | 2.065 | 61.511 | 30.852 | 91.614 | 15 29 19.3 | 5 | 09 | 34.9 |
| 180 | 0.6944 | 86.086 | 86.302 | 6.948 | 43.319 | 1.741 | 58.048 | 29.096 | 86.581 | 13 48 55.9 | 4 | 36 | 10.5 |
| 190 | 0.6579 | 82.237 | 81.853 | 5.913 | 41.054 | 1.481 | 54.960 | 27.535 | 82.066 | 12 23 58.3 | 4 | 07 | 53.5 |
| 200 | 0.6250 | 78.125 | 77.828 | 5.072 | 39.013 | 1.270 | 52.188 | 26.137 | 77.993 | 11 11 26.1 | 3 | 43 | 44.4 |
| 210 | 0.5952 | 74.405 | 74.172 | 4.384 | 37.163 | 1.097 | 49.685 | 24.876 | 74.301 | 10 09 00.7 | 3 | 22 | 57.0 |
| 220 | 0.5682 | 71.023 | 70.838 | 3.814 | 35.481 | 0.954 | 47.413 | 23.733 | 70.941 | 9 14 54.3 | 3 | 04 | 55.6 |
| 230 | 0.5435 | 67.935 | 67.787 | 3.339 | 33.943 | 0.835 | 45.342 | 22.692 | 67.869 | 8 27 42.1 | 2 | 49 | 12.1 |
| 240 | 0.5208 | 65.104 | 64.984 | 2.940 | 32.532 | 0.735 | 43.455 | 21.739 | 65.051 | 7 46 16.5 | 2 | 35 | 24.0 |
| 250 | 0.5000 | 62.500 | 62.402 | 2.601 | 31.234 | 0.651 | 41.701 | 20.864 | 62.457 | 7 09 43.1 | 2 | 23 | 13.2 |
| 280 | 0.4464 | 55.804 | 55.748 | 1.852 | 27.983 | 0.463 | 37.222 | 18.619 | 55.779 | 5 24 34.1 | 1 | 54 | 10.8 |
| 300 | 0.4167 | 52.083 | 52.044 | 1.506 | 26.035 | 0.377 | 34.736 | 17.374 | 52.066 | 4 58 24.9 | 1 | 39 | 27.9 |
| 320 | 0.3906 | 48.828 | 48.800 | 1.241 | 24.409 | 0.310 | 32.562 | 16.285 | 48.815 | 4 22 16.8 | 1 | 27 | 25.3 |
| 340 | 0.3676 | 45.956 | 45.935 | 1.035 | 22.974 | 0.259 | 30.645 | 15.325 | 45.947 | 3 52 19.8 | 1 | 17 | 26.4 |
| 350 | 0.3571 | 44.643 | 44.625 | 0.949 | 22.318 | 0.237 | 29.768 | 14.887 | 44.635 | 3 39 14.6 | 1 | 13 | 04.7 |
| 380 | 0.3289 | 41.118 | 41.106 | 0.741 | 20.557 | 0.185 | 27.416 | 13.710 | 41.113 | 3 05 59.6 | 1 | 01 | 59.8 |
| 400 | 0.3125 | 39.063 | 39.063 | 0.636 | 19.530 | 0.159 | 26.045 | 13.024 | 39.058 | 2 47 51.5 | 0 | 55 | 57.1 |
| 420 | 0.2976 | 37.202 | 37.195 | 0.549 | 18.600 | 0.137 | 24.804 | 12.403 | 37.195 | 2 32 15.2 | 0 | 50 | 45.0 |
| 450 | 0.2778 | 34.722 | 34.717 | 0.446 | 17.360 | 0.112 | 23.150 | 11.576 | 34.720 | 2 12 37.7 | 0 | 44 | 12.5 |
| 475 | 0.2632 | 32.895 | 32.891 | 0.380 | 16.447 | 0.095 | 21.931 | 10.966 | 32.893 | 1 59 02.1 | 0 | 39 | 40.7 |
| 500 | 0.2500 | 31.250 | 31.247 | 0.325 | 15.624 | 0.081 | 20.834 | 10.418 | 31.249 | 1 47 25.8 | 0 | 35 | 48.6 |
| 525 | 0.2381 | 29.762 | 29.760 | 0.281 | 14.881 | 0.070 | 19.842 | 9.921 | 29.761 | 1 37 26.5 | 0 | 32 | 20.8 |
| 550 | 0.2273 | 28.409 | 28.407 | 0.245 | 14.204 | 0.061 | 18.940 | 9.470 | 28.408 | 1 28 47.1 | 0 | 29 | 35.7 |
| 575 | 0.2174 | 27.174 | 27.172 | 0.214 | 13.587 | 0.054 | 18.116 | 9.058 | 27.173 | 1 21 13.9 | 0 | 27 | 04.6 |

*Short radius (i.e., <150 m) may require a correction to $\Delta_s/3$ to determine the precise value of $\theta_s$.
Source: "Metric Curve Tables," Table IV, Roads and Transportation Association of Canada (RTAC). A = 125 m.

Step 3: From Equation 13.22, we have:

$$T_s = (R + p)\tan\frac{\Delta}{2} + q$$

$$= 300.377\tan 8° + 26.035 = 68.250 \text{ m}$$

Step 4:

$$\Delta_c = \Delta - 2\Delta_s$$
$$= 16° - 2(4°58'24.8'') = 6°03'10.2''$$
$$\frac{\Delta_c}{2} = 3°01'35.1''$$

Step 5: From Equation 13.5:

$$L_c = \frac{2\pi R\Delta_c}{360}$$

$$= \left(2\pi \times 300 \times \frac{6.052833}{360}\right) = 31.693 \text{ m}$$

Step 6: Key station computation:

$$
\begin{array}{lr}
\text{PI at} & 1 + 086.271 \\
-T_s & 68.250 \\
\hline
\text{T.S.} = & 1 + 018.021 \\
+L_s & 52.083 \\
\hline
\text{S.C.} = & 1 + 070.104 \\
+L_c & 31.693 \\
\text{C.S.} = & 1 + 101.797 \\
+L_s & 52.083 \\
\text{S.T.} = & 1 + 153.880 \\
\end{array}
$$

Circular curve deflections (see Table 13.13):

$$\Delta_c = 6°03'10''$$

$$\frac{\Delta_c}{2} = 3°01'35'' = 181.58'$$

From Section 13.4, the deflection angle for one unit of distance is $(\Delta/2)/L$. Here, the deflection angle for 1 m of arc is:

$$\frac{\Delta_c/2}{L_c} = \frac{181.58}{31.693} = 5.7293'$$

The required distances (deduced from Table 13.13) are:

$(1 + 080) - (1 + 070.104) = 9.896$; deflection angle $= 5.7293 \times 9.896 = 56.70'$

**Table 13.13**  CURVE SYSTEM DEFLECTION ANGLES

| Station | Distance from T.S. (or S.T.) $l$ (m) | $l^2$ | $\dfrac{\theta_s \times 60}{L_s^2}$ | $\dfrac{l^2\,(\theta_s \times 60)}{L_s^2}$ Deflection (minutes) | Deflection |
|---|---|---|---|---|---|
| T.S. 1 + 018.021 | 0 | 0 | | | 0°00′00″ |
| 1 + 020 | 1.979 | 3.9 | 0.036667 | 0.1436 | 0°00′09″ |
| 1 + 040 | 21.979 | 483.9 | 0.036667 | 17.71 | 0°17′43″ |
| 1 + 060 | 41.979 | 1762.2 | 0.036667 | 64.62 | 1°04′37″ |
| S.C. 1 + 070.104 | 52.083 | 2712.6 | 0.036667 | 99.464 | 1°39′28″ |

| | Circular curve data | | | Deflection angle (cumulative) | |
|---|---|---|---|---|---|
| S.C. 1 + 070.104 | $\Delta_c = 6°03′10″,\ \dfrac{\Delta_c}{2} = 3°01′35″$ | | | 0°00.00′ | 0°00′00″ |
| 1 + 080 | Deflection for 9.896 m = 56.70″ | | | 0°56.70′ | 0°56′42″ |
| 1 + 100 | Deflection for 20 m = 114.59′ | | | 2°51.29′ | 2°51′17″ |
| C.S. 1 + 101.797 | Deflection for 1.797 m = 10.30″ | | | 3°01.59′ | 3°01′35″ |

| Station | $l$ (m) | $l^2$ | $\dfrac{\theta_s \times 60}{L_s^2}$ | Deflection (minutes) | Deflection (cumulative) |
|---|---|---|---|---|---|
| C.S. 1 + 101.797 | 52.083* | 2,712.6 | 0.036667 | 99.464 | 1°39′28″ |
| 1 + 120 | 33.880 | 1,147.9 | 0.036667 | 42.09 | 0°42′05″ |
| 1 + 140 | 13.880 | 192.7 | 0.036667 | 7.06 | 0°07′04″ |
| S.T. 1 + 153.880 | 0 | 0 | 0.036667 | 0 | 0°00′00″ |

*Note that $l$ is measured from the S.T.

Even interval = 20.000; deflection angle = 5.7293 × 20 = 114.59′

(1 + 101.797) − (1 + 100) = 1.797; deflection angle = 5.7293 × 1.787 = 10.30′

These values are now entered cumulatively in Table 13.13.

# 13.20  Approximate Solution for Spiral Problems

It is possible to lay out spirals by using the approximate relationships illustrated in Figure 13.25. Since $L_s \approx LC$ (long chord), the following can be assumed:

$$\frac{Y}{L_s} = \sin\theta_s \qquad Y = L_s \sin\theta_s \tag{13.33}$$

$$X^2 = L_s^2 - Y^2$$
$$X = \sqrt{L_s^2 - Y^2} \tag{13.34}$$

$$q = \frac{1}{2}X \tag{13.35}$$

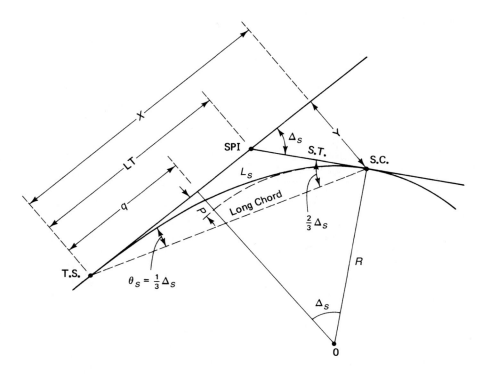

Basic Assumption: $L_s \approx$ Long Chord

**FIGURE 13.25**  Sketch for approximate formulas.

**Table 13.14**  DATA SUMMARY

| Parameter | Precise methods | | Approximate methods | |
|---|---|---|---|---|
| | Example 13.7 (ft) | Example 13.8 (m) | Example 13.7 | Example 13.8 |
| $Y$ | 5.88 | 1.506 | 5.89 | 1.507 |
| $X$ | 149.79 | 52.044 | 149.88 | 52.061 |
| $q$ | 74.97 | 26.035 | 74.94 | 26.031 |
| $P$ | 1.47 | 0.377 | 1.47 | 0.377 |
| LT | 100.07 | 34.736 | 100.13 | 34.744 |
| ST | 50.07 | 17.374 | 50.10 | 17.379 |

$$p = \frac{1}{4} Y \qquad (13.36)$$

Using the sine law, we obtain the following equation:

$$LT = \sin\left(\frac{2}{3}\right)\Delta_s \times \frac{\sin L_s}{\sin \Delta_s} \qquad (13.37)$$

Using the sine law yields:

$$ST = \sin\left(\frac{1}{3}\right)\Delta_s \times \frac{L_s}{\sin \Delta_s} \qquad (13.38)$$

For comparison, the values in Examples 13.7 and 13.8 are compared to the values obtained by the approximate methods. From Table 13.14, we can see that the precise and approximate values for $Y$, $X$, $q$, $P$, LT, and ST are quite similar. The largest discrepancy shows up in the $X$ value, which is not required for spiral layout. The larger the $\Delta_s$ values, the larger will be the discrepancy between the precise and approximate values. For the normal range of spirals in use, the approximate method is adequate for the layout of an asphalt-surfaced, ditched highway. For curbed highways or elevated highways, precise methods should be employed.

## 13.21  Superelevation: General Background

If a vehicle travels too fast on a horizontal curve, the vehicle may either skid off the road or overturn. The factors that cause this phenomenon are based on the radius of curvature and the velocity of the vehicle: the sharper the curve and the faster the velocity, the larger will be the centrifugal force requirement. Two factors help to stabilize the radius and velocity factors: (1) side friction, which is always present to some degree between the vehicle tires and the pavement, and (2) superelevation ($e$), which is a banking of the pavement toward the center of the curve.

The side friction factor ($f$) has been found to vary linearly with velocity. Design values for $f$ range from 0.16 at 30 mph (50 km/h) to 0.11 at 80 mph (130 km/h). Superelevation must satisfy normal driving practices and climatic conditions. In practice, values for superelevation range from 0.125 (that is, 0.125 ft/ft or 12.5% cross slope) in relatively ice-free southern states to 0.06 in the northern states and Canadian provinces. Typical values for superelevation can be found in Tables 13.8 and 13.9.

## 13.22  Superelevation Design

Figure 13.26 illustrates how the length of spiral ($L_s$) is used to change the pavement cross slope from normal crown to full superelevation. Figure 13.26(b) illustrates that the pavement can be revolved about the centerline (the usual case), or the pavement can be revolved about the inside or outside edges, a technique that is often encountered on divided four-lane highways where a narrow median restricts drainage profile manipulation.

Figures 13.28(b) and 13.29 clearly show the technique used to achieve pavement superelevation when revolving the pavement edges about the centerline (℄) profile. At points $A$ and $A'$, the pavement is at normal crown cross section—with both edges (inside and outside) of the pavement a set distance below the ℄ elevation. At points S.C. ($D$) and C.S. ($D'$), the pavement is at full superelevation—with the outside edge a set distance above the ℄ elevation and the inside edge the same set distance below the ℄ elevation. The transition from normal crown cross section to full superelevation cross section proceeds as follows.

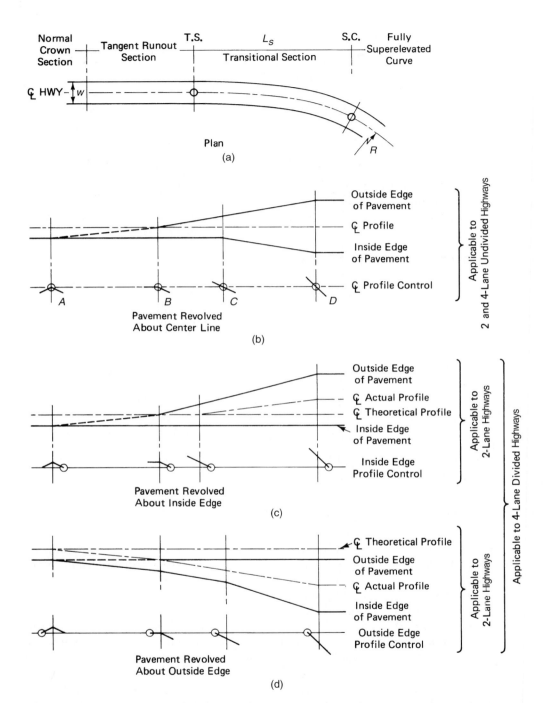

**FIGURE 13.26** Methods of attaining superelevation for spiraled curves. (From *Geometric Design Standards for Ontario Highways,* Ministry of Transportation, Ontario)

### OUTSIDE EDGE

- From *A* to the T.S. (*B*), the outside edge rises at a ratio of 400:1 (relative to the ℄ profile) and becomes equal in elevation to the ℄.
- From the T.S. (*B*), the outside edge rises (relative to the ℄ profile) at a uniform rate from being equal to the ℄ elevation at the T.S. (*B*) until it is at full superelevation above the ℄ elevation at the S.C. (*D*).

### INSIDE EDGE

- From *A*, through the T.S. (*B*), to point *C*, the inside edge remains below the ℄ profile at normal crown depth.
- From *C* to the S.C. (*D*), the inside edge drops at a uniform rate from being at normal crown depth below the ℄ profile to being at full superelevation depth below the ℄ profile.

The transition from full superelevation at the C.S. (*D'*) to normal cross section at *A'* proceeds in a manner reverse to that just described.

■ **EXAMPLE 13.9** *Superelevation Problem (Foot Units)*
See Figure 13.27 for vertical curve computations and Figures 13.28 and 13.29 for pavement superelevation computations. This example uses the horizontal curve data of Example 13.7:

$$V = 40 \text{ mph}$$
$$\Delta = 25°45' \text{ RT}$$
$$D = 9°$$

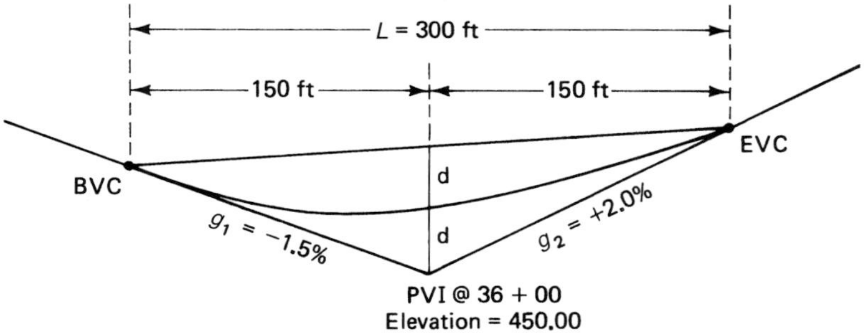

$$\text{BVC} = (36 + 00) - 150 = 34 + 50$$
$$\text{EVC} = (36 + 00) + 150 = 37 + 50$$
$$\text{Elevation BVC} = 450.00 + (150 \times 0.015) = 452.25$$
$$\text{Elevation EVC} = 450.00 + (150 \times 0.020) = 453.00$$
$$\text{Midchord Elevation} = \frac{452.25 + 453.00}{2} = 452.63$$
$$\text{Tangent Offset: } d = \frac{452.63 - 450.00}{2} = 1.315 \text{ ft}$$

**FIGURE 13.27** Vertical curve solution for the problem of Example 13.9.

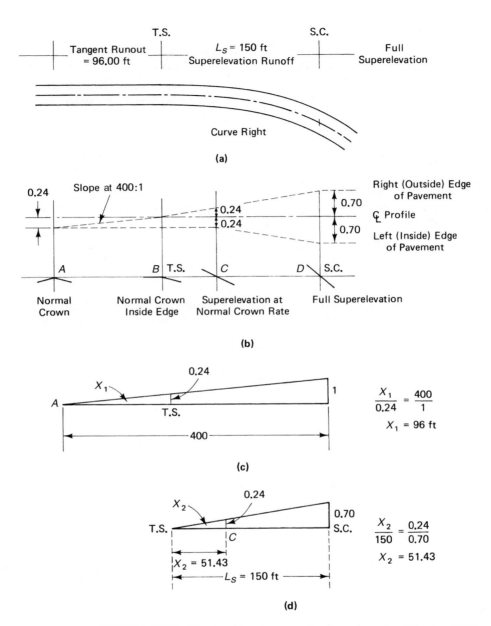

**FIGURE 13.28** Sketches for the superelevation example of Section 13.22 and Example 13.9. (a) Plan. (b) Profile and cross sections. (c) Computation of tangent runout. (d) Location of point C.

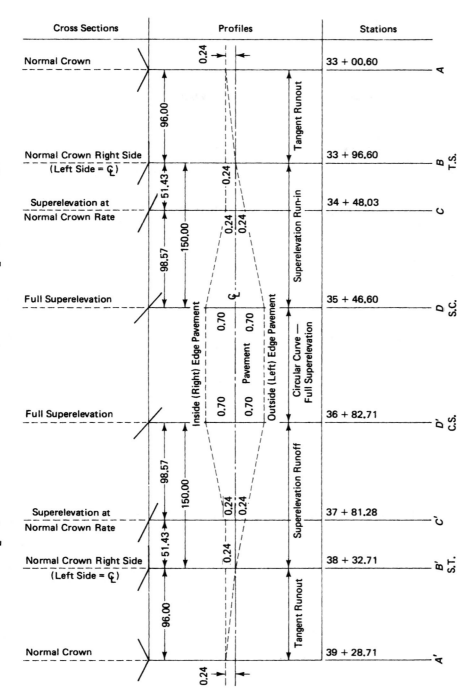

**FIGURE 13.29** Superelevated pavement profiles and cross sections for the problem of Example 13.9.

PI at 36 + 17.42

Two-lane highway, 24 ft wide, each lane 12 ft wide

Additional data are as follows:

PVI at 36 + 00

Elevation PVI = 450.00

$g_1 = -1.5\%$

$g_2 = +2\%$

$L = 300$ ft

Tangent runout at 400:1

Normal crown at 2%

Pavement revolved about the ℄

From Tables 13.8 and 13.9, we have:

$$L_s = 150 \text{ ft}$$
$$e = 0.058$$

Chainage of low point:

$$X = \frac{-g_1 L}{A} = \frac{1.5 \times 300}{2 - (-1.5)} = 128.57 \text{ ft}$$

BVC at 34 + 50

$$X = 1 \quad 28.57$$

Low point = 35 + 78.57

You must determine the ℄ and edge-of-pavement elevations for even 50-ft stations and all other key stations.

**Solution**

1. Compute the key horizontal alignment stations. (These stations have already been computed in Example 13.7.)
2. Solve the vertical curve for ℄ elevations at 50-ft stations, the low point, **plus any horizontal alignment key stations that may fall between the BVC and EVC.**
3. Begin preparation of Table 13.15, showing all key stations for both horizontal and vertical alignment. List the ℄ grade elevation for each station.
4. Compute station $A$; see Figure 13.28(c):

$$\text{Cross fall at 2\% for 12 ft} = 0.02 \times 12 = 0.24 \text{ ft}$$

$$\text{Tangent runout} = \frac{400}{1} \times 0.24 = 96 \text{ ft}$$

**Table 13.15** ℄ PAVEMENT ELEVATIONS

| Station | | Tangent elevation | Tangent offset $\left(\dfrac{X}{L/2}\right)^2 d$ | | | ℄ elevation |
|---|---|---|---|---|---|---|
| A | 33 + 00.60 | 454.49 | | | | 454.49 |
| | 33 + 50 | 453.75 | | | | 453.75 |
| T.S. (B) | 33 + 96.60 | 453.05 | | | | 453.05 |
| | 34 + 00 | 453.00 | | | | 453.00 |
| C | 34 + 48.03 | 452.28 | | | | 452.28 |
| BVC | 34 + 50 | 452.25 | $(0/150)^2 \times 1.32 =$ | | 0 | 452.25 |
| | 35 + 00 | 451.50 | $(50/150)^2 \times 1.32 =$ | | 0.15 | 451.65 |
| S.C. (D) | 35 + 46.60 | 450.79 | $(96.6/150)^2 \times 1.32 =$ | | 0.55 | 451.35 |
| | 35 + 50 | 450.75 | $(100/150)^2 \times 1.32 =$ | | 0.58 | 451.33 |
| Low point | 35 + 78.57 | 450.32 | $(128.6/150)^2 \times 1.32 =$ | 0.97 | | 451.29 |
| PVI | 36 + 00 | 450.00 | $(150/150)^2 \times 1.32 =$ | | 1.32 | 451.32 |
| | 36 + 50 | 451.00 | $(100/150)^2 \times 1.32 =$ | | 0.58 | 451.58 |
| C.S. (D') | 36 + 82.71 | 451.65 | $(67.3/150)^2 \times 1.32 =$ | | 0.27 | 451.92 |
| | 37 + 00 | 452.00 | $(50/150)^2 \times 1.32 =$ | | 0.15 | 452.15 |
| EVC | 37 + 50 | 453.00 | $(0/150)^2 \times 1.32 =$ | | 0 | 453.00 |
| C' | 37 + 81.28 | 453.63 | | | | 453.63 |
| | 38 + 00 | 454.00 | | | | 454.00 |
| S.T. (B') | 38 + 32.71 | 454.65 | | | | 454.65 |
| | 39 + 00 | 456.00 | | | | 456.00 |
| A' | 39 + 28.71 | 456.57 | | | | 456.57 |

$$\text{T.S.} = 33 + 96.60 \text{ ft}$$
$$X_1 \text{ (tangent runout)} = \underline{\quad 96.00 \quad}$$
$$A = 33 + 00.60$$

Compute station A' (the tangent runout at the higher chainage spiral):

$$\text{S.T.} = 38 + 32.71$$
$$\text{Tangent runout} \quad \underline{+\ 96.00}$$
$$A' = 39 + 28.71$$

5. Compute station C; see Figure 13.28(d):

$$\text{Cross fall at 5.8\% for 12-ft lane} = 0.058 \times 12 = 0.70 \text{ ft}$$

$$\text{Distance from T.S. to } C = 150 \times \frac{0.24}{0.70} = 51.43 \text{ ft}$$

$$\text{T.S.} = 33 + 96.60$$
$$X \text{ distance} = \underline{\quad 51.43 \quad}$$
$$C = 34 + 48.03$$

Compute station C' (at the higher chainage spiral):

$$\text{S.T.} = 38 + 32.71$$

$$X_2 \text{ distance} = 51.43$$

$$C' = 37 + 81.28$$

6. Figure 13.29 shows that right-side pavement elevations are 0.24 ft below ℄ elevation from $A$ to $C$ and from $C'$ to $A'$, and 0.70 ft below ℄ from S.C. to C.S. Right-side pavement elevations between $C$ and S.C. and C.S. and $C'$ must be interpolated. Figure 13.29 also shows that left-side pavement elevations must be interpolated between $A$ and T.S., between T.S. and S.C., between C.S. and S.T., and between S.T. and $A'$. Between S.C. and C.S., the left-side pavement elevation is 0.70 higher than the corresponding ℄ elevations.

7. Fill in the left- and right-edge pavement elevations (Table 13.16), where the computation simply involves adding or subtracting normal crown (0.24) or full superelevation (0.70).

8. Perform the computations necessary to interpolate for the missing pavement-edge elevations in Table 13.16 (values are underlined). See Figures 13.30 and 13.31.

**Table 13.16** PAVEMENT ELEVATIONS FOR THE PROBLEM OF SECTION 13.22

|  | Station | ℄ grade | Left-edge pavement Above/below ℄ | Left-edge pavement Elevation | Right-edge pavement Below ℄ | Right-edge pavement Elevation |
|---|---|---|---|---|---|---|
| $A$ | 33 + 00.60 | 454.49 | −0.24 | 454.25 | −0.24 | 454.25 |
|  | 33 + 50 | 453.75 | −0.12 | 453.63 | −0.24 | 453.51 |
| T.S. ($B$) | 33 + 96.60 | 453.05 | 0.00 | 453.05 | −0.24 | 452.81 |
|  | 34 + 00 | 453.00 | +0.02 | 453.02 | −0.24 | 452.76 |
| $C$ | 34 + 48.03 | 452.28 | +0.24 | 452.52 | −0.24 | 452.04 |
| BVC | 34 + 50 | 452.25 | +0.25 | 452.50 | −0.25 | 452.00 |
|  | 35 + 00 | 451.65 | +0.48 | 452.13 | −0.48 | 451.17 |
| S.C. ($D$) | 35 + 46.60 | 451.35 | +0.70 | 452.05 | −0.70 | 450.65 |
|  | 35 + 50 | 451.33 | +0.70 | 452.02 | −0.70 | 450.62 |
| Low pt. | 35 + 78.57 | 451.29 | +0.70 | 451.99 | −0.70 | 450.59 |
| PVI | 36 + 00 | 451.32 | +0.70 | 452.02 | −0.70 | 450.62 |
|  | 36 + 50 | 451.58 | +0.70 | 452.28 | −0.70 | 450.88 |
| C.S. ($D'$) | 36 + 82.71 | 451.92 | +0.70 | 452.62 | −0.70 | 451.22 |
|  | 37 + 00 | 452.15 | +0.62 | 452.77 | −0.62 | 451.53 |
| EVC | 37 + 50 | 453.00 | +0.39 | 453.39 | −0.39 | 452.61 |
| $C'$ | 37 + 81.28 | 453.63 | +0.24 | 453.87 | −0.24 | 453.39 |
|  | 38 + 00 | 454.00 | +0.15 | 454.15 | −0.24 | 453.76 |
| S.T. ($B'$) | 38 + 32.71 | 454.65 | 0.00 | 454.65 | −0.24 | 454.41 |
|  | 38 + 50 | 455.00 | −0.04 | 454.96 | −0.24 | 454.76 |
|  | 39 + 00 | 456.00 | −0.17 | 455.83 | −0.24 | 455.76 |
| $A'$ | 39 + 28.71 | 456.57 | −0.24 | 456.33 | −0.24 | 456.33 |

Interpolated values are underlined.
Pavement revolved about the centerline (℄).

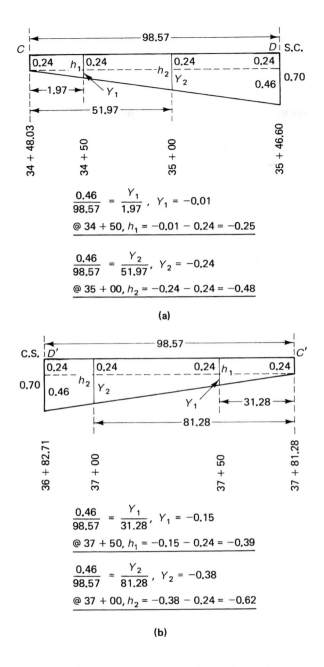

$$\frac{0.46}{98.57} = \frac{Y_1}{1.97}, \ Y_1 = -0.01$$

@ 34 + 50, $h_1 = -0.01 - 0.24 = -0.25$

$$\frac{0.46}{98.57} = \frac{Y_2}{51.97}, \ Y_2 = -0.24$$

@ 35 + 00, $h_2 = -0.24 - 0.24 = -0.48$

(a)

$$\frac{0.46}{98.57} = \frac{Y_1}{31.28}, \ Y_1 = -0.15$$

@ 37 + 50, $h_1 = -0.15 - 0.24 = -0.39$

$$\frac{0.46}{98.57} = \frac{Y_2}{81.28}, \ Y_2 = -0.38$$

@ 37 + 00, $h_2 = -0.38 - 0.24 = -0.62$

(b)

*Note:* Pavement Edge Differentials (with ℄) Between C and D or D' and C' Are Identical at Each Station.

**FIGURE 13.30** Right-edge pavement elevation interpolation for the problem of Example 13.9. (a) Tangent run-in. (b) Tangent run-out.

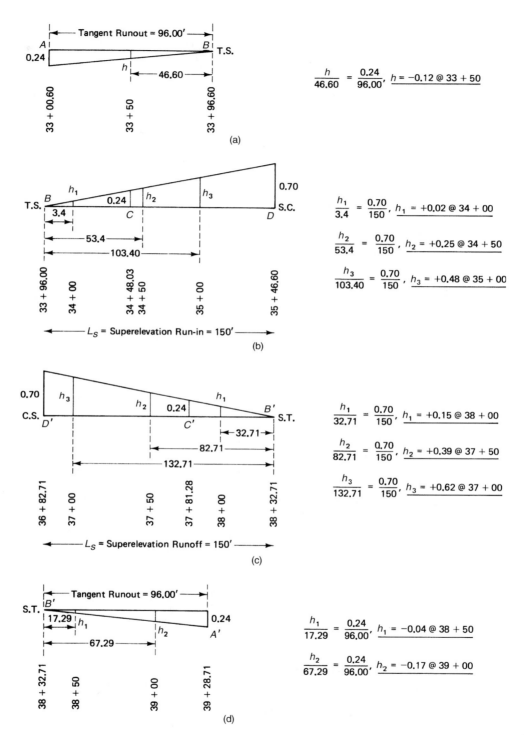

**FIGURE 13.31**  Left-edge pavement elevation interpolation for the problem of Example 13.9.

# Questions

1. Why are curves used in roadway horizontal and vertical alignments?

2. Curves can be established by occupying ℄ or offset stations and then turning off appropriate deflection angles, or they can be established by occupying a central control station and then turning off angles and measuring out distances–as determined through coordinates analyses. What are the advantages and disadvantages of each technique?

3. Why do chord and arc lengths for the same curve interval sometimes appear equal in value?

4. What characteristic do parabolic curves and spiral curves have in common?

5. Describe techniques that can be used to check the accuracy of the layout of a set of interchange curves using polar techniques (that is, angle/distance layout from a central control station).

6. Why do construction surveyors usually provide offset stakes?

# Problems

**13.1** Given PI at 9 + 27.26, $\Delta = 29°42'$, and $R = 700$ ft, compute tangent ($T$) and length of arc ($L$).

**13.2** Given PI at 15 + 88.10, $\Delta = 7°10'$, and $D = 8°$, compute tangent ($T$) and length of arc ($L$).

**13.3** From the data in Problem 13.1, compute the stationing of the BC and EC.

**13.4** From the data in Problem 13.2, compute the stationing of the BC and EC.

**13.5** A straight-line route survey, which had PIs at 3 + 81.27 ($\Delta = 12°30'$), and 5 + 42.30 ($\Delta = 10°56'$), later had 600-ft-radius circular curves inserted at each PI. Compute the BC and EC stationing (chainage) for each curve.

**13.6** Given PI at 5 + 862.789, $\Delta = 12°47'$, and $R = 300$ m, compute the deflections for even 20-m stations.

**13.7** Given PI at 8 + 272.311, $\Delta = 24°24'20''$, and $R = 500$ m, compute $E$ (external), $M$ (midordinate), and the stations of the BC and EC.

**13.8** Given PI at 10 + 71.78, $\Delta = 36°10'30''$ RT, and $R = 1,150$ ft, compute the deflections for even 100-ft stations.

**13.9** From the distances and deflections computed in Problem 13.6, compute the three key ℄ chord layout lengths, that is, (1) BC to first 20-m station, (2) chord distance for 20-m (arc) stations, and (3) from the last even 20-m station to the EC.

**13.10** From the distances and deflections computed in Problem 13.8, compute the three key ℄ chord layout lengths, that is, (1) BC to first 100-ft station, (2) chord distance for 100-ft (arc) stations, and (3) from the last even 100-ft station to the EC.

**13.11** From the distances and deflections computed in Problem 13.8, compute the chords (6) required for layout directly on offsets 50-ft right and 50-ft left of ℄.

**13.12** Two highway ℄ tangents must be joined with a circular curve of radius 1,000 ft. See Figure 13.32. The PI is inaccessible because its location falls in a river. Point $A$ is established near the river on the back tangent, and point $B$ is established near the river on the forward tangent. Distance $AB$ is measured to be 615.27 ft. Angle $\alpha = 51°31'20''$, and angle $\beta = 32°02'45''$. Perform the calculations required to locate the BC and the EC in the field.

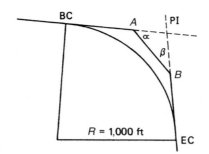

FIGURE 13.32

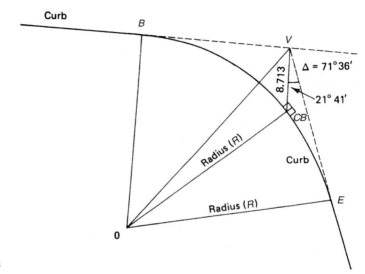

FIGURE 13.33

**13.13** Two street curb lines intersect with $\Delta = 71°36'$. See Figure 13.33. A curb radius must be selected so that an existing catch basin (CB) will abut the future curb. The curb-side of the catch basin ℄ is located from point $V$: $V$ to CB = 8.713 m and angle $E$-$V$-CB = $21°41'$. Compute the radius that will permit the curb to abut the existing catch basin.

**13.14** Given the following compound curve data: $R_1 = 200$ ft, $R_2 = 300$ ft, $\Delta_1 = 44°26'$, and $\Delta_2 = 45°18'$, compute $T_1$ and $T_2$ (see Figure 13.15).

**13.15** Given the following vertical curve data: PVI at 7 + 25.712, $L = 100$ m, $g_1 = -3.2\%$, $g_2 = +1.8\%$, and elevation of PVI = 210.440, compute the elevations of the curve low point and even 20-m stations.

**13.16** Given the following vertical curve data: PVI at 19 + 00, $L = 500$ ft, $g_1 = +2.5\%$, $g_2 = +1\%$, and elevation at PVI = 723.86 ft, compute the elevations of the curve summit and even full stations (that is, 100-ft even stations).

**13.17** You are given the following vertical curve data: $g_1 = +3\%$, $g_2 = -1\%$, design speed = 110 km/hr (from Table 13.6, $K = 90$ m), PVI at 0 + 360.100, with an elevation of 156.663 m. Compute the curve elevations at the high point (summit) and the even 50-m stations.

**13.18** Given the following spiral curve data: $D = 8°$, $V = 40$ mph, $\Delta = 16°44'$, and PI at 11 + 66.18, determine the value of each key spiral and circular curve component ($L_s$, $R$, $P$, $q$, LT, ST, $X$, $Y$, $\Delta_s$, $\Delta_c$, $T_c$, and $L_c$) and determine the stationing (chainage) of the T.S., S.C., C.S., and S.T.

**13.19** Given the same data as in Problem 13.18, use the approximate equations (Equations 13.33 to 13.38) to compute $X$, $Y$, $q$, $P$, LT, and ST. Enter these values in a table with equivalent values as determined in Problem 13.18 and compare the results.

**13.20** Use the data from Problem 13.18 to compute the deflections for the curve system (spirals and circular curves) at even 50-ft stations.

# 14 Construction Surveys

## 14.1 General Background

Construction surveys provide the horizontal and vertical layout for every key component of a construction project. This provision of *line and grade* can be accomplished only by experienced surveyors familiar with both the related project design and the appropriate construction techniques. A knowledge of related design is essential for interpreting the design drawings effectively for layout purposes, and a knowledge of construction techniques is required to ensure that the layout is optimal both for line and grade transfer and for construction scheduling.

We have seen that data can be gathered in various ways for engineering and other works. Modern practice favors total station surveys for high-density areas of limited size, and aerial techniques for high-density areas covering large tracts. Additionally, GPS techniques are now being implemented successfully in areas of moderate density. The technique chosen by a survey manager will usually be influenced by the costs (per point) and the reliability of the various techniques.

With regard to surveying applications, modern practice has become more dependent on the use of total stations and recently on the use of global positioning system (GPS) receivers working in real time (RTK techniques). In theory, GPS techniques seem to be ideal because roving receiver–equipped surveyors move quickly to establish precise locations for layout points in which both line and grade are promptly determined and marked.

Surveyors have found that to utilize RTK surveying successfully in construction surveying, much care must be taken to establish sufficient horizontal and vertical control monuments. In addition to the more stringent control requirements, surveyors must depend on an RTK system that has many components, which can be cause for concern. Some of the disadvantages are short observation times, problems with radio transmissions, problems with satellite signal reception due to canopy obstructions (dual constellation receivers can help here), instrument calibration, multipath errors, and other errors (some of which will not be evident in error displays).

For these reasons, points located through the use of GPS techniques must be verified, if possible, through independent surveys (for example, check GPS surveys based on different control stations, tape measurements from point to point where feasible, etc.). In the real world of construction works, the problems surrounding layout verification are compounded by the fact that the surveyor often doesn't have unlimited time to perform measurement checks because the contractor may actually be waiting on site to commence construction. A high level of planning and a rigid and systematic method (proven successful in past projects) are necessary for performing the GPS survey.

Unlike other forms of surveying, construction surveying is often associated with an accelerated speed of operation. Once contracts have been awarded, contractors often wish to commence construction immediately because they will probably have commitments for their employees and equipment. They will not accept delay. A hurried surveyor is more likely to make mistakes in measurements and calculations, and thus even more vigilance than normal is required. Construction surveying is not an occupation for the faint of heart; the responsibilities are great and the working conditions often less than ideal. However, the sense of achievement when viewing the completed facility can be very rewarding.

## 14.1.1 Grade

The word **grade** has several different meanings. In construction work alone, it is often used in three distinctly different ways to refer to:

1. A proposed elevation.
2. The slope of profile line (i.e., gradient).
3. Cuts and fills—vertical distances below or above grade stakes.

The surveyor should be aware of these different meanings and always note the context in which the word is used.

## 14.1.2 Machine Guidance and Control

Regardless of the layout technique, layout activity often takes up much of the surveyors' time and attention. Recent advances in machine guidance have resulted in techniques that significantly improve the efficiency in providing construction line-and-grade control. By reducing the need for as many layout surveyors and grade checkers near the working equipment, these techniques also provide an increased measure of safety.

Large tracts (for example, airports, parking lots) can be brought to grade through the use of rotating lasers and machine-mounted laser detectors, which convey to the machine operator (bulldozer, grader, or scraper) the up and down operations required to bring the facility to the designed grade elevations. Rotating lasers can be set to define a horizontal plane or a sloped plane. The laser plane is referenced at some distance above the design grade.

Earthwork operations can now be performed using backhoe excavators controlled by lasers. The signals received by the machine-mounted detectors are displayed in the machine cab, where the operator can observe the location of the bucket's teeth with respect to the design grade in real time. In addition, audible tones permit the operator to keep focused on the work while guiding the excavation process up or down as needed. Accuracies are said to be as reliable as those used in most earthwork techniques. See Figure 14.1(a).

Some manufacturers produce software that can integrate motorized theodolites and appropriately programmed PC computers to target machine-mounted reflecting prisms. These radio-controlled systems can monitor work progress and give real-time direction for line-and-grade operations of various construction equipment in a wide selection of engineering works (for example, tunnels, road/railway construction, drilling). Manufacturers claim measurement standard deviations of 2 mm in height and 5 mm in position. See Figure 14.1(b).

In addition to laser- and computer-controlled total station techniques, machine guidance is also available, in real time, with the use of layout programs featuring GPS receivers. As with the total station techniques, receptors are mounted on the various construction equipment, with the readings transmitted to the GPS controller or integrated PC computers. In-cab displays tell the operator how much up and down movement is needed on the cutting edge of the blade (grader or bulldozer) to maintain design alignment. This technique is used successfully in site preparation work, subbase placement, leveling, and even on superelevated curves.

The sections in this chapter present methods of construction line-and-grade determination. With machine guidance techniques, these line-and-grade determinations still have to be made, but instead of placing grade stakes, the surveyor may input the required data into guidance programs that operate directly from PC computers or from program design cards that are updated as the work progresses.

## 14.2  Accuracy and Mistakes

The elimination of mistakes and the achievement of required accuracy have been stressed in this text. In no area of surveying are these qualities more important than in construction surveying. All field measurements and calculations are suspect until they have been verified by independent means or by repeated checks. Mistakes have been known to escape detection in as many as three independent, conscientious checks by experienced personnel. These comments apply to all tape, EDM, total station, and GPS layouts.

## 14.3  Construction Control

Depending on the size and complexity of the project, the survey crew should arrive on site one day or several days prior to the commencement of construction. The first on-site job for the construction surveyor is to relocate the horizontal and vertical control used in the preliminary survey (see Chapter 8). Usually, several months and sometimes even years have passed since the preliminary survey, the project design based on the preliminary survey, and the budget decision to award a contract for construction.

It may be necessary to reestablish the horizontal and vertical control in the area of proposed construction. If this is the case, extreme caution is advised because the design plans are based on the original survey fabric, and any deviation from the original control could well lead to serious problems in construction. If the original control (or most of it) still exists in the field, it is customary to check and verify all linear and angular dimensions that could directly affect the project.

The same rigorous approach is required for vertical control. If local benchmarks have been destroyed (as is often the case), the benchmarks must be reestablished accurately. Key existing elevations shown on design drawings (for example, connecting invert

(a)

**FIGURE 14.1** (a) BucketPro Excavator cab display system used in machine-controlled excavation. (Courtesy of Spectra Precision, Dayton, Ohio) (b) Paving machine operation controlled by a motorized total station/radio control modem/PC computer instrumentation package. (Courtesy of Leica Geosystems Inc., Norcross, Ga.)

(b)

elevations for gravity-flow sewers, or connecting beam seat elevations on concrete structures) must be resurveyed to ensure that (1) the original elevation shown on the plan was correct, and (2) the new and original vertical control are both referenced, in fact, to the same vertical datum. In these areas, absolutely nothing is taken for granted.

Once the original control has been reestablished or verified, the control must be extended over the construction site to suit the purposes of each specific project. This operation and the giving of line and grade are discussed in detail for most types of projects in subsequent sections.

## 14.4   Measurement for Interim and Final Payments

On most construction projects, partial payments are made to the contractor at regular intervals, and final payment is made upon completion and acceptance of the project. The payments are based on data supplied by the project inspector and the construction surveyor. The project inspector records items such as daily progress, staff and equipment in use, and materials used, whereas the construction surveyor records items that require a surveying function (for example, excavation quantities, concrete placed in structures, placement of sod).

The discussion in Chapter 1 covered field book layout and stressed the importance of diaries and thorough note taking. These functions are important in all survey work but especially so in construction surveying. Since a great deal of money can depend on the integrity of daily notes and records, it is essential that the construction surveyor's notes and diaries be complete and accurate with respect to dates, times, locations, quantities, methods of measurement, personnel, design changes, and so on.

## 14.5   Final Measurements for As-Built Drawings

On completion of a project, it is essential that a final plan showing the actual details of construction be drawn. The final plan, known as the *as-built drawing,* is usually quite similar to the design plan, with the exception that revisions are made to reflect changes in design that invariably occur during the construction process. Design changes result from problems that become apparent only after construction is under way. It is difficult, especially on complex projects, to plan for every eventuality that may be encountered; however, if the preliminary surveyor and the designer have both done their jobs well, the design plan and the as-built plan are usually quite similar.

## 14.6   Municipal Roads Construction

### 14.6.1   Classification of Roads

The plan shown in Figure 14.2 depicts a typical municipal road pattern. The *local roads* shown have the primary purpose of providing access to individual residential lots. The *collector roads,* both major (for example, John Street) and minor (for example, Green Lane) provide the dual service of lot access and traffic movement. The collector roads connect the local roads to *arterial roads* (for example, Bayview Avenue and Woodbine Avenue). The main purpose of the arterial roads is to provide a relatively high level of traffic movement service.

Municipal works engineers base their road design on the level of service to be provided. The proposed cross sections and geometric alignments vary in complexity and cost

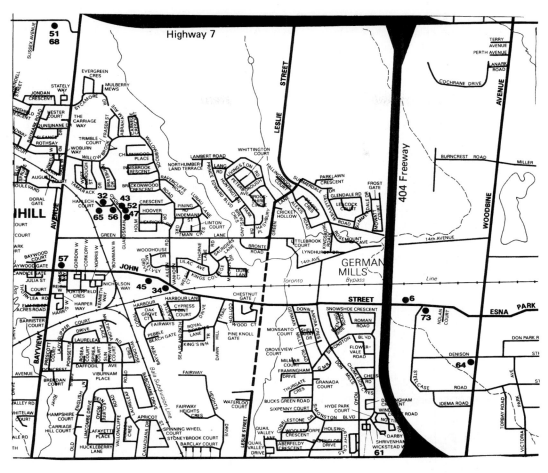

**FIGURE 14.2** Municipal road pattern. (Courtesy of Fine Line Graphic and Cartographic Services, Toronto)

from the fundamental local roads to the more complex arterials. The highest level of service is given by the *freeways* (for example, the 404 Freeway), which provide high-velocity, high-volume routes with limited access (interchanges only), ensuring continuous traffic flow when design conditions prevail.

## 14.6.2 Road Allowances/Rights of Way

The road allowance varies in width from 40 ft (12 m) for small locals to 120 ft (35 m) for major arterials. In parts of North America, the local road allowances originally were 66 ft wide (one Gunter's chain). When widening was required due to increased traffic volumes, it was common to take 10-ft widenings on each side, initially resulting in an 86-ft road allowance for major collectors and minor arterials. Additional widening left major arterials at 100- and 120-ft widths.

### 14.6.3 Road Cross Sections

A full-service municipal road allowance usually has asphalt pavement, curbs, storm and sanitary sewers, water distribution pipes, hydrants, catch basins, and sidewalks. Additional utilities such as natural gas pipelines, electrical supply cables, and cable TV are also often located on the road allowance. The essential differences between local cross sections and arterial cross sections are the widths of pavement and the quality and depths of pavement materials. The construction layout of sewers and pipelines is covered in subsequent sections. See Figure 14.3 for a typical municipal road cross section.

The crossfall (height of crown) used on the pavement varies from one municipality to another, but is usually close to a 2% slope to provide adequate drainage. The curb face is often 6 in. (150 mm) high, except at driveways and crosswalks, where the height is restricted to about 2 in. (50 mm) for vehicle and pedestrian access. The slope on the boulevard from the curb to the street line usually rises at a 2% minimum slope, thus ensuring that roadway storm drainage does not run onto private property.

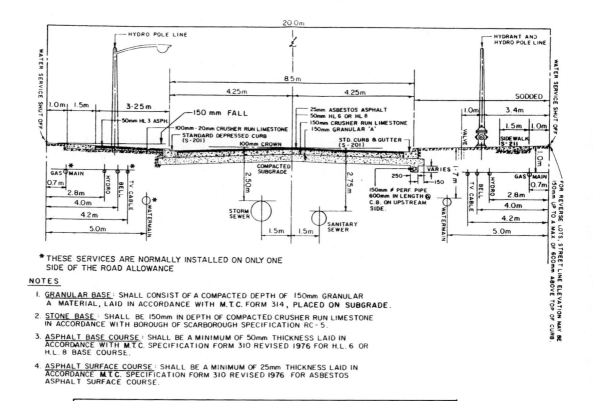

**FIGURE 14.3** Typical cross section of a local residential road.

## 14.6.4 Plan and Profile

A typical plan and profile is shown in Figure 14.4. The plan and profile, which usually also shows the cross-section details and construction notes, is the "blueprint" from which the construction is accomplished. The plan and profile and cross section, together with the contract specifications, spell out in detail precisely where and how the road (in this example) is to be built.

The plan portion of the plan and profile gives the horizontal location of the facility, including curve radii, whereas the profile portion shows the key elevations and slopes along the road centerline, including vertical curve information. The cross section shows cross slopes, vertical dimensions, and cross horizontal dimensions for all municipal services. The plan and profile relates all data to the project stationing established as horizontal control.

## 14.6.5 Establishing a Centerline (℄)

For this task, we will use the example of a ditched residential road being upgraded to a paved and curbed road. The first job for the construction surveyor is to reestablish the centerline (℄) of the roadway. Usually this entails finding several property markers delineating street line (℄). Fence and hedge lines can be used initially to guide the surveyor to the approximate location of the property markers. When the surveyor finds one property marker, he or she can then measure frontage distances shown on the property plan (plat) to locate a sufficient number of additional markers.

Usually, the construction surveyor has the notes from the preliminary survey showing the location of property markers used in the original survey. If possible, the construction surveyor will use the same evidence used in the preliminary survey, taking the time, of course, to verify the resulting alignment. If the evidence used in the preliminary survey has been destroyed, as is often the case when a year or more elapses between the two surveys, the construction surveyor will take great care to ensure that his or her results are not appreciably different from those of the original survey, unless, of course, an error occurred on the original survey. If the evidence used in the original survey was coordinated, a global positioning system (GPS) receiver can be used to navigate to the correct location.

The property markers can be square or round iron bars (including rebars), or round iron or aluminum pipes, magnetically capped. The markers can vary from 18 in. to 4 ft in length. It is not unusual for the surveyor to have to use a shovel because the tops of the markers are often buried. The surveyor can use an electronic or magnetic metal detector to aid in locating buried markers.

Sometimes even an exhaustive search of an area will not turn up a sufficient number of markers to establish ℄. The surveyor must then extend the search to adjacent blocks or backyards to reestablish the missing markers. The surveyor can also approach the homeowners in the affected area and inquire about the existence of a mortgage survey plan or house survey (see Figure 14.5) for the specific property. Such a plan is required in most areas before a financial institution will provide mortgage financing. The mortgage survey plan shows dimensions from the building foundation to the street line and to both sidelines. Information thus gained can be used to narrow the search for a missing marker, or it can be used directly to establish points on the street line.

Once several points have been established on both sides of the roadway, the ℄ can be marked from each of these points by measuring (at right angles) half the width of the road allowance. The surveyor then sets up a theodolite on a ℄ mark near one of the project extremities and sights in on the ℄ marker nearest the other project extremity. The surveyor

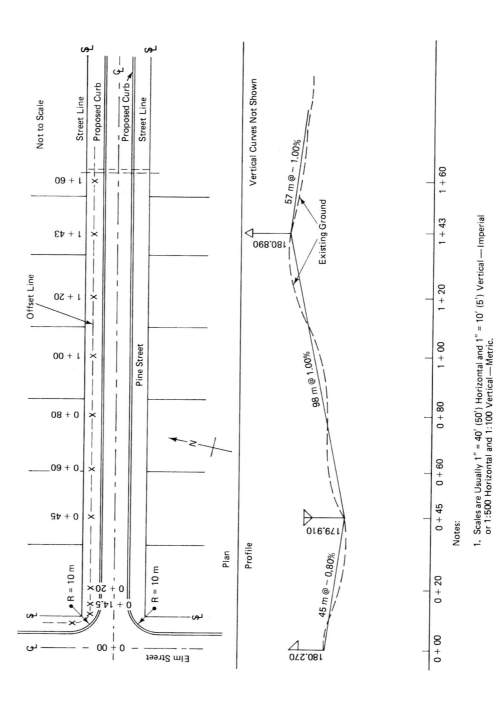

**Plan**

**Profile**

Vertical Curves Not Shown

Notes:

1. Scales are Usually 1" = 40' (50') Horizontal and 1" = 10' (5') Vertical —Imperial or 1:500 Horizontal and 1:100 Vertical—Metric.

2. 0 + 00 can be Assigned to any Convenient Point, but is Usually Assigned to the Intersection of the Two Center Lines.

3. See Cross Section Shown in Figure 14.7.

**FIGURE 14.4** Plan and profile.

556

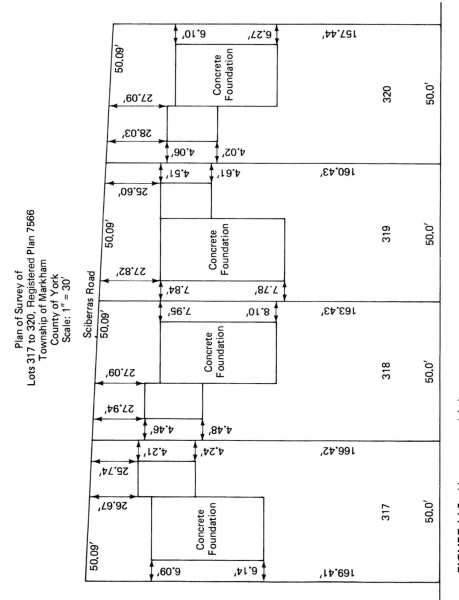

**FIGURE 14.5** House survey (plat).

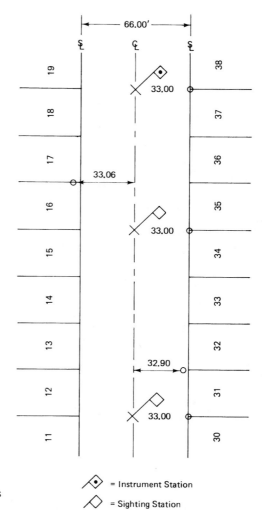

**FIGURE 14.6** Property markers used to establish centerline.

◇• = Instrument Station

◇ = Sighting Station

can then see if all markers line up in a straight line, assuming tangent alignment (see Figure 14.6). If the markers do not all line up, the surveyor checks the affected measurements. If discrepancies still occur (as is often the case), the surveyor can make the "best fit" of the available evidence. Depending on the length of the roadway involved and the quantity of ℄ markers established, the number of markers lining up perfectly will vary. Three well-spaced, perfectly aligned markers is the absolute minimum number required for the establishment of ℄. The reason that all markers do not line up is that, over the years, most lots are resurveyed; some lots may be resurveyed several times. The land surveyor's prime area of concern is that area of the plan immediately adjacent to the client's property, and the surveyor must ensure that the property stakeout is consistent both for evidence and plan intentions. Over several years, cumulative errors and mistakes can significantly affect the overall alignment of the street lines.

If the ℄ is being marked on an existing road, as in this example, the surveyor will use nails with washers and red plastic flagging to establish marks. The nails can be driven into gravel, asphalt, and in some cases, concrete surfaces. The washers keep the nails from sinking below the road surface, and the red flagging helps in relocation.

If the project had involved a new curbed road in a new subdivision, the establishment of the ℄ would have been much simpler. The recently set property markers would, for the most part, be intact, and discrepancies between markers would be minimal (because all markers would have been set in the same comprehensive survey operation). The ℄ in this case would be marked by wood stakes 2″ by 2″ or 2″ by 1″ wide and 18″ long.

## 14.6.6   Establishing Offset Lines

In this example, the legal fabric of the road allowance as given by the property markers constitutes the horizontal control. Construction control would consist of offset lines referenced to the proposed curbs with respect to line and grade. In the case of ditched roads and most highways (see Section 14.7), the offset lines are referenced to the proposed centerline with respect to line and grade.

The offset lines are placed as close to the proposed location of the curbs as possible. It is essential that the offset stakes do not interfere with equipment and form work; it is also essential that the offset stakes be far enough removed so that they are not destroyed during cut or fill operations. Ideally, the offset stakes, once established, will remain in place for the duration of construction. This ideal can often be realized in municipal road construction, but it is seldom realized in highway construction due to the significant size of cuts and fills. If cuts and fills are not too large, offset lines for curbs can be 3 to 5 ft (1 to 2 m) from the proposed face of the curb. An offset line this close allows for very efficient transfer of line and grade. In the case of a ditched gravel road being upgraded to a curbed paved road, the offset line will have to be placed far enough away on the boulevard to avoid the ditch-filling operation and any additional cut and fill that may be required. In the worst case, it may be necessary to place the offset line on the street line, an 18- to 25-ft (6- to 8-m) offset.

## 14.6.7   Determining Cuts and Fills

The offset stakes (with nails or tacks for precise alignment) are usually placed at 50-ft (20-m) stations and at any critical alignment change points. The elevations of the tops of the stakes are usually determined by rod and level, or total station, based on the vertical control established for the project. It is then necessary to determine the proposed elevation for the top of the curb at each offset station. In Figure 14.4, you could see that elevations and slopes have been designed for a portion of the project. The plan and profile were simplified for illustrative purposes, and offsets were shown for one curb line only.

Given the ℄ elevation data, the construction surveyor must calculate the proposed curb elevations. The surveyor can proceed by calculating the relevant elevations on ℄ and then adjusting for crown and curb height differential or by applying the differential first and working out curb elevations directly.

To determine the difference in elevation between ℄ and the top of the curb, the surveyor must analyze the appropriate cross section. In Figure 14.7, you can see that the cross

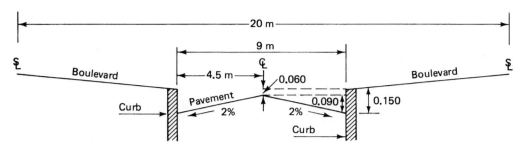

**FIGURE 14.7** Cross section showing the relationship between the centerline and the top of the curb elevations.

**Table 14.1** GRADE COMPUTATIONS

| Station | ℄ elevation | | Curb elevation |
|---------|------------|--|----------------|
| 0 + 00 | 180.270 | | |
| | −0.116 | | |
| BC 0 + 14.5 | 180.154 | +0.060 | 180.214 |
| | −0.044 | | |
| 0 + 20 | 180.110 | +0.060 | 180.170 |
| | −0.160 | | |
| 0 + 40 | 179.950 | +0.060 | 180.010 |
| | −0.040 | | |
| 0 + 45 | 179.910 | +0.060 | 179.970 |
| | +0.150 | | |
| 0 + 60 | 180.060 | +0.060 | 180.120 |
| | +0.200 | | |
| 0 + 80 | 180.260 | +0.060 | 180.320 |
| | +0.200 | | |
| 1 + 00 | 180.460 | +0.060 | 180.520 |
| | +0.200 | | |
| 1 + 20 | 180.660 | +0.060 | 180.720 |
| | +0.200 | | |
| 1 + 40 | 180.860 | +0.060 | 180.920 |
| | +0.030 | | |
| 1 + 43 | 180.890 | +0.060 | 180.950 |
| etc. | | | |

fall is $4.5 \times 0.02 = 0.090$ m (90 mm). The face on the curb is 150 mm; therefore, the top of the curb is 60 mm above the ℄ elevation.

A list of key stations (see Figure 14.4) is prepared, and ℄ elevations at each station are calculated (see Table 14.1). The ℄ elevations are then adjusted to produce curb elevations. Since superelevation is seldom used in municipal design, it is safe to say that the curbs on both sides of the road are normally parallel in line and grade. A notable exception can occur when intersections of collectors and arterials are widened to allow for turn lanes or bus lanes.

**Table 14.2** GRADE SHEET

| Station | Curb elevation | Stake elevation | Cut | Fill |
|---------|---------------|-----------------|-----|------|
| 0 + 14.5 | 180.214 | 180.325 | 0.111 | |
| 0 + 20 | 180.170 | 180.315 | 0.145 | |
| 0 + 40 | 180.010 | 180.225 | 0.215 | |
| 0 + 45 | 179.970 | 180.110 | 0.140 | |
| 0 + 60 | 180.120 | 180.185 | 0.065 | |
| 0 + 80 | 180.320 | 180.320 | On grade | |
| 1 + 00 | 180.520 | 180.475 | | 0.045 |
| 1 + 20 | 180.720 | 180.710 | | 0.010 |
| 1 + 40 | 180.920 | 180.865 | | 0.055 |
| 1 + 43 | 180.950 | 180.900 | | 0.050 |
| etc. | | | | |

The construction surveyor can then prepare a grade sheet (see Table 14.2), copies of which are given to the contractor and project inspector. The top of stake elevations, determined by level and rod, (or total station) are assumed in this example. The grade sheet, signed by the construction surveyor, also includes the street name, date, limits of the contract, and, most important, the offset distance to the face of the curb. Note that the construction grades (cut and fill) refer only to the vertical distance to be measured down or up from the grade stake to locate the proposed elevation. Construction grades do not define with certainty whether the contractor is in a cut or fill situation at any given point. In Figure 14.8, for example, at 0 + 20, a construction grade of cut 0.145 is given, whereas the contractor is actually in a fill situation (that is, the proposed top of the curb is **above** the existing ground at that station). This lack of correlation between construction grades and the construction process can become more pronounced as the offset distance lengthens. For example, if the grade stake at station 1 + 40 had been located at the street line, the construction grade would have been cut, whereas the construction process is almost entirely in a fill operation.

When the layout is performed using foot units, the basic station interval is 50 ft. The dimensions are recorded and calculated to the closest one hundredth (0.01) of a foot. Although all survey measurements are in feet and decimals of a foot, for the contractors' purposes, the final cuts and fills are often expressed in feet and inches. The decimal–inch relationships are soon committed to memory by surveyors working in the construction field (see Table 14.3). Cuts and fills are usually expressed to the closest ⅛ in. for concrete, steel, and pipelines, and to the closest ¼ in. for highway, granular surfaces, and ditch lines. The grade sheet in Table 14.4 illustrates the foot–inch relationships. The first column and the last two columns are all that are required by the contractor, in addition to the offset distance, to construct the facility properly.

In some cases, the cuts and fills (grades) are written directly on the appropriate grade stakes. This information, written with lumber crayon (keel) or permanent markers, is always written on the side of the stake facing the construction. The station is also written on each stake and is placed on that side of each stake facing the lower chainage.

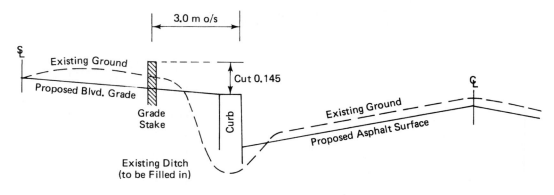

Station 0 + 20 Cut Grade

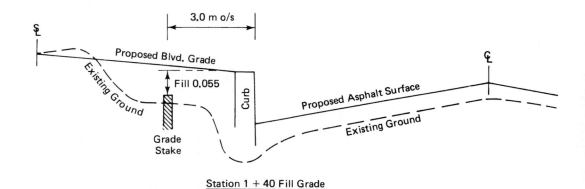

Station 1 + 40 Fill Grade

**FIGURE 14.8**  Cross sections showing cut and fill grades.

**Table 14.3**  DECIMAL FOOT/INCH CONVERSION

| | | |
|---|---|---|
| $1' = 12''$, | $1'' = 1/12' = 0.083$ ft | |
| $1'' = 0.08(3)'$ | $7'' = 0.58'$ | $1/8'' = 0.01'$ |
| $2'' = 0.17'$ | $8'' = 0.67'$ | $1/4'' = 0.02'$ |
| $3'' = 0.25'$ | $9'' = 0.75'$ | $1/2'' = 0.04'$ |
| $4'' = 0.33'$ | $10'' = 0.83'$ | $3/4'' = 0.06'$ |
| $5'' = 0.42'$ | $11'' = 0.92'$ | |
| $6'' = 0.50'$ | $12'' = 1.00'$ | |

## 14.6.8  Treatment of Intersection Curb Construction

Intersection curb radii usually range from 30 ft (10 m) for two local roads intersecting to 60 ft (20 m) for two arterial roads intersecting. The angle of intersection is ideally 90°; however, the range from 70° to 110° is allowed for sight design purposes.

**Table 14.4**  GRADE SHEET SHOWING FOOT–INCH CONVERSION[a]

| Station | Curb elevation | Stake elevation | Cut | Fill | Cut | Fill |
|---------|---------------|-----------------|-----|------|-----|------|
| 0 + 30 | 470.20 | 471.30 | 1.10 | | 1′1¼″ | |
| 0 + 50 | 470.40 | 470.95 | 0.55 | | 0′6⅝″ | |
| 1 + 00 | 470.90 | 470.90 | On grade | | On grade | |
| 1 + 50 | 471.40 | 471.23 | | 0.17 | | 0′2″ |
| 2 + 00 | 471.90 | 471.46 | | 0.44 | | 0′5¼″ |
| 2 + 50 | 472.40 | 472.06 | | 0.34 | | 0′4⅛″ |

[a]Refer to Table 14.3 for foot–inch conversion.

The curb elevation at the BC (180.214) is determined from the plan and profile of Pine Street (see Figure 14.4 and Table 14.2). The curb elevation at the EC is determined from the plan and profile of Elm Street (assume that the EC elevation = 180.100). The length of the curb can be calculated from Equation 13.5:

$$L = \frac{\pi R \Delta}{180}$$

$$= 15.708 \text{ m}$$

The slope from BC to EC can be determined as follows:

$$180.214 - 180.100 = 0.114 \text{ m}$$

The fall is 0.114 over an arc distance of 15.708 m, which is −0.73%.

These calculations indicate that a satisfactory slope (0.5% is the usual minimum) joins the two points. The intersection curve is located by four offset stakes, BC, EC, and two intermediate points. In this case, 15.708/3 or 5.236 m is the distance measured from the BC to locate the first intermediate point, the distance measured from the first intermediate point to the second intermediate point, and the distance used as a check from the second intermediate point to the EC.

In actual practice, the chord distance rather than the arc distance is used. Since the curve deflection angle $\Delta/2 = 45°$, and we are using a factor of ⅓, the corresponding deflection angle for one-third of the arc would be 15°:

$$C = 2R \sin (\text{deflection angle})$$

$$= 2 \times 10 \times \sin 15° = 5.176 \text{ m}$$

These intermediate points can be deflected in from the BC or EC, or they can be located by the use of two tapes: one surveyor at the radius point (holding 10 m, in this case) and the other surveyor at the BC or intermediate point (holding 5.176), while the third surveyor holds the zero point of both tapes. The latter technique is used most often on these small-radius problems. The only occasions when these curves are deflected in by theodolite occurs when the radius point (curve center) is inaccessible (fuel pump islands, front porches, etc.).

The proposed curb elevations on the arc are as follows:

$$
\begin{array}{llll}
\text{BC} & 0 + 14.5 & = 180.214 \\
& & \underline{-\ 0.038} \\
\text{Stake 1} & & = 180.176 \\
& & \underline{-\ 0.038} \\
\text{Stake 2} & & = 180.138 \\
& & \underline{-\ 0.038} \\
\text{EC} & & = 180.100 & \text{Check} \\
\text{Arc interval} & & = \phantom{0}5.236\ \text{m}
\end{array}
$$

Difference in elevation $= 5.236 \times 0.0073 = 0.038$

Grade information for the curve can be included on the grade sheet. The offset curve can be established in the same manner, after making allowances for the shortened radius (see Figure 14.9).

For an offset (o/s) of 3 m, the radius will become 7 m. The chords required can be calculated using Equation 13.8:

$$C = 2R \sin (\text{deflection})$$
$$= 2 \times 7 \times \sin 15^\circ = 3.623 \text{ m}$$

## 14.6.9 Sidewalk Construction

The sidewalk is constructed adjacent to the curb or at some set distance from the street line. If the sidewalk is adjacent to the curb, no additional layout is required because the curb itself gives line and grade for construction. In some cases, the concrete for this curb and sidewalk is placed in one operation.

When the sidewalk is to be located at some set distance from the street line (₵), a separate layout is required. Sidewalks located near the ₵ give the advantages of increased pedestrian safety and boulevard space for the stockpiling of a winter's accumulation of plowed snow in northern regions. Figure 14.10 shows the typical location of a sidewalk on the road allowance.

Sidewalk construction usually takes place after the curbs have been built and the boulevard has been brought to sod grade. The offset distance for the grade stakes can be quite short (1 to 3 ft). If the sidewalk is located within 1 to 3 ft of the ₵, the ₵ is an ideal location for the offset line. In many cases, only a line layout is required for construction because the grade is already established by boulevard grading and because the permanent elevations at ₵ are seldom adjusted in municipal work. The cross slope of the sidewalk (toward the curb) is usually given as ¼ in./ft (2%).

When the sidewalk is located as near as 1 ft to the ₵, greater care is required by the surveyor to ensure that the sidewalk does not encroach on private property throughout its

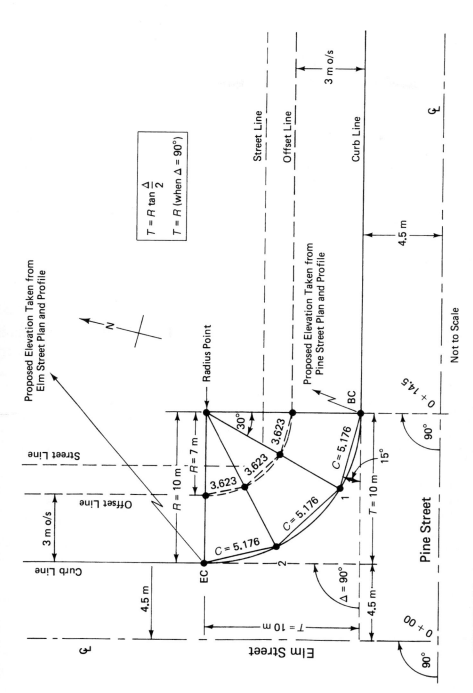

**FIGURE 14.9** Intersection geometrics (one quadrant shown).

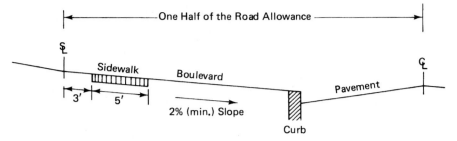

One Half of the Road Allowance

₵

Sidewalk  Boulevard

₵

Pavement

3'  5'

2% (min.) Slope

Curb

*Note:* The Sidewalk is Always Constructed so that it Slopes Toward the Road — Usually @ 1/4″ per foot (2%).

**FIGURE 14.10**  Typical location of a sidewalk on the road allowance.

length. Due to numerous private property surveys performed by different surveyors over the years, the actual location of the ₵ may no longer conform to plan location.

## 14.7  Highway Construction

Highways, like the municipal roads, are classified as *locals, collectors, arterials,* and *freeways.* The bulk of the highways, in mileage, are arterials that join towns and cities together in a state or provincial network. Unlike municipal roads, highways do not usually have curbs and storm sewers, relying instead on ditches for the removal of storm drainage. In municipal work, the construction layout and offsets are referenced to the curb lines; in highway work, the layout and offsets are all referenced to the centerline of construction.

The construction surveyor must first locate the right-of-way (ROW) legal markers and set up the construction ₵ in a manner similar to that described in the preceding section. Mistakes can be eliminated if the surveyor, armed with a complete set of construction and legal plans, takes the time to verify all evidence by checking plan measurements against field measurements. The construction surveyor next reestablishes the stationing used for the project. Stations established in the preliminary survey can be reestablished from reference monuments or crossroad intersections. Stations are reestablished from at least three independent ties to ensure that verification is possible.

Highways are laid out at 100-ft (30- or 40-m) stations, and additional stations are required at all changes in horizontal alignment (including BC, EC, TS, and ST) and at all changes in vertical direction (including BVC, EVC, and low points). The horizontal and vertical curve sections of highways are often staked out at 50-ft (15- to 20-m) intervals to ensure that the finished product conforms closely to the design. When using foot units, the full stations are at 100-ft intervals (for example, 0 + 00, 1 + 00). In metric units, municipalities use 100-m full station intervals (0 + 00, 1 + 00), whereas most highway agencies use 1,000-m (kilometer) intervals for full "stations" (for example, 0 + 000, 0 + 100, . . . , 1 + 000).

The ₵ of construction is staked out using a steel tape, plumb bobs, or electronic distance measurement (EDM) and using specifications designed for 1/3,000 accuracy (minimum). The accuracy of ₵ layout can be verified at reference monuments and road intersections, and by GPS positioning.

Highways can also be laid out from random coordinated stations using total station polar layouts. Most interchanges are now laid out using polar methods, whereas most of the highways between interchanges are laid out using rectangular layout offsets. The methods of polar layout, which are covered in Chapters 7 and 10, require higher-order control survey precision (for example, 1:10,000). Highways can also be laid out using the real-time differential GPS surveying techniques described in Sections 11.11 and 11.12.

The profile grade, shown on the contract drawing, can refer to the top of granular elevation or it can refer to the top of asphalt elevation. The surveyor must ensure that the proper reference is used before calculating subgrade elevations for the required cuts and fills. Resultant cuts and fills must also be identified clearly with respect to the reference feature, for example, the top of subgrade, the top of granular, or the top of asphalt or concrete.

## 14.7.1 Clearing, Grubbing, and the Stripping of Topsoil

*Clearing* and *grubbing* are the terms used to describe the cutting down of trees and the removal of all stumps and rubbish. The full highway width is staked out, approximating the limits of cut and fill, so that the clearing and grubbing can be accomplished. The first construction operation after clearing and grubbing is the stripping of topsoil. The topsoil is usually stockpiled for later use. In cut sections, the topsoil is stripped for full width, which extends to the points at which the far-side ditch slopes intersect the original ground (OG) surface (see Figure 14.11). In fill sections, the topsoil is usually stripped for the width of the highway embankment (see Figure 14.12). Most highway agencies do not strip the topsoil where heights of fill exceed 4 ft (1.2 m), believing that this water-bearing material cannot damage (frost) the road base below that depth. The bottom of fills (toe of slope) and the

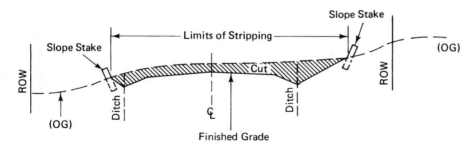

**FIGURE 14.11** Highway cut section.

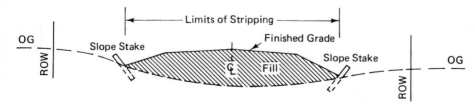

**FIGURE 14.12** Highway fill section.

top of cuts (top of slope) are identified by slope stakes. These stakes, which are driven in angled away from ℄, delineate not only the limits of stripping but also indicate the limits for cut and fill, such operations taking place immediately after the stripping operation. Lumber crayon (keel) or permanent markers are used to mark station and slope stake (s/s).

## 14.7.2 Placement of Slope Stakes

Figure 14.13 shows typical cut and fill sections in both foot and metric dimensions. The side slopes shown are 3:1 (that is, three horizontal to one vertical), although most agencies use a steeper slope (2:1) for cuts and fills over 4 ft (1.2 m). To locate slope stakes, the difference in elevation between the profile grade at ℄ and the invert of ditch (cut section) or the toe of embankment (fill section) must first be determined. In Figure 14.13(a), the difference in elevation consists of:

| | |
|---|---|
| Depth of granular | = 1.50 ft |
| Subgrade crossfall at 3% over 24.5 ft | = 0.74 ft |
| Minimum depth of ditch | = 1.50 ft |
| Total difference in elevation | = 3.74 ft |

The ℄ of this minimum depth ditch would be 29.0 ft from the ℄ of construction. In cases where the ditch is deeper than minimum values, the additional difference in elevation and the additional distance from the ℄ of construction can be calculated easily using the same slope values.

In Figure 14.13(b), the difference in elevation between the ℄ and the invert of the ditch consists of:

| | |
|---|---|
| Depth of granular | = 0.45 m |
| Fall at 3% over 7.45 m | = 0.22 m |
| Minimum depth of ditch | = 0.50 m |
| Total difference in elevation | = 1.17 m |

The ℄ of this minimum depth ditch would be 8.95 m from the ℄ of construction. In these two examples, only the distance from the highway ℄ to the ditch ℄ has been determined. See Example 14.1 for additional information.

In Figure 14.13(c), the difference in elevation consists of:

| | |
|---|---|
| Depth of granular | = 1.50 ft |
| Fall at 3% over 24.5 ft | = 0.74 ft |
| Total difference in elevation | = 2.24 ft |

The difference from the ℄ of construction to this point, where the subgrade intersects the side slope, is 24.5 ft.

In Figure 14.13(d), the differences in elevation consists of:

| | |
|---|---|
| Depth of granular | = 0.45 m |
| Fall at 3% over 7.45 m | = 0.22 m |
| Total difference in elevation | = 0.67 m |

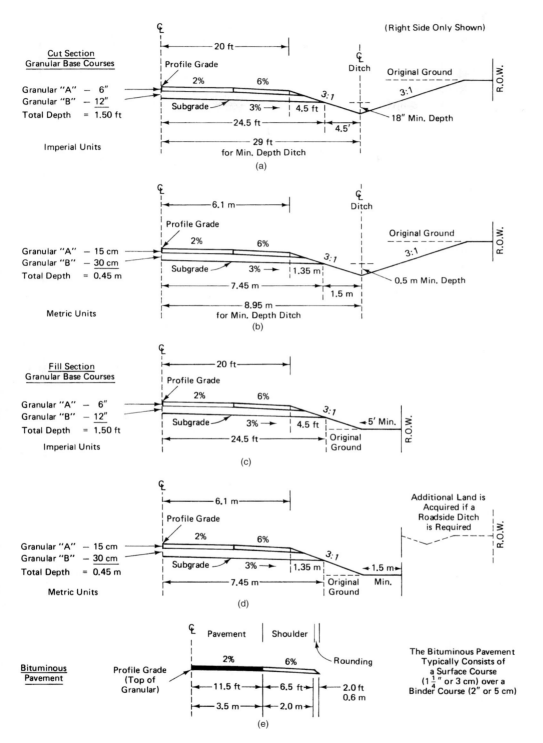

**FIGURE 14.13** Typical two-lane highway cross section. (a) Cut section—foot units. (b) Cut section—metric units. (c) Fill section—foot units. (d) Fill section—metric units. (e) Bituminous pavement section.

The distance from the ℄ of construction to this point, where the subgrade intersects the side slope, is 7.45 m. In the last two examples, the computed distance locates the slope stake.

■ **EXAMPLE 14.1** *Location of a Slope Stake in a Cut Section*
Refer to Figures 14.13(a) and 14.14. If the profile grade (top of granular) is 480.00 and HI = 486.28:

$$\text{Ditch invert} = 480.00 - 3.74 = 476.26$$
$$\text{Grade rod} = 486.28 - 476.26 = 10.02$$
$$\text{Depth of cut} = \text{grade rod} - \text{ground rod}$$

The following equation must be satisfied by trial-and-error ground rod readings:

$$X = (\text{depth of cut} \times 3) + 29.0$$

**Solution**
The surveyor, holding a cloth tape as well as the rod, estimates the desired location and gives a rod reading. For this example, assume that the rod reading was 6.0 ft at a distance of 35 ft from ℄.

$$\text{Depth of cut} = 10.02 - 6.0 = 4.02$$
$$X = (4.02 \times 3) + 29.0 = 41.06 \text{ ft}$$

Since the surveyor was only 35 ft from the ℄, he or she must move farther out. At the next point, 43 ft from ℄, a reading of 6.26 was obtained.

$$\text{Depth of cut} = 10.02 - 6.26 = 3.76$$
$$X = (3.76 \times 3) + 29.0 = 40.3 \text{ ft.}$$

At 43 ft, the surveyor was too far out. He or she moves closer and gives a rod reading of 6.10 at 41 ft from the ℄. Now:

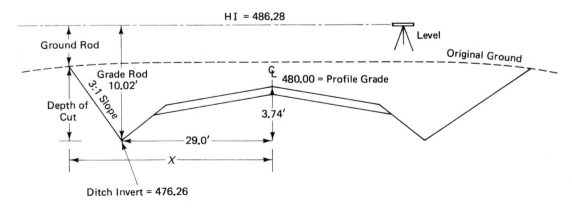

**FIGURE 14.14** Location of a slope stake in cut section.

$$\text{Depth of cut} = 10.02 - 6.10 = 3.92$$
$$X = (3.92 \times 3) + 29 = 40.8 \text{ ft}$$

This location is close enough for placing the slope stake; the error of 0.2 ft is not significant in this type of work. Usually, two or three trials are required to locate the slope stake properly.

Figures 14.15 and 14.16 illustrate the techniques used when surveying in slope stakes in fill sections. The slope stake distance from the centerline can also be scaled from cross sections or topographic plans. In most cases, cross sections (see Chapter 8) are drawn at even stations (100 ft or 30 to 40 m). The cross sections are necessary to calculate the volume estimates used in contract tendering. The location of the slope stakes can be scaled from the cross-section plan. In addition, highway contract plans are now usually developed photogrammetrically from aerial photos; these plans show contours that are precise enough for most slope stake purposes. You can usually scale off the required distances from the ℄ by using either the cross-section plan or the contour plan to the closest 1.0 ft or 0.3 m. The cost savings gained from determining this information in the office should usually outweigh any resultant loss of accuracy. The precision is usually greater now because

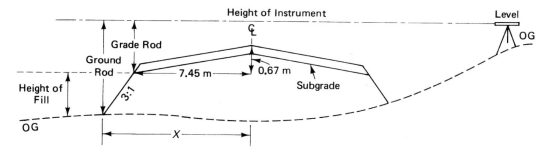

**FIGURE 14.15**  Location of slope stakes in a fill section. Case 1: instrument HI above subgrade.

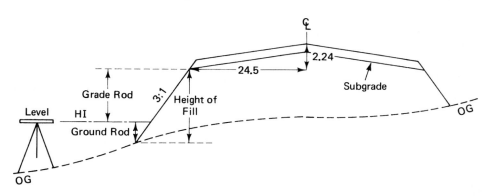

**FIGURE 14.16**  Location of a slope stake in a fill section. Case 2: instrument HI below subgrade.

Sec. 14.7    Highway Construction

of the advances in computers and photogrammetric equipment. Occasional field checks can be used to check on these scale methods. Lidar imaging also holds great potential for these types of ground surface measurement applications (see Section 12.24).

If scale methods are employed, total stations can be used to establish the horizontal distance from the ℄ to the slope stake. These methods will be more accurate than using a cloth tape on deep cuts or high fills, where "breaking tape" may be required several times.

## 14.7.3 Layout for Line and Grade

In municipal work, it is often possible to put the grade stakes on offset, issue a grade sheet, and then continue with other work. The surveyor may be called back to replace the odd stake knocked over by construction equipment, but usually the layout is thought to be a one-time occurrence.

In highway work, the surveyor must accept the fact that the grade stakes will be laid out several times. The repetitive nature of this layout work makes it a natural choice for the use of machine guidance techniques (Section 14.1). The chief difference between the two types of work is the large values for cut and fill. For the grade stakes to be in a "safe" location, they must be located beyond the slope stakes. This location is used for the initial layout, but as the work progresses, this distance back to the ℄ becomes too cumbersome to allow for accurate transfer of alignment and grade. As a result, as the work progresses, the offset lines are moved ever closer to the ℄ of construction, until the final location for the offsets is 2 to 3 ft (1 m) from each edge of the proposed pavement. The number of times that the layout must be repeated is a direct function of the height of fill or depth of cut involved.

In highway work, the centerline is laid out at the appropriate stations. The centerline points are then offset individually at convenient distances on both sides of the ℄. For the initial layout, the ℄ stakes, offset stakes, and slope stakes are all put in at the same time. The cuts and fills are written on the grade stakes and referenced either to the top of the stake or to a mark on the side of the stake that will give even foot (even decimeter) values. The cuts and fills are written on that side of the stake facing the ℄, whereas the stations are written on that side of the stake facing the 0 + 00 location, as noted previously.

As the work progresses and the cuts and fills become more pronounced, care should be taken in breaking tape when laying out grade stakes so that the horizontal distance is maintained. The centerline stakes are offset by turning them 90°, either with a right-angle prism or, more usually, by the swung arm method. Cloth tapes are used to lay out the slope stakes and offset stakes. Once a ℄ station has been offset on one side, care is taken when offsetting to the other side to ensure that the two offsets and the ℄ stake are all in a straight line.

When the cut and/or fill operations have brought the work to the proposed subgrade (bottom of granular elevations), the subgrade must be verified by cross sections before the contractor is permitted to place the granular material. Usually, a tolerance of 0.10 ft (30 mm) is allowed. Once the top of the granular profile has been reached, layout for the pavement (sometimes a separate contract) can commence. The final layout for pavement is usually on a very close offset (3 ft or 1 m). If the pavement is to be concrete, more precise alignment is provided by nails driven into the tops of the stakes.

When the highway construction has been completed, a final survey is performed. The final survey includes cross sections and locations that are used for final payments to the contractor and for the completion of an as-built drawing. The final cross sections are taken at the same stations used in the preliminary survey.

The description in this chapter referred to two-lane highways. The procedure for layout of a four-lane divided highway is very similar. The same control is used for both sections; grade stakes can be offset to the center of the median and used for both sections. When the lane separation becomes large and the vertical alignment is different for each direction, the project can be approached as though it were two independent highways. The layout for elevated highways, which are often found in downtown urban areas, follows the procedures used for structures layout and entails the use of more precise methods and instrumentation that will provide the higher accuracy required by these types of surveys

## 14.7.4 Grade Transfer

The grade stakes can be set so that the tops of the stakes are at "grade." Stakes set to grade are colored red or blue on the top to differentiate them from all other stakes. This procedure is time-consuming and often impractical except for final pavement layout. Generally, the larger the offset distance, the more difficult it is to drive the tops of the stakes to grade.

As noted earlier, the cut and fill can refer to the top of the grade stake or to a mark on the side of the grade stake that represents an even number of feet (decimeters) of cut or fill. The mark on the side of the stake is located by sliding the rod up and down the side of the stake until a value is read on the rod that will give the cut or fill to an even foot (decimeter). This procedure of marking the side of the stake is best performed by two people, one to hold the rod and the other to steady the bottom of the rod and then to make the mark on the stake. The cut or fill can be written on the stake or entered on a grade sheet, one copy of which is given to the contractor.

To transfer the grade (cut or fill) from the grade stake to the area of construction, a means of transferring the stake elevation in a horizontal manner is required. When the grade stake is close (within 6 ft or 2 m), the grade transfer can be accomplished using a carpenter's level set on a piece of sturdy lumber [see Figure 14.17(a) and (b)]. The recently developed laser torpedo level permits the horizontal reference (laser beam) to extend beyond the actual location of the level itself (that is, right across the grade). When the grade stake is far from the area of construction, a string line level may also be used to transfer the grade of cut or fill (see Figure 14.18). In this case, a fill of 1 ft 0 in. (as well as the offset distance) is marked on the grade stake. A guard stake has been placed adjacent to the grade stake, and the grade mark is transferred to the guard stake. A 1-ft distance is measured up the guard stake, and the grade elevation is marked.

A string line is then attached to the guard stake at the grade elevation mark. Then a line level is hung from the string (near the halfway mark), and the string is pulled taut to eliminate most of the sag (it is not possible to eliminate all the sag). The string line is adjusted up and down until the bubble in the line level is centered; with the bubble centered, you can see quickly at ℄ how much more fill may be required to bring the highway, at that point, to grade. This technique is not as precise as the laser beam techniques. Use of rotating construction lasers allows one person, working alone, to transfer and check grades much more quickly and efficiently.

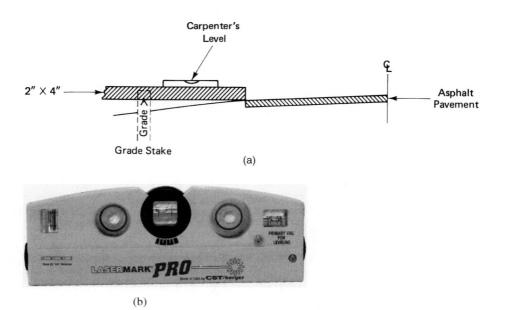

Carpenter's
Level

2" × 4"

Grade Stake

Asphalt
Pavement

(a)

(b)

**FIGURE 14.17** (a) Grade transfer using a conventional carpenter's level. (b) 8" laser torpedo level, featuring accuracy up to ¼" (0.02') at 100 ft (6 mm at 30 m); 3
precision glass vials—horizontal, vertical, and adjustable; and three AA cell
batteries providing approximately 40 hours of intermittent use. (Courtesy
of CST/Berger, Ill.)

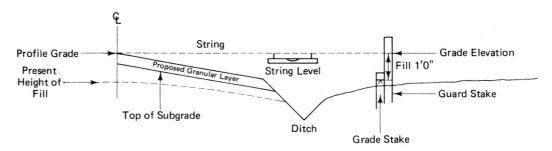

Profile Grade

Present
Height of
Fill

Top of Subgrade

String

Proposed Granular Layer

String Level

Ditch

Grade Stake

Grade Elevation

Fill 1'0"

Guard Stake

**FIGURE 14.18** Grade transfer using a string level.

You can see in Figure 14.18 that more fill is required to bring the total fill to the top
of the subgrade elevation. The surveyor can convey this information to the grade inspector
so that the fill can be increased. As the height of fill approaches the proper elevation (top of
subgrade), the grade checks become more frequent.

In the preceding example, the grade fill was 1 ft 0 in. Had the grade been cut 1 ft, the procedure with respect to the guard stake would have been the same; that is, you would measure
up the guard stake 1 ft so that the mark now on the guard stake would be 2 ft above the ₵ grade.

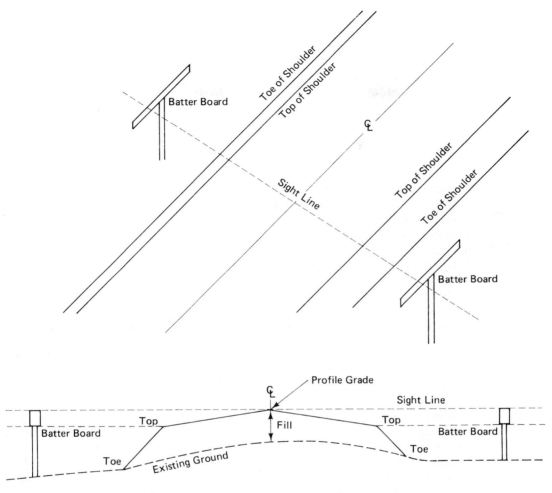

**FIGURE 14.19** Grade transfer using batter boards.

The surveyor or grade inspector at ℄ would simply measure down 2 ft using a tape measure from the level string at ℄. If the measurement down to the "present" height of fill exceeded 2 ft, it would indicate that more fill was required; if the measurement down to the "present" height of fill were less than 2 ft, it would indicate that too much fill has been placed and that an appropriate depth of fill must be removed.

Another method of grade transfer used when the offset is large and the cuts or fills significant is the use of batter boards. Batter boards are horizontal crosspieces attached to grade stakes or reference stakes and are set to an even number of feet or meters above the proposed grade elevation so referenced. Batter boards permit visual sightings to monitor the construction process. See Figure 14.19 (road layout) and Figures 14.23 and 14.24 (pipeline layout). In the preceding example, a fill grade is transferred from the grade stake to the guard stake. The fill grade is measured up the guard stake and the grade elevation is marked (any even foot/decimeter cut or fill mark can be used as long as the relationship to the profile grade is marked clearly). A crosspiece is nailed on the guard stake at the grade mark and parallel to the ℄. A similar guard stake and crosspiece are established on the opposite side of the ℄. The surveyor or grade inspector can then sight over the two cross-pieces to establish a profile grade datum at that point. Another worker can move across the section with a rod, and the progress of the fill (cut) operation can be checked visually. In some cases, two crosspieces are used on each guard stake, one indicating the ℄ profile grade and the lower one indicating the shoulder elevation.

### 14.7.5 Ditch Construction

The ditch profile often parallels the ℄ profile, especially in cut sections. When the ditch profile does parallel the ℄ profile, no additional grades are required to assist the contractor in construction. However, it is quite possible to have the ℄ profile at one slope (even 0%) and the ditch profile at another slope (0.3% is often taken as a minimum slope to give ade-quate drainage). If the ditch grades are independent of the ℄ profile, the contractor must be given these cuts or fill grades, either from the existing grade stakes or from grade stakes specifically referencing the ditch line.

In the extreme case (e.g., a spiraled highway going over the brow of a hill), the con-tractor may require five separate grades at one station (that is, ℄, two edges of pavement, and two different ditch grades). It is even possible in this extreme case to have the two ditches flowing in opposite directions for a short distance.

## 14.8   Sewer and Tunnel Construction

Sewers are usually described as being in one of two categories. Sanitary sewers collect res-idential and industrial liquid waste and convey these wastes (sewage) to a treatment plant. Storm sewers are designed to collect runoff from rainfall and to transport this water (sewage) to the nearest natural receiving body (for example, a creek, river, lake). The rain-water enters the storm sewer system through ditch inlets or through catch basins located at the curb line on paved roads. The design and construction of sanitary and storm sewers are similar because the flow of sewage is usually governed by gravity. Since the sewer grade lines (flow lines) depend on gravity, it is essential that the construction grades are given precisely.

Figure 14.20 shows a typical cross section of a municipal roadway. The two sewers are typically located 5 ft (1.5 m) either side of the ℄. The sanitary sewer is usually deeper than the storm sewer because it must be deep enough to allow for all house connections. The sanitary house connection is usually at a 2% (minimum) slope. If sanitary sewers are being added to an existing residential road, the preliminary survey must include the base-ment floor elevations. The floor elevations are determined by taking a rod reading on the windowsill and then, after getting permission to enter the house, measuring from the win-dowsill down to the basement floor. As a result of deep basements and long setbacks from the ℄, sanitary sewers often have to be at least 9 ft (2.75 m) below the ℄ grade.

In the southern United States, the depth of storm sewers below the ℄ grade depends on the traffic loading. In the northern United States and most of Canada, it depends on the

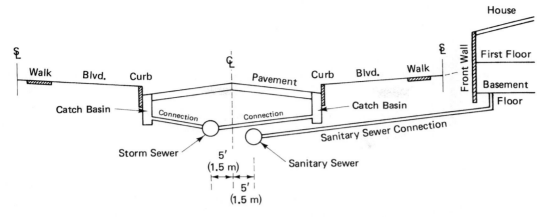

**FIGURE 14.20** Municipal road allowance showing typical service locations (see also Figure 14.3).

depth of traffic loading or frost penetration, whichever is larger. The minimum depth of storm sewers ranges from 3 ft (1 m) in some areas of the south to 8 ft (2.5 m) in the north. The design of the inlets and catch basins depends on the depth of the sewer and the type of effluent. The minimum slope for storm sewers is usually 0.50%, whereas the minimum slope for sanitary sewers is often set at 0.67%. In either case, the designers try to achieve self-cleaning velocity at 2.5 to 3 ft/s (0.8 to 0.9 m/s) to avoid excessive sewer maintenance costs.

Manholes (maintenance holes, MHs) are located at each change in direction, slope, or pipe size. In addition, manholes are located at 300- to 450-ft (100- to 140-m) intervals maximum. Catch basins are located at 300-ft (100-m) maximum intervals; they are also located at the high side of intersections and at all low points. The 300-ft (100-m) maximum interval is reduced as the slope on the road increases.

For construction purposes, sewer layout is considered only from one manhole to the next. The stationing (0 + 00) commences at the first (existing) manhole (or outlet) and proceeds only to the next manhole. If a second leg is also to be constructed, that station of 0 + 00 is assigned to the downstream manhole and proceeds upstream only to the next manhole. Each manhole is described by a unique manhole number to avoid confusion with the stations for extensive sewer projects. Figure 14.21 shows a section of sewer pipe. The *invert* is the inside bottom of the pipe. The invert grade is the controlling grade for construction and design. The sewer pipes may consist of vitrified clay, metal, some of the newer plastics, or, as is usually the case, concrete. The pipe wall thickness depends on the diameter of the pipe. For storm sewers, 12 in. (300 mm) is often taken as the minimum diameter. The *springline* of the pipe is at the halfway mark, and house connections are made above this reference line. The crown is the outside top of the pipe. Although this term is relatively unimportant (sewer cover is measured to the crown) for sewer construction, it is important for pipeline (pressurized pipes) construction because it gives the controlling grade for construction.

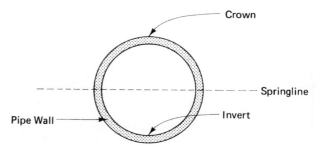

**FIGURE 14.21** Sewer pipe section.

## 14.8.1 Layout for Line and Grade

As in all other construction work, offset stakes are used to provide line and grade for the construction of sewers. Before deciding on the offset location, it is wise to discuss the matter with the contractor. The contractor will be excavating the trench and casting the material to one side or loading it into trucks for removal from the site. Additionally, the sewer pipe will be delivered to the site and positioned conveniently alongside its future location. The position of the offset stakes should not interfere with either of these operations.

The surveyor will position the offset line as close to the pipe centerline as possible, but seldom is it possible to locate the offset line closer than 15 ft (5 m) away; 0 + 00 is assigned to the downstream manhole or outlet, the chainage proceeding upstream to the next manhole. The centerline of construction is laid out with stakes marking the location of the two terminal points of the sewer leg. The surveyor will use survey techniques giving 1/3,000 accuracy as a minimum for most sewer projects. Large-diameter (6-ft or 2-m) sewers require increased precision and accuracy.

The two terminal points on the ℄ are occupied by a theodolite, and right angles are turned to locate precisely the terminal points at the assigned offset distance; 0 + 00 on offset is occupied by a transit or theodolite, and a sight is taken on the other terminal offset point. Stakes are then located at 50-ft (20-m) intervals, with the surveyor checking in at the terminal point to verify accuracy.

The tops of the offset stakes are surveyed and their elevations determined, and the surveyor ensures that the leveling is accurate; the invert elevation of MH 3 (see Figure 14.22) shown on the contract plan and profile is verified at the same time. The surveyor next calculates the sewer invert elevations for the 50-ft (20-m) stations. He or she then prepares a grade sheet showing the stations, stake elevations, invert grades, and cuts. The following examples will illustrate the techniques used.

Assume that an existing sewer (see Figure 14.22) is to be extended from existing MH 3 to proposed MH 4. The horizontal alignment will be a straight-line production of the sewer leg from MH 2 to MH 3. The vertical alignment is taken from the contract plan and profile (see Figure 14.22). The straight line is produced by setting up the transit or theodolite at MH 3, sighting MH 2, and double-centering to the location of MH 4. The layout then proceeds as described previously.

The stake elevations, as determined by differential leveling, are shown in Table 14.5. At station 1 + 50, the cut is 8'3⅛" (see Figure 14.23). To set the cross-trench batter

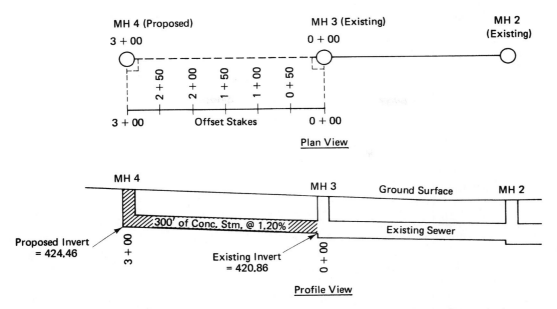

**FIGURE 14.22** Plan view (a) and profile view (b) of a proposed sewer (foot units).

**Table 14.5** SEWER GRADE SHEET: FOOT UNITS[a]

| Station | Invert elevation | Stake elevation | Cut | Cut |
|---|---|---|---|---|
| MH 3 0 + 00 | 420.86 | 429.27 | 8.41 | 8′4⅞″ |
| 0 + 50 | 421.46 | 429.90 | 8.44 | 8′5¼″ |
| 1 + 00 | 422.06 | 430.41 | 8.35 | 8′4¼″ |
| 1 + 50 | 422.66 | 430.98 | 8.32 | 8′3⅞″ |
| 2 + 00 | 423.26 | 431.72 | 8.46 | 8′5½″ |
| 2 + 50 | 423.86 | 431.82 | 7.96 | 7′11½″ |
| MH 4 3 + 00 | 424.46 | 432.56 | 8.10 | 8′1¼″ |

[a]Refer to Table 14.3 for foot–inch conversion.

board at the next even foot, measure up 0′8⅛″ to the top of the batter board. The offset distance of 15 ft can be measured and marked at the top of the batter board over the pipe ₵, and a distance of 9 ft measured down to establish the invert elevation. This even foot measurement from the top of the batter board to the invert is known as the grade rod distance. A value can be picked for the grade rod so that it is the same value at each station. In this example, 9 ft appears to be suitable for each station because the value is larger than the largest cut. The arithmetic shown for station 1 + 50 is performed at each station so that the batter boards can be set at 50-ft intervals. The grade rod (a 2 in. by 2 in. length of lumber held by a worker in the trench) has a foot piece attached to the bottom at a

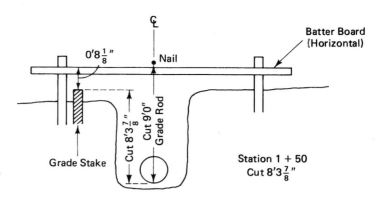

**FIGURE 14.23** Use of cross-trench batter boards.

right angle to the rod so that the foot piece can be inserted into the pipe, which will allow measurement precisely from the invert.

This method of line-and-grade transfer has been shown first because of its simplicity; it has **not,** however, been widely used in the field in recent years. With the introduction of larger and faster trenching equipment, which can dig deeper and wider trenches, this method would only slow the work down because it involves batter boards spanning the trench at 50-ft intervals. Most grade transfers are now accomplished by freestanding offset batter boards or laser alignment devices. Using the data from the previous example, we can illustrate how the technique of freestanding batter boards is used (see Figure 14.24).

These batter boards (3 ft or 1 m wide) are erected at each grade stake. As in the previous example, the batter boards are set at a height that will result in a grade rod that is an even number of feet (decimeters) long. With this technique, however, the grade rod distance will be longer because the top of the batter board should be at a comfortable eye height for the works inspector. The works inspector usually checks the work while standing at the lower chainage stakes and sighting forward to the higher chainage stakes. The line of sight over the batter boards is a straight line parallel to the invert profile, and in this example (see Figure 14.22), the line of sight over the batter boards is rising at 1.20%.

As the inspector sights over the batter boards, he or she can include in the field of view the top of the grade rod, which is being held on the most recently installed pipe length. The top of the grade rod has a horizontal board attached to it in a fashion similar to the batter boards. The inspector can determine visually whether the line over the batter boards and the line over the grade rod are at the same elevation. If an adjustment up or down is required, the worker in the trench makes the necessary adjustment and has the work rechecked. Grades can be checked to the closest ¼ in. (6 mm) in this manner. The preceding example is now worked out using a grade rod of 14 ft (see Table 14.6).

The grade rod of 14 ft requires an eye height of 5′ 7⅛″ at 0 + 00; if this is considered too high, a grade rod of 13 ft can be used, which would result in an eye height of 4′ 7⅛″ at the first batter board. The grade rod height is chosen to suit the needs of the inspector.

In some cases, an additional station is put in before 0 + 00 (i.e., 0 − 50). The grade stake and batter board refer to the theoretical pipe ₵ and invert profile produced back

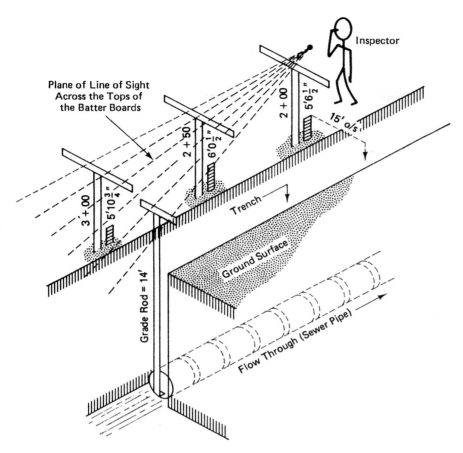

**FIGURE 14.24** Freestanding batter boards.

through the first manhole. This batter board will, of course, line up with all the others and will be useful in checking the grade of the first few pipe lengths placed. Many agencies use 25-ft (10-m) stations, rather than the 50-ft (20-m) stations used in this example. The smaller intervals allow for much better grade control.

One distinct advantage to the use of batter boards in construction work is that an immediate visual check is available on **all** the survey work involved in the layout. The line of sight over the tops of the batter boards (which is actually a vertical offset line) must be a straight line. If, upon completion of the batter boards, all the boards do not line up precisely, it is obvious that a mistake has been made. The surveyor will check the work by first verifying all grade computations and, second, by releveling the tops of the grade stakes. Once the boards are in alignment, the surveyor can continue with other projects. See Figure 14.25 and Table 14.7 for a sewer grade sheet example stated in metric units.

**Table 14.6** SEWER GRADE SHEET FOR BATTER BOARDS

| Station | Invert elevation | Stake elevation | Cut | Stake to batter board | Stake to batter board |
|---------|------------------|-----------------|-----|----------------------|----------------------|
| MH 3 0 + 00 | 420.86 | 429.27 | 8.41 | 5.59 | 5′7⅛″ |
| 0 + 50 | 421.46 | 429.90 | 8.44 | 5.56 | 5′6¾″ |
| 1 + 00 | 422.06 | 430.41 | 8.35 | 5.65 | 5′7¾″ |
| 1 + 50 | 422.66 | 430.98 | 8.32 | 5.68 | 5′8⅛″ |
| 2 + 00 | 423.26 | 431.72 | 8.46 | 5.54 | 5′6½″ |
| 2 + 50 | 423.86 | 431.82 | 7.96 | 6.04 | 6′0½″ |
| MH 4 3 + 00 | 424.46 | 432.56 | 8.10 | 5.90 | 5′10¾″ |

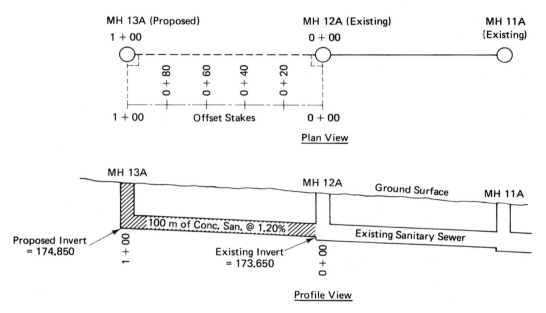

**FIGURE 14.25** Plan view (a) and profile view (b) of a proposed sewer (metric units).

## 14.8.2 Laser Alignment

Laser devices are now in use in most forms of construction work. Lasers are normally used in a fixed direction and slope mode or in a revolving, horizontal pattern. One such device [see Figure 14.26(a) and (b)] can be mounted in a sewer manhole, aligned for direction and slope, and used with a target for the laying of sewer pipe. The laser beam can be deflected by dust or high humidity, and care must be taken to overcome these factors.

Lasers used in sewer trenches sometimes are accompanied by blowers that remove the humid air. To overcome the humidity problem, the laser can be used above grade with a signal-sensing target rod. Working above ground not only eliminates the humidity factor, it allows for more accurate and quicker horizontal alignment. These devices allow for setting slope within the

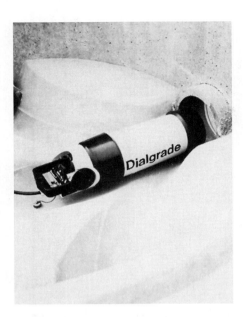

(a)

(b)

**FIGURE 14.26** (a) Pipeline laser-mounted in a stormpipe manhole. (Courtesy of Spectra-Physics, Inc., California) (b) Pipe-laying laser featuring red or green visible laser beam, working range of 650 ft, grade range settings of $-15\%$ to $+50\%$ vertical, self-leveling range of $\pm 10\%$ vertical, and accompanying pipe targets sized to fit various pipe diameters. (Courtesy of CST/Berger, Ill.)

(a)

**FIGURE 14.27** Rotating lasers. (a) Site grade control. (b) Laser sensor mounted on backhoe gives a proper trenching depth for field tile installation. (Courtesy of Laser Alignment, Inc., Michigan)

(b)

limits of $-10°$ to $30°$. Some devices have automatic shutoff capabilities when the device is disturbed from its desired setting. Figures 14.27 and 14.28 illustrate additional laser applications.

## 14.8.3 Catch Basin Construction Layout

Catch basins (CBs) are constructed with the storm sewer or at a later date, just prior to curb construction. Usually, the catch basin is located by two grade stakes, one on each side of the CB. The two stakes are on the curb line and are usually 5 ft (2 m) from the center of the

**FIGURE 14.28** Laser transit supplies a reference laser beam and a reference laser plane (horizontal or vertical). It is used here to control a dredging operation. (Courtesy of Spectra-Physics, Inc., California)

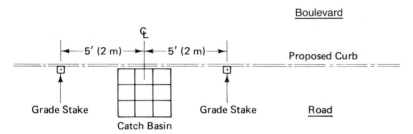

**FIGURE 14.29** Catch basin layout (plan view).

catch basin. The cut or fill grade is referenced to the CB grate elevation at the curb face. The ₵ pavement elevation is calculated, and from it the crown height is subtracted to arrive at the top of the grate elevation (see Figures 14.29 and 14.30).

At low points, particularly at vertical curve low points, it is usual practice for the surveyor to lower the catch-basin grate elevation (below design grade) to ensure that ponding does not occur on either side of the completed catch basin. We noted in Section 13.15 that the longitudinal slope at vertical curve low points is almost flat for a significant distance. The catch basin grate elevation can be lowered arbitrarily as much as 1 in. (25 mm) to ensure that the gutter drainage goes directly into the catch basin without ponding. The catch basin, which can be of concrete poured in place, is now more often prefabricated concrete that is delivered to the job site and set below finished grade until the curbs are constructed. At the time of curb construction, the finished grade for the catch basin grate is achieved by installing one or more courses of brick on top of the concrete walls.

## 14.8.4 Pipeline Construction

Pipelines are designed to carry water, oil, or natural gas under pressure. Because pressure systems do not require close attention to grade lines, the layout for pipelines can proceed at

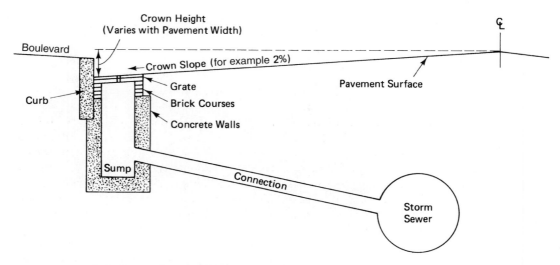

**FIGURE 14.30** Typical catch basin (with sump).

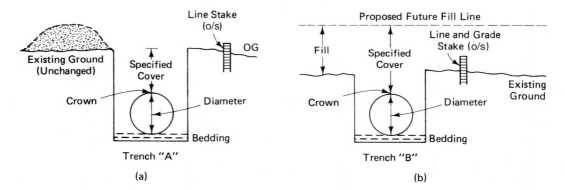

**FIGURE 14.31** Pipeline construction. (a) Existing ground to be unchanged. (b) Existing ground to be altered.

a much lower order of precision than is required for gravity pipes. Pipelines are usually designed so that the cover over the crown is adequate for the loading conditions expected and is also adequate to prevent damage due to frost penetration, erosion, and the like.

The pipeline location can be determined from the contract drawings; the grade stakes are offset an optimal distance from the pipe ₵ and are placed at 50- to 100-ft (15- to 30-m) intervals. When existing ground elevations are not being altered, the standard cuts required can be simply measured down from the ground surface. Required cuts in this case would equal the specified cover over the crown plus the pipe diameter plus the bedding, if applicable (see Figure 14.31).

In the case of proposed general cuts and fills, grades must be given to establish suitable crown elevation so that **final** cover is as specified. Additional considerations and higher precisions are required at major crossings (for example, rivers, highways, utilities). Final surveys show the actual location of the pipe and appurtenances (valves and the like). As-built drawings, produced from final surveys, are especially important in urban areas, where it seems there is no end to underground construction.

## 14.8.5 Tunnel Construction

Tunnels are used in road, sewer, and pipeline construction when the cost of working at or near the ground surface becomes prohibitive. For example, sewers are tunneled when they must be at a depth that would make the open cut technique too expensive (or operationally unfeasible), or sewers may be tunneled to avoid disruption of services on the surface, such as would occur if an open cut was put through a busy expressway. Roads and railroads are tunneled through large hills and mountains to maintain optimal grade lines. Control surveys for tunnel layouts are performed on the surface, joining the terminal points of the tunnel. These control surveys use GPS positioning or precise traverse survey methods and allow for the computation of coordinates for all key points (see Figure 14.32).

In the case of highway (railway) tunnels, the ℄ can be run directly into the tunnel and is usually located on the roof either at the ℄ or at a convenient offset (see Figure 14.33). If the tunnel is long, intermediate shafts can be sunk to provide access for materials, ventilation, and alignment verification. Conventional engineering theodolites are illustrated in

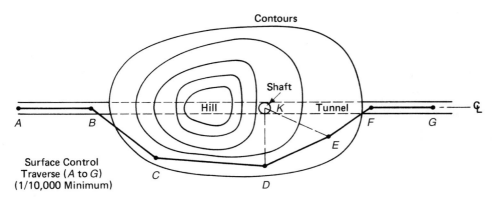

(a)

Direction and Length of *B–F, D–K,* and *E–K*
can be Computed from Traverse Data

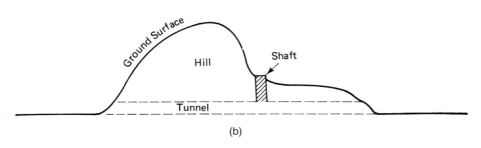

(b)

**FIGURE 14.32** Plan view (a) and profile view (b) of tunnel location.

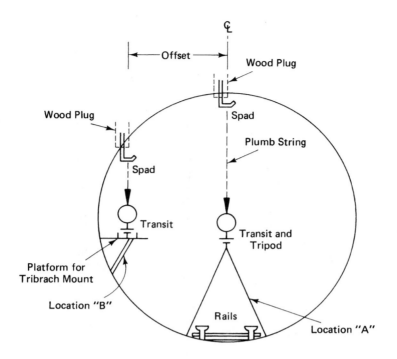

Tunnel ₵ is Usually Located in the Roof (Location "A") and then can be
Offset (Location "B") to Provide Space for Excavation and Materials Movement.
Line and Grade can be Provided by a Single Laser Beam which has been
Oriented for Both Alignment and Slope.

**FIGURE 14.33**   Establishing line in a tunnel.

Figure 14.33; for cramped quarters, a suspension theodolite (Figure 14.34) can be used. Levels can also be run directly into the tunnel, and temporary benchmarks are established in the floor or roof of the tunnel. In the case of long tunnels, work can proceed from both ends and meet somewhere near the middle. Constant vigilance with respect to errors is of prime importance.

In the case of a deep sewer tunnel, mining surveying techniques must be employed to establish line and grade (see Figure 14.35). The surface ₵ projection *AB* is carefully established on beams overhanging the shaft opening. Plumb lines (piano wire or aircraft cables) are hung down the shaft, and the tunnel ₵ is developed by overaligning the transit or theodolite in the tunnel. A great deal of care is required in overaligning—this very short backsight will be produced over a relatively long distance, thus magnifying any sighting errors.

The plumb lines usually employ heavy plumb bobs (capable of taking additional weights if required). The plumb bobs are sometimes submerged in heavy oil to dampen the swing oscillations. If the plumb line swing oscillations cannot be totally eliminated, the oscillations must be measured and then averaged. Lasers have been used for the vertical alignment of shafts, but because of the time and effort required to set and aim the laser precisely, some mining firms have gone back to the simpler and easier techniques utilizing plumb bobs.

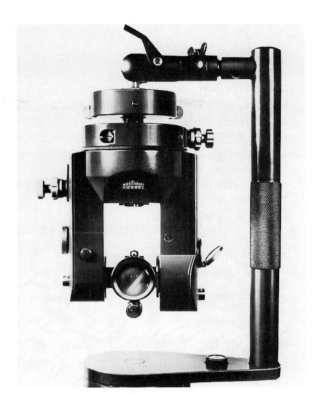

**FIGURE 14.34** Breithaupt mining suspension theodolite. It can be used with a tripod or can be suspended from a steel punch in the ceilings of cramped galleries or drifts. (Courtesy of Keuffel & Esser Co.)

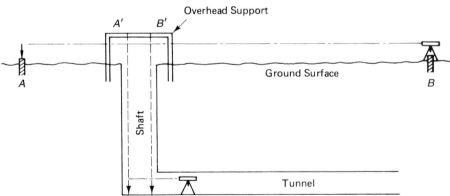

Tunnel ℄ AB is Carefully Marked on the Overhead Support at A' and B'. These Two Marks are Set as Far Apart as Possible for Plumbing into the Shaft.

The Transit in the Tunnel Over-aligns the Two Plumb Lines (Trial and Error Technique); ℄ is then Produced Forward using Double-Centering Techniques.

Precision can be Improved by Repeating this Process when the Tunnel Excavation has Progressed to the Point where a much Longer Backsight is Possible.

**FIGURE 14.35** Transfer of surface alignment to the tunnel.

Some tunnels are pressurized to control ground water seepage. The air locks associated with pressure systems cut down considerably on the clear dimensions in the shaft, making the plumbed line transfer even more difficult.

Transferring line from ground surface to underground locations by use of plumb lines is an effective although outdated technique. Modern survey practice favors the use of precise optical plummets to accomplish the line transfer. These plummets are designed for use in zenith or nadir directions (see Figure 14.35). The accuracy of this technique can be as high as 1 or 2 mm in 100 m. (In addition to tunnel-shaft applications, these instruments are very useful in controlling high-rise construction through elevator shafts or through-floor ports.) Precise optical plummets, together with laser light directed through the eyepiece, have been used with success in positioning target helicopters over control points for angle and distance (EDM) measurements.

## 14.9   Culvert Construction

The plan location and invert grade of culverts are shown on the construction plan and profile. The intersection of the culvert ℄ and the highway ℄ is shown on the plan and is identified by its highway station. In addition, when the proposed culvert is not perpendicular to the highway ℄, the skew number will be shown (see Figure 14.36).

The construction plan shows the culvert location (℄ station), skew number, and length of culvert. The construction profile shows the inverts for each end of the culvert. One grade stake is placed on the ℄ of the culvert, offset a safe distance from each end (see Figure 14.37).

The grade stake references the culvert ℄ and gives the cut or fill to the top of the footing for open footing culverts, to the top of the slab for concrete box culverts, or to the invert of pipe for pipe culverts. If the culvert is long, intermediate grade stakes may be required. The stakes may be offset 6 ft (2 m), or longer distances if site conditions warrant.

In addition to the grade stake at either end of the culvert, it is customary when laying out concrete culverts to place two offset line stakes to define the end of the culvert. These end lines are normally parallel to the ℄ of construction or perpendicular to the culvert ℄. See Figure 14.38 for types of culverts.

## 14.10   Building Construction

All buildings must be located with reference to the property limits. Accordingly, the initial stage of the building construction survey involves the careful retracing and verification of the property lines. Once the property lines are established, the building is located according to plan, with all corners marked in the field. At the same time, original cross sections are taken, perhaps using one of the longer wall lines as a baseline.

The corners already established are offset an optimum distance, and batter boards are erected (see Figure 14.39). The crosspieces are set either to first-floor elevation (finished) or to a set number of feet (decimeters) above or below the first-floor elevation. The contractor is always informed of the precise reference datum. The batter boards for each wall line are joined by string or wire running from nails or saw-cuts at the top of each batter board. The string (wire) is at (or referenced to) the finished first floor. After the excavation for footings and basement has been completed, final cross sections can be taken to determine excavation quantities and

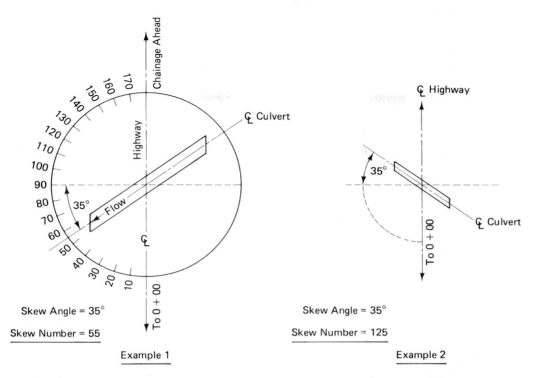

Skew Angle = 35°

Skew Number = 55

Example 1

Skew Angle = 35°

Skew Number = 125

Example 2

The <u>Skew Number</u> is Obtained by Measuring Clockwise to the Nearest 5°, the Angle Between the Back Tangent ₵ of the Highway and the ₵ of the Culvert.

**FIGURE 14.36**  Culvert skew numbers, showing the relationship between the skew angle and the skew number.

costs. In addition to layout for walls, it is customary to stake out all columns or other critical features, given the location and proposed grade.

Once the foundations are complete, it is necessary only to check the contractor's work in a few key dimension areas on each floor. Optical plummets, lasers, and theodolites can all be used for high-rise construction (see Figures 14.40 and 14.41).

# 14.11   Other Construction Surveys

The techniques for survey layout of heavy construction (for example, dams, port facilities, and other large-scale projects) are similar to those already described. Key lines of the project are located according to plan and referenced for the life of the project. All key points are located precisely, and in many cases these points are coordinated and tied to a state or provincial coordinate grid. The two key features of construction control on large-scale projects are (1) high precision and (2) durability of the control monuments and the overall control net.

Prior to construction, horizontal and vertical controls are established over the project site. Most of the discussion in this chapter has dealt with rectangular layout techniques, but as noted earlier, some projects lend themselves in whole or in part to polar

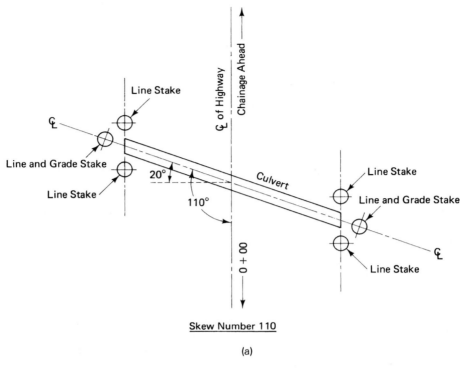

Skew Number 110

(a)

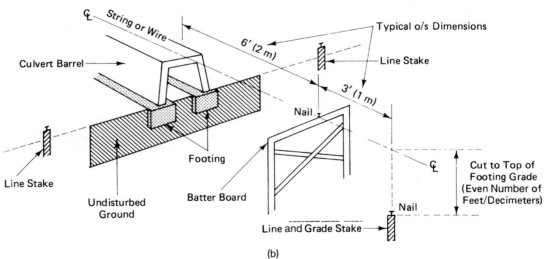

(b)

**FIGURE 14.37** Line and grade for culvert construction. (a) Plan view. (b) Perspective view. (Courtesy of the Ministry of Transportation, Ontario)

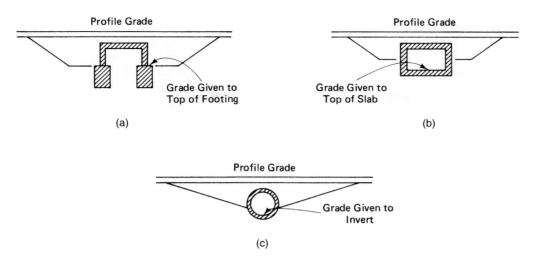

**FIGURE 14.38** Types of culverts. (a) Open footing culvert. (b) Concrete box culvert. (c) Circular, arch, etc., culvert.

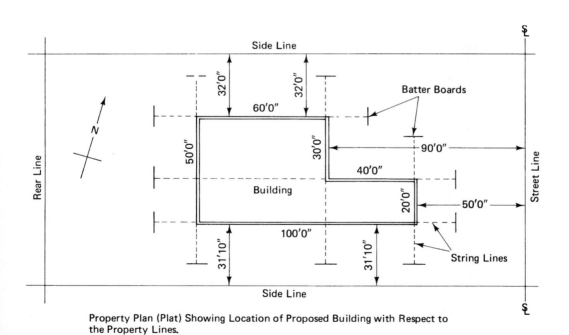

Property Plan (Plat) Showing Location of Proposed Building with Respect to the Property Lines.

This Plan also Shows the Location of the Batter Boards and the String Lines for Each Building Wall Footing.

**FIGURE 14.39** Building layout.

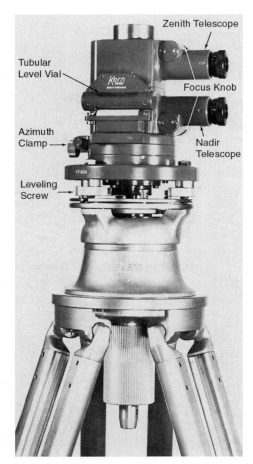

**FIGURE 14.40** Kern OL precise optical plummet. SE in 100 m for a single measurement (zenith or nadir) = ±1 mm (using a coincidence level). Used in high-rise construction, towers, shafts, and the like. (Courtesy of Kern Instruments—Leica, Inc.)

layout techniques using coordinated control and coordinated construction points. Heavy construction is one project area usually well suited for polar layouts and/or GPS layouts.

## 14.12   Construction Survey Specifications

The bulk of all construction work is laid out meeting 1/3,000 (for example, sewers, highways) or 1/5,000 (for example, curbed roads, bridges) specifications. The foregoing is true for rectangular layouts, but as noted in Chapter 10, the control for layout by polar techniques is accomplished meeting survey techniques allowing for 1/10,000 to 1/20,000 accuracy ratios. Section 10.9 gives the specifications now used internationally in construction surveying.

**FIGURE 14.41** Rotating laser positioned to check plumb orientation of construction wall. (Courtesy of Laser Alignment, Inc.)

## Questions

1. Measurement and calculation mistakes are to be avoided in all forms of surveying. Why do construction surveyors need to be even more vigilant about recognizing and correcting mistakes?

2. How can water be used to check building footings for level?

3. Describe factors that may affect surveyors' safety in each of the following areas: highway construction surveying, pipeline surveying, and municipal street surveying.

## Problems

**14.1** A new road is to be constructed beginning at an existing road (℄ elevation = 472.70 ft) for a distance of 600 ft. The ℄ gradient is to rise at 1.32%. The elevations of the offset grade stakes are as follows: 0 + 00 = 472.60, 1 + 00 = 472.36, 2 + 00 =

473.92, 3 + 00 = 475.58, 4 + 00 = 478.33, 5 + 00 = 479.77, and 6 + 00 = 480.82. Prepare a grade sheet (see Table 14.4) showing the cuts and fills in feet and inches.

**14.2** A new road is to be constructed to connect two existing roads. The ℄ intersection with the east road (0 + 00) is at an elevation of 210.500 m, and the ℄ intersection at the west road (1 + 32.562) is at an elevation of 209.603 m. The elevations of the offset grade stakes are as follows: 0 + 00 = 210.831, 0 + 20 = 210.600, 0 + 40 = 211.307, 0 + 60 = 210.114, 0 + 80 + 209.772, 1 + 00 = 209.621, 1 + 20 = 209.308, and 1 + 32.562 = 209.400. Prepare a grade sheet (see Table 14.2) showing cuts and fills in meters.

**14.3** In Figure 14.13(a), if the ditch invert is to be 3′6″ deep (below subgrade), how far from the highway ℄ would the ℄ of the ditch be?

**14.4** Refer to Figure 14.13(b):
  **(a)** If the ditch invert is to be 2.0 m deep (below subgrade), how far from the highway ℄ would the ℄ of the ditch be?
  **(b)** If the original ground is level with the ℄ of the highway right across the width of the highway, how far from the ℄ would be the slope stake marking the far side of the ditch at original ground?

**14.5** A storm sewer is to be constructed from existing MH 8 (invert elevation = 360.44) at +1.20% for a distance of 240 ft to proposed MH 9. The elevations of the offset grade stakes are as follows: 0 + 00 = 368.75, 0 + 50 = 368.81, 1 + 00 = 369.00, 1 + 50 = 369.77, 2 + 00 = 370.22, and 2 + 40 = 371.91. Prepare a grade sheet (see Table 14.5) showing the stake-to-batter-board distance in feet and inches. Use a 14-ft grade rod.

**14.6** A sanitary sewer is to be constructed from existing MH 4 (invert elevation = 150.666) at +0.68% for a distance of 115 meters to proposed MH 5. The elevations of the offset grade stakes are as follows: 0 + 00 = 152.933, 0 + 20 = 152.991, 0 + 40 = 153.626, 0 + 60 = 153.725, 0 + 80 = 153.888, 1 + 00 = 153.710, and 1 + 15 = 153.600. Prepare a grade sheet (see Table 14.7) showing the stake-to-batter-board distances in meters. Use a 4-m grade rod.

**Table 14.7**  GRADE SHEET: METRIC UNITS

| Station | Invert elevation | Stake elevation[a] | Cut | Stake to batter board, grade rod (GR) = 5.0 m |
|---|---|---|---|---|
| MH 12A 0 + 00 | 173.650 | 177.265 | 3.615 | 1.385 |
| 0 + 20 | 173.890 | 177.865 | 3.975 | 1.025 |
| 0 + 40 | 174.130 | 177.200 | 3.070 | 1.930 |
| 0 + 60 | 174.370 | 178.200 | 3.830 | 1.170 |
| 0 + 80 | 174.610 | 178.005 | 3.395 | 1.605 |
| MH 13A 1 + 00 | 174.850 | 178.500 | 3.650 | 1.350 |

[a]Stake elevations and computations are normally carried out to the closest 5 mm.

# CHAPTER

# 15 Land Surveying

## 15.1 General Background

Land surveying involves the establishment of boundaries for public and/or private properties. It includes both the measurement of existing boundaries and the laying out of boundaries. Land surveys (performed by professional surveyors) are made for one or more of the following reasons:

1. To subdivide the public lands (United States) or crown lands (Canada) into townships, sections or concessions, and quarter-sections or lots, thus creating the basic fabric to which all land ownership and subsequent surveys will be directly related.

2. To attain the necessary information for writing a legal description and for determining the area of a particular tract of land.

3. To reestablish the boundaries of a parcel of land that has been previously surveyed and legally described.

4. To subdivide a parcel of land into two or more smaller units in agreement with a plan that dictates the size, shape, and dimensions of the smaller units.

5. To establish the position of particular features such as buildings on the parcel with respect to the boundaries.

Land surveys are required whenever real property or real estate is transferred from one owner to another. The location of the boundaries must be established to ensure that the parcel of land being transferred is properly located; acceptably close to the size and dimensions indicated by the owner; and free of encroachment by adjacent buildings, roadways, and the like. The boundary must be related directly to a preestablished point in the township survey fabric, or tie line, to determine the location of the land tract properly. It is often necessary to determine the location of buildings on the property relative to the boundaries for the purpose of arranging mortgages and ensuring that building bylaws concerning location restrictions have been satisfied.

This chapter describes the techniques employed and the modes of presentation used for various types of land surveys. Familiarity with the methods employed is essential for anyone involved in any aspect of surveying. For example, construction surveying (see Chapter 14) involving the layout for new road construction within an allowance for road on the original township survey necessitates the reestablishment of the legal boundaries of the road allowance. Bends and/or jogs in the road allowance alignment, attributable to the methods employed in the original township survey, occur frequently. An understanding of the survey system used not only explains why these irregularities exist, but also warns the surveyor in advance where they may occur.

A recently surveyed subdivision provides ample evidence of property boundary locations. As soon as any construction commences, however, the lot markers may be removed, bent, misplaced, or covered with earth fill. Therefore, reestablishment of the street and lot pattern becomes an essential yet demanding task. It must be carried out before further work may proceed. The use of previous surveys that showed the positioning of buildings on the lots, known as title or mortgage surveys, greatly assists in reestablishing the property boundaries.

## 15.1.1 Surveyor's Duties

The professional land surveyor must be knowledgeable in both the technical and legal aspects of property boundaries—she or he must have passed state or provincial exams and be properly licensed. Considerable experience is also required, particularly with regard to deciding on the "best evidence" of a boundary location. It is not uncommon for the surveyor to be exposed to conflicting physical as well as legal evidence of a boundary line. Consequently, a form of apprenticeship is often required, in addition to academic qualifications, before the surveyor is licensed to practice by the state, province, or territory.

Regulations are usually required, by law, to assist in standardizing procedures and requirements. Most states and provinces have organizations or associations that are corporate bodies operating under conditions set out in legislative acts. The objectives of a typical surveying association are:

1. To regulate the practice of professional land surveying and to govern the profession in accordance with this act, the regulations, and the bylaws.
2. To establish and maintain standards of knowledge and skill among its members.
3. To establish and maintain standards of professional ethics among its members so that the public interest may be served and protected.

## 15.1.2 Historical Summary

The first North American land surveys were performed in Ontario in 1783 and north of the Ohio River in 1785. These public land surveys divided the land for settlers in rectangular patterns, with most of the lines following one of the cardinal directions as determined by compass. Prior to the establishment of public land surveys, land in the northern and eastern United States (the original thirteen colonies) and parts of Canada were obtained by purchase or as a gift from the British crown.

Early titles were described vaguely, but as time went on, description of these holdings was accomplished by metes and bounds. The term **metes** referred to the distances (originally measured in chains or rods) and bearings, referenced to magnetic north. The term **bounds** meant the boundary references that helped define the property. Many of these early parcels followed natural features (for example, river banks, trails, roads, etc.) rather than the cardinal directions later adopted in the public lands system. Bounds also included the names of adjacent property owners when that data was available.

Modern resurveys of these lands show distances in feet and bearings referenced to astronomical north. Since the U.S. adoption of the metric system in 1993, it is possible, in the future, that some descriptions will show distances in meters when these properties are resurveyed and redescribed.

A metes and bounds survey, or property description, started at a key point on the property boundary, known as the point of beginning (POB), and then proceeded around each side of the property in turn, giving the distance and bearing, together with boundary references (including survey markers such as blazes, rock cairns, wood posts, metal bars and tubes, etc.). In public land surveys, originally only the township lines were run, and section corners were established along these lines at intervals of 1 mile. In 1805, a congressional act directed that each section corner should be marked and that the public lands should be divided into quarter-sections on the township maps, or *plats,* as they were termed legislatively. In 1832, Congress ruled that the public lands should be subdivided into quarter-sections. In 1909, the Secretary of the Interior was directed to resurvey the boundaries of previously surveyed public lands at his or her discretion. This applied only to lands that were still public and thus had no effect upon the boundaries of privately owned lands. In 1946, the Bureau of Land Management in the Department of the Interior was made responsible for public land surveys, which had been administered by the General Land Office in the Treasury Department since 1812.

Prior to 1910, when the contract system of surveying the public lands was abolished, most of the land surveying had been done by private surveyors under government contract. These early surveys were made with crude instruments such as a compass and a chain, often under adverse field conditions. Consequently, some were incomplete and others showed field notes for lines that were never run in the field. Therefore, the corners and lines are often found in other than their theoretical locations. The original corners as established during the original survey, however inaccurate or incomplete, stand as the true corners. The surveyor must therefore use these corners for all subsequent survey work.

In 1789, the surveyor general of Canada was directed to prepare plans of each district using townships 9 miles wide by 12 miles long. Prior to 1835, various nonsectional or "special" township survey systems were authorized. Each presented particular techniques for the establishment of individual lines and generated difficulties for resurveys and access along public road allowances. These difficulties are discussed in this section. This confusion was partially ended in 1859, when sectional townships 6 miles square and divided into 36 sections, each 1 mile square without road allowances, were authorized through federal legislation.

The complexities of survey systems based on French common law, used in states such as Louisiana and provinces like Quebec (or those influenced by Mexican law in California and Texas), are beyond the scope of this section. Some of these systems are based on the importance of frontage ownership along water bodies, such as rivers, for purposes of water access and transportation. Consequently, the irregularities resulting from following natural boundaries present a totally different resurvey concept from the systems based on English common law.

Because various regions of the United States and Canada have been surveyed under different sets of instructions from 1783 to the present, important changes in detail have occurred. The local surveyor should become familiar with the exact methods in use at the time of the original survey before commencing to retrace land boundaries.

## 15.2 Public Land Surveys (North America)

### 15.2.1 General Background

The most common methods for public land surveys in the United States and Canada provide for townships that are 6 miles square, each containing 36 sections. In the United States, each section is thus 1 mile square and is numbered from 1 to 36, as illustrated in Figure 15.1. Section 1 is in the northeast corner of the township. The sections are then numbered consecutively from east to west and from west to east alternately, ending with section 36 in the southeast corner, as illustrated. In Canada, the sections are bounded and numbered as shown in Figure 15.2. Each section is 1 mile square, as in the United States.

Initially, only the exterior boundaries of the township were surveyed and mile corners were established on the township lines. However, the plats or original township maps showed subdivisions that were divided into sections 1 mile square, numbered as just described. Under these conditions, subsequent surveys had to be carried out to establish the corners and boundaries of sections in the interior of the townships. Changes in the procedures for township surveys led successively to each section corner being marked, then to each quarter section corner being established. Because the methods of resurvey differ, depending on the corners that were originally established, it is essential that the surveyor understand these techniques.

This section discusses both the American system and the principles of the various sectional systems used in Canada. The Canadian systems were based on the general principles of the American system.

| | | | | | |
|---|---|---|---|---|---|
| 6 | 5 | 4 | 3 | 2 | 1 |
| 7 | 8 | 9 | 10 | 11 | 12 |
| 18 | 17 | 16 | 15 | 14 | 13 |
| 19 | 20 | 21 | 22 | 23 | 24 |
| 30 | 29 | 28 | 27 | 26 | 25 |
| 31 | 32 | 33 | 34 | 35 | 36 |

**FIGURE 15.1** Numbering of sections in the United States.

| 31 | 32 | 33 | 34 | 35 | 36 |
|----|----|----|----|----|----|
| 30 | 29 | 28 | 27 | 26 | 25 |
| 19 | 20 | 21 | 22 | 23 | 24 |
| 18 | 17 | 16 | 15 | 14 | 13 |
| 7  | 8  | 9  | 10 | 11 | 12 |
| 6  | 5  | 4  | 3  | 2  | 1  |

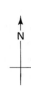
N

**FIGURE 15.2**  Numbering of sections in Canada.

## 15.2.2  Standard Lines

**15.2.2.1 Initial points**  The point at which a survey commences in any area is known as the initial point. A meridian, called the principal meridian, and a parallel of latitude, called the baseline, are run through the initial points, as illustrated in Figure 15.3. After the initial point has been established, the latitude and longitude of the point are determined using field astronomical observations.

Many of the original township surveys were carried out simultaneously. Therefore, several initial points have been established. The principal meridian through an initial point is given a name, and the original surveys governed by each initial point are recorded. For example, the initial point for the Mount Diablo principal meridian, governing surveys in the states of California and Nevada, has a longitude of 121°54′47″W and a latitude of

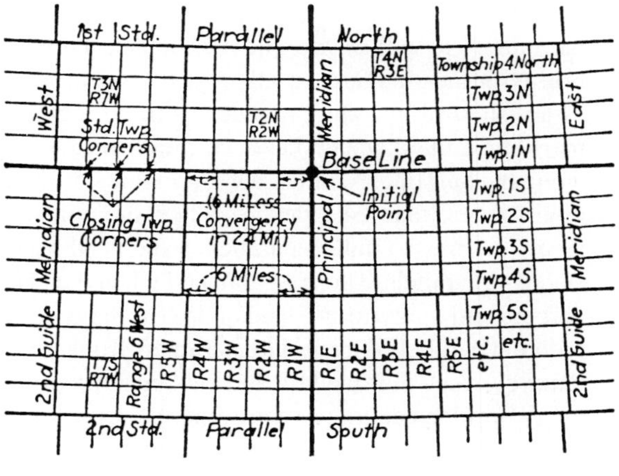

**FIGURE 15.3**  Initial point, parallels, and meridians.

37°52′54″N. The original surveys referred to a particular initial point shown on a map entitled "United States, Showing Principal Meridians, Base Lines, and Areas Governed Thereby," published by the Bureau of Land Management (U.S. Government Printing Office, Washington, D.C.).

In the Canadian system, the international boundary (latitude 49°00′N) is used as the baseline, where appropriate, such as in the western provinces. The principal meridian has an approximate longitude of 97°27′09″W and is located about 12 miles west of the city of Winnipeg, Manitoba. The second meridian is located close to longitude 102°W; the third near 106°W, and so on. Therefore, each initial meridian after the second is located four degrees west of the preceding one. The coast meridian of British Columbia is in a special location due to the configuration of the Pacific Ocean's coastline.

### 15.2.2.2 Meridians

The principal meridian is a true north/south line that is extended in either direction from the initial point to the limits of the area covered by the township surveys. This line is monumented at 40-chain (½-mile) intervals in both the United States and Canada. Additional monumentation was provided in the United States at intersections with streams 3 chains (198 ft) or more wide, navigable water bodies, and lakes having an area of 25 acres or more.

In the United States, two independent linear measurements of the meridian were made. When the difference in these measurements was greater than 20 links (13.2 ft) per 80 chains (1 mile), the line was remeasured until the difference between two of the measurements was less than 20 links. The corners were placed at the mean distances. If the alignment was found to be over 3 ft off the north/south course, the alignment was corrected.

In Canada, no accuracy tolerances were given in the early instructions and no penalties were levied if the work was incorrect. There was no suggestion that the work should be redone. A common source of error was miscounting the number of chains (66 ft) across the front of a section or lot. Consequently, it is not uncommon to find the older township surveys differing from the intended dimensions by approximate multiples of 66 ft. Because the only equipment available to carry out the early surveys was a compass and chain, differences much greater than those stated previously will be found in doing resurveys.

Guide meridians are located at intervals of 24 miles east and west of the principal meridian. These lines are true meridians and extend north of the baseline to their intersection with the standard parallel, as illustrated in Figure 15.4. These guide meridians are established in the same manner as the principal meridians. Due to the convergence of meridians, the distance between these lines will be 24 miles only at the starting points along the baseline. As illustrated in Figure 15.4, the distance between meridians at all other points is less than 24 miles. As a new monument is established where the guide meridian meets the next standard parallel to the north, two sets of monuments are located on the standard parallels. Those established when the parallel was first located are called standard corners and apply to the lands north of the parallel. Those established by the intersection with the parallel of the guide meridians from the south are called closing corners. The distance between the standard and closing corners should be recorded in the field notes.

Similar accuracy requirements apply to the guide meridians as to the principal meridians. Monuments are placed at half-mile (40-chain) intervals. All measurement discrepancies are placed in the last half-mile. Consequently, the distance from the first monu-

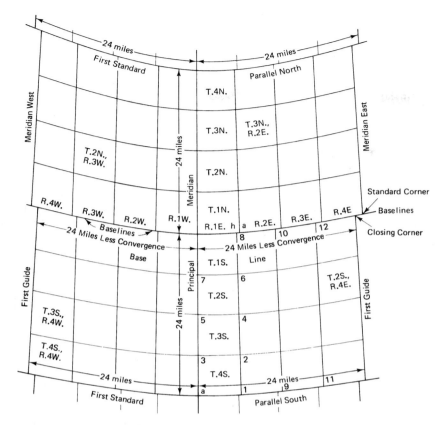

**FIGURE 15.4** Standard parallels and guide meridians.

ment south of the standard parallel to the closing monument on the parallel may differ from 40 chains (½ mile).

### 15.2.2.3 Convergence of meridians

Because all meridians form a great circle through both the North and South poles, these lines converge toward a pole as they proceed northerly or southerly from the equator. Consequently, a line at right angles (90°) with a meridian will be an east-west line for an infinitely small distance from the meridian. If the line at 90° to the meridian is extended, it will form a great circle around the earth that will not be an east-west line except along the equator. The true east-west line is called a parallel of latitude, which is represented by a small circle, illustrated by line *AB* in Figure 15.5. The true parallel, due to convergence, will gradually curve to the north (when located north of the equator) of the great circle at right angles to the meridian.

In Figure 15.5, *DAG* and *EBG* represent two meridians. *P* is the earth's North Pole, *F* is the center of the earth, *DE* is an arc of the equator, *AB* is the arc of a parallel of latitude at latitude $\varphi$, and $\lambda$ is the difference in longitude between the meridians. The angular and linear convergency of the two meridians is to be determined. (Convergence is also discussed in Chapter 10.)

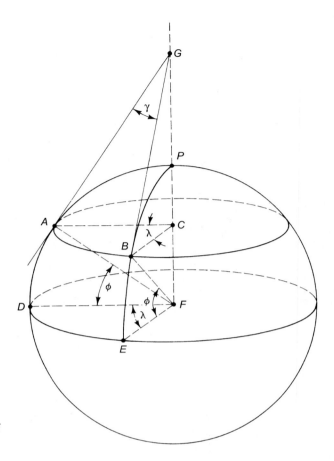

**FIGURE 15.5** Convergence of meridians.

The difference in longitude between the meridians is:

$$\lambda \text{ (radians)} = \frac{AB}{BC}, \text{ therefore } AB = BC \times \lambda \text{ (radians)} \qquad (15.1)$$

The latitude of the circle, of which $AB$ is an arc, is:

$$\varphi = \text{angle } BFE = \text{angle } BGC \qquad (15.2)$$

Therefore:

$$\sin \varphi = \frac{BC}{BG} \qquad \text{and} \qquad BG = \frac{BC}{\sin \varphi}$$

The angle of convergency, for all practical purposes, is:

$$\gamma \text{ (radians)} = \frac{AB}{BG}$$

Substituting for *AB* and *BG* from Equations 15.1 and 15.2 gives:

$$\gamma = \frac{BC \times \lambda}{BC/\sin \varphi} = \lambda \sin \varphi \qquad (15.3)$$

where $\gamma$ and $\varphi$ are in radians. If *AB*, the distance measured along a parallel between two meridians, is *d*, and the radius of the earth at the parallel is *R*, then from Equation 15.1, we have:

$$\lambda = \frac{AB}{BC} = \frac{d}{R \cos \varphi}$$

Substitution of this equation into Equation 15.3 gives:

$$\gamma \text{ (radians)} = \frac{d \sin \varphi}{R \sin \varphi} = \frac{d \tan \varphi}{R} \qquad (15.4)$$

If *d* is in miles and $R = 20{,}960{,}000$ ft (the mean radius of the earth), then from Equation 15.4:

$$\gamma \text{ (seconds)} = 52.09 \, d \tan \phi \qquad (15.5)$$

If *d* is in kilometers, then:

$$\gamma \text{ (seconds)} = 32.370 \, d \tan \varphi \qquad (15.6)$$

If the distance between parallels along the meridians, represented by *AD* and *BE* in Figure 15.5, is *y*, and if the difference in arc length along the two parallels (that is, $DE - AB$ in Figure 15.5) is *p*, then for all practical purposes:

$$\gamma = \frac{p}{y}$$

where $\gamma$ is the mean angle of convergency of the two meridians. If the mean latitude is $\varphi$, substituting in Equation 15.4 gives:

$$p = \frac{dy \tan \varphi}{R} \qquad (15.7)$$

Therefore, the reduction in arc distance along the northerly parallel due to convergence can be calculated using Equation 13.7.

If *d* and *y* are in miles and *R* is the mean radius of the earth, then:

$$p \text{ (feet)} = 1.33 dy \tan \varphi \qquad (15.8)$$

$$p \text{ (chains)} = 0.0202 dy \tan \varphi \qquad (15.9)$$

$$p \text{ (meters)} = 0.4055 dy \tan \varphi \qquad (15.10)$$

If $d$ and $y$ are in kilometers, then:

$$p \text{ (meters)} = 0.1565dy \tan \varphi \qquad (15.11)$$

## ■ EXAMPLE 15.1

Find the angular convergency between two guide meridians 24 miles (38.63 km) apart at latitude 47°30′.

**Solution**

1. Using Equation 15.5:
   $\gamma = 52.09 \times 24 \times \tan 47°30′ = 1{,}364″ = 0°22′44″$
2. Using Equation 13.6:
   $\gamma = 32.37 \times 38.63 \times \tan 47°30′ = 1{,}365″ = 0°22′45″$

## ■ EXAMPLE 15.2

Find the convergency in feet, chains, and meters of two guide meridians 24 miles apart and 24 miles long if the **mean** latitude is 47°30′.

**Solution**

1. Using Equation 15.8:
   $p = 1.33 \times 24 \times 24 \times \tan 47°30′ = 836 \text{ ft}$
2. Using Equation 15.9:
   $p = 0.0202 \times 24 \times 24 \times \tan 47°30′ = 12.70 \text{ chains}$
3. Using Equation 15.10:
   $p = 0.4055 \times 24 \times 24 \times \tan 47°30′ = 255 \text{ m}$
4. Using Equation 15.11:
   $p = 0.1565 \times 38.63 \times 38.63 \times \tan 47°30′ = 255 \text{ m}$

As discussed in the preceding section, two sets of monuments are established on the standard parallels due to convergence of the meridians. Using Example 15.2, the distance between these monuments would be 12.70 chains.

### 15.2.2.4 Parallel of latitude
Due to this convergence, the baseline, being a true parallel, must be run as a curve having chords 40 chains (½ mile) long. There are three methods of establishing a parallel of latitude: (1) the solar method; (2) the tangent method; and (3) the secant method, which is the most commonly used.

*15.2.2.4.1 Solar method*   The sun is used to determine the true meridian every 40 chains. The true parallel is then established by turning 90° from the meridian. A slight error will be incurred using this method because observations are taken at 40-chain intervals rather than at small increments along the parallel. However, the line defined using this method will be well within acceptable accuracies for original surveys.

*15.2.2.4.2 Tangent method*   The direction of the tangent is determined by turning a horizontal angle of 90° to the east or west with the meridian. Points on the parallel are established at 40-chain (½-mile) intervals by offsets to the north from the tangent. The establishment of a baseline for a latitude of 47°30′ is illustrated in Figure 15.6. The illustration

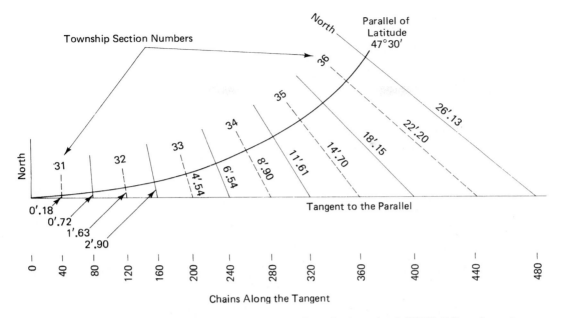

**FIGURE 15.6** Baseline using tangent offsets for latitude of 47°30′ (offsets from the tangent to the parallel of latitude are shown in feet).

**Table 15.1** OFFSETS FROM TANGENT TO PARALLEL (FEET) FOR LATITUDES FROM 30° TO 50° INCLUSIVE

| Latitude | 1 mile | 2 miles | 3 miles | 4 miles | 5 miles | 6 miles |
|----------|--------|---------|---------|---------|---------|---------|
| 30° | 0.38 | 1.54 | 3.46 | 6.15 | 9.61 | 13.83 |
| 35° | 0.47 | 1.86 | 4.19 | 7.45 | 11.65 | 16.77 |
| 40° | 0.56 | 2.23 | 5.02 | 8.93 | 13.95 | 20.09 |
| 45° | 0.66 | 2.66 | 5.98 | 10.64 | 16.62 | 23.94 |
| 50° | 0.79 | 3.17 | 7.13 | 12.68 | 19.81 | 28.52 |

is exaggerated to illustrate the offset lengths properly. In fact, the small magnitude of the offset distances compared with the distances along the tangent leads to the conclusion that distances measured along the tangent are essentially equal to those measured along the parallel within the accuracy requirements for baseline surveys.

The values of the offsets depend on the latitude and the distance from the starting meridian. These values are proportional to the square of the distances from the starting meridian, as illustrated in Table 15.1.

The values of the tangent offsets significantly exceed the width of normal cut lines, as illustrated in Figure 15.6. Because the true parallel must be blazed and the landmarks noted, it may be necessary to clear two lines: the tangent and the true parallel. Therefore, this method is more costly and time-consuming than the secant method.

***15.2.2.4.3 Secant method*** The secant used for laying out a parallel of latitude passes through the 1- and 5-mile points on the parallel, as illustrated in Figure 15.7. The offset is

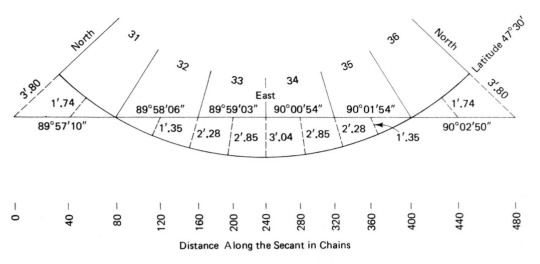

**FIGURE 15.7** Baseline using secant offsets for latitude 47°30′ (offsets from the secant to the parallel of latitude are shown in feet).

measured southerly from the initial point to the secant and the angle turned to determine the direction of the secant easterly. The secant is the line actually run, the points on the parallel being located at 40-chain (½-mile) intervals by offsets from the secant. As illustrated in Figure 15.2, all offsets to the true parallel are southerly and those at the ½, 5½, and 6-mile points are to the north.

The secant method is advantageous because the offsets are much smaller than those required for the tangent method, as you can see by comparing Figures 15.6 and 15.7. Therefore, a cleared line of reasonable width will contain both the secant and the parallel. The measurements made to landmarks along both lines will be essentially the same, thus requiring no modifications in the field notes.

Both the tangent and secant are straight lines on the plan view. Due to the convergency of meridians, however, the azimuths of these lines vary along the line. The changes in azimuths along these lines are determined using Equation 15.5, where $d$ is the distance along the parallel from the starting meridian.

The tangent commences at an azimuth of 90° from the meridian and bends gradually southerly, as shown on Figure 15.6. The azimuth of the tangent 6 miles from the starting meridian is therefore 90°05′41″, the additional 5′41″ being the convergence for a $d$ of 6 miles. Using the tangent method, the 90° azimuth would be reestablished every 6 miles, and the process of laying out the parallel would be repeated as illustrated in Figure 15.6.

The azimuths of the secant are shown in Table 15.2. Assuming that the secant is laid out toward the east, as illustrated in Figure 15.7, the direction of the secant from the starting meridian to the end of the third mile is north of true east. From the 3-mile to the 6-mile points, the azimuth is south of true east. At the 3-mile point, the azimuth of the secant is 90°. At the starting meridian, the secant has an azimuth of 89°57′10″ at a latitude of 47°30′, as illustrated in Figure 15.7 and interpolated from Table 15.2. The difference

**Table 15.2** AZIMUTHS OF THE SECANT

| Latitude | 0 mile | 1 mile | 2 miles | Deflection angle 6 miles |
|----------|---------|---------|---------|------------------|
| 30 | 89°58.5′ | 89°59.0′ | 89°59.5′ | 3′00″ |
| 35 | 89°58.2′ | 89°58.8′ | 89°59.4′ | 3′38″ |
| 40 | 89°57.8′ | 89°58.5′ | 89°59.3′ | 4′22″ |
| 45 | 89°57.4′ | 89°58.3′ | 89°59.1′ | 5′12″ |
| 50 | 89°56.9′ | 89°57.9′ | 89°59.0′ | 6′12″ |

*Source:* U.S. Bureau of Land Management.

between the starting azimuth and that at the 3-mile point is 02′50″; this is the angular convergency for meridians 3 miles apart.

By the same reasoning, the secant azimuth at the 6-mile point is 90°02′50″. The transit is set up at the 0-mile offset point, and the azimuth of the secant line is laid off using the azimuths given in Table 15.2. For our example, at a latitude of 47°30′, the azimuth is 89°57′10″. The secant is then directed in a straight line for 6 miles, and the points are established at ½-mile (40-chain) intervals using the offsets as described previously. At the end of 6 miles, the succeeding secant line may be established by either (1) establishing the true meridian and laying off the same azimuth angle as before or (2) turning off a deflection angle, from the preceding secant to the succeeding secant, equal to the convergency of meridians 6 miles apart. These deflection angles are given in the last column of Table 15.2.

## 15.2.3   Township Boundaries

Most township boundaries in the United States and Canada were established using the sectional systems, wherein the boundary lines were oriented north-south and east-west. Because this was the most common method, it is emphasized in this section.

**15.2.3.1 Sectional systems**   The normal method of establishing township boundaries is best understood by referring to Figure 15.4. The procedure is set out as follows:

1. Commencing at point 1, located on the first standard parallel south (a baseline) 6 miles to the east of the principal meridian (or guide meridian), a line is run due north for 6 miles to point 2. Monuments are established at intervals of 40 chains (½ mile).

2. From point 2, a line is run westerly to intersect the principal meridian (or guide meridian) at or near point 3. Because this is a trial line, only temporary monuments are set at 40-chain (½-mile) intervals. Since point 3 has previously been set during the running of the principal (or guide) meridian, the amount by which the trial line fails to intersect point 3 is measured.

3. The line from point 3 to point 2 is run along the correct course, and the temporary monuments are replaced by permanent monuments in the correct pattern. The true line is properly blazed, and the topographic and vegetation features are recorded along the true line. Due primarily to the convergence of meridians, the length of the line between points 2 and 3 will be less than 6 miles. This difference, resulting from

convergence and measurement errors, is placed in the most westerly 40 chains (½ mile). All other distances are therefore 40 chains.

4. The eastern boundary of the next township to the north is run northerly from point 2 to point 4.

5. The procedure in step 2 is repeated to establish the north boundary of the next township between points 4 and 5. Any discrepancies are again left in the most westerly 40 chains.

6. The preceding steps are continued, establishing easterly and northerly township boundaries in that order, that is, points 6 and 7.

7. From point 6, the meridian is run to its intersection with the baseline (or standard parallel) at point 8. A closing corner is established at point 8. The distance from the closing corner to the nearest standard corner is measured and recorded. Since all errors in measurement up the meridian from point 1 to point 8 are placed in the line from point 6 to point 8, the last 40 chains on the meridian may be less or more than 40 chains.

8. The two other meridians, points 9 to 10 and 11 to 12 in Figure 15.4, in the 24-mile-square block, are run in a manner similar to that described for points 1 to 8. Therefore, any east-west discrepancies are placed in the westerly 40 chains of each township as before, and the northerly 40 chains of each meridian will absorb the measurement errors.

A thorough understanding of this procedure is important because all 36 sections in a township are not of equal size. Therefore, the legal requirements relating to the rectangular surveys of the public lands should be examined. Due to the procedures employed in carrying out the township boundary surveys, combined with the effect of the convergence of meridians, certain sections within each township will vary in area, a situation illustrated in Figure 15.8.

Of the 36 sections in each standard township, 25 are considered to contain 640 acres because these sections are not affected by the convergence of meridians or the placing of measurement errors. The sections containing less than 640 acres are located along the

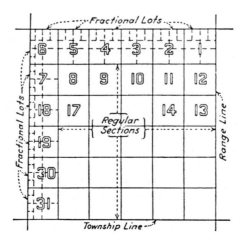

**FIGURE 15.8** Relative sizes of sections in sectional townships.

westerly township boundary, primarily due to the convergence of meridians, and along the northerly boundary, primarily due to the measurement errors concentrated in the northerly 40 chains (½ mile) along the meridian. Therefore, sections 6, 7, 18, 19, 30, and 31 will contain lesser acreages, and sections 1 to 5 will be 640 acres more or less.

**15.2.3.2 Numbering and naming of townships**   In a sectional system, the townships of a survey district are numbered into ranges and tiers (townships) in relation to the principal meridian and the baseline used for the district. As illustrated in Figure 15.4, the fourth township south of the baseline is in tier four south (T.4S.). The fourth township west of the principal meridian is located in range 4 west. Using this method of numbering, any township is located if its range, tier, and principal meridian are stated. The example shown in Figure 15.4 and discussed previously illustrates this system: tier (township) 4 south, range 4 west of the sixth principal meridian. The abbreviation for this township would be T.4S., R.4W., 6th P.M.

## 15.2.4   Reestablishing Boundaries

The aim of both the American and Canadian governments was to monument the corners using the procedures discussed in Section 15.2.3. However, for a multitude of reasons (some of the more common are listed later), many of these corner marks have been obliterated. Consequently, the modern surveyor is required to relocate a missing corner. The basic requirements for this process are a thorough understanding of the methods used in establishing the original boundaries of the particular township in question, combined with good judgment regarding the best evidence of the corner location, including copies of the original field notes.

A lost corner is a survey point whose position cannot be determined because no reasonable evidence of its location exists. The only means of reestablishment involves clearly defined surveying procedures using the closest related existing corners. The main reasons for lost corners are:

- Obliteration of the marked lines and wooden corner posts by forest fires and logging, which often cover large areas.
- Improper marking of the lines and/or monuments during the original township or subdivision surveys.
- Inaccurate placing of lines and monuments.
- Lack of concern for preservation of the original corners and lines, particularly by early settlers.

The surveyor must first determine if the survey corner is really lost. If the original monuments were wooden, the decaying of the stake will often leave a brownish rust color in the soil. You can look for this telltale color by carefully slicing the earth horizontally using a thin shovel blade. Blazes on trees used as witness points for survey corners, also called **bearing trees,** as well as blazes marking the survey lines, will become totally covered by subsequent tree growth and enlargement of the tree diameter. For example, I reestablished a corner located along a township boundary, along which much of the evidence had been obliterated by a forest fire. Using the original survey field notes and the terrain features described thereon (see Section 15.2.7), a trial line was run for a distance of 3¾ miles, where a bearing tree (witness point) had been blazed and inscribed BT during the original survey. Because this tree was located outside the forest fire area, the most likely tree, based on the original notes, was selected for investigation. No evidence was visible on the outside of this tree, now 4 ft in diameter. After the tree was felled, the most likely location of the inscribed BT was determined by checking the date of the original survey in the field notes. The survey was carried out in midwinter, so I assumed that the BT would be inscribed approximately 7 ft off the ground, rather than the normal 4 ft, due to snow cover. It was necessary to remove thin slabs of wood, starting from the bark of the appropriate face recorded on the original survey notes. This laborious process was rewarded by finding the initials BT approximately 1 ft inside the tree. Based on direction and distance from the true corner to this witness post, the original corner was reestablished.

Fence lines placed by early settlers were commonly erected with a combination of post and wire and wire stapled to trees on or close to the intended line. Some line fences were installed using only the wire stapled on trees, depending upon the density of growth. With the passing years, the original fences rusted and were not replaced for various reasons. Therefore, under the worst conditions, the only remaining evidence is the wire stapled to the tree, preserved by subsequent growth. The presence of the wire causes a slight bulge in the outside bark of the tree, which diminishes in size relative to the length of time since the fence was stapled. The surveyor should look for these bulges in the trees along the suspected location of the line up to approximately 4 ft above the ground surface. In addition, magnetic locators or the more accurate battery-operated bar detectors should be used to verify the presence of fence wire within the trees. If the wire is detected, it is necessary to notch the tree and uncover the wire. The number of growth rings outside the wire should be counted carefully because they will help you determine the year of the fence installations. I found the use of these investigative methods to be instrumental in the reestablishment of an original survey line. The net result was the proving of ownership of 6 acres of valuable land.

The preceding examples illustrate the intensity of investigation required to determine if the survey corner is truly lost. If all avenues of best evidence are not explored in their entirety, the surveyor will likely be put in the embarrassing and expensive position of defending his or her lack of thoroughness in a court of law. Experience in reestablishing original survey points and boundaries is essential. A young and/or inexperienced surveyor would be well advised, under these circumstances, to carry out such surveys under the direction of an experienced surveyor. This is often arranged by hiring the experienced surveyor in a consultative capacity for the particular survey, searching for evidence under his or her direction, accepting his or her analysis of the results, and requiring his or her explanation leading to these decisions. To understand the reestablishment process, the surveyor must be familiar with the original survey procedures described in this chapter because the reestablishment of original survey points is based on the intent of the original survey.

## 15.2.5   Canadian Sectional Systems

A total of six sectional systems were used to subdivide most of Canada. The townships were commonly 6 miles square, containing 36 sections of 640 acres each. Other variations based on section areas, such as 1,000 acres and 800 acres, were used prior to May 1, 1871.

The first, second, and third Canadian sectional systems are illustrated in Figure 15.9. The effects of convergency were offset by running in supplementary baselines used as correction lines. These lines were located every two townships north and south of the main baseline, as shown in Figure 15.9. Guide meridians were run north and south every four townships west of the principal meridian, the second meridian shown in Figure 15.9. Thus, convergence was "corrected," resulting in a high irregularity of township configurations and sizes, as illustrated immediately east of the third meridian in Figure 15.9.

The main points of difference between the U.S. and Canadian sectional systems are:

- The numbering of townships is different, as illustrated under the "first system" section on the right side of Figure 15.9. The townships number northerly from the international baseline, for example, from 1 to 24 in Figure 15.9. The ranges number westerly from the nearest principal meridian, for example, from I to XXX between the second and third meridians in Figure 15.9. The number for the township marked by the circular dot in the first system section of Figure 15.9 is Township 11, Range 30, west of the first meridian. The abbreviation would be Tp.11, R.30, 1st P.M. This is similar to but not identical to the U.S. system, discussed in Section 15.2.3.
- The numbering of sections is different, as illustrated in Figure 15.2. Refer to Figure 15.1 for the U.S. system. The numbering of quarter-quarter sections is also different.
- The Canadian systems provide for road allowances from 1 to 1½ chains in width on either all or some of the township and section lines. The U.S. system often did not set aside specific road allowances but made an allowance of 5% of the total area for roads. Where allowances were specified, they were usually one-half chain on either side of the section line in width.

These differences between the two systems significantly affect the resurvey techniques. The surveyor should consult the publications covering the aspects of every Canadian system in detail (*Dominion Land Surveyors Manual,* Department of Energy, Mines, and Resources, Ottawa, Ontario, Canada).

## 15.2.6   Corner Monumentation and Line Marking

Manuals covering these topics are available from the Bureau of Land Management, Washington, D.C., and from the Surveys and Mapping Branch, Department of Energy, Mines, and Resources, Ottawa, Ontario, Canada. In addition to specifying the methods of township subdivision and reestablishment techniques for each survey system, details on corner monumentation and line marking are provided. The information given in this section of the textbook has been selected to assist the modern surveyor in locating the corner monuments and the survey lines for purposes of reestablishment.

**15.2.6.1 Corners**   It is unfortunate that most of the public lands were surveyed before the present monumentation regulations went into effect. Consequently, most of the monuments used consisted of wood (often cedar) posts. If nothing else was available, mounds of earth, earth-covered charred stakes, or charcoal, boulders, and the like, were used. These monuments were not permanent, and considerable skill is required to relocate them. For example, many of the wooden posts have either rotted or burned in forest fires, so careful

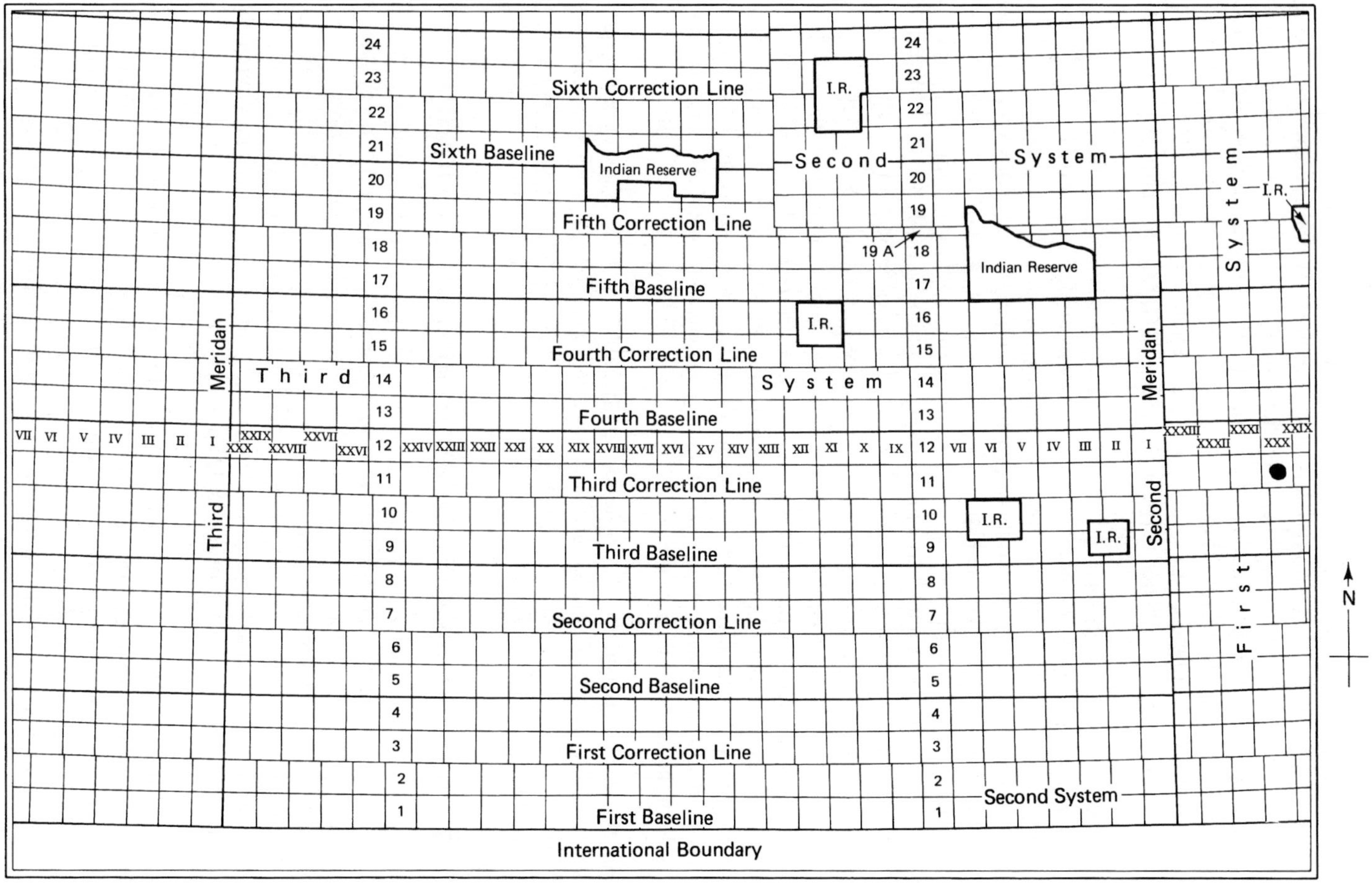

**FIGURE 15.9** Subdivision of country into blocks and townships, illustrating the Canadian first system, second system, and third system. (From the *Dominion Land Surveyors Manual*, Department of Energy, Mines, and Resources, Ottawa.)

slicing of the soil in the area with a sharp shovel will sometimes reveal a rust-colored stain from the underground portion of the post.

Corner markings for sectional survey systems are complex, and you can find detailed information in the *Manual of Surveying Instructions* from the Bureau of Land Management, Washington, D.C., or the Canadian equivalent from the Department of Energy, Mines, and Resources, Ottawa, Ontario. Because the variety of markings is beyond the scope of this book, only general characteristics will be discussed, and two typical examples will be given.

All monuments are marked using a system that will provide accurate information regarding the type of monument and its location. Metal caps placed on top of iron posts are marked with capital letters and numbers. The township, section, range numbers, and the year of the survey are all inscribed. Stone monuments were marked with notches and grooves on the edges, which indicate the distances in miles from the township boundaries.

The markings on the caps of iron post monuments are illustrated in Figure 15.10. The sketch in part (c) illustrates the position of the points in parts (a) and (b). Point (a) is a township corner marked by the symbol SC (standard corner). The markings are set to be viewed from the south, so the township to the north is shown: T20N. The ranges on each side of the township line are shown, in this case, range 6 east (R6E) and range 7 east (R7E). The section numbers to the northwest (S36) and to the northeast (S31) are shown below the respective ranges, thus fixing the point. The date of survey (1908) is shown as the bottom number, which assists the modern surveyor in obtaining the original field notes from the appropriate state government authority. Point (b) is a section corner. The town-

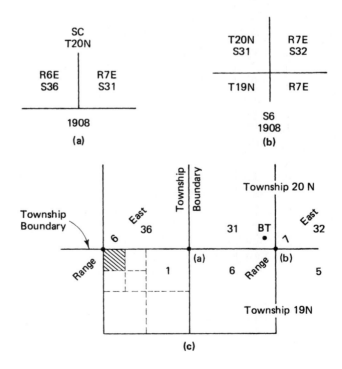

**FIGURE 15.10** Example markings on iron monuments. (a) Township corner. (b) Section corner. (c) Location of points from points (a) and (b).

ship number (T20N) is shown on the upper left of the symbol, and the section to the north-west is indicated below the township number (S31). The range number, in this case, range 7 east (R7E), is shown on the right side, with the northeast section corner (S32) indicated below. The township (T19N) and the range (R7E) to the south of the corner marker are shown as indicated in Figure 15.10(b).

In addition to setting the monuments on the actual section or lot corners in the original survey, additional monuments known as witness points were within 5 chains (330 ft) of the monuments. These witness points consisted of bearing trees, designated as BT, and bearing objects, designated as BO, used where there were no trees. Trees used as witnesses are blazed (cut to the smooth wood surface), and the smooth wood surface on the blaze is inscribed with letters and figures to aid in the identification of the locations. A tree used as a witness for a section corner, such as point (b) in Figure 15.10, would be inscribed T20N R7E S31 BT, which indicates that the bearing tree (BT) is located as shown in Figure 15.10. The true bearing and horizontal distance are determined, including a description of the tree, and recorded in the field notes. Normally, at least one and usually two bearing trees are established for each corner set in the original survey. Due to changing regulations and/or lack of diligence by the original surveyor, the only markings on a bearing tree are often BT. This does not create a practical problem, however, because the surveyor doing the retracement can usually deduce the location of the found bearing tree referred to in the original field notes. This becomes a problem only when two bearing trees close together have been marked to witness the same monument. Two important facts regarding bearing trees should be appreciated by the modern surveyor:

- The tree continues to grow around the original blaze, thus covering the blaze and the inscriptions thereon. Consequently, it is necessary to cut carefully into the tree until the inscription BT is found.
- The blaze and inscription may be up to 5 ft higher on the tree if the original monument was set and witnessed in the northern United States and Canada during winter. Therefore, it is necessary to determine the month of survey in snowfall areas to determine that portion of the tree vertically from the ground where the BT was originally carved.

Bearing objects within 5 chains (330 ft) of the monument are used where no substantial trees exist. These consist of one or more of the following: (1) significant cliffs or large boulders, (2) stone mounds, and (3) pits dug into the ground. Where the bearing object consists of rock, the point used for the measurements to the monument is marked, using a chisel, with a cross (×), the letters BO, and the section number (the latter only for sectional survey systems). Stone mounds are used where loose stone is readily available. Where no rocks, stones, or trees are available, the corners may be witnessed by digging pits 18 in. (45 cm) square and 12 in. (30 cm) deep. One side (not corner) of the pit should face the monument. Depending upon the country (United States or Canada) and the regulations in force at the time, up to four pits are sometimes required (placed on all four sides of the monument), and the distance of the pits from the monument varies, although it is normally 3 ft. Because the pit will usually fill in gradually with a different soil, and often revegetates with a different species, the location of the pit(s) may be identified many years or decades later.

**15.2.6.2 Lines** The marking of the survey lines on the ground was done to preserve the lines between monuments. In addition to setting the monuments and witness points as described in the previous section, natural terrain features along the line were recorded in the field notes, as discussed in Section 15.2.7, and blazes or "hack marks" were made on living timber at regular intervals along the line. The regulations pertaining to public land surveys in the United States and crown land surveys in Canada have always required blazing and hack marks along lines through timber. Trees directly on the line, called line trees, are marked with two horizontal V-shaped notches, called hack marks, on each side of the tree facing along the line in both directions. Trees along the line within one-half chain (50 links, 33 ft) are blazed at breast height, the flat side of the blaze being placed parallel to and facing the line. The frequency of blazes along the lines varies widely, depending on the density of the trees and the thoroughness of the original surveyors.

The modern surveyor should be aware of the following practical aspects of line reestablishment:

- Forest fires and settlers have destroyed much of the timber. Therefore, the surveyor should check the age of a mature tree in the area by counting the growth rings. If the tree examined could not have existed at the time of the last known original or retracement survey, there is no point in wasting time looking for evidence of hack marks or blazes on the trees near the suspected line location.
- If the original blazed trees still exist, a keen eye is required to observe evidence of old blazes. After determining the expected height of the blazes above the ground surface from the month of the year of the last survey and allowing for snow depths, if applicable, the surveyor should look carefully for any vertical bark scar, unnatural flat spots, or bulges on the outside of the tree. Any unnatural marking at the appropriate height should be investigated.

## 15.2.7 Field Notes and Survey Records

Field notes along all run survey lines are often of great value in reestablishing lines where no physical ground evidence exists. In many cases, no other evidence exists. The present-day surveyor should bear in mind the conditions under which the original field notes were made. The chain may have been missing one or even two links. The number of chains to a particular feature may have been miscounted, thus creating potential discrepancies of approximately 66 ft or 132 ft. The use of aerial photographs and comparison with the field notes, prior to attending in the field, are usually of great assistance in identifying the discrepancies mentioned (see Chapter 12). This is particularly true for streams, rivers, swamps, and geological features such as ridges or cliffs. Office and subsequent field adjustments of the line on the aerial photographs, bearing the possible discrepancies in mind, will save the modern surveyor considerable time in line reestablishment.

The information to be included in field notes, according to the manuals, is similar in both the United States and Canada. A summary list of this information follows:

1. Course and length of each line run, including offsets, the reason, and the method used.

2. The type, diameter, and bearing and distance from the monument of all bearing trees and bearing objects (see Section 15.2.6), including the material used for the monuments and depth set into the ground.

3. Line trees—their species name, diameter, distance along the line, and markings.

4. Line intersections with either natural or manufactured features, such as the line distance to Native American or Canadian reservations, mining claims, railroads, ditches, canals, electric transmission lines; changes of soil types, slopes, vegetation, and geological features such as ridges, fractures, outcrops, and cliffs. All pertinent information, such as the bearings of intersecting boundaries, including the margin of heavy timber lines, are recorded.

5. Line intersections with water bodies such as unmeandered rivers and creeks, and intermittent water courses such as ravines, gullies, and the like. The distance along the line is measured to the center of the smaller water courses, and to each bank for larger rivers.

6. Lakes and ponds on line, describing the type and slopes of banks, water quality (clear or stagnant), and the approximate water depth.

7. Towns and villages, post offices, Native American or Canadian occupancy, houses or cabins, fields, mineral claims, mill sites, and all other official monuments other than survey monuments.

8. Stone quarries and rock ledges, showing the type of stone.

9. All ore bodies, including coal seams, mineral deposits, mining surface improvements, and salt licks.

10. Natural and archeological features, such as fossils, petrifactions, cliff dwellings, mounds, and fortifications.

Two types of field notes were kept. One type listed the chainages (stationing) to pertinent points down the left side of the page, with each pertinent feature listed shown on the right side opposite the appropriate chainage. The other type was termed split line, in which the centerline was widened to accommodate the chainage figures, and the features to the left or right of the line as run were shown on the side of the page where they were located. A typical example of the latter is shown in Figure 15.11 (and Figure 8.12).

Copies of the field notes and the township plat or original survey maps are kept on record at the Bureau of Land Management, Washington, D.C.; the Department of Energy, Mines, and Resources, Ottawa, Ontario; and at the majority of the state and provincial government offices. The departments storing these records in the state or provincial governments have various names (Auditor of State; Public Survey Office; Register of State Lands, Natural Resources, Lands, and Forests, etc.). Consequently, the present-day surveyor must determine the appropriate government agency in the state or province where the records are kept.

### 15.2.7.1 Resurveys and real property boundaries

The storage of township monument and line resurveys varies considerably, depending on the regulations of the federal, state, and provincial jurisdictions in which the property is located. The normal situation is that the original field notes and plans must, by law, be made available to other surveyors or members of the public for a reasonable fee. The maximum fee is usually

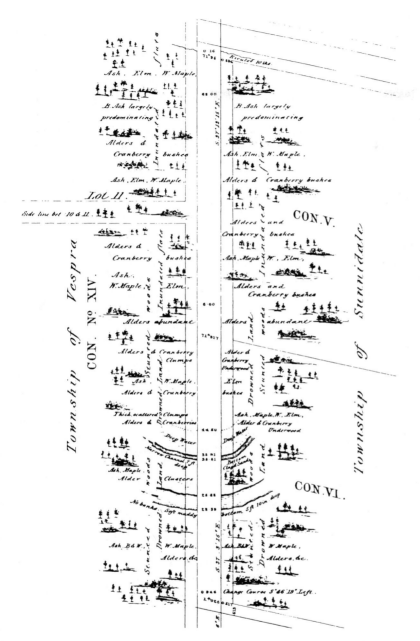

**FIGURE 15.11**  Split-line field notes for township subdivision. (Courtesy of Ontario Ministry of Natural Resources)

stipulated by the federal, state, or provincial land surveyors' association. The fee is determined by the time required to locate the proper file and plans in the surveyors' office, combined with the costs of reproduction of the notes and plans.

The same system is generally used for field notes and plans relating to real property boundary surveys. Plans for subdivision are kept on record in the county registry office. These are numbered consecutively as received by the registrar. The degree to which these plans are examined for reliability and accuracy varies greatly between jurisdictions. Some county registry offices will accept plans of subdivision without any investigation, while others will go to great lengths to verify or check key measurements through field investigation.

## 15.3   Property Conveyance

When any piece of land changes ownership, it cannot be by word of mouth and must be by a written document, usually called a deed. The deed includes a legal description of the property, for which some type of survey is usually required. The purchaser normally wants to ensure that he or she is in fact acquiring the land(s) described in the offer to purchase. It is also important to establish that any structures included in the offer are located entirely on the land. Knowledge of any rights-of-way, easements, highway widenings, and the like, are also essential. Such title encumbrances are important because the owner's rights on these lands are usually severely curtailed by them. For example, erection of any structure (on the encumbrance portion), even a small building, is usually not allowed, even though the land is still owned by the owner of the lands adjacent to the encumbrance.

The principles of establishing boundaries are well established. They are based on set definitions of legal terms, deed descriptions, riparian rights (for lands bordering on water bodies), and adverse possession. I have selected these topics for discussion in this section because they are common to most property boundary surveys. The survey techniques for carrying out rural land surveys, urban land surveys, and city surveys are discussed in Sections 15.4, 15.5, and 15.6, respectively.

## 15.3.1   Definitions of Legal Terms

Some of the most common legal terms relating to conveyance of land are defined next. The definitions are presented as a practical interpretation of the formal definitions found in legal dictionaries. The real meanings of the terms as they affect the modern surveyor are more important than those couched in formal legal language.

1. Adverse possession: When land is used by a person other than the owner for an extended period of time (usually 20 years), the land may be claimed from the owner by the user under certain circumstances. This term is discussed in more detail in Section 16.3.4.

2. Alluvium: When land along the bank of a river or shore of a lake or sea is increased by any form of wave or current action or by dropping of the water level, the additional land is called alluvium. This process is usually gradual and the rate of addition cannot be accurately or easily determined in relation to small increments of time.

Because the owner of the lands along the river bank or shoreline may gain or lose land by these processes, the additional lands become the property of the owner of the shoreline.

3. Avulsion: This process involves the sudden removal of the land of one owner to the land of another caused by water forces. When avulsion happens, the transferred property belongs to the original owner. The main difference between avulsion and alluvium is the rate at which the transfer of soil and land occurs. Avulsion can be attributed to a sudden movement caused by an identifiable event, such as a violent storm or flood.

4. Deed description: The deed is the legal document transferring land(s) from one owner to another. The most important documentation in the deed, from the surveyor's perspective, is the description of the property being transferred. The description is intended to describe the details of the property boundaries, including bearings, distances, and appropriate corner markers. Because the interpretation of the description is of great importance, this topic is covered in detail in Section 15.3.2.

5. Fee simple: The word **fee** indicates that the land and structures thereon belong to their owner and may be transferred to those heirs chosen by the owner or, if necessary, that the law appoints. The word **simple** means that the owner may transfer the property to whomever he or she chooses. Therefore, to hold the title of land in "fee simple" is the most straightforward and simplest form. It places no restrictions on the owner regarding the sale or disposition of the land.

6. High-water mark: The high-water mark occurs where the vegetation changes from aquatic species to terrestrial species. If no vegetation is present, such as a bare rock shoreline, the high-water mark is usually indicated clearly by a distinctive change in the color or tone of the rock along a level line representing the appropriate water level. This line may appear either above or below the existing water level at the time of the survey, depending on local water-level conditions.

7. Metes and bounds: A method of describing property by listing boundary distances and directions, together with a note of adjacent property owners and relevant natural features.

8. Mortgage: The purchaser usually obtains a mortgage, involving financing by a bank or loan corporation, for the remainder of the purchase price of the property and structures thereon, if applicable. Most mortgage-lending institutions require survey documentation to ensure that the buildings are not only entirely on the property but are also within the acceptable clearances from the property lines as established by the local municipality. These surveys are discussed in Section 15.5.

9. Patent: When property is conveyed by federal, state, or provincial governments to institutions, companies, or individuals, it is called a patent. This is usually the first entry made in the registry office books kept for sections and lots or concessions.

## 15.3.2 Deed Descriptions

Deed descriptions include the directions and distances of all lines along the property boundaries of the parcel of land. The types of corner monumentation and the area of the parcel may or may not be included. The description is usually in written form, rather than a survey plan.

The property is described as starting or commencing at a point, and the description continues either clockwise or counterclockwise around the property, returning to the starting point. The starting point, or *point of beginning* (POB), must be directly related by both distance and direction to a point established in the original township subdivision survey or a lot corner in a registered plan of subdivision. In the latter case, the plan of subdivision is already located with respect to the township subdivision fabric.

Note that deed descriptions have been written by people from every walk of life, particularly during the early development of the United States (especially in the original colonial states) and Canada. Consequently, the deed description may contain errors and mistakes in measurement, direction, and calculations of areas. The units used in descriptions vary considerably. Chains (66 ft), links (0.01 chain), and rods (16.5 ft) were commonly used in older deeds in both the United States and Canada. The measurements were subsequently given in feet in both countries and more recently in meters in Canada. As a result, inconsistencies with the deed description and the boundary evidence on the ground are difficult and sometimes impossible to resolve. When these conflicts occur, the law states that the surveyor should establish the boundaries to match the intentions of the parties involved in the property conveyances.

Figure 15.12 shows a typical property that requires a detailed deed description. It also provides examples of mistakes and omissions common to many deed descriptions.

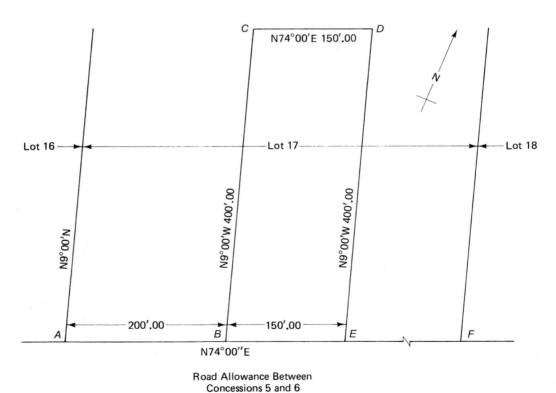

**FIGURE 15.12** Typical land parcel requiring detailed deed description.

This example is used to provide you with some exposure to a survey system different from both the American and Canadian sectional systems. These special or nonsectional systems occur in various jurisdictions. The "county," Leeds, in this case, contains a number (usually between 6 and 12) of "named townships," Bastard, in this case. "Concessions" are laid out in one direction (numbered from north to south in this example) and lots are laid out in the other direction (numbered from west to east in this example). Therefore, a description of the **whole** lot would be lot 17, concession 6, Township of Bastard, County of Leeds, Province of Ontario. The following example describes a portion of lot 17, concession 6:

> All and singular that certain parcel, tract of lands and premises situate, lying and being in lot 17, concession 6, Township of Bastard, County of Leeds, being more particularly described as follows:
>
> Commencing at a point in the southerly limit of lot 17, concession 6, distant 200.00 feet measured easterly from the southwest corner of the said lot 17; thence N9°00′W, 400.00 feet, more or less, to a point in a post and wire fence, along a course parallel with the westerly limit of lot 17; thence N74°00′E along a post and wire fence a distance of 150.00 feet; thence S9°00′E, 400.00 feet, more or less, to a point in the southerly limit of the said lot 17; thence S74°00′W, 150.00 feet, more or less, to the point of commencement.

The following comments on this example description will explain some of the wording, establish the priorities for the surveyor, and point out common errors in description writing. Reference is made to the corners and boundaries lettered from *A* to *E* inclusive in Figure 15.12.

1. Point *A* is a fixed point (sometimes referred to as point of commencement [POC]) because it was originally established during the township subdivision. As mentioned previously, the deed description must refer to an established corner in the township fabric.

2. Point *B* is the point of beginning (POB), which is always the first point mentioned in the deed description and is an actual corner of the property being described.

3. The distance *BC* is intended to be 400.00 ft. The "more or less" is shown after the measurement in the preceding description because the intent is that point *C* should lie at the base of the fence. Therefore, the fence, not the 400.00 ft, governs.

4. The line *CD* runs along the post and wire fence, as stated in the description, and is therefore not necessarily a straight line from *C* to *D*. Consequently, as the fence bends, the line also bends accordingly.

5. The distance along the easterly boundary of the parcel, line *DE,* is governed by the distance from the fence to the south limit of the township lot, for the same reasons in comment 3. The bearing is indicated as S9°00′E without any other qualifications. This indicates that the line *DE* may not be parallel with the line *BC* and hence the westerly lot line. Therefore, point *E* could actually be east or west of the point shown in Figure 15.12.

6. The southerly boundary *BE* was likely intended to be 150.00 ft, but this distance may be greater or less depending on the actual location of point *E.* The "more or less"

shown after this measurement in the description does not have as much significance as the "more or less" phrase mentioned previously. The reason for this is complex and beyond the scope of this text. Suffice it to say that "more or less" is commonly attached to the last measurement mentioned in the deed description.

In Figure 15.12, the distance *AB* is known as the tie distance because it represents the length from the point of commencement to point *A,* which is fixed within the township survey fabric. It is not uncommon for the tie distance to be stated incorrectly in the description. This problem is compounded when subsequent descriptions, such as the parcel immediately east of line *DE,* use a tie distance of 200.00 ft, plus 150.00 ft, or 350.00 ft. This perpetuation of the error in tie distance has been known to continue over a large number of parcels as the lands are sold over the years.

## 15.3.3   Riparian Rights

Riparian rights refer to those rights of a property owner of land that borders on a water body. The rights include the use of the shore and ownership of land under the water surface and therefore use of the water. The definition of riparian rights varies somewhat from state to state. The main difficulties in surveys involving properties along water bodies are as follows:

- The boundaries are both irregular and subject to change with time due to alluvial processes (see Section 15.3.1).
- The ownership may extend only to the high-water mark (see Section 15.3.1) or to the center of a stream or river. This determination depends on the laws of the state or province in which the land is located. These laws vary widely and are very inconsistent.
- Certain survey systems incorporated a publicly owned strip of land, usually 1 chain (66 ft) wide, parallel with the shoreline or high-water mark. Because the owner normally wants to locate buildings as close to the water as possible, the net result is that all or a portion of a private residence is located on public lands.

### 15.3.3.1 Property lines in areas of alluvium   Where the shoreline location has been changed by alluvial processes, the existing property boundaries intersect the new shoreline. This situation is illustrated by Figure 15.13. The following list is one survey procedure that has been employed to solve this problem:

1. The distances along the frontage where the shoreline has been altered are determined. Distance *AF* along the original shoreline will usually have to be determined from either existing monument evidence or from the deed descriptions. The distance *AF* along the new shoreline can be measured using a traverse and offset measurements to bend points in the shoreline, as illustrated in Figure 15.13. The new shoreline is plotted from this information, and the distance *AF* is scaled as accurately as possible. Where the frontage of alluvium is large and/or difficult to survey on the ground, existing or newly acquired aerial photographs will provide an accurate and economical positioning of the new shoreline (see Chapter 12).

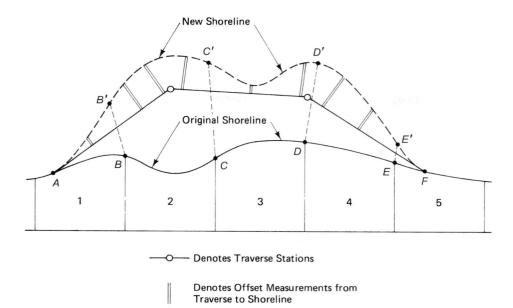

─○─ Denotes Traverse Stations

‖ Denotes Offset Measurements from
Traverse to Shoreline

**FIGURE 15.13**  Riparian boundaries for areas added by alluvium.

2. The ratio between the distances $AF$ (new shoreline) to $AF$ (original shoreline) is determined. In this example, the ratio is 1:1.25.

3. Locate point $B'$ so that $AB':AB = 1:1.25$. This same ratio is used to determine the locations of points $C'$, $D'$, and $E'$. Therefore, the new shoreline is proportioned among the five parcels affected by the alluvium.

4. Note that the sidelines of the affected lots now bend at the original shoreline where they did not previously. Thus, the original points $A$ to $F$ must be located on the ground and the angles measured to determine the directions of the lines crossing the alluvium, such as $BB'$ and $CC'$.

## 15.3.4  Adverse Possession

The use of land by other than the registered owner for a sufficiently long and uninterrupted time (usually 20 years) may lead to a land transfer to the user from the registered owner. The legalities of adverse possession vary considerably among states and provinces. The general principles are discussed herein to warn the surveyor of the responsibilities and the investigative techniques to be employed. Some common legal topics are given next. These points do not hold in all jurisdictions, and it is the surveyor's responsibility to investigate their validity for the property under investigation.

1. Public property, such as unpatented lands, streets, and highways, cannot be acquired by adverse possession.

2. Usually the land use, whether it involves agriculture, erection of buildings, or fencing, is known to the owner of the land. In many cases, the landowner is not aware that adverse possession exists and, if these other land uses on the land do not interfere with the owner, he or she commonly chooses to ignore them.

3. These land uses under adverse possession must be against the interests of the owner under most jurisdictions. This issue has to be interpreted carefully. At the beginning of the adverse land uses, the owner could not have been hostile or he or she would have put a stop to the adverse uses of the land. Therefore, the owner becomes hostile when he or she decides to stop the adverse land uses and finds out that, by law, he or she cannot.

4. The adverse possession may consist of public use of a private right-of-way on private lands. In other words, private land can become public if extended usage is permitted by the owner.

5. If the landowner informs those carrying out the adverse land uses that he or she is the owner of these lands before the adverse land use has continued for the number of years required by law, the time period for adverse possession starts over again. For example, if the legal period for continuous use is 20 years, the adverse land uses started in 1975, and the owner informs those conducting the adverse land uses that he or she is the owner of the lands in 1983, no action can be undertaken for adverse possession until 2003, assuming that the owner does not mention his or her ownership to the user again. The best form of notification is by registered mail, which provides a record that the letter exists and was received. Verbal notification should be carried out in front of witnesses and the date noted.

## 15.4  Rural Land Surveys

Rural land is considered to be land outside the boundaries of cities, towns, villages, and the like. It usually consists of relatively large areas, in excess of 2 and commonly 10 acres. These larger land tracts usually differ from urban lands and city lands in the following ways:

- Many of the original land grants in the United States and Canada were not regular in shape because the boundaries were often natural features such as ridges, streams, or river banks. Manufactured features and the names of adjacent owners were often used as an aid in locating property boundaries. The property descriptions using these features and names did not contain any definitive bearings and distances. Many of the features have since disappeared and, of course, the adjacent owners have changed many times since.

- Rural lands are not as valuable as urban or city lands on a per-unit basis. Therefore, the property descriptions and surveys have not been done with the same care because the survey costs would be high in proportion to the land values.

- Control survey networks, such as those discussed in Chapter 10, have not been extended into some rural areas at this time because the priorities for control systems are for urban and city surveys. Therefore, the boundary markers will not be incorporated into the statewide or provincewide horizontal and vertical coordinate system. As a result, each rural land survey basically stands on its own. Errors accumulate, and no overall control system is available to correct or proportion the errors between coordinate control points.

- Most public lands were originally surveyed and patented as rural lands (agricultural), especially all homesteads (160 acres). The accuracy of such surveys were at best 1:400 and, for many, less than 1:100.

## 15.4.1   Descriptions

Descriptions of rural lands take several forms, mainly depending on when the description was written and the value of the land. These different types are briefly discussed next.

1. Descriptive only: These relate all property locations to natural and manufactured features, as discussed earlier.

2. Metes and bounds: A typical metes and bounds description is given in Section 15.3.2 and illustrated in Figure 15.12, wherein only the bearings and lengths of the sides are given. This example is given to the nearest 0.01 ft and the degrees to the nearest minute, thus indicating that the survey was done with a transit and tape. However, many property descriptions were based on compass and chain surveys and are described using chains and links for measurements, and directions are given to the nearest degree. The meaning of the wording used in deed descriptions and some of the common errors are discussed in Section 15.3.2.

3. Township subdivision: Parts of lots, called *aliquot parts,* are easily described for sectional systems. The legal description of a 40-acre (16-hectare) tract for the hatched area in Figure 15.10 (c) and the example principal meridian used in Section 15.2.2 is as follows: The northwest quarter of the northwest quarter of section one (1), Township nineteen (19) North, Range six (6) East, of the Initial Point of the Mount Diablo Meridian, containing forty (40) acres, more or less, as set out in the United States Public Lands Survey.

4. Coordinates: For economic reasons previously mentioned in this subsection, coordinates have not achieved common usage for rural land surveys. One exception to this is the use of coordinate systems by state or provincial highway departments. Therefore, lands bordering a newly constructed highway may be sufficiently close to coordinated monuments to incorporate this information into the deed description. The description is similar in wording to the example given in Section 15.3.2, with the addition of north and east coordinates stated in brackets after the point location of each corner. For example, point *B* in Figure 15.12 would show "N638,014.08, E160,269.69" in brackets after the first mention of point *B*. The coordinates quoted are in feet, and the metric equivalent would be used in countries where the metric system is already in use or where the conversion process has actually been completed and sanctioned by law. The other corners on the property boundary would have the appropriate coordinates indicated in brackets after the first mention of the corner in the description.

The use of coordinates related to a state- or provincewide system is, in my opinion, the ultimate solution to presenting an accurate description of a parcel of land. The description would clearly give the name of the state or province, followed by: "The lands enclosed by the following coordinates," followed by a simple tabulation of north and east coordinates. This would result in truly fixing the property corners and would avoid references to oblique statements such as those concerning the post and wire fence discussed in Section 15.3.2. The technology to achieve this simple solution exists. The savings in lawsuits between or among adjacent landowners would be tremendous. The only real requirements are an extension of the state or provincial coordinates to establish enough coordinated monuments, combined with the laws to ensure that all descriptions are directly related to the state or provincial coordinate systems.

## 15.4.2 Boundary Surveys

Two general types of boundary surveys are carried out in rural lands. One is the original survey, whereby new property lines are created. The other is a resurvey, which results in relocating property lines that have been previously surveyed. The principles for both types are similar because both have to be located with respect to the original township survey fabric. However, the procedures are somewhat different. Due to the similarities of approach, you are encouraged to read both subsections.

**15.4.2.1 Original**   An original survey is necessary when a tract of land, which has not previously been surveyed, is being transferred from one owner to another. The land is usually defined in an informal description in the offer to purchase. The form of description may be set out using the general format of any one of the four description types discussed in Section 15.4.1.

The following procedure is necessary to carry out an original survey properly:

1. A copy of the offer to purchase or any other document relating to the property boundaries should be obtained. For example, if the westerly portion of the property illustrated in Figure 15.12 is to be surveyed, it is important to determine if the parcel is "the westerly half of the parcel" or "the westerly 75 ft (22 m) of the parcel." The difference will be apparent from examining the wording of the description and subsequent explanation given in Section 15.3.1. Half the parcel will be 75 ft (22 m) more or less, and the westerly 75 ft (22 m) will be exactly 75 ft. At this time, it is also wise for the surveyor to establish the intent of the purchaser (who is usually the client) regarding what he or she thinks the property should consist of.

2. If the description in the offer mentions any registered deed numbers, such as the "westerly half of the lands described in instrument number 45792," a copy of this document must be obtained from the county registry office because it bears direct reference to the survey results. It may also be necessary to obtain deed descriptions of adjacent properties on each side of the parcel being surveyed. These deed descriptions will indicate the field measurements that should be held and those that should be proportioned.

3. The reference monument or corner in the township subdivision fabric, for example, point *A* in Figure 15.12, must be located or reestablished. Often, this point is not easily located, and the techniques discussed in Section 15.2.4 must be used. These methods are time consuming and therefore costly. Discussions with local residents regarding the corner location are useful only if all else fails. The surveyor should be aware that the local citizens seldom have any real conception of distance and/or direction in terms of

measurement, have little or no knowledge of surveying, and may have a vested interest in the location of property boundaries. A properly signed, witnessed, and legally worded affidavit (statement) of the local person's length of residence in the area and any other pertinent facts relating to why he or she should know the location of the corner should definitely be obtained by the surveyor. This safeguard applies only where this local knowledge is to be used in any way to assist in defining the location of the corner.

4. The property line adjacent to the street or highway, commonly called the street line (for example, the line on which points *B* and *E*, Figure 15.12, are located), must be determined. This requires knowledge of the township subdivision system originally used. For the sectional system, where 5% of the area was allotted for roads, the best evidence may be in adjacent boundary surveys or deed descriptions because the roads may follow a circuitous route. If the road allowance happens to follow along a section boundary in sectional systems, or along a concession or side road in nonsectional or special systems, the surveyor must be aware that the corner to be reestablished (if possible) is the adjacent section, quarter-section, or lot corner on the opposite side of the parcel (for example, point *F* in Figure 15.12). In certain cases, the only existing evidence is the location of the traveled road. In this case, the center of the road is determined by measurement, and the two street lines are located 33 ft (10 m) on either side.

5. The property corners on the street line are established and monumented. Because fences, trees, and other obstructions are usually located on this line, it is common to use an offset line parallel with the street line for ease in measuring distances and angles. This is illustrated in Figure 15.14. Points *A′* and *B′* are set using temporary markers, such as nails with flagging, on the offset line, which usually is located along the shoulder or ditch of the road. The property corners on the street line *A* and *B* are set by turning the appropriate angle (90° is safest) and measuring the offset distance (*A′A* and *B′B*.)

6. The other corners of the property are established by various field techniques, most of which are illustrated in Figure 15.14. Based on the boundary requirements and existing evidence, as discussed later, the surveyor normally uses a combination of offset lines incorporated within a closed traverse (*EFGHIB′E*). This assumes that obstacles to running the property boundaries directly exist. Some examples relating to Figure 15.14 are listed below:

   a. If the distance *AD* is fixed, then the offset line *EF* can be run to point *F*, and *D* is subsequently set by turning the appropriate angle *EFD*.

   b. If point *C* is located at an identifiable point in the field, such as a fence intersection, the monument is set at point *H* and tied to the traverse by measuring the angle off the traverse lines to point *C* and the distance *HC*. This distance should be measured at least twice and verified because subsequent calculations of the position of point *C* will not provide a check on this measurement.

7. The distances and angles measured are recorded carefully in the field notes. The traverse is then closed for latitudes and departures using the techniques described in Chapter 6. The governing bearing, to which all other traverse bearings are related, must be established. Most present-day survey regulations require that this be related to true north, referenced as passing through a well-defined point nearby, such as a

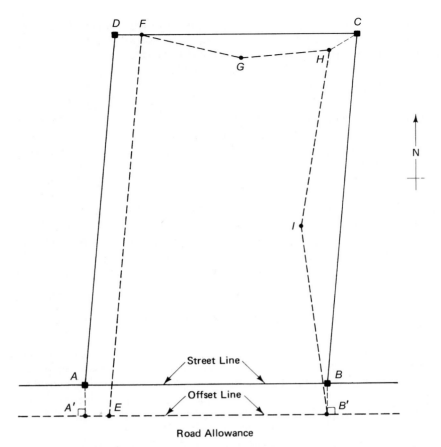

**FIGURE 15.14** Rural land survey techniques and field note format.

main section or lot corner. The true north or "astronomical" bearing of *AB* or *A′B′* may have been established by a survey of adjacent lands involving this same line. If this information is not available, it may be necessary to determine the astronomical bearing through observations of Polaris, or through GPS techniques as described in Chapters 10 and 11. If state or provincial coordinate control points are within a reasonable distance, only an open traverse measuring angle could be used to transfer, through azimuth or bearing calculations, the bearing along the line between the control points to one of the property boundaries.

8. The rectangular coordinates of each property boundary corner are calculated using the methods given in Chapter 6. Subsequently, the bearing and distance of each property boundary are calculated, for example, *AB, BC, CD,* and *DA* in Figure 15.14.

9. A plan of the property boundaries, showing the bearings and distances of each line, is drawn; the monumentation is set; and any relevant factors, such as existing

fences, are noted. Depending on the degree of supervision within the local jurisdiction, the surveyor is advised to contact the registrar of deeds regarding details such as drawing size and whether an Imperial scale or metric (in Canada) is required.

10. The survey plan is submitted to the client and, if required, to the local county registry office. If the latter is necessary, the inspector of surveys at the registry office will examine the plan for errors and omissions, and the exchange of revised plans will continue until the survey plan is approved. These details often delay the acceptance of the survey, thus possibly postponing the closing date of the property transaction. The surveyor is well advised to warn the client beforehand of this possibility.

11. The area is calculated, if required, using the methods given in Chapter 6.

12. A deed description, if required, is prepared. Metes and bounds and/or coordinates are the preferred systems, depending on the jurisdiction. It is becoming common practice to attach the survey plan to the deed and to identify clearly the property and its boundaries. The description in the deed can then merely indicate "the property shown as Part 1 on the attached reference plan No. 59R 4047," for example. In the province of Ontario, the 59 is the registry office number, R indicates reference, and 4047 is the survey plan number. This system avoids most of the disadvantages of deed descriptions and the common errors and misunderstandings discussed in Section 15.3.2.

### 15.4.2.2 Resurvey
A resurvey means that previously surveyed boundaries have to be reestablished in their original locations. Resurveys are required for various reasons. Transfer of land from one owner to another is a common reason because the new owner usually requires documentation of the holdings. The location of a new highway, railway, hydro power line, or gas distribution line also requires resurveys. Tables 10.3 and 10.4 showed the positional tolerances and closure requirements as adopted by the American Land Title Association (ALTA) and the American Congress for Surveying and Mapping (ACSM).

The surveyor should be aware that many rural properties have never required survey work since the original township subdivision. For example, if the property has remained in the same family for several generations, the need for a resurvey has never arisen.

Resurveys are considerably more challenging to the surveyor than original surveys. In fact, resurveys in rural lands require more experience, investigative capabilities, imagination, and perseverance than any other type of survey. Many of the factors involved were discussed previously. The main reasons for the difficulties in resurveys are summarized below:

- Most of the evidence has been destroyed by forest fires, disintegration of wooden posts, removal of monuments, and so on.
- The original surveys contained many errors, particularly if the survey was carried out using a compass and link chain. The magnetic declination (difference between magnetic north and true north) at the time of the survey was usually different than it is now. Although link chains originally contained 100 links, either wear at the link connections and/or the loss of one or more links off one end during the original survey resulted in chains of other than 66 ft long.

- Information transferred from one record to another, such as from the field notes to the plat or original survey plan, was often in error.
- Evidence from persons presumably familiar with the location of corners or lines often conflicts. Selfish interests and conflicts with adjoining property owners are but two common causes.

The surveyor must also be a detective and judge in carrying out resurveys. Conflicting evidence both in the field and on the original records is the norm. The surveyor is responsible for sorting through all available evidence; accepting all, portions, or none of that evidence; and defending his or her decisions to all involved parties, including the presentation of expert evidence in a court of law. The surveyor is required to report his or her decisions to the client. Therefore, the surveyor is well advised to keep a detailed log of decisions and the reasons for each. It should be assumed from the beginning that the evidence may be examined by a formal body, such as a court, at any future time.

The following steps are usually required in carrying out a resurvey. It is impossible to cover all the possibilities within the scope of this text. However, the principles are essentially the same.

1. The surveyor obtains the descriptions of the property, as well as descriptions of all adjacent lands. He or she reviews the descriptions critically for gross errors (see Section 15.3.2) and corrects them, where possible, to match the apparent intent of the description.
2. The descriptions are plotted to scale on a plan. At this point, the property boundaries in conflict with adjacent lands as described become apparent. For example, the same property lines may overlap or leave gaps due to discrepancies in the descriptions. This identifies the described boundaries requiring further intensive investigation, through reviewing both the deed descriptions and fieldwork. Those lines along which the descriptions of adjacent lands agree are identified as the most reliable starting points for the field survey work.
3. If the bearings shown on the records are magnetic, the magnetic declination at the time of the survey is determined through past records, and the bearings are corrected to true north. This provides a crude approximation, particularly in areas of magnetic anomalies, such as rocks containing iron compounds. If the date of the survey is unknown and at least one boundary can be identified, astronomical observations are made to determine the true bearing of this line. All other lines are then referred to this bearing.
4. Several situations may confront the surveyor when the detailed field investigations have been undertaken. The three usual circumstances, and the procedures to be followed, are discussed next.
   a. *At least one boundary is established:* The established boundary line and the remaining boundary lines are measured and compared with the measurements stated in the deed descriptions. The proportionate lengths of the other sides of the parcel are calculated based on this comparative value. The property boundaries are then rerun as described and/or mapped on the original township plat. The approximate locations of each corner are thus established. The surveyor looks carefully for field evidence of, first, the corner and related witness points and, second, the lines originally run between monuments, using the methods described

in Section 15.2.4. If positive evidence is found regarding the location of a corner, the old monument is left if it is in good condition. If it is not, it is replaced by a new monument. If no evidence of either the parcel corners or lines exists beyond the one established boundary, the corner is temporarily established based on the deed description. The area around the temporary corner is examined thoroughly for any evidence of the monuments and/or lines. If no evidence is found, the temporary corner becomes the permanent corner, provided that the distance measurements have been proportioned correctly prior to setting the temporary corner, because this is the best evidence available.

b. *Only one corner is established.* The surveyor has no choice but to establish the true bearings of the lines in the deed description from the original survey using the magnetic declination at the time of the original survey, if the date can be established. The survey is rerun on the basis of the single corner and the surveyor's best estimate of the bearings from or to that point. Proportional correction is impossible to determine; therefore, the other parcel boundaries must be established based only on deed descriptions.

c. *No corners or lines are evident.* The situation is extremely difficult. Descriptions of adjacent properties must be given greater credence under these conditions. The plotting of the description of the parcel and adjacent tracts becomes more significant. The evidence of local residents is highly questionable for the reasons stated previously. The surveyor must realize that agreement on the corners and boundaries by all affected owners is critical under these conditions. After having carried out the detailed investigation described previously and having reached no conclusion, the surveyor is well advised to call a meeting of all involved parties. Notice should be given by registered mail and preferably through personal delivery, if possible. The meeting should be held in the field at each potentially contentious corner and a resolution of the location resolved, if possible. It is important to prepare the required documents carefully and in advance, stating that those involved agree to the applicable corner location. This procedure involves all concerned parties through formal notice. If a consensus is achieved, the surveyor has solved the problem, and the required documentation is summarily signed and witnessed. One or more property owners may not attend, but when all are given reasonable notice, the majority rules. I have found this method to be extremely effective, and the results are more than gratifying. Because all parties are or should be involved, the resulting agreements carry considerable weight. Properly witnessed signatures agreeing to the common boundaries established provide valuable legal evidence. The surveyor must realize that, in this type of situation, the key word is "agreement," not "theory." In my experience, the owners involved should be convinced that compromising on boundary locations will avoid both hard feelings and expensive lawsuits in the future.

5. Once the corners and boundaries have been established by field evidence and/or agreement of owners, the surveyor should continue with step 6, as described in Section 15.4.2.1.

6. The remaining procedure consists of implementing steps 7 to 12, as described in Section 15.4.2.1.

The key factor in rural surveying is the acquisition of sufficient evidence, field or otherwise, to designate the boundaries as agreed on by the owners involved.

## 15.4.3 Subdivisions

Rural land is subdivided for reasons other than proportional or aliquot parts of quarter-sections or lots. When rural land is subdivided irregularly, the purpose is commonly the creation of large lots, usually between 0.5 acre (0.2 hectare) and 2 acres (0.8 hectare). The houses subsequently built on these lots use wells for a water supply and have sewage disposal systems for each house located on the lot. In areas where this type of subdivision is being developed, the rural road system is established, and most original township subdivision boundaries have been fenced.

Certain principles are involved in surveying the irregular boundaries of subdivisions in rural lands. The surveyor should be aware of the more important principles, which are discussed next. Fences are defined as those that have existed long enough to meet the requirements of adverse possession, as defined in Section 15.3.4.

- Fences along either side of road allowance boundaries are not used as property lines if these road allowances were established as part of the township subdivision. Therefore, lines between quarter-section corners and between lot corners along concession roads, and side-line allowances between concessions are governed by the lines between adjacent corners, regardless of the fence location. Consequently, the monumentation along a fence adjacent to a road allowance is often located some distance from the fence. This fact is also useful in relocating previous monumentation along road allowance fence lines.

- Fences along lines other than road allowances that form boundaries of these subdivisions usually predominate over the direct corner-to-corner boundaries. This fact is important because subdivision lot corners intersecting these lines should be set in the fence line, regardless of the number of bends in the fence. The surveyor should be aware that the fence line represents an informal, yet agreed upon, boundary between the property owners.

## 15.5 Urban Land Surveys

Urban land surveys differ from rural land surveys as follows:

- The lands are located within or adjacent to the city or town boundary. A more practical definition of **location** would be the proximity of the lands to existing or potential water supply and sewage collection systems. The costs of these sewers dictate that the lot sizes be much smaller than those in rural land surveys to permit the distribution of costs over a larger number of lots for a comparable land area. The lot sizes are usually between 0.10 acre (0.04 hectare) and 0.20 acre (0.08 hectare).

- The land value is greater than that of rural lands because of the smaller dimensions per lot. Therefore, the surveys must be carried out with greater precision (see Tables 10.3 and 10.4). For example, the mispositioning of a house on a lot may not satisfy the requirements of a mortgage company or municipality. Because the lot sizes are small, a slight variation in the subdivision lot boundary has more effect.

- Resurveys are simpler and easier than those in rural lands because monumentation is more recent and more permanent, but the conflict between adjacent property owners may be more intensive because of the higher cost of the land involved.

## 15.5.1 Descriptions

The boundaries of a tract of land can be described within or adjacent to city or town boundaries in relation to registered plans, blocks, or lots. The original township subdivision boundaries have usually been well established, as have subsequent aliquot parts and/or irregular subdivisions (discussed in Section 15.4). Consequently, deed descriptions of urban lands usually relate to street locations and lots within a registered plan of subdivision. Examples of such situations and the deed descriptions are stated next and illustrated in Figure 15.15.

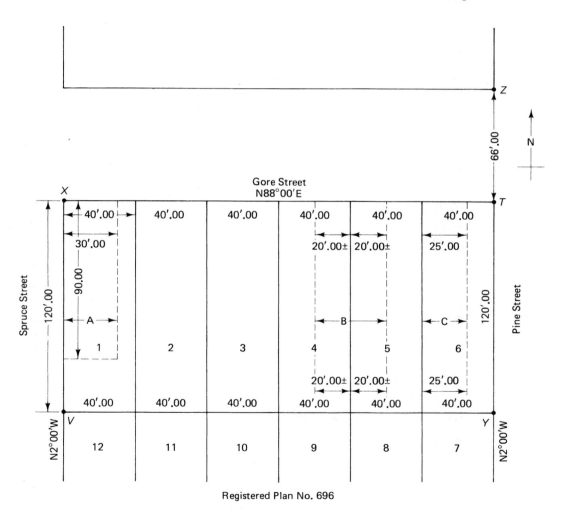

**FIGURE 15.15** Urban land descriptions.

1. Boundaries coincide with lot(s) on a plan of subdivision. If the subdivision is registered and given a plan number, the description may read "Lot 16, Registered Plan No. 969, City of Toronto, Formerly County of York," or "Lot 8 in Block B, as said lots and blocks are delineated upon a map entitled Townsend Shores, filed in the office of the County Recorder for the County of Sarasota, State of Florida."

2. Boundaries do not coincide with lot(s) on a plan of subdivision. The properties are described by metes and bounds, with the point of commencement referred to a lot or block corner shown on the plan (parcel A, Figure 15.15); by aliquot parts of lots such as half-lots (parcel B, Figure 15.15, east half of lot 4 and west half of lot 5); or by fixed portions of lots, such as the westerly 25 ft (8 m) of a certain lot (parcel C, Figure 15.15).

3. Boundaries related to coordinated monuments. Control surveys (see Chapter 10) have been completed over larger American and Canadian cities. The monuments resulting from such surveys are coordinated precisely, with respect to either a state or provincial coordinate system or to an arbitrarily selected initial point within the city. These initial points are given large enough coordinates for both north and east directions so that negative coordinates are not encountered. The boundaries may be defined by the following:

   a. Positioning the point of commencement with respect to a coordinated reference point by bearing and distance (or calculated coordinates) and describing the property by metes and bounds (see Section 15.3.2).

   b. The same procedure as described in step 3(a) but with a corner on the boundary, other than the point of commencement, described in relation to another coordinated reference point in the city control network. This provides a useful check on the property location.

   c. Positioning all property boundary corners by listing the coordinates of each in order (clockwise or counterclockwise) around the property. The surveyor should be aware that the transposition of numbers in listing these coordinates is not uncommon. The surveyor is well advised to plot the coordinates as given in the description to scale and to use this as a check for the intended property dimensions.

   d. Deeds or certificates of title avoid written descriptions through the attachment of survey plans that show the bearings and distances of the property boundaries. Where coordinate systems, either state, provincial, or city, have been established, these may also be shown on the plan for each property corner.

## 15.5.2 Boundary Surveys

**15.5.2.1 Original**   Original boundary surveys fall into two categories. The first is the establishment of the boundary of the area proposed for subdivision, such as lots 1 to 12 inclusive in Figure 15.15. In this case, the original survey would have defined the boundaries of Gore, Spruce, and Pine streets. This would have been done by determining the overall boundaries of the lands to be subdivided and relating the street boundaries to these limits. The original boundary is established using the best-evidence rules discussed in

Section 15.4.2. The surveyor should note that much more evidence usually exists for urban surveys than for rural surveys.

The second category of original boundary survey is the establishment of the lot lines such as those shown in Figure 15.15. These are usually laid out on paper by a town or urban planner, and the approximate dimensions are shown on a proposed or "draft" plan of subdivision. The planner normally fits as many lots as possible into the available area at this stage. This planning work is based on the overall subdivision boundaries and minimum lot frontages and areas as regulated by the municipality, so the surveyor is often faced with the problem of fitting the number of lots shown on the draft plan into the final surveyed plan. This fact should be made clear to the planner and client before the survey work begins. In addition, the usual required minor modifications in lot sizes and pattern should be discussed with the client and planner as the project proceeds. This discussion should avoid the possibility of moving lot-boundary monuments after they have been set.

### 15.5.2.2 Resurvey
Before techniques of resurveying urban boundaries are discussed, the surveyor should be aware of the lack of permanence of the original street-line and lot boundaries created. The urban subdivision is monumented under close to ideal conditions. The land is vacant at the time and no construction has taken place. Once construction of roads and houses as well as the installation of water mains and sewers begins, however, the survival rate of lot corner monumentation decreases substantially.

The vast majority of the survey markers are eventually removed, severely bent, or covered by up to 3 ft of fill. Consequently, the surveyor will usually be confronted with an incredible lack of survey evidence. This situation is very disconcerting when the survey plan of subdivision indicates, neatly and clearly, the position of original monuments set at each lot corner. Thus, the surveyor will expect to find monuments that either do not exist or have been misplaced.

Resurveying a subdivision is a considerable challenge that requires perseverance and understanding. In my experience, it is common to locate only between 5% and 15% of the lot corners in their original position. For example, in Figure 15.15, the surveyor would be relatively fortunate to find undisturbed monuments at points X, Y, and Z. If the object of the survey involves the boundary establishment of parcel B, the entire boundaries of lots 4 and 5 must be determined. In this example, a procedure similar to the following would have to be undertaken:

1. The line YZ would be measured. This distance should be 186.00 ft (120 ft, plus 66 ft) according to plan but measures 186.04 ft in the field.
2. Point T is set 66.00 ft south of point Z on the line YZ. Road allowances always retain their original width when resurveyed.
3. The distance XT is measured at 240.12 ft, although it is 240.00 ft according to the plan. This discrepancy means that the frontage of the lots on Gore Street must be adjusted by proportioning to 240.12/ 6, or 40.02 ft.
4. The street-line locations of lots 4 and 5 are set using the frontage of 40.02 ft for each.
5. Because parcel B consists of the east half of lot 4 and the west half of lot 5 by description, the midpoints of lots 4 and 5 are set along the street line (line XT), a distance of 20.01 ft both west and east of the 4–5 lot boundary.
6. Because no further evidence of the easterly boundary of Spruce Street other than point Z exists, the plan angle of 90° is turned off at X from T to establish this street line.

7. Line *YV* is run parallel to Gore Street to intersect the easterly boundary of Spruce Street at point *V*. Therefore, the actual lengths of both *YT* and *VX* are 120.04 ft, rather than the plan distance of 120.00 ft.

8. The rear corners of parcel B are set proportionately in the same way as the front corners. Thus, the boundaries of parcel B have been established using survey techniques based on the best evidence available. By proportioning, the dimensions of this parcel are 40.02 ft by 120.04 ft.

The example described is quite straightforward. If horizontal curves, including reverse curves (see Chapter 13), exist between two found points on a street line, the establishment of the street line involves considerable calculations, more fieldwork, and some trial and error measurements.

Resurveys must often be carried out for lots or parts thereof on urban subdivisions originally monumented by perishable markers such as wooden stakes. Under these conditions, resurveys become more difficult due to lack of monumentation but are easier because occupational boundaries such as fence lines have been firmly established. Resurveys in urban lands are seldom as easy as they may appear. The existence of a neatly presented registered plan of subdivision does not, in any way, guarantee the current existence of the monuments shown. Title or mortgage surveys, discussed next, often assist greatly in establishing street and property lines.

## 15.5.3 Title or Mortgage Surveys

These surveys involve the detailed positioning of the existing buildings on a parcel of land in relation to the boundaries. The surveys are performed for two primary reasons:

- The finance company or bank granting a mortgage on a property, and usually the buildings thereon, requires proof that the buildings are within the property boundaries.
- Most municipalities have bylaws stating minimum distances to the street line and the side lines of the lots. The title or mortgage surveys show whether these bylaws have been satisfied or not. Surveys for this purpose are usually carried out as soon as the basement of the house has been constructed up to the first floor level. Hence, if the building location does not satisfy the bylaws and if negotiations for exemptions from these regulations with the municipality are unsuccessful, the building can be moved before construction is completed.

Figure 15.16 illustrates a typical title or mortgage survey (see also Figure 14.5). The steps in conducting such a survey include the following:

1. The lot boundaries, as discussed in Section 15.5.2, are reestablished. Note that the lot patterns in Figures 15.15 and 15.16 are identical.

2. The distances from the outside basement walls to the street line and both lot lines are measured, usually by reading the measurement on the tape through the theodolite

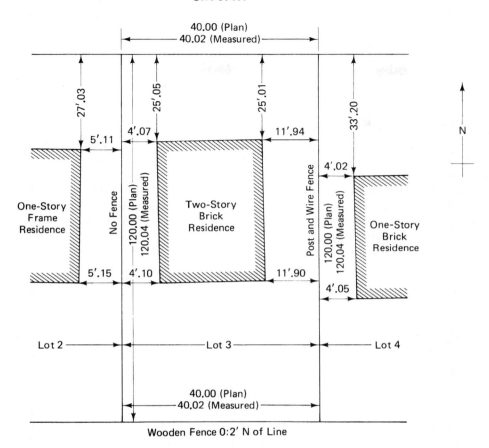

**FIGURE 15.16**   Typical title or mortgage survey.

telescope. The distances required are those at right angles to the lot line, in other words, the shortest distance between the lot line and the building corner.

3. The measurements to the street line, called setbacks, and those to the lot lines, called sideyards, are also measured for the buildings on both sides of the lot or parcel being surveyed.

4. Occupation lines such as fences are positioned and shown on the survey plan. If the fence is not on the property line, such as the southerly fence in Figure 15.16, its position is noted.

5. All lot distance measurements are shown. It is common to show both the "plan" and "measured" distances for each boundary, as illustrated in Figure 15.16. It is necessary to measure the outside dimensions of the buildings to plot them to scale. The corner markers may or may not be replaced. Often they are not replaced because this increases the cost of the survey.

The surveyor should note that title or mortgage survey measurements are very useful for reestablishing property boundaries because the distances from the buildings are measured to the true property lines. Often, the residents have a copy of the survey among their valuable papers in the house. It is well worth the surveyor's time to ask local residents on nearby properties for a loan of these surveys. The surveyor's name and date of the title or mortgage survey should be recorded and shown in the resurvey field notes.

## 15.6 Cadastral Surveying

Cadastral surveying is a general term applied to several different types of surveys. It is mentioned here only to make the reader aware of the expression and the broad aspects of its use. A rigid definition of a cadastral survey involves only the information required to define the legal boundaries of a parcel of land, whether it is rural or urban. Therefore, the monumentation, bearings, distances, and areas would be shown. This definition has now been expanded through common usage to include cultural features, such as building location; drainage features; and topographic information, such as spot elevations or contours.

## Problems

**15.1** Calculate the angular convergency for 2 meridians 6 miles (9.66 km) apart at latitude 36°30′ and 46°30′.

**15.2** Find the convergency in feet, chains, and meters of 2 meridians 24 miles apart if the latitude for the southern limit is 40°20′ and the latitude for the north limit is 40°41′.

**15.3** If the tangent offset is 3.28 ft (1.00 m) at 3 miles (4.83 km) from the meridian, calculate the offsets for 5 miles (8.05 km), 7 miles (11.27 km), and 10 miles (16.10 km) from the same meridian.

**15.4** For a 6-mile-square sectional township, calculate the area of section 6 if the mean latitude through the middle of the township is 46°30′. Take into account only the effects of convergence in this calculation.

**15.5** In Figure 15.10, show how the iron monument would be marked for:
   **(a)** The northwest corner of township T.20N., R.7E.
   **(b)** The southeast corner of section 32 of township T.20N., R.6E.

**15.6** Plot the following description of property that is located in a standard U.S. sectional system to a scale of either 1:5,000 or 1 in. = 400 ft: commencing at the southwest corner of Section 35 in Township T.10N., R.3W., thence N0°05′W along the westerly boundary of Section 35, 2,053.00 ft to a point therein; thence N89°45′E, 1,050.00 ft; thence southerly, parallel with the westerly limit of Section 35, 670.32 ft; thence N89°45′E, 950.00 ft; thence southerly, parallel with the westerly limit of Section 35, 1,381.68 ft, more or less, to the point of intersection with the southerly boundary of Section 35; thence westerly along the southerly boundary of Section 35, 2,000.00 ft, more or less, to the point of commencement.

**15.7** The locations of the original and new shoreline are shown in Figure 15.17.
   **(a)** Describe how you would establish points *B, C,* and *D* along the new shoreline.

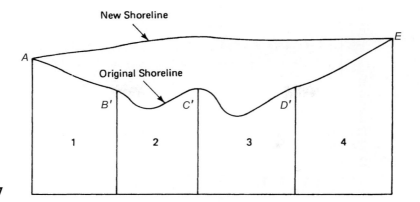

**FIGURE 15.17**

(b) Sketch the locations of these points along the new shoreline on a clear plastic overlay.

**15.8** Prepare a legal description for parcel B in Figure 15.15.

**15.9** If the measured bearing of Pine Street in Figure 15.15 was N1°50′W instead of N2°00′W, and the distance *XT* remains the same as shown in the figure, calculate the rear dimensions of lots 1 through 6.

# 16 Hydrographic Surveys

## 16.1  General Background

Why do we need hydrographic surveys? Offshore engineering and the shipping industry have continued to expand. Drilling rigs, located up to 125 mi (200 km) offshore, search for resources, particularly oil and gas. Offshore islands are constructed (sometimes under severe weather conditions) of dredged material to support marine structures. Harbor depths up to 80 ft (25 m) are required to accommodate larger ships and tankers. Containerization has become an efficient and preferred method of cargo handling. The demand for recreational transportation ranges from large pleasure cruise ships to small sailboats. Hydrographic surveys are made to acquire and present data on oceans, lakes, bays, or harbors. In addition to harbor construction and offshore drilling, these surveys are carried out for one or more of the following activities:

- Determining the water depths and locations of rocks, sandbars, and wrecks for navigation channel openings and salvage operations.
- Dredging for harbor deepening, maintenance, mineral recovery, and navigation channel access.
- Evaluating areas of sedimentation and erosion for coastline protection and offshore structures.
- Measuring areas subject to siltation or scouring to determine the effects on water quality and existing structures, such as bridge abutments and storm sewage outfalls.
- Providing recreational facilities such as beaches and marinas.
- Determining site locations for submarine cables and underwater pipelines and intakes.
- Determining pollution sources.
- Evaluating the effects of corrosion, particularly in salt water.
- Determining the extent of wetland areas.

This chapter describes the procedures required to obtain the necessary data for hydrographic surveys, hydrographic plans, and electronic charts.

## 16.2 Objectives of Hydrographic Mapping and Electronic Charting

The primary requirement involves showing the topographic configuration of the underwater features, both natural and built. The resulting product is therefore similar to a topographic map of land areas. See Figure F.1. However, the methods used to obtain the information for hydrographic surveys are vastly different.

In the horizontal plane, the position of a survey vessel must be fixed to the required accuracy. The location of the vessel is complicated by weather conditions, particularly wind, waves, and fog. The depth of the seabed below the survey vessel, known as a *sounding,* is subject to variations caused by wave and tidal action. After the original sounding has been corrected, the resulting depth is called a reduced sounding. See Figure 16.1.

The surveyor must also be aware that the costs and accuracies of hydrographic surveys are normally not comparable to land surveys. While the land surveyor can see the features, the hydrographic surveyor cannot, except in shallow, clear waters. This may result in the omission of important features, such as rocks or wrecks, that vitally affect the proposed undertaking.

The objective of the hydrographic survey must be considered in light of these issues. For example, cost overruns may be justified to locate important underwater features through an increased number of soundings. Therefore, the proper planning of a hydrographic survey, as discussed in the following section, is critical for the final product to satisfy the project requirements at a cost that is acceptable.

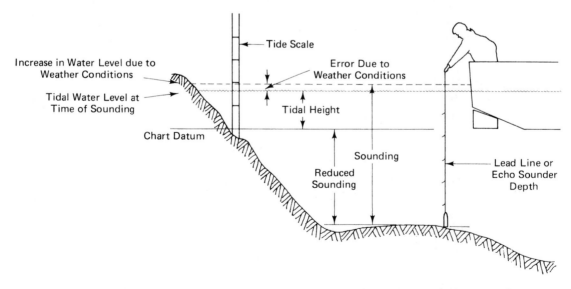

**FIGURE 16.1**   Reduced soundings and errors due to wave action and water-level fluctuations.

## 16.3   Planning

Careful planning and preparation are essential for any undertaking. Flexibility in the plan allows for delays due to weather and equipment breakdowns. In the preplanning stage, all available and applicable information should be examined, and copies should be obtained whenever possible. Hydrographic charts of the general area provide indications of the sounding depths and depth variations that are likely to be encountered. This information is useful for sounding equipment selection and the design of the sounding pattern.

Topographic maps indicate the configuration of the shoreline and natural or built features that may be used as control stations for horizontal position fixing. Aerial photographs viewed stereoscopically (in three dimensions) will provide this information, as well as offshore bar and shore formations (see Chapter 12), in greater detail. Color aerial photographs and lidar images are particularly useful because of their high penetration capabilities through water.

Navigational directions and boating restrictions, including channel locations, normal and storm wave heights, prevailing wind directions, and areas of restricted vessel use, assist in sounding vessel selection and in identifying sources for obtaining permits in restricted areas. Tide tables are essential for the design of recording gauges. If existing gauges are operational, their locations, frequency of water level recordings, base datum used, and the availability of the data to the surveyor should be known in advance. Horizontal control data from previous land and/or hydrographic surveys will reduce the effort and cost of the survey measurements among shoreline control stations. Previous knowledge of existing coordinate control networks will allow the survey data to be tied to the survey system, if required.

If the survey is to be controlled by global positioning system (GPS) techniques, attention must be given to the availability of Coast Guard DGPS radio beacons so that differential techniques can be utilized. Software that will coordinate all data collection (soundings and positionings) and integrate with onboard electronics must be acquired. If necessary, a decision must be made about whether to buy or rent the equipment.

## 16.4   Survey Vessels

General considerations should include the following:

1. Overall purpose of the survey, particularly the need for geophysical survey equipment or additional survey requirements.
2. Weather conditions, such as wave heights.
3. Size of the survey team and whether team members are to live on the craft.

Specific conditions that will always apply include the following:

1. Sufficient space for position-fixing and plotting. The plotting board should be under cover and relatively free from engine vibration.
2. An all-around view for visual position-fixing techniques.
3. Sufficient electrical power at the required voltages for all equipment needs.

4. Compatibility of fuel capacity and storage for supplies within the range and operational requirements.

5. Stability and maneuverability at slow speeds (up to 6 km/h, or 4 knots).

6. Cruising speeds of at least 15 km/h (10 knots) to minimize time loss from the base to the survey area and to provide sufficient speed to return safely to port in the event of sudden storms.

## 16.5 Vertical Control: Depth and Tidal Measurements

The depth of the point below the water surface or sounding must be related to the desired datum or reference level. This will normally involve corrections for seasonal water levels under nontidal conditions, and for tidal variations where tides are a factor. The relationship between soundings and corrected or reduced soundings is shown in Figure 16.1.

### 16.5.1 Depth Measurements

A weighted line, graduated in meters, feet, or both, is used only for projects involving a small number of soundings. However, it is a valuable addition to the surveyor's equipment for calibrating echo-sounders and also for use as a backup system. The echo-sounder provides depth measurements by timing the interval between transmission and reception of an acoustic pulse, which travels to the bottom and back at a rate of approximately 1,500 m/s (5,000 ft/s). Separate transmissions are made at rates of up to six per second. The beamwidth that emanates from the vessel is typically about 30°, as illustrated in Figure 16.2(a). The portion of the seabed within the beamwidth is termed the **isonified area.**

In depth measurement, the most significant point is directly below the transducer, which is the vibratory diaphragm that controls the frequency of transmission. However, the echo sounder records the earliest return from its transmission (that which has traveled the shortest distance). Within a beamwidth of 30°, this return may not be from a target directly beneath the transducer, but from seabed anomalies within the isonified area [see Figure 16.2(a)]. This will lead to anomalies in the soundings, which may be differentiated by an experienced observer. Highly reflective targets such as bare rock and shipwrecks, located near the edges of the beam, show as narrow, clearly defined bands on the read-out, compared with thick, poorly defined bands over soft sediments, weedbeds, and the like, as illustrated in Figure 16.3. Constant monitoring of the transmission returns and notes of anomalies should be incorporated in the hydrographic survey.

Sound velocity in water is a function of temperature, salinity, and density. These factors vary daily and seasonally, and as a result of periodic occurrences such as heavy rainfalls and tidal streams. Any attempt to correct the soundings with respect to these variables is both unsatisfactory and cost-ineffective. As a result, it must be recognized that accuracies in acoustic measurements in seawater will not be better than 1 part in 200.

Calibration of echo-sounders is carried out either by comparison with direct measurements, using weighted lines, or by a bar check in depths less than 30 m, as illustrated in Figure 16.2(b). The latter involves setting a bar or disc horizontally beneath the transducer at various depths. The echo-sounder recorder is adjusted to match the directly measured depths. If the sounder is not adjustable, the differences are recorded for regular depth

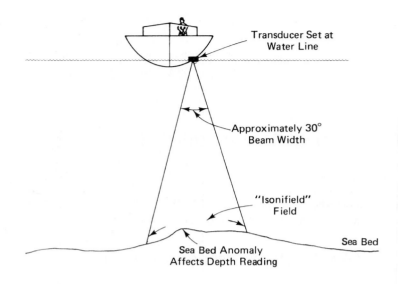

Transducer Set at Water Line

Approximately 30° Beam Width

"Isonifield" Field

Sea Bed

Sea Bed Anomaly Affects Depth Reading

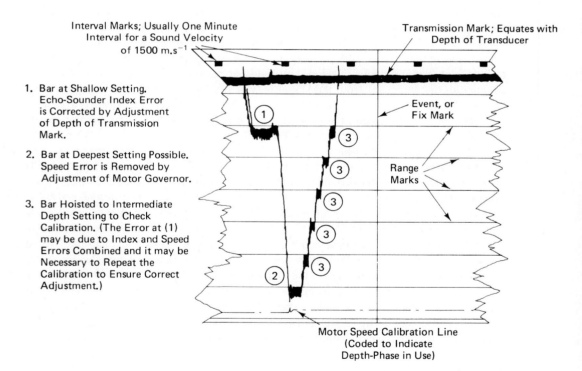

Interval Marks; Usually One Minute Interval for a Sound Velocity of 1500 m.s⁻¹

Transmission Mark; Equates with Depth of Transducer

1. Bar at Shallow Setting. Echo-Sounder Index Error is Corrected by Adjustment of Depth of Transmission Mark.

2. Bar at Deepest Setting Possible. Speed Error is Removed by Adjustment of Motor Governor.

3. Bar Hoisted to Intermediate Depth Setting to Check Calibration. (The Error at (1) may be due to Index and Speed Errors Combined and it may be Necessary to Repeat the Calibration to Ensure Correct Adjustment.)

Event, or Fix Mark

Range Marks

Motor Speed Calibration Line (Coded to Indicate Depth-Phase in Use)

**FIGURE 16.2**   Isonified area and bar check for echo-sounder depths. Transducer and isonified area (top). Typical bar check (bottom).

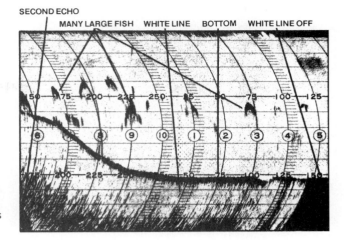

**FIGURE 16.3** Variations in echo-sounder read-out characteristics. Note that the poorly defined bottom read-out in topographic depression indicates soft bottom sediments.

intervals, and the resulting corrections are applied to each sounding. It is advisable to calibrate the echo-sounder at the beginning and end of each day's use, particularly at 10%, 50%, and 80% of the maximum depths measured.

Recent improvements to depth measurements include the now widespread use of multibeam echo-sounding in shallow waters. Because of the fast rate of data acquisition (900 depth points per second), manual editing is no longer feasible. This system requires an onboard computer (color monitor and plotter) for data logging, navigation, quality control, multibeam calibration, data editing, and plotting. The computer software can also integrate the data collected by the sensors on pitch, heave, and roll.

Weighted (hand) sounding lines are seldom used for depths over 30 m (100 ft). The lines may be small-linked steel chain, wire, cotton, hemp cord, or nylon rope. A weight, usually made of lead, is attached to one end. Markers are placed at intervals along the line for depth reading. Lines constructed of link chains are subject to wear through abrasion. Wire lines will stretch moderately when suspended, depending on the size of the bottom weight. The weights vary from 2.3 kg (5 lb) to 32 kg (75 lb), although 4.5 kg (10 lb) is usually sufficient for moderate depths and low velocities. Cotton or hemp lines must be stretched before use and graduated when wet. They must be soaked in water for at least one hour before use to allow the rope to assume its working length. Nylon lines stretch appreciably, and unpredictably, and they are not recommended for other than very approximate depth measurements. The hydrographic surveyor should calibrate the sounding lines against a steel survey tape regularly under the conditions most similar to actual usage, such as hemp lines after soaking.

## 16.5.2 Tidal Gauging

Observations of tidal variations from the datum are required throughout the sounding operation for the reduction of soundings. Any datum may be selected, as discussed previously. It is common practice, however, to use the level of the lowest predicted tide, known as the

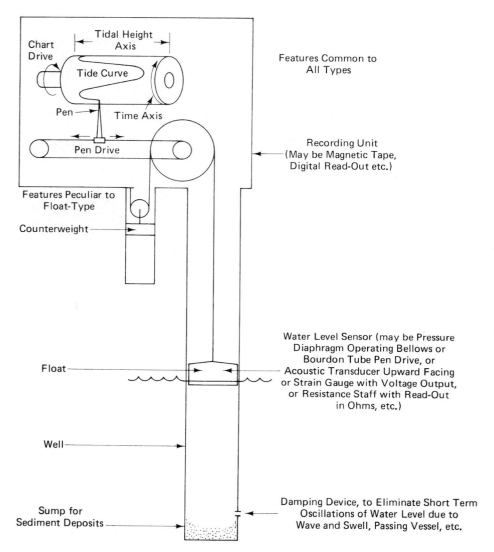

**FIGURE 16.4** Typical tidal gauge.

lowest astronomical tide (LAT). This datum can be obtained from available information and existing benchmarks in developed countries.

A tide pole or recording tide gauge is required to obtain the necessary information during the sounding period. A simple graduated pole, erected with its zero mark below the lowest expected water level and of sufficient length to cover the tidal range, may be used. However, an observer is required to record the water levels and corresponding times, which may be costly. The observer must also be trained to allow for local disturbances, such as wakes from passing boats, so that only the tidal variations are measured. The recording tide gauge involves higher capital costs, which may be justified on the grounds of not requiring an observer. A typical tidal gauge is illustrated in Figure 16.4.

The difficulties of tidal observation relate primarily to the location of the observation gauges. Difficulties include:

1. Proximity to the survey area.
2. Configuration of the coastline: Indentions or embayments result in tidal variations between the back of the bay and the straighter portion of the shoreline. Therefore, a survey encompassing such an embayment should provide tidal recording stations at both locations.
3. Slope of the seabed: Gently sloping seabeds immediately offshore will affect the real time of tidal variations. This is not significant in most cases and can be corrected only by placing the measuring pole in deeper waters outside this zone, which is usually not practical.
4. Impounding of water due to offshore bars and/or islands: The measuring rod or tidal gauge should be placed outside the area thus affected. Tidal variation measurements taken where impoundment occurs will be worthless for reducing soundings.

Location of the tide-measuring device is extremely important in acquiring meaningful data for the reduction of soundings. Accurate time records of these measurements are essential for correlation with the actual time of each sounding.

## 16.6   Position-Fixing Techniques

The location of the survey vessel in the horizontal plane when a particular sounding has been measured is a fundamental requirement for the hydrographic survey. Directional control of the vessel along the sounding lines is an important factor for ensuring that the survey area is covered sufficiently to meet the specifications.

Before discussing each position-fixing technique, some generalities in this field should be recognized. Three overall methods of position-fixing techniques are described in this section: manual, electronic, and GPS. The manual operations involve more basic equipment, such as theodolites, sextants, and the like, as well as larger field crews for taking and recording the large number of visual readings necessary. The electronic techniques involve more sophisticated equipment and correspondingly smaller field crews because many of the readings are recorded automatically. GPS techniques include differential GPS (DGPS) for submeter precision and real-time kinematic (RTK) for centimeter precision (useful in engineering works).

The factors governing the selection of the technique to be used relate primarily to the location of the site, the complexity of the site area, the volume of data to be collected, and the necessity of collecting similar data over the same area on a weekly, monthly, or seasonal basis. Also keep in mind that the electronic devices are rapidly becoming easier to operate, and they provide greater accuracies and are more easily available. You should be familiar with the manual techniques for two main reasons. First, an understanding of these techniques is essential if one recognizes the need for comprehending completely the basic requirements for position-fixing. Second, these techniques are still used regularly for local projects that are limited in scope.

## 16.6.1 Double-Sextant Angles Observed from the Vessel

Simultaneous horizontal sextant angles are observed among three shore stations, as illustrated in Figure 16.5. The accuracies attained at distances from shore of between 200 m and 7 km depend largely on the operator's experience, which is an important factor. At 200 m offshore, an accuracy of 0.5 m can be realized. At 7 km offshore, this level of precision could well become 10 to 30 m.

The vessel should be equipped with a plotting board and appropriate equipment for fixing the position of the sounding as soon as the two angles have been read by the observers. A 360° protractor with three legs pivoting about the center point, as illustrated in Figure 16.6, can be constructed easily. Setting the angles between the three legs to match the observed sextant angles and then placing all three legs on the plotting sheet over the shore stations observed ensures that the position of the vessel is at the center of the protractor. Because it is common to allow an interval of one minute between position fixes, the operator of this plotting instrument (sometimes called a station pointer) should be able to read the depth and plot the fix and depth within this period.

The vessel is kept on the course, predetermined by the sounding plan (see Section 16.7), through a combination of compass bearings and minor course corrections after each

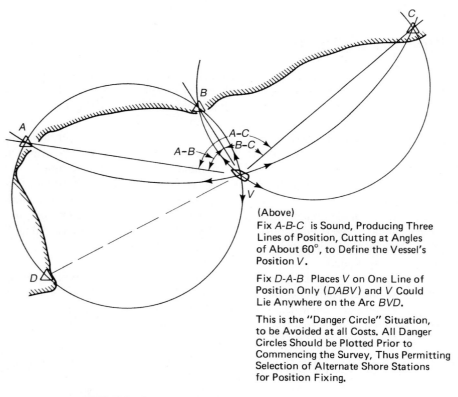

(Above)
Fix *A-B-C* is Sound, Producing Three Lines of Position, Cutting at Angles of About 60°, to Define the Vessel's Position *V*.

Fix *D-A-B* Places *V* on One Line of Position Only (*DABV*) and *V* Could Lie Anywhere on the Arc *BVD*.

This is the "Danger Circle" Situation, to be Avoided at all Costs. All Danger Circles Should be Plotted Prior to Commencing the Survey, Thus Permitting Selection of Alternate Shore Stations for Position Fixing.

**FIGURE 16.5** Double-sextant method.

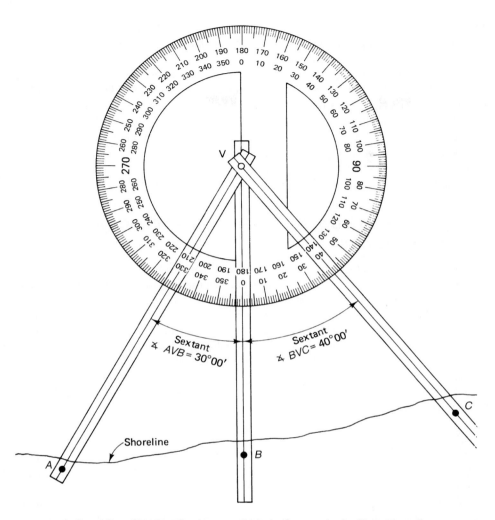

A, B and C are Shoreline Stations on which the Sextant Angles Shown have Been Observed. The Location of Each Station is Accurately Plotted on Mylar and the Fix is Carried Out on the Vessel At "V".

Three Clear Plastic Strips with Center Marking Lines as Shown Above are Pivoted About the Center Point of the Protractor.

**FIGURE 16.6** Station pointer for double-sextant angle-fixing.

fix is plotted. Continuous plotting of fixes onboard the vessel thus ensures the intended coverage of the sounding area with the least number of soundings, which results in maximum efficiency. The survey team requirements are normally met by four persons: the driver of the vessel, two sextant angle observers, and a plotter and depth recorder.

The sextant angle observers should stand close together and be positioned over the depth-measuring instrument to minimize positioning errors. Immediately after reading the sextant angle for one fix, each observer should realign the sextant with the shore stations and keep the images constantly superimposed. This method ensures correct readings at any time that a fix is requested by the driver.

Each sextant angle should be between 20° and 110°. To ensure further the accuracy of the fix, the sum of the two angles should exceed 50°. The danger circle occurs when the vessel and all three shore stations lie on the circle's perimeter. This situation must be avoided because the boat's position may lie at any point on the circle and is therefore indeterminate. Figure 16.5 illustrates this situation using shore stations *D, A,* and *B.* When the vessel is on or near this circle, an alternative shore station, such as *C,* should be used to solve the problem. All danger circles should be preplotted before commencing the survey. Although outdated, this technique is included to provide perspective.

## 16.6.2   Intersection from Theodolite Stations on Shore

The position of the vessel is determined by two simultaneous horizontal angles measured by theodolites set up on shore stations (three shore stations provide for error analysis). The theodolites are zeroed on any station that is part of the horizontal control network. As the boat proceeds along the sounding lines, the theodolite observers track the vessel's path, sighting a target on the boat mounted over the echo-sounder. At the instant that a fix is required, the boat driver raises a prearranged signal or gives a radio signal; the sounding is recorded on the vessel; and each shore observer records the measured angle. Each fix is numbered consecutively in the field notes by both theodolite operators and the echo-sounder reader in the vessel. Plotting of the fixes is undertaken after the data from the vessel and the shore station have been correlated.

## 16.6.3   Plotting of Data

The fix numbers and, if necessary, the recorded times should be compiled by the survey team after completion of a maximum of four range lines or 50 fixes. At this time, the farthest points offshore on each sounding line should be plotted to ensure that the spacing between the lines satisfies the specifications. The plotting of fixes using this technique is time consuming at best. Positioning of a properly oriented 360° protractor over each theodolite station and a leg fixed at the center of each accelerates the plotting of the angle intersection points. The plotting apparatus is therefore constructed like the station pointer (see Figure 16.6). Two protractors, each having two legs, are required, rather than one protractor with three legs, as illustrated in the figure. Alternately, the use of total stations permits the computation of sighted location coordinates.

## 16.6.4   Known Range Line and Single Angle

The range line markers control the course of the vessel, as shown in Figure 16.7. The fix is obtained by taking a horizontal angle from shore with a theodolite or from the vessel using a sextant. The latter is preferable for the reasons stated in Section 16.6.2. A three-person team is required: a boat driver using range poles for line, a sextant angle observer, and an

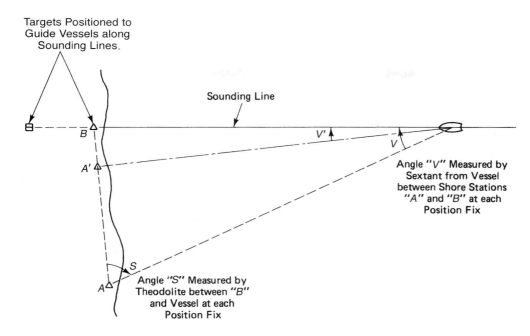

Targets Positioned to Guide Vessels along Sounding Lines.

Sounding Line

Angle "*V*" Measured by Sextant from Vessel between Shore Stations "*A*" and "*B*" at each Position Fix

Angle "*S*" Measured by Theodolite between "*B*" and Vessel at each Position Fix

Note: If Shore Station Located at *A'* Instead of *A*, Angle *V'* is less than 10° thus Reducing Accuracy of Fix Below Acceptable Survey Standards.

Only One of the Two Angles Shown is Required for the Position Fix, that is <u>Either</u> "*S*" <u>or</u> "*V*."

**FIGURE 16.7** Range line and single angle.

echo-sounder reader. Two lines are normally fixed, and the targets are then moved as the work progresses.

This method is usually restricted to within 3 km (approximately 2 miles) of the shoreline, depending on the size of the targets and the size of the horizontal angles. The accuracy of the fix drops below normally acceptable standards when the angle from the vessel is below 10°. This should be considered in the location of the shore stations, a topic discussed in Section 16.8.

## 16.6.5   Constant Vessel Velocity

The vessel travels at a constant velocity between two shore stations. After an initial trial run to determine the optimum speed, soundings are taken at regular time intervals varying from 15 s to 60 s, depending on the level of detail required for the survey. The boat is kept on course by a team member situated at the station being approached by the vessel. The line of sight between the two stations on the line is visual, and signal flags are used for direction. Therefore, the accuracy and reliability of location along the line may vary between points due to unavoidable variations in vessel velocity. The distances offshore from the stations at each end of the lines where the boat starts and stops should be measured. A driver and echo-sounder reader are also required. If the sounder has an automatic read-out, only two persons are required for the survey team. This method is particularly applicable to lake surveys and centerline profiles of rivers and streams, as illustrated in Figure 16.8.

It is usually important to locate the deepest areas in lake surveys because these areas may be missed in the original sounding line layout. Cruising the lake at higher vessel velocities or sweeping (see Section 16.6.8) while constantly monitoring the soundings locates deep areas as well as shoals. With the use of GPS techniques, the need for constant speed is now less important.

## 16.6.6   Intersecting Range Lines

This method is used when it is necessary to repeat the soundings at the same points. The determinations of dredging quantities and of changes in the bottom due to scour of silt or sand are two common applications.

Fixed range lines are established on shore and are located to intersect as closely as possible to right angles, as shown in Figure 16.9. The shore stations are permanently marked, usually by iron bars driven into the ground, mortared stone cairns, or painted crosses on bedrock. Targets are erected over the shore stations during the survey and are stored for reuse.

The boat proceeds to the intersection and takes the sounding, as required. A common difficulty is keeping the vessel stationary long enough to obtain an accurate sounding at the intersection point, particularly under strong wind conditions. It is therefore advisable to use a boat capable of good maneuverability at low speeds. The point of intersection should be approached into the direction of the wind.

Poor weather conditions must be anticipated using this method because the depth measurements are taken at preselected intervals: monthly, weekly, and so on. Since the surveyor cannot wait for more suitable weather conditions and the soundings must be compared with previous readings, the following procedure is useful:

1. Swells caused by wave action mean that the sounding referred to the mean water level or mean low-water level could be in error by as much as half the wave height. This error will be minimized by recording at least three soundings at both the wave crest and the wave trough, and averaging the figures. The vessel may have to reapproach the intersection point each time to avoid rapid drifting.

2. Strong winds blowing in one direction for periods of over 24 hours will cause the mean water level to rise or lower during and after this period. The resulting error in all soundings taken under these conditions must be corrected. Permanent marking of the mean datum elevation should be established, preferably on a shoreline having a slope toward the water of over 25%. This will minimize the error caused by breaking waves offshore. The change in water level is measured with a graduated rod. Take the average of the trough and crest readings, and compare this average to the mean datum elevation. All soundings are corrected accordingly.

3. Tidal variations, discussed in Section 16.5.2, must be accounted for in addition to the preceding considerations.

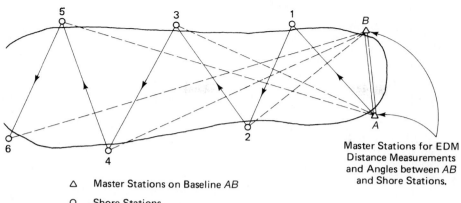

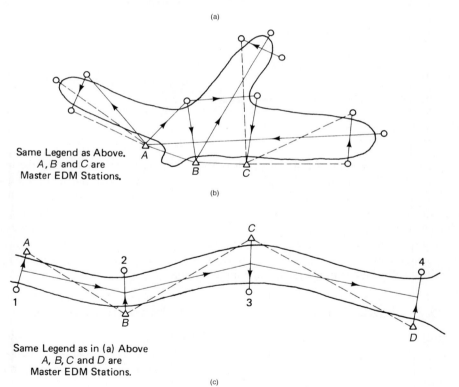

**FIGURE 16.8** Layout for constant vessel velocity soundings. (a) Inland lake with regular shoreline. (b) Inland lake with irregular shoreline. (c) River.

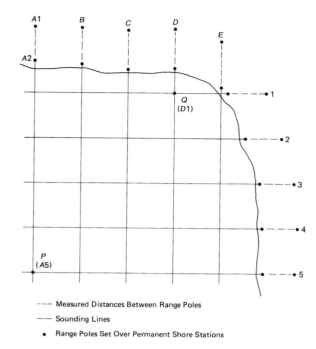

**FIGURE 16.9** Intersecting range lines.

--- Measured Distances Between Range Poles

— Sounding Lines

• Range Poles Set Over Permanent Shore Stations

Position of "Q" Located with Greater Accuracy than "P"
due to Proximity of Shoreline Stations.
Position Fixes Designated by Letter + Number System,
for Example "P" is "A5" and "Q" is "D1."

The precision of this method depends primarily on the success of locating the intersection points. This, in turn, depends on the distance between the two range poles at each shore station, as shown in Figure 16.9. The desired level of accuracy for surveys of this type is 1:1,000. To achieve this accuracy, experience and practice have shown that the offshore distance to the point of intersection (A2 to P) should not be greater than 10 times the distance between the two range poles (A1 to A2). This factor is often limited by existing land uses on shore and/or shoreline topography. When GPS is used to locate positions, soundings will be taken more quickly and more accurately.

## 16.6.7 Electromagnetic Position-Fixing Systems

Electromagnetic position-fixing (EPF) systems determine the vessel's location by the intersection of a minimum of two range distances measured to shore stations (distances 1 and 3, Figure 16.10). The systems are classified into short-, medium-, and long-range based on the different characteristics of radio-wave propagation used. Each is described briefly, but greater emphasis is placed on the short-range systems because these tools are more commonly available to the hydrographic surveyor and they also provide greater accuracies. The wavelengths used penetrate through rain, thus making these systems relatively weather-independent.

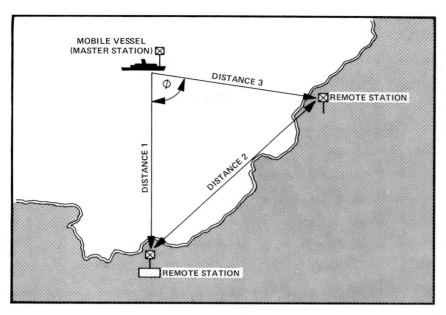

**FIGURE 16.10** Tracking of a remote mobile unit. The base station calculates the position of the vessel using the distance shown. Master measures to two remote stations (distances 1 and 3). The distance between remotes is measured using standard survey techniques (distance 2).

Before discussing any EPF system, the various motions of the vessel should be considered. **Roll** (sideways movement), **pitch** (stern to bow movement), **heave** (vertical displacement), **yaw** (sideways displacement), and combinations thereof are present except for the rare condition of **dead calm seas.** Consequently, the antenna on the vessel masthead is subject to constant movement, which affects the accuracy of the position determination.

Short-range (up to 70 km offshore) and medium-range (up to 700 km offshore) systems are described together due to the similarities in equipment, operation, and environmental effects. (See Figures 16.11 and 16.12.) Long-range systems are discussed briefly; GPS systems are described in Chapter 11.

### 16.6.7.1 Practical considerations
The majority of areas where hydrographic surveying is to be undertaken involves aboveground natural or built features along the shoreline. The microwave signals are transmitted in large angular cones. Published cone sizes or beamwidths by manufacturers are not to be taken as the limit of the signal. The chances for reflections from these shoreline features are significant; thus, they have the potential of causing errors. Consequently, the proper selection of shore remote stations and certain operational procedures becomes critical. Signal fading due to atmospheric conditions; cancellations, commonly known as range holes; and multipath effects are discussed next. In addition, the applications and selections of range-range versus range-angle techniques are discussed.

Figure 16.13 presents a situation not uncommon in areas requiring hydrographic surveys. Reflections of the carrier beams by the water, the ground surface near the ray paths,

**FIGURE 16.11** Setup of a microwave range/angle shore station. In this case, a Microfix unit is mounted on the theodolite. On the vessel, an identical Microfix is typically mast-mounted. (Courtesy of Telefix Canada, Markham)

**FIGURE 16.12** Pulse-type transponder, the key component at the master station. (Courtesy of Davis Canada Engineering Products)

and/or buildings (as illustrated in Figure 16.13) cause position-fixing errors. These effects are commonly known as **multipath.** Due to the beamwidth, the outer portions of the beams are reflected by the earth's surface and nearby objects. Random reflections caused by ships, buildings, topographic features, and surface water conditions can be factors in hydrographic surveying, particularly in harbors. Gross effects can occur, and the surveyor should examine the geometry of the remote and master stations.

As mentioned previously, some components of a received signal are reflected and therefore travel a longer path than that of the direct beam. However, if the difference in path lengths equals an even number of half-wavelengths of the carrier wave, the energy content of that beam component cancels that of the direct beam. The net effect is the lack

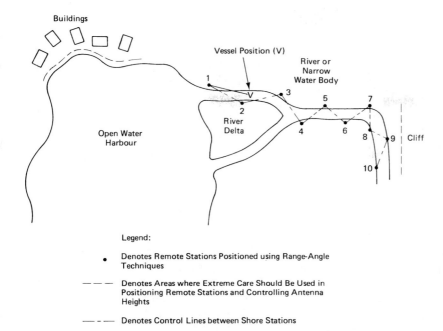

Legend:

●    Denotes Remote Stations Positioned using Range-Angle Techniques

— — —    Denotes Areas where Extreme Care Should Be Used in Positioning Remote Stations and Controlling Antenna Heights

— - —    Denotes Control Lines between Shore Stations

**FIGURE 16.13**   Reflection due to natural and built features and example of range-angle technique applications.

of any distance reading, commonly known as range holes, cancellation zones, or signal fade. The position of these zones or holes can be calculated using formulas provided in the manufacturer's operating manual. The two most critical variables are antenna height and carrier frequency. The carrier frequency is usually fixed within a small range. Consequently, it may be necessary to adjust initial antenna heights correctly to prevent cancellation zones falling within the intended survey area. Antenna heights may also have to be adjusted during the survey as the operating area changes location to avoid these same effects. Newer systems and adaptations to older systems provide much greater flexibility now because of antenna design improvements. See also Section 16.6.8, which describes the use of GPS in hydrographic positioning.

Based on the angular limitations at the vessel illustrated in Figure 16.10, weak triangular configurations, sometimes called triangles of uncertainty, are usually present within the survey area offshore. On many coastlines, it is not possible to position remote stations to maintain proper triangle configuration. Therefore, if accuracy is important, consider placing one or more of the remote stations farther inland or onboard a solidly moored vessel or other offshore platform. For example, the angle $\varphi$ in Figure 16.10 should be between 30° and 150°.

Under certain conditions, a series of remote stations must sometimes be placed progressively along the coast or river shoreline, mainly to increase survey efficiency, as illustrated by stations 1 to 10 inclusive in Figure 16.13. Thus, the vessel may proceed without delay instead of waiting while one set of remote stations is removed and repositioned.

Weather conditions, primarily the refractive index of air, affect instrument accuracy, and can cause errors as much as 40 ppm. This index depends on the prevailing atmospheric pressure, temperature, and humidity along the beam path. It is normal practice to measure these variables periodically at each end of the line, average the results, and make the necessary measurement corrections using charts or nomographs supplied by the manufacturer. Certain weather conditions are not favorable for accurate measuring. One example is a warm offshore wind, which will disproportionately distort the effects of normal air temperatures over the water. Under normal weather conditions, this is not a concern, particularly for small-range systems, because the 40 ppm becomes a very small measurement error.

The position of the vessel is usually determined by the two or more distances, or the multirange method. For example, this technique would be used in the open-water harbor shown in Figure 16.13. Hydrographic surveying along narrow bodies of water, such as rivers, requires a different approach, known as the range-angle method. The remote station locations shown in Figure 16.13 are located close to the banks to minimize vegetation cutting for clear lines of site. The stations are located using angle and distance, and using the type of instrument setup illustrated over a theodolite (see Figure 16.11).

As the vessel proceeds along the river, it is located by determining the distance 1–V and the angle V–1–2, as illustrated in Figure 16.13. This method requires a master station aboard the vessel, constant tracking of the vessel by the theodolite, and a prearranged signal system or time interval for fixing. The remote stations are usually prelocated, and several units are set up in groups and then moved farther along as the survey proceeds.

Improvements are continuously being made to merge range-range and range-angle systems. Therefore, the operator can select the most efficient system using the same computer hardware. Also, several range-angle approaches have been designed for adaptation to older equipment. These approaches provide for totally manual to completely automatic techniques. Loran-C is still used by many pleasure crafts and ships because receivers are available at reasonable prices. Hydrographic charts that display Loran-C Lettices are still produced. The navigator can use them to plot position.

**16.6.7.2 Long-range systems** The permanent long-range EPF systems are more useful for navigation than for hydrographic surveying. Worldwide coverage is available using eight stations, transmitting at wavelengths approximately 100 times those of the short-range systems. The system is known as Omega, and a vessel can expect to be positioned within 2 km (approximately 1.3 miles). Therefore, the applications are primarily navigational and are used for very preliminary location surveys for marine features such as areas having sufficient water depths for large oil tankers.

## 16.6.8   Hydrographic Surveying and the Global Positioning System (GPS)

As noted in Chapter 11, this remarkable positioning development is revolutionizing the way we determine our geographical location at any moment in time. Its impact on marine positioning and navigation will probably be even greater than on land-based surveys. Marine positioning involves few obstructions to the reception of the satellite signals, and the electronic nature of the technology permits simultaneous capture of position, headings, and sounding data.

**FIGURE 16.14**  Leica GPS antenna and receiver on a small craft, providing positioning data for echo-soundings in a differential kinematic mode. The data collector here is a notebook computer. (Courtesy of Leica Inc. and Swissair Photo-surveys Ltd.)

Figure 16.14 shows a small craft using differential GPS techniques to record river-sounding positions. The same equipment used with newly developed handheld total stations (see Figure 16.15 ) permits simultaneous collection of positioning, sounding, and shoreline details. Various commercial data collectors can be used for this multi-technology data capture. A notebook computer with three serial ports would be particularly useful; onboard applications software can be expanded to include layout capabilities for marine construction, thus giving the user a very powerful surveying capability.

As we noted in Chapter 11, the U.S. Coast Guard has created the DGPS system, which enables coastal, Great Lakes, and major river radio beacons to transmit differential GPS code corrections continuously to an unlimited number of working surveyors and sailors—within ranges of 100 km to 400 km. Canada has a similar service for its coastal regions. Surveyors working onboard ships can use the radio beacon transmissions (in the worldwide RTCM standard) with onboard GPS receivers to locate themselves to within submeter accuracy, and to provide a differential speed accuracy of about 0.1 knot. The Radio Technical Commission for Maritime Services, Special Committee 104 (RTCM SC-104), which created standards for DGPS transmission, has also created RTK messages; because their length is almost double that available from equipment manufacturers, the current trend is to utilize the manufacturers' standards for RTK radio transmission. Trimble Inc. has released a compact measurement record (CMR) for general use to encourage more efficient base station data transfer.

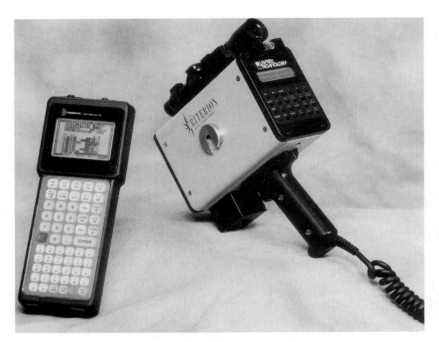

(a)

**FIGURE 16.15** (a) Criterion handheld survey laser #300, with data collector; angles by flux-gate compass; and distances without a prism to 1,500 ft (to 40,000 ft with a prism). This instrument is used to collect data with an accuracy of ±0.3° and ±0.3 ft. for mapping and GIS data bases. It provides a good extension for canopy-obstructed GPS survey points. (Courtesy of Laser Technology Inc., Englewood, Colorado)

Figure 16.16 shows an L1-frequency C/A code, 6-channel GPS receiver. Other receivers have as many as 12 channels, and some dual-frequency receivers can also process carrier observations, which allows for real-time kinematic (RTK) surveys (1 cm accuracy in position and 0.5 m/s accuracy in differential speed) when they are referenced to shore-based receivers radio-transmitting differential corrections. Current RTK radio transmitters have a range of only 10 to 20 km. Most receivers require five or more satellites to accomplish initialization quickly. After initialization, the survey can continue with just four satellites. Postprocessed solutions are also available by utilizing the differential data transmitted by the dual-frequency CORS stations (see Sections 11.8 and 11.9).

For areas outside the DGPS range, manufacturers have developed base stations (single- and dual-frequency) capable of tracking 12 channels of continuous code and carrier data at a rate of 0.5 seconds, with accuracies of 10 cm for code and 0.005 m for carrier observations. These base stations can transmit differential corrections using RTCM standards (for code corrections) to onboard receivers. As noted earlier, when transmitting carrier data, radios have a range of 10 m to 20 km.

(b)

**FIGURE 16.15 (continued)** (b) Prosurvey 1000 handheld survey laser: used (without prisms) to record distances and angles to survey stations. Shown here being used to determine river width in a hydrographic survey. (Courtesy of Laser Atlanta, Norcross, Georgia)

Onboard considerations for hydrographic surveying include the measurement from the mast-mounted GPS antenna to the GPS receiver on the bridge, and from there to the sounding transducer on the hull. If the distance from the antenna to the receiver is greater than 30 m, an amplifier may be needed to boost the signals. Another consideration is the applications software, which should be capable of performing all needed processing and the linking of all peripheral electronic equipment. For example, Trimble Inc. HYDRO software can link positioning with electronic sensors such as echo-sounders, compasses, tide gauges, sidescan sonar, and acoustic positioning. Additional modules include contouring, profiles, volumes, and digitizing. This software also displays an electronic chart of the area showing the planned range lines together with the location (distance in feet or meters right or left of the range line) and the heading of the vessel. Figure 16.17 is a screen display showing the vessel on sounding line CH00140. The vessel is 1.1 m off-line to the right. Also shown are the point coordinates (latitude/longitude) and a displayed depth of roughly 26½ m.

It is possible to mount two separate GPS receivers on large survey vessels to reduce the effects of sounding errors caused by the roll, pitch, heave, and yaw of the vessel. Hydrographic maps are now giving way to onboard electronic charts. As new data on soundings, tides, currents, etc., are collected into a central database, the upgraded data can

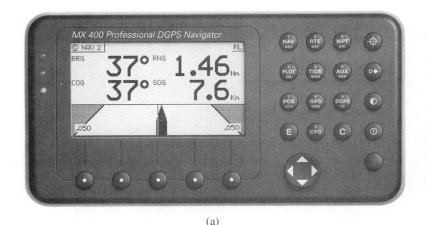

(a)

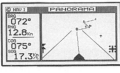

(b)

**FIGURE 16.16** (a) Receiver. (b) Typical displays. Leica MX400 DGPS Navigator—a single-frequency, 6-channel GPS receiver equipped with an optional DGPS beacon receiver. Positions can be displayed as latitude/longitude, Loran-C, Decca and UTM. (Courtesy of Leica Geosystems, Norcross, Georgia)

then be transferred electronically to a vessel to update that vessel's electronic chart, giving it some real-time characteristics.

### 16.6.9 Sweeping

**Sweeping** is the term applied to taking additional soundings to locate underwater features in areas not covered by the original sounding plan. Figure 16.18 illustrates the problem. The isonified area of the seabed below the echo-sounder is proportional to the water depth. As discussed in Section 16.5.1, the cone beneath the transducer of the echo-sounder is approximately 30°. Consequently, the shallower depths along the sounding lines $A$ and $B$ in Figure 16.18 leave a gap between the two lines that has not been sounded. As illustrated, an important seabed feature can be missed during the survey. A gap exists between lines $B$ and $C$, while the area between lines $C$ and $D$ is covered adequately.

The difficulty comes from the fact that the surveyor does not know the water depths until the survey is completed. Therefore, the sweeping operation is the last requirement of the project. Areas requiring sweeping must be identified. Using the cone of 30° beneath the echo-sounder, depths less than 1.85 times the distance between the sounding lines may require sweeping. For example, if the sounding lines are 50 m (165 ft) apart, depths less than 93 m (305 ft) will have gaps. At the discretion of the surveyor, extra sounding lines may be used to sound the gaps. The same position-fixing techniques employed during the survey, as illustrated in solution (b) of Figure 16.18, are used. A cost-effective compromise

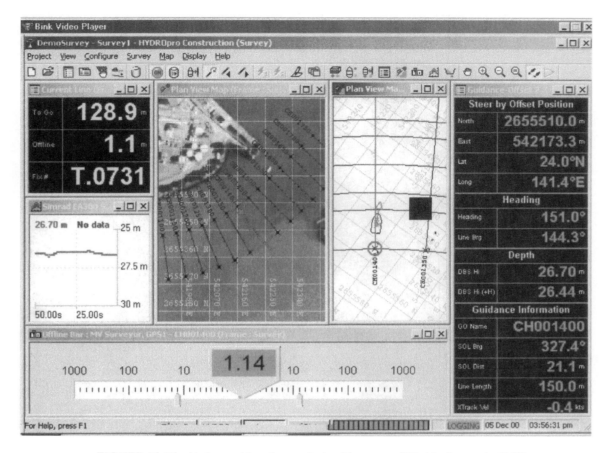

**FIGURE 16.17**  Hydrographic software display. (Courtesy of Trimble, Sunnyvale, Calif.)

involves running the vessel at higher speeds parallel to the shoreline in sounding out lines to the depths where coverage is ensured. See solution (c) of Figure 16.18. Note the location of any depth anomalies, and position-fix only these unusual occurrences.

Improvements to sweeping include (1) using an array of transducers that are lowered from booms projecting from the sides of the vessel—each transducer can obtain depth measurements every second, all of which are logged; and (2) using swath sounders to give a fan-shaped acoustic beam. This latter technique is a side-scan sonar that can detect the angle of arrival of incoming acoustic energy.

## 16.7   Sounding Plan

The most economical coverage of the seabed is achieved through a series of equally spaced sounding lines over the survey area. Specific considerations are:

- Appropriate scale of the survey.

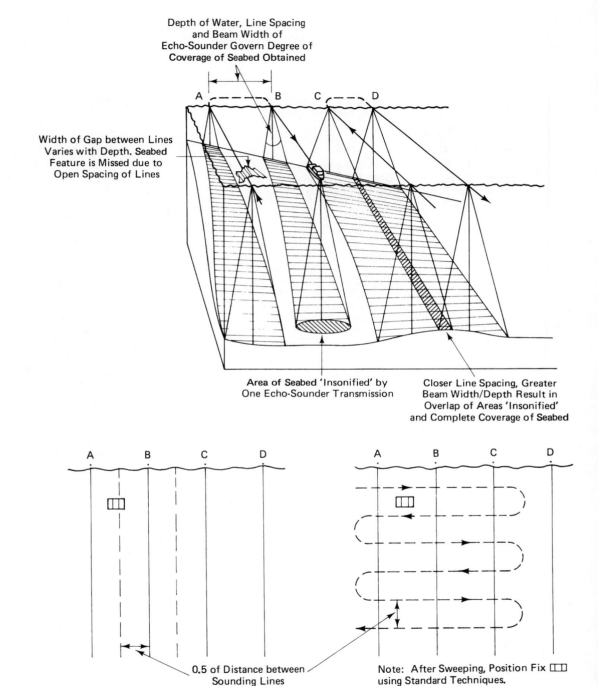

Depth of Water, Line Spacing
and Beam Width of
Echo-Sounder Govern Degree of
Coverage of Seabed Obtained

Width of Gap between Lines
Varies with Depth. Seabed
Feature is Missed due to
Open Spacing of Lines

Area of Seabed 'Insonified' by
One Echo-Sounder Transmission

Closer Line Spacing, Greater
Beam Width/Depth Result in
Overlap of Areas 'Insonified'
and Complete Coverage of Seabed

0.5 of Distance between
Sounding Lines

Note: After Sweeping, Position Fix ▭▭
using Standard Techniques.

**FIGURE 16.18**   Sweeping to ensure complete seabed coverage.

- Spacing between the sounding lines and their orientation with the shoreline.
- Interval between fixes along a sounding line.
- Speed of the vessel.
- Direction in which the sounding lines are run.

The scale of the survey is set by the degree of thoroughness and the precision of the soundings. Therefore, the scale determines the number of sounding lines and fixes along each line. Depending on the preceding factors, scales for surveys within 5 km (approximately 3 miles) from the shoreline range between 1:1,000 (1 in. = ±83 ft) and 1:20,000 (1 in. = ±1,666 ft). The distance between the sounding lines is based on the rule that it should not exceed 10 mm or 1 cm (approximately 0.4 in.) on the drawing. Therefore, at a scale of 1:1,000, the lines should not be greater than 5,000 × 0.01 m, or 50 m apart.

The Canadian Hydrographic Service's line spacing is a half centimeter (0.005) at any scale, for example:

$$1:20,000 \text{ line spacing} = 100 \text{ m}$$
$$1:10,000 \text{ line spacing} = 50 \text{ m}$$
$$1:5,000 \text{ line spacing} = 25 \text{ m}$$
$$1:1,000 \text{ line spacing} = 5 \text{ m}$$

Drop the two zeros and divide by 2 to learn the line spacing.

The speed of the vessel during sounding is determined by the realistic assumption that the time interval between fixes will be a minimum of 1 minute. For a scale of 1:5,000, the speed of the vessel would be 7 km/h (approximately 4 knots).

The sounding lines are run in a direction that is nearly at right angles with the direction of the depth contours. The effects of geological conditions, offshore bars, and the like, as discussed in Section 16.3.7, should be considered in determining the most efficient and economical direction for the angle of the sounding lines with the shoreline.

The sounding plan shown in Figure 16.19 illustrates these principles. In addition, the location of shore stations for using the double-angle sextant method (see Section 16.6.1) is shown, as well as the required ties to the horizontal control network, which is discussed in Section 16.8.

Trial lines, also known as check lines, are usually run in the area to be surveyed to determine the best sounding pattern for the existing bottom conditions. Soundings may be taken on parallel lines, radiating lines, and grid lines in both directions—that is, any pattern that will ensure complete bottom coverage.

## 16.8  Horizontal Control

The specific considerations of target design and location are discussed in Section 16.3.4. The overall control survey system should meet the specifications set out in Chapter 10. If a provincial or state control survey system has been established, the hydrographic shore stations should be tied to the overall system using trilateration, triangulation, supplementary traverses, or GPS positioning. For example, in Figure 16.19, shore station numbers 2, 5, and 10 should be tied accurately to control stations *A, B,* and *C,* respectively. Shore stations 2, 5, and 10 should be monumented to provide for hydrographic resurvey possibilities in

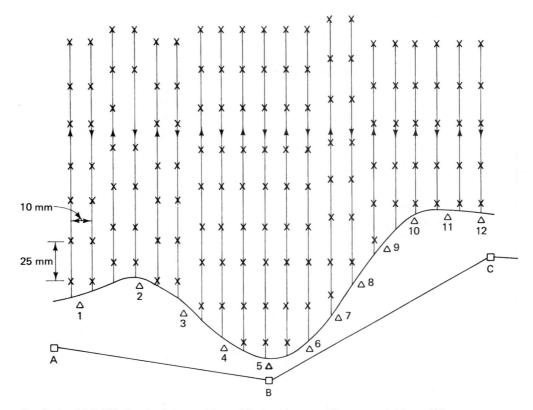

For Scale of 1:5,000, Spacing between Line = 50 m and between Fixes on each Line = 125 m

△ Shoreline Stations Placed to Satisfy Sextant Angle Requirements from Each Fix: Also in Linear Pattern along Shoreline to Minimize Occurrence of Danger Circles in Offshore Sounding Area.

□ Overall Horizontal Control System: May be Established Provincial/State Coordinate System Monuments or Traverse set up for Particular Hydrological Survey being Conducted. Shoreline Stations Tied to Control System and Coordinated to Required Accuracy.

**FIGURE 16.19**  Sounding plan and shore stations for double-sextant method.

the future. This low cost of monumenting will pay large dividends because you can avoid repeating the connections with the overall control system.

The other shoreline stations should be tied to stations 2, 5, and 10 using less accurate survey methods. Normally, 1:5,000 or 1:3,000 precision techniques will suffice. Because the shoreline itself provides some horizontal control to the survey, it requires special consideration. Shorelining depends on (1) the nature of the coast, (2) the range of the tide, and (3) the scale of the survey. The shoreline can be located using aerial surveys, helicopter/GPS surveys, existing base maps and topographic maps, a coastline traverse, and even stadia surveys for small harbors.

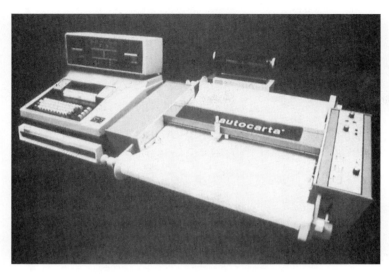

**FIGURE 16.20**  Computer-based data acquisition and processing system with real-time plotting. (Courtesy of Racal Decca Survey, Inc., Houston, Texas)

## 16.9  Processing and Presentation of Data

Prior to commencing the fieldwork for manual surveys, the sounding plan is drawn to the desired scale, similar to that illustrated in Figure 16.19. This plan should show accurately the location of all shore stations and each sounding line. Ideally, the plotting of individual fixes and depth should take place in the vessel immediately after the information has been acquired, as previously discussed. Electronic and GPS-based data capture, being digital in nature, permit the storage of the data in the computer, and permit the presentation to be provided by digital plotters or in electronic chart formats.

Tidal variations above or below the chosen datum are recorded against time to provide the information necessary in obtaining the reduced soundings. The soundings are then corrected on the plan, and the reduced sounding is shown in brackets beside the field sounding. If a constant-recording echo-sounder is used, the tidal variations are marked directly on the trace, and the reduced soundings are subsequently read directly from the trace. If depth contours are required, they are obtained through interpolation between the individual reduced soundings and plotted on the plan.

Several automatic plotting instruments, such as that illustrated in Figure 16.20, have been developed. These are computer-based data acquisition and processing systems for offshore survey operations. A visual plot of all information must be analyzed before leaving the survey area.

## 16.10  Airborne Laser Bathymetry

In the past few years, airborne laser bathymetry (ALB) has become operational in the field of shallow-water hydrographic surveying. Most systems employ two spectral bands: one to detect the water surface (1,064 nm infrared band) and the other to detect the bottom (532

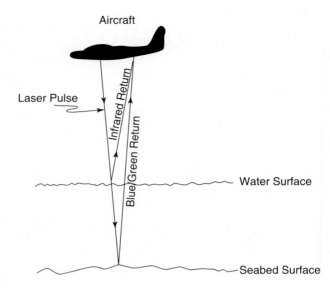

Aircraft

Laser Pulse

Infrared Return

Blue/Green Return

Water Surface

Seabed Surface

**FIGURE 16.21** Airborne laser bathymetry (ALB) depth measurement.

nm blue/green band). The depth of the water is determined from the time difference of laser returns reflected from the surface and from the seabed. See Figure 16.21. Although this technology is still in its infancy, it is predicted that its short mobilization times (compared to shipboard echo-sounding), efficient area coverage, lower costs, and relatively fast processing of data, will make it the mainstay of shallow-water bathymetry.

The ability to penetrate water depends to a high degree on the clarity of the water. Very turbid water may permit penetration of only a few meters, and clear water may permit penetration up to 30 or 40 meters, or more. Typical shallow-water lidar surveys are operated from helicopters or fixed-wing aircraft flying at 200 meters altitude and at speeds of between 60 and 120 knots (110 to 220 km/hr). They collect depth-soundings on a four-meter horizontal grid, giving the position accurate to 3 meters horizontally and 15 cm vertically (when controlled by GPS measurements). See the SHOALS website at http://sam.usae.army.mil/op/shoals/pages/airborne.htm.

ALB can produce more effective coverage of shallow water soundings because, given the altitude of the lidar instrument package, the cone of signal emissions has the room to spread and thus to cover consistently a much wider area of the seabed than can conventional launch-based multibeam echo-sounders, which are operating on the surface of the water. The shallower the water, the more pronounced is this advantage. In very shallow water, the launch-based multibeam echo-sounder can cover only a very narrow swath of seabed and runs the continual risk of hull-bottom damage.

# Problems

**16.1** Calculate the reduced sounding for each of the conditions tabulated below.

| | Depth using echo sounder | Tidal height above (+) or below (−) chart datum | Error due to weather conditions above (+) or below (−) tidal water level at time of sounding |
|---|---|---|---|
| (a) | 10.2 m | +1.5 m | −0.3 m |
| (b) | 15.7 m | −0.8 m | +0.5 m |
| (c) | 32.7 ft | +3.8 ft | −1.4 ft |
| (d) | 50.2 ft | −2.3 ft | −1.8 ft |

**16.2** Using a transparent overlay, plot the locations of shoreline stations 3 through 7 in Figure 16.19. Draw the danger circle for stations 4, 5, and 6. Identify the sounding locations, from those shown in Figure 16.19, that are on or close to the danger circle. Number the sounding locations affected and tabulate the three shore stations that should be used to position-fix each of these points.

**16.3** The reduced soundings for each of the offshore sounding points illustrated in Figure 16.9 are tabulated below in meters (the equivalent depth in feet is given in parentheses).

| Location | Depth | Location | Depth | Location | Depth |
|---|---|---|---|---|---|
| A1 | 1.3 (4.3) | B4 | 5.4 (17.8) | D2 | 1.5 (4.9) |
| A2 | 3.0 (9.9) | B5 | 5.6 (18.4) | D3 | 2.3 (7.6) |
| A3 | 5.0 (16.5) | C1 | 0.8 (2.6) | D4 | 2.0 (6.6) |
| A4 | 7.0 (23.1) | C2 | 2.0 (6.6) | D5 | 1.8 (5.9) |
| A5 | 8.7 (28.5) | C3 | 3.3 (10.8) | E2 | 0.6 (2.6) |
| B1 | 1.0 (3.3) | C4 | 3.5 (12.5) | E3 | 1.1 (3.6) |
| B2 | 2.5 (8.2) | C5 | 3.5 (12.5) | E4 | 0.9 (3.0) |
| B3 | 4.0 (13.2) | D1 (Q) | 0.6 (2.6) | E5 | 1.2 (3.9) |

(a) If the horizontal distance between adjacent points (for example, B1 and B2) on the sounding grid is 50 m, plot the soundings at a scale of 1:2,000. (If the Imperial system is used, use a horizontal distance of 150 ft between points and plot at a scale of 1 in. = 200 ft)

(b) Determine and plot the location of the depth contours through interpolation. Assume the water elevation to be zero. Use 1-m contour intervals (3 ft for the Imperial system).

**16.4** For sweeping an area with additional soundings, calculate the maximum depth at which there would be no gaps in the original soundings if the sounding lines are 30 m (100 ft) apart.

**16.5** Calculate the minimum distances between sounding lines and the intervals between fixes along a line for each of the following drawing scales:
(a) 1:2,000
(b) 1 in. = 100 ft

**16.6** State which type of electromagnetic position-fixing system you would use for the following circumstances and give three main brief reasons for your selection.

Accuracy requirements: ±0.25 m (0.8 ft)
Maximum distance offshore: 10 km (6 mi)

**16.7** Figure F.1 is a hydrographic map compilation of the lower Niagara River. See also Figures 12.12 (aerial image) and 12.13 (satellite image), which show the same general geographic area. Compare and contrast the information available from this hydrographic map with the information available from the remotely sensed images. List the general uses to which each of these same-area, images can be put.

# APPENDIX A  Random Errors

## A.1  General Background

When a very large number of measurements is taken to establish the value of a specific dimension, the results will be grouped around the true value, much like the case of the range target illustrated in Figure A.1. When all systematic errors and mistakes have been removed from the measurements, the residuals between the true value (dead center of the bull's-eye) and the actual measurements (shot marks) will be due to random errors.

The rifle target shown in Figure A.1 illustrates some of the characteristics of random errors:

- Small random errors (residuals) occur more often than large random errors.
- Random errors have an equal chance of being plus (right) or minus (left).

The number of rifle shots hitting the left and right side of each ring are shown in the ring frequency summary. These results are then plotted directly below in the form of a bar chart called a histogram. You can see that the probability of any target shot hitting a ring (or half-ring) is directly proportional to the area of the histogram rectangles. For example, the probability of one of the target shots hitting the bull's-eye (for a specific rifle and specified conditions) is $(28 + 27)/265 = 0.21$ (or 21%).

Table A.1 shows that the total of the ring probabilities is, of course, unity. Geometrically, it can be said that the area under the probability curve is equal to 1, and the probability that an error (residual) falls within certain limits is equal to the area under the curve between those limits. The probabilities for the hits in each ring are shown calculated in Table A.1. For example, given the same conditions (that is, the same precision rifle and same range conditions) as when the shots in Figure A.1 were fired, one would expect that 40% of all future rifle shots would hit the middle two rings $(0.208 + 0.192 = 0.400)$.

Any discussion of probability and probable behavior implies that a very large (infinite) number of observations have been taken. The larger the number of observations, the closer the results will conform to the laws of probability. In the example used, if the number of rifle shots were greatly increased and the widths of the rings greatly narrowed, the

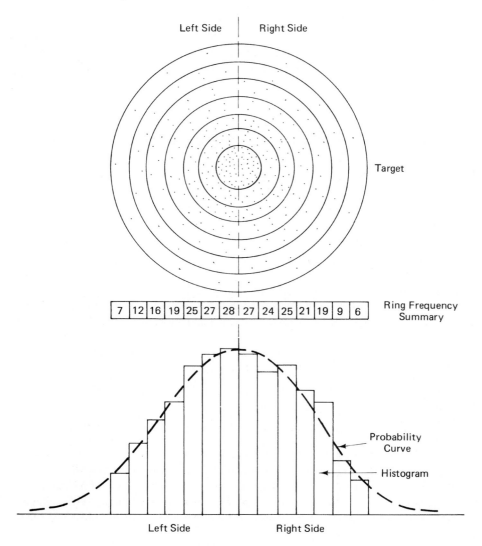

**FIGURE A.1**   Range target: 265 shots on target.

resultant plot would take the form of a smooth, symmetrical curve known as the probability curve. This curve is shown superimposed on the histogram in Figure A.1.

In surveying, you cannot take a large number of repetitive measurements. But if you use survey techniques that normally give results that, when plotted, take the form of a probability curve, it is safe to assume that the errors associated with the survey measurements can be treated using random error distribution techniques.

Before leaving the example of the rifle target shot distribution, it is worthwhile to consider the effect of different precisions on the probability curve. If a less precise rifle (technique) is used, the number of shots hitting the target center will be relatively small,

**Table A.1** TARGET RING PROBABILITIES

| Ring number | Probability |
|---|---|
| 1 (bull's-eye) | $\dfrac{28 + 27}{265} = 0.208$ |
| 2 | $\dfrac{27 + 24}{265} = 0.192$ |
| 3 | $\dfrac{25 + 25}{265} = 0.189$ |
| 4 | $\dfrac{19 + 21}{265} = 0.151$ |
| 5 | $\dfrac{16 + 19}{265} = 0.132$ |
| 6 | $\dfrac{12 + 9}{265} = 0.079$ |
| 7 | $\dfrac{7 + 6}{265} = 0.049$ |
| | Total  1.000 |

and the resultant probability curve [see Figure A.2(a)] will be relatively flat. On the other hand, if a more precise rifle (technique) is used, a larger number of shots will hit the target center and the resultant probability curve will be much higher [see Figure A.2(b)], indicating that all the rifle shots are grouped more closely around the target center.

If the sights of the high-precision rifle were out of adjustment, the target hits would consistently be left or right of the target center. The shape of the resulting probability curve would be similar to that shown in Figure A.2(b), except that the entire curve would be shifted left or right of the target center plot point. This situation illustrates that precise methods can give inaccurate results if the equipment is not adjusted properly.

## A.2   Probability Curve

The probability curve shown in Figure A.1 and A.2 has the following equation:

$$y = \frac{1}{\sigma\sqrt{2\pi}} e^{-v^2/2\sigma^2} \tag{A.1}$$

where $y$ is the ordinate value of a point on the curve (frequency of a residual of size occurring); $v$ is the size of the residual; $e$ is the base of natural logarithms (2.718); and $\sigma$ is a constant known as the standard deviation or standard error, a measure of precision. Since $\sigma$ is associated with an infinitely large sample size, the term **standard error (SE)** will be used when analyzing finite survey repetitions.

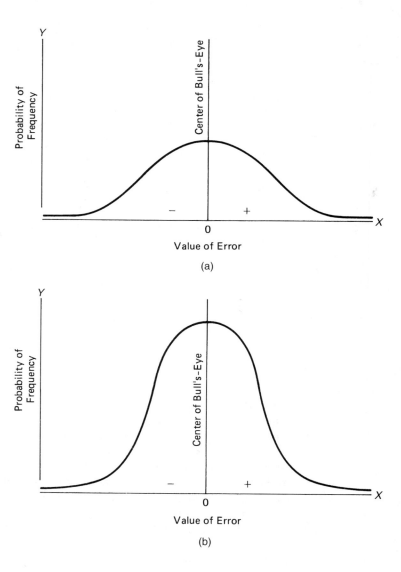

**FIGURE A.2** Precision comparisons. (a) Probability curve for target results from a low-precision rifle. (b) Probability curve for target results from a high-precision rifle.

## A.3 Most Probable Value

In the preceding section, the concept of a residual ($v$) was introduced. A residual is the difference between the true value or location (for example, a bull's-eye center) and the value or location of one occurrence or measurement. When the theory of probability is applied to survey measurements, the residual is in fact the error, that is, the difference between any field measurement and the true value of that dimension. In Section 1.13, the topic of errors was first introduced. It was noted that the true value of a measurement was never known, but that for the purpose of calculating errors, the arithmetic mean was taken to be the true, or most probable, value. Since we do not have large (infinite) numbers of repetitive measurements in surveying, the arithmetic mean will itself contain an error (discussed later as the error of the mean):

$$\text{Mean:} \qquad \bar{x} = \frac{\Sigma x}{n} \qquad\qquad (A.2)$$

where $\Sigma x$ is the sum of the individual ($x$) measurements, and $n$ is the number of individual measurements.

## A.4 Standard Error

We saw in Figure A.2 that precision can be depicted graphically by the shape of the probability curve. In statistical theory, precision is measured by the standard deviation (also called standard error or root mean square error). Theoretically:

$$\sigma = \pm\sqrt{\Sigma v^2/n} \qquad\qquad (A.3)$$

where $\sigma$ is the standard deviation of a very large sample, $v$ is the true residual, and $n$ is the very large sample size. Practically:

$$\text{SE} = \pm\sqrt{\Sigma v^2/(n-1)} \qquad\qquad (A.4)$$

where SE is the standard error of a set of repetitive measurements; $v$ is the error ($x - \bar{x}$), and $n$ is the number of repetitions. Since the use of $\bar{x}$ ($\bar{x}$ = mean) instead of the true value always results in an underestimation of the standard deviation, ($n - 1$) is used in place of $n$. The term ($n - 1$) is known in statistics as degrees of freedom and represents the number of extra measurements taken. That is, if a line were measured 10 times, it would have 9 ($10 - 1$) degrees of freedom. Obviously, as the number of repetitions increases, the difference between $n$ and ($n - 1$) becomes less significant. The concepts just described are being used increasingly to define and specify the precision of various field techniques.

As we noted earlier, the arithmetic mean contains some uncertainty; this uncertainty can be expressed as the standard error of the mean ($\text{SE}_m$). The laws of probability dictate that the error of a sum of identical measurements be given by the error multiplied by the square root of the number of measurements: $\text{SE}_{sum} = \text{SE}\,\sqrt{n}$. The mean (standard error) is given by the sum divided by the number of occurrences; therefore:

$$\text{SE}_m = \frac{\text{SE}\,\sqrt{n}}{n} = \frac{\text{SE}}{\sqrt{n}} \qquad\qquad (A.5)$$

This expression shows that the standard error of the mean is inversely proportional to the square root of the number of measurements; that is, if the measurement is repeated by a factor of 4, the standard error of the mean is cut in half. This relationship demonstrates that, beyond a realistic number, continued repetitions of a measurement do little to reduce uncertainty.

Many instrument manufacturers now specify the precision of their equipment by stating the standard error associated with the equipment use. The terms **standard error, standard deviation,** and **mean square error (MSE)** are all used to specify the identical concept of precision.

## A.5 Measures of Precision

Figure A.3 shows the SE, 2SE, and 3SE plotted under the probability curve. It can be shown that the area under the curve between the limits shown is as follows:

$$\bar{x}(\text{mean}) \pm 1\text{SE} = 68.27\% \text{ of area under the curve}$$

$$\bar{x}(\text{mean}) \pm 2\text{SE} = 95.46\% \text{ of area under the curve}$$

$$\bar{x}(\text{mean}) \pm 3\text{SE} = 99.74\% \text{ of area under the curve}$$

We saw in Section A.1 that the area under the probability curve is directly proportional to the probability of expected results. The preceding relationship can be restated by noting that the probability of measurements deviating from the mean is as follows:

$$
\left.\begin{array}{l} 68.27\% \\ 95.46\% \\ 99.74\% \end{array}\right[ \quad \text{of all measurements will be in range of} \quad \left.\begin{array}{l} \bar{x}(\text{mean}) \pm \text{SE} \\ \bar{x}(\text{mean}) \pm 2\text{SE} \\ \bar{x}(\text{mean}) \pm 2\text{SE} \end{array}\right]
$$

A term used in the past, **probable error,** was the 50% error (that is, the limits under the curve representing 50% of the total area). Those limits are $\pm 0.6745$ SE. Today's surveyors are more interested in the concept of maximum anticipated error, which varies from 90% to the 95% probability limits.

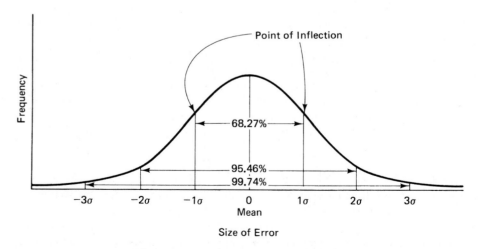

**FIGURE A.3** Graph of probability curve showing standard errors.

| Error | Certainty (%) | |
|---|---|---|
| Probable (0.6745 SE) | = 50% | (A.6) |
| Standard (SE) | = 68.27% | |
| 90% (1.6449 SE) | = 90% | (A.7) |
| 95% (1.9599 SE) | = 95% | (A.8) |

## A.6 Illustrative Problem

To illustrate the concepts introduced thus far, consider the data in Table A.2. The results of 15 measurements of a survey baseline are shown together with the probability computations. It is assumed that all systematic errors have already been removed from the data.

### PROBABILITY COMPUTATIONS

1. Mean (most probable value), $\bar{x} = \Sigma x/n = 3994.612/15 = 266.3075$ m (Equation A.2)
2. Standard error, $SE = \sqrt{\Sigma v^2/(n - 1)} = \sqrt{0.0003565/15} = 0.0050$ m (Equation A.4)
3. Standard error of the mean, $SE_m = SE/\sqrt{n} = 0.0050/\sqrt{15} = 0.0013$ m (Equation A.5)
4. Probable error (50% error) $= 0.6745\ SE = 0.0034$ m (Equation A.6)

**Table A.2** ANALYSIS OF RANDOM DISTANCE ERRORS ($v = x - \bar{x}$)

| $n$ | Distance $x$ (m) | Residual, $v$ | $v^2$ |
|---|---|---|---|
| 1 | 266.304 | −0.0035 | 0.0000123 |
| 2 | 266.318 | +0.0105 | 0.0001103 |
| 3 | 266.312 | +0.0045 | 0.0000203 |
| 4 | 266.304 | −0.0035 | 0.0000123 |
| 5 | 266.313 | +0.0055 | 0.0000303 |
| 6 | 266.307 | −0.0005 | 0.0000003 |
| 7 | 266.309 | +0.0015 | 0.0000023 |
| 8 | 266.303 | −0.0045 | 0.0000203 |
| 9 | 266.301 | −0.0065 | 0.0000423 |
| 10 | 266.305 | −0.0025 | 0.0000063 |
| 11 | 266.302 | −0.0055 | 0.0000303 |
| 12 | 266.310 | +0.0025 | 0.0000063 |
| 13 | 266.314 | +0.0065 | 0.0000423 |
| 14 | 266.307 | −0.0005 | 0.0000003 |
| 15 | 266.303 | −0.0045 | 0.0000203 |
| | $\Sigma x = 3994.612$ | $\Sigma v = -0.0005$ | $\Sigma v^2 = 0.0003565$ |

5. 90% error = 1.6449 SE = 0.0082 m (Equation A.7)
6. 95% error = 1.9599 SE = 0.0098 m (Equation A.8)

The following observations are taken from the data in Table A.2:

1. The most probable distance is 266.308 m.
2. The standard error of any one measurement is ±0.005 m.
3. The standard error of the mean is ±0.001 m; that is, there is a 68.27% probability that the true length of the line lies between 266.308 ± 0.001m. There is a 90% probability that the true length of the line lies between 266.308 ± 0.002 m (0.0013 × 1.6449 = 0.002). There is a 95% probability that the true length of the line lies between 266.308 ± 0.003 m (0.0013 × 1.9599 = 0.00254).
4. With the probable error (50%) at ±0.0034, it is expected that half of the 15 measurements will lie between 266.308 ± 0.003 (from 266.305 to 266.311). In fact, only 5 (⅓) measurements fall in that range.
5. With the 90% error at ±0.008, it is expected that 90% of the measurements will lie between 266.308 ± 0.008 (from 266.300 to 266.316). In fact, 93% (14 out of 15) fall in that range.
6. With the 95% error at ±0.098, it is expected that 95% of the measurements will lie between 266.308 ± 0.0098 (from 266.298 to 266.318). In fact, all the measurements fall in that range.

Note that expected frequencies are entirely valid only for randomly distributed data. When the number of observations is small, as is the case in surveying measurements, you will often encounter actual data that are marginally inconsistent with predicted frequencies. If the field data differ significantly from probable expectations, however, it is safe to assume that the data are unreliable, due either to untreated systematic error or to undetected mistakes. As a rule of thumb, measurements that fall outside the range of $\bar{x}$ ± 3.5 SE (see Figure A.3) either are rejected from the set of measurements or are repeated in the field.

## A.7 Propagation of Errors

This section deals with the arithmetic manipulation of values containing errors (for example, sums, products, etc.).

### A.7.1 Sums of Varied Measurements

The sum of any number of measurements that have individual mean and SE values is determined as follows. If distance $K$ is the sum of two distances, $A$ and $B$, then:

$$\text{SE}_K = \sqrt{\text{SE}_A^2 + \text{SE}_B^2} \tag{A.9}$$

■ **EXAMPLE A.1**
If distance $A$ were found to be 101.318 ± 0.010 m and distance $B$ were found to be 87.200 ± 0.008 m, what is the distance $K$ $(A + B)$?

**Solution**

Use Equation A.9:

$$SE_K = \sqrt{0.010^2 + 0.008^2} = 0.013 \text{ m} \qquad (A.9)$$
$$K = 188.518 \pm 0.013 \text{ m}$$

### ■ EXAMPLE A.2

If from the preceding data, distance $L$ is the **difference** in the two distances $A$ and $B$, then find the value of $L$.

**Solution**

Use Equation A.9:

$$SE_L = \sqrt{SE_A^2 + SE_B^2}$$
$$= \sqrt{0.010^2 + 0.008^2} = \pm 0.013$$
$$L = (101.318 - 87.200) \pm 0.013$$
$$= 14.118 \pm 0.013 \text{ m}$$

### ■ EXAMPLE A.3

If the difference in elevation between two points is determined by taking two rod readings, each having an SE of 0.005 m, what is the SE of the difference in elevation?

**Solution**

Use Equation A.9 or Equation A.10:

$$SE \text{ (diff. of elev.)} = \sqrt{0.005^2 + 0.005^2} = 0.007 \text{ m}$$

or

$$SE \text{ (diff. of elev.)} = 0.005 \sqrt{2} = 0.007 \text{ m}$$

## A.7.2   Sums of Identical Measurements

The sum of any number of measurements, each one having the same SE, is as follows:

$$SE_{sum} = \sqrt{n \times SE^2}$$
$$SE_{sum} = SE \sqrt{n} \qquad (A.10)$$

### ■ EXAMPLE A.4

A distance of 700.00 ft is laid out using a 100.00-ft steel tape that has an SE = 0.02 ft. Find the standard error of the 700.00-ft distance.

**Solution**

Use Equation A.10:

$$0.02 \sqrt{7} = 0.05 \text{ ft}$$

## A.7.3 Products of Measurements

The product of any number of measurements that have individual SE values can be given by the following relationship:

$$SE_{product} = \pm\sqrt{A^2 SE_B^2 + B^2 SE_A^2}$$ (A.11)

where A and B are the dimensions to be multiplied.

### ■ EXAMPLE A.5

Consider a rectangular field having $A = 250.00$ ft $\pm 0.04$ ft and $B = 100.00$ ft $\pm 0.02$ ft. Find the area of the field and the SE of the area.

**Solution**

Use Equation A.11:

$$SE_{product} = \pm\sqrt{250^2 \times 0.02^2 + 100^2 \times 0.04^2}$$
$$= \pm 6.40 \text{ ft}$$

$$\text{Area of field} = 250 \times 100 = 25,000 \pm 6 \text{ ft}^2$$

## A.8 Weighted Observations

If the reliability of different sets of measurements varies one to the other, then equal consideration cannot be given to those sets. Some method (weighting) must be used to arrive at a best value. For example, measurements may be made under varying conditions, by people with varying levels of skills, and they may be repeated a varying number of times.

## A.8.1 Weight by Number of Repetitions

The simplest concept of weighted values can be illustrated by the following method, where the weighted mean is calculated. A distance was measured six times; the values obtained were 6.012 m, 6.011 m, 6.012 m, 6.012 m, 6.011 m, and 6.013 m. The value of 6.012 was observed three times; 6.011, two times; and 6.013, one time.

| Distance, $x$ | Weight, $w$ | $x \times w$ |
|---|---|---|
| 6.012 | 3 | 18.036 |
| 6.011 | 2 | 12.022 |
| 6.013 | 1 | 6.013 |
| | $\Sigma w = 6$ | $\Sigma xw = 36.071$ |

$$\text{Weighted mean} = \frac{36.6071}{6} = 6.012 \text{ m}$$

That is:

$$\bar{x}_w = \frac{\Sigma\, xw}{\Sigma w} \tag{A.12}$$

where $\bar{x}_w$ is the weighted mean, $x$ is the individual measurement, and $w$ is the weight factor.

If the distance had been measured six times and six different results had occurred, each measurement would have received a weight of 1, and the computation would simply be the same as for the arithmetic mean.

## A.8.2  Weight by Standard Error of the Mean ($SE_m$)

The standard error of the mean $SE_m$ was introduced in Section A.4. This measure tells us about the reliability of a measurement set and supplies a weight for the mean of a set of measurements. A set with a small $SE_m$ should receive more weight than a set with a large (less precise) $SE_m$. We saw from Equation A.5:

$$SE_m = \frac{SE}{\sqrt{n}}$$

that the error varies inversely with the square root of the number of measurements; it is also true that the number of measurements varies inversely with the $SE_m^2$.

In the previous section, we saw that weights were proportional to the number ($n$) of measurements; that is, generally:

$$W_k \;\alpha\; \frac{1}{SE_k^2} \tag{A.13}$$

## A.8.3  Adjustments

When the absolute size of an error is known, and when weights have been assigned to measurements having varying reliabilities, corrections to the field data will be made so that the error is eliminated by applying corrections that reflect the various weightings. It is obvious that measurements having large weights will be corrected less than measurements having small weights. (The more certain the measurement, the larger the weight.) It follows that correction factors should be in inverse ratio to the corresponding weights.

■ **EXAMPLE A.6**

The angles in a triangle were determined—with $A$ being measured three times, $B$ being measured two times, and $C$ being measured once—for a closure error of 20″. What are the correction factors and the adjusted angles?

**Solution**

The correction factor is simply the inverse of the weight, and the actual correction for each angle is simply the ratio of the correction factor to the total correction factor, all multiplied by the total correction. See Table A.3.

**Table A.3** ANGLE ADJUSTMENTS USING WEIGHT FACTORS

| Angle | Mean value | Weight | Correction factor | Correction | Adjusted angle |
|-------|-----------|--------|-------------------|------------|----------------|
| A | 45°07′32″ | 3 | 1/3 = 0.33 | 0.33/1.83 × 20 = +4 | 45°07′36″ |
| B | 71°51′06″ | 2 | 1/2 = 0.50 | 0.50/1.83 × 20 = +5 | 71°51′11″ |
| C | 63°01′02″ | 1 | 1 = 1.00 | 1/1.83 × 20 = +11 | 63°01′13″ |
| | 179°59′40″ | | 1.83 | 20 | 179°59′60″ |
| | | | | | = 180°00′00″ |

Error = −20″     Correction = +20″

## ■ EXAMPLE A.7

Consider the same angles, except in this case the weights will be related to the SE characteristics of three different theodolites. What are the correction factors and the adjusted angles?

**Solution**

See Table A.4.

**Table A.4** ANGLE ADJUSTMENTS USING SE[a]

| Angle | Mean value | SE | (SE²) Correction factor | Correction | Corrected angle |
|-------|-----------|-----|-------------------------|------------|-----------------|
| A | 45°07′34″ | ±0.50″ | 0.25 | 0.25/29.25 × 20 = 0 | 45°07′40″ |
| B | 71°51′06″ | ±2.00″ | 4.00 | 4/29.25 × 20 = 3 | 71°51′09″ |
| C | 63°01′00″ | ±5.00″ | 25.00 | 25/29.25 = 17 | 63°01′17″ |
| | 179°59′40″ | | 29.25 | 20 | 179°59′60″ |
| | | | | | = 180° |

Error = −20″     Correction = +20″0

[a]In this case Equation A.13 was used.

## ■ EXAMPLE A.8   *Adjustment of a Level Loop*

Errors are introduced into level surveying each time a rod reading is taken. It stands to reason that corrections to elevations in a level loop should be proportional to the number of instrument setups (that is, the weights should be inversely proportional to the number of instrument setups). Furthermore, since there is normally good correlation between the number of setups and the distance surveyed, corrections can be applied in proportion to the distance surveyed. (If a part of a level loop were in unusual terrain, corrections could then be proportional to the number of setups.) What are the correction factors and the adjusted elevations?

**Solution**

Consider Table A.5, where temporary benchmarks (TBMs) are established in the area of an interchange construction (see also Figure A.4).

**Table A.5**  ELEVATION ADJUSTMENTS USING WEIGHT FACTORS

| Station | Elevation | Number of setups between stations | Correction factor | Corrected elevation |
|---|---|---|---|---|
| BM 506 | 172.865 (fixed) | | | 172.865 |
| TBM A-1 | 168.303 | 5 | 5/16 × 0.011 = 0.003 | 168.306 |
| TBM A-2 | 168.983 | 2 | 7/16 × 0.011 = 0.005 | 168.988 |
| TBM A-3 | 170.417 | 2 | 9/16 × 0.011 = 0.006 | 170.423 |
| BM 506 | 172.854 | 7 | 16/16 × 0.011 = 0.011 | 172.865 |
| | | 16 | | |

$$\text{Error} = 172.854 - 172.865 = -0.011 \text{ m}$$

$$\text{Correction} = +0.011 \text{ m}$$

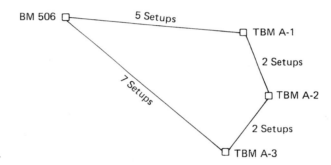

**FIGURE A.4**  Level loop adjustment.

## A.9  Principle of Least Squares

The data in Table A.2 showed that the smaller the sum of the squared errors, $\Sigma (x - \bar{x})^2$, the more precise will be the data (that is, the more closely the data are grouped around the mean $\bar{x}$). If such data were to be assigned weights, it is logical to weight each error $(x - \bar{x})$ so that the sum of the squares of the errors is a minimum. This is the principle of least squares: $\Sigma \, Wa \, (x - \bar{x})^2$ is a minimum.

The development of the principle of least squares and the adjustments based on that principle can be found in texts on surveying adjustments. For a least squares adjustment to be valid, a reliable estimate of the SEs of various measuring techniques must be available to identify the individual weights properly.

## A.10  Two-Dimensional Errors

The concept of two-dimensional errors was first introduced in Section 6.7 and Figure 6.12. When the concept of position is considered, two parameters ($x$ and $y$ or $r$ and $\theta$) must be analyzed. In Chapter 6, we saw that traverse closures were rated with respect to relative accuracies (1/5,000, or 1/10,000, etc.).

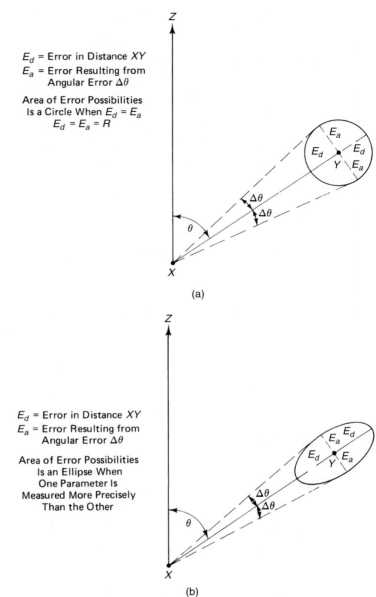

$E_d$ = Error in Distance $XY$

$E_a$ = Error Resulting from Angular Error $\Delta\theta$

Area of Error Possibilities Is a Circle When $E_d = E_a$

$$E_d = E_a = R$$

(a)

$E_d$ = Error in Distance $XY$

$E_a$ = Error Resulting from Angular Error $\Delta\theta$

Area of Error Possibilities Is an Ellipse When One Parameter Is Measured More Precisely Than the Other

(b)

**FIGURE A.5** Area of uncertainty. (a) Error circle. (b) Error ellipse.

Figure A.5(a) and (b) shows the two-dimensional concept, with an area of uncertainty generated by the uncertainty in distance ($\pm E_d$) in combination with the uncertainty ($E_a$) resulting from the uncertainty in angle $\pm\Delta\theta$. The figure of uncertainty is usually an ellipse with the major and minor axes representing the standard errors in distance and direction. When the distance and the direction have equal standard errors, the major axis equals the minor axis, resulting in a circle as the area of uncertainty, where $E_d = \sigma x$ and $E_a = \sigma y$; $r^2 = \sigma x^2 + \sigma y^2$ is the equation of such a circle of uncertainty. See Figure A.6.

In the previous discussion of one-dimensional accuracy, the probability that the true value was within $\pm 1\sigma$ (one standard deviation) was 68%. In the case of the standard ellipse ($r^2 = \sigma x^2 + \sigma y^2$), the probability that the true value is within the ellipse is 39%. If a larger probability is required, a constant $K$ is introduced so that:

$$(Kr)^2 = \sigma x^2 + \sigma y^2$$

represents the larger area (see Figure A.6). Values for $K$ are shown in Table A.6.

**Table A.6**

| Probability, $P(\%)$ | $K$ |
|---|---|
| 39.4 | 1.000 |
| 50.0 | 1.177 |
| 90.0 | 2.146 |
| 95.0 | 2.447 |
| 99.0 | 3.035 |
| 99.8 | 3.500 |

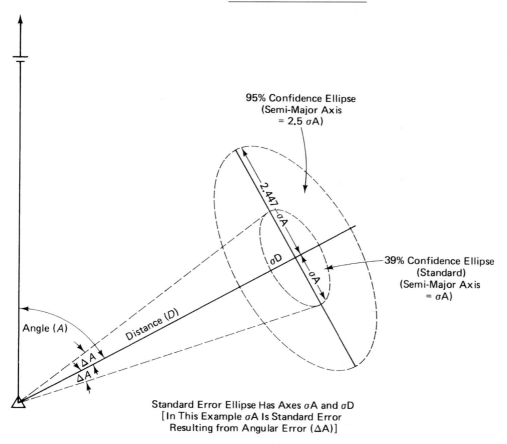

**FIGURE A.6**    Standard error ellipse and the 95% confidence ellipse.

## ■ EXAMPLE A.9

Assume that a station $(A)$ to be set for construction control is 450.00 ft from a control monument with a position accuracy of $\pm 0.04$ ft. What level of accuracy is indicated for angle and distance?

**Solution**

$$r = \pm 0.04 = \sqrt{\sigma x^2 + \sigma y^2}$$

Since this case represents a circle, $\sigma x = \sigma y$:

$$\pm 0.04 = \sqrt{2 \sigma x^2}$$

$$\sigma x = \frac{0.04}{\sqrt{2}} = 0.028 \text{ ft}$$

Therefore, for an error due to a distance measurement of 0.028, an accuracy of $0.028/450 = 1/16{,}000$ is indicated. And since the error due to angle measurement is also 0.028, the allowable angle error can be determined as follows:

$$\frac{0.028}{450} = \text{tan of the angle error}$$

Therefore, the allowable angle error is $\pm 0°00'13''$. Furthermore, at the 39.4% probability level, the distance must be measured to within $\pm 0.028$ ft; however, if we wish to speak in terms of the 95% level of probability that our point is within $\pm 0.04$ ft, we must use the $K$ factor (Table A.6 and Figure A.6) of 2.45. Thus, the limiting error is now:

$$\frac{0.028}{2.45} = 0.011 \text{ ft for both distance and angle}$$

The angle limit is given by $0.011/450 = \text{tan angle error}$. Therefore, the maximum angle error is now $\pm 0°00'05''$

# B Trigonometric Definitions and Identities

## B.1 Right Triangles

### B.1.1 Basic Function Definitions

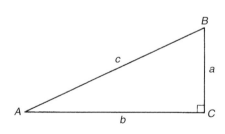

$$\sin A = \frac{a}{c} = \cos B \qquad (B.1)$$

$$\cos A = \frac{b}{c} = \sin B \qquad (B.2)$$

$$\tan A = \frac{a}{b} = \cot B \qquad (B.3)$$

$$\sec A = \frac{c}{b} = \operatorname{cosec} B \qquad (B.4)$$

$$\operatorname{cosec} A = \frac{c}{a} = \operatorname{cosec} B \qquad (B.5)$$

$$\cot A = \frac{b}{a} = \tan B \qquad (B.6)$$

### B.1.2 Derived Relationships

$$a = c \sin A = c \cos B = b \tan A = b \cot b = \sqrt{c^2 - b^2}$$

$$b = c \cos A = c \sin B = a \cot A = a \tan B = \sqrt{c^2 - a^2}$$

$$c = \frac{a}{\sin A} = \frac{a}{\cos B} = \frac{b}{\sin B} = \frac{b}{\cos A} = \sqrt{a^2 + b^2}$$

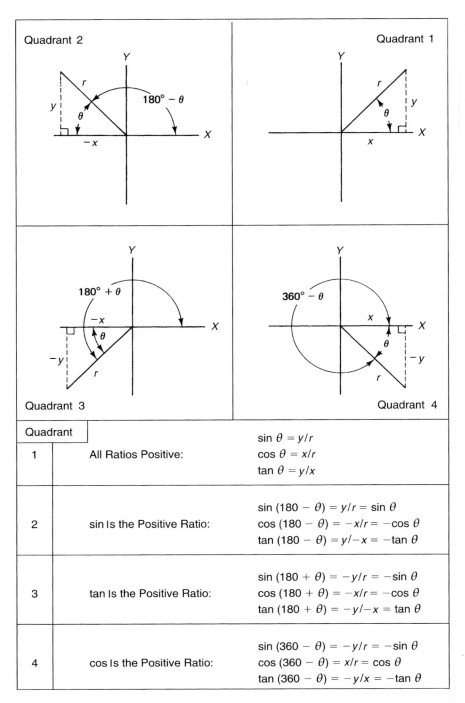

| Quadrant | | |
|---|---|---|
| 1 | All Ratios Positive: | $\sin \theta = y/r$ <br> $\cos \theta = x/r$ <br> $\tan \theta = y/x$ |
| 2 | sin Is the Positive Ratio: | $\sin (180 - \theta) = y/r = \sin \theta$ <br> $\cos (180 - \theta) = -x/r = -\cos \theta$ <br> $\tan (180 - \theta) = y/-x = -\tan \theta$ |
| 3 | tan Is the Positive Ratio: | $\sin (180 + \theta) = -y/r = -\sin \theta$ <br> $\cos (180 + \theta) = -x/r = -\cos \theta$ <br> $\tan (180 + \theta) = -y/-x = \tan \theta$ |
| 4 | cos Is the Positive Ratio: | $\sin (360 - \theta) = -y/r = -\sin \theta$ <br> $\cos (360 - \theta) = x/r = \cos \theta$ <br> $\tan (360 - \theta) = -y/x = -\tan \theta$ |

## B.2    Algebraic Signs for Primary Trigonometric Functions

The quadrant numbers reflect the traditional geometry approach (counterclockwise) to quadrant analysis. In surveying, the quadrants are numbered 1 (N.E.), 2 (S.E.), 3 (S.W.), and 4 (N.W.). The analysis of algebraic signs for the trigonometric functions (as shown) remains valid. Handheld calculators will automatically provide the correct algebraic sign if the angle direction is entered in the calculator in its azimuth form.

## B.3    Oblique Triangles

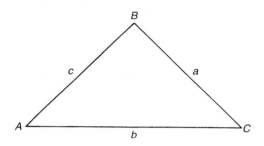

### B.3.1    Sine Law

$$\frac{a}{\sin A} = \frac{b}{\sin B} = \frac{c}{\sin C} \qquad (B.7)$$

### B.3.2    Cosine Law

$$a^2 = b^2 + c^2 - 2bc \cos A \qquad (B.8)$$

$$b^2 = a^2 + c^2 - 2ac \cos B \qquad (B.9)$$

$$c^2 = a^2 + b^2 - 2ab \cos C \qquad (B.10)$$

| Given | Required | Formulas |
|-------|----------|----------|
| $A, B, a$ | $C, b, c$ | $c = 180 - (A + B);\ b = \dfrac{a}{\sin A} \sin B;\ c = \dfrac{a}{\sin A} \sin C$ |
| $A, b, c$ | $a$ | $a^2 = b^2 + c^2 - 2bc \cos A$ |
| $a, b, c$ | $A$ | $\cos A = \dfrac{b^2 + c^2 - a^2}{2bc}$ |
| $a, b, c$ | Area | Area $= \sqrt{s(s - a)(s - b)(s - c)}$ where $s = \frac{1}{2}(a + b + c)$ |
| $C, a, b$ | Area | Area $= \frac{1}{2} ab \sin C$ |

## B.4 General Trigonometric Formulas

$$\sin A = 2 \sin \tfrac{1}{2}A \cos \tfrac{1}{2}A = \sqrt{1 - \cos^2 A} = \tan A \cos A \tag{B.11}$$

$$\cos A = 2 \cos^2 \tfrac{1}{2}A - 1 = 1 - 2 \sin^2 \tfrac{1}{2}A = \cos^2 \tfrac{1}{2}A$$
$$- \sin^2 \tfrac{1}{2}A = \sqrt{1 - \sin^2 A} \tag{B.12}$$

$$\tan A = \frac{\sin A}{\cos A} = \frac{\sin 2A}{1 + \cos 2A} = \sqrt{\sec^2 A - 1} \tag{B.13}$$

## B.5 Addition and Subtraction Identities

$$\sin (A \pm B) = \sin A \cos B \pm \sin B \cos A \tag{B.14}$$

$$\cos (A \pm B) = \cos A \cos B \pm \sin A \sin B \tag{B.15}$$

$$\tan (A \pm B) = \frac{\tan A \pm \tan B}{1 \pm \tan A \tan B} \tag{B.16}$$

$$\sin A + \sin B = 2 \sin \tfrac{1}{2}(A + B) \cos \tfrac{1}{2}(A - B) \tag{B.17}$$

$$\sin A - \sin B = 2 \cos \tfrac{1}{2}(A + B) \sin \tfrac{1}{2}(A - B) \tag{B.18}$$

$$\cos A + \cos B = 2 \cos \tfrac{1}{2}(A + B) \cos \tfrac{1}{2}(A - B) \tag{B.19}$$

$$\cos A - \cos B = 2 \sin \tfrac{1}{2}(A + B) \sin \tfrac{1}{2}(A - B) \tag{B.20}$$

## B.6 Double-Angle Identities

$$\sin 2A = 2 \sin A \cos A \tag{B.21}$$

$$\cos 2A = \cos^2 A - \sin^2 A = 1 - 2 \sin^2 A$$
$$= 2 \cos^2 A - 1 \tag{B.22}$$

$$\tan 2A = \frac{2 \tan A}{1 - \tan^2 A} \tag{B.23}$$

## B.7 Half-Angle Identities

$$\sin \frac{A}{2} = \sqrt{\frac{1 - \cos A}{2}} \tag{B.24}$$

$$\cos \frac{A}{2} = \sqrt{\frac{1 + \cos A}{2}} \tag{B.25}$$

$$\tan \frac{A}{2} = \sqrt{\frac{\sin A}{1 + \cos A}} \tag{B.26}$$

**absolute positioning**    Also called point positioning. The direct determination of a station's coordinates by receiving positioning signals from a minimum of four GPS satellites.

**absorption**    The process by which radiant energy is retained by a substance. The absorbing medium itself may emit energy, but only after an energy conversion has taken place.

**accuracy**    The conformity of a measurement to the "true" value.

**accuracy ratio**    The error in a measurement divided by the overall value of the measurement, expressed as a fraction with a numerator of 1 and a denominator rounded to the closest 100 units. For example, an error of .01 ft in 30.00 ft would result in an accuracy ratio of 1:3,000.

**active control station (ACS)**    *See* CORS.

**alignment**    The location of the centerline of a survey or a facility.

**ambiguity**    The integer number of carrier cycles between the GPS receiver and a satellite.

**area**    A GIS term describing a surface polygon having two dimensions, and enclosed by a set of lines or chains.

**arithmetic check**    A check on the reductions of differential leveling involving the sums of the backsights and the foresights.

**arterial road (highway)**    A road designed primarily for traffic mobility, with some property access consideration.

**as-built (final) surveys**    Postconstruction surveys that confirm design execution and record in-progress revisions.

**atmospheric window**    The ranges of wavelengths at which water vapor, carbon dioxide, and other atmospheric gases only slightly absorb radiation.

**automatic level**    A surveyor's level in which line of sight is maintained automatically in the horizontal plane, once the instrument is roughly leveled.

**azimuth**     The angle to a line of sight, measured clockwise (usually) from a north meridian.

**backsight (BS)**     A sight taken with a level to a point of known elevation, thus permitting the surveyor to compute the elevation of the HI. In transit work, the backsight is a sighting taken to a point of known position to establish a reference direction.

**baseline**     A line of reference for survey work; often the legal centerline, the street line, or the centerline of construction is used, although any line could be selected arbitrarily or established. In GPS, a baseline joins two GPS receivers engaged in relative positioning.

**batter boards**     Horizontal crosspieces on grade stakes or grade rods that refer to proposed elevations.

**bearing**     Direction of a line given by the acute angle from a meridian and accompanied by a cardinal compass direction.

**benchmark**     A fixed solid reference point with a precisely determined published elevation.

**borrow pit**     A source of fill material that is located off the right of way.

**break line**     A linear series of elevations that define a change in the slope of a surface. Examples are ridge lines, valley lines, top and bottoms of slope, ditch lines, etc.

**bucking-in (interlining)**     A trial-and-error technique of establishing a theodolite on a line between two points that themselves are not intervisible. Also known as *wiggling in.*

**catch basin**     A structure designed to collect surface water and transfer it to a storm sewer.

**central meridian**     A reference meridian in the center of the zone covered by the plane coordinate grid; at every 6 degrees of longitude in the UTM grid.

**circular curve**     A curve with a constant radius.

**clearing**     The cutting and removal of trees from a construction site.

**COGO (coordinate geometry)**     Software programs that facilitate coordinate geometry computations; used in surveying and civil engineering design.

**collector road (highway)**     A road designed to provide property access with some traffic mobility; it connects local roads to arterials.

**compound curve**     Two or more circular arcs turning in the same direction that have common tangent points and different radii.

**construction survey**     Provision of line and grade.

**contour**     A line on a map joining points of similar elevation.

**control surveys**     Surveys taken to establish reference points, elevations, and lines for preliminary and construction surveys.

**coordinates (plane)**     A set of numbers ($X, Y$) defining the two-dimensional position of a point, given by the distances measured north and east of an origin reference point having coordinates of (0, 0).

**CORS**    Continuously operating reference station (GPS). CORS transmitted data can be used by single-receiver surveyors or navigators to permit higher precision differential positioning.

**cross section**    A profile of the ground and surroundings taken at right angles to a reference line.

**culvert**    A structure designed to provide an opening under a road, etc., usually for the transportation of storm water.

**cut**    In construction, the excavation of material; also the measurement down from a grade mark.

**cycle slip**    A temporary loss of lock on satellite carrier signals causing a miscount in carrier cycles. Lock must be reestablished to continue positioning solutions.

**data collector**    An electronic field book designed to store field data—both measured and descriptive.

**datum**    An assumed or fixed horizontal reference plane.

**deflection angle**    The angle between the prolongation of the back line measured right (R) or left (L) to the forward line.

**departure**    The change in easterly displacement of a line ($\Delta E$).

**differential leveling**    Determining the differences in elevation between points using a surveyor's level.

**differential positioning (DGPS)**    Obtaining measurements at a known base station to correct simultaneous measurements made at rover receiving stations.

**diurnal**    Something occurring over 24 hours (that is, during one rotation of the earth).

**doppler effect**    The apparent change in frequency of sound or light waves varying with the relative velocities of both the source and the observer; if the source and the observer come closer together, the emitted frequency appears to be increased.

**double centering**    A technique of turning angles or producing straight lines involving a minimum of two sightings with a theodolite: once with the telescope direct and once with the telescope inverted.

**drainage**    The collection and transportation of ground- and storm water.

**DTM (digital terrain model)**    A three-dimensional depiction of a ground surface, usually produced by computer software (sometimes referred to as a DEM—digital elevation model).

**DXF (drawing exchange format)**    An industry-standard format that permits graphical data to be transferred among various CAD, GIS, and soft-copy photogrammetry applications programs.

**EDM**    Electronic distance measurement.

**EFB**    Electronic field book. *See* Data collector.

**elevation**    The vertical distance above or below a given datum; also known as *orthometric height*.

**elevation factor**  The factor used to convert ground distances to sea-level distances.

**end area**  The area of a cross section. When the areas of two adjacent station cross sections are averaged and then multiplied by the distance between them, the volume of cut or fill between those stations is determined.

**engineering surveys**  Preliminary and layout surveys used for design and construction.

**eolian**  Surface features or materials created by the wind.

**EOS (earth observing system)**  NASA's study of the earth scheduled to cover the period 2000 to 2015, in which a series of small to intermediate earth observation satellites will be launched to measure global changes. The first satellite (experimental) in the series (TERRA) was launched in 1999.

**epoch**  An observational event in time that forms part of a series of GPS observations.

**error of closure**  The difference between the measured location and the theoretically correct location.

**ETI$^+$ (enhanced thematic mapper)**  An 8-band multispectral scanning radiometer, onboard Landsat 7, that is capable of providing relatively high resolution (15 m) imaging information about the earth's surface.

**external distance**  The distance from the midcurve to the PI in circular curves.

**fiducial marks**  Reference marks on the edges of aerial photos, used to locate the principal point on the photo.

**fill**  Material used to raise the construction level; also, the measurement up from a grade mark.

**final survey**  *See* as-built survey.

**forced centering**  The interchanging of theodolites, prisms, and targets into tribrachs, which have been left in position over the station.

**foresight (FS)**  In leveling, a sight taken to a BM or TP to obtain a check on a leveling operation or to establish a transfer elevation.

**free station**  A conveniently located instrument station used for construction layout, the position of which is determined after occupation through resection techniques.

**freeway**  A highway designed for traffic mobility in which access is restricted to interchanges with arterials and other freeways.

**GDOP (general dilution of precision)**  A value that indicates the relative uncertainty in position, using GPS observations, caused by errors in time (GPS receivers) and satellite vector measurements. A minimum of four widely spaced satellites at high elevations usually produce good results (that is, lower GDOP values).

**geodetic datum**  A precisely established and maintained series of benchmarks referenced to adjusted mean sea level (MSL).

**geodetic height ($h$)**  The distance from the ellipsoid surface to the ground surface.

**geodetic survey**    A survey of such high precision and/or covering such a large geographic area that computations must be based on the ellipsoidal shape of the earth.

**geographic information system (GIS)**    Analysis and display of selected layers of a spatially and relationally referenced database.

**geographic meridian**    A line on the surface of the earth joining the poles, in other words, a line of longitude.

**geoid**    A surface that is approximately represented by mean sea level (MSL) and is, in fact, the equipotential surface of the earth's gravity field.

**geoid undulation ($N$)**    The distance between the geoid surface and the ellipsoid surface. $N$ is negative if the geoid surface is below the ellipsoid surface. Also known as *geoid height.*

**geospatial data**    Data describing both the geographic location and attributes of features on the earth's surface.

**geostationary (geosynchronous) orbit**    A satellite orbit in which the satellite appears stationary over a specific location on earth. A formation of geostationary satellites presently provides communication services worldwide.

**glacial**    Pertaining to surface features and materials produced by the formation and movement of glaciers.

**global positioning system (GPS)**    A ground positioning ($Y$, $X$, and $Z$) technique based on the reception and analysis of NAVSTAR satellite signals.

**gon**    A unit of angular measure in which 1 revolution = 400 gon and 100.000 gon = a right angle. Also known as *grad.*

**grad**    *See* gon.

**grade sheet**    A construction report giving line and grade (offsets) and cuts/fills at each station.

**grade stake**    A wood stake (usually) with a cut/fill reference mark to that portion of a proposed facility adjacent to the stake.

**grade transfer**    A technique of transferring cut/fill measurements to the facility using a carpenter's level, stringline level, laser, and batter boards.

**gradient**    The slope of a grade line.

**grid distance**    A distance on a coordinate grid.

**grid factor**    A factor used to convert ground distances to grid distances.

**grid meridian**    Meridians parallel to a central meridian on a coordinate grid.

**ground distance**    A distance as measured on the ground surface.

**grubbing**    The removal of stumps, roots, etc., from a construction site.

**gunter's chain**    Early (1800s) measuring device consisting of 100 links, measuring 66 ft long.

**haul**    In highway construction, the distance that 1 cubic yard (meter) of cut material is transported to a fill location.

**hectare**    10,000 square meters.

**height of instrument (HI)**     Height of the line-of-sight of an instrument above a datum; used in leveling.

**hi**     Height of instrument (optical axis) above the instrument station; used in GPS, theodolite/EDM, and stadia surveying.

**horizontal line**     A straight line perpendicular to a vertical line.

**hydrographic surveys**     Surveys designed to define shoreline and underwater features.

**igneous rock**     Surface features and materials resulting in the solidification of magma.

**interlining (bucking-in)**     A trial-and-error technique of establishing a theodolite on a line between two points that themselves are not intervisible. Also known as *wiggling in.*

**intermediate sight (IS)**     A sight taken with a level or transit to determine a feature elevation and/or location.

**invert**     The inside bottom of a pipe or culvert.

**ionosphere**     The section of the earth's atmosphere that is about 50 km to 1,000 km above the earth's surface.

**ionospheric refraction**     The impedance in the velocity of signals (GPS) as they pass through the ionosphere.

**lacustrine**     Surface features or materials resulting from original deposition in lakes.

**laser alignment**     Horizontal and/or vertical alignment given by a fixed or rotating laser.

**latitude (geographic)**     Angular distance from the earth's center, measured northerly or southerly from the equatorial plane.

**latitude (of a course)**     The change in northerly displacement of a line ($\Delta N$).

**level line**     A line in a level surface.

**lidar (light detection and ranging)**     This technique, used in airborne and satellite imagery, utilizes timed laser pulses that are reflected from surface features to obtain DTM mapping detail.

**line**     A GIS term describing the joining of an ordered set of coordinated points, or by a grid of cells, and having one dimension.

**line and grade**     The horizontal and vertical position of a facility.

**linear error of closure**     The line of traverse misclosure representing the result of the measuring errors.

**littoral**     Surface features and materials produced by coastal wave action.

**local road (highway)**     A road designed for property access, connected to arterials by collectors.

**longitude**     Angular distance measured in the plane of the equator from the reference meridian through Greenwich, England. Lines of longitude are indicated on globes as meridians.

**magnetic declination**    The horizontal angle between the direction given by a compass needle and geographic north.

**mask angle**    The vertical angle below which satellite signals are not recorded or not processed; often a value of 10° or 15° is used. Also known as the *cutoff angle.*

**mass diagram**    A graphic representation of cumulative highway cuts and fills.

**mean sea level (MSL)**    A reference datum for leveling.

**meridian**    A north-south reference line; or the line formed by the intersection of the earth's surface with a plane containing the earth's axis of rotation.

**metamorphic**    Surface features and materials resulting from sedimentary or igneous rock that has been subjected to geoforces of pressure, heat, and/or water.

**midordinate distance**    The distance from the midchord to the midcurve in circular curves.

**mistake**    A poor result due to carelessness or a misunderstanding.

**monument**    A permanent surveying reference marker (usually concrete, steel, or aluminum) for horizontal and vertical positioning.

**multispectral scanner**    Scanning device, used for satellite and airborne imagery, that records reflected and emitted energy in two or more bands of the electromagnetic spectrum.

**nadir angle**    A vertical angle measured from the nadir direction (straight down) upward to a point.

**NAVSTAR**    A set of orbiting satellites used in navigation and positioning.

**normal tension**    The amount of tension required in taping to offset the effects of sag.

**original ground**    The position of the ground surface prior to construction.

**orthometric height (H)**    The distance from the geoid surface to the ground surface. Also known as *elevation.*

**page check**    Arithmetic check.

**parabolic curve**    A curve used in vertical alignment to join two adjacent grade lines.

**parallax**    An error in sighting that occurs when the object and/or the cross hairs of a telescope are focused improperly.

**photogrammetry**    The science of making measurements from aerial photographs.

**plan**    Bird's-eye view of a route location.

**plane survey**    A survey of such limited size (most surveys) that computations can be based on plane geometry and trigonometry for all horizontal positioning.

**planimeter**    A mechanical or electronic device used to measure areas by tracing the outline of the area on the map or plan.

**plat**    A plan of survey usually showing property information.

**point of beginning (POB)**    A referenced point (corner) or a property line from which a description of the property deed commences and at which the description closes.

**point**    A GIS term describing a single spatial entity represented by a set of northing/easting coordinates, or by a single pixel location, and having zero dimension.

**polar coordinates**    The location of a feature by angle and distance.

**polygon**    A GIS term for a closed chain of points representing an area.

**precision**    The degree of refinement (repeatability) with which a measurement is made.

**pre-engineering survey**    A preliminary survey that forms the basis for engineering design.

**preliminary survey**    The gathering of a data (distance, position, and angles) to locate physical features so that data can be plotted to scale on a map or plan.

**profile**    A series of elevations along the direction of a survey line (for example, along a road or watercourse ℄).

**property survey**    A survey to retrace or establish property lines, or to establish the location of buildings within property limits.

**pseudorange**    The uncorrected distance from a GPS satellite to a GPS ground receiver determined by comparing the code transmitted from the satellite to the replica code residing in the GPS receiver. When corrections are made for clock and other errors, the pseudorange becomes the range.

**random errors**    Errors associated with the skill and vigilance of the surveyor.

**real time positioning (real time kinematic, RTK)**    RTK requires a base station to measure the satellites' signals, process the baseline corrections, and then broadcast the corrections (differences) to any number of roving receivers that are simultaneously tracking the same satellites.

**rectangular coordinates**    The location of a feature by two distances, 90 degrees opposed.

**relative positioning**    The determination of position through the combined computations of two or more receivers simultaneously tracking the same satellites, resulting in the determination of the baseline vector ($X$, $Y$, $Z$) joining the two receivers.

**remote object elevation**    The determination of the height of an object using total station sightings together with onboard applications software.

**remote sensing**    Geodata collection and interpretive analysis for both airborne and satellite imagery.

**resection**    The solution of the coordinated position of an occupied station by the sighting of angles to three or more coordinated reference stations—two or more stations, if both angles and distances are measured.

**right of way (ROW)**    The legal property limits of a utility or access route.

**route survey**    Preliminary, control, and construction surveys that cover a long but narrow area, as in highway and railroad construction.

**sag**    The error caused when a tape is supported only at its ends.

**scale factor**    The factor used to convert sea-level distances to plane grid distances.

**sea-level correction factor**    The factor used to convert ground distances to sea-level equivalent distances.

**sedimentary**    Surface features and materials first formed by water, wind, or glaciers.

**shaft**    An opening of uniform cross section joining a tunnel to the surface; used for access and ventilation.

**sidereal day**    The time taken for one complete revolution of the earth with reference to an infinitely faraway object, for example, a star.

**skew number**    A clockwise angle (closest 5 degrees) turned from the back tangent to the centerline of a culvert or bridge.

**slope stakes**    Stakes placed to locate the top or bottom of a slope.

**solar day**    The time taken for one complete revolution of the earth with reference to the sun.

**soundings**    The measurement of water depths in rivers, lakes, and oceans.

**spiral curve**    A transition curve of constantly changing radius placed between a high-speed tangent and a central curve; it permits a gradual speed adjustment.

**springline**    The horizontal bisector of a storm or sanitary pipe.

**station**    A point on a baseline that is a specified distance from the point of commencement. The point of commencement is identified as 0 + 00; 100 feet or 100 meters are known as full stations (1,000 m in some highway applications); 1 + 45.20 identifies a point distant 145.20 ft/m away from the point of commencement (0 + 145.20 in some highway applications).

**superelevation**    The banking of a curved section of road to help overcome the effects of centrifugal force.

**systematic errors**    Errors whose magnitude and algebraic sign can be determined.

**tangent**    A straight line, often referred to with respect to a curve.

**temporary benchmark**    A semipermanent point of known elevation.

**tension error**    An error caused by other than standard tension.

**three-wire leveling**    A more precise technique of differential leveling in which rod readings are taken at the stadia hairs in addition to the main cross hair.

**toe of slope**    Bottom of slope.

**total station**    An electronic theodolite combined with an EDM and an electronic data collector capable of measuring and recording horizontal and vertical distances and angles and then computing N, E, and elevation values.

**traverse**    A continuous series of measured (angles and distances) lines.

**troposphere**    The part of the earth's atmosphere that stretches from the surface to about 80 km upward (includes the stratosphere as its upper portion).

**turning point (TP)**    In leveling, a solid point where an elevation is temporarily established so that the level may be relocated.

**universal time**    Mean solar time at the meridian of Greenwich, England, and kept by atomic clocks.

**UTM**    Universal transverse Mercator grid system.

**vertical angle**    An angle in the vertical plane measured up ($+$) or down ($-$) from horizontal.

**vertical curve**    A parabolic curve joining two grade lines.

**vertical line**    A line from the surface of the earth to the earth's center. Also referred to as a plumb line or a line of gravity.

**waving the rod**    The slight waving of the leveling rod to and from the instrument that permits the surveyor to take a precise (lowest) rod reading.

**zenith angle**    A vertical angle measured downward from the zenith (upward plumb line) direction.

# D Answers to Selected Chapter Problems

## Chapter 2

2.4 (a) $177.31 \times 66 = 11{,}702.46$ ft $\times .3048 = 3{,}566.91$ m

2.4 (d) $1.90 \times 66 = 125.4$ ft $\times .3048 = 38.22$m

2.8 Tan slope angle $= .02$; angle $= 1.14576°$
$H = 122.57 \cos 1.14576° = 122.55$ ft

2.11 Error per tape length $= -0.03$ ft; tape used 365.28/100 times
error $= -.03 \times 3.6528 = -0.08$ ft
corrected distance $= 365.28 - 0.11 = 365.17$ ft

2.12 Error per tape length $= +0.004$ m; tape used 137.888/30 times,
error $= +0.004 \times 4.59627 = +0.018$m
corrected distance $= 137.888 + 0.018 = 137.906$ m

2.15 $(10 + 45.26) - (8 + 62.63) = 182.63$ ft
$C_T = 0.00000645(90 - 68) 182.63 = 0.03$ ft
$C_L = 0.02 \times 1.8263 = -0.04$ ft
$C = .03 - .04 = -0.01$ ft
Layout 182.64 ft

2.21 $C_T = .00000645(100 - 68)488.38 = +0.10$ ft
$C_L = +0.02 \times 4.8838 = +0.10$ ft
$C = +0.10 + 0.10 = +0.20$ ft
Corrected slope distance $= 488.38 + 0.20 = 488.58$ ft
Tan slope angle $= .008$; slope angle $= 0.458356°$
$H = 488.58 \cos 0.458356° = 488.56$ ft

2.27 $C_S = -w^2L^3/24p^2 = -0.32^2 \times 48.888^3/(24 \times 100^2) = -.050$ m
Corrected distance $= 48.888 - .050 = 48.838$ m

# Chapter 3

3.2 (a) iii    1.57    (b)    iii    0.987
     (c) i    3.06    (d)    i    1.145

3.6

| STATION | BS | HI | FS | ELEVATION |
|---------|------|--------|------|-----------|
| BM 100 | 2.71 | 614.50 | | 611.79 |
| TP 1 | 3.62 | 613.24 | 4.88 | 609.62 |
| TP 2 | 3.51 | 612.78 | 3.97 | 609.27 |
| TP 3 | 3.17 | 613.14 | 2.81 | 609.97 |
| TP 4 | 1.47 | 612.99 | 1.62 | 611.52 |
| BM100 | | | 1.21 | 611.78 |

BS = 14.48      FS = 14.49

611.79 + 14.48 − 14.49 = 611.78      Check

3.16 a) True difference = 8.72 − 5.61 = 3.11 ft
     b) Correct rod reading = 5.42 + 3.11 = 8.53 ft; on A
     c) Error is +0.04 in 300 ft, or .0001 ft/ft
     d) Cross hair adjusted downward to read 8.53 on A

# Chapter 4

4.2 (a) S20°58′W
     (b) S43°09′E
     (c) N87°11′W

4.5 (a) S42°46′W
     (b) S 2°21′E
     (c) N 9°41′W

4.9 Clockwise Solution:

| | | |
|---|---|---|
| Azimuth AB = | | 44°44′40″ |
| | + | 180 |
| Azimuth BA = | | 224°44′40″ |
| | −B | 140°28′50″ |
| Azimuth BC = | | 84°15′50″ |
| | + | 180 |
| Azimuth CB = | | 264°15′50″ |
| | −C | 101°30′20″ |
| Azimuth CD = | | 162°45′30″ |
| | + | 180 |
| Azimuth DC = | | 342°45′30″ |
| | −D | 72°48′10″ |
| Azimuth DE = | | 269°57′20″ |
| | + | 180 |
| Azimuth ED = | | 449°57′20″ |
| | −E | 161°25′40″ |

Azimuth EA =  288°31'40"
          −  180
Azimuth AE =  108°31'40"
        −A  63°47'00"
Azimuth AB =  44°44'40"     Check

# Chapter 6

6.2 (b), (c), and (d)

| COURSE | AZIMUTH | BEARING | DISTANCE | LATITUDE | DEPARTURE |
|--------|---------|---------|----------|----------|-----------|
| AB | 193°56' | S 13°56'W | 636.45 | −617.72 | −153.32 |
| BC | 84°24' | N84°24'E | 654.45 | 63.86 | 651.33 |
| CD | 350°33' | N 9°27'W | 382.65 | 377.46 | − 62.83 |
| DA | 292°03' | N67°57'W | 469.38 | 176.21 | −435.04 |
|  |  |  | 2,142.93 | −0.19 | +0.14 |

$E = \sqrt{0.19^2 + 0.14^2} = 0.24$ ft

Accuracy = E/P = 0.24/2143 = 1/8,929 = 1/8,900

6.3 (b) Coordinates:

| STATION | NORTH | EAST |
|---------|-------|------|
| B | 1,000.00 | 1,000.00 |
|  | + 63.92 | +651.29 |
| C | 1,063.92 | 1,651.29 |
|  | +377.49 | −62.86 |
| D | 1,441.41 | 1,588.43 |
|  | +176.25 | −435.07 |
| A | 1,617.66 | 1,153.36 |
|  | −617.66 | −153.36 |
| B | 1,000.00 | 1,000.00 | Check |

6.4 (a) Area by coordinates:

$X_B(Y_C - Y_A) = 1,000.00(1,063.92 - 1,617.66) = -553,740$

$X_C(Y_D - Y_B) = 1,651.29(1,441.41 - 1,000.00) = +728,896$

$X_D(Y_A - Y_C) = 1,558.43(1,617.66 - 1,063.92) = +862,965$

$X_A(Y_B - Y_D) = 1,153.36(1,000.00 - 1,441.41) = -509,105$

$$2A = 529,016$$
$$A = 264,508 \text{ ft}^2$$

(1 acre = 43,560 ft$^2$) or A = 6.1 acres

6.9 (a) CD = 852.597 m

DE = S74°30'23"W

6.17 Coordinates of E = 1977.519N, 2002.900E

6.19 EA = N 7°20'52"W, 22.675 m; DE = N64°47'56"W, 41.273 m

# Chapter 7

7.1 Prism constant = EG − EF − FG

$$= 586.645 − 298.717 − 287.958 = −0.030 \text{ m}$$

7.3 (a) Horizontal distance = (1878.610 + 1878.633)/2 = 1878.622 m

(b) Elevation at B = 181.302 + (47.462 + 47.353)/2 = 228.71 m

7.5 H = 387.603 cos 4°18′57″ = 386.504 m

Elevation at B = 110.222 + 1.601 + (387.603 sin 4°18′57″) − 1.915 = 139.077 m

# Chapter 10

10.1 <u>A to B</u>; ΔN = −77.773: ΔE = −280.126

Distance AB = 290.722; Bg = S74°29′00.4″W

*Average Factors*

| Elevation | Scale |
|---|---|
| 9997166 | 99990182 |

10.3 CD = 206.064

10.4

| COURSE | GRID BEARING | GEODETIC BEARING |
|---|---|---|
| CD | N.89°15′59.0″E. | N.89°22′08.7″E |

10.7 Azimuth of line 332–331 = 299°14′43″

# Chapter 12

12.1 (a) H = SR.f = 20,000 × .153 = 3,060 m

Altitude = 3060 + 180 = 3,240 m

(b) SR = 20,000 × 12 = 240,000

H = SR.f = 240,000 × 6.022/12 = 120,440 ft

Altitude = 120,400 + 520 = 120,920 ft

12.2 (a) Photo scale = 23.07 × 1:50,000/4.75 = 1:10,295

12.3 (c) SR is 1:500 × 12 or 1:6,000

Number of photos required = $10 \times 47/0.4 \dfrac{(10,000)^2}{(6,000)^2} = 3265$

12.5 (a) (i) Ground speed of aircraft = 350 km/hr

$$= \dfrac{350 \times 1,000}{60 \times 60} = 97.2 \text{ m/s}$$

Therefore, the camera would move $97.2 \times \dfrac{1}{100} = .972$ m during exposure.

12.9 On the ground, the dimensions of the area covered by one photograph are 70 mm × 500 = 35,000 mm = 350 m (1,150 ft). For a forward overlap of 60%, the distance along the direction of the flight line = 350 × 0.60 = 210 m. Therefore, the "new" area to be photographed between successive exposures is 350 − 210 = 140 m. Hence, an exposure must be taken every 140 m along the flight line. The ground speed of the aircraft is 160 km/hr = 160 × 1,000/(60 × 60) = 44.4 m/s. Time between exposures thus equals 140/44.4 = 3.15, say, 3.2 seconds.

# Chapter 13

13.3 PI at   9 + 27.26
    −T   1   85.60
    BC =  7 + 41.66
    +L   3   62.85
    EC = 11 + 04.51

13.5 $EC_2$ = 5 + 98.85

13.7 $E = 500 \left( \dfrac{1}{\cos 12°12'10''} \right) - 1 = 11.558$ m

    $M = 500\,(1 - \cos 12°12'10'') = 11.297$ m

    $T = 500 \tan 12°12'10'' = 108.129$ m

    $L = 500\,\pi \times \dfrac{24.40556}{180} = 212.979$ m

13.8 Deflection at 13 + 00 + 15°02′31

13.16 Summit at 20 + 07.14, elevation = 722.07 ft

# Chapter 14

14.1

| Station | ₵ Grade | Stake elevation | Cut | Fill | Cut | Fill |
|---|---|---|---|---|---|---|
| 0 + 00 | 472.70 | 472.60 | | 0.10 | | 0′1 ¼″ |
| 1 + 00 | 474.02 | 472.36 | | 1.66 | | 1′8″ |

14.2

| Station | ₵ Grade | Stake elevation | Cut | Fill |
|---|---|---|---|---|
| 0 + 00 | 210.500 | 210.831 | 0.331 | |
| 0 + 20 | 210.365 | 210.600 | 0.235 | |

14.5

| | | | | Stake to batterboard (grade rod = 14′) | |
|---|---|---|---|---|---|
| Station | Invert Elevation | Stake Elevation | Cut | Feet | Ft/in |
| MH8 0 + 00 | 360.44 | 368.75 | 8.31 | 5.69 | 5′8 ¼″ |
| 0 + 50 | 361.04 | 368.81 | 7.77 | 6.23 | 6′2¾″ |

# Chapter 15

15.1 For latitude 36°30′: γ(seconds) = 52.09 $d$ tan ϕ
    = 52.09 × 6 × 0.73996 = 231″ = 0°03′51″
    γ(seconds) = 32.37 $d$ tan ϕ = 32.37 × 9.66 × .73996 = 231″ = 0°03′51″

15.2 $p$ (chains) = 0.0202 $dy$ tan ϕ = 10.0 chains (Equation 15.9)
    $p$ (meters) = 0.1565 $dy$ tan ϕ = 201 m (Equation 15.11)
    $p$ (meters) = 0.4055 $dy$ tan ϕ = 201 m (Equation 15.10)

15.4 Area of section 6 = 1 mi. × (1.000 + 0.9904)/2 = 0.9952 mi.$^2$ = 636.9 ac.

15.9 a. Length of rear boundary is reduced by 5.04 − 4.97 = 0.07 ft
    Therefore, new length = 25.06 − 0.07 = 24.99 ft
    The bearing is the same.

b. Change in bearing is calculated as follows:

$$\tan (\text{bearing change}) = \frac{0.07}{26.75} = 0.00262$$

Therefore, bearing change $= 0°09'00''$
Therefore, new bearing $= N10°12'00''E + 0°09'00'' = N10°21'00''E$
The distance is unchanged.

# Chapter 16

16.1

| Depth Using Echo sounder | Tidal Height[a] | Weather Conditions[b] | Reduced Sounding |
|---|---|---|---|
| 10.2 m | 1.5 m | −0.3 m | 9.0 m |

[a] Tidal height above (+) or below (−) chart datum.

[b] Error due to weather conditions above (+) or below (−) tidal water level at time of sounding.

16.5

| SCALE | DISTANCE BETWEEN SOUNDING LINES | DISTANCE BETWEEN FIXES |
|---|---|---|
| (a) 1:2,000 | 2000 × 0.01 m = 20 m | 1,000 × 0.025 m = 50 m |
| (b) 1 in. = 100 ft | 100 ft/in. × 0.4 in. = 40 ft | 100 ft/in. × 1.0 in. = 100 ft |

# E Internet Websites

The websites listed here cover surveying, GPS, photogrammetry, GIS, and mapping. Some sites include web links to various related sites. Although the websites shown here were verified at the time of publication, some changes are inevitable. Corrected site locations and new sites may be accessed by searching the web links shown at the sites listed in this appendix.

American Association of Geographers (AAG): www.aag.org

American Association of State Highway and Transportation Officials (AASHTO): www.aashto.org

American Congress on Surveying and Mapping (ACSM): http://www.acsm.net

American Society for Photogrammetry and Remote Sensing: http://www.asprs.org

ARCINFO tutorial home page: http://boris.qub.ac.uk/shane/arc/ARChome.html

Ashtech (Magellan): http://www.ashtech.com

Association for Geographic Information: www.agi.org.uk/

Australian Surveying and Land Information Group: http://www.auslig.gov.au/acres/facts.htm

Beadle's (John) Introduction to GPS Applications: http://ares.redsword.com/gps/apps

Bennett (Peter) NMEA-0183 and GPS Information: http://vancouver-webpages.com/pub/peter/

Berntsen International, Inc. (surveying markers): http://www.berntsen.com

Brody's home page (GIS Internet Index): www.index-site.com/gis.html

BYU's distributed geographic information links: www.geog.byu.edu/gisonline/links/main.htm

Canada Centre for Remote Sensing: www.ccrs.nrcan.gc.ca/ccrs/

Canada Centre for Remote Sensing (tutorial): www.ccrs.nrcan.gc.ca/ccrs/educate.html

Canadian Geodetic Survey: http://www.geod.nrcan.gc.ca

Clark Labs (IDRISI): www.clarklabs.org

CORS information: http://www.ngs.noaa.gov/CORS/cors-data.html

Corvallis Microtechnology: http://www.cmtinc.com

Dana (Peter H.) global positioning overview:
   http://www.colorado.Edu/geography/gcraft/notes/gps/gps.html

EagleScan remote sensing devices: http://www.3dillc.com/rem-lidar.html

Earth Science Information Center: http://ask.usgs.gov/

ESRI: http://www.esri.com

Flatirons surveying site: http://www.flatsurv.com

Geotronics—Spectra Precision—Trimble: http://www.geotronics.se/

GIS—Kingston University Center (UK): http://www.kingston.ac.uk/geog/gis

Global Positioning System Resources (Sam Wormley):
   http://www.cnde.iastate.edu/staff/swormley/gps.html

Glonass home page (Russian Federation): http://rssi.ru/SFCSIC/english.html

GPS World Magazine: http://www.gpsworld.com

Landsat 7 Science Data Users Handbook:
   http://ltpwww.gsfc.nasa.gov/IAS/handbook

Land Surveying and Geomatics: http://homepage.interaccess.com/~maynard/

Land Surveyor Reference Page (Stan Thompson): http://www.lsrp.com/index.html

Leica Geosystems Inc.: http://www.leica.com/

Leick GPS GLONASS GODESY home page:
   http://www.spatial.maine.edu/~leick/gpshome.htm

L H Systems (digital photogrammetry): http://www.lh-systems.com/

MAPINFO (mapping): http://www.mapinfo.com

MicroSurvey (surveying and design software): http://www.microsurvey.com/

National Center for Geographic Information and Analysis: www.ncgia.ucsb.edu/

National Imagery and Mapping Agency (NIMA): www.nima.mil/

National Wetlands Inventory, U.S. Fish and Wildlife Service: www.nwi.fws.gov/

NASA, EROS Data Center: http://edcwww.cr.usgs.gov

NASA, GPS applications page: http://gpshome.ssc.nasa.gov

NASA, lidar satellite sensing: http://essp.gsfc.nasa/vcl/

NASA, remote sensing tutorial: http://rst.gsfc.nasa.gov

Natural Resources, Canada: www.ccrs.nrcan

Natural Resources Canada, remote sensing tutorial:
   http://www.ccrs.nrcan.gc.ca/ccrs/eduref/tutorial

NGS home page: http://www.ngs.noaa.gov/

Nikon: http://www.nikonusa.com

Optech: (airborne laser terrain mapper): www.optech.on.ca

Penn State Geographic Visualization Science, Technology and Applications Center:
   www.geovista.psu.edu/

POB, Point of Beginning Magazine: http://www.pobonline.com/

Professional Surveyor Magazine: http://www.profsurv.com

SHOALS (U.S. Army Corps of Engineers):
   http://sam.usae.army.mil/op/shoals/pages/airborne.htm

Sokkia: http://www.sokkia.com/

Spectra Precision (Geodimeter): http://www.geodat.com

Spectra Precision (Terrasat—GPS/GIS): http://www.terrasat.com

Sun/Polaris Ephemeris (Jerry Wahl): http://www.cadastral.com

Surveyors Module International (SMI): http://www.smi.com/
Tarr's (Paul) GPS WWW resources list: http://www.inmet.com/~pwt/gps_gen.html
Topcon GPS (including tutorial): http://www.topconps.com
Topcon Instrument Corporation: http://www.topcon.com
Trimble: http://www.trimble.com
Trimble—GIS: www.trimble.com/gis/index.htm
Trimble GPS tutorial: www.trimble.com/gps/index.htm
Tripod Data Systems (TDS): http://www.tdsway.com
United States Bureau of Land Management (BLM): www.blm.gov/gis/nsdi.html
United States Census Bureau: www.census.com
United States Coast Guard and Navigation Center: http://www.navcen.uscg.gov
United States Geological Survey: http://www.usgs.gov/
United States Spatial Data Transfer Standard Information (SDTS):
www.mcmcweb.er.usgs.gov/sdts/
University Navstar Consortium: www.unavco.ucar.edu/
University of Maine: http://www.spatial.maine.edu/
Urban and Regional Information Syustems Association (URISA): www.urisa.org
Zeiss (Carl) Surveying: http://www.zeiss.com/survey/
ZI Imaging Corp. (Intergraph/Zeiss): www.ziimaging.com

# Examples of Current Geomatics Technology

Appendix F appears at the end of this textbook in a full-color insert. The figures include examples of traditional mapping and GIS mapping, aerial photography, soft-copy photogrammetry equipment and presentations, and an example of a state-of-the-art total station.

# G Typical Field Projects

The following projects can be performed in either foot units or metric units and can be adjusted in scope to fit the available time.

## G.1   Field Notes

Survey field notes can be entered into a bound field book or on looseleaf field notepaper; if a bound field book is used, be sure to leave room at the front of the book for a title, index, and diary—if they are required by your instructor. The following list of instructions will guide you in the proper use and layout of a field book:

1. Write your name in ink on the outside cover.
2. Page numbers (for example, 1 to 72) are to be on the right side only.
3. All entries are to be in pencil, 2H or 3H.
4. See Figure G.1 for examples of pages 1–7.
5. All entries are to be printed (uppercase, if permitted).
6. Calculations are to be checked and initialed.
7. Sketches are to be used to clarify field notes. Orient the sketch so that the included north arrow is pointing toward the top of the page.
8. All field notes should be updated daily.
9. Show the word **copy** at the top of all copied pages.
10. Field notes are to be entered directly in the field book—not on scraps of paper to be copied later.
11. Mistakes in entered data are to crossed out—not erased.
12. Spelling mistakes, calculation mistakes, and the like, should be erased and reentered correctly.
13. Lettering is to be read from the bottom of the page or the right side.
14. The first page of each project should show the date, temperature, project title, crew duties, and so on.

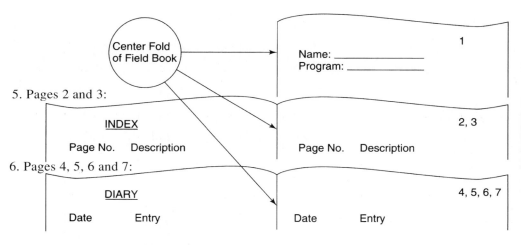

FIGURE G.1   Field book layout.

15.  The diary should show absentees, weather, description of work, and so on.

## G.2   Project 1: Building Measurements

**Description**   You will measure the selected walls of an indicated campus building with a cloth or fiberglass tape, and record the measurements on a sketch in the field book, as directed by the instructor (see Figure G.2 for sample field notes).

**Equipment**   Cloth or fiberglass tape (100 ft or 30 m).

**Purpose**   To introduce you to the fundamentals of note keeping and survey measurement.

**Procedure**   Use the measuring techniques described in class prior to going out.

One crew member will be appointed to take notes for this first project. At the completion of the project (same day), the other crew members will copy the notes (ignoring erroneous data) into their field books, including the diary and index data. (Crew members will take equal turns acting as note keeper over the length of the program.)

Using a straightedge, draw a large sketch of the selected building walls on the right-hand (grid) side of your field book. Show the walls as they would appear in a plan view. For example, ignore overhangs, or show them as dashed lines. Keep the tape taut to remove sag, and try to keep the tape horizontal. If the building wall is longer than one tape length, make an intermediate mark (do not deface the building), and proceed from that point.

After completing all the measurements in one direction, start from the terminal point, and remeasure all the walls. If the second measurement agrees with the first measurement, put a check mark beside the entered data. If the second measurement agrees acceptably (for

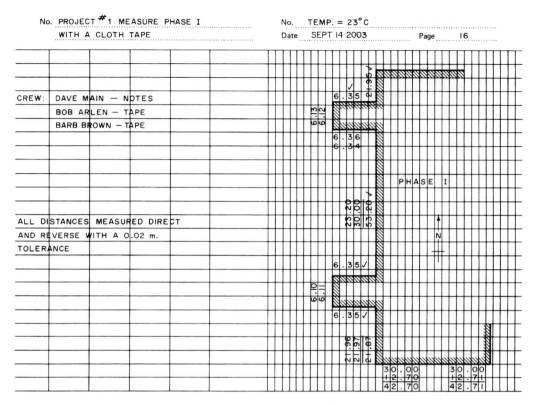

**FIGURE G.2**  Sample taping field notes for building dimensions—Project I.

example, within $\pm 0.10$ ft or 0.02 m), enter that measurement directly above or below the first entered measurement. If the second measurement disagrees with the first (for example, by more than 0.10 ft or 0.02 m), enter that value on the sketch, and measure that dimension a third time. Discard the erroneous measurement by drawing a line (using a straightedge) through the erroneous value.

**Discussion**  If the class results are summarized on the chalkboard, it will be clear that all crews did not obtain the same results for specified building wall lengths. There will be much more agreement among crews on the lengths of the shorter building walls than on the lengths of the longer building walls (particularly the walls that were longer than one tape length). Discuss and enumerate the types of mistakes and errors that can account for measurement discrepancies among survey crews working on this project.

Sec. G.2    Project 1: Building Measurements    **715**

# G.3   Project 2: Experiment to Determine "Normal Tension"

**Description**   Project 2 is an experiment in which you will determine the tension required to eliminate errors due to tension and sag for a 100-ft or 30-m steel tape supported only at the ends. This tension is called normal tension.

**Equipment**   Steel tape (100.00 ft or 30.000 m), two plumb bobs, and a graduated tension handle.

**Purpose**   To introduce you to measurement techniques requiring the use of a steel tape and plumb bobs and to demonstrate the "feel" of the proper tension required when using a tape that is supported only at the ends (the usual case).

## Procedure

- With a 100-ft or 30-m tape fully supported on the ground and under a tension of 10 lbs or 50 N (standard tension), as determined by use of a supplied tension handle, measure from the initial mark and place a second mark at exactly 100.00 ft or 30.000 m.

- Check this measurement by repeating the procedure (while switching personnel) and correcting if necessary. If this initial measurement is not performed correctly, much time will be wasted.

- Raise the tape off the ground and keep it parallel to the ground to eliminate slope errors.

- Using plumb bobs and the tension handle, determine how many pounds or Newtons of tension (see Table 2.1) are required to force the steel tape to agree with the previously measured distance of 100.00 ft or 30.000 m.

- Repeat the process after switching crew personnel. (Acceptable tolerance is $\pm 2$ lbs.)

- Record the normal tension results (at least two) in the field book, as described in the classroom.

- Include the standard conditions for the use of steel tapes in your field notes. See Table G.1

**Discussion**   If the class results are summarized on the chalkboard, it will be clear that not all survey crews obtained the same average value for normal tension. Discuss the reasons for the tension

**Table G.1**   STANDARD CONDITIONS FOR THE USE OF STEEL TAPES[a]

| English System | or | Metric System |
|---|---|---|
| Temperature = 68°F | | Temperature = 20°C |
| Tension = 10 lbs | | Tension = 50 N (11.2 lbs) |
| Tape is fully supported. | | Tape is fully supported. |

[a]For this project, you can assume that the temperature is standard, 68°F or 20°C.

measurement discrepancies and agree on a working value for normal tension for subsequent class projects.

# G.4   Project 3: Field Measurements with a Steel Tape*

**Description**   You will measure the sides of a five-sided closed field traverse using techniques designed to permit a precision closure ratio of 1:5,000 (see Table 2.2). The traverse angles will be obtained from Project 5. See Figure G.3 for sample field notes.

**Equipment**   Steel tape, two plumb bobs, hand level, range pole or plumb bob string target, and chaining pins or other devices to mark the position on the ground.

**Purpose**   To develop some experience in measuring with surveying equipment (see also Project 5).

**Procedure** for Steel Taping

- Each course of the traverse will be measured twice—forward (direct) and then immediately back (reverse)—with the two measurements agreeing to within 0.03 ft or 0.008 m. If the two measurements do not agree, they will be repeated until they do and before the next course of the traverse is measured.

*Projects 3 and 5 can be combined, and you can use EDM-equipped theodolites or total stations. The traverse courses can be measured using EDM and a prism (pole-mounted or tribrach-mounted). Each station will be occupied with a theodolite-equipped EDM instrument, or total station, and each pair of traverse courses can be measured at each setup. Traverse computations will use the mean distances thus determined and the mean angles obtained from each setup. Refer to Chapters 6 and 7.

No. PROJECT #3
TRAVERSE DISTANCES

No.
Date MARCH 29, 2003          Page   10

| COURSE | DIRECT | REVERSE | MEAN | MEAN ($C_T$) |
|--------|--------|---------|------|--------------|
| 111–112 | 164.96 | 164.94 | 164.95 | 164.97 |
| 112–113 | 88.41 | 88.43 | 88.42 | 88.43 |
| 113–114 | 121.69 | 121.69 | 121.69 | 121.70 |
| 114–115 | 115.80 | 115.78 | 115.79 | 115.80 |
| 115–111 | 68.36 | 68.34 | 68.35 | 68.36 |

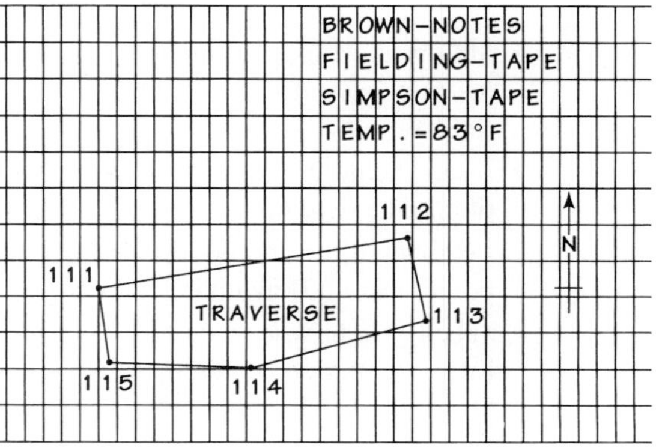

BROWN–NOTES
FIELDING–TAPE
SIMPSON–TAPE
TEMP. =83°F

TRAVERSE

**FIGURE G.3**   Sample field notes for Project 3 (traverse distances).

- When measuring on a slope, the high-end surveyor normally holds the tape directly on the mark, and the low-end surveyor has to use a plumb bob to keep the tape horizontal.
- The low-end surveyor uses the hand level to keep the tape approximately horizontal by sighting the high-end surveyor and noting how much lower she or he is in comparison. The plumb bob is then set to that height differential. Use chaining pins or other markers to mark intermediate measuring points on the ground temporarily. Use scratch marks or concrete nails on paved surfaces.
- If a range pole is first set behind the far station, the rear surveyor can keep the tape aligned properly by sighting at the range pole and directing the forward surveyor on line.
- Record the results as shown in Figure G.3, and then repeat the process until all five sides have been measured and booked. When booked erroneous measurements are to be discarded, cross them out with a straightedge—don't erase.
- If the temperature is something other than standard, correct the mean distance for temperature. ($C_T$); that is, $C_T = .00000645(T - 68)L_{ft}$ or $C_T = .0000116 (T - 20)L_m$.

**Reference**     Chapter 2.


## G.5   Project 4: Differential Leveling

**Description**     You will use the techniques of differential leveling to determine the elevations of a temporary benchmark (TBM), and of the intermediate stations identified by the instructor (if any). See Figure G.4 for sample field notes.

**Equipment**     Survey level, rod, and rod level (if available).

**Purpose**     To give you experience using levels and rods and recording all measurements correctly in the field book.

**Procedure** (Refer to Figure G. 4.)

- Start at the closest municipal or college benchmark (BM) (description given by the instructor), and take a backsight (BS) reading to establish a height of instrument (HI).
- Insert the description of the BM (and all subsequent TPs), in detail, under Description in the field notes.
- Establish a turning point (TP 1) generally in the direction of the defined terminal point (TBM 33) by taking a foresight (FS) on TP 1.
- When you have calculated the elevation of TP 1, move the level to a convenient location, and set it up again. Take a BS reading on TP 1, and calculate the new HI.
- The rod readings taken on any required intermediate points (on the way to or from the terminal point) will be booked in the Intermediate Sight (IS) column, unless

| STA | BS | HI | IS | FS | ELEV | DESCRIPTION |
|---|---|---|---|---|---|---|
| | | | | | | BROWN-INST. |
| | | | | | | SMITH-ROD |
| | | | | | | TEMP.=65°F |
| BM 21 | 0.54 | 182.31 | | | 181.77 | BM. BRONZE PLATE ON E. WALL OF S.E. |
| | | | | | | STAIRWELL OF PHASE 1 BLDG., ABOUT |
| | | | | | | 1 m ABOVE THE GROUND. |
| TP 1 | 0.95 | 175.04 | | 8.22 | 174.09 | N. LUG ON TOP FLANGE OF HYD.@ |
| | | | | | | E/SIDE OF BUS SHELTER |
| TP 2 | 0.80 | 168.76 | | 7.08 | 167.96 | SPIKE IN S/SIDE OF HP @ 237 FINCH |
| | | | | | | AVE. |
| TP 3 | 0.55 | 160.20 | | 9.11 | 159.65 | SPIKE IN S/SIDE OF HP @ 245 FINCH |
| | | | | | | AVE. |
| 111 | | | 4.22 | | | TRAVERSE STATION I.B. |
| 112 | | | 4.71 | | | TRAVERSE STATION I.B. |
| 113 | | | 2.03 | | | TRAVERSE STATION I.B. |
| 114 | | | 1.22 | | | TRAVERSE STATION I.B. |
| TP 4 | 3.77 | 163.45 | | 0.52 | 159.68 | TOP OF I.B. @ STA. 115 |
| TBM 3 | | | | 1.18 | 162.27 | BRASS CAP ON CONC. MON.-CONTROL |
| | | | | | | STATION 1102 |
| TBM 33 | 1.23 | 163.50 | | | 162.27 | |
| TP 4 | 2.71 | 162.39 | | 3.82 | 159.68 | |
| TP 3 | 8.88 | 168.53 | | 2.74 | 159.65 | |
| TP 5 | 11.86 | 177.38 | | 3.01 | 165.52 | TOP OF N.E. CORNER OF CONCRETE |
| | | | | | | STEP @ 233 FINCH AVE. |
| TP 1 | 10.61 | 184.72 | | 3.27 | 174.11 | |
| BM 21 | | | | 2.94 | 181.78 | (e=+0.01) |
| ΣBS | = 41.90 | | ΣFS | = 41.89 | | |
| | | | | | | |
| | ΣBS, | 41.90 | − ΣFS, | 41.89 = | 0.01 | 181.77 + .01 = 181.78, CHECK |

After the arithmetic check has been successfully applied, compute the elevations for the intermediate readings—I.S.

**FIGURE G.4**  Sample field notes for Project 4 (differential leveling).

some of those intermediate points are also being used as turning points (TPS). See, for example, TP 4.

- If you can't "see" the terminal point (TBM 33) from the new instrument location, establish additional turning points (TP 2, TP 3, etc.), and repeat the above steps until you can take a reading on the terminal point.
- After you have taken a reading (FS) on the terminal point (TBM 33) and calculated its elevation, move the level slightly and set it up again. Now, take a BS on the terminal point (TBM 33), and prepare to close the level loop back to the starting benchmark.

Sec. G.5     Project 4: Differential Leveling          **719**

- Repeat the leveling procedure until you have surveyed back to the original BM. If you use the original TPs on the way back, book them by their original numbers—you do not have to describe them again. If you use new TPs on the way back, describe each TP in detail under Description, and assign each one a new number.
- If the final elevation of the starting BM differs by more than 0.04 ft or 0.013 m from the starting elevation (after the calculations have been checked for mistakes by performing an "arithmetic check," also known as a "page check"), repeat the project. Your instructor may give you a different closure allowance, depending on the distance leveled and/or the type of terrain surveyed.

**Notes**

- Keep BS and FS distances from the instrument roughly equal.
- "Wave" the rod (or use a rod level) to ensure a vertical reading.
- Eliminate parallax for each reading.
- Use only solid (steel, concrete, or wood) and well-defined features for TPs. If you cannot describe a TP precisely, do not use it!
- Perform an arithmetic check on the notes before assessing closure accuracy.

    **Reference**    Chapter 3.

## G.6  Project 5: Traverse Angle Measurements and Closure Computations

| | |
|---|---|
| **Description** | You will measure the angles of a five-sided field traverse (see also Project 3), using techniques consistent with the desired precision ratio of 1/5,000. |
| **Equipment** | Theodolite or total station and a target device (range pole, plumb bob string target, or prism). |
| **Purpose** | To introduce you to the techniques of setting up a theodolite or total station over a closed traverse point, turning and "doubling" interior angles, and checking your work by calculating the geometric closure. Then compute (using latitudes and departures) a traverse closure to determine the precision ratio of your field work. (If you are using a total station with a traverse closure program, use that program to check your calculator computations.) For traverse computation purposes, assume a direction for one of the traverse courses, or use one supplied by your instructor. See Figure G.5 for sample field notes. |

**Procedure**

- Using the same traverse stations that were used for Project 3, measure each of the five angles (direct and double).
- Read all angles from left to right. Begin the first (of two) angles at 0°00′00″ ("direct"), and begin the second angle ("double") with the value of the first angle reading.

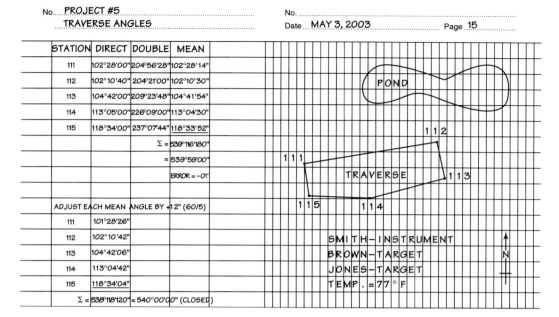

| STATION | DIRECT | DOUBLE | MEAN | | | | | | | | | | | | | | | |
|---|---|---|---|---|---|---|---|---|---|---|---|---|---|---|---|---|---|---|
| 111 | 102°28'00" | 204°56'28" | 102°28'14" | | | | | | | | | | | | | | | |
| 112 | 102°10'40" | 204°21'00" | 102°10'30" | | | | | | POND | | | | | | | | | |
| 113 | 104°42'00" | 209°23'48" | 104°41'54" | | | | | | | | | | | | | | | |
| 114 | 113°05'00" | 226°09'00" | 113°04'30" | | | | | | | | | | | | | | | |
| 115 | 118°34'00" | 237°07'44" | 118°33'52" | | | | | | | | 112 | | | | | | | |
| | | Σ = | 539°116'180" | | | | | | | | | | | | | | | |
| | | = | 539°59'00" | | | 111 | | | | | | | | | | | | |
| | | ERROR = | -01' | | | | | TRAVERSE | | | | 113 | | | | | | |
| | | | | | | | | | | | | | | | | | | |
| ADJUST EACH MEAN | ANGLE BY | +12" (60/5) | | | | 115 | | | 114 | | | | | | | | | |
| 111 | 101°28'26" | | | | | | | | | | | | | | | | | |
| 112 | 102°10'42" | | | | | SMITH-INSTRUMENT | | | | | | | | | | | | |
| 113 | 104°42'06" | | | | | BROWN-TARGET | | | | | | N | | | | | | |
| 114 | 113°04'42" | | | | | JONES-TARGET | | | | | | | | | | | | |
| 115 | 118°34'04" | | | | | TEMP. = 77°F | | | | | | | | | | | | |
| Σ = | 539°118'120" | = 540°00'00" (CLOSED) | | | | | | | | | | | | | | | | |

**FIGURE G.5**  Sample field notes for Project 5 (traverse angles).

- Transit the telescope between the direct and double readings.
- Divide the double angle by 2 to obtain the "mean" angle. If the mean angle differs by more than 30" (or a value given by your instructor) from the direct angle, repeat the procedure.
- When all the mean angles have been booked, add the angles to determine the geometric closure.
- If the geometric closure exceeds 01' $(30''\sqrt{N})$, find the error.
- Combine the results from Projects 3 and 5 to determine the precision closure of the field traverse (1/5,000 or better is acceptable). Use an assumed direction for one of the sides (see above).

# G.7   Project 6: Topographic Field Surveys

Topographic field surveys can be accomplished in several ways, for example:

- Cross sections and tie-ins, with a manual plot of the tie-ins, cross sections, and contours.
- Transit/EDM, with a manual plot of the tie-ins and contours.
- Total station, with a computer-generated plot on a digital plotter.

**Purpose**     Each type of topographic survey shown in this section is designed to give you experience in collecting field data (location details and elevations) using different specified surveying equipment and surveying procedures. These different approaches to topographic surveying have the same objective: the production of a scaled map or plan showing all relevant details and height information (contours and spot elevations) of the area surveyed. Time and schedule constraints will normally limit most programs to include just one or two of these approaches.

## G.7.1 Cross Sections and Tie-Ins Topographic Survey

**Description**   Using the techniques of right-angled tie-ins and cross sections (both referenced to a baseline), you will locate the positions and elevations of selected features on the designated area of the campus. (See Figures G.6, G.7, and G.8.)

**Equipment**   Cloth or fiberglass tape, steel tape, and two plumb bobs. A right-angle prism is optional.

**Procedure**

- Establish your own baseline using wood stakes or pavement nails. You can also use a curb line, as shown in Figure G.6, as the survey baseline (use keel or other nonpermanent markers to mark the baseline).

- The point of intersection of your baseline with some other line (or point, as defined by your instructor) will be 0 + 00.

- Measure the baseline stations (for example, 50 ft or 20 m) precisely with a steel tape, and mark them clearly on the ground. Use a keel marker, nails, or wood stakes.

- Determine the baseline stations of all features left and right of the baseline by estimating 90° (swung-arm technique) or by using a right-angled prism.

- When you have recorded the baseline stations of all the features in a 50- to 100-ft, or 20- to 30-m interval (the steel tape can be left lying on the ground on the baseline), determine and record the offset (o/s) distances left and right of the baseline to each feature using a cloth tape. Tie in all detail to the closest 0.10 ft or 0.03 m. (A fiberglass tape can be used for these measurements.)

- Do not begin the measurements until the sketches have been made for the survey area.

- Elevations should be determined using a level and a rod. The level should be set up in a convenient location where a benchmark (BM) and a considerable number of intermediate sights (ISs) can be "seen." See Figure G.7.

- Hold the rod on the baseline at each station and at all points where the ground slope changes (e.g., top and bottom of curb, edge of walk, top of slope, bottom of slope, limit of survey). See the typical cross section illustrated in Figure G.8.

- When all the data (that can be "seen") have been taken at a station, the rod holder then moves to the next (50-ft or 20-m) station and repeats the process.

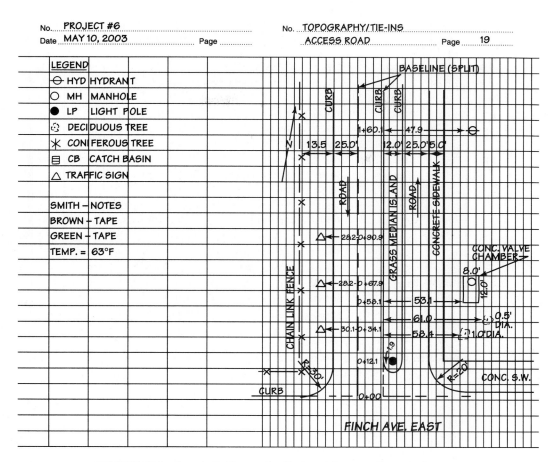

**FIGURE G.6** Sample field notes for Project 6 (topography tie-ins).

- When the rod can no longer be seen, the instrument operator calls for the establishment of a turning point (TP). After taking a foresight to the new TP, the instrument operator moves the instrument closer to the next stage of work and a backsight is taken to the new TP before continuing with the cross sections. In addition to cross sections at the even-station intervals (for example, 50 ft., 20 m), take full or partial sections between the even stations if the lay of the land changes significantly.

## G.7.2 Theodolite/EDM Topographic Survey

**Description**    Using electronic distance measurement (EDM) instruments and optical or electronic theodolites, you will locate the positions and elevations of all topographic detail and a sufficient number of additional elevations to enable a representative contour drawing of the selected areas. See the sample field notes in Figure G.9.

| STA. | B.S. | H.I. | I.S. | F.S. | ELEV. | DESCRIPTION |
|------|------|------|------|------|-------|-------------|
| BM 3 | 8.21 | 318.34 | | | 310.13 | S.W. CORNER OF CONC. VALVE CHAMBER |
| | | | | | | @ 0+53.1 |
| 0+00 | | | 3.34 | | 315.00 | ₵, ON ASPH. |
| | | | 0.03 | | 318.31 | 75.0' LT, ON ASPH. |
| | | | 7.35 | | 310.99 | 50.0' RT, ON ASPH. |
| | | | | | | |
| 0+50 | | | 6.95 | | 311.39 | ₵, ON ASPH. |
| | | | 7.00 | | 311.34 | 25' LT, BOT. CURB |
| | | | 0.3 | | 318.0 | 38.5' LT, @ FENCE, ON GRASS |
| | | | 7.5 | | 310.8 | 6' RT, ₵ OF ISLAND, ON GRASS |
| | | | 8.32 | | 310.02 | 12' RT, BOT. CURB |
| | | | 8.41 | | 309.93 | 37.0' RT, BOT. CURB |
| | | | 8.91 | | 309.43 | 37.0' RT, TOP OF CONC. WALK |
| | | | 9.01 | | 309.33 | 42.0' RT, TOP OF CONC. WALK |
| | | | 9.3 | | 309.0 | 46.9' RT, TOP OF HILL, ON GRASS |
| | | | 11.7 | | 306.6 | 56.6' RT, @ BUILDING WALL, ON GRASS |
| | | | | | | |

**FIGURE G.7**    Sample field notes for Project 6 (topography cross sections).

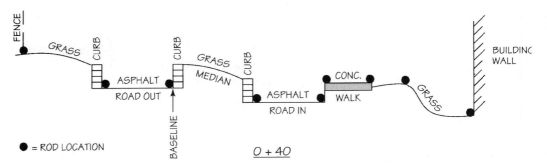

**FIGURE G.8**    Cross-section plot for Project 6.

**Equipment**      Theodolite, EDM, and one or more pole-mounted reflecting prisms.

### Procedure

- Set the theodolite at a control station (northing, easting, and elevation known), and backsight on another known control station.
- Set an appropriate reference angle (for example, 0°00'00" or some assigned azimuth) on the horizontal circle.

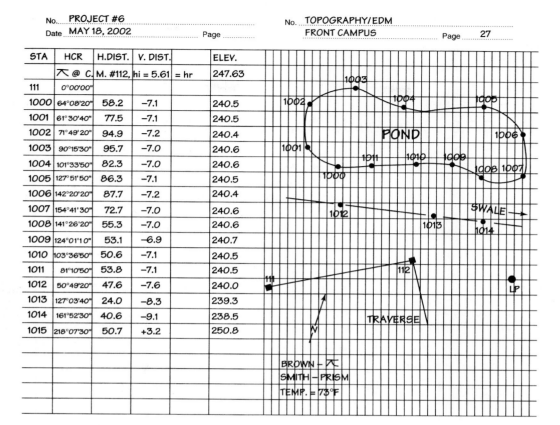

| STA | HCR | H.DIST. | V. DIST. | | ELEV. |
|-----|-----|---------|----------|---|-------|
| | ⊼ @ C.M. #112, | | hi = 5.61 | = hr | 247.63 |
| 111 | 0°00'00" | | | | |
| 1000 | 64°08'20" | 58.2 | −7.1 | | 240.5 |
| 1001 | 61°30'40" | 77.5 | −7.1 | | 240.5 |
| 1002 | 71°49'20" | 94.9 | −7.2 | | 240.4 |
| 1003 | 90°15'30" | 95.7 | −7.0 | | 240.6 |
| 1004 | 101°33'50" | 82.3 | −7.0 | | 240.6 |
| 1005 | 127°51'50" | 86.3 | −7.1 | | 240.5 |
| 1006 | 142°20'20" | 87.7 | −7.2 | | 240.4 |
| 1007 | 154°41'30" | 72.7 | −7.0 | | 240.6 |
| 1008 | 141°26'20" | 55.3 | −7.0 | | 240.6 |
| 1009 | 124°01'10" | 53.1 | −6.9 | | 240.7 |
| 1010 | 103°36'50" | 50.6 | −7.1 | | 240.5 |
| 1011 | 81°10'50" | 53.8 | −7.1 | | 240.5 |
| 1012 | 50°49'20" | 47.6 | −7.6 | | 240.0 |
| 1013 | 127°03'40" | 24.0 | −8.3 | | 239.3 |
| 1014 | 161°52'30" | 40.6 | −9.1 | | 238.5 |
| 1015 | 218°07'30" | 50.7 | +3.2 | | 250.8 |

**FIGURE G.9**   Sample field notes for Project 6 (topography by theodolite/EDM).

- Set the height of the reflecting prisms (HR) on the pole equal to the height of the optical center of the theodolite/EDM (hi). If the EDM is not coaxial with the theodolite, set the height of the target (target/prism assembly) equal to the optical center of the instrument (see the left illustration in Figure 7.7). Take all vertical angles to the prism target, or to the center of the prism if the EDM is coaxial with the theodolite.

- Prepare a sketch of the area to be surveyed.

- Begin taking readings on the appropriate points and enter the data in the field notes (see Figure G.9) and enter the "shot" number in the appropriate spot on the accompanying field-note sketch. Keep shot numbers sequential, perhaps beginning with 1,000. Work is expedited if two prisms are employed. While one prism-holder is walking to the next "shot" location, the instrument operator can take a reading at the other prism-holder.

- When all field shots (horizontal and vertical angles and horizontal distances) have been taken, sight the reference backsight control station again to verify the original angle setting; also verify that the height of the prism is unchanged.

- Reduce the field notes to determine station elevations and course distances, if required.
- Plot the topographic features and elevations at $1'' = 40'$ or 1:500 metric (or at another scale, as given by your instructor).
- Draw contours over the surveyed areas. See Chapter 8.

## G.7.3 Total Station Topographic Survey

**Description**     Using a total station and one or more pole-mounted reflecting prisms, you will tie in all topographic features and any additional ground shots (including break lines) that are required to define the terrain accurately. See Sections 7.10, 7.11, and 7.12, as well as and Figure G.10.

**Equipment**     Total station and one or more pole-mounted reflecting prisms.

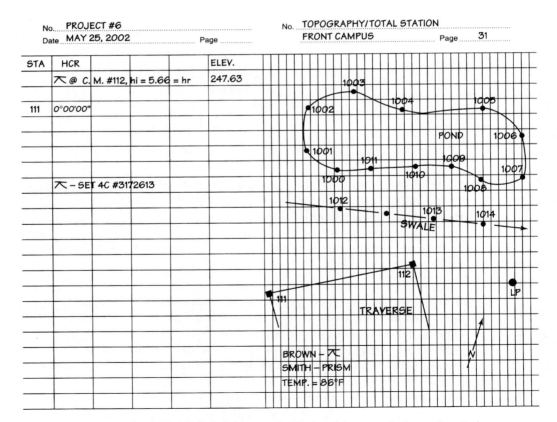

**FIGURE G.10**   Sample field notes for Project 6 (topography by total station).

**Procedure**

- Set the total station over a known control point (northing, easting, and elevation known).* Turn on the instrument, and index the circles if necessary (by transiting the telescope and revolving the instrument 360°). Some newer total stations do not require this operation.

- Set the program menu to the type of survey (topography) being performed and to the required instrument settings. Select the type of field data to be stored (for example, N, E, and Z; E, N, and Z; etc.). Set temperature and pressure settings, if required.

- Check the configuration settings [tilt correction, coordinate format, zenith vertical angle, angle resolution (for example, 5″), $c + r$ correction (no.), units (ft/m, degree, mm Hg), auto power off (say, 20 minutes)].

- Identify the instrument station from the menu. Insert the date, station number coordinates, elevation, and hi. It may have been possible to upload all control station data prior to going out to the field. In that case, scan through the data, and select the appropriate instrument station and backsight station(s). Enter the height of the instrument (hi), and store or record all the data.

- Backsight to one or more known control point(s) (point number, north and east coordinates, and known elevation). Set the horizontal circle to 0°00′00″ or to some assigned reference azimuth for the backsight reference direction. Store or record the data.

- Set the initial topography point number in the instrument (for example, 1,000), and set for automatic point number incrementation. Adjust the height of the reflecting prism (HR) equal to the instrument hi.

- Begin taking intermediate sights. Provide an attribute code (consistent with the software code library; see Table G.2 for an example) for each reading. Some software programs enable attribute codes to provide automatically for feature "stringing" (for example, curb1, edge of water1, fence3), whereas other software programs require the surveyor to prefix the code with a character (Z) that turns on the stringing command. See Section 7.12 and Figure 7.22(a) and (b). Most total stations have an automatic mode for topographic surveys, where one button-push will measure and store all the point data as well as the code and attribute data. The code and attribute data of the previous point are usually presented to the surveyor as a default setting. If the code and attribute data are the same for a series of readings, the surveyor only has to press "enter" and not enter all that identical data.

- Put all or some selected point numbers on the field sketch. These field notes will be of assistance later in the editing process if mistakes have occurred in the numbering or the coding.

- When all required points have been surveyed, check into the control station originally backsighted to ensure that the instrument orientation is still valid.

- Transfer the field data into a properly labeled file in a computer.

---

*As an alternative, the station can be set in any convenient location, and its position can be determined using the onboard resection program after the required number of visible control stations are sighted.

**Table G.2**  TYPICAL CODE LIBRARY

| | Control | | Utilities |
|---|---|---|---|
| TCM | Temporary control monument | HP | Hydro pole |
| CM | Concrete monument | LP | Lamp pole |
| SIB | Standard iron bar | BP | Telephone pole |
| IB | Iron bar | GS | Gas valve |
| RIB | Round iron bar | WV | Water vavle |
| NL | Nail | CABLE | Cable |
| STA | Station | | |
| TBM | Temporary benchmark | | |

| | Municipal | | Topographic |
|---|---|---|---|
| ℄ (CL) | Centerline | GND | Ground |
| RD | Road | TB | Top of bank |
| EA | Edge of asphalt | BB | Bottom of bank |
| BC | Beginning of curve | DIT | Ditch |
| EC | End of curve | FL | Fence line |
| PC | Point on curve | POST | Post |
| CURB | Curb | GATE | Gate |
| CB | Catch basin | BUSH | Bush |
| DCB | Double catch basin | HEDGE | Hedge |
| MH | Manhole | BLD | Building |
| STM | Storm sewer manhole | RWALL | Retaining wall |
| SAN | Sanitary sewer manhole | POND | Pond |
| INV | Invert | STEP | Steps |
| SW | Sidewalk | CTREE | Coniferous tree |
| HYD | Hydrant | DTREE | Deciduous tree |
| RR | Railroad | | |

- After opening the data-processing program, import the field data file and begin the editing process and the graphics generation process (this is automatic for many programs).
- Create the TIN and contours.
- Either finish the drawing with the working program or create a dxf file for transfer to a CAD program. Then finish the drawing.
- Prepare a plot file, and then plot the data (to a scale assigned by your instructor) on the lab digital plotter.

## G.8  Project 7: Building Layout

| | |
|---|---|
| **Description** | You will lay out the corners of a building and reference the corners with batter boards. See Figure G.11. |
| **Equipment** | Theodolite, steel tape, plumb bobs, wood stakes, light lumber for batter boards, C-clamps, keel or felt pen, level, and rod. (A theodolite/EDM, or total station and prism can replace the theodolite and steel tape.) |

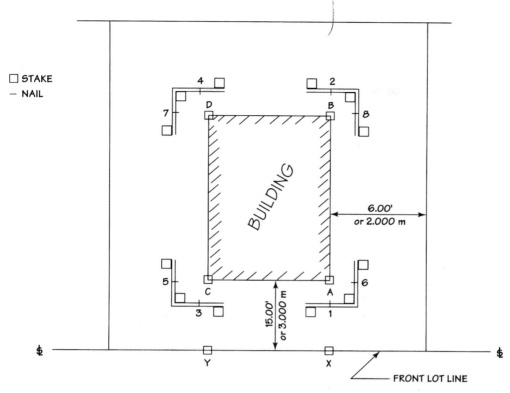

STAKE
NAIL

**FIGURE G.11** Sample field notes for Project 7 (building layout).

**Purpose**     To give you experience in laying out the corners of a building according to dimensions taken from a building site plan and in constructing batter boards, referencing both the line and grade of the building walls and floor.

**Procedure**

- After the front and side lines have been defined by your instructor and after the building dimensions have been given, set stakes *X* and *Y* on the front property line, as shown in Figure G.11.
- Set up the theodolite at *X*, sight on *Y*, turn 90° (double), and place stakes at *A* and *B*.
- Set up the theodolite at *Y*, sight on *X*, turn 90° (double), and place stakes at *C* and *D*.
- Measure the building diagonals to check the accuracy of the layout. Adjust and remeasure if necessary.
- After the building corners have been set, offset the batter boards a safe distance (for example, 6 ft or 2 m), and set the batter boards at the first-floor elevation, or as given by your instructor.

- After the batter boards have been set, place line nails on the top of the batter boards as follows:
  1. Set up on *A*, sight *B*, place nail 2, transit the telescope, and set nail 1.
  2. From the setup on *A*, sight *C*, place nail 5, transit the telescope, and place nail 6.
  3. Set up on *D* and place nails 3, 4, 7, and 8 in a similar fashion.

## G.9    Project 8: Horizontal Curve

| | |
|---|---|
| **Description** | Given the centerline alignment of two intersecting tangents (including a stationing reference stake), you will calculate and lay out a horizontal curve. |
| **Equipment** | Theodolite, steel tape, plumb bobs, wood stakes, and range pole or string target. (A theodolite/EDM, or total station and prism can replace the theodolite and steel tape.) |
| **Purpose** | To give you experience in laying out a circular curve at specified station intervals after first calculating all the necessary layout measurements from the given radius and the measured location of the PI and the $\Delta$ field angle. |

**Procedure**

- Intersect the two tangents to create the PI.
- Measure the station of the PI.
- Measure (and double) the tangent deflection angle ($\Delta$).
- After receiving the radius value from your instructor, compute $T$ and $L$. Then compute the station of the BC and EC. See Section 14.3.
- Compute the deflections for even stations at 50-ft or 20-m intervals. See Section 14.4.
- Compute the equivalent chords. See Section 14.5.
- Set the BC and EC by measuring out $T$ from the PI along each tangent.
- From the BC, sight the PI and turn the curve deflection angle ($\Delta/2$) to check the location of the EC. If the line of sight does not fall on the EC, check the calculations and measurements for the BC and EC locations. Make any necessary adjustments.
- Using the calculated deflection angles and appropriate chord lengths, stake out the curve.
- Measure from the last even station stake to the EC to verify the accuracy of the layout.
- Walk the curve, looking for any anomalies (for example, two stations staked at the same deflection angle). The symmetry of the curve is such that even minor mistakes are obvious in a visual check.

## G.10    Project 9: Pipeline Layout

| | |
|---|---|
| **Description** | You will establish an offset line and construct batter boards for line and grade control of a proposed storm sewer from MH 1 to |

MH 2. Stakes marking those points will be given for each crew in the field.

**Equipment**   Theodolite, steel tape, wood stakes, and light lumber and C-clamps for the batter boards. (A theodolite/EDM, or total station and prism can replace the theodolite and steel tape.)

**Purpose**   To give you experience in laying out offset line and grade stakes for a proposed pipeline. You will learn how to compute a grade sheet and construct batter boards, and check the accuracy of your work by sighting across the constructed batter boards.

## Procedure

- Set up at the MH 1 stake and sight the MH 2 stake.
- Turn off 90°, measure the offset distance (for example, 10 ft or 3 m), and establish MH 1 on the offset.
- Set up at the MH 2 stake, sight the MH 1 stake, and establish MH 2 on the offset. Refer to Figure 15.24 for guidance.
- Give the MH 1 offset stake a station of 0 + 00, measure to establish grade stakes at the even stations (50 ft or 20 m), and check the distance from the last even station to the MH 2 stake to check that the overall distance is accurate.
- Using the closest benchmark (BM), determine the elevations of the tops of the offset grade stakes. Close back to the benchmark within the tolerance given by your instructor.
- Assume that the invert of MH 1 is 7.97 ft or 2.430 m (or another assumed value given by your instructor) below the top of the MH 1 grade stake.
- Compute the invert elevations at each even station, and then complete a grade sheet similar to those shown in Tables 15.6 and 15.7. Select a convenient height for the grade rod.
- Using the "stake to batter board" distances in the grade sheet, use the supplied light lumber and C-clamps to construct batter boards similar to those shown in Figure 15.24. Use a small carpenter's level to keep the cross pieces horizontal. Check to see that all cross pieces line up in one visual line. A perfect visual check (all batter boards line up behind one another) is a check on all the measurements and calculations.

# Four-Screw Surveying Instruments: The Dumpy Level and the Engineer's Vernier Transit

## H.1  Dumpy Level

The dumpy level (see Figure H.1) was at one time used extensively on all leveling surveys. Although this simple instrument has been replaced, to a large degree, by more sophisticated instruments, it is shown here in some detail to aid in the introduction of the topic. For purposes of description, the level can be analyzed with respect to its three major components: telescope, level tube, and leveling head.

The telescope assembly is illustrated in Figure H.2(a), (b), and (c). These schematics also describe the telescopes used in theodolites/transits. Rays of light pass through the objective (1) and form an inverted image in the focal plane (4). The image thus formed is magnified by the eyepiece lenses (3) so that the image can be seen clearly. The eyepiece lenses also focus the cross hairs, which are located in the telescope in the principal focus plane. The focusing lens (negative lens; 2) can be adjusted so that images at varying distances can be brought into focus in the plane of the reticle (4). In most telescopes designed for use in North America, additional lenses are included in the eyepiece assembly so that the inverted image can be viewed as an erect image. The minimum focusing distance for the object ranges from 1 to 2 m, depending on the instrument.

**FIGURE H.I** Dumpy level. (Courtesy of Keuffel & Esser Co.)

The line of collimation (line of sight) joins the center of the objective lens to the intersection of the cross hairs. The optical axis is the line taken through the center of the objective lens and perpendicular to the vertical lens axis. The focusing lens (negative lens), which is moved by focusing screw C [Figure H.2(a)], has its optical axis the same as the objective lens.

The cross hairs [Figure H.2(a), 4] can be thin wires attached to a cross-hair ring or, as is more usually the case, the cross hairs are lines etched on a circular glass plate enclosed by a cross-hair ring. The cross-hair ring, which has a slightly smaller diameter than does the telescope tube, is held in place by four adjustable capstan screws. The cross-hair ring (and the cross hairs) can be adjusted left and right or up and down simply by loosening and then tightening the two appropriate opposing capstan screws.

Four leveling foot screws are utilized to set the telescope level. The four foot screws surround the center bearing of the instrument [Figure H.2(a)] and are used to tilt the level telescope using the center bearing as a pivot.

Figure H.3 illustrates how the telescope is positioned during the leveling process. The telescope is first positioned directly over two opposite foot screws. The two screws are kept only snugly tightened (overtightening makes rotation difficult and could damage the threads) and are rotated in opposite directions until the bubble is centered in the level tube. Loose foot screws indicate that the rotations have not proceeded uniformly. At worst, the foot screw pad can rise above the plate, making the telescope wobble. The solution for this condition is to turn the loose screw until it again contacts the base plate and provides snug friction when turned in opposition to its opposite screw.

The telescope is first aligned over two opposing screws, and the screws are turned in opposite directions until the bubble is centered in the level tube. The telescope is then turned 90° to the second position, which is over the other pair of opposite foot screws, and the leveling procedure is repeated. This process is repeated until the bubble remains centered in those two positions. When the bubble remains centered in these two positions, the telescope is then turned 180° to check the adjustment of the level tube.

If the bubble does not remain centered when the telescope is turned 180°, the level tube is out of adjustment. The instrument can still be used, however, by simply noting the number of divisions that the bubble is off center and by moving the bubble half the number

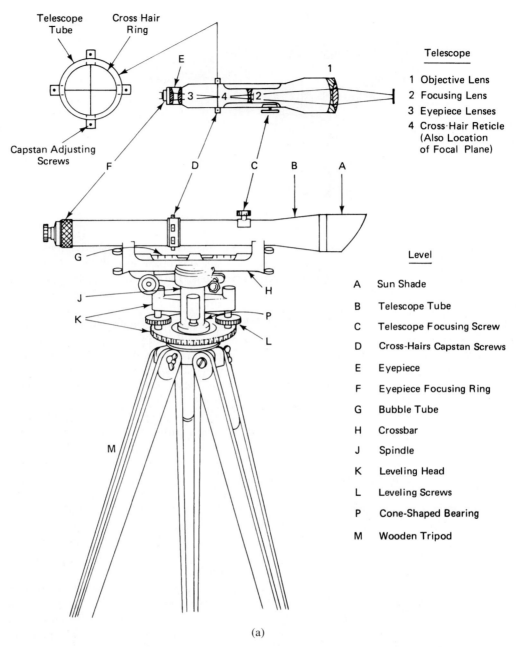

Telescope Tube

Cross Hair Ring

Capstan Adjusting Screws

**Telescope**

1 Objective Lens
2 Focusing Lens
3 Eyepiece Lenses
4 Cross-Hair Reticle
(Also Location of Focal Plane)

**Level**

A   Sun Shade

B   Telescope Tube

C   Telescope Focusing Screw

D   Cross-Hairs Capstan Screws

E   Eyepiece

F   Eyepiece Focusing Ring

G   Bubble Tube

H   Crossbar

J   Spindle

K   Leveling Head

L   Leveling Screws

P   Cone-Shaped Bearing

M   Wooden Tripod

(a)

**FIGURE H.2**   (a) Dumpy level. (Adapted from *Construction Manual,* Ministry of Transportation, Ontario)

734

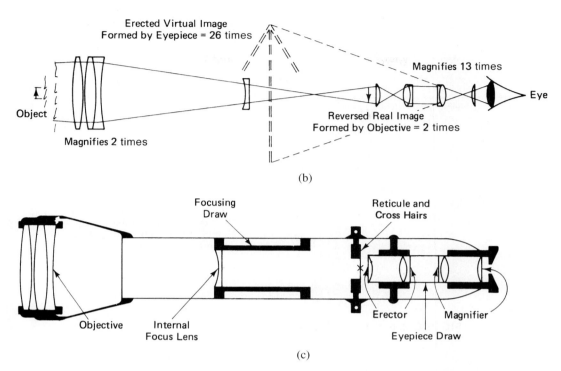

**Magnifies 13 times**

**Erected Virtual Image**
**Formed by Eyepiece = 26 times**

Eye

Object

**Reversed Real Image**
**Formed by Objective = 2 times**

**Magnifies 2 times**

(b)

Focusing
Draw

Reticule and
Cross Hairs

Objective

Internal
Focus Lens

Erector

Magnifier

Eyepiece Draw

(c)

**FIGURE H.2** (b) Diagram of an optical system for a level or theodolite telescope. (Courtesy of Sokkia Co. Ltd. (c) Telescope. (Courtesy of Sokkia Co. Ltd.)

of those divisions. For example, if you turn the leveled telescope 180° and note that the bubble is four divisions off center, the instrument can be leveled by moving the bubble to a position of two divisions off center. The bubble will remain two divisions off center, no matter which direction the telescope is pointed. It should be emphasized that the instrument is, in fact, level if the bubble remains in the same position when the telescope is revolved, regardless of whether or not that position is in the center of the level vial. See Section 5.9.2 for adjustments used to correct this condition.

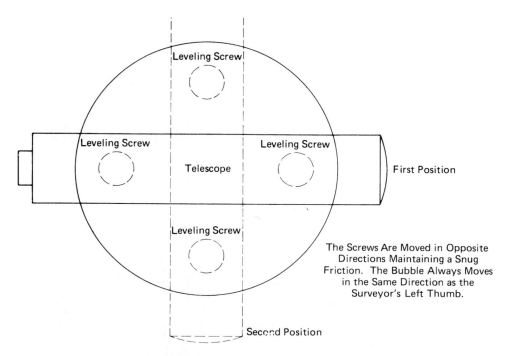

The Screws Are Moved in Opposite
Directions Maintaining a Snug
Friction. The Bubble Always Moves
in the Same Direction as the
Surveyor's Left Thumb.

**FIGURE H.3**   Telescope positions when leveling a four-screw level instrument.

## H.2    The Engineer's Vernier Transit

### H.2.1    The Engineer's Transit: General Background

Prior to the mid-1950s, and before the development and/or widespread use of electronic and optical theodolites, most engineering surveys for topography and layout were accomplished using the engineers' transit (see Figure H.4). This instrument had open circles for horizontal and vertical angles; angles were read with the aid of vernier scales. This four-screw instrument was positioned over the survey point by using a slip-knotted plumb bob string attached to the chain hook hanging down from the instrument.

Figure H.5 shows the three main assemblies of the transit. The upper assembly, called the alidade, includes the standards, telescope, vertical circle and vernier, two opposite verniers for reading the horizontal circle, plate bubbles, compass, and upper-tangent (slow-motion) screw. The spindle of the alidade fits down into the hollow spindle of the circle assembly. The circle assembly includes the horizontal circle that is covered by the alidade plate except at the vernier windows, the upper clamp screw, and the hollow spindle previously mentioned.

The hollow spindle of the circle assembly fits down into the leveling head. The leveling head includes the four leveling screws; the half-ball joint, about which opposing screws are manipulated to level the instrument; a threaded collar that permits attachment to

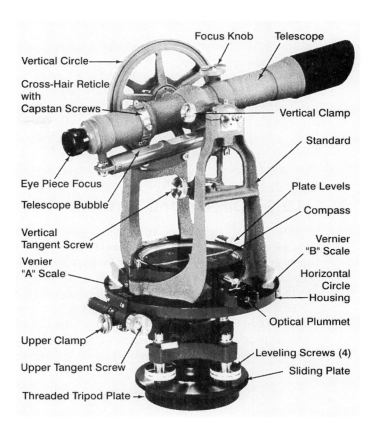

Focus Knob — Telescope

Vertical Circle

Cross-Hair Reticle with Capstan Screws

Vertical Clamp

Standard

Eye Piece Focus

Plate Levels

Telescope Bubble

Compass

Vertical Tangent Screw

Vernier "B" Scale

Venier "A" Scale

Horizontal Circle Housing

Optical Plummet

Upper Clamp

Leveling Screws (4)

Upper Tangent Screw

Sliding Plate

Threaded Tripod Plate

**FIGURE H.4** Engineer's transit. (Courtesy of Keuffel & Esser Co.)

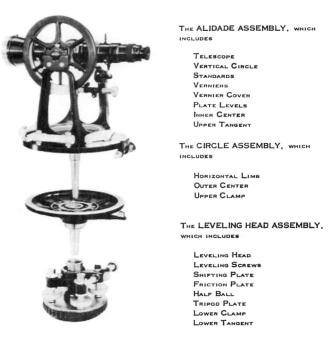

The ALIDADE ASSEMBLY, which includes

> Telescope
> Vertical Circle
> Standards
> Verniers
> Vernier Cover
> Plate Levels
> Inner Center
> Upper Tangent

The CIRCLE ASSEMBLY, which includes

> Horizontal Limb
> Outer Center
> Upper Clamp

The LEVELING HEAD ASSEMBLY, which includes

> Leveling Head
> Leveling Screws
> Shifting Plate
> Friction Plate
> Half Ball
> Tripod Plate
> Lower Clamp
> Lower Tangent

**FIGURE H.5** Three major assemblies of the transit. (Courtesy of Sokkia Co. Ltd.)

The Inner Center of the Alidade Assembly fits into the Outer Center of the Circle Assembly and can be rotated in the Outer Center. The Outer Center fits into the Leveling Head and can be rotated in the Leveling Head.

a tripod; the lower clamp and slow-motion screw; and a chain with an attached hook for attaching the plumb bob.

The upper clamp tightens the alidade to the circle, whereas the lower clamp tightens the circle to the leveling head. These two independent motions permit angles to be accumulated on the circle for repeated measurements. Transits that have these two independent motions are called repeating instruments. Instruments with only one motion (upper) are called direction instruments. Since the circle cannot be previously zeroed (older instruments), angles are usually determined by subtracting the initial setting from the final value. It is not possible to accumulate or repeat angles with a direction theodolite.

## H.2.2 Circles and Verniers

The horizontal circle is usually graduated into degrees and half-degrees or 30 minutes (see Figure H.6), although it is not uncommon to find the horizontal circle graduated into degrees and one-third degrees (20 minutes). To determine the angle value more precisely than the least count of the circle (i.e., 30 or 20 minutes), vernier scales are employed.

Figure H.7 shows a double vernier scale alongside a transit circle. The left vernier scale is used for clockwise circle readings (angles turned to the right), and the right vernier scale is used for counterclockwise circle readings (angles turned to the left). To avoid confusion about which vernier (left or right) scale to use, recall that the vernier to be used is the one whose graduations are increasing in the same direction as are the circle graduations.

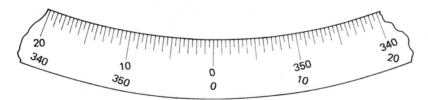

**FIGURE H.6**   Part of a transit circle showing a least count of 30 minutes. The circle is graduated in both clockwise and counterclockwise directions, permitting the reading of angles turned to both the left and the right.

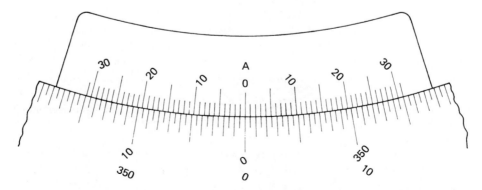

**FIGURE H.7**   Double vernier scale set to zero on the horizontal circle.

The vernier scale is constructed so that 30 vernier divisions cover the same length of arc as do 29 divisions (half-degrees) on the circle. The width of one vernier division is $(29/30) \times 30' = 29'$ on the circle. Therefore, the space difference between one division on the circle and one division on the vernier represents $01'$. In Figure H.7, the first division on the vernier (left or right of the index mark) fails to line up exactly with the first division on the circle (left or right) by $01'$. The second division on the vernier fails to line up with the corresponding circle division by $02'$, and so on. If the vernier were moved so that its first division lined up exactly with the first circle division ($30'$ mark), the reading would be $01'$. If the vernier were moved again the same distance of arc ($1'$), the second vernier mark would now line up with the appropriate circle division line, indicating a vernier reading of $02'$. Generally, the vernier is read by finding which vernier division line coincides exactly with any circle line, and then by adding the value of that vernier line to the value of the angle obtained from reading the circle to the closest $30'$ (in this example).

In Figure H.8(a), the circle is divided into degrees and half-degrees ($30'$). Before even looking at the vernier, we know that its range will be $30'$ (left or right) to cover the least count of the circle. Inspection of the vernier shows that 30 marks cover the range of $30'$, indicating that the value of each mark is $01'$. (Had each of the minute marks been further subdivided into two or three intervals, the angle could then have been read to the closest $30'$ or $20'$.) If we consider the clockwise circle readings (field angle turned left to right), we see that the zero mark is between $184°$ and $184°30'$; the circle reading is therefore $184°$. Now to find the value to the closest minute, we use the left-side vernier. Moving from the zero mark, we look for the vernier line that lines up exactly with a circle line. In this case, the $08'$ mark lines up; this is confirmed by noting that both the $07'$ and $09'$ marks do not line up with their corresponding circle mark, both by the same amount. The angle for this illustration is $184° + 08' = 184°08'$.

If we consider the counterclockwise circle reading in Figure H.8(a), we see that the zero mark is between $175°30'$ and $176°$ the circle reading is therefore $175°30'$. To that value, we will add the right-side vernier reading of $22'$, to give an angle of $175°52'$. As a check, the sum of the clockwise and counterclockwise readings should be $360°00'$.

All transits are equipped with two double verniers (A and B) located $180°$ apart. Although increased precision can theoretically be obtained by reading both verniers for each angle, usually only one vernier is employed. Furthermore, to avoid costly mistakes, most surveying agencies favored the use of the same vernier, the A vernier, at all times.

As noted earlier, the double vernier permits angles to be turned to the right (left vernier) or to the left (right vernier). By convention, however, field angles are normally turned only to the right. The exceptions to this occur when deflection angles are being employed, as in route surveys, or when construction layouts necessitate angles to the left, as in some curve deflections. There are a few more specialized cases (e.g., star observations) when it is advantageous to turn angles to the left, but as stated earlier, the bulk of surveying experience favors angles turned to the right. This type of consistency provides the routine required to foster a climate in which fewer mistakes occur, and in which mistakes that do occur can be recognized readily and eliminated.

The graduations of the circles and verniers as illustrated were in wide use in the survey field. However, there are several variations to both circle graduations and vernier graduations. Typically, the circle is graduated to the closest $30'$ (as illustrated), $20'$, or $10'$ (rarely). The vernier will have a range in minutes covering the smallest division on the cir-

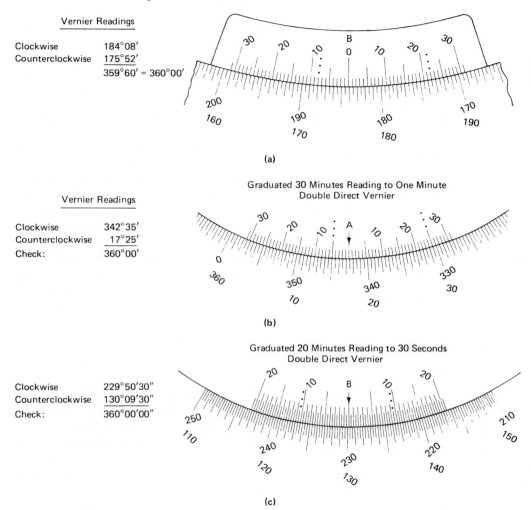

**FIGURE H.8** Sample vernier readings. Triple dots identify aligned vernier graduations.

*Note:* Appropriate vernier scale graduation numerals are angled in the same direction as the referenced circle graduation numerals.

cle (30', 20', or 10'), and can be further graduated to half-minute (30") or one-third minute (20") divisions. A few minutes spent observing the circle and vernier graduations of an unfamiliar transit will easily disclose the proper technique required for reading [see also Figure H.8(b) and (c)].

The use of a magnifying glass (5×) is recommended for reading the scales, particularly for the 30' and 20' verniers. Vernier transits were largely replaced by optical theodolites in the 1970s and 1980s; optical theodolites were largely replaced by electronic transits/theodolites in the 1990s.

## H.2.3  Telescope

The telescope [see Figure H.2(b) and (c)] in the transit is somewhat shorter than that in a level with a reduced magnifying power (26× versus the 30× often used in the level). The telescope axis is supported by the standards, which are of sufficient height to permit the telescope to be revolved (**transited**) 360° about the axis. A level vial tube is attached to the telescope so that, if desired, it may be used as a level.

The telescope level has a sensitivity of 30" to 40" per 2-mm graduation, compared to a level sensitivity of about 20" for a dumpy level. When the telescope is positioned so that the level tube is under the telescope, it is said to be in the direct (normal) position. When the level tube is on top of the telescope, the telescope is said to be in a reversed (inverted) position. The eyepiece focusing ring is always located at the eyepiece end of the telescope, whereas the object focus knob can be located on the telescope barrel just ahead of the eyepiece focus, midway along the telescope, or on the horizontal telescope axis at the standard.

## H.2.4  Leveling Head

The leveling head supports the instrument. Proper manipulation of the leveling screws allows the horizontal circle and telescope axis to be placed in a horizontal plane, which forces the alidade and circle assembly spindles to be placed in a vertical direction. When the leveling screws are loosened, the pressure on the tripod plate is removed, thus permitting the instrument to be shifted laterally a short distance (3/8 in.). This shifting capability permits the surveyor to position the transit center precisely over the desired point.

## H.2.5  Transit Adjustments

See also the theodolite adjustments in Section 5.9.

**H.2.5.1  Standards Adjustment**   The horizontal axis should be perpendicular to the vertical axis. The standards are checked for proper adjustment by first setting up the theodolite and then sighting a high (at least 30° altitude) point [point A in Figure 5.13(c)]. After clamping the instrument in that position, the telescope is depressed and point B is marked on the ground. The telescope is then transited (plunged), a lower clamp is loosened, and the transit is turned and once again set precisely on point A. The telescope is again depressed, and if the standards are properly adjusted, the vertical cross hair will fall on point B; if the standards are not in adjustment, a new point C is established. The discrepancy between B and C is double the error resulting from the standards maladjustment.

Point $D$, which is now established midway between $B$ and $C$, will be in the same vertical plane as point $A$. The error is removed by sighting point $D$ and then elevating the telescope to $A'$, adjacent to $A$. The adjustable end of the horizontal axis is then raised or lowered until the line of sight falls on point $A$. When the adjustment is complete, retighten the upper friction screws carefully so that the telescope revolves with proper tension.

**H.2.5.2 Telescope Bubble** If the transit is to be used for leveling work, the axis of the telescope bubble and the axis of the telescope must be parallel. To check this relationship, the bubble is centered with the telescope clamped, and the peg test (Section 3.11) is performed. When the proper rod reading has been determined at the final setup, the horizontal cross hair is set on that rod reading by moving the telescope with the vertical tangent (slow-motion) screw. The telescope bubble is then centered by means of the capstan screws located at one (or both) end(s) of the bubble tube.

**H.2.5.3 Vertical Circle Vernier** When the transit (plate bubbles) has been carefully leveled, and the telescope bubble has been centered, the vertical circle should read zero. If a slight error (index error) exists, the screws holding the vernier are loosened, the vernier is tapped into its proper position, and then the screws are retightened so that the vernier is once again just touching, without binding, the vertical circle.

## H.2.6  Plate Levels

Transits come equipped with two plate levels set at 90° to each other. Plate levels have a sensitivity range of 60″ to 80″ per 2-mm division on the level tube, depending on the overall precision requirements of the instrument.

## H.2.7  Transit Setup

The transit is removed from its case, held by the standards or leveling base (never by the telescope), and placed on a tripod by screwing the transit snugly to the threaded tripod top. When carrying the transit indoors or near obstructions (e.g., tree branches), the operator carries it cradled under the arm, with the instrument forward, where it can be seen. Otherwise, the transit and tripod can be carried on the shoulder. (Total stations [see Chapter 7] should always be removed from the tripod and carried by the handle or in the instrument case.)

The transit is placed roughly over the desired point, and the tripod legs are adjusted so that (1) the instrument is at a convenient height and (2) the tripod plate is nearly level. Usually, two legs are placed on the ground, and the instrument is roughly leveled by manipulation of the third leg. If the instrument is to be set up on a hill, the instrument operator faces uphill and places two of the legs on the lower position; the third leg is placed in the upper position and then manipulated to level the instrument roughly. The wing nuts on the tripod legs are tightened and a plumb bob is attached to the plumb bob chain, which hangs down from the leveling head. The plumb bob is attached by means of a slip knot, which allows placement of the plumb bob point immediately over the mark. If it appears that the instrument placement is reasonably close to its final position, the tripod legs are pushed into the ground without jarring the instrument.

If necessary, the length of the plumb bob string is adjusted as the setting-up procedure advances. If after pushing the tripod legs, the instrument is not centered, one leg is either pushed in farther or pulled out and repositioned until the plumb bob is very nearly over the point, or until it becomes obvious that manipulation of another leg would be more productive. When the plumb bob is within ¼″ in. of the desired location, the instrument can then be leveled.

Now, two adjacent leveling screws are loosened so that pressure is removed from the tripod plate and the transit can be shifted laterally until it is precisely over the point. If the same two adjacent leveling screws are retightened, the instrument will return to its level (or nearly so) position. Final adjustments to the leveling screws at this stage will not be large enough to displace the plumb bob from its position directly over the desired point.

The actual leveling procedure is a faster operation than that for a dumpy level. The transit has two plate levels, which means that the transit can be leveled in two directions, 90° opposed, without rotating the instrument. When both bubbles have been carefully centered, it remains only for the instrument to be turned through 180° to check the adjustment of the plate bubbles. If one or both bubbles do not center after turning 180°, the discrepancy is noted and the bubble brought to half the discrepancy by means of the leveling screws. If this procedure has been done correctly, the bubbles will remain in the same position as the instrument is revolved, indicating that the instrument is level.

## H.2.8 Measuring Angles by Repetition (Vernier Transit)

Assuming that the instrument is over the point and level, the following procedure is used to turn and "double" an angle. Turning the angle at least twice permits the elimination of mistakes and increases precision because of the elimination of most instrument errors. It is recommended that only the A vernier scale be used.

1. **Set the scales to zero.** Loosen both the upper and lower motion clamps. While holding the alidade stationary, revolve the circle by pushing on the circle underside with the fingertips. When the zero on the scale is close to the vernier zero, tighten (snug) the upper clamp. With the aid of a magnifying glass, turn the upper tangent screw (slow-motion screw) until the zeros are set precisely. It is good practice to make the last turn of the tangent screw against the tangent screw spring so that spring tension is ensured.

2. **Sight the initial point** (see Figure 5.6 and assume the instrument is at *A,* and an angle is from *B* to *E*). With the upper clamp tightened and the lower clamp loose, turn and point at station *B,* and then tighten the lower clamp. At this point, check the eyepiece focus and object focus to eliminate parallax (see Section 3.7). If the sight is given by a range pole, or even a pencil, always sight as close to the ground level as possible to eliminate plumbing errors. If the sight is given with a plumb bob, sight high on the plumb bob string to minimize the effect of plumb bob oscillations. Using the lower tangent screw, position the vertical cross hair on the target, once again making the last adjustment motion against the tangent screw spring.

3. **Turn the angle.** Loosen the upper clamp and turn clockwise to the final point (*E*). When the sight is close to *E,* tighten the upper clamp. Using the upper tangent screw,

set the vertical cross hair precisely on the target using techniques already described. Read the angle by using (in this case) the left-side vernier, and record the value in the appropriate column in the field notes (see Figure 5.6).

4. **Repeat the angle.** After the initial angle has been recorded, **transit (plunge) the telescope,** loosen the lower motion, and sight at the initial target, station *B*. The simple act of transiting the telescope between two sightings can eliminate nearly all the potential instrument errors associated with the transit, when turning angles or producing a straight line.

The procedure described in the first three steps is now repeated, the only differences being that the telescope is now inverted and the initial horizontal angle setting is $101°24'$ instead of $0°00'$. The angle that is read as a result of this repeated procedure should be approximately double the initial angle. This "double" angle is recorded and then divided by two to find the mean value, which is also recorded.

If the procedure has been executed properly, the mean value should be the same as the direct reading or half the least count ($30''$). In practice, a discrepancy equal to the least count ($01'$) is normally permitted. Although doubling the angle is sufficient for most engineering projects, precision can be increased by **repeating** the angle several times. Due to personal errors of sighting and scale reading, this procedure has practical constraints for improvement in precision. It is generally agreed that repetitions beyond six or perhaps eight times will not further improve the precision.

When multiple repetitions are used, only the first angle and the final value are recorded. The final value is divided by the number of repetitions to arrive at the mean value. It may be necessary to augment the final reading by $360°$ or multiples of $360°$ prior to determining the mean. The proper value can be roughly determined by multiplying the first angle recorded by the number of repetitions.

# Index

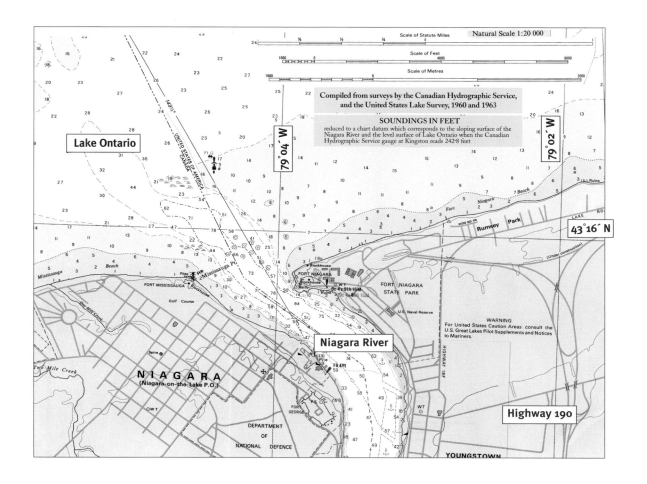

**Hydrographic map of the lower Niagara River. This map is adapted from one produced by the Canadian Hydrographic Service and the United States Lake Survey, 1960 and 1963. Also, refer to figures 12.12 and 12.13 for the same area coverage.**

FIGURE F.1

## Seismic Vulnerability of the Puget Sound Region

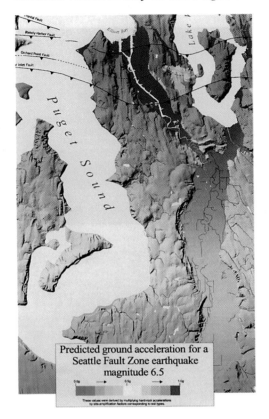

Predicted ground acceleration for a
Seattle Fault Zone earthquake
magnitude 6.5

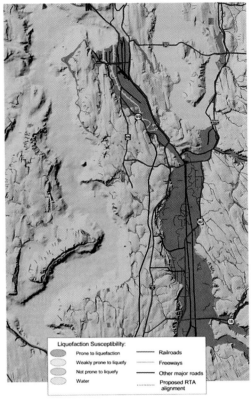

Liquefaction Susceptibility:

Prone to liquefaction        Railroads

Weakly prone to liquefy      Freeways

Not prone to liquefy        Other major roads

Water                   Proposed RTA
                                    alignment

**An illustration of the vulnerability of the
transportation system in King County, Washington.
(Courtesy of ESRI, Calif., and Michael Jenkins,
King County GIS Center, Seattle, Wash.)**

King County GIS
Seattle, Washington

*By Michael Jenkins*

**Contact**
Michael Jenkins
michael.jenkins@metrokc.gov

**Software**
ArcInfo 7.1.2, ARC GRID, ArcView GIS
3.1, and ArcView Spatial Analyst
**Hardware**
Pentium-based PC
**Printer**
HP DesignJet 2500CP
**Data Source(s)**
U.S. Geological Survey, King County
GIS, and Pierce County GIS

## FIGURE F.2

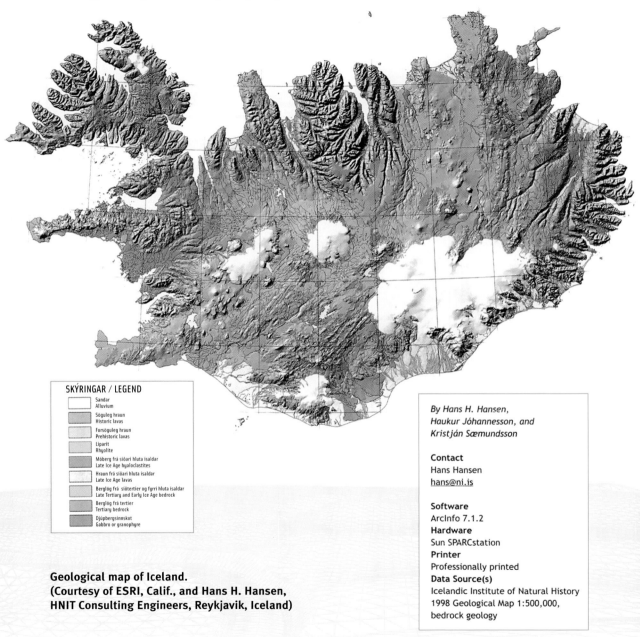

# Geological Map of Iceland, 1:1,000,000

## SKÝRINGAR / LEGEND

- Sandar
  Alluvium
- Söguleg hraun
  Historic lavas
- Forsöguleg hraun
  Prehistoric lavas
- Liparít
  Rhyolite
- Móberg frá síðari hluta ísaldar
  Late Ice Age hyaloclastites
- Hraun frá síðari hluta ísaldar
  Late Ice Age lavas
- Berglög frá síðtertíer og fyrri hluta ísaldar
  Late Tertiary and Early Ice Age bedrock
- Berglög frá tertíer
  Tertiary bedrock
- Djúpbergsinnskot
  Gabbro or granophyre

By Hans H. Hansen,
Haukur Jóhannesson, and
Kristján Sæmundsson

**Contact**
Hans Hansen
hans@ni.is

**Software**
ArcInfo 7.1.2
**Hardware**
Sun SPARCstation
**Printer**
Professionally printed
**Data Source(s)**
Icelandic Institute of Natural History
1998 Geological Map 1:500,000,
bedrock geology

**Geological map of Iceland.
(Courtesy of ESRI, Calif., and Hans H. Hansen,
HNIT Consulting Engineers, Reykjavik, Iceland)**

# FIGURE F.3

Aerial photograph, at 20,000 ft, showing the
Niagara Falls area.
(Courtesy of U.S. Geological Survey,
Sioux Falls, S. Dak.)

FIGURE F.4

SOCET SET Unix workstation. Shown here is the
host computer and L H System's three-dimensional
hand controller, which gives XYZ control of the
floating mark in the stereo model. The XY motion
is just like that produced by a mouse, and a
thumbwheel performs Z operations.
(Courtesy of L H Systems, San Diego, Calif.)

FIGURE F.5

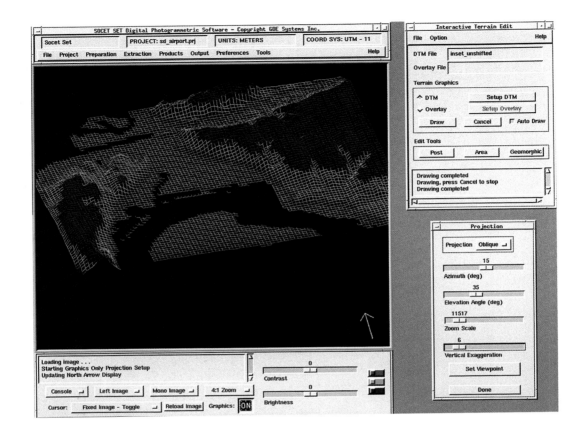

Computer screen printout developed using SOCET®
software. This screen shot shows a typical oblique
projection of a digital terrain model (DTM).
(Courtesy of L H Systems, San Diego, Calif.)

FIGURE F.6

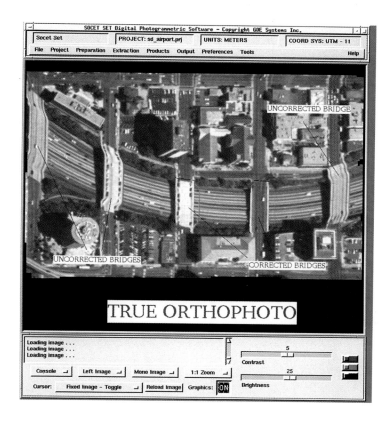

Computer screen printout developed using
SOCET® software. This screen shot shows a
partially corrected orthophoto.
(Courtesy of L H Systems, San Diego, Calif.)

FIGURE F.7

Trimble dual-frequency GPS total station 4800,
shown here with a data logger, RTK radio modem,
and radio antenna. All units are attached to the
pole.
(Courtesy of Trimble, Sunnyvale, Calif.)

FIGURE F.8